Now Proudly Published by Prentice Hall

THE SCOTT FORESMAN HANDBOOK FOR WRITERS has proven that a comprehensive handbook is easy, practical—even fun—to use. Each bestselling edition has provided complete, up-to-date material needed for today's Composition Classroom. And as the authors anticipate developments in writing influenced by new theories and technologies, each new edition has led the field in addressing emerging trends. As a result of this forward-looking philosophy, writers using **THE SCOTT FORESMAN HANDBOOK** know what college writing means today and what writers will need to know tomorrow.

"What did you write today?"
"What will you write tomorrow?"

To preview the highlights and new features of **THE SCOTT FORESMAN HANDBOOK FOR WRITERS, SEVENTH EDITION,** please see the Preface, which provides complete and detailed descriptions of each new feature.

Do you want to provide your students with meaningful technology that enhances the handbook and is an exciting, useful tool for the Composition Classroom?

Always on the cutting edge, Prentice Hall is pleased to now offer **The Scott Foresman Handbook Premium Companion Website™** and **Research Navigator™**. Turn the page for details!

Companion Website™

The New Premium Companion Website™ for THE SCOTT FORESMAN HANDBOOK FOR WRITERS, SEVENTH EDITION, offers instant online access to every page of the text plus the opportunity for students to create a personalized handbook, **My Handbook,** simply by logging on using the FREE access code included with every new copy of the Seventh Edition.

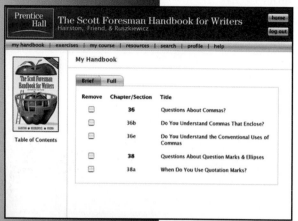

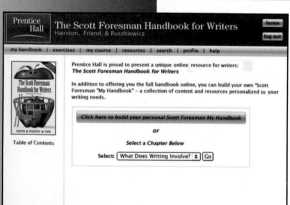

Sample screens from the Companion Website™ are accurate as of press time. © 2004 Pearson Education, Upper Saddle River, NJ.

To log on, go to
www.prenhall.com/hairston
where you'll find:

🍎 **The Scott Foresman E-Book.** A complete electronic version of **THE SCOTT FORESMAN HANDBOOK** that gives quick, easy access to every topic via a Table of Contents search, a key-word search, and a search-by-rule number feature. Plus, there are links to thousands of interactive exercises.

🍎 **My Handbook.** A comprehensive, automatically graded diagnostic test helps identify problem areas and creates a personalized online handbook for each student. Students can add and delete topics from their personalized online handbook, cutomized to meet their individual needs. Self-assessment tests are also available so that students can check their progress.

🍎 **Interactive, self-graded exercises.** Editing exercises are keyed to every chapter of the handbook, using multiple choice, essay, fill-in-the-blank, and paragraph-editing formats.

🍎 **Research Navigator™.** Simplifies research for your students by including extensive information on the research process and use of three exclusive databases. *See the back cover for more details.*

Prentice Hall — The Scott Foresman Handbook for Writers
Hairston, Friend, & Ruszkiewicz

home | log out

my handbook | exercises | my course | resources | search | profile | help

Diagnostic Test for Writers: Results

Congratulations! You have completed the diagnostic test. Below are the results for each section. You may click on any topic to see how you did on each question in that section.

If your score is less than 80%, the "Add To My Handbook" box is checked for that topic. You may check or uncheck boxes to add or remove topics. If you wish to use these results to build your *My Handbook*, click the button below.

Table of Contents

overall results

correct = 70%
incorrect = 25%
unanswered = 5%

Topic	Percent Correct	Correct/ Total	Add To My Handbook
Capital Letters	80	8/10	☐
Commas	67	8/12	☑
Apostrophes	100	7/7	☐
Quotation Marks	67	4/6	☑
Verb Tense	67	6/9	☑
Pronoun Case	90	9/10	☐
Subject Verb Agreement	44	4/9	☑

The Scott Foresman
Handbook for Writers

SEVENTH EDITION

MAXINE HAIRSTON
University of Texas at Austin

JOHN RUSZKIEWICZ
University of Texas at Austin

CHRISTY FRIEND
University of South Carolina

PEARSON

Prentice
Hall

Upper Saddle River, New Jersey 07458

Library of Congress Cataloging-in-Publication Data

HAIRSTON, MAXINE.
The Scott Foresman handbook for writers / Maxine Hairston,
John Ruszkiewicz, Christy Friend.—7th ed.
  p. cm.
Includes index.
ISBN 0-13-114681-5
1. English language—Rhetoric—Handbooks, manuals, etc. 2. English
language—Grammar—Handbooks, manuals, etc. 3. Report writing—
Handbooks, manuals, etc. I. Ruszkiewicz, John J. II. Friend, Christy.
III. Title.

PE1408.H2968 2003
808'.042—dc21   2002044571

Editor in Chief: Leah Jewell
Senior Acquisitions Editor: Stacy Best Ruel
Production Editor: Joan E. Foley
Copyeditor: Kathryn Graehl
Assistant Manufacturing Manager:
  Mary Ann Gloriande
Prepress and Manufacturing Buyer:
  Brian Mackey
Executive Marketing Manager:
  Brandy Dawson
Marketing Assistant: Christine Moodie
Text Permissions Specialist:
  Kathleen Karcher
Media Editor: Christy Schaack

Director, Image Resource Center:
  Melinda Reo
Image Rights and Permissions Manager:
  Zina Arabia
Interior Image Specialist:
  Beth Boyd-Brenzel
Image Researcher: Yvonne Gerin
Creative Design Director: Leslie Osher
Interior Designer:
  Laura Gardner/Wendy Ann
  Fredericks/Robert Farrar-Wagner
Cover Designer: Laura Gardner
Cover Artist: Theo Rudnak

This book was set in 10/12 Garamond by Carlisle Communications, Ltd., and was printed
and bound by R. R. Donnelley & Sons Company. The cover was printed by Coral Graphics.

Printed in the United States of America
10 9 8 7 6 5 4 3 2

ISBN 0-13-114681-5

Pearson Education LTD., London
Pearson Education Australia PTY, Limited, Sydney
Pearson Education Singapore, Pte. Ltd
Pearson Education North Asia Ltd, Hong Kong
Pearson Education Canada, Ltd., Toronto
Pearson Educación de Mexico, S.A. de C.V.
Pearson Education-Japan, Tokyo
Pearson Education Malaysia, Pte. Ltd
Pearson Education, Upper Saddle River, New Jersey

Contents

PART **II**

Writing for Academic and Public Forums   101

PART **III**

Style 229

PART IV

Design and Shape of Writing 367

PART **VI**

Punctuation and Mechanics 587

PART **VII**

Research and Writing 673

Preface

If you are teaching first-year composition, you have a diverse classroom of students from ambitious chemistry majors or aspiring poets to budding entrepreneurs. Regardless of your students' interests, odds are that they'll write every day. Whatever their goals as writers, the seventh edition of *The Scott Foresman Handbook* will help your students achieve them. Do your students need step-by-step advice for surviving their first college research paper assignment? Instructions for crafting a Web page or a PowerPoint presentation? Tips on literary analysis for a senior thesis? Formatting guidelines for a business letter? They will find it all in this handbook.

Since the best-selling first edition, *The Scott Foresman Handbook* has proven again and again that a comprehensive handbook can be easy, practical, even fun to use. Each new edition has provided complete, up-to-date material on writing processes, argumentation, style, grammar, mechanics, and punctuation, in friendly and accessible language. Yet we've also broken new ground, anticipating developments in writing influenced by innovative theories and technologies. For example, earlier editions of this handbook have led the field in addressing document design, online research, service learning, and other emerging trends. As a result of our forward-looking philosophy, writers using *The Scott Foresman Handbook* know what college writing means today and what it will mean tomorrow.

What's New

This seventh edition continues our commitment to preparing students for college writing as well as writing beyond college. In keeping with this goal, we have added new material that writers need for today, and we have expanded and updated familiar sections. Here are the highlights:

More on Visual and Multimedia Literacy. *The Scott Foresman Handbook* was the first handbook acknowledging that college writers now produce many different kinds of documents in a variety of media including visual and aural "texts." We have updated our popular document design material (Chapters 21, 22, and 24), and our chapters on writing processes (Chapters 1-5) now explore design issues at every stage of a project. Our coverage of visual literacy also includes several entirely **new chapters and sections:**

- The **NEW Chapter 13, "How Do You Prepare an Oral or Multimedia Report?"** helps writers prepare traditional oral reports as well as presentations that incorporate technological elements, including presentation software. Full-color examples of PowerPoint slides illustrate effective ways to present information visually.

- The **NEW Chapter 23, "How Do You Create a Web Site?"** represents our first full chapter on writing for the Web. This detailed chapter presents step-by-step instructions for crafting a Web page from start to finish. Designed to serve both Web novices and more experienced Web writers, this beautifully illustrated chapter offers assistance to writers for working with a basic HTML editor or with more helpful Web-authoring software. Web design has never looked so easy!

- Because many college courses now include online components, we've added to **Chapter 8** a practical **NEW section on using courseware such as Blackboard.** Full-color illustrations introduce students to the basic features and uses of course management software enabling students to approach online assignments with confidence.

- **Chapter 11, "How Do You Interpret and Use Visual Texts?"** has been updated and expanded, incorporating many **NEW examples of visual rhetoric** and a **NEW student paper that analyzes a print advertisement,** demonstrating critical visual literacy in action.

- **Chapter 14, "How Do You Write About Literature?"** now includes **sections on analyzing films and television** as literary artifacts.

- **NEW photos and images appear throughout the book** and many were created by the text authors themselves in order to reinforce key points about writing, style, and mechanics.
- **NEW, extensive Companion Website™** at www.prenhall.com/hairston offers:
  - An E-Book available 24/7 that contains the entire *The Scott Foresman Handbook, Seventh Edition,* in a searchable format, which enables students to find information quickly and easily.
  - A self-graded diagnostic test that assists students in identifying problem areas and creates a personalized handbook, *My Handbook.* Students are provided with information and exercises in order to improve their problem areas. Competency tests are also available so students can assess their own progress.
  - Hundreds of interactive, text-tied, and self-graded exercises including editing activities.
  - Additional information on research and documentation styles.

More Examples of Real Writers at Work. The pages of *The Scott Foresman Handbook* are filled with **photos of student and professional writers at work,** as we're happy to give a human face to this reference book. For the seventh edition, we showcase even more writers, representing a wider range of academic, civic, and professional projects and writing situations. These include the following:

- **NEW "ESL Tips" appear throughout Chapters 34, 35, and 36,** each offering advice from successful ESL writers on negotiating problematic areas of academic English. These chapters have also been revised to include more **discussion of rhetorical and cultural dimensions of college writing in the U.S.,** supplementing our coverage of grammatical and mechanical conventions.
- **A NEW section on writing centers in Chapter 8** introduces students to this important campus resource for improving their writing and gives advice on getting the most from a writing center consultation.

- **NEW student samples throughout the book, including an APA paper originally published in an undergraduate online research journal.** Also, to reinforce our emphasis on real-world writing, there are updated "Going Public" examples showing students engaged in public and community writing.

Updated and Expanded Research Coverage. No part of *The Scott Foresman Handbook* has been more widely admired (or imitated) than its chapters on research and documentation. As in previous editions, we provide everything instructors and writers need to prepare traditional academic research papers, as well as thorough guidelines for electronic, service-oriented, and community-oriented projects. In this edition, we have rearranged and enhanced this material so that it's even more user-friendly. Examples of this include the following:

- **Research coverage is regrouped into six smaller, more accessible chapters (46–51)** enabling students to locate this information easily at each stage of a project.
- **The NEW Chapter 52, "What Is Documentation?"** answers basic questions students often ask about documentation, explaining, for example, why most writing instructors teach MLA style and how MLA, APA, and CMS styles differ.

- All research and documentation material has been freshly updated, and a **NEW sample APA paper** appears in Chapter 54.

What's Familiar

A Respected, Proven Resource. Although we've made many revisions to this new edition, the most important features of *The Scott Foresman Handbook* haven't changed. The handbook retains its authoritative discussion of the writing process; its full coverage of critical thinking and reading, argumentation, and academic writing; its engaging and thorough treatment of grammar, mechanics, and usage; its lively discussion of research; and its exhaustive treatment of documentation. Because we teach undergraduate writing courses year after year, we know that student writers need accurate, current information. We've applied this knowledge in the creation of *The Scott Foresman Handbook*.

Serving Students Best. Since its first edition, *The Scott Foresman Handbook* has strived to serve students better and help them achieve their writing goals. With this in mind, each chapter is framed around the questions students commonly ask about writing, rather than presenting rules and terminology out of context. Our research materials have been carefully refined, edition after edition, and are clear, easy, and manageable. As in past editions, we continue to tackle thorny issues such as evaluating electronic sources, plagiarism, civil language, and, uniquely, grades. Perhaps most important, we continue to address student writers in language that is both personal and encouraging. We recognize that writing is hard work and that even a volume as thick as this one only begins to address the complexities writers face in sharing their ideas. We are committed to students' writing success.

Extending Beyond the Classroom. Our support for student writing extends beyond the classroom. *The Scott Foresman Handbook* provides support for writers moving from academic assignments to work in their local communities. In addition to **Chapter 9, "How Do You Write for the Public?"** the handbook emphasizes civic and public issues throughout, in the many "Going Public" examples, the **discussions of service-learning and online courses,** and the many sample **student papers focused on civic and public issues.** We want writers to know and believe that their "writing matters."

Supplements

Resources for Instructors

- **The Instructor's Resource Manual: Creating a Community of Writers** offers guidance to new and experienced instructors for teaching in the composition classroom. ISBN 013-182392-2

- **Answer Key** to the exercises within *The Scott Foresman Handbook, Seventh Edition.* ISBN 013-182390-6
- Our course management solutions, **Blackboard, Course Compass™,** and **WebCT** adapted for *The Scott Foresman Handbook, Seventh Edition,* provide extensive book-specific content including **the entire *The Scott Foresman Handbook* online as a searchable E-Book** as well as **online exercises for each chapter.** Access Code Cards for these course management solutions are available. VALUE PACK FREE with new copies of *The Scott Foresman Handbook, Seventh Edition.* Contact your Prentice Hall representative for complete information.
- **Prentice Hall Resources for Teaching Writing**—individual booklets covering some of the most effective approaches and important concerns of composition instructors today—are available to use with your students and teaching assistants. Contact your Prentice Hall representative for sample copies of the following:
  - **Distance Learning** by W. Dees Stallings. ISBN 013-088656-4
  - **Computers and Writing** by Dawn Rodriguez. ISBN 013-084034-3
  - **Classroom Strategies** by Wendy Bishop. ISBN 013-572355-8
  - **Portfolios** by Pat Belanoff. ISBN 013-572322-1
  - **Journals** by Christopher C. Burnham. ISBN 013-572348-5
  - **Collaborative Learning** by Harvey Kail and John Trimbur. ISBN 013-028487-4
  - **English as a Second Language** by Ruth Spack. ISBN 013-028559-5
  - **Teaching Writing Across the Curriculum** by Art Young. ISBN 013-081650-7

Resources for Students

- **Premium Companion Website™** at www.prenhall.com/hairston offers an **E-Book** available 24/7 that contains the entire *The Scott Foresman Handbook, Seventh Edition,* in a searchable format; a self-graded **diagnostic test** to assist students in identifying their specific problem areas and then in creating their individualized handbook, *My Handbook;* hundreds of **interactive exercises,** text-tied and self-graded; and **research and documentation information.**
- **Evaluating Online Sources with Research Navigator™** helps students make the most of their research time, offering help with the research process and three exclusive databases full of relevant and reliable source material, including EBSCO's **ContentSelect™**

Academic Journal Database, *The New York Times* Search-by-Subject Archive, and the *Best of the Web* Link Library. VALUE PACK FREE with *The Scott Foresman Handbook, Seventh Edition.* Visit www.researchnavigator. com to learn more.

- **The New American Webster Handy College Dictionary** or **The New American Roget's College Thesaurus in Dictionary Form** is available to VALUE PACK FREE with *The Scott Foresman Handbook, Seventh Edition.* Contact your Prentice Hall representative for ordering information.
- **A Writer's Guide to Research and Documentation** by Kirk G. Rasmussen features the most recent information on MLA, APA, CBE, and CM formats and covers the research process. VALUE PACK FREE with *The Scott Foresman Handbook, Seventh Edition.* ISBN 013-032641-0
- **A Writer's Guide to Writing in the Disciplines and Oral Presentations** by Christine Manion helps students write successfully in different academic disciplines, as well as offers advice and information on preparing oral presentations. VALUE PACK FREE with *The Scott Foresman Handbook, Seventh Edition.* ISBN 013-018931-6
- **A Writer's Guide to Document and Web Design** by Lory Hawkes offers students additional information on document and Web design. VALUE PACK FREE with *The Scott Foresman Handbook, Seventh Edition.* ISBN 013-018929-4
- **A Writer's Guide to Writing About Literature** by Edgar V. Roberts prepares students for writing about literature with information on research and literature, as well as additional sample student papers. VALUE PACK FREE with *The Scott Foresman Handbook, Seventh Edition.* ISBN 013-018932-4

Acknowledgments

Since a project of this size and scope is necessarily (and fortunately) a collaborative effort, we have many people to thank for their work on *The Scott Foresman Handbook.* First and foremost, we are grateful to the editorial staff at Prentice Hall, who have enthusiastically welcomed and supported this project. We thank Leah Jewell, Editor in Chief, for her guidance throughout the revision process and our Acquisitions Editors, Stacy Best Ruel and Corey Good, for their hard work and energetic support. Production manager Joan Foley patiently and efficiently coordinated the many changes we made for this edition. Art editor

Guy Ruggiero helped us to incorporate new images and graphic elements, and the eye-catching new cover was designed by Laura Gardner. Kathleen Karcher and Yvonne Gerin worked tirelessly to procure permissions for the text and images that appear throughout the book.

We owe a special debt to Jocelyn Steer and Carol Rhoades, who drafted the original ESL chapters that we've expanded and updated for this edition. Thanks also go to Dan Seward, who updated Chapters 23 and 24, drafted the new material on courseware that appears in Chapter 8, and created the streamlined new graphics that appear in Chapter 3. We could not have completed this edition nearly as quickly without the help of two talented research assistants, Lee Bauknight and R. Brian Wellborn, who searched for images, proofread drafts, and formatted manuscript. We thank Lee especially for helping to prepare the new material on literary devices in Chapter 14; we appreciate Brian's digital magic in enhancing several photographs. (No, he didn't make the authors look younger.) Thanks, too, to the student actors at Shakespeare at Winedale whose images appear at several places in the book.

We also extend our sincere thanks to the many students whose papers, projects, and photos appear throughout the book; we feel honored to publish their work. Finally, we thank all the instructors who have used *The Scott Foresman Handbook* throughout its many editions, especially those reviewers whose comments enable us to refine each new edition. We owe much to all of you: J. Robert Baker, Fairmont State College; Sue Beebe, Southwest Texas State University; Bill Bolin, Texas A&M University, Commerce; Andrew Burke, University of Georgia; Peggy Cheng, Southern Oregon University; John M. Clark, Bowling Green State University; John Coakley, New Jersey Institute of Technology; Deborah Core, Eastern Kentucky University; Lauren S. Coulter, University of Tennessee at Chattanooga; Aleta J. Crockett, Bluefield State College; Laurie Delaney, Kent State University; Dawn L. Elmore-McCrary, San Antonio College; April Fallon, Kentucky State University; Jim Frazer, University of Arkansas at Little Rock; Cassy Gilson, Broward Community College; Tami Haaland, Montana State University, Billings; Ashan Hampton, Morehouse College; Candy A. Henry, Penn State University, New Kensington; Mary Lynch Kennedy, State University of New York at Cortland; Judith Kerman, Saginaw Valley State University; Scott Orme, Spokane Community College; Jennifer Palmgren, University of Kansas; Pennie Pflueger, Louisiana State University; Susan Pratt, Concordia University, St. Paul; William Provost, University of Georgia; Dave Rieder, University of Texas at Arlington; David Sandell, University of Texas; Karah Stokes, Kentucky State University; Jennifer Turley, DeVry Institute of Technology; Pauline Uchmanowicz, State University of

New York at New Paltz; Ted Walkup, Clayton College and State University; Lori Watts, McLennan Community College; June West, Bates Technical College.

Writing Processes

CHAPTER 1

What Does Writing Involve?

1a Why write?

- Students at the University of Arizona designed and created Web sites for local nonprofit agencies as part of a business writing class.
- A first-year English student at Midlands Technical College regularly attends a community writers' group to get feedback on papers she's drafting for classes and poetry she writes for fun.
- An education major at Trinity University wrote a letter that alerted her employer to dangerous staffing shortages at the children's summer camp where she worked.
- A psychology major at the University of Oklahoma shared her research with professionals in her field when she presented a paper she had written at a statewide academic conference.

As these examples suggest, writing is not a mysterious activity at which only a talented few can succeed. Nor is it a purely academic skill that you will leave behind at graduation. On the contrary: in our

information-based society, almost everyone writes. Through writing, people share what they know, debate issues, promote their beliefs, and advocate change. Whether you are drafting a letter to your senator about student loan funding or posting an online notice to recruit players for your intramural volleyball team, writing gives you a public voice.

Writing is also a rich medium for intellectual inquiry. As the novelist E. M. Forster put it, "How do I know what I think until I see what I say?" Many people use writing to work through their ideas on an issue or to help organize complex material they learn in school or on the job.

The ability to write has become even more important with the explosion of electronic media during the past decade. People once could get along in school by writing papers that would be seen only by their teachers, or at work by writing an occasional memo to the boss. But today writers address wider audiences as part of a typical day's work. In school, you may communicate with classmates and instructors online—in fact, if you are taking distance education courses, email may be your primary mode of communication. At work, computerized conferencing software makes it easy to network with colleagues worldwide. Citizens now also have online access to many government agencies and archives.

Years ago, futurists predicted that computers would make writing obsolete. Now we know that new technologies have only expanded its possibilities. As you begin this handbook, then, don't approach it as a dusty collection of rules that you can forget at the end of the term. Instead, read it knowing that writing is a powerful medium for communication and for learning. Writing matters.

E-Tips To see more examples of student writing projects, go to <www.prenhall.com/hairston>.

1b What does it take to write well?

To take full advantage of the opportunities writing offers, you first need to *see* yourself as a writer. Many people underestimate their potential because they don't realize that writing is a skill that almost anyone can master.

Resist discouraging myths about writing. The following myths about writing have been around for a long time; don't let them fool you.

- **Myth:** *Good writers are born, not made.*
  Fact: People become good writers by working at it. If you want to write well, you can if you invest the time.
- **Myth:** *Good writers know what they want to say before they start writing.*
  Fact: Many good writers begin with only a general notion of what they want to say. They know that the process of writing can help them generate new ideas and rethink what they already know.
- **Myth:** *Good writers get it right the first time.*
  Fact: Although experienced writers sometimes produce polished work on the first try, they usually must work through several drafts.
- **Myth:** *Good writers work alone.*
  Fact: Writers often rely on colleagues for ideas and help, even if they do much of the actual composing alone. They may also co-author articles, reports, or essays.
- **Myth:** *Writing won't be important once you leave school.*
  Fact: Most people write every day, whether or not they are in school. Even professionals in technical fields like engineering, medicine, and computer science spend a significant portion of their time communicating their expertise through reports and proposals.
- **Myth:** *Writing means putting words on a page—nothing more.*
  Fact: Most writers do produce traditional written or printed texts, like letters or reports. However, composing documents like Web sites, brochures, or presentations often also means working with images, graphics, layouts, and other multimedia elements.
- **Myth:** *Only professional authors publish their work.*
  Fact: Now that computers make it easy to preserve and distribute documents, even the writing you do in school may reach large audiences via the Internet or campus publications.

EXERCISE 1.1 Make a list of everything you've written in the past three days. Then discuss these questions with your classmates: What activities in your everyday life require writing? What kinds of tasks do you accomplish through writing? With whom do you communicate when you write? Do you do most of your writing in or outside school?

EXERCISE 1.2 When you hear the term *writer,* what kind of person comes to mind? Many people reserve the terms *author* and *journalist* for those who make their living solely by writing. But can you think of other people who write frequently? What kinds of writing do they do? Discuss your answers with your classmates.

1c How does writing work?

It's tempting to believe that there's a secret formula for writing well and that if you could just discover it, your life would be much easier. Unfortunately, no such formula exists—there's no quick or foolproof way to turn an initial idea into a polished final text. However, researchers do agree that most people, when they write, follow general thinking patterns similar to those that occur in other creative activities. Chart 1.1 on page 6 outlines these general stages and describes some of the activities writers engage in during each.

Remember, though, that any formal diagram can only hint at what writers really do. Writing is a complex activity that involves rich and mutually reinforcing skills. A chart can't show nuances in the process or overlap among the various stages, nor can it differentiate among individual writers and varied writing situations. Some successful writers—like Justin Cone, whose paper draft appears at the end of Chapter 5—shift freely among the preparing, researching, planning, and revising stages as they work. Others, like Barbara Westbrook, whose work appears in Chapter 12, delay major revisions until they have a first draft. Still others—like Christy Friend, co-author of this book—revise as they go along. For complex projects, writers may need to repeat steps in the process several times.

Writers also adjust their approach to their purpose, their audience, and the specific demands of the project. Writing a 15-page term paper for a professor requires extensive planning and research; sending an email to ask your lab partner about an upcoming homework assignment may require very little. So don't think of the writing process as a lockstep march from outlining to proofreading. It's a dynamic, flexible network of choices that writers adapt to suit their needs.

Chart 1.1

Stages of Writing

- **Preparing:** Read, brainstorm, browse online, and talk to people in order to decide what you want to write about and to generate ideas about it.

- **Researching:** Gather facts or examples from reading, conversations with others, field research, or your own experiences to support your ideas.

✓ • **Planning:** Develop and organize your ideas further, perhaps preparing working lists, outlines, or note cards or sketching out visual elements.

- **Drafting:** Begin to put words (and images or other visual elements, if you're using them) onto a page or screen. Compose one or more drafts, rethinking and reshaping your materials as necessary.

- **Incubating:** Take time off to let your ideas simmer. New ideas may come to you after you've taken a break.

✓ • **Revising:** Critically review what you have written and make any large-scale changes you need in topic, organization, content, design, or audience adaptation.

- **Editing:** Critically review your draft to make smaller-scale changes in style, clarity, and readability.

- **Proofreading:** Read carefully to rid your project of mechanical problems such as spelling, punctuation, and formatting errors.

EXERCISE 1.3 Think back to a piece of writing you were proud of— perhaps a letter to the editor that was published, a personal statement that won you a scholarship, or an *A* paper in a difficult class—and write a paragraph describing the preparation you put into it, how many times you revised it, and why you think it was successful.

EXERCISE 1.4 Write a paragraph or two candidly describing your most hectic writing experience, when you were most pressed to get a project done. What did you have to do to finish the project? Was it successful? Why or why not? What, if anything, would you do differently if you had the chance to do it again?

1d How do you define a writing situation?

Writing is a *social activity,* a way of interacting with others. Every time you write, you enter into a *writing situation* in which

✓ • *You*
✓ • Say *something*
✓ • To *somebody*
✓ • For *some purpose.*

Experts on *rhetoric,* the art of persuasive communication, believe that people communicate more effectively when they think in these terms: *what* do I want to say, to *whom,* and *why?* Every time you write, you should think carefully about your purpose, your audience, and how you want to come across to your readers. Probably no other single habit will do more to help you become a skilled writer.

1e How do you define your purpose(s) for writing?

When you begin a writing project, consider why you are writing in the first place. Do you need to show an instructor that you've mastered a difficult concept or reading assignment? Do you have an idea you care about and want others to care about too? Is there an ongoing debate you wish to enter? We don't mean that every time you write you have to come up with an earth-shattering idea or that everything you write must aim at a serious and lofty goal. Nonetheless, having a general purpose in mind will help you to focus and to think about the kinds of supporting materials you will need.

1 Decide what you hope to accomplish. You will usually write more effectively if you think about your purpose ahead of time and use it to shape your first draft. Centuries ago, theorists of rhetoric identified three basic purposes for writing: writing *to inform,* or writing that teaches readers new information; writing *to persuade,* or writing that convinces readers to believe or act in new ways; and writing *to entertain,* writing that diverts and engages readers.

Often you may want to achieve more than one of these goals within a single paper. To review a restaurant for a campus magazine, for example, your primary aim might be to *evaluate* the food and service, but you would also want to *persuade* readers to visit or avoid the restaurant and perhaps to *entertain* them as well. See Section 3b for specific methods of organizing projects to suit particular purposes.

Thinking about these purposes isn't just an exercise; it's a practical matter. When you don't know why you're writing, you can't produce a coherent paper. If you find that you are starting a draft without any idea of your goals, you may need a clearer explanation of the task.

Sometimes you may not be completely sure of your purpose until you've explored the topic by writing a first draft. You may look into several angles on an idea before you figure out what you want to say. Eventually, though, even the most exploratory essay must articulate a purpose that satisfies both writer and readers. Checklist 1.1 will help you think about your writing goals.

Checklist 1.1

Purpose

1. If you are writing a paper for a course, list any description of purpose in the assignment. Target words like *narrate, explain, argue, evaluate.*

2. What do you want readers to get from your piece? Do you want to inform, persuade, or entertain? If you have multiple goals, which is the most important, and which are secondary?

3. What supporting materials will you draw on to achieve your goal(s)? What research, examples, or personal experiences will you use?

4. How will you present these supporting materials in your paper? Will you narrate, define, describe, compare and contrast, explain, or argue? Will you incorporate tables, images, or other visual elements?

5. What form will this project take? Will you write a letter, an editorial, a report, a Web page, or a review, for example? Where might you publish this piece?

2 Consider how other elements in the writing situation shape your purpose(s). Although we discuss each aspect of the writing situation separately in this chapter, in practice it's difficult to consider any of these elements in isolation. For any project, your purpose(s) will help you define your audience, the form in which you present your ideas, and the impression you want to make. Suppose, for example, that you are angry about a proposal to stop offering evening courses at your college. If you want to convince people that these courses should continue, you have a choice of audiences. Here is where your purpose becomes important.

If you want direct action, you need to write to the person in charge of scheduling courses—the campus registrar, for example. For this audience, your purpose might be to construct a calm, well-supported argument demonstrating the harmful effects of cancellation—potential graduation delays for working students who can attend class only in the evening, shrinking college enrollment if angry evening students transfer to other local colleges, and so on. If, however, you want to get fellow students to join your cause, you might draft and circulate a petition or publish a newspaper editorial condemning the proposed cancellation in more passionate terms.

1f   How do you write for an audience?

Suppose that you are concerned about the lack of after-school programs for children in your city.

- You write a research paper for a government course, documenting that such programs help prevent juvenile crime.
- The next week, your city council debates whether to enter into a partnership with the local YMCA to pilot an after-school program at a local elementary school. You compose a short statement supporting the project and present it during the town-hall portion of the meeting.
- Months later, as part of a volunteer team, you prepare a flyer to distribute to elementary school students, encouraging them to sign up for the YMCA program.

Although the topic and your viewpoint remain the same, your three pieces of writing will differ dramatically. The academic paper will use technical terminology, academic source materials, and a sophisticated organizational structure. The statement to the city council might draw on the same sources, but it will be shorter and it will argue a position more strongly. The children's flyer will rely on simple language and visual elements. All these differences represent *audience adaptations,* the ways in which a writer tailors a piece to appeal to readers' interests and needs.

Each time you write, you will have to think carefully about who your audience might be and how they will respond to the material you are writing about. Perhaps the examples above—the differences among writing for a college professor, a panel of city officials, and a group of fourth graders—make audience adaptation seem simple. It's not. Even seasoned writers sometimes misjudge their readers, offering material that baffles or bores them.

Sometimes writers have to contend with multiple and possibly conflicting audiences: men and women; young, middle-aged, and older people; liberals and conservatives; teacher and classmates. In other cases, identifying an audience at all seems nearly impossible. When you create a Web page, for example, literally anyone in the world who has access to the Internet might read it.

Don't let these complexities discourage you. Even though you cannot always pinpoint your readers or predict their responses, knowing even a few parameters will help you focus. Try the following two-step process.

1. **Analyze your audience.** Brainstorm a list of all the groups who are likely to read your work. Then, for each group, consider what knowledge, attitudes, and needs they are likely to bring to your piece.

2. **Tailor your work to respond to these characteristics.** With your audience in mind, decide how much background information you need to provide, whether you can use specialized terminology or visual elements, and whether readers will need to be persuaded to accept your ideas. Think about what kinds of examples and arguments might appeal to and what kinds might alienate them.

Learning how to appeal to an audience takes time and practice, but it is a skill that any writer can master. As you begin to think about your readers, consult Checklist 1.2 on audience. If within a single project you will reach several potential audiences, run through the checklist for each group. Then you'll need to reconcile the differences among those groups as you write—admittedly not an easy task. But at least you'll have a clearer understanding of the challenge.

Checklist 1.2

Audience

1. Does the assignment specify a particular audience? If so, describe that audience. If not, whom do you visualize as the audience(s) for this project?

2. What do they already know about your subject? What kinds of information will they need you to provide?

3. What values and beliefs are important to them? To what kinds of examples and arguments are they likely to respond?

4. What is their attitude about your subject? How will you convince them of the value of your ideas?

5. Will they feel most comfortable with a formal or more casual approach to the topic? What kind of formats, layouts, or visuals will they accept?

EXERCISE 1.5 Briefly analyze what you think readers would want to know if you were writing

1. a personal statement for a scholarship application.

2. a letter disputing a charge on your credit card account.

3. a description of an experiment you carried out for a chemistry class.

4. a flyer advertising a benefit performance by your best friend's blues band.

EXERCISE 1.6 Working with a classmate, look through a magazine—some possibilities are *Sports Illustrated, Spin, Harper's, Maxim, Money, Wired, Good Housekeeping, Source*—and study the advertisements and the kinds of articles it carries. Then draft a description of the kinds of people you think the editor and publisher of the magazine assume its readers to be. Use Checklist 1.2 on page 10 to guide your work.

1g How do you present yourself to readers?

Just as important as audience and purpose is the impression you make on your readers. Readers respond most favorably when they trust and respect the person sending the message. This is why we see Olympic athletes pitching athletic shoes on television and successful entrepreneurs selling books about investment strategies. But presenting an

The justices of the Supreme Court strive to present an image that is trustworthy and credible.

effective image isn't just about "selling" something. It's also about showing readers that you are a person whose ideas are worth listening to.

1 Show readers that you are credible. Would you take driving lessons from someone whose license has been revoked? Or let someone with no computer training replace your hard drive? Of course not. It's a question of credibility, of having enough knowledge about or experience with the topic to be believable. Readers expect you to show that you know what you are talking about before they will give your ideas serious consideration.

One way to achieve credibility is to learn everything you can about a topic before you begin writing. Do your homework. Find out who the authorities are on your subject and become familiar with their work. Browse through background sources to get a sense of key terminology, concepts, and ongoing debates about the subject. Once you have this knowledge, you will be able to write with confidence—and you will project this confidence to readers. See Chapters 47 and 48 for more on researching a topic.

Your personal experiences can also build credibility. If you are writing about U.S. immigration policy, for example, don't hesitate to share your own experience—perhaps, for example, your family came to this country from Taiwan. Even though your experience doesn't make you an authority on every aspect of the subject, it gives you knowledge that is richer and in some ways more powerful than what you can learn from books. Of course, there are forums—such as scientific writing—in which personal expression is generally inappropriate. But when the assignment allows it, readers will respect your close involvement with a topic.

Finally, to win readers' respect, you must come across as a professional. Use an appropriate format, edit carefully, and proofread thoroughly to show your audience that you are serious about your work.

Checklist 1.3 will help you to credibly present yourself to readers.

Checklist 1.3

Presenting Yourself to Readers

1. How can you show readers that you are knowledgeable about your subject? What research, reading, or personal experience will you draw upon?
2. How will you show readers that you are trustworthy? What will you do to present information accurately and fully?
3. How will you show readers that you are reasonable and fair? What tone will you adopt, and how will you talk about opposing views?

2 Present material fairly and honestly. Some television commercials make grand claims about a product or denigrate competitors without sufficient supporting evidence. If you're like most people, this kind of dishonesty turns you off.

Readers believe writers whom they perceive as trustworthy, so you'll need to present material accurately and fairly in a paper. Base your arguments on reputable sources, and be open about any gaps or limitations in what you know. Suppose you're writing a paper arguing that day care negatively affects young children. You will need to acknowledge that some studies indicate that day care is not especially harmful. Otherwise, readers who have heard of such studies may think that you are trying to hide something.

You will also need to cite the sources of your information, to show that the materials you've consulted are reliable and authoritative. When readers see that you treat your subject honestly, they'll be more open to your ideas. See Chapters 49 and 50 for more about evaluating and documenting sources.

3 Use a civil tone. Being polite to those who disagree with you may seem a bit naive given the hostile tone of much public discussion in our society. It sometimes seems that the more outrageous the statement, the more attention it gets, and you may be tempted to follow this trend in your writing. Don't be fooled—the loudest voices aren't always the ones that people end up listening to.

When animal rights activists deride meat eaters as "murderers" or yell obscenities at medical researchers whose experiments involve animals, they offend far more of their audience than they convince. When a radio talk-show host jokes about shooting a politician whose views annoy him, more listeners are disgusted than impressed. Readers don't want to identify with a bully. They will resist your ideas if you come across as mean-spirited.

You will project a more credible image when you treat different viewpoints fairly and generously. It's fine to disagree strongly with another's ideas; without vigorous disagreement, neither democracy nor intellectual exchange can thrive. But confine your criticism to the issues rather than attack your opponent's worth as a human being. Avoid name-calling ("idiot," "religious right fanatic," "tax-and-spend liberal"), inflammatory language (calling a viewpoint "evil," "stupid," "un-American"), and ethnic or gender stereotypes. Not only will you sound more professional, but your fairness will lay the groundwork for ongoing conversation with readers who hold different views.

1g
image

See Section 18e for more on avoiding bias in your language and Section 11b for spotting bias in graphic and visual elements of a document. For advice on addressing opposing views, see Section 12c.

EXERCISE 1.7 Writers of political advertisements are especially sensitive to the importance of creating a positive image for their candidates. Obtain copies of campaign advertisements and literature from a recent election, or look up an elected official's home page on the Internet. Then, working with a group of classmates, discuss how successfully the politician presents himself or herself as credible, honest, and likable. Circle words, phrases, and details that suggest these qualities. Are you persuaded by this image?

EXERCISE 1.8 Select a subject that you know a lot about, and imagine that you have been asked to write about it for several different venues: a college research paper, a televised public-service announcement, and a letter for the editorial page of a local newspaper. How would each element of the writing situation—your purpose, your audience, and the image you want to project as a writer—affect the written product? Which task appeals to you the most? Discuss your responses with your classmates.

CHAPTER 2

How Do You Find and Explore a Topic?

2a How do you find a topic?

Sometimes you will start a writing project knowing exactly what you want to write about. When you don't have to find your topic, you can begin immediately to generate ideas, plan, and start a draft.

Often, however, college instructors encourage students to choose their own topics, believing that students write better when they can investigate subjects that interest them. "Having a choice is great," you may say, "but how do I find a topic that both my readers and I will enjoy?"

■ **1 Think beyond broad, traditional topics.** Too often students think that they should always write about issues of earthshaking importance. Does this list look familiar?

Abortion	Gun Control	Euthanasia
Terrorism	Capital Punishment	Pollution

These issues *are* important. And if you feel passionately enough about one of them to do the research that will add something current, fresh, or informative to the debate on that issue, don't shy away from it. However, be aware that because so much has already been written about these issues, you risk bogging down in generalities and clichés. Tired old material won't impress readers, no matter how serious its subject.

If you do choose one of these broad topics, make your paper unique by focusing on a recent controversy or a local case. Rather than write a general paper on terrorism, you might concentrate on the controversy surrounding ethnic profiling as a law enforcement tool. Similarly, while a generic paper on capital punishment would probably rehash arguments that are decades old, one that investigates a local death penalty case might yield new insights. Checklist 2.1 can help you find original angles on a traditional issue.

Checklist 2.1

To Find a Topic, Ask Yourself . . .

- **What three subjects do you enjoy reading about most?** What magazines do you pick up? What kinds of books do you browse through? Which newspaper headlines catch your eye?

- **What three subjects do you know the most about?** What topics could you discuss for half an hour without notes? What problems lead people to seek your advice or expertise? What could you teach someone else to do?

- **What three subjects are you most curious about?** What issues or subjects have you always wanted to learn more about, but never had the time? On what topics would you like to become an expert?

- **What three subjects do you enjoy arguing about most?** On what subjects can you hold your own with just about anyone? What opinions do you advocate most strongly?

- **What three issues in your community do you care about the most?** What issues affect you or people you know? For what causes do you volunteer? What opinions and ideas would you like to communicate to government officials or to the community at large?

2 Consider your interests and strengths. When you have to invest as much energy in a task as you do in a writing project, be good to yourself. Choose a topic that interests you, preferably one that you already have some knowledge and ideas about. Begin by brainstorming a list of possibilities: current issues on campus or in your neighborhood, activities you enjoy, experiences you've had, or subjects that have always made you curious. Look over your list and select one or two ideas that seem best suited for the assignment and the amount of time you have to complete the project. Checklist 2.1, shown above, will help you discover such topics.

James Prosek turned his interests in painting and fishing into a writing career. His first book, Trout: An Illustrated History *(1996), was published while he was an undergraduate at Yale.*

3 Choose a topic in your world. You may be used to heading straight for the library or the Internet when you receive a paper assignment. But some of the best issues for writing are unfolding right in front of you. Perhaps your local school board is debating whether to require uniforms in city high schools, or maybe you're concerned about increased gang activity in your grandparents' neighborhood.

Even if your instructor has assigned a general topic, try to connect that topic to your own experience or to issues in your community. For example, an assignment to research the civil rights movement for your history class could lead you to inquire about local concerns: Was your school or community ever segregated? How did your city or town react to civil rights initiatives or legislation? Do contemporary concerns for women's or gay rights have roots in this earlier political movement?

Any one of these issues could make a promising paper topic. Because such topics connect to your everyday life, you're bound to have a strong interest in finding out more about them. Additionally, when you concentrate on local events, you are more likely to do original research; expert sources of information—newspapers, community organizations, government offices, and interested citizens—are close at hand. And should you decide to publish your writing outside the classroom, perhaps as a guest newspaper editorial or as a letter to an elected official, you may even influence public opinion on your topic.

4 Browse in the library. If you have a general subject area in mind, try looking it up in the library catalog or in the directory of the Library of Congress (better known as the *Subject List*). Just the way a broad subject is broken down into headings and subheadings should suggest many topic possibilities. Consult such reference sources as specialized encyclopedias, too. If you want to learn about endangered animal species in your state, for example, a glance at the *Encyclopedia of the Environment* might provide several topic ideas.

Even when you don't have a general subject area to direct your library search, try browsing in the periodicals room or the new book section for topics that spark your curiosity. For more on finding library sources, see Chapter 47.

E-Tips   Now that most college libraries have put some or all of their card catalogs and reference databases online, you can browse the library without leaving your desk. Visit your college or university's Web site to find out how to access your library's resources.

■ **5 Look for ideas online.** In addition to the library materials your school offers online, the Internet houses many resources for writing. If you have a general subject in mind, look for newsgroups to see what others are saying about it. Usenet newsgroups exist for almost every conceivable topic, and they are convenient places to browse because they are open to everyone.

Listservs are more difficult to browse because you have to subscribe to a list in order to participate in its discussions. However, some listservs maintain archives of past exchanges that are open to anyone; these can be excellent resources.

You can usually access newsgroups from your Web browser and explore them with a search engine. See <http://www.liszt.com> for a directory of electronic mailing lists, newsgroups, and IRC chat groups. To search Usenet groups, try <http://groups.google.com>.

To explore a wider variety of materials, conduct an Internet search. A keyword search on a subject that interests you will elicit a wealth of diverse and interesting material. But be forewarned: it may also call up materials you find irrelevant or distracting. And because it's so easy to link from one site to another, you may spend hours following an unproductive trail of associations. To ensure that you don't lose valuable information, save bibliographic information for any useful sources you encounter on the Internet. For more advice on using online resources, see Chapter 47.

E-Tips
A powerful way to search for topic ideas is to use a Web search engine that is arranged by categories, such as *Yahoo* <www.yahoo.com>, *Google* <www.google.com>, or *Lycos* <www.lycos.com>. The groupings themselves offer a range of general topic areas ("Arts & Humanities," "Health," "Science"), but the topics get more intriguing when you explore them more deeply, especially *Yahoo*'s "Society and Culture." Check out "Issues and Causes" at <http://dir.yahoo.com/Society_and_Culture/Issues_and_Causes/>.

2b How do you refine your topic?

Once you have found a promising topic, you'll probably need to narrow it down. If you don't focus your efforts, you may end up writing a superficial paper of little interest to anyone, no matter how promising your initial subject seemed to be. Problems of focus happen when writers try to cover more material than they can within the parameters of their project—for example, attempting to present a history of the feminist movement in a short course paper, or a summary of current tax policy in a letter to the editor. This kind of overreaching can result in a project long on generalities but short on lively details and thoroughly developed ideas.

1 Don't try to cover everything. You may be excited about your subject and eager to learn more about it. But remember that your time to develop a project is usually limited. You can't discover all there is to know about a topic such as single parenthood in a few weeks. Even if you could, you wouldn't be able to fit all that material into one paper. It's better to narrow your research to something more manageable, perhaps the difficulties involved in being an unmarried teenage father. Better yet, focus on whether providing counseling and parent-education classes can help single fathers stay more involved in their children's lives.

Does that kind of topic reduction seem too drastic? It's probably not, especially when you consider that any paper you write should contain only a portion of what you know about its subject.

2 Make a tree diagram. One way to narrow a topic to manageable size is to draw a tree diagram. To do this, make a chart on which you divide and subdivide the topic into smaller and smaller parts, each of which branches out like an inverted tree. The upside-down tree helps you see many potential areas within each division as well as the relationships among them.

Refining your writing is like using a spotlight; it puts the focus on a smaller area, allowing you to concentrate on the details.

Suppose you've become interested in writing about college student debt after watching your roommate run up several thousand dollars in credit-card bills during a single semester. Your tree diagram exploring this topic might look something like this:

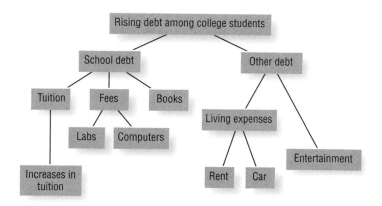

Now select the most promising branch from your first diagram and make a new diagram to refine that idea further.

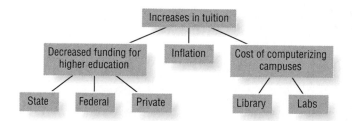

3 Make an idea map. Another way to narrow a topic is to look within the subject for patterns of related ideas worth exploring. Making an idea map is an easy way to do this. In the middle of a blank sheet of paper, write down a phrase that describes your general subject. Circle that term—say, *college expenses*—and then, for about ten minutes, attach every word you can think of either to that original term or to others that you have linked to it. Circle all those additional words as you write them, and draw lines connecting them to the words that triggered them.

Your finished map might look something like the one on page 21. When you're done, examine the map to see whether any clusters of words suggest topics you might develop. For example, one group of ideas (tuition—increases—state funding cuts—fees—student loans)

suggests a paper about government funding for higher education. Another (credit cards— "student card" promotions—spring break trip—football weekends—clubbing) might lead you to explore the kinds of luxuries that easy credit allows students to purchase. As with tree diagrams, you can use any promising concept from your first idea map as the focal point of a second exercise, starting again with the narrowed subject to develop more ideas.

(4) Investigate an interesting question or hypothesis.

Another way to narrow a topic is to pursue an interesting problem involving your topic for which you do not yet have a satisfactory answer—much as investigative reporters look for "leads" that will turn into breaking news stories.

Sometimes a promising issue will take the form of a question. Reading a headline about decreased national crime rates, for example, might spur you to ask this question.

QUESTION   Why is violent crime increasing among juveniles at a
            time when the overall crime rate is decreasing?

Rather than ask an open-ended question, some writers prefer to start a project with a hypothesis, a statement that makes a tentative claim to be tested in a paper. Scientists often begin research projects with these kinds of educated guesses. Here is an initial hypothesis on the topic of juvenile violence.

> HYPOTHESIS   Despite a drop in the overall crime rate, violence among juveniles is increasing because of the harmful influence of television.

A guiding question or hypothesis will usually help you focus your topic. But at this stage it is probably too early to commit to a definite position. Until the evidence comes in and you have more information, remain flexible in your thinking and be willing to revise your focus and approach.

How can you find a promising question or hypothesis to focus on? In your preliminary reading and discussion about the topic, look for clues.

- Titles and focal points of published pieces on the topic
- Names of important people, experts, events, or institutions related to the topic
- Issues or questions that come up repeatedly
- Issues about which people disagree

5 State a tentative goal. If you are working on a topic that you understand well, or are engaged in an informational or service-learning project for which you already know the purpose or goal, you might compose a brief mission statement. Here is an example.

> **Goal:** This Web site will create an environment in which users can interact with proposals for the new city veterans' monument, thus helping to shape its design, its function, and associated community outreach programs.

Remember, though, that even when you begin a paper with a well-established goal, you should be prepared to shift your focus as your knowledge about the topic and the writing situation grows.

EXERCISE 2.1 Suppose you want to write a short paper for a composition course on one of the following subjects. Write down several promising subtopics that you might focus on; then use a tree diagram or an idea map to generate ideas about the subtopic that you find most interesting.

> Preventing terrorism
> Crime on college campuses
> Illegal drug use
> "Reality" television

EXERCISE 2.2 Obtain a copy of today's editorial page from your local or campus newspaper. Working with a group of your classmates, identify the topic of each piece. Then answer these questions: How broad is the writer's topic? How do you think the writer decided on that focus? How adequately does he or she cover the topic?

2c How do you explore and develop a topic?

You have a topic. What's the next step? Now you need to push your idea further by exploring its implications, finding supporting evidence, and filling in specific details. Since classical times rhetoricians have looked for ways to stimulate this kind of thinking. They came up with the term *invention* to describe the techniques writers use to generate subject matter for a paper.

This section explains invention techniques that can help you explore and develop a thesis. You can use any of these techniques at any point in your writing process. Although it's logical to review them before starting a draft, you may want to return to them while writing or revising—anytime you need to expand and develop your ideas.

1 Freewrite about the topic. Freewriting is writing nonstop for ten or fifteen minutes on a topic in order to explore what you already know and to discover areas you'd like to learn more about. Don't worry about grammar, spelling, or other niceties while you're freewriting—the point of freewriting is to generate ideas. Continue to write as long as ideas come, and don't cross out or reject anything prematurely. But be alert for phrases and concepts that extend your thesis in promising directions.

Here is a sample from a freewrite that Justin Cone did before writing the paper that appears in Section 5d. Note that he has not always capitalized, that he doesn't always write complete sentences, and that his style is very informal. But note also how many ideas even this short excerpt articulates.

> I want to write about the Internet. that is, is it a threat to our society? . . . I mean, why books when you can have full-color, action packed, digital sound, excitement at the click of the button? why take part in the painstakingly slow process of reading when there are so many other quicker ways to gather information, the nightly news for instance? there are answers to these whys, but what? get

back to that later. the point is, new media technology is far more appealing to society than books. and as technology grows, books as we know them today would logically die out. actually I don't believe that books will ever die out, they will merely switch, people will read books for different reasons. . . .

2 Use the journalist's questions. Beginning journalists are taught to keep six questions in mind when writing a news story.

Who?   What?   Where?
When?   Why?   How?

Simple as they seem, these questions can help you be sure you have covered all the bases, especially when you are writing an informative paper (though not every question will apply to every topic).

3 Look at your topic from different perspectives. One way to do this is to consider some frameworks people have traditionally used to organize and generate ideas. Among the oldest are the four categories of questions that classical rhetoricians used to explore topics: questions of *fact, definition, value,* and *policy.* Originally designed to develop speeches for the law courts of ancient Greece and Rome, these questions move from simple to more complex ways of examining an issue.

- Questions of **fact** involve things already known about your topic: What has already happened? What factual information is already available? What policies are already in place?
- Questions of **definition** interpret these facts and place them in a larger context: What category does your topic fit into? What laws or approaches apply?
- Questions of **value** ask you to make a judgment: Is the idea you're talking about a good thing or a bad thing? Is it ethical or unethical? Workable or unworkable?
- Questions of **policy** allow you to consider specific courses of action: What exactly should be done in response to the issue? Are old solutions working, or is a new approach needed?

You won't be able to answer all these questions in a single paper, but they are useful for comprehensively examining a topic. Here, for example, are ways a writer might use these questions to find material for a paper on whether the fashion industry's use of thin models in advertising indirectly encourages eating disorders among young women. Once you've run through all the questions, decide which one(s) you want to treat most fully in your paper. For example, an editorial on this topic might focus on the definitional question "How does our culture define 'beauty'?" A report, however, might gather information that answers the factual question "How many fashion ads feature unusually thin models?" For more on how these questions can help you construct a thesis statement, see Section 51a.

HIGHLIGHT *Looking at a Topic from Different Perspectives: Fashion and Body Image Among Young Women*

- **Questions about the facts:** To what extent do young women draw their beauty ideals from fashion ads? How many fashion ads feature unusually thin models? How many young women have eating disorders?

- **Questions about key definitions:** How docs our culture define "beauty"? How preoccupied with thinness must one be to be defined as having an "eating disorder"?

- **Questions about values:** Is it ethical for fashion designers to display their clothes on models who are much thinner than most women can ever be? Is it sensible for the industry to produce clothing that doesn't look good on most people? Does the artistic value of fashion trends outweigh any harmful social effects they may cause?

- **Questions about policy:** What could the fashion industry do to promote a healthier ideal of beauty? How might young women be discouraged from trying to look like models?

---

4 Write a zero draft. You may find that your best device for generating material is just to start a draft. The very act of writing will often get the creative juices flowing and help you to organize your thoughts. Think of this first try as a "zero draft," a trial run that doesn't really count. Zero drafts are easy to write, and after they're complete, you can select the best material to use in your next draft. Some experts suggest writing several zero drafts to try out several possible approaches to a project.

5 Read up on your topic. No one ever said you have to come up with all your ideas on your own. Get to the library or get on the Internet, look up your subject, and read. You'll find detailed instructions on doing library research in Section 47a.

But don't read just to find facts; read to discover how other writers have treated topics like yours. Perhaps you want to write about a bicycle trip you took across the American Northwest. Look up some travel literature. Your eyes may be opened by the sheer variety of approaches available to record your adventures, everything from serious field accounts written by anthropologists to the rollicking narratives in travel magazines. The same might be true if you're writing a review of a book or a movie. Seeing how others have reviewed works for different kinds of publications will suggest possibilities for your own review.

■ 6 Talk to others about your topic. From the start, invite others to join in exploring your topic. Look for campus events, clubs, or forums that might be connected to the subject. Check the local papers for information about lectures, films, or community meetings where you might meet people interested in your work. And when you find such people, network with them to find more people and organizations tied to your subject.

Online newsgroups and listservs offer instant access to an even wider network of contacts. Once you have a good sense of the issues you want to write about, consider posting to one of these forums a short description of your project and a request for input. You may get valuable suggestions from experts in the field that will guide your reading and research. However, at this stage in your work, you must be cautious about online exchanges: most are unmonitored, so the accuracy and quality of information will vary. You should also be careful to observe the etiquette appropriate to online forums. See Section 47c-2 for more on entering online discussions.

Classmates are another useful resource. In many writing classes, the instructor arranges for groups of students to meet before they start work on a project so they can help each other generate ideas. Even if there's no standing arrangement, you can talk informally or exchange email with classmates who share an interest in your topic. Even if you haven't decided exactly what your paper will cover, you'll find that as you start to explain your ideas to others, more ideas will come to you. You may see arguments you hadn't considered and learn about new examples or sources.

EXERCISE 2.3 Use any two of the techniques described in this section to generate ideas about one of your writing projects in progress. Then discuss your experience with your classmates: Which strategy yielded the best ideas? Which are you likely to use again as a regular part of your writing process?

EXERCISE 2.4 Choose a controversy currently under debate in your neighborhood, campus, or city. (If no ideas come to mind, consult a local or campus newspaper.) Use the four categories outlined on page 24 to identify questions about facts, definitions, values, and policies regarding that issue. Which questions generate the most disagreement? Which have already been settled? Which ones could provide the focus for an interesting paper? Discuss your responses with your classmates.

2d
topic

2d How do you write a topic proposal?

Occasionally an instructor may ask you to write a preliminary proposal defining your topic and analyzing the writing situation for a course paper. Even when it's not assigned, such a proposal can help you refine your ideas about your topic, audience, purpose, and tone early so that your decisions can guide your research and shape your first draft.

When your instructor asks you to write a topic proposal, you should typically include the following elements. Also be sure to check with your instructor to find out if he or she has additional requirements.

Checklist 2.2

Writing a Topic Proposal

1. Identify your topic.
2. Articulate a working thesis statement, research question, hypothesis, or key issue that you plan to focus on in the project (see Section 2a).
3. Indicate what kinds of research you plan to do and what supporting materials you will use (see Section 7a).
4. Offer a brief analysis of your writing situation (see Section 1d).

Going Public *A Topic Proposal* ————————————————

In the following sample proposal, first-year composition student Justin Cone describes his goals for the paper shown in draft form on pages 79–84. The assignment asked him to write a research paper explaining and exploring a current controversy for the instructor and the class. Cone begins his proposal by explaining his topic and purpose, and then he identifies his audience. He ends by considering the kind of impression he wants to make on readers.

Note that while he has done a lot of thinking about his topic, at this point in the process Cone is still refining and developing his ideas. He hasn't yet formulated a definite thesis statement or identified specific research materials—and his language is less formal than his instructor will expect to see in the finished paper.

Justin Cone

Topic Proposal

          Where Exactly Are We Surfing To?

          The Information Superhighway. The Net. The

World Wide Web. Cyberspace. These are the buzzwords

of the fastest growing technological craze since

floppy disks. Yet although an estimated 30 million

users of the Internet can wield these words

skillfully, a question remains unanswered: What *value*

does this new technology possess? How can society

benefit from the cyber-revolution? How can individuals

benefit? Is there something good for everyone on the

Internet? Or is it a quick, cheap substitute for real

knowledge? Is it bad that my peers would rather surf

the Net than read classic novels?

          In an attempt to speak above the growing

chatter of keyboards across the planet, I hope to

find some answers to these questions. Although I

will do library and online research, I can also draw

on my own personal experience here. I was born into

this age of information. My mother admits to

plopping me down in front of a computer game while

she did laundry; I grew up teaching myself to

program in BASIC and trading lingo with computer

store clerks like I was Bill Gates.

My audience will be my classmates, who, like me and the rest of our generation, have been shaped by media technology. By drawing on our common experience, I hope to write a paper that will engage their interest and make them look closely at our lifestyle—without coming across as moralistic.

CHAPTER **3**

How Do You Focus and Organize a Writing Project?

Now you have an interesting, workable topic for your writing project. You've thought about it carefully, talked with others about it, and gathered a satisfyingly rich collection of information about it. What's next? It's time to sort through these raw materials and make some decisions about the direction your paper will take.

This chapter offers strategies to guide you from the invention stage through the planning and organizing stages of a paper, so that when you sit down to write that first draft, you can do so with purpose and confidence.

3a How do you craft a thesis?

As you explore your topic, you will likely discover one or two issues that you know you want your paper to focus on. These issues will shape your *thesis statement.* A *thesis* is a sentence (or sometimes two or three sentences) that explicitly identifies the point of a paper. Depending on the project, it may be a conclusion you draw as a result of doing research, your answer to a puzzling question about your topic, or a claim you will spend the rest of the paper explaining or supporting.

Many writers like to construct a tentative thesis statement early in their writing process and use it as a framework for organizing their first draft. By keeping your tentative thesis in mind, you can be sure of covering all the important points. This section will help you develop a solid thesis and incorporate it effectively into your paper.

1 Make a strong point. A thesis statement is more than just an observation; it is a statement that might be questioned or challenged. This means that your thesis should not be so obvious that most readers already agree with it ("Domestic violence harms families"), so wishy-washy that readers can't tell where you stand ("There are many strengths and weaknesses in our town's current zoning law"), or so subjective that you can't cite credible evidence to support it ("My child is the most beautiful child in his preschool"). Rather, it should offer a clearly stated analysis, critique, or position on your topic that readers will find new and significant.

When you construct a thesis, ask yourself whether an intelligent member of your audience might respond to it with a hostile "So what's your point?" or a disappointed "Big deal!" If you suspect he or she might, look for a more significant idea or sharpen the point you intend to make. The following examples illustrate the difference.

BORING   Brought to Boston as a slave in 1761, Phillis Wheatley would become the first African-American woman recognized for her poetry. So what's your point? What makes this fact interesting?

BETTER   Because Phillis Wheatley was the first African-American woman to achieve fame as a poet, it is surprising that her work contains so few references to slavery and racial injustice.

BORING   Boxing is one of the most dangerous sports. Everyone knows that. What's new?

BETTER   Because professional boxers often sustain severe injuries or brain damage in the ring, the sport should be subject to stricter safety regulations.

In argument papers, the thesis statement often makes a *claim* that the rest of the paper is devoted to supporting. For more on claims, see Sections 12a and 12b. Checklist 3.1 contains guidelines for constructing a strong thesis.

Checklist 3.1

What Makes a Strong Thesis?

- Does it focus on a **substantive issue,** one that deserves readers' attention?

- Is the thesis **debatable**—could reasonable people disagree with it?

- Does it address an issue that affects the public? Is the issue **current**? **Will readers care** about this thesis?

- Is your thesis **clearly stated**? Can readers tell where you stand?

- Can you **support** your thesis adequately, using research or your own experiences? Do you need to narrow or qualify your claim?

■ **2 Sharpen your focus.** For many writers, developing a manageable thesis is a challenge. Especially when you are exploring a broad or complicated topic, it may be tempting to settle for a thesis statement that breaks a sprawling subject into several parts rather than present a focused idea. Take these examples.

> SPRAWLING   Child abuse is a serious problem with three major aspects: causes, detection, and prevention.
>
> SPRAWLING   Among the most commonly prescribed medications in the United States are antidepressant, weight-loss, and behavior-altering drugs.

Broad categories like these can, in fact, work well if you *need* to divide an issue into basic components—as you might when designing a home page on the Internet. The home page introducing a Web site on child abuse might quite logically link to additional pages that separately explore causes, detection, and prevention. The simplicity of the design would help to make the site user-friendly and coherent.

But for projects that require more extensive development and discussion of ideas, like an academic research paper or an argumentative piece, such a thesis might seem more like a shopping list than a compelling claim. Broad statements like these deaden the argument by preventing readers (and writers too) from examining underlying concepts fully, whereas a more sharply focused thesis allows for extended examination of an issue.

> FOCUSED   Since most citizens know little about how to respond appropriately when they suspect someone of abusing a child, better public education in this area could significantly reduce child abuse.
>
> FOCUSED   Doctors are increasingly willing to prescribe antidepressant drugs to populations other than the clinically depressed, including people who undergo minor mood swings. This trend raises troubling questions about whether normal levels of unhappiness have become unacceptable in our culture.

One way to avoid an unmanageably broad thesis is to limit it to one or two of the most urgent questions connected to your topic. In your reading and conversations, look for issues that demand strong evidence from you but that also encourage readers to rethink their ideas about the topic. For general advice on narrowing your topic, see Section 2b. For help finding compelling research questions related to your topic, see Chapter 46.

Checklist 3.1 on page 31 offers guidelines for constructing a strong thesis statement.

3 Preview the direction your paper will take. Write a complete sentence or two that forecasts in some detail the ideas you expect to write about, in roughly the same order in which you plan to address them. Your thesis sentence(s) should be *succinct* yet *comprehensive*—that is, it should be short yet indicate the major points you want to make. Suppose you are writing an article for the pre-law student newsletter on your campus. This thesis tells readers what to expect:

> When you start looking for that summer job or
> internship, you need to think beyond high pay and
> congenial working companions and seek out jobs where
> you can learn something about the law.

4 Place your thesis effectively. Don't assume that your thesis must be the first sentence of your paper, although it can be. Your decision about where to put your thesis depends on the writing situation: your audience, your purpose, and the position you want to take on the topic.

When you are presenting information or arguments in a straightforward, no-nonsense fashion—as you should in an essay examination or a business letter—you'll want to state your thesis early. It may even be your first sentence. At other times you'll need to provide a context for your thesis, by defining key terms or giving background information. That's why, in academic papers, the thesis statement often appears at the end of the introductory paragraph.

In other situations, you may want to delay your thesis even more. You may be writing to explore a question rather than to present a settled opinion on it. Or, if your thesis is controversial, you may want to present your evidence first, then lead readers gradually to your point. In the social sciences, writers often begin research reports by describing their methods and data and end with their larger conclusions. In such cases, your thesis may not be stated until the last paragraph.

Remember, though, that a delayed thesis doesn't give you license to write an unfocused paper. Even if you don't clarify your specific claim until late in the essay, readers should understand what central ideas your paper will address from its very beginning, or they won't be able to follow your discussion.

Suppose you interviewed a group of children about their television viewing habits for a communications course. Your introductory paragraph might contain a framing statement like this.

> My interviews with 22 second graders explored this question: Do children really like the kinds of programs that the networks and the general public assume are their favorites?

This question sets the stage for a more developed thesis statement later in the paper, one that might look something like this:

> My data indicate that these children gravitate toward educational and family-oriented programming rather than the violent cartoons that many people assume children like—a finding that has important implications for parents and the television networks.

5 Revise your thesis as your project evolves. Don't be surprised if your thesis shifts as you continue to explore, research, and plan your project. Most writers will revise their working thesis statement to make it more precise or to reflect changes in the paper's direction. Don't worry about such changes. This is the time when you should be testing your preliminary assumptions and ideas so that your final paper will be stronger. Learn from every part of the process, and don't be discouraged easily. Your final thesis may be nothing like what you imagined at the outset—and that's okay.

EXERCISE 3.1 Review the guidelines for an effective thesis, and then rate the following thesis statements as "good," "not too bad," or "needs a lot of work." Revise the statements that don't merit a "good" rating to make them stronger.

1. In trying to promote meaningful campaign finance reform, organizations like Common Cause run into opposition from lobbyists, major companies, the news media, and, most of all, the candidates themselves.

2. Scientists will soon possess enough information about genes to cure virtually all diseases.

3. Recent films like *Spider-Man* and *Men in Black II* show that today's action movies rely more than ever on high-tech special effects.

4. Some drivers are too dangerous to be allowed on the road.

Going Public   *An Opening Paragraph with Thesis* _____

Sometimes a thesis statement pulled out of context, like the previous examples in this chapter, can seem pretty bland. Fortunately, in a real paper, a thesis isn't solely responsible for shaping a reader's first impression. The sentences that surround it also play an important part. In this opening paragraph for a course paper, Justin Cone uses personal experiences to set his thesis into context and to spark his instructor's and classmates' interest in his topic. Cone's thesis is highlighted. See pages 79–83 for a finished draft of this paper.

> Technology's Children: Has Media Technology
> Intellectually Stunted Our Generation?
>
> I was the 5-year-old learning ABCs from Kermit
> the Frog. I was the 7-year-old programming in BASIC at
> 5:30 in the morning, just before Bugs Bunny aired. I
> was the 10-year-old successfully installing a modem,
> sans instructions. But I was also the 16-year-old who
> couldn't finish reading Thomas Hardy's Tess of the
> D'Urbervilles for junior English because I didn't have
> the mental stamina to read anything longer than a
> computer screen. I was raised during the computer
> craze. Now my peers and I stand on a shore as
> technology's children, looking across the growing
> technological divide to a chunk of land sliding into
> the sea, where our parents swim, where our teachers
> worry, and where traditional kinds of literacy sink—
> dragging much of our culture and history with it. My
> experience is part of a larger phenomenon in our
> culture. Media technology has shaped young adults'
> ways of processing knowledge in ways that make books
> seem slow and out of date. In leaving books behind,
> our generation may lose priceless cultural archives,
> but we may also pioneer exciting new ways of learning.

3b How do you organize a writing project?

No matter how good your ideas are, if you don't make the effort to organize them, readers will get lost and blame you for their confusion. Coherent organization is the foundation of any writing project.

It is true that many writers never consciously select a design before they start a paper. They may know intuitively what events they want a story to contain or what order the information in a report should follow. Still, understanding the options available when you organize a paper can help you. When you begin a writing project, look for models that show how other writers have approached similar tasks. Whether you are writing a biology lab report or a research paper for your world literature course, examples give you valuable clues about how to organize your argument. (If you're not sure where to find such models for a course assignment, ask your instructor. For documents you write at work or in the community, ask an experienced colleague.) See Chapters 7 and 9 for more on writing within particular genres.

Some basic patterns for organizing papers are discussed below, arranged from the simplest to the most complex.

1 Consider an introduction/body/conclusion structure.

This basic pattern works for many kinds of projects. Lawyers, scientists, and writers in many academic fields favor this design because it suggests a logical movement from statement to proof.

- In the **introduction** you begin by telling your readers clearly and simply what topics your paper will cover.

Frank O. Gehry's Guggenheim Museum Bilbao (Spain) has been hailed as a triumph of contemporary architecture. Its unusual structure both challenges and delights visitors.

- In the **body** of the paper you follow with examples and explanations for each of your main points.
- In your **conclusion** you tie your points together and leave readers with a sense of closure.

Another way of describing this basic structure is to call it a commitment and response pattern. That's because in the first section of the paper a writer promises to cover certain issues or address particular questions. The opening commitment can be direct or indirect. In a *direct commitment,* the writer addresses an issue squarely, almost as if making an announcement. Such an opening obliges the writer to cover every point mentioned.

> While there is some evidence that modern-day reptiles and dinosaurs are genetically related, recent fossil finds in China and Mongolia suggest that birds may be the closest links to our dinosaur predecessors.

A commitment can also be made *indirectly* by narrating an anecdote or an incident.

> Did you leave fall registration today with a rearranged schedule because two of the courses you planned to take had been canceled and three others were already full? If so, welcome to the biggest club on campus.

Through this indirect commitment, the writer has clearly indicated without actually saying so that the subject of the paper will be registration problems.

Papers that result from the basic introduction/body/conclusion pattern will usually take a simple shape.

Basic Introduction-Body-Conclusion Pattern

Introduction	I. First-year students need a rep.
Present thesis . . .	on the board of the student union.
◆ *First argument*	II. Other years have representation
❑ Support: examples,	A. All students need a voice
reasons, evidence, etc.	B. First-years have special needs
◆ *Second argument*	III. First-years need to be welcomed
❑ Support: examples,	A. Student union can be friendlier
reasons, evidence, etc.	B. Good to socialize outside dorms
◆ *Other arguments . . .*	IV. Welcoming campus helps retention
Conclusion	V. An inviting student union can help
Closing summary . . .	first-years join campus communities.

(Body)

Such papers can also incorporate significant variations. When you make a point or support an argument, for example, you must usually deal with opposing views; if you don't address them, the paper will seem to evade key questions. Counterarguments—discussions of opposing views—inevitably make the structure of the paper more complex. They can be addressed immediately, near the beginning of the paper, or they can be dealt with as they arise in the body of the piece (but don't end with a counterargument, or you'll weaken your own case).

Here's how the basic model might look when counterarguments are added to the mix. (See Section 12c for more on handling different views in a paper.)

Introduction-Body-Conclusion Pattern with Counterarguments

Introduction *Present thesis . . .*	I. First-year students need a rep. on the board of the student union.

◆ *First argument*
❑ Support . . .
❑ Counterarguments addressed by rebuttal
◆ *Second argument*
❑ Support . . .
❑ Counterarguments addressed by rebuttal
◆ *Other arguments . . .*
	II. Other years have representation
	  A. First-years need a voice
	  B. First-years may not understand the system, but can learn it
	III. First-years need to be welcomed
	  A. Student union better than dorms
	  B. Dorm rec-rooms are good but not for meeting older students
	IV. Welcoming campus helps retention

Conclusion *Closing summary . . .*	V. An inviting student union can help first-years join campus communities.

(Body labels along left of body rows)

This pattern—or any of its numerous variations—works especially well for essay exams or other impromptu writing when you have to organize your ideas quickly. It's easy to outline and readily expandable.

2 Consider a narrative or a process design. When you narrate a story, you usually describe events in the order they occurred. The structure can be quite straightforward.

Narrative Pattern

Introduction *Present thesis . . .*	I. Our town's public buildings reflect the architectural styles of several different historical periods.
◆ *First event* ◆ *Second event* ◆ *Third event* ◆ *Other events . . .*	II. Colonial town hall (1793) III. Victorian courthouse (1846) and post office (1888) IV. Art-deco library (1932)
Conclusion *Closing summary . . .*	V. These buildings tell a story about our town's gradual development.

If for an astronomy course you wanted to narrate the discovery of pulsar stars, you might begin with the scientists at Bell Laboratories who thought that they were receiving messages from extraterrestrial beings when they first intercepted radio signals from pulsars. A narrative can also be more complicated—for instance, by moving back in time as a movie does with flashbacks.

A process pattern is essentially the same as a narrative pattern, but instead of telling a story you are explaining how something works. You list and describe each step in the process.

Process Pattern

Introduction *Present thesis . . .*	I. Winning a reality-TV game show requires patience and cunning.
Body ◆ *First step* ◆ *Second step* ◆ *Third step* ◆ *Other steps . . .*	II. First, display trustworthiness III. Second, form a small coalition IV. Third, lie low for a while V. Last, betray coalition members
Conclusion *Closing summary . . .*	VI. To win the big bucks, you need to remember it is only a game.

Be careful to include all the necessary steps in the proper order. You can find good examples of process patterns in instructional and technical manuals.

3 Consider a comparison and contrast structure. In many kinds of papers you will have to examine different objects or ideas in relation to each other, especially when you are evaluating or arguing. In organizing such papers you can use one or two basic plans, either describing the things you are comparing one at a time (*subject by subject*) or describing them in an alternating sequence (*feature by feature*). The models here are followed by sample outlines.

Comparison and Contrast Pattern: Subject by Subject

Introduction *Present thesis . . .*	I. Sport-utility vehicles, though currently more popular than family sedans, have environmental and safety drawbacks that should make potential buyers beware.

Body ◆ *First subject examined*
◻ First feature
◻ Second feature
◻ Other features . . .
◆ *Second subject*
◻ First feature
◻ Second feature
◻ Other features . . .
	II. Pros and cons of SUVs
	    A. Popularity
	    B. Environmental impact
	    C. Safety
	III. Pros and cons of family sedans
	    A. Popularity
	    B. Environmental impact
	    C. Safety

Conclusion *Closing summary . . .*	IV. Buyers who value safety and the environment over style should bypass sport-utility vehicles in favor of traditional sedans.

Subject by Subject:
Sport-Utility Vehicles (SUVs) vs. Family Sedans

I. **Thesis:** SUVs, while currently more popular than family sedans, have environmental and safety drawbacks that should make potential buyers beware.

II. **Subject 1:** Features of SUVs
   A. *Feature A: Popularity of SUVs*
   B. *Feature B: Environmental impact of SUVs*
   C. *Feature C: Safety of SUVs*

III. **Subject 2:** Features of family sedans
   A. *Feature A: Popularity of family sedans*
   B. *Feature B: Environmental impact of family sedans*
   C. *Feature C: Safety of family sedans*

IV. **Conclusion:** Buyers who value safety and the environment over style should bypass SUVs in favor of a traditional family sedan.

Comparison and Contrast Pattern: Feature by Feature

Introduction *Present thesis . . .*	I.	Sport-utility vehicles, though currently more popular than family sedans, have environmental and safety drawbacks that should make potential buyers beware.
Body ◆ *First feature examined* ◻ In first subject ◻ In second subject	II.	Popularity A. Of sport-utility vehicles B. Of family sedans
◆ *Second feature* ◻ In first subject ◻ In second subject	III.	Environmental impact A. Of sport-utility vehicles B. Of family sedans
◆ *Other features . . .* ◻ In first subject ◻ In second subject	IV.	Safety A. Of sport-utility vehicles B. Of family sedans
Conclusion *Closing summary . . .*	V.	Buyers who value safety and the environment over style should bypass sport-utility vehicles in favor of traditional sedans.

Feature by Feature:
Sport-Utility Vehicles (SUVs) vs. Family Sedans

I. **Thesis:** SUVs, while currently more popular than family sedans, have environmental and safety drawbacks that should make potential buyers beware.

II. **Feature A:** *Popularity*
   A. Popularity of SUVs
   B. Popularity of family sedans

III. **Feature B:** *Environmental impact*
   A. Environmental impact of SUVs
   B. Environmental impact of family sedans
IV. **Feature C:** *Safety*
   A. Safety of SUVs
   B. Safety of family sedans
 V. **Conclusion:** Buyers who value safety and the environment over style should bypass SUVs in favor of a traditional family sedan.

The subject-by-subject plan works best in short papers involving only a few comparisons; in such pieces readers don't have to recall a large quantity of information to make the necessary comparisons. When you're doing a longer paper, however, use the feature-by-feature pattern; otherwise readers may lose track of the features you're comparing.

4 Consider a division or classification structure. These two ways of organizing a paper are quite different, though both involve creating categories to make material more manageable. A paper organized according to the principle of *division* breaks a topic into its components—its separate parts. A paper on the solar system might devote a section to each planet; a paper on a political candidate might describe her positions on several major issues in an order that seems appropriate.

Division Pattern

Introduction *Present thesis . . .*	I. Candidate Everson's platform is based on four main issues.
Body ◆ *First division* ◆ *Second division* ◆ *Third division* ◆ *Other divisions . . .*	II. Crime prevention III. Local tax rates IV. Traffic control V. Environment
Conclusion *Closing summary . . .*	VI. Everson will devote the most resources to crime prevention.

Classification involves breaking a large subject into categories according to some consistent and useful principle of division. Classification must follow rules that don't apply to division. First, classifications must be *exhaustive:* every member of the class must fit into a category. A classification of the planets might divide those that have significant moons from those that do not; obviously all of the nine planets fall into one of these classes.

With no moon

With one moon

With more than one moon

Any principle of division you use must also be *consistent*. You can't classify by more than one principle at a time—for example, if you group planets according to the number of moons they have *and* whether or not they have rings, you are not really classifying. Finally, classes *must not overlap*. That means you should be able to place an object in only one category.

Classification Pattern

Introduction *Present thesis . . .*	I.	This year's most popular bands represent many musical genres.
Body ◆ *First classification*	II.	Modern rock
◆ *Second classification*	III.	Reggae and ska
◆ *Third classification*	IV.	Hip-hop and "new soul"
◆ *Other classifications . . .*	V.	Folk, bluegrass, and country
Conclusion *Closing summary . . .*	VI.	Young music fans appreciate a variety of musical styles.

Yet most systems of classification break down at one point or another, like the one in the model above. What do you do with acts—such as Ricky Martin or Bruce Springsteen—who play more than one kind of music? Well, you can create yet another class (Latin-pop or folk-rock), or you can classify by the musician's major body of work. But you won't always be able to eliminate every exception.

5 Consider a cause-and-effect design. This design is appropriate when you write a paper explaining why something has happened. The typical cause-and-effect paper moves from an explanation of some existing condition to an examination of its particular causes. In other words, you see what has happened and you want to know why. For example, you might wonder why so many people did their Christmas shopping online last year. Possible causes might include the increased number of shopping outlets on the Web, the fact that more people have access to the Internet, and unusually cold winter weather that kept shoppers indoors.

Typically you'll see more than one explanation for a given event, so a cause-and-effect paper may examine various causes, from the least important to the most important.

Cause-and-Effect Pattern

Introduction *Present thesis . . .*	I.	Animated films have succeeded recently due to good writing.
Body ◆ *Effects explained*	II.	Animated films have made money and gained critical accolades
◆ *Least important causes*		
◆ *More important causes . . .*	III.	Because animation is better
◆ *Most Important cause*	IV.	Because scripts have broad appeal
Conclusion *Closing summary . . .*	V.	Plots and dialogue of new animated films entertain both young & old.

You can begin your essay by identifying an effect and then go on to hypothesize about the causes, or you can start by listing a number of causes and then show how they contribute to a particular effect.

6 Consider a problem-and-solution pattern. You can use this pattern effectively for papers in which you argue for change or propose an idea to settle a problem.

Problem-and-Solution Pattern

Introduction *Present thesis . . .*	I. All business school graduates should be required to take a course on professional ethics.
Body ◆ *Problem and need for solution established* ◆ *Rejected solutions* ❑ First rejected solution • Advantages • Disadvantages ❑ Other rejects . . . ◆ *Proposed solution* ❑ Feasibility ❑ Disadvantages ❑ Advantages ❑ Implementation	II. Public distrust following recent scandals is bad for business III. Threat of punishment not enough A. May deter some illegal actions B. But damage is done whether or not crime is punished, and C. Unethical actions may be legal VI. Ethics class prevents problems A. Easy to add a new requirement B. Some want fewer requirements C. Focus on ethics not legalities D. Principles addressed via debate
Conclusion *Closing summary . . .*	V. A discussion of principles will help graduates balance obligations to public, customers, & investors.

The first part of this pattern says, "We've got a problem and we've got to solve it—now." Here's how one student began a problem-and-solution essay.

> In <u>Bowling Alone</u>, sociologist Robert Putnam argues that Americans who live in areas where there is little social cohesion--where individuals feel isolated and neighbors don't trust each other--have a higher risk of disease and a shorter average life span.

The nature of the problem is evident from just this single sentence.

The second part of the problem-and-solution pattern steers the reader through proposals for solving the problem. Since most of these ideas will be rejected (or furnish only a part of the recommended solution), the advantages and limitations of each are examined carefully. This section of the essay assures readers that no plausible approach has been ignored.

In the third part of this pattern you propose a solution to the problem. You may then want to discuss the disadvantages and advantages of this proposal, highlighting the advantages. Readers need to feel that nothing is under wraps and that no hidden agendas guide your proposal. You can then conclude by explaining how the change can be put into place.

7 Use formatting and visual elements to reinforce your paper's organization. When the assignment allows it, don't hesitate to use visual devices like bulleted and numbered lists, headings, color, and images to help readers see at a glance how you've organized your project. For detailed advice on incorporating visual elements into a text, see Chapters 21 and 22.

EXERCISE 3.2 Working with a group of classmates, consider what patterns you might use for writing about two of the topics listed below. Give reasons why you think those patterns would work well in each case.

> Where to eat out near your campus
> The popularity of *The Simpsons*
> Your experience volunteering at a local agency
> Whether corporate oil drilling should be permitted in wildlife preserves

3c How do you outline a paper?

No question about it, an outline can help you keep a writing project on track, whether you are following one of the patterns described in Section 3b or following one of your own. But a blueprint for your essay doesn't have to be a full-sentence outline. You can choose from a number of organizational devices, including the working list and the scratch outline. Just be sure that if you're writing a paper for a class, you follow any instructions on outlining given by your instructor.

As you begin to plan your essay, remember that no approach to outlining is necessarily "right." Experiment with several techniques until you find out what works best for you.

1 Try a working list. The working list is the most flexible of all outlining devices. Start by jotting down the key points you want to make, leaving plenty of room under each major idea. This strategy works best as a preliminary planning technique because it allows you to add examples and points under the main ideas they support as they occur to you.

Here are headings you might use for a cause-and-effect paper titled "The Case for Reviving the Family Dinner."

- How family eating patterns have changed
- Benefits of family dinners for children
- Benefits of family dinners for parents

Working from a brainstorming list or perhaps from freewriting on the subject, you select subpoints to fit under these major headings. You might also want to jot "cue notes" in the margin of the working list to remind yourself of anecdotes that illustrate specific points, as in the following example.

EXAMPLE 3.1   Working List

The Case for Reviving the Family Dinner

- **How family eating patterns have changed** *vs. families in 1960s-1970s*
  More single-parent families and
  two-career families
  Increase in fast-food intake *microwave dinners, delis*
  More prepackaged single-portion foods in stores
  Family members often eat separately or in front
  of TV
- **Benefits of family dinners for children**
  Spend more time with family *use story about dad's spaghetti dinners?*
  Better nutrition
  Learn table manners
  Participate in cooking and cleanup
- **Benefits of family dinners for parents**
  Quality time with children
  More economical
  Can be sure that children are eating well
  Research study: children who eat with
  families fare better in school and are
  better-adjusted *Check article in last Sun newspaper*

When you think you have enough material, look over your list and decide which points you want to treat first and how you can arrange the others. Then start writing and, as you work, refer to your list to check that you are staying on track. Add and delete items from the list as you need to—nothing in a working list is untouchable.

2 Make an informal (scratch) outline. Many writers like working from careful plans but dislike the formality and restrictions of formal outlines. For them the informal or scratch outline—which arranges points into categories and subcategories—provides a happy medium.

A scratch outline should begin with a thesis that states your claim or main idea. Then decide what major points you'll use to support that thesis. For each major point you'll need subpoints that support, explain, or illustrate the main point. However, your statement of points and subpoints can be quite loose since the conventions of the full-sentence outline need not be followed. Here's a sample scratch outline on reviving family dinners, following a cause-and-effect pattern of the sort described in Section 3b-5. Note that the scratch outline is considerably fuller than the working list; thus it provides more organizational guidance.

EXAMPLE 3.2   Scratch Outline

The Case for Reviving the Family Dinner

Thesis: Because eating meals together offers so many social and emotional benefits, parents need to restore family dinner as a top priority in their homes.

1. Contemporary American families eat meals together much less frequently than previous generations did.
   • Most families used to eat breakfast and dinner together—now both children and parents may be away from home for long hours and hardly see each other.
   • Statistics show that fast-food intake and restaurant sales have risen steadily since 1980.
   • Even grocery stores offer a variety of single-portion convenience foods, microwave dinners, and other items designed for people eating alone.
2. While eating alone may be convenient, family meals offer important benefits for children.
   • Family dinners ensure that children spend time with their parents and siblings each day. (childhood examples)
   • A recent study showed that children whose families eat dinner together at least once a week

```
        do better in school and have fewer behavioral
        problems. (cite article)
      • Children who eat with their families have a
        chance to learn table manners and basic cooking
        and cleanup skills.
   3. Parents also benefit from family meals.
      • Parents can ensure that children are eating a
        healthy diet.
      • Family dinners allow parents to spend quality
        time with children.
      • Cooking and eating at home is cheaper than eat-
        ing out.
```

3 Make a formal (sentence) outline. A formal outline is a fairly complex structure that compels you to think rigorously about how the ideas in a piece of writing will fit together. (That's why instructors often require them.) If your major points really aren't compatible or parallel, a formal outline will expose the problems. When your supporting evidence is thin or inconsistent, those flaws may show up too.

In a formal sentence outline you state every point in a complete sentence, and you make sentences within each grouping parallel, according to the following scheme.

Chart 3.1

Framework of a Formal Outline

I. ....
    A. ....
        1. ....
        2. ....
    B. ....
        1. ....
        2. ....
        3. ....
    C. ....
II. ....

Here's how a formal outline of the article on family dinner might begin. We haven't detailed the entire argument, but you can see from this excerpt how the material would be organized.

EXAMPLE 3.3 Formal Outline

The Case for Reviving the Family Dinner

Thesis: Because eating meals together offers so many social and emotional benefits, parents need to restore family dinner as a top priority in their homes.

I. Contemporary American families eat meals together much less frequently than previous generations did.
   A. Most families in the 1960s and 1970s ate dinner and breakfast together.
      1. Dad's Sunday-night spaghetti dinners were a tradition in my family.
      2. Popular TV shows from the era, such as *The Brady Bunch,* frequently feature family meals.
   B. However, today families' schedules are so complicated that family members often eat separately.
      1. According to the federal government, nearly one-third of families are headed by a single working parent, and more than 60 percent of mothers now work outside the home.
      2. Children also participate in more extracurricular activities, including sports leagues and after-school programs, so they spend less time at home.
      3. When family members' schedules conflict, it is difficult to plan shared mealtimes. . . .

4 Use an outlining program on a computer. What makes outlining on a computer preferable to doing the job on paper is the ease with which an on-screen outline can be expanded, contracted, rearranged, and otherwise altered. Rather than constraining ideas, a computer outline encourages a writer to be flexible because adding and rearranging ideas is as easy as moving the cursor and pressing a few keys.

EXERCISE 3.3 Make a working list for a writing project you're currently working on. When you are done, make a formal outline of the same project. What additions and changes did you make to construct the formal outline? Which outline will you find most helpful when you sit down to begin a draft of the project? Why?

3d How do you choose a title?

It may seem odd to choose a title while you are still planning and organizing a project. But titles are surprisingly important. Readers want and expect them. In fact, they may be annoyed if they don't find one that helps them anticipate what they will be reading—so don't make your title an afterthought.

1 Experiment with a working title. Choose a working title (one you can change as the work progresses) that will keep you on track as you move through the planning and drafting stages of your project. For example, when Justin Cone wrote the topic proposal that appears on pages 28–29, he knew that he wanted his paper to explore the positive and negative effects of the Internet, so he crafted this initial title: "Where Exactly Are We Surfing To?"

This title contains cues that helped Justin to shape his first draft: *surfing* focuses the paper on the Internet; *where* suggests that the paper will explore the effects and implications of Internet use. These focuses led him to choose a cause-and-effect pattern of organization.

2 Revise the working title to reflect your finished product. As you plan and draft, check your working title periodically to be sure it still fits the paper. Justin made exactly these kinds of revisions as his research progressed, when he decided to shift his focus from the Internet to the intellectual effects of all electronic gadgets, including television, computers and video games, on his generation. His final title—"Technology's Children: Has Media Technology Intellectually Stunted Our Generation?"—reflects this new focus. Justin's full paper appears on pages 79–83.

3 Keep your readers in mind. Be sure your title accurately reflects the content of your paper. No cute titles, please. People doing computer searches look for keywords that help to identify the content of a book or an article and direct the researcher to the place where he or she can find it. An essay on Napoleon called "Short Guy, Big Ego" would be hard to find. So it's essential that your title let readers know what your paper is really about.

If you have your heart set on a clever phrase that's not particularly descriptive, try a two-part title. Start with the unconventional phrase

3d
title

and follow it with a colon. The second part of the title, after the colon, should clarify exactly what the paper is about, as in "Short Guy, Big Ego: A Psychological Analysis of Napoleon's Military Strategy."

EXERCISE 3.4 Which of these titles seem as if they'd be good predictors of content in a paper? Why?

1. Cruising the Universe with Physicist Stephen Hawking

2. The Growing Crime Problem

3. College Students and Public Service: A New Trend

4. What's in a Name?

5. Cowboys and Commies: Politics in the Hollywood Western, 1942–1973

CHAPTER 4

How Do You Write a Draft?

4a How do you start a draft?

For many people, getting started is the hardest part of writing. Even professional authors describe the paralyzing anxiety they sometimes feel as they sit and stare at a blank page or computer screen. Beginnings *are* hard, but remember that a first draft doesn't have to be perfect. It's simply a place to start. In this section we offer suggestions to help you through the drafting process—so that you can stop worrying, take the plunge, and *start writing*.

1 Find a place to write and gather the things you'll need. If you can, find a spot away from friends, family, and noise, where you won't be distracted. Collect your materials—computer disks, notes, source materials, dictionary, and a copy of the assignment—and lay them out where you can see them. Turn your computer on and let it hum. In making preparations like these, you're not procrastinating; you're creating a working environment.

2 Keep the ideas coming. Some people agonize over their first few sentences, tinkering endlessly in a quest to get them just right. Don't let an awkward beginning stall the entire draft. Remember that what appears in a draft won't necessarily become part of the finished essay. So treat your first paragraph as a device to get rolling. Write three or four sentences nonstop to build momentum, no matter how imperfect they may be. You may be surprised at how quickly words begin to flow once you've warmed up to your topic.

Remember too that you don't have to write the opening paragraph first. You can always begin with whatever section of the paper seems easiest to write and come back to the introduction later, after you have a better sense of where your argument is headed. See Section 16a for more on writing opening paragraphs.

3 Don't criticize yourself or edit your writing prematurely. As you work on a first draft, cut yourself some slack. Don't moan, "This is awful!" or "I hate my writing!" Writing can be a slow and difficult business; you should congratulate yourself when you're making any progress at all. Most pieces of good writing develop over time. You can't expect something to be perfectly polished when you first start working on it.

Nor should you fiddle with problems of mechanics, formatting, or style in your early drafts. You can go back and fix difficulties with spelling, punctuation, parallelism, word choice, and the like *after* you've gotten your ideas down on paper. If you bog down in details of form too early, you may lose your momentum for writing, letting your brightest ideas fade while you hunt for the spelling of *nitpicker.* Worse, you may find yourself always playing it safe, writing only the kinds of sentences you can compose easily, never pushing yourself to grapple with difficult ideas or to try out a more interesting style.

4 Set your own pace. When you're not sure what pace best suits you, try writing quickly at first. If you hit a snag or can't produce the specific phrase or example you need, skip the troublesome spot and move on. Above all, keep writing. A draft in hand, even a sketchy one, will give you a sense of accomplishment. You'll have material to develop and refine.

But if you're the kind of writer who isn't comfortable composing quickly, don't feel that you must change your routine. Especially when they are working on a project that incorporates a lot of research, many skilled writers do work slowly. They may take several hours to turn out a few paragraphs, but their first drafts are often quite polished. In the long run, slow writers may not spend much more time completing a project than writers who produce material faster but rework that material through more drafts.

Composer Ludwig van Beethoven (1770–1824) typically revised his compositions through numerous drafts. His Ninth Symphony, shown at left, was written and revised over a period of more than twenty years.

5 Get feedback from other writers. One of the best ways to get writing done is to share ideas with other people. In college courses, in the work force, and in community forums, groups of writers routinely brainstorm for ideas, compare findings, evaluate organizational strategies, and test arguments. Such groups serve as important first audiences for drafts and keep writers motivated—after all, no one wants to let colleagues down. Many college writers consult the writing center on their campus for help as they develop a first draft of a project.

In Section 4e you'll find tips for approaching collaborative writing projects; Section 46b-6 offers suggestions for doing collaborative research. See Section 5d for guidelines on helping another writer revise a draft and Section 8b for more on visiting a writing center.

6 Draft on a computer. Even before you begin a draft, you can use your computer to accumulate and store material for your paper. For example, you can start a file that records your initial impressions about a project days or weeks before the deadline. You can bookmark online sources that you want to refer to in your paper or download and store copies of relevant articles or images. Over time you'll accumulate a surprising amount of material to use in your draft. (Be sure, however, to keep track of and to cite material in your draft that comes from other sources. See Chapter 47 for more details.)

With a computer it's also easy to take risks. You can experiment with major changes without losing the work you've already done, by saving alternative versions of your draft until you decide which one you want to use. (Revising a text doesn't automatically improve it.)

Finally, computers make it easy to experiment with different formats and to incorporate graphic or multimedia elements. See Chapters 21 and 22 for more on visual dimensions of writing.

4b How do you keep a draft on track?

When you begin a draft, you will probably have a thesis and a general organizational plan in mind. You may have gathered the resources you plan to use in the paper (articles, interview data, Web sites, statistics) and even developed an outline. But the real work of writing a draft doesn't start until you begin putting words onto a screen. Only then can you see precisely how your plan may have to be altered to fit the particular material and your particular writing situation. As a writer you have to be both focused and flexible: focused enough to guide readers through your material and flexible enough to shift strategies when necessary. This section will help you keep your draft on track.

1 Highlight key ideas. Know what main points you want to cover and keep them in mind as you compose the draft. One way to do this is to summarize your thesis up front, in the first paragraph. Beginning with key points gives readers a notion of what to expect; then you can follow with supporting material. For example, here is an opening paragraph that forecasts what the rest of the paper will be about. The thesis sentence is underlined.

> At the beginning of this decade, one-third of the doctors graduating from medical schools were women. Now the figure is around 40 percent. Women doctors will soon be in the majority in specialties such as obstetrics-gynecology, pediatrics, and psychiatry, and they are rapidly making inroads into traditionally male territories such as surgery and orthopedics. This shifting balance in what up to now has been a male-dominated profession is changing American medicine in a number of ways. <u>One can already see changes in medical education as the number of women professors in medical school increases.</u>

Even if you choose to ease your readers into your thesis by opening the paper with background information or an attention-getting anecdote (see Section 16a), you still need to keep your main point in mind so that the opening doesn't wander too far astray.

Continue to highlight main ideas throughout the draft. Use phrases like these to snap readers to attention.

> The main points to consider are . . .
>
> The chief issue, however, is . . .
>
> Now we have come to the crucial question.

You can also keep readers focused on key points with constructions that express your own thoughts about the topic or that draw their attention to contrasting viewpoints.

> I believe that . . .
>
> Other researchers say . . .
>
> Critics of this view have argued . . .

Even cues as simple as *first, second,* and *third* can help readers follow the structure of your paper. For more guidance on using transitional words and phrases, see Section 17b.

2 Keep the amount you write about each point roughly proportionate to its importance in the paper.

Be careful not to write a lopsided draft that misleads readers. If what you intend as an introduction takes up half the paper, it's no longer an introduction. If your thesis promises to develop a new solution to a problem yet mentions this solution only in the last paragraph, you haven't fulfilled that promise. Should you find yourself writing at length on a minor point, or quoting at length from one source while neglecting others, step back and return to your central argument.

However, while you should respect the principle of proportion, don't be too stingy with words and ideas in a first draft. You'll discover in editing that it is easier to prune material you don't like than it is to fill in where your ideas are thin. Obviously you don't want to stray too far from your thesis. But you do want to capture any fresh thoughts that emerge as you write. The same is true of examples, illustrations, facts, figures, and details: if they don't work, you can always cut them later or find a better place in the draft to use them.

3 Allow yourself enough time to draw conclusions.

Conclusions are important. Don't put so much energy into the introduction and body of a paper that you skimp on the final paragraphs. You can weaken your paper badly if you do, since the ending often determines what impression readers will take from your piece.

When you approach the end of a draft, take time to reread what you have written. Then consider what remains to be done: What are the larger implications of the ideas you've discussed? What do you want readers to know, believe, or do as a result of your piece? What loose ends need to be tied up? Let these concerns help shape your concluding paragraph(s). If you have time, try out several endings and choose the one that you think best fits your audience and purpose. See Section 16b for more on closing paragraphs.

4c   When should you take a break?

In the middle of a writing project you may suddenly find yourself stumped. You gaze at your computer screen or look at a blank page, but nothing happens. No ideas come. Such a lull can be scary, especially when a deadline looms. But don't panic; you may simply need to kick back and let your thoughts *incubate.*

Incubation is an interval during which a writer stops composing for a time to let ideas germinate or develop. You can't force or rush incubation; you can only be ready to grab a new idea when it surfaces.

1 Allow time for both long and short incubation periods.

When possible, start a writing project well before its deadline, since you may need several incubation periods. For authors who work consistently, such rest periods are absolutely necessary. When they've written themselves out for the day, they know it's fruitless to sit at the desk any longer.

The periods that lapse between writing the first, second, and even third drafts of a paper can be similarly productive. But shorter incubation periods help too. When you are stuck for a word or can't think of the example you need to illustrate a point, get away from the desk long enough to do an errand or chat with someone. Even such a brief pause can trigger an insight. So you don't have to keep yourself glued to the chair all the time in order to write—minor interruptions can actually be productive.

2 Don't use incubation as an excuse for procrastination.

You should take occasional breaks while writing, but you can't afford to wait forever for inspiration. If you're still having problems with a project after a few hours (or a weekend) of rest, get back to work anyway. Review your notes or outlines; consult your research; reread what you've already written; try focusing on a new section of the paper. Most important, just write!

Going Public   *One Writer's Drafting Process* _____

Even professional writers typically compose documents in several stages. When communication specialist Brad Stratton was asked to write a brochure publicizing a workshop sponsored by his employer, he spent parts of three days working toward his first draft. Note how often Brad moved back and forth among writing, researching, incubating, and revising during the drafting process.

Monday-Day 1

3:00–3:25	Reviewed content information and handwrote introduction
3:25–3:30	Shared draft of introduction with colleague
3:30–4:45	Put draft away; focused on other work
4:45–5:00	Typed introduction draft into computer, making some changes

Tuesday-Day 2

9:30–10:00	Reviewed other brochures for ideas
10:00–11:00	Made scratch outline of entire brochure in a new document
11:00–11:25	Reviewed outline; did additional research on Internet to fill gaps in previous research
11:25–12:05	Wrote main text
12:05–1:45	Imported introduction from other document; experimented with layout; added photos from last year's workshop
1:45–2:00	Reviewed text and corrected typos
2:00	Printed draft of brochure and gave copies to colleagues for review

Wednesday-Day 3

9:00–9:30	Made additions and changes to text based on readers' suggestions
9:30–11:00	Worked on design: added logo, borders, and background graphics
11:00–12:00	Break
12:00–12:30	Proofread draft; printed out and submitted copy to boss

4d How do you know when you have a solid draft?

Many writing instructors ask students to submit a draft of an assignment for feedback before turning in the final version. You might also be asked to share a preliminary version of a report or memo with co-workers or to show a first version of an editorial to a news editor. As the deadline to turn in your draft approaches, relax. Although the paper you are laboring over may not be as good as you'd like, remember that you'll have a chance to revise and polish later. Don't relax too much, though: you'll waste your readers' time if you settle for a draft that's incomplete or rushed.

How do you know when you've made a solid effort? When you've met the three standards listed in Checklist 4.1, you can probably rest assured that readers will find your draft worth reading and responding to.

Checklist 4.1

Knowing When You Have a Solid Draft

Before you give a draft to your instructor, colleague, or peer reviewer for comments, be sure you've met these standards.

1. **Have you made a good-faith effort?** Be sure you've invested substantial time and thought in your paper. If you haven't, you're passing up an opportunity you may not get again: the chance to get useful criticism of your paper while it's still in progress.

2. **Is the draft reasonably complete?** Have you stated a thesis, developed it with supporting arguments and examples, and finished with a defensible conclusion? Have you included any charts, tables, or images that will appear in the final project? A few paragraphs don't qualify as a working draft. Nor does a carefully written opening followed by an outline of what the rest of the paper will cover.

3. **Is the draft readable?** You can't expect instructors, classmates, or colleagues to respond carefully to a paper that's hard to read.

   • Double-space your draft, leaving ample margins all the way around the page for comments.

   • Be sure that your printer or photocopier has made dark, legible copies.

   • If you must handwrite a draft, *print* in ink on every other line.

   • Write or print on one side of the paper only and number your pages.

EXERCISE 4.1 Evaluate a draft you have recently written against the three criteria in Checklist 4.1. Does your paper meet the standards? If not, what changes would you have to make to remedy the problems?

4e   How do you work on a draft collaboratively?

It's hard enough to stay focused when you're writing a draft by yourself. But the challenges multiply when you co-author a paper with classmates or colleagues. Being able to write collaboratively is an important skill. In business, project teams prepare presentations; in college, instructors sometimes ask groups of students to undertake service-learning or other joint writing projects; and in community settings, groups must create statements of their policies or goals.

It's always a relief to share the workload. But pundits don't joke about the ineffectiveness of committees for no reason. Without a shared focus and careful planning, group efforts can become frustrating exercises.

The kind of collaborative drafting we discuss in this section is different from the work of peer revision groups that meet to help individual writers improve an already written draft. For more on peer revision, see Section 5d.

1 Decide on shared goals. Suppose your instructor has asked you and several classmates to develop a promotional Web site for a local historical museum as part of a service-learning project. Before you even turn on the computer, you should come to a consensus on what your group hopes to accomplish.

- Do you want to construct a primarily informational site where readers can find out the museum's address, hours of operation, major exhibits, and admission fees?
- Will your site also try to persuade readers to serve as volunteer tour leaders or to donate funds to build a new children's wing?
- Will your Web site be technically sophisticated or very basic?

Once you've agreed on general goals, you can plan the actual research and writing. See Section 46b-6 for specific advice on doing collaborative research.

Of course, you may not be able to sharply define your project in a first meeting. You may need to brainstorm or do background research. If group members have different ideas about the project, you'll need to negotiate these differences. You'll also need to consider the goals of your instructor and of the museum staff. It may take time to hammer out a shared purpose, but it's time well spent. If you rush to begin a

4e
collab

project when each person has different ideas, you'll end up with a mishmash of material that no one can agree how to put together.

2 Consider assigning separate sections of the project to each writer. You may find it efficient to divide a group assignment into sections. Ask each writer to research and compose a section individually, and then schedule a group meeting to combine and edit the sections into a coherent document. Students working on the museum Web site might ask one writer to take responsibility for constructing an informational home page, another to compose pages on current exhibits, and another to create a list of external links to other Web sites of interest to museum patrons.

When you compose a group project in this way, set aside plenty of time to pull the pieces together. You'll need to eliminate overlap, address gaps in your coverage, and revise for consistency. The finished product shouldn't read like several short pieces awkwardly cobbled together.

Splitting a document into individually authored parts is the quickest way to complete a group writing assignment. However, this approach doesn't work well for texts that aren't easily separated into components or for a document that you want to represent the perspective of the entire group.

3 Consider writing the document collaboratively. Collaborative drafting—when an entire group participates in composing a text—can yield impressive results. Many powerful public documents, including the Declaration of Independence, were written in this way. The advantage of this method is that several ideas and viewpoints are often better than one: you'll have diverse input and ideas at every point in the composing process.

The primary disadvantage of this method, of course, is the amount of time required. You'll need to schedule plenty of group meetings or

Collaboration often means working together through the entire writing process. Here, writers from the Split P Soup: Poetry for the Community project at the University of South Carolina discuss the layout of a poem they're preparing for publication.

frequent email exchanges to write and discuss the text in progress. Consider assigning one person to be the group's "recorder," in charge of maintaining the draft in progress and recording new text and ideas.

4 Address disagreements promptly. Like most group activities, collaborative writing isn't always smooth sailing. Many students resist group work because they've had bad experiences with classmates who monopolized a project or neglected their responsibilities.

The best way to deal with such problems is to do your best to prevent them in the first place. After you've decided on your group's goals, work out a schedule of meetings and deadlines that everyone can agree on. Distribute a copy of the schedule to each group member and to your instructor, if possible. If one writer fails to abide by the agreement, raise the issue in your next meeting. Remind him or her of the schedule and offer encouragement. You may need to ask your instructor to help if the problem persists.

Other difficulties arise when group members disagree about the direction a project is taking. Suppose that in a persuasive paper for an English composition course, some members of a group want to create a multimedia presentation on the health risks of body piercing while the rest want to write a traditional report. Or one group member strongly opposes using school taxes for private school vouchers while the others favor it. If you can't settle on an approach that satisfies everyone, consult your instructor. He or she may allow you to compose two smaller subprojects or to incorporate a statement of minority views into your document.

CHAPTER 5

How Do You Revise, Edit, and Proofread?

Why make a fuss distinguishing among terms as similar as *revising, editing,* and *proofreading?* It's because revising, editing, and proofreading are different phases of the writing process, each of which involves thinking about a different aspect of the paper.

Chart 5.1

Revising, Editing, Proofreading		
		Focus on
Revision (first draft)		Purpose, audience, content organization
Editing (later draft)		Style, emphasis, tone
Proofreading (final draft)		Mechanics, format

When you start *revising* your draft, don't think in terms of *fixing* or *correcting* your writing—that's not really what you are doing. Rather you are *shaping a work in progress,* reviewing what you have written and looking for ways to improve it. You may get new ideas and shift the focus of the paper; you may cut, expand, and reorganize. At this point you are making large-scale changes.

When you *edit* a paper, you are less concerned with the big issues. Instead, you turn your attention to matters of style that affect clarity, emphasis, and tone. You may rewrite sentences you find awkward or correct problems with parallelism and repetition. Your goal is to create sentences and paragraphs that present your ideas effectively. These are small-scale changes.

When you *proofread* a paper, you go back over it line by line to correct typographical errors, check for omissions, verify details, eliminate inconsistencies, and remove gaffes. This is the fix-it stage, when you're preparing the paper to appear in public. It's a good idea to postpone proofreading until the end of a project. If you begin to correct errors while you are composing or revising, you could waste time repairing sentences that later might be deleted.

5a What does revising involve?

When you revise a draft, don't try to work through it paragraph by paragraph, making changes as you go. The problems of a first draft are likely to involve large-scale issues of content and rhetorical strategy that affect every paragraph, concerns that must be addressed before you can polish individual sentences. That's the point of serious revision—to reconsider everything you have written. At this point, THINK BIG! Don't tinker.

Large-scale changes include revising for focus, purpose, proportion, commitment, adaptation to audience, organization, and content. Begin by printing out a copy of your first draft and reading it from start to finish, thinking about these major elements.

1 Read your draft thoughtfully. Review the assignment and any feedback you have received from your instructor, classmates, or colleagues. Ask yourself how you feel about the draft. What's good that you definitely want to keep? Where does it seem weak?

Ideally you should appraise your draft several days (or at a minimum several hours) after you have completed it so that you can read it more objectively. Obviously you can enjoy the advantages of setting a draft aside only if you start on a project early.

Prototypes of vehicles like this Honda Insight often first appear at auto shows to test consumer reactions. In response, manufacturers then modify their products the same way you might revise a first draft after showing it to readers.

One bold option to consider at this point is writing an entirely new draft. Take this path when you dislike what you've written, when editors have found little to praise, or when you just need a fresh start. Creating a new draft may seem discouraging, but in the long run, starting from scratch may be easier than repairing a draft that just won't work. Even then, your first draft need not be a waste of effort. Often an unsuccessful version points a writer toward what he or she really wanted to write.

2 Refine the focus of the paper. Once you've determined that your draft is workable, be sure that it makes and develops a central point. You have a problem with focus if the draft makes a lot of general statements without supporting and developing them. Check your examples and supporting material. Have you relied mostly on common knowledge? If so, your draft may lack the credibility that comes from specific information. To check for focus, ask yourself these questions.

Checklist 5.1

Revising for Focus

- Have you taken on a larger topic than you can handle?
- Are you generalizing instead of stating a specific claim or thesis?
- Have you supported your ideas with sufficient evidence and examples?

See Section 2b for more on focusing a topic and Section 3a for advice on creating and refining a thesis.

3 Consider your purpose. Ask yourself whether someone reading your draft would understand what you're trying to achieve. If you lacked a sense of purpose when you began drafting the paper, you now need to decide exactly what you want to accomplish. Be sure that your intentions are evident to yourself and to your readers. Here are three questions to ask yourself.

Checklist 5.2

Revising for Purpose

- Do you clearly state in the first paragraph or two what you plan to do?
- Does the draft develop all the main points you intended to make?
- After reading the draft, will most readers be able to summarize your main idea?

See Section 1e for more on refining your purpose.

4 Examine your paper's proportions. *Proportion* means the distribution and balance of ideas. You should develop your ideas in relation to their importance. Ask yourself these questions.

Checklist 5.3

Revising for Proportion

• Are the parts of the paper out of balance? For example, have you gone into too much detail at the beginning and then skimped on the rest?

• Can your readers tell what points are most important by the amount of attention you've given to them?

• Does the conclusion do justice to the ideas it summarizes?

5 Check that you have kept your promises to readers. The introduction and thesis of your paper will evoke certain expectations in your readers. When you revise, check your response to the commitments you've made. Now is the time to tie up loose ends, so ask these questions.

Checklist 5.4

Revising for Commitment

• What exactly do you promise your readers at the beginning of the paper? Do you fulfill those promises?

• Do you support all the points you made in your thesis?

• Do you finish what you started? Have you inadvertently raised issues that you can't or don't intend to cover in the paper?

• Does your conclusion agree with your opening?

6 Check for adaptation to audience. Sometimes a first draft is what we call *writer-centered;* that is, the writer has concentrated on expressing his or her ideas without thinking much about the audience. Such an approach can be productive in a first draft, but a major goal of revising should be to change *writer-centered* writing to *reader-centered* writing. You do that by trying to put yourself in the place of your readers. Consider these questions.

Checklist 5.5

Revising for Audience

- Do you spend too much time discussing material that most of your readers already know?
- Do you answer important questions that readers might have about your topic?
- Do you define all the concepts and terms your readers need to know?
- Do you use language your readers will understand?

See Checklist 5.2 on audience (p. 64) for more advice.

7 Check the organization. A well-organized project has a plan and a clear direction. Readers can move from the beginning to the end of a paper without getting lost. To revise the structure of a draft, you'll need a printed copy because organizational problems can be hard to detect on a computer screen. You need a sense of the whole to see how the parts are meshing. To check your organization, ask these questions.

Checklist 5.6

Revising for Organization

- Does your paper state a clear thesis or claim? Does it then develop key points related to that thesis?
- Does the development of your points follow a pattern readers will recognize?
- Do the transitions move readers sensibly from point to point?
- Would the paper work better if you moved some paragraphs around?

See Section 3b for more detailed tips on organization and Section 17b for more on making smooth transitions between ideas.

8 Evaluate your design and check images and graphics. Now that you have a complete draft, you can assess how well the document is working visually: Have you used an appropriate format for the writing situation? Are the pages readable? Are sections logically arranged and easy for readers to locate? Check any tables, charts, and images to be sure that they add something substantive to the text and that they are accurate and legible. For more information about revising design elements, consult Chapter 22.

■ **9 Check the content of the paper.** When you revise, you may need to add information to give a paper more substance. A college paper needs the weight of evidence to advance its argument. Ask yourself these questions.

Checklist 5.7

Revising for Content

- Do you fully develop and support each main idea?

- Do you need to add specific information and concrete examples that will make your case stronger? Do you need to do more research?

- Do you cite reliable, credible sources to back up your ideas?

- Does the title of your paper reflect its content?

If the content of your draft seems thin, return to the library or to other sources. See Chapter 47 for more on doing research.

■ **10 Revise from a printed copy, not from a computer screen.** Whether you are revising, editing, or proofreading, you'll probably work best from a hard copy of your paper. Problems that seem all but invisible on a screen (weak organization, sprawling paragraphs, poor transitions, repeated words) show up more clearly in print.

After you've marked problems on your draft, transfer all corrections made on the printed version to the computer file.

EXERCISE 5.1 Apply the criteria for large-scale revision described above to a draft you have written.

Going Public *A Revised Opening Paragraph* _____

Carl Jackson wanted to write a paper for his first-year composition course exploring the corrupt practices used by some colleges to recruit high school basketball players. Here's the opening paragraph of his first draft exactly as he wrote it.

```
        Basketball is one of the most exciting games to
watch because of the nonstop action at every minite
of the game. Unlike football where time is taken to
huddle and the average play last only about five
seconds, or even worse, baseball which is America's
sport, seems to drag on forever until something
exciting happens. My opinion of basketball being the
most exciting sport to watch is arguable but what is
not arguable is the amount of unethical practices
found in the sport. It seems that every year another
team has been placed on probation or a school has had
to suspend its program. Among these are recruiting
violations and payments to recruits and active
players by alumni. These are the areas on which I
would like to focus and possibly give a few
suggestions on how to clean up college basketball.
```

If Jackson were to begin editing and proofreading this paragraph before undertaking larger-scale revisions, he'd probably make these corrections: (1) change *minite* to *minute;* (2) change *average play last* to *average play lasts;* (3) simplify the sentence that begins *Unlike football;* (4) change *amount* to *number.*

But Jackson's classmates who reviewed the paper thought that the paragraph had bigger problems. For one thing, they were confused about Jackson's focus. If he is interested in basketball, why does he comment on football and baseball? The first few sentences seem unrelated to the conclusion of the paragraph, and that conclusion isn't very intriguing. They doubted that this opener would keep readers interested. Clearly, Jackson needed to overhaul the paragraph.

Here's the heavily revised paragraph that opened his second draft. The new version gets to the point more quickly and catches readers' attention with the possibility of a solution to the recruitment problem. Though open to additional changes, this new paragraph demonstrates what we mean by large-scale revision.

```
        Basketball is one of the most exciting games to
watch, with its fast-paced, nonstop action, but even
avid fans might be hard-pressed these days to keep up
```

with NCAA investigations of the sport. It seems that
every year another college basketball program has
been placed on probation by the NCAA for recruiting
violations. This widespread problem has generated
much debate on what should be done to clean up the
sport of basketball. The suggestions range from
cutting athletic scholarships to paying the athletes
to play. Although a case can be made for both of
these extreme measures, I believe that there is a
better way to bring back the integrity of basketball.

Notice that the mechanical and grammatical errors of the first version are not present in the second. To have spent time fixing them before making the revisions would have been a waste of time.

5b What does editing involve?

Revision should have given you a better-focused, better-organized, more interesting draft. If you're reasonably satisfied with your revised paper, you're ready to *edit,* that is, to make the small-scale changes that you put on hold while you were adding, cutting, and rearranging material. Now you will consider concrete and specific language, word choice, wordiness, transitions, and a better introduction and conclusion.

Now is the time to use the handbook to check on style (Part III), grammar and usage (Part V), and mechanics (Part VI).

1 Make your language concrete and specific. Language is *concrete* when it describes things as they are perceived by the senses: colors, textures, sizes, sounds, actions. Language is *specific* when it names particular people, places, and things.

Although generalizations and abstract terms are appropriate in some writing situations, readers usually need vivid descriptions that bring concepts to life. As you edit, look for ways to add people to your discussions, to illustrate generalizations with examples, and to supply your readers with facts and images. Give your writing texture. See Chapters 18 and 20 for more on adding detail and variety to your writing.

The Washington monument got some TLC during a recent restoration project. Changes were small in scale, but still significant.

2 Strive for a readable style. Look at your word choices. Do you achieve the right level of formality for the writing situation? Do you balance technical terms with everyday language? Are your subjects specific, and do your verbs express powerful actions? Are your modifiers vivid and accurate?

Different writing styles are appropriate in different settings. When in doubt about what kind of language you should use in a piece, take a look at similar pieces others have written. For example, if you are writing a textbook review for an education course, look at similar reviews in education journals to see whether their authors use contractions and first-person pronouns, or whether more formal constructions are the rule.

Finally, look carefully at any questions your instructors or colleagues have raised about word choice. Check words you're not sure of in a dictionary to be certain the meaning you intend is appropriate and contemporary. Careful use of a thesaurus is appropriate at this stage. See Chapters 18 and 20 for more detailed suggestions on style.

3 Be sure that your tone is appropriate. For most writing projects, you'll want to avoid polarizing or hostile language that might alienate readers. Replace any name-calling ("bleeding-heart liberal," "lazy government bureaucrats," "so-called expert"), stereotypes, or unduly extreme descriptions ("man-hating ideology" to describe feminism or "religious fanatics" to describe members of an evangelical movement) with more moderate references.

If you want to make a reasoned argument, beware of relying too much on intensely emotional language ("I am unspeakably disgusted by the tobacco industry's greed because . . . "). Although a well-timed expression of feeling can move readers, your personal anger shouldn't become the focus of an argument. Of course, such language might be perfectly suitable in other kinds of writing, such as an autobiographical narrative.

For more information about tone, consult Sections 12c and 18c. Section 1g discusses the importance of presenting a fair and responsible image in a paper.

4 Cut wordiness. Many writers produce wordy first drafts, especially when generating ideas. In subsequent drafts, however, it's time to cut. In particular, go after sprawling verb phrases ("make the evaluation" → "evaluate"), redundancies ("initial start-up" → "start-up"), and boring strings of prepositional phrases ("in the bottle on the shelf in the refrigerator" → "in the bottle on the refrigerator shelf"). Be ruthless. You can often cut up to a fourth of your prose without losing anything but verbiage (see Section 20b).

5 Test your transitions. *Transitions* are words and phrases that connect sentences, paragraphs, and whole passages of writing. When transitions are faulty, a paper will seem choppy and disconnected. To decide whether that's the case, read your draft aloud. If you pause, stumble, and detect gaps, you should improve the connections between ideas. Often you'll just need to add words or phrases to the beginnings of sentences and paragraphs—expressions such as *on the other hand, however,* and *finally.* In some cases you'll have to edit more deeply, rearranging whole sections of the piece to put ideas in a more coherent order. See Chapters 15 and 17 for additional suggestions.

6 Polish the introduction and the conclusion. Most of us know that the introduction of a draft is important enough to merit special attention. It makes sense, however, not to edit the first paragraph until you know precisely how your paper is going to come out. Then you can make sure that the introduction is accurate and interesting.

Conclusions also warrant special care, but they may be even harder to write than introductions. So don't fuss too much with the conclusion until you have the main part of the paper under control. Then try to work out a strong ending that pulls the paper together and leaves your readers satisfied.

For more specific suggestions on how to improve introductory and concluding paragraphs, see Chapter 16.

7 Use a computer style checker—carefully. Style checkers and editing programs have various functions: they may calculate the readability level of sentences in a paper, locate expletive constructions (*it is, there is*), spot clichés, detect repetitions, and so on. But for all their cleverness, such programs deal with stylistic problems chiefly by counting items. They can't assess context. And it is usually context that determines, for example, whether expletives or repetitions are appropriate. If you have access to a style checker, use it, but don't assume that it can create a polished paper for you.

When you don't have access to a commercial style checker, you can create a simple version on your own. Use the search command in your word-processing program to look for specific weaknesses in your writing. For example, if you use *to be* verbs too frequently, direct the computer to find all uses of *be, is, are, was,* and *were* so that you can replace them, when appropriate, with action verbs. The longer your paper, the more helpful the search command can be.

8 Refine your layout and design. Although you made major decisions about format, graphics, and other visual elements during the drafting and revision stages, now is the time to fine-tune and polish your document's design. For example, would adding color or changing font size make the project more readable? Do you need to adjust the position of images or tables? Do the different parts of your paper look consistent? See Chapters 21 and 22 for more detailed advice on design issues.

Checklist 5.8

When Editing . . .

- Sharpen your language—make it concrete and specific.

- Check your word choice—make it readable and clear.

- Lop out wordiness.

- Be sure your tone is appropriate.

- Test your transitions.

- Polish your opening and closing.

- Use a style checker if you find it helpful.

- Fine-tune design and layout.

Going Public *Edited Sentences from Student Papers* _____

Here are sentences from student papers that have been improved by judicious editing. Notice that the changes do not greatly alter the meaning of the selections.

ORIGINAL

wordy, passive opening
It has been maintained throughout history by some of
hyphen needed   wrong connotation
the most well-trained and (notorious) nutritionists and
redundant?
(specialists) that a vegetarian diet is superior to a

nonvegetarian diet.

EDITED

Over the years, many well-trained and respected

nutritionists have maintained that a vegetarian diet

is superior to a nonvegetarian diet.

ORIGINAL

Be specific. Which border?
The immigrants cross the **border** believing that they
where?
will not be here forever. They come to make more
"to" repeated too often
money to take home to Mexico to build a better life.

EDITED

These immigrants cross the Texas-Mexico border

believing that they will not be in the United States

forever. They hope to make enough money in the

United States to return to Mexico and build better

lives.

EXERCISE 5.2 Apply the criteria for editing to a draft you are working on. Give your paper all the attention to detail it deserves. And don't back away from making more complicated changes when they are necessary.

5c   What does proofreading involve?

When you are reasonably satisfied with the content, organization, and style of your paper, you're ready to put it in final form. Like checking your appearance in the mirror before an important meeting, *proofreading* provides a final measure of quality control. The more you care about the impression a paper makes, the more important it is *not* to neglect this last step.

Use Parts III, V, and VI of the handbook to check punctuation, usage, and the conventions of edited American English.

1   Check your weakest areas. If you are a poor speller, consult a dictionary frequently. If you are inclined to put commas where they're not needed, check to be sure they don't interrupt the flow of ideas. And see that you have used the correct forms of troublesome words such as *its/it's, your/you're, there/their/they're.*

2   Check for inconsistencies. Have you switched your point of view in ways that might be confusing—for example, addressing readers initially as *you* and later referring to them as *we* or *they?* Do you use contractions in some parts of the paper but avoid them in others? Are headings in boldface on some pages and italics on other pages? Is the tone consistent throughout (not inappropriately casual in some places and formal in others)?

3   Check punctuation. Look for comma splices—that is, places where a pair of independent clauses are mistakenly joined with a comma instead of a semicolon. Take a moment to review all semicolons. See that proper nouns and adjectives (*England, African*) and *I* are capitalized. And check that you have used quotation marks and parentheses in pairs. (See Chapters 37–45.)

4   Run your computer's spelling checker. But keep in mind that a spelling checker won't catch many serious misspellings, such as *where* for *were* or *no* for *know.* Thus you'll need to follow up with a final check of your own.

5   Check for typographical errors. Look especially for transposed letters, dropped endings, faulty word division, and omitted apostrophes.

6 Check the format of your paper. Be sure to number your pages, to italicize or underline titles of sources as needed, to put other titles between quotation marks (see Chapters 41 and 44), and to clip your pages together. Be sure that you've cited outside sources appropriately and listed them in your bibliography (see Chapters 49 and 52–57). Set the margins correctly and review the page breaks. You don't want the computer to leave a heading at the bottom of a page or to separate an illustration from its caption.

Checklist 5.9

When Proofreading . . .

* Check spelling, grammar, and usage.

* Eliminate inconsistencies.

* Get the punctuation right.

* Double-check spelling.

* Eliminate typographical errors.

* Check the format of your paper.

EXERCISE 5.3 Proofread a writing project you've recently completed, looking at all the areas listed in Checklist 5.9. Which problems do you spot most often? How do you think you might avoid them in future projects?

5d How do you help another writer revise, edit, and proofread?

It's common these days for students in writing classes to work together on their papers. Meeting in small groups, writers read photocopies of each other's drafts and respond to them. The instructor may also comment on the drafts and make suggestions.

This method of responding to drafts (sometimes called *peer revision*) makes it possible for each writer in the class to receive feedback from several readers. Classmates, acting as friendly editors, can tell you whether you've included all the information you need and whether your argument is clear; they may also suggest alternative approaches or point out where you can rein in ideas that have gone too far. Even if you don't have the chance to participate in a formal peer editing session, try to get several readers' reactions to your work in progress. You can only profit from their responses—just as a professional author profits from an editor's comments before a book goes into print.

It takes skill to respond to another person's writing critically and honestly. When you do so, remember that you aren't taking the place of the writing teacher: you're an editor, not a grader. You can help a fellow writer most by showing an interest in what he or she has written, asking questions, giving encouragement, and making constructive suggestions on drafts.

Similarly, you should use peers' criticism of your own drafts constructively, listening closely and selecting the comments that best suit your goals for the project. This section provides tips to help you get the most out of a revision session.

1 Read the writer's draft straight through once. Read it as a piece of writing intended to inform, persuade, or entertain. Get a feel for the big issues before worrying about details of mechanics and usage. Do you understand what the writer is trying to achieve? Could you summarize the point of the paper? Do you find it informative, persuasive, or interesting? First impressions are important; if you don't think the draft works, try to explain why.

2 Read the paper a second time. Use the guidelines in Checklist 5.10 on page 77 to help you formulate specific responses. It's important that you say more than "I really like your paper" or "A few of your points are confusing." Explain *what* you like about it, such as well-researched facts or colorful turns of phrase. Show *where* you believe the paper needs development. At this stage keep your focus on large-scale issues, not on misspellings or editing problems to be dealt with later.

3 Make marginal comments. If you are working with a photocopy of the draft, jot comments in the margins as you read it the second time. Editorial comments should be genuine queries or pointed observations, not stinging criticisms. Even when you're pointing out a weakness in a paper, use a courteous and supportive tone, not a sarcastic or unkind one. A question can sometimes be the most helpful remark: Can you say more about this? Have you left something out here? How does this idea relate to your claim? Be as specific as you can about your reaction to the paper, and let the writer know where something is working well.

4 Write out your responses to the paper. After you have read the paper carefully and annotated it in the margins, you still want to give the writer a general comment—something to ponder. That comment should come in a paragraph at the end of the paper, and it should be a thoughtful note summarizing your reaction to the draft. It often helps if you begin by saying what you think the paper has accomplished. That way the writer knows whether the paper has achieved at least part of what he or she hoped. Then you can say something about how well the paper works. Conclude your comment with suggestions for revision, stressing what you believe the writer's priorities might be.

The response memo to Justin Cone's essay (see page 84) is a good example of this kind of written response.

5 Use a limited number of proofreading symbols. When reading a first draft, you don't want to waste time editing minor points of mechanics and usage that the writer can deal with in later versions. On the other hand, you may occasionally be asked to read a late draft of a paper, or you may know that the writer wants special help with a weakness such as spelling or punctuation. In such cases give the draft one last careful reading and look for mechanical problems only. At this time circle misspelled words (but don't correct them). Place words you think should be deleted in parentheses (but don't cross them out). Put a wavy line under words or phrases you think don't represent the writer's best choice.

> Books have detailed our culture since it began. When
> we wonder what life was like in eighteenth-century
> American we turn to volumes written then. Historical
> events are preserved in print documents, and where
> history leaves blanks, literature (and poetry) step
> in. Can the new media take over this function?

To mark other items, consult the back of this book for proofreading symbols.

Checklist 5.10

Responding to a Draft

- What do you like most about the paper?

- How well does the paper achieve its purpose? Where does the purpose come through clearly?

- How well does the writer tailor the piece to the audience? What suggestions might you make for better adapting the paper for its intended readers?

- What suggestions can you make about focusing the topic? Should the focus be narrower? Does the paper need a sharper thesis?

- Does the writer come across as credible? What suggestions can you make that might add greater authority to the paper?

- What questions does the paper raise? What additional information, discussion, or examples would you like to have?

- How effectively does the writer use language? Are sentences clear and readable? How appropriate is the tone? What recurring problems with grammar, usage, and mechanics do you notice?

- What general comments do you have for the writer?

Going Public   *Draft with Peer Comments*

Here is a draft of a paper by a first-year composition student, Justin Cone. The assignment asked him to write a research paper exploring an ethical or social issue relevant to his classmates. It's a fine draft in many respects, interesting and thoughtful. It uses personal experiences and clever turns of phrase to catch readers' attention, drawing them into the argument. The paper also incorporates source materials effectively.

The draft also has some weaknesses. To get at them we've written comments in the margins and a concluding memo of the sort you might prepare in responding to a colleague's draft. These comments are a composite of real responses Cone received from several classmates and his instructor; we've combined them in a single response from "Maria." Notice that most of the comments target large issues for revision rather than editing and mechanical problems.

Note too that Cone's paper cites and documents sources in MLA format. Some writers prefer to use Columbia Online Style for citing electronic sources. Check with your instructor to find out which style he or she prefers. You'll find information about MLA Style in Chapter 53 and on Columbia Online Style in Chapter 57.

Justin Cone

Topics in Writing

Technology's Children: Has Media Technology
Intellectually Stunted Our Generation?

I was the 5-year-old learning ABCs from
Kermit the Frog. I was the 7-year-old programming
in BASIC at 5:30 in the morning, just before Bugs
Bunny aired. I was the 10-year-old successfully
installing a modem, sans instructions. But I was
also the 16-year-old who couldn't finish reading
Thomas Hardy's <u>Tess of the D'Urbervilles</u> for   *Interesting opening!*
junior English because I didn't have the
concentration or mental stamina to read anything
longer than a computer screen.

I was raised during the computer craze. Now
my peers and I stand on a shore as technology's
children, looking across the growing technological   *Nice image,*
divide to a chunk of land sliding into the sea,   *but I get a*
                                                        little con-
where our parents swim, where our teachers worry,   *fused be-*
                                                        cause the
and where traditional kinds of literacy sink--   *sentence is*
                                                        so long &
dragging much of our culture and history with it.   *complicated*
In this paper, I will explore how media technology
has shaped young adults' ways of processing   *Clear,*
                                                        interesting
knowledge so that books seem slow and out of date.   *thesis*
In leaving books behind, our generation may lose
priceless cultural archives amassed over thousands
of years. But we may also pioneer exciting new ways
of learning.

When exploring a cause-and-effect relationship, the first thing I try to do is identify the
cause. But in this case the cause is hard to tag.

If there were some way to round up all the music videos, TV programs, fax transmissions, Internet sites, email, and online conversations (to name a few), we could heap the entire blinking, vibrating mass into a corner and point our fingers as if to say, "That's what did it." I am not foolish enough to blame media technology for all America's problems, but I can see the amazing impact it has had on my generation. As Boston area school superintendent Robert Calabrese notes, "You have to remember that the children of today have grown up with the visual media. . . . They know no other way" (qtd. in Birkerts 125). Fifty years ago, children did not grow up with computers in their homes or remote control access to instant news, sports, music videos, cartoons, and video games. But in 2002, more than 70 percent of U.S. homes with children younger than 19 used computers, and most of those had Internet access (Sellers).

This difference is the foundation for both advantages and disadvantages for my generation. We are (privileged) in that we are familiar with new forms of communication. Kids and computers "click"-- we "revel in having mastered a medium that often befuddles [our] parents" (Silver and Perry). As new media promise to move us faster and farther into the future, "to surmount impedances and hasten transitions," we embrace them (Birkerts 121).

Why is this an advantage?

Yet we are disadvantaged because much of the world still plods along the old, slow route of print. Thus our schools still demand that we be able to read and comprehend lengthy writings from heavy books. In an online article titled "Obsolete Skill Set: The 3 R's," professor Seymour Papert observes:

A child who has grown up with the freedom to explore provided by. . . machines will not sit quietly through the standard curriculum dished out in most schools today. Already, children are made increasingly restive by the contrast between the slowness of school and the more exciting pace they experience in video games and television. (2)

This quiet war between print and new media will, like all wars, claim casualties. Leaving behind books means walking away from a storehouse of cultural treasures. Books have <u>detailed</u> our culture since it began. When we wonder what life was like in eighteenth-century (American,) we turn to volumes written then. Historical events are preserved in print documents, and where history leaves blanks, literature (and poetry) step in. Can the new media take over this function? James *Will you answer this question?* Morris notes that while books are physical artifacts that can survive for many years, "Hardware and software mutate at a giddy pace and leave their forebears in the dust. The new machines cannot read the old software" (11). Books provide us with a continuity that electronic media cannot.

Sven Birkerts explains another quality associated with books, which he argues is found only in reading books. He explains, "As we read we are gradually engulfed by a half-familiar set of sensations. Because the characters walk, we walk; because they linger by roadsides or market squares, we do too. And by subtle stages we are overwhelmed" (25). I can remember reading <u>One Flew Over the Cuckoo's Nest</u> for a couple of hours and then taking a break. Leaning back in my chair for a stretch, I was surprised to see that I wasn't in a mental hospital, observing all the patients through Chief's eyes. The book had helped me build an imaginary world, but I believed in the world because I had experienced it.

Yet regardless of their merits, books are dying. Their death is not a choice, but the inevitable result of an unstoppable technological momentum carrying us into the future. Writer Neil Postman fears such a future, prophesying, "When a culture becomes overloaded with pictures; when *Why? Explain.* logic and rhetoric lose their binding authority *I'm confused.* . . . then a culture is in serious jeopardy." Such pessimistic predictions weigh heavily on our social conscience. Yet while scholars like Birkerts and Postman define the problems with technology beautifully, they offer no alternatives or suggestions, not even a "good luck" pat on the back *Good point* for my generation. Are we to allow ourselves to plummet into cultural despair? Or can we use our unique knowledge to go upward instead of down? I'll go out on a limb and say it: Yes, we can.

On a recent Sunday I decided to surf the Internet and found myself looking at a page on Shakespeare. After browsing some online pictures of Stratford-upon-Avon, I clicked a tiny icon and read a short biography of him. A list of play titles *This is fun,* blinked at the bottom of the screen, and I clicked *but does it really have* on <u>Hamlet.</u> An hour later I was reading Act II, Scene *learning* 1 with my roommate. When we happened upon a strange *value? I'm* word, we clicked over to the online glossary. Once, *not convinced.* we surfed all the way to ancient Rome before realizing that we had abandoned the play. With a

simple click, we leaped back into the dialogue at
<http://the-tech.mit.edu/Shakespeare/ works.html>.

No matter how large or well indexed, a book
simply cannot offer such a rich experience. As
Papert describes it, "the knowledge I gained was *I'm confused by this quote.*
not the collection of propositions I read in books, *Is this a good thing or*
but the web of connections that formed as my mind *a bad thing?*
bounced here and there in a non-linear fashion"
(2). The point of all this is simply that we can,
through the hypertextual visual media, learn *What is "hypertextual"?*
effectively: differently, maybe, but effectively
just the same.

Granted, the transition from books to *I think you need a fuller conclusion.*
"bookless" may be a difficult one. But it is one
that will not be completely good or completely bad
until our generation makes it so.

Works Cited

Birkerts, Sven. The Gutenberg Elegies: The Fate of
   Reading in an Electronic Age. New York:
   Ballantine, 1995.

Morris, James M. "The Human Touch." Wilson Quarterly
   22.4 (Autumn 1998): 11–12.

Papert, Seymour. "Obsolete Skill Set: The 3 R's."
   HotWired. 8 Dec. 1996 <http://www.feedmay.com/
   95.05dialog4.html>.

Postman, Neil. Conscientious Objections: Stirring Up
   Trouble About Language, Technology, and
   Education. New York: Knopf, 1988.

Sellers, Dennis. "Personal Computers on the Rise Among
   Households with Kids." 24 May 2002. MacCentral.
   10 July 2002. <http://maccentral.macworld.com/
   news/0205/24.computers.php>.

Silver, Marc, and Joellen Perry. U.S. News and World
   Report 22 Mar. 1999: 57.

Here is Maria's memo with additional comments.

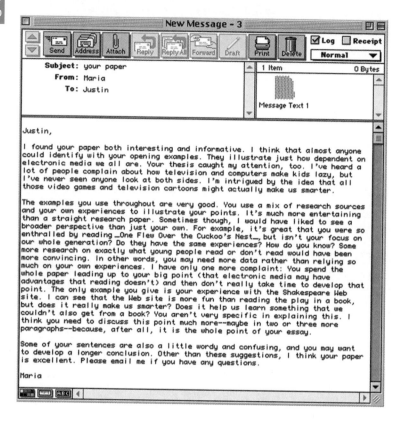

EXERCISE 5.4 Review Maria's comments on Justin's draft. If you had written this paper, would you find the advice helpful? Does it give enough guidance for improving the next draft? Working with a classmate, make a list of additional suggestions you might have made if Justin had asked you for feedback on his draft.

EXERCISE 5.5 Exchange drafts of a writing assignment or project with a classmate. Use the guidelines in Section 5d to write a memo responding to each other's drafts. Refer to your classmate's memo as you revise and edit the paper.

CHAPTER 6

How Is Writing Evaluated?

No matter how interesting or satisfying a project may be, most writers, sooner or later, ask the inevitable question: How will this be evaluated? Most of the academic, public, and professional writing you do will be judged by someone. In a college course, evaluation may certify that you have reached a specific level of proficiency, describe the progress you have made, or signal your readiness for new challenges. In public and professional settings, evaluation may simply assess how well your project was received by its intended audience. In fact, evaluations can be as varied and complex as any other part of the writing process.

But evaluations need not be mysterious or anxiety-producing. This chapter explains some of the most common methods college instructors use to evaluate writing and suggests strategies for successfully dealing with them. We recognize, of course, that different instructors bring different ideas, strategies, and expectations to the courses they teach—and that's as it should be. You should adapt our general suggestions to fit the particular requirements of your courses and instructors. We realize too that you'll face evaluation outside the classroom, when you write in workplace and community settings; however, the assessment methods used in these settings vary widely and are generally less explicitly defined than those you'll encounter in college courses—so we don't address them here. Fortunately, the strategies you learn for dealing with grades in college may help you anticipate the standards your writing must reach outside school.

Mr. Lowe *by Mark Pett*

6a How do you deal with letter grades?

Letter grades are so familiar to us all that they seem like a natural part of the academic landscape. Yet you shouldn't assume that you have nothing to learn about the marks assigned to your work. You may be surprised to discover that you have more control over the process of evaluation than you suspect.

1 Understand your school's and your instructor's grading criteria.

At the beginning of any graded writing course, gather as much information as you can about the standards your work will be expected to meet. For instance, how does your instructor or school define an *A* or a *C* or an *F*? Does the system regard *D* as a passing mark? Can a course be taken pass/fail for credit?

Typically, a college or university will have fairly general criteria for coursework. Many—but not all—schools offer some version of the following scale.

A	excellent	D	below average
B	above average	F	unsatisfactory
C	average		

Some institutions add plus and minus grades (*A−*, *C+*) or assign numerical equivalents to the letter grades. There are no nationwide standards for writing evaluation; in fact, even on a single campus, standards may vary from department to department and from one instructor to another. That's why it's so important to find out which standards will apply to you.

Some writing instructors distribute their own detailed grading criteria for the courses they teach. One instructor provides this description of a *C* paper to his first-year composition students:

AN EXCERPT FROM ONE INSTRUCTOR'S GRADING CRITERIA

C Paper (Average)

A *C* paper responds adequately to the assignment. Its treatment of an appropriate topic is thoughtful and reasonably well developed. A clear claim or thesis is supported by logical warrants and adequate, reliable evidence. The writer anticipates counterarguments and offers appropriate rebuttals. The structure of the paper is solid and logical. Paragraphs are organized around clear topic sentences. Transitions connect sentences to sentences and paragraphs to paragraphs. Sentences are correctly structured and reasonably varied. The handling of documentation (if any) is adequate. A *C* paper is generally correct though it may have a few comma splices, common subject-verb agreement errors, or difficulties with pronoun agreement/reference. The paper is double spaced, paginated, titled, printed on clean white paper, and either clipped or stapled.

Such a description is more helpful than the term *average* in explaining what an instructor expects in a *C* paper. But it may still be too broad to explain exactly what features an instructor looks for in a particular assignment. For instance, not all papers will have paragraphs introduced by topic sentences or make claims that require evidence or documentation. For this reason, some instructors provide grading standards tailored to each assignment. Here's a list of criteria one instructor developed for a researched argument assignment in a first-year composition course:

RHE 309S Critical Reading and Persuasive Writing
Professor Ruszkiewicz
Paper #1—Identity

Name: _____   Date: _____

Title of Paper: _____

1. Quality of your discussion of *identity*   Excellent___:___:___:___:___Poor

2. Clarity of your claim & argument   Excellent___:___:___:___:___Poor

3. Persuasiveness of your evidence   Excellent___:___:___:___:___Poor

4. Use of appropriate sources   Excellent___:___:___:___:___Poor

5. Handling of rebuttal/qualifiers   Excellent___:___:___:___:___Poor

6. Organization
   (including paragraph structures)   Excellent___:___:___:___:___Poor

7. Interest/adaptation to audience   Excellent___:___:___:___:___Poor

8. Sentence structures and style   Excellent___:___:___:___:___Poor

9. Handling of quotations/documentation   Excellent___:___:___:___:___Poor

10. Grammar/mechanics/word choice   Excellent___:___:___:___:___Poor

11. Presentation/format   Excellent___:___:___:___:___Poor

GRADE   _____

In schools that use "contract grading" in writing courses, the expectations will be markedly different. In this system, students and instructor agree beforehand that a particular grade will be earned by doing specified kinds of work or by completing a specific set of assignments. In such a course, a student might contract to earn an *A* by satisfactorily completing six papers or a *B* by satisfactorily completing five. The terms of the contract may be quite detailed and may involve activities such as participation in online forums in distance learning courses. If a project submitted is deemed acceptable and meets the contracted types and amounts of work, the grade follows automatically. Under a contract system, you have considerable power to determine your final grade.

2 Work to clarify any criteria that seem confusing.

Whatever the system of evaluation you are working with, you should examine it critically and ask questions *before* and *while* you prepare your projects, not after. If you are told that an average paper will earn a *C,* you might ask your instructor these questions.

- What does a *C* (or *B,* or *A*) paper or project do?
- What does a *C* paper look like? May I see models?
- What does "average" in this case mean—an average performance in the section, in the first-year class as a whole, in the entire school?

When your instructor hands out detailed grading criteria, go over them with each new assignment, perhaps with a highlighting pen so you don't overlook important requirements.

Even when instructors don't spell out clear-cut standards, you can still learn much about their evaluation strategies by observing what they do in class. Did your instructor spend days teaching forms of argument or transitional phrases? She will likely pay attention to these features in your papers. Does the assignment sheet for a project mention "audience awareness," "cumulative sentences," or "MLA documentation"? Be sure you understand these concepts and handle them well in your project. Again, when you don't understand your instructor's expectations, don't be shy—ask for help.

3 Understand which portions of your work will be evaluated.

The grade you receive on any assignment may depend on more than the quality of the final project. You should read any assignment sheet like a contract, to be sure you know what will count in the evaluation. Many instructors evaluate an entire writing process, assigning credit, for example, to your topic proposal, working bibliography, peer editing, first draft, and so on. Don't dismiss early stages of the writing process as busywork; your instructor may see them, with good reason, as points at which much learning takes place.

Similarly, examine carefully the formulas used to compute your final course mark. Sometimes an instructor designs a grading formula to place heavier emphasis on work produced later in the term. That way, he or she can reward students who make substantial progress. Here is one example.

Paper #1	10%
Paper #2	20%
Paper #3	30%
Paper #4	30%
Quizzes/participation	10%

In other cases the grading formula may include elements that carry the same weight throughout a term—items such as quizzes, exams, class participation, and credit for peer editing. Even faithful attendance may play a role in determining your final grade.

You should also be sure you know exactly who will be evaluating your work. You'll find it easier to satisfy your evaluators when you know precisely who they are. If your writing course includes a service-learning or internship component, will your supervisor in that setting help to decide on your grade? At some institutions, grades in writing courses may be decided by a panel of instructors so that standards stay consistent across course sections. In courses that include collaborative writing projects, your team members may have a voice in determining your grade.

4 Read your instructor's responses carefully. Your instructor and your colleagues may comment in a variety of ways on your drafts and final essays. It's important to read and respond to those comments appropriately.

Most papers come back from instructors (or peer editors) with comments in the margin. Whether written on paper or added electronically, these brief comments are usually directed at specific issues in your writing.

Some comments may just be proofreading symbols of the kind you'll find in this handbook at the beginning of the chapters on grammar and mechanics: *sp, cs, no* ¶. These symbols tell you that the text contains a specific mechanical problem, one you should be able to fix by consulting a corresponding chapter in a handbook. Many instructors simply place an *X* next to a line that contains a slip in grammar, mechanics, or usage, leaving it to you to discover the particular problem. When you encounter an *X* or its equivalent and don't immediately detect a problem, you might review a list of proofreading symbols (see inside the back cover of this book). Consider, too, those problems instructors have noted before in your work: Do you typically have difficulty with subject-verb agreement? With pronoun references? With wordiness? Look for patterns in the errors marked by teachers or peer editors, and then work to eliminate your most persistent problems.

Some marginal comments may be aimed at larger issues. Look especially at any questions posed by an instructor or peer editor: *Where's your thesis? Can you provide a better example? Have you considered possible rebuttals to your case?* Such questions tell you that a serious reader expects more from your writing and that serious revision should follow. Even if you won't have an opportunity to revise that assignment, you can use such comments to improve your next project.

Finally, look carefully at any summary comments you receive at the end of a draft or graded project. Some instructors write lengthy responses to a paper; others offer briefer feedback. Typically, instructors use their final comments to describe the overall strengths and weaknesses of a draft and to suggest strategies for revision or future work. Don't be defensive when you read these remarks—you can learn a lot from them.

Chart 6.1

Interpreting Marginal Comments

Marginal comments tend to be brief, even when they are attached to a paper electronically. Standard proofreading symbols and comments are reprinted on the inside back cover of this handbook. But you may encounter other, more cryptic remarks on your drafts. Following are suggestions for dealing with a few of them. (Remember, however, that different instructors may use correction symbols in different ways. Be sure to ask your instructor if you have questions about his or her comments.)

AWK   means AWKWARD

Your sentence or phrase doesn't read quite right. The language may be grammatical, but the item needs to be reworked for clarity. See Chapter 19.

WDY   means WORDY

State the idea more directly. Cut *be* verbs, eliminate passive verbs, excise redundancies. See Chapter 20.

LOG?   means LOGIC?

Your editor is challenging your thinking in this passage. Maybe you've made an unsupported (or unsupportable) claim, committed a logical fallacy, or offered unreliable evidence. See Chapter 12.

?   means HUH?

Your reader is puzzled by something you've said, not by a problem in mechanics or usage. Review how you've phrased your ideas, or reconsider the evidence you have offered.

X   means PROBLEM

Your reader has found a problem in mechanics or usage somewhere in the line next to the *X*. You'll have to find it on your own.

✓   means GOOD

Your reader likes the point you've made or the way you have phrased an idea. Be happy.

EXERCISE 6.1

1. Check your school's official handbook or catalog for its statement about evaluation and grading. How does it define and measure success in a course? How detailed are the criteria of evaluation? How well do those criteria fit written work?

2. On a Web search engine such as *Google* <http://www.google.com> use a search term such as "grading standards" or "evaluating writing" to locate statements about grading policy from several writing courses. Compare the policies: How do they differ? How are they alike? What do they emphasize? Which do you find most helpful as a writer?

6b   How do you prepare a portfolio?

In the last decade, many writing instructors have moved to *portfolio* evaluation of their students' progress as writers. Portfolio systems can vary as much as conventional grading, but they do share consistent elements. Writers are typically asked to assemble printed or online collections of their work produced over a term to show how they have developed. The writers may even control some aspects of the evaluation, such as choosing which projects to include in their final portfolios.

As you might guess, the emphasis in portfolio systems, in theory at least, is on the process of writing rather than solely on final products and grades. Portfolios are designed to make evaluation a fuller and richer experience, one that focuses on a body of work rather than on individual assignments. Portfolios also emphasize the relationship between writers, their colleagues, and their instructors. Yet grades still play a role in portfolio systems because most institutions still demand them.

1 Understand what writing portfolios do.

Portfolios can be shaped in many ways, so it's important to know the purpose of a portfolio you are asked to prepare. Will it be used for course placement or to certify that you have met a specific writing requirement? Will it serve as a record of your work over an extended period of time, perhaps an entire college career? Or will it be a component of your grade for a specific writing course?

Because portfolios serve different purposes, their contents vary enormously. Portfolios designed to provide a look at a writer's development over an extended period of time might include the following:

- Materials generated at the invention stage of writing, including freewriting, scratch outlines, topic proposals, and in-class or homework exercises
- Multiple drafts of papers
- Peer editing and instructors' comments on projects
- Transcripts from online forums or MOO sessions
- Creative work in multiple genres and forms
- Final versions of projects
- Self-assessments of written work

Other types of portfolios may be more restrictive; your instructor may specify exactly what the final portfolio should include. It's not unusual for an evaluation project to include two portfolios: a *working portfolio,* which includes all the relevant material generated during a specific time, and a briefer *final portfolio,* in which writers select their best or most representative materials to demonstrate what they've learned both about themselves and the process of writing. These choices are often the most revealing aspect of presenting a portfolio.

2 Design your portfolio to create a record of learning.

A good portfolio not only demonstrates that you have progressed as a writer; it actually contributes to that development by making you think more about your learning. That's why portfolios often incorporate so many kinds of items. You may not take the invention stage of writing or peer editing seriously until you see it fitted into the overall process of writing. Portfolios encourage this kind of reflection.

Portfolios should also encourage you to think of yourself as a writer, not as a student graded for each item you produce. As a result, portfolios sometimes include items you don't create yourself, such as the remarks of peers and instructors on your work. And some of that work may be tentative or open-ended. While a final portfolio typically includes several polished final products, your instructor may encourage you to select fragmentary pieces or exercises that ended up as interesting dead ends. The overall package should represent a full range of your talents.

3 Comment thoughtfully and honestly on your work.

In many portfolio projects, writers are asked to prepare statements in which they reflect on their writing and learning process. These statements, often required at specific stages, demand a self-scrutiny that may not be instinctive, especially since such reflection is not a typical part of most college courses. Your statements should be thoughtful and scrupulously honest. If you try to write what you think your instructor wants to hear, or if you exaggerate in order to make your progress sound more impressive, you won't learn much about yourself as a writer and you probably won't fool your instructor either. If you aren't sure what to write, focus on specific aspects of your experience as a writer in the course: how you found a topic for a paper; why you made specific revisions to a piece; what you discovered in the library. Begin with the details of composing and consider, too, the connections you have made with other writers. Such statements will often be informal, even colloquial in tone, but they should be serious too.

Going Public *One Student's Self-Assessment* _____

Here is a self-assessment written at the end of a semester by student Sarah Davis, who had just completed a nonfiction writing course. Christy Friend, her instructor, had asked her to write a two- to three-page letter explaining the items in her portfolio, evaluating her progress during the term, and estimating her course grade.

May 3, 2002

Final Portfolio

English 460

Dear Dr. Friend,

The reason I enrolled in English 460 was simply to become a better writer. I considered writing to be a weak area for me, since my background is in biology and health sciences. As a biology major, I have written numerous lab reports and scientific research papers, and I consider that my strength. These papers are easy for me because I already have the information; I just have to arrange it. The challenge occurs when I have to write about a book I read, a character, or what an idea means to me. However, the strategies I have learned in this class (freewriting, thought questions, journal, constant feedback) have helped me tremendously. As I explain below, during the semester I have greatly improved my ability to collaborate, write in a variety of genres, and revise and polish my work.

Collaboration has helped me improve the most. I enjoy consulting with different people on each draft in progress. My revision group can tell me if my essay makes sense to them, does it flow, is there anything they don't understand. Although I participated in all the workshops, peer feedback helped me especially in writing my final draft of "The Track" because they gave me a sense of which words and details worked to further my theme. I have also worked hard to incorporate your feedback in all of my finished papers and to provide detailed advice to my group members.

Practicing with a range of nonfiction genres has also been a challenging and helpful experience.

In my portfolio, you will see humor writing, place writing, a memoir essay, an argumentative piece, and a draft of a profile. I had the most success with the argument genre, as you will see in my editorial, "Response to Edward Lewis," where I collect all the facts about the topic of athletes' scholastic record on campus, take a stance, and defend it against the opposition.

I have also improved my revision and editing skills this semester. The continual revisions to my memoir piece, "The Track," were overwhelming at times. I had so many memories and it was tough to condense the material into one essay. As the final structure developed (using vignettes organized within the framework of a single workout) it was a lot easier to streamline. I am proud of the way I was able to incorporate flashbacks to deepen the focus while still keeping the events clear. The most important thing in this revision was explaining the importance of running, my overriding focus, to my readers. I had to keep asking myself, "Does my passion interest the reader?" and "How can I make them understand why this is important to me?"

While the other pieces I've included here are finished, I slashed the idea of finishing the profile piece I started about my Dad, because it is too personal a topic to deal with for this audience. Instead, I opted to include a humor piece about college life and time management. I first suggested this piece to Allen and Katie in a revision workshop, and they helped me to brainstorm ideas that eventually led up to this piece. The final piece in the portfolio, "Hospital," has incorporated your suggestion to bring my own voice in and acquire a clearer focus. In my final draft, I have clarified why I was at the hospital and focused on the irony of the ICU. For awhile, the conclusion of this piece gave me trouble, but by taking your advice to focus on the ironies of the hospital, I was able to maintain my focus and successfully conclude the piece.

Finally, this class has helped me as a writer to express myself more clearly and fully on paper. I am more confident not just about my own writing, but also about helping others improve their work. I have worked hard in this class to improve and polish the papers selected here, participate in all the in-class writing activities and journal, experiment with new forms of writing, and participate in the revision workshops. Taking all these things into consideration, I believe I deserve an "A" for my work in this class.

Sincerely,

Sarah Davis

4 Work steadily on your portfolio. A portfolio system of evaluation doesn't demand less from you than more traditional systems. To prepare a substantial portfolio, you'll have to work steadily and consistently over a full school term (or longer). You can't expect to make up all your deferred work in a burst of energy at the last minute—portfolios don't work that way. You need to determine at the start what items your portfolio will have to contain and when they must be in place. Often, portfolios are submitted several times during a term, not just at the end. Remember, too, that you'll likely be asked to work with other writers in the construction of their portfolios. Be just as conscientious in responding to their work as you want them to be with your own.

Finally, take the time to present a handsome portfolio, whether the work you produce is on paper or online. "Handsome" doesn't mean overproduced or slick; rather, your portfolio ought to show that you have given every element the time it merits—documents should be organized, clearly labeled, and displayed in a folder, notebook, or other format recommended by your instructor.

 Some instructors use a *learning record*, a systematic way of evaluating progress in literacy over extended periods of time. Created originally to serve students in elementary and secondary schools, learning records have begun to appear in college courses as well, especially in an online form. For detailed information on the *Learning Record, Online*, see <http://www.cwrl.utexas.edu/~syverson/olr>. For more general information about using a learning record system, see <http://www.learningrecord.org>.

EXERCISE 6.2 Write a self-assessment of a recent writing project or series of projects you've written in a single course. What are the strengths and satisfactions of the piece(s)? What do you think you might have managed better?

6c What are your rights and responsibilities in the evaluation process?

Evaluating writing may not be a hard science, but neither is it a completely mysterious, subjective process—even though it might sometimes seem so when you are puzzling over why the American literature paper you thought was great received a *C*, or why your first history essay got an *A* but the second rated only a *B−*.

Because writing is a human activity, it provokes human responses that are subtle and variable. Yet evaluations under such conditions can also be rigorous and consistent. If you take responsibility for your part in the process and assume good faith on the part of those who are assessing your work, your experiences with evaluation will be more productive.

1 Bring reasonable expectations to the evaluation process. When your writing is evaluated in a college course, you can reasonably expect your instructor to give you some basic information. You should know what work you're expected to complete, which assignments

will be graded, and how your final mark will be computed. Many instructors provide this information in a course syllabus or policy statement handed out during the first few days of class.

You should also receive periodic feedback on your work, in the form of grades or evaluative comments on your writing, and sometimes both. When an instructor returns a graded project, you should receive some indication of why your work received the mark it did. Not all instructors provide such justifications in written comments, but most are willing to meet with you to talk about a grade. It's part of your instructor's job to give this kind of information and feedback—and you have a right to expect it.

But just as your instructor should set reasonable policies, you should be sure that your own expectations are reasonable. First, recognize that standards are typically much higher in college courses than they are elsewhere—especially in high school English courses. Complaining that you don't deserve a *C* on a paper because you always got *A*'s before is a fallacy of argument that you probably don't want an instructor to point out. Similarly, don't blame a lower-than-expected grade on details in the assignment you should have paid more attention to (such as due dates or the form of documentation required).

Understand, too, that teachers will usually give you feedback at some stages of your project, from the topic proposal to the first draft. But they can't and shouldn't do everything. They can't comment on every underdeveloped thought, sharpen every unfocused paragraph, catch every error, reword every less-than-sterling sentence. To do so would intrude upon your rights as an author. At some point you must take charge of the writing project and move it beyond what others might have imagined. You won't always succeed on your own, but you will learn more about writing when you take responsibility for your work—both the failures and the successes.

2 Question a grade responsibly. There will be times when you wish to inquire about a grade. When this is the case, don't run up to your instructor and demand satisfaction immediately after an assignment is returned. Instead, take time to weigh the mark and any comments on your paper against the specific grading criteria, the performance you may have seen from other students, and your own frank assessment of what you have achieved.

It may be hard to do, but you should approach a grade inquiry as an opportunity to learn more about your writing. Ask yourself what might account for the difference between your perception of the work and your instructor's. If you think you did everything an instructor required, would merely doing what was required earn the kind of evaluation you hoped to receive? You also have to be honest about *effort.* Some instructors will reward writers for the time put into a project, but effort alone cannot be the entire story. All writers have the experience at times of laboring mightily to produce average or unsatisfying work.

If you decide to pursue a grading inquiry, build a reasonable argument (see Chapter 12): be sure you have a substantive claim to make, good reasons to support it, and specific evidence to draw upon. Many instructors expect inquiries about grades to be put into writing. (It's a good exercise even when such a statement is not required.) If you can draw attention to genuine strengths or strategies in a project that your teacher might have overlooked or undervalued, you may have a case. Be as specific as possible and focus on large-scale rhetorical issues such as your response to the assignment, your sensitivity to an audience, or the quality of your thinking and research. Make your case on substantive claims, not on quibbles or technicalities.

SUMMARY *When Your Writing Is Evaluated in a Course . . .*

You have the *right* to

- Know what work you need to complete and what assignments will be graded.

- Know how your course mark will be computed.

- Receive periodic feedback to tell you how well your writing matches your instructor's standards.

You have the *responsibility* to

- Assume that your instructor is acting in good faith.

- Recognize that you can learn from evaluations of your writing.

- Bring reasonable expectations to the grading process.

- Pay attention to instructions and grading criteria.

- Pay attention to instructor's comments on your work.

- Pursue grading inquiries responsibly.

PART

11

Writing for Academic and Public Forums

CHAPTER 7

How Do You Write in College?

7a How do you write a successful academic paper?

As a college student, you can count on having to write. That's a fact of life, regardless of your major. But if you wrote only a few papers in high school, or if you have been out of school for several years and have written little during that time, you may feel uncertain when you think about starting to write again, not only in English classes but in history, philosophy, and science courses. Understandably, you wonder what instructors expect.

The answer is that academic writing is not necessarily tricky, but it differs from high school writing because college instructors have unique requirements in mind. While expectations vary somewhat from instructor to instructor and from subject to subject, most projects will ask you to approach topics with a critical eye, to justify your ideas with logical reasons and evidence, and to cite the sources of your information. These expectations are not optional; they are the *responsibilities* of any college writer. Once you understand these responsibilities, you can address academic audiences with confidence.

1 Review the assignment. When instructors assign a writing project, they usually have specific expectations in mind: a certain approach to a topic, certain kinds of research, a set number of pages, and a particular due date. Take all these instructions into account as you plan your paper. Think about what you can realistically accomplish, and focus your work accordingly.

Before you get too far into a topic, ask yourself these practical questions: How much research will you have to do? What special materials will you need? How much time do you have? Some books may not be immediately available, or the library may not carry the periodical you want. If you need to do interviews, you'll have to allot time to contact people and keep appointments. And if the paper is due in the same week as two papers for other courses, you'll need to start extra early.

In other words, assess the requirements and think ahead, just as you would for any other big project—planning a family reunion or mailing your income tax forms by the deadline—so you can avoid last-minute snags.

2 Don't take on too much in a writing project. When you make a claim in a paper, think of yourself as having staked out a piece of territory: you've asserted what you believe and drawn lines around it, and now you have to defend it. You don't want to find out when you're halfway through that your claims are overextended and you can't back up the commitments you've made. You'll do better to stake out a smaller topic that you can manage. Then you'll have a chance to think and write about it in detail. See Section 2b for advice on how to narrow a topic.

7a
college

3 Support your claims with reasons and evidence. If one word could describe college instructors and professors, it would be *skeptical*, especially when they read an explanation or an argument. Unless you're doing an informal assignment like a journal entry or writing a personal piece for a creative writing course, it's usually not enough to claim on the basis of personal opinion or feelings that something is true or that something should be done. In most courses, instructors want students to support their claims with reasons and evidence. Thus the best topics for academic assignments are generally those that are amenable to factual evidence and research. A passionate account of your belief in the afterlife, your relationship with your spouse, or your love for the great outdoors is better suited to personal writing than to most academic assignments.

4 Understand what constitutes good reasons and acceptable evidence in academic writing. We've all read popular magazine articles that generalize about a trend or a phenomenon on the basis of a single perspective or a few dramatic examples: "How Learning Phonics Made My Child an 'A' Student" and "Dangerous Cults Infiltrating Campus, Say Local Citizens." These kinds of pieces dramatize issues vividly; however, their approach wouldn't satisfy an instructor seeking a thorough academic treatment of a topic. Academic writing has its own standards of argument and proof that are more rigorous than what's expected in many other kinds of writing.

In academic writing, readers expect you to support your arguments with logical reasons and sufficient evidence. These supporting materials should come from reliable, recent sources, and you should be

Popular and academic publications often report on similar topics, such as diet and health, but they usually support their claims quite differently.

able to produce enough of them to show that you're knowledgeable about the topic. This often means doing research. Depending on the paper you're writing, you might look for the following kinds of data.

- Historical documents
- Research findings
- Case studies
- Eyewitness accounts
- Statements from experts on the subject
- Statistics

You'll find such evidence in reference volumes, scholarly books and articles, government archives, and publications produced by professional organizations.

When undergraduate student Matt Valentine decided to write a research paper about the Holocaust, he already had general opinions about the subject. But he didn't stop there; he did research to compile reputable data. In the library he consulted historical books and articles; he asked a history professor to direct him to relevant government documents from World War II; he consulted Web sites maintained by non-profit organizations concerned with the Holocaust; and he interviewed a local Holocaust survivor. When he sat down to write his paper, Valentine had on hand an impressive amount of supporting evidence that he knew would satisfy his readers.

However, academic evidence isn't "one size fits all." Some arguments and evidence are more appropriate to some writing tasks than to others. If Valentine were writing his paper for a history class, his historical sources would be the most relevant. If he were writing a survivor's profile for a journalism course, he might draw primarily on material he collected in personal interviews. For his writing course he decided to examine the language that people use to talk and write about the Holocaust, so he concentrated on literary and popular works about the topic. The Going Public section below summarizes some sources he incorporated into his final paper. (See Sections 47b and 47c for more on finding and selecting academic sources.)

7a
college

Going Public *Writing an Annotated Bibliography* _____

An instructor may ask you to turn in an *annotated bibliography* that briefly describes and evaluates the sources you plan to use in a paper. This excerpt from Matt Valentine's annotated bibliography details some of the materials he eventually included in his term paper about the Holocaust. Note the breadth and variety of his sources. Do you think he's chosen materials that his instructor will find valid and reliable? Are they the right kinds of evidence for an academic paper?

WORKING BIBLIOGRAPHY FOR

"THE RHETORIC OF ATROCITY:

HOW PEOPLE WRITE AND TALK ABOUT THE HOLOCAUST"

American Jewish Committee. The Jews in Nazi Germany:

A Handbook of Facts Regarding Their Present

Situation. 1935. New York: Fertig, 1982. This

republished book gives perspectives held by

American Jews in the years preceding the

Holocaust.

Keegan, John. "Code of Silence." New York Times 25

Nov. 1996: A13. This news article reports on the

release of government records suggesting that

officials of the Allied forces were aware of the

Holocaust death camps but chose to keep the

information away from the public and not to act

upon it.

Meyer, Walter. Personal interview. 24 Nov. 1996.
First a member of the Hitler Youth and later a
concentration camp prisoner, Dr. Meyer talks
about propaganda, attitudes in urban Germany and
in the camps, and the reactions of the Allied
occupation forces after the war.

7a
college

Pehle, Walter H. From "Reichskristallnacht" to
Genocide. Nov. 1938. Trans. William Templer. New
York: Berg, 1991. This book, which contains
scholarly essays by historians, deals with the
development of anti-Semitic sentiments in
Germany leading to the Holocaust. Also, some
essays explore the civilian population: to what
extent were the German citizens aware of what
was going on?

Spiegelman, Art. Maus II: A Survivor's Tale. New
York: Pantheon, 1991. This best-selling,
Pulitzer Prize-winning comic book tells the
story of one survivor's experience of the
Holocaust.

---

5 Document your sources and give credit to others where appropriate.

College instructors expect writers to cite their sources and to give credit for any words or ideas that have come from someone else. If you write, "It is generally believed that . . . " or "Experts agree on . . . ," your instructor is likely to ask, "By whom? Where?" When you cite statistics or research, your teacher will want to know where you got your data. And if you use *any* material that someone else thought of or wrote first, you're obligated to give that source credit. If you don't, you're committing plagiarism, a serious offense. (See Section 49d for more about plagiarism.)

Documenting sources takes time, but it's an essential part of college writing. It's not difficult to do once you know where to look for guidelines. Sections 49a and 49c offer comprehensive information on documenting sources.

6 Follow research and writing conventions appropriate to your subject area. While the guidelines we discuss in this chapter apply generally to the writing you'll do in any course, be aware that some expectations differ from subject area to subject area. Suppose that you wanted to write a paper on alcoholism. Imagine the various forms it might take in different courses: In a creative writing course you might craft a poem about a character's struggle with recovery. In a sociology course you might write a formal case study based on interviews with a member of Alcoholics Anonymous. In a biology course you might collect and report on data about the physical effects of alcohol on laboratory rats. All three projects would require critical thought, research, and the ability to construct a clear argument. Their differences grow out of the different *goals* and *approaches* valued in each discipline—the humanities, the social sciences, and the natural sciences.

7a
college

- **Goals:** What kinds of questions interest scholars in this discipline? What do they want to find out? Do they want to know how physical objects and processes work? Are they interested in discovering how people have interpreted the world at different times or in different cultures?
- **Methods:** How do scholars in a particular discipline go about finding out what they want to know? Do they test hypotheses systematically and empirically? Do they critically interpret texts and other artifacts?
- **Evidence:** What kinds of materials do scholars in a subject area typically use to support their arguments—numerical data, historical artifacts, quotations from literary or philosophical texts?
- **Genres:** What kinds of documents do scholars in a field typically produce—lab reports, critical analyses, case studies, personal commentaries? What organizational and stylistic conventions are typical? Is it appropriate to use first person pronouns or passive verb constructions, for example?
- **Documentation:** What system do scholars in the field use for citing and documenting sources?

The chart on page 108 lists some basic characteristics of research and writing in the humanities, social sciences, and natural sciences. Keep these in mind as you approach your writing in other courses, and ask your instructor when you're unsure about what rules apply.

7 Remember that college instructors expect professional-looking work. When you turn in a paper, you send your instructor a message about the kind of student you are. Just as you

HIGHLIGHT	*Writing in Academic Disciplines*	
HUMANITIES	SOCIAL SCIENCES	NATURAL SCIENCES
Subject areas		
Literature, philosophy, history, classics	Sociology, psychology, anthropology, social work, education	Astronomy, botany, chemistry, physics, zoology
Purposes		
To study how people use language or other symbols to interpret experience	To study how people create and live within social systems	To study the structure and workings of the physical world
Methods		
Close reading and analysis of texts	Field work and other observational research; statistical analysis of data	The scientific method, experimental testing of hypotheses
Sources		
Literary, philosophical, and historical works and critical commentaries on them	Data collected from interviews, surveys, field observations; previous research by other scholars	Data collected through systematic observation in controlled settings
Formats		
Critical and interpretive essays, book reviews, personal and reflective pieces, creative writing	Field notes, case studies, research reports, reviews of research	Lab reports; research reports; summaries of research; process analyses
Documentation		
Usually MLA	Usually APA	Often CBE

wouldn't come to class barefoot or smoke cigars during a lecture, you shouldn't tarnish your image with a poorly presented essay. Even if your instructors have been lenient about usage or punctuation errors when they read your drafts or haven't issued special warnings about grammatical correctness, they care about such details in the final product. If your paper looks good, it will make a good impression.

Before you submit an essay for a grade, proofread for faulty punctuation, agreement errors, and spelling. If you have trouble with any of these areas, get a second opinion from a friend or consult the grammar and usage portions of this book. Run your computer's spelling checker. Then check to see that your paper complies with any formatting instructions included in the assignment: Has the instructor specified MLA or APA style? a particular font size? single or double spacing? See Section 5c for advice on proofreading and Chapters 53 through 57 for help with particular formats.

7a
college

Instructors hate to get papers they can barely read. Word-process all writing projects, double spaced, with numbered pages. Be sure your printer produces quality output. Fasten with a staple or paper clips.

If the assignment allows it, you may want to experiment with layout, typefaces, and other graphic elements to create an even more attractive finished product. Chapters 21 and 22 provide comprehensive advice on document design.

Checklist 7.1

Writing for College Assignments

When you write in college, remember to

- Assess the assignment and plan to meet its requirements.
- Limit your thesis to one that you can adequately cover and support.
- Support your claims with reasons and evidence.
- Keep in mind what constitutes acceptable evidence in academic writing.
- Follow conventions appropriate for the subject area.
- Document your sources.
- Hand in only carefully edited, proofread, professional-looking papers.

EXERCISE 7.1 Here are several claims from undergraduate writing assignments. For each claim, suggest specific kinds of supporting evidence you think the writer's instructor would find appropriate and convincing.

1. *From a research project for a social work course:* For children who come from severely abusive families, high-quality institutional care is a better option than programs that try to reform the parents in an effort to keep the family together.

2. *From a research paper for a first-year writing course:* Professional athletes are poor role models because so many of them engage in unsportsmanlike or illegal behavior, on and off the playing field.

3. *From an essay exam for an ethics course:* Circuses are unethical because they exploit animals purely for entertainment.

4. *From a research review for a human biology course:* A growing body of data suggests that asthma has a strong genetic component.

EXERCISE 7.2 From a popular magazine, select an article on a current topic. Then go to the library and find a scholarly journal article on the same topic. Compare and contrast the kinds of evidence used in the two pieces: How much evidence does each writer cite? What kinds of sources does each draw on? Which piece do you find more interesting? more convincing?

EXERCISE 7.3 Evaluate a paper you've recently written for a college course against Checklist 7.1 on page 109. Then ask yourself these questions: Does your paper meet the standards? Where does it fall short? If you could write the paper over again, to which item on the list would you pay the most attention? Why?

7b How do you write on essay examinations?

If you're like many writers, you'll do most of your writing outside the classroom—in your room, the library, or another familiar and relatively comfortable setting. However, when you write in a test situation, your approach will be drastically different. Whether you're taking a midterm exam in a history course or a competency examination required by your job, you can count on less flexibility and more pressure. You may have to write in response to questions that you have not chosen and have never seen before. You'll compose in a classroom setting, and you'll usually have only an hour or two to shape your ideas into a single draft that convinces readers you know the material.

Every writer should know how to compose under pressure. Researchers estimate that up to half the writing you do during college will occur on exams. After you leave school, you'll find that many jobs require the ability to write quickly and efficiently. Journalists must create news stories on tight deadlines. Engineers and other technical workers fre-

quently write on-the-spot progress reports. And many government agencies base promotions for police officers, social workers, and other employees partly on competency test scores. Unfortunately, many writers resign themselves to failure at this kind of writing, believing, "I freeze under pressure."

Don't give up before you start. You *can* write well in an exam setting if you understand the unique skills involved and work to master them.

1   Know the material. Preparation is half the battle in an essay exam. Lay the foundation for success well in advance by attending class regularly, keeping up with required readings, and participating actively in class discussions.

But simply absorbing the material is not enough. You also need to organize and think critically about what you know. Look for clues in course lectures and readings about what ideas and examples are important (*Three basic arguments for . . . ; A central figure in . . .*) and organize your notes accordingly. As you read, summarize important theories and concepts in your own words to be sure that you understand them. Review your notes periodically and ask yourself how new material fits with the old. And when you have questions, speak up.

If your teacher often asks students to express their views on course material or apply it to new situations, you can bet that he or she will include these kinds of questions on the exam. Prepare yourself by rehearsing your views about key points in the lecture and readings: Do you agree? Do you disagree? What approaches or theories make the most sense to you?

To practice applying your knowledge, look occasionally at the newspaper and imagine how the material you're studying might relate to a current event or controversy. For example, that article you read in your U.S. history course about the debates between the Federalists and the Anti-Federalists in the Revolutionary period might help you understand what's at issue in a contemporary Supreme Court decision about states' rights. See Chapter 10 for detailed advice on getting the most out of your reading.

2 Find out as much as you can about the exam. Because many exams cover hundreds or even thousands of pages of material, focus your preparation on those portions most likely to appear on the exam. As the exam date approaches, ask your instructor for details: How many questions will the test include? What kinds of questions? What topics will be emphasized? Will you get to choose from several questions? Knowing some parameters will help guide your study: for instance, if the test consists of four short essays, you won't have time to list many examples or details, so you should concentrate on learning main ideas.

If your instructor provides copies of exams from previous semesters, seize the opportunity. An old exam can help you anticipate what kinds of items will appear, and you can use it for a practice run. If your instructor does not offer sample exams, many schools maintain test files that archive exams from a variety of courses. The more you know about what to expect, the more comfortable you'll feel.

3 Use your study time intelligently. This advice may seem obvious, but it's true. An exam requires you to quickly pull together what you know—so you'll need to be in top academic form. Forgo extreme studying techniques, such as cramming or pulling all-nighters, that leave you exhausted at the time of the test. And don't try to learn every piece of information covered in class; you'll only feel overwhelmed.

Instead, spend your time practicing the thinking and writing skills that exam essays require. Make scratch outlines of important theories or arguments you think are likely to be covered, along with one or two key examples or details, and use these as the basis for your review. Once you have a solid command of the material, devise questions similar to those you think might appear on the exam and practice answering them. Use a timer to accustom yourself to thinking under pressure.

Classmates can be another valuable resource. If you enjoy working collaboratively, try forming a study group with colleagues. Meet once or twice before the exam to compare notes, puzzle out gaps in your knowledge, and practice explaining key points to each other. But don't substitute group meetings for individual study. Allow yourself plenty of time to go over group insights and integrate them with your own knowledge.

4 Devise strategies for coping with pressure. Many writers have trouble adapting their writing process to a stressful, inflexible

test environment. But don't panic. You can anticipate certain difficulties and decide beforehand how you will deal with them.

First, eliminate unnecessary stress. Get a good night's sleep, eat a healthful meal, and keep anxiety-producing cramming to a minimum before the exam. Gather all your materials—examination booklets, pens, calculator, and notes or books when the instructor allows them—well in advance. Arrive a few minutes early, but not too early; sitting in an empty classroom for too long may make you nervous.

Plan also to head off specific problems that can happen during the exam: if you haven't had much experience writing under pressure, time yourself on practice questions beforehand so that you won't stall during the exam. If you tend to panic when you see an unfamiliar question, plan to work on the easiest items first, then come back to the more challenging ones. If you fall apart when time runs short, give yourself a safety net by outlining each response before you start writing, so you can attach the outline to any unfinished response. And if you will write the exam on a computer, remind yourself to save frequently so that you don't inadvertently lose something important. This kind of troubleshooting will free you to focus on the actual writing.

5 Figure out what the question is asking you to do.

Exam questions generally give writers much more specific instructions than out-of-class paper assignments do. So it's vital that you analyze each exam question carefully before you begin writing.

Start by locating all the key terms—usually nouns or noun phrases—that *identify* or *limit* the subject: "Discuss the *major components* of *Plato's educational ideal* as elaborated in *The Republic*"; "Explain *four kinds of confounding* that can occur in *observational research*"; "What are the *clinical indications* of *bipolar disorder,* and how do they differ from *cyclothymia?*" Next, underline key verbs that tell you what to do with the topic: *analyze, compare, discuss, explain, trace.* Each of these instructions means something a bit different, as Chart 7.1 on pages 115–116 shows.

Finally, cross out any material that does not seem relevant to the question. Instructors sometimes begin an exam with a quotation, an example, or an introductory discussion that serves primarily to clarify the main question. Such material may make the question look intimidatingly long, but you need to pay attention to it only if it helps you focus. In this rather daunting example from a British literature course, for instance, the core question is stated only in the last sentence.

> Since the beginning of the semester, we have seen thinkers such as Freud, Marx, and Nietzsche describe the philosophical contradictions that inhabit the twentieth century. *Choose one major text we have read this semester and trace the ways that work describes contradictions in private, public, or intellectual activities.*

Here the references to Freud, Marx, and Nietzsche only introduce the idea of "contradiction," the focus of the main question. To answer this question, you don't need to comment on any of these thinkers; you just have to explain how contradiction shows up in one of the literary texts you studied for the class.

EXERCISE 7.4 Identify key terms in an examination question from another course or from a standardized test for college admission, job certification, or another purpose. What specific topics does the question stake out? Which verbs tell you what to do with those topics? If you have a copy of your response, analyze how well you fulfilled these instructions.

6 Budget your time. Keep the amount of time you spend on each question roughly proportionate to its importance. If you squander all your time on a single question, you're likely to jeopardize your chance for a good grade. Here is a simple way to figure out how to allocate your time: Divide the number of points each question is worth by the number of points on the whole exam. The result equals the percentage of time you should devote to that question. For example, suppose you have a 50-point question on a one-hour test that is worth 200 total points. You should probably spend about 15 minutes, or 25 percent of the hour, on that response.

If you run out of time in the middle of a response, resist the temptation to steal time set aside for other questions. Instead, jot a note to your instructor explaining that you ran out of time, and attach your outline. Many instructors will give partial credit for outlined responses.

Chart 7.1

Common Exam Terms

Analyze: Break an argument or a concept into parts and explain the relationships among them; evaluate or explain your interpretation or judgment.

> Analyze the effects of ketosis on the digestive system.

Apply: Take a concept, formula, or theory and adapt it to another situation.

> Apply Bernard's elements of sound executive management to President Ronald Reagan's management practices during his first term.

Argue, prove: Take a position on an issue and provide reasons and evidence to support that position.

> Argue whether or not you believe it is possible to run government agencies like private sector businesses.

Compare: Point out similarities between two or more concepts, theories, or situations.

> Compare the educational philosophies of Dewey and Rousseau. How did each conceptualize the learner? the function of education? the role of the teacher?

Contrast: Point out differences between two or more concepts, theories, or situations.

> Contrast the uses of imagery in Yeats's "The Second Coming" and Hardy's "The Darkling Thrush."

Critique, evaluate: Make and support a judgment about the worth of an idea, theory, or proposal, accounting for both strengths and weaknesses.

> Evaluate spanking as a method of discipline for each of these age groups: infants, preschoolers, school-age children, and adolescents.

Define: State a clear, precise meaning for a concept or object, and perhaps give an illustrative example.

> Define the three measures of central tendency (mean, median, mode); then explain which would provide the most accurate gauge of annual income in a given community.

Discuss, explain: Offer a comprehensive presentation and analysis of important ideas relating to a topic, supported with examples and evidence. These questions usually require detailed responses.

> Discuss the Ebonics controversy, drawing on the research we have studied this semester to clarify key points of difference.

(Continued)

Common Exam Terms *(Continued)*

Enumerate, list: Name a series of ideas, elements, or related objects one by one, perhaps giving a brief explanation of each.

> List Jean Piaget's developmental stages, and give an example of how moral choices are negotiated at each stage.

Review, summarize: Briefly lay out the main points of a larger theory or argument.

> Summarize the definitions of legal discrimination presented in the decisions *Sweatt v. Painter* and *Hopwood v. The University of Texas.*

Trace: Explain chronologically a series of events or the development of a trend or idea.

> Trace the pathway of a nerve impulse from stimulus to response.

7 Make a plan. A test setting doesn't allow false starts. In order to pack as much writing as possible into the allocated time, you'll need a good sense of where you're going before you begin. Once you've determined what kind of response an essay question requires, take five minutes or so to map out your answer. If the question asks for independent argument or analysis, consider brainstorming or freewriting to generate ideas. If the question asks you to synthesize course material, try an idea map that organizes information under key categories. (See Section 2b for more on prewriting techniques.)

Use these initial ideas as the foundation for a list or scratch outline of the full response. Whatever format you choose, it should include your thesis, main supporting ideas, and important examples. Once your outline is in place, you are ready to begin the actual writing. See Sections 3b and 3c for more on organizing and outlining an essay.

8 Understand what a good response looks like. Because grading standards vary from course to course and from instructor to instructor, no single formula can guarantee you perfect marks on every test you take. Nonetheless, a study by the researcher Randall Popken found that instructors across disciplines share some similar expectations. Most want a tightly organized response that contains the following elements.

- **A clear thesis statement** in the first paragraph or, better yet, in the first sentence. Don't worry about crafting a dramatic introduction—there isn't time.

- **Logical organization** with a single key idea developed in each paragraph and with clear transitions between points.
- **Adequate support and evidence** for each point, drawn from course readings and lectures.
- **Your own views or analysis** when the question asks for them. Remember, though, to justify your ideas with evidence and support.
- **A conclusion** that ties together main points and summarizes their importance, even if you have time for only a sentence or two.
- **Clear prose** free of major grammatical and mechanical errors.

If you have covered these basics, don't worry about adding creative flourishes. A powerful introduction, a scintillating style, or an encyclopedic coverage of a topic beyond what the question requires may dazzle, but your instructor doesn't expect them. A realistic goal in a test setting is to produce a solid first draft that demonstrates your command of the material.

Finally, before you set aside a lot of time for editing and proofreading, ask your instructor how he or she deals with grammatical and mechanical problems. Many teachers don't penalize minor mistakes unless they hinder the clarity of your argument, but others are sticklers for correctness.

Going Public *Framing a Successful Examination Essay* ———

Undergraduate writer Jena Gentry encountered this question on the midterm for a U.S. history course: "Discuss some important causes of the Great Crash of 1929. How did Presidents Hoover and Roosevelt try to deal with the resulting Great Depression? How successful were they?" Note how the opening paragraph of her response, excerpted here, summarizes basic concepts and forecasts the direction of her argument.

> The economic boom of the 1920s had a dramatic impact on the U.S. economy. While corporate profits were large, they weren't being recycled into the consumer market, but rather invested into an inflated stock market whose prices were continually increasing. The terrible result—the Great Crash of 1929—came as a result of four main causes: the saturation of the consumer market, a rigid price structure and speculative market, an unequal distribution of wealth, and Republican public policies that favored the rich. Two presidents, Hoover and Roosevelt, tried to deliver Americans out of the subsequent Great Depression. However, Hoover believed that the government should stay out of the economy, and his modest program of

legislation didn't do much. Roosevelt's ambitious New Deal was more successful, bringing many Americans a measure of relief, recovery, and reform.

The rest of Gentry's essay contains twelve paragraphs: one devoted to each cause of the Great Crash, three discussing Hoover's efforts to deal with the Depression, four explaining and evaluating Roosevelt's New Deal, and a brief conclusion.

Here is a less successful beginning, written in response to the same question. This writer knows the material but has not framed her observations within the terms laid out in the question. There is no explicit reference to causes of the Great Crash, and there is no mention of Hoover or Roosevelt. As a result, the instructor has no framework for understanding the facts and details the writer includes.

Throughout the 1920s, everything was produced at much speed and production increased 40 percent. Wages increased a slight 12 percent while corporate profits went up an incredible 70 percent. So much money was kept out of the market that the economy began to fail. Wage increases weren't enough to allow workers to be economically stable when prices were so high, and the wealthy were only putting their money into the stock market. When all this occurred, terrible results followed. The economy crashed and America went into the biggest depression in its history.

CHAPTER 8

How Do You Use Course Web Sites and Campus Writing Centers?

8a How do you use course Web sites?

Does your English syllabus include a Web address alongside its list of course policies and assignments? Don't be surprised if it does. Many college courses now use Web sites to do things traditionally done in a classroom. Your instructor, for example, might ask you to submit academic writing online as part of an assignment or class discussion. The guidelines that follow will help you take advantage of the benefits that class Web sites offer and, in the process, prepare you for a means of interacting that has become standard in many academic, professional, and social communities.

1 Visit your class Web site early and often. Doing so allows you to see early on how online resources will fit in with other course activities. The site might simply be a place to post handouts, supplementary material, or announcements. But many instructors now use Web sites to extend class discussion and foster group writing activities. These online activities can provide rewarding outlets for ideas that can't be explored within the limits of a one-hour classroom session.

But don't think of the class Web site as a way to avoid the classroom. Your online activities should extend and complement your face-to-face interactions with instructors and classmates. Class Web sites can also lead back into classroom activities by providing reading prompts, response forums, and detailed assignment guidelines. These resources can help instructors focus class time on material that has garnered attention or caused confusion.

E-Tips Many class Web sites are *password-protected*, meaning that users must log in to access them. Your instructor should inform you how to set up your username and password. Be sure not to share your username and password with others. Doing so compromises your privacy and the security of the site. It might also jeopardize your grade, since some instructors automatically assign credit for assignment postings based on students' login names.

2 Keep in mind your instructor's purpose for using the site. Ask these questions:

- Is the site a forum for posting announcements?
- Is the site the primary tool for class-related email?
- What features of the site are used in required assignments?
- Will students post assignments to the site?
- Is access to the site limited to people enrolled in the class, or is it available to anyone who browses the Internet?

Obviously you'll want to visit the class Web site often if it will be your primary means of communicating with instructors and classmates outside class time. Remember also to observe appropriate conventions for online communication. See Section 24f and Checklist 24.8 for more information about posting to online forums.

Avoid using the class Web site for activities that your instructor hasn't approved. Don't, for example, turn in papers to an online "drop box" if your instructor wants printed documents. He or she may not accept papers turned in online for every assignment.

3 Familiarize yourself with the site's interactive features.
Like any piece of computer software, the interactive features of class Web sites can take some getting used to. Fortunately, these sites often feature easy-to-use online forms. Web forms consist of one or more fields into which you enter information (text boxes, checklists, etc.) and a means of saving your entries, often a button labeled "Submit," "Reply," or "Update."

The following list describes some of the most common interactive tools you'll find on class Web sites.

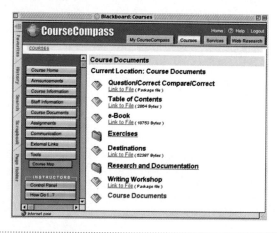

Figure 8.1   *This Web page for a first-year composition course includes several interactive features.*

- **Threaded discussion forums.** These online discussion tools offer a flexible means for extending dialogue beyond an individual class meeting. You can deliberate more about each comment than in an oral debate because responses to a single topic (a *thread*) are posted over an extended period of time. Section 24f provides more guidelines for online forums.

- **Class email.** Some class sites offer their own form of email, allowing you to address messages either to specific individuals or to the entire group. Be aware that these email features don't always work with standard Internet email systems. You may need to check both your regular email inbox and the one on your class Web site. Ask your instructor which email address you're expected to use for class activities.

- **Online questionnaires.** These can help your instructor assess what students know before each class meeting so that he or she can review confusing areas and discuss topics of interest in class. Many instructors also give quizzes online so that class time can be spent on other activities.

- **Home page builders.** Your class site may allow you to create your own personal home page using Web forms. While this method of creating a Web page won't allow you as much flexibility as if you created an HTML document from scratch, it does cover the basics. You can often enhance the appearance of your page by using HTML codes, uploading images, or uploading entire HTML documents. See Chapter 23 for more on HTML documents.

E-Tips

Many Web forms allow you to enter HTML codes in your entries to enhance the appearance of your writing. You can often, for example, make a sentence bold, italicize an unfamiliar word, or even enter a hyperlink to a Web address. See Section 23b for an explanation of HTML codes.

---

4 Build your own online writing space. The interactive tools on your class Web site can help you manage tasks and information throughout the writing process. Unlike the work space on your home computer, the writing space you create on your class Web site will be accessible wherever you have Internet access—whether you're studying in your dorm room, visiting your parents for the weekend, researching at the library, or working casually at an Internet café. Here are some suggestions.

- **Bookmark online references.** "Bookmarks" or "favorites" store addresses of Web pages you want to visit regularly. When you create them on your class Web site, you can consult them from any computer with Internet access. You might, for example, bookmark an address to an online grammar reference or store a list of U.S. census Web pages that provide statistics for a research paper.
- **Create "to do" lists.** Some class Web sites help you manage activities with personalized task lists or online calendars. At the beginning of an assignment, enter due dates for drafts. Then add intermediate deadlines for individual steps of the writing process—proposing a thesis, researching, composing an introduction, and so on.
- **Take research notes without a notebook.** If you don't have pen and paper handy, a class Web site can serve as a virtual notebook. At the library, try logging into your class Web site using an Internet-accessible computer and typing your notes in a self-addressed email. Be sure to include bibliographic and citation information in your notes (see Chapter 49), especially if you don't plan to check out the printed source.
- **Transport and back up important files.** Since most class Web sites allow you to attach files to email messages, you can use self-addressed messages to transport important files, such as working drafts, from one computer to another without using a diskette. As long as you don't delete the self-addressed message from your in box, you will also have a backup of your file.

5 Work with others throughout the writing process.

Class Web sites are a form of "groupware"—computer software designed to help people complete shared tasks. Here are just a view ways of using your class Web site to complete collaborative writing projects.

- **Freewrite together through online chat.** Online chat tools capture the dynamic interaction of face-to-face conversation in a written format. Since you can typically review the transcript of a chat session afterwards, you can treat such exercises as freewriting (see Section 2c-1). You might voice ideas you can use later in your project, and you'll also get immediate feedback on ideas you would not otherwise be able to test until a formal peer review.
- **Develop topics in threaded discussions.** In a *topic forum,* you can post topic proposals (see Section 2d) as individual discussion forum threads. Participants can then respond to topic proposals posted by others, providing valuable feedback in what might otherwise be a lonesome quest for ideas. Critical comments early in

the writing process can help you anticipate counterarguments and confirm readers' interest in your topic. Commenting on others' proposals may also help you better understand the assignment.

- **Share research efforts with online bibliographies.** Some topics cover a wide range of sources, not all of which can be efficiently researched by one person. By assigning each individual one area to cover thoroughly, you can divide the research effort—assuming each member composes annotated bibliographies (see Section 7a), letting others know sources that might be of value. Share these bibliographic notes via threaded discussion forums or email lists.

- **Thoroughly explore an issue with a group Web site.** If your class Web site allows you to upload Web pages, you can link together a number of people's writing on a single broad topic. This kind of project allows writers to take sides, fill in gaps, and thoroughly investigate issues of common interest.

8b How do you use a writing center?

Are you having a terrible time deciding on a topic for your history term paper? Has your biology professor told you that you need to work on making your sentences clearer and more concise? Would you like a second opinion on the admissions essay you're submitting for law school? Odds are, your campus houses a place where you can find all these things: the writing center.

If your campus has a writing center, you should make it part of your writing process. Some labs are small-scale operations that emphasize one-on-one consultations between instructors and students; others are much larger facilities with their staffs including peer tutors; still others do

part of their work online and reach out to local communities as well. Each center will have its own philosophy, methods, and priorities. But all writing centers share one goal: to help writers do their *own* work better.

1 Find out where your writing center is and what it does. Don't wait until you are about to graduate to discover that there is a writing lab on your campus waiting to help you prepare job application letters or format a handsome résumé. That's the experience of too many students who think that a writing center is just for first-year students with grammar problems (see Section 8b-4). A quick visit to your school's writing lab or its Web site might reveal a surprising place where writers get together for all sorts of reasons.

Naturally, most centers do focus on student writing assignments in composition courses, but many also offer a full range of services. You might find help with technical writing projects and Web or document design, or there may be tutorials for writers whose native language is not English. An increasing number of centers are reaching out to writers interested in composing fiction and poetry. And most labs help students from across the curriculum, without respect to major or field.

So find out where your local writing center is located and how to use its services. Some centers take drop-in clients; others require appointments. Note, too, the hours of operation of the lab and whether it offers online help or even a telephone advice line. A few writing centers may charge for their services, but most are supported by student tuition or fees.

> **E-Tips**
>
> The best known and most comprehensive online writing lab (or OWL) site belongs to Purdue University. Visit it at <http://owl.english.purdue.edu>.

2 Use a writing center throughout the writing process. Perhaps nothing helps writers more than having knowledgeable people to talk with as they develop their projects. Yet many students will muddle through the early stages of writing entirely on their own without realizing how much a writing center tutor might assist them in finding a topic, discovering reputable sources, creating a structure, and more. These are precisely the moments in the writing process when it helps to have a second opinion, and most staffers in a writing lab are trained to offer one. Even when an assignment is fairly specialized, an experienced tutor can raise basic questions, especially about audience and purpose, that may make a difference in the quality of a first draft.

You can get more specific help, too, in evaluating or positioning your sources, for example, or overcoming writer's block or figuring out what system of documentation to use if an instructor hasn't identified one. But you cannot take advantage of this support if you wait until the last moment to visit a writing lab.

8b
service

3 Be an active learner in the writing center. When you make a writing center appointment, be sure you know what you want to accomplish so you can help the consultant help you. For example, if you received an assignment sheet for a paper, bring it with you, or at least know what the hard points of the paper are: length, due dates, audience, form of documentation, and so on. A teacher may not always supply all this information, but don't keep a consultant guessing. Similarly, if you are working on a different kind of project, let's say a personal statement for a medical school application, bring the instructions or the application itself to the session.

If you want a tutor to look at the draft of a paper after a teacher or peer editors have commented at it, bring those comments with you and be sure you've read them closely yourself. When possible, come to the consultation with a clean draft of your project and specific questions. Expect to participate actively in the session. Experienced tutors will encourage you to do much of the talking. They may even ask you to begin the session by reading your paper aloud: you'll be surprised by how much you learn from that simple exercise. Take notes throughout the discussion, make marginal comments on your draft, and engage in plenty of give-and-take. Don't be afraid to ask what seem like "dumb" questions. Such queries often go right to the heart of an issue or help a tutor understand better how to help you.

Well-trained tutors won't attempt to cover every aspect of longer projects in a single session or try to correct all the problems they see. Instead they'll end a session by giving you a manageable strategy for developing your project further or revising it. If you are concerned by problems with grammar, mechanics, and usage, the tutor may set priorities for you. In many cases, you may want to schedule follow-up sessions. Don't think you have to accomplish all your goals in a single session.

4 Don't treat a writing center as a repair shop or an editing service. The purpose of a writing center is to make you a better writer, not to get you a better grade on a particular assignment. That may strike you as a peculiar notion, but it shouldn't. Unfortunately, most students (and not a few instructors) still harbor the notion that the point of a writing lab is to fix problems with grammar and mechanics too big to handle in class. They expect the writing center to offer drill and practice on all those "fine points" somehow missed in high school: subject-verb agreement, comma splices, parallelism, and so on. Unfortunately, research suggests that much of what is learned from such exercises doesn't transfer to actual writing. So if you go to a writing center expecting a few grammar modules on a computer to clear up your difficulties with writing, you are misinformed. And you are underestimating what a writing center can do. Getting the grammar and mechanics right is often the *easy* part—at least for native speakers of English. Your mechanical skills will improve when writing projects engage you enough to care about them. You'll suddenly have a motive for learning the fine points of language that just is not there when you're grinding through exercises.

For the same reason, you shouldn't come to a writing center expecting the tutors or consultants to proofread the final draft of your papers or projects. That is your responsibility as a writer. It is appropriate for tutors to teach you how to edit carefully and to suggest areas where you need work. They might explain to you why titles should be italicized or why spelling checkers can't be trusted. But don't ask them to point out specific errors or misspellings.

Nor should you expect a savvy tutor to grade a paper or draft. Only a classroom instructor, who knows the full context of the assignment and has read the full range of response to it, can assess a project. Don't embarrass yourself or a consultant in a writing center by asking what grade your paper deserves. That's not a question a consultant should answer.

Checklist 8.1

Getting Help at a Writing Center

• Bring any assignment sheet with you to a writing center consultation. It may help a tutor better understand the paper you are developing.

• Bring any comments you have received from your instructor or from peer editors. Read the comments carefully yourself.

• Come to the session with specific goals. Don't expect a tutor to "fix" everything.

• Be on time for your appointment.

• Decide whether you want a report of the session sent to your instructor. Some writing centers will give you this option.

CHAPTER 9

How Do You Write for the Public?

How do you write outside the classroom?

Knowing how to write a solid academic paper is crucial to your success in college. However, college writers often need to adapt their writing to settings outside the classroom. You may write letters to friends or elected officials, applications for jobs or scholarships, publicity materials for campus groups, or editorials for local publications. What do all these tasks have in common? They are all *public* statements of one kind or another.

Yet what impresses readers in one setting may offend them in another, just as the same joke might get a big laugh at a family dinner but raise eyebrows at a church banquet. When you adapt your writing to different situations, think about what those readers expect and what seems appropriate under the circumstances. This chapter will help you understand important conventions of nonacademic writing so that you will come across as a skilled, responsible writer—no matter whom you find yourself addressing.

1 Understand the range of writing you may do outside the classroom. Most college students write for many audiences and purposes beyond the classroom. Writing instructors at many universities now require students to compose documents for nonprofit groups, to publish pieces in local media, or to post their writing on the Internet, in addition to writing traditional papers. You may also have to produce documents as part of your job or for campus or community groups. At other times, you may become so excited about a topic you've studied in class that you want to express your views more publicly.

You'll be better prepared to use your skills as a writer when you understand the range of situations you'll address and the kinds of documents you may be asked to produce. To give you a sense of this range, we asked several of the student writers featured in this book to list projects they'd recently completed that weren't part of a course assignment. Their list appears in the box below.

2 Learn to spot opportunities for public writing. Writing can be a powerful way to make your views heard and to get things done. But not all situations lend themselves equally well to it. Before

---

HIGHLIGHT *Examples of Public Writing Projects*

WRITING AT WORK

- Articles for employee newsletter
- Information updates to office Web site
- Responses to complaint letters from customers
- Research report for boss on a legal issue
- Memo requesting vacation time

WRITING FOR CAMPUS GROUPS

- Letter inviting governor to speak at banquet
- Dramatic sketch for campus acting troupe
- Scholarship application essay for alumni association
- Funding proposal for speaker series

WRITING ON CIVIC AND COMMUNITY ISSUES

- Letter to the editor on proposed library closure
- Guest editorial on proposed capital punishment legislation
- Message to student listserv about proposed cuts in financial aid
- Letter to senator on whether the Confederate flag should fly over the state capitol
- Lesson plans for nonprofit after-school program

PERSONAL WRITING PROJECTS

- Personal Web page
- Poems to share with local writers' group
- Article on dance submitted to magazine
- Messages to newsgroup on go-cart racing

you undertake a writing project, ask yourself these questions to decide whether the circumstances are right.

- **Is writing the most effective response to this situation?** Some problems call for direct or immediate action. Suppose that your neighbor's dog has just bitten the mail carrier. Would it be more effective to write a letter to your neighbor warning her to keep her dog inside or to simply pry the dog off the mail carrier's ankle? The answer is obvious (at least, we know which answer the mail carrier would prefer). However, if you believe that your neighbor's dog is part of a larger problem caused by lax leash laws in your city, that problem might be addressed by writing letters to the city council or circulating a citizen petition.

- **Is there an audience who cares (or can be persuaded to care) about your message?** Each year thousands of preteens write love letters to pop idols like the Backstreet Boys and Britney Spears. Are these letters examples of effective public writing? No, because no matter how passionately the writers feel about their arguments, neither the stars to whom the letters are directed nor any other audience has strong feelings about the issue. The question of who wins Backstreet Boy Howie D's heart is unlikely to have significant effects either on the larger community or on the letter writers. On the other hand, a group of students might successfully write to request that Howie D make an appearance at a school fund-raiser since he and his agent would presumably be interested in the opportunity to help a good cause.

- **Is the timing right?** Public writing is most effective if it appears when an issue seems most relevant to readers. April 14, the night before income taxes are due and the busiest day of the year at the accounting firm where you work, is not the best time to confront your boss with a memo calling for more stylish upholstery on the office chairs. (Best hold your proposal until budget deliberations later in the year.) Nor does a newspaper editor want to print a letter responding to a column that appeared nine months ago, though she might print responses submitted within a week or two.

Writing is challenging and time-consuming—too much so to be wasted where it's unlikely to have an impact. When you choose to write, choose the setting and the timing carefully to make sure that every word counts.

■ **3 Find out as much as you can about your readers' expectations.** When you write in a public setting—especially a setting new to you—don't automatically fall back on familiar academic conventions. The kind of writing your instructors reward in college will not always be received with enthusiasm in other forums.

Say that you've just received an *A* on an English paper you wrote on a recent police brutality case in your city and you've decided to write an editorial for the campus newspaper on the same topic. You'll quickly find that the news editors expect a piece that is much shorter, more attuned to the events in that week's news, more partisan, and simpler in organizational structure than your course paper. You'll also discover that the conventions for citing sources are simpler in journalism than in academic writing. If you take the time to learn these conventions, you'll be able to produce a publishable editorial.

Before you begin any project for an unfamiliar audience or situation, find out what is expected.

- What genres and topics are typical for this forum?
- What are the typical length, style, and tone of documents published in this setting?
- What kinds of arguments and evidence do writers typically draw on?
- What are the expectations for formatting and for citing sources?

Many publications make submission guidelines available to prospective writers. In other cases, you'll have to ask someone in charge what the accepted practices are. See Section 1f for more tips on adapting your writing to particular audiences.

4 Seek out models and advice. One of the best ways to discover your readers' expectations in a new setting is to look at examples of similar documents. If you're entering an essay to win a scholarship, request a copy of the previous year's winning essay. If you hope to publish an article in a local music magazine, skim previous issues to get a feel for the kinds of topics and stories it prints. Find a couple of pieces that appeal to you and use them as models for organizing your own. You shouldn't imitate every sentence, but a familiarity with your models will help you get started. You can and should add individual touches once you've laid out your basic argument. Chapter 24 contains models of several kinds of academic and nonacademic writing projects.

Also feel free to ask experienced writers for advice. Call on colleagues, instructors, friends, and the staff of your university writing center to read your draft and offer general feedback. When you're unsure, it's better to head off a potential mistake than to recover from one that appears in print.

Garbl's Writing Center at <http://garbl.home.attbi.com> offers advice, templates, and links for writing a variety of public documents, including letters to the editor, letters to legislators, and editorials.

5 Recognize that public writing offers benefits and risks that academic writing does not. Although you may feel anxious when you turn in a course paper, your instructor and classmates are a relatively private audience. Slips in logic or punctuation won't usually damage anything other than your grade, and you can generally experiment with new ideas without fear of offending your instructor. But when you write for larger public audiences, responses may be more direct and less predictable. If you write an email message to your office listserv criticizing the company scheduling policy, your boss, unlike your writing instructor, may take your complaints personally—and may be less sympathetic the next time you ask for a night off.

For this reason, it's especially important to consider the impression you hope to make on readers when you undertake a public writing project. When Jesse Faleris wrote the letter advocating gun control that appears on pages 133–136—a letter he submitted to National Rifle Association (NRA) leadership at their annual convention—he faced a tricky rhetorical situation. As a longtime member of the organization, he understood their entrenched resistance to gun control measures of any kind and knew that such arguments would have to be carefully presented in order to be heard. Moreover, he valued his membership and wanted to avoid antagonizing fellow members in ways that would be unproductive. He solved this problem by prefacing his arguments with a statement of his commitment to gun ownership rights and to the organization's general goals, a statement that he hoped would build consensus with his audience. He recognized that his letter might nonetheless evoke negative responses, but he felt that the argument was important enough to justify the risk. (See Section 1g for more on creating a positive impression on readers.)

Knowing that your ideas have reached and affected others is precisely what makes public writing so rewarding. While Faleris's English instructor probably wouldn't penalize him for his views on gun control, neither does she have the power to change NRA policy. So don't allow the directness of writing to a public audience scare you into confining your ideas to the classroom. But be prepared: *Before* you publish or mail your piece, think through the possible responses your writing might elicit. When you've anticipated these consequences, you can decide how you want to address them.

6 Be professional. You'll be taken seriously as a writer if you submit attractive, polished, and carefully edited and proofread documents. That rule applies to virtually every writing situation. See Section 5a-6 for more on this topic.

Going Public   *Shaping an Argument for a Public Audience* ___

9a
public

As you read this letter that student writer Jesse Faleris addressed to NRA leaders at the group's annual national convention, note how he shapes his argument to defuse potential negative responses from his readers. Consider, too, the ways in which his letter differs from an academic research paper on gun control.

To Fellow Members of the National Rifle Association:

I am greatly concerned about the current escalation of gun legislation and how our organization's position may affect the rights of American citizens to own firearms. Unfortunately, I believe that our organization's current philosophy of "Guns do not kill--people do" is no longer an effective stance, and that if the Second Amendment is to survive future abolition legislation, our organization must transform its image.

Before I continue with my suggestions, let me offer a summary of my background. I am a military careerist with ten years' United States armed forces active duty service. I am the son of an accomplished gunsmith who is actively involved in Canadian firearms legislation. I have four years' experience in military public relations, and I am currently a public relations and law philosophy student at the University of South Carolina. I am the coach of the USC ROTC pistol team. Most importantly, I am a gun owner and an advocate of all Americans' right to bear arms.

It is this last concern that prompts me to write to you today. While I have not found a succinct mission statement of the NRA, the literature produced by our organization defines us as the protectors of Americans' rights to own and use firearms for sport as well as self-defense. But the majority of our literature centers around the media's exploitation of the gun debate, and the government's misdirected attempts at firearms legislation. For example, the August issue of the NRA's American Guardian magazine criticizes a bill introduced into the U.S. Senate, which would ban "Saturday night specials." Senator Barbara Boxer introduced this bill in hopes of ridding cities of the small inexpensive handguns that are often used in crimes. The NRA rebuts by saying that the government wants to stop America's impoverished peoples from protecting themselves.

I understand why the NRA maintains the Second Amendment posture that "the right of the people to keep and bear arms, shall not be infringed," but at what cost do we deny any infringement? I understand that need for a firm conviction from a philosophical standpoint, but philosophy does not solve social problems any more than misdirected legislation does. This is because the general populace will no longer accept "guns don't kill" logic. In the midst of heightened awareness to hate crimes and random violence, the handgun is quickly becoming the social icon of America's violence problem. Polls from the Gallup Organization, the Associated Press, and others reveal that upwards of 95 percent of Americans favor further gun legislation.

For these reasons, the NRA must drop our current antilegislation attitude in favor of a "responsible gun owner" persona. We must demand that not only our members, but also the gun owners outside our membership, as well as the manufacturers, actively advance responsible gun ownership. As gun owners, we must take responsibility to safeguard our firearms against use by irresponsible persons with the following steps.

- We must protect unsupervised minors from access to firearms. Yes, trigger locks! If used, trigger locks are a responsible means of regulating who uses a firearm. Again, I understand the NRA's slippery slope argument that any infringement will lead to abolition, but if we look at Canada as an example we may find voluntary compliance unrealistic.

- The manufacturers must contribute to the effort of safeguarding the public from firearm products. Including trigger locks with the purchase of new firearms is a necessity. Providing additional trigger locks for existing guns at manufacturers' cost is reasonable and would be recognized as a positive and responsible response to consumer America's concerns.

- Finally, we must work with legislators, particularly those supportive of gun owners, to draft and introduce effective and responsible gun legislation. This legislation should focus on criminal use of guns. We must find a way to keep criminals from using guns, without limiting the law-abiding citizens' right to keep and bear arms.

As a linchpin between gun owners, Congress, and gun manufacturers, the NRA possesses the influence to arbitrate these responsible proposals. These are our guns, our streets, our children and our legislatures-- let us take responsible action to safeguard all we hold precious.

I hope that my honest intentions are clear. I do not want to lose my rights, nor my children's, nor my grandchildren's rights to keep and bear arms. I am convinced that the NRA and Gun Owners of America organizations want to protect our rights in a changing social atmosphere. What I hope is that we can use our influence to effect positive changes in the average American's beliefs about gun ownership.

Respectfully,

Jesse M. Faleris

SUMMARY | *When You Write for the Public . . .*

- Choose an appropriate audience and forum.
- Be sure the timing is right.
- Learn your readers' expectations.
- Use models to help you get started.
- Recognize that your writing may elicit responses.
- Be professional.

EXERCISE 9.1 Here is a list of four public writing projects completed by undergraduate students. For each project answer these questions: How do you think the piece differs from an academic treatment of the same topic? What kinds of adjustments do you think the writer made for audience, purpose, and setting? Discuss your responses with classmates.

1. An article on aging and nutrition for a nursing-home newsletter.

2. A proposal directed at the city arts commission requesting funding for Diversity Week activities sponsored by a local cultural organization.

3. An informational Web site that rates local landlords and apartment complexes according to the number of renters' complaints filed against them.

4. A review of the latest Eddie Murphy film for the local paper.

9b How do you write in service-learning courses?

While much of the writing you do in college will never leave the classroom, an increasing number of composition courses nationwide now incorporate one or more *service-learning projects*—projects that ask students to apply what they've learned by writing "real" documents for community agencies or groups. Service learning can take many shapes. Composition students at Carnegie Mellon University, for example, work with inner-city teenagers to produce newsletters and videos that explore the young people's views on drug use, violence, and gender issues. Students at Michigan State University are placed in community agencies for which they write newsletters, publicity materials, reports, and other documents. Business writing students at the University of Arizona collaborate with local nonprofit groups to write grant proposals. And students in other programs across the country serve in tutoring programs, homeless shelters, local arts agencies, and many other public settings as part of their academic work in a writing course.

If you're taking a writing class that includes a service-learning component, you can look forward to valuable opportunities: You'll learn more about organizations in your community and the work they do. You'll have a chance to do work that affects your community. You'll gain experience working collaboratively with others, and you'll make contacts that may help you find future volunteer work or a job after graduation. And perhaps most important, you'll have a chance to test your research and writing skills on real audiences.

But because they combine several audiences, purposes, and sets of expectations for writing, service-learning projects pose special challenges. This section offers general guidance for dealing with these challenges and introduces you to Ray McManus, a student writer who completed a service-learning project at the University of South Carolina.

ε-Tips   Consult your university's Web page to learn more about service-learning programs on your campus. Campus Compact, a national alliance of colleges and universities committed to community service, has compiled information on service-learning opportunities nationwide at <www.compact.org>.

1 Understand the dual purpose of service learning.
Service-learning projects differ from strictly academic writing projects because they involve real writing for community audiences. They also differ from the volunteer work that you do outside school, even when that work involves writing. Service learning always involves an academic dimension—your instructor asks you to write for the community not just because it's a civic-minded thing to do but so that you can also explore concepts and strategies that you're learning in the course. In service-learning projects, both the service and the academic dimensions of the course are equally important: one reinforces the other.

When you begin a service-learning course, ask yourself:

• How does my work in the community reflect, reinforce, or problematize the material I'm learning in class?
• How does the material I'm learning in class help me to effectively approach the work I'm doing in the community?

Ray McManus, the student writer whose work is featured in this section, engaged in a service-learning project as part of a course on teaching writing. The project, in which he and other students designed and led several poetry workshops for teenagers at the local library, had both practical and academic components. On the one hand, his experiences with the workshops allowed him and his classmates to test strategies and approaches to teaching poetry that they'd read about in class. On the other, the workshops gave Ray, who hopes to become a teacher of creative writing, valuable experience in his chosen field and useful contacts with interested local librarians, teachers, and schools.

2 Be aware of the different audiences your writing will address.
The dual purpose of service learning means that you'll be writing for at least two audiences—your instructor and the community readers of any document you produce. Sometimes you'll write for both audiences simultaneously. Be aware of their differences and tailor your work accordingly, since the expectations in one setting are likely to differ from those in another. If you have questions about what's expected, don't hesitate to ask.

The chart below gives you an idea of the kinds of audiences and documents Ray McManus produced over the course of his project.

HIGHLIGHT *Writing Projects for One Service-Learning Course*

9b
service

During the course of Ray McManus's service-learning project, he created a variety of documents for a variety of audiences. Some work was turned in to his professor, some was seen only by library staff and patrons, and some was directed to both audiences.

WORK PRODUCED FOR PROFESSOR
Annotated bibliography of resources on children's poetry writing
Reflective journal entries on workshop sessions
Lesson plans for workshop sessions
Final research paper reporting on and analyzing experience

WORK PRODUCED FOR LIBRARY STAFF OR PATRONS
Collaboratively written publicity flyers
Interview with newspaper
Thank-you letter to library director

WORK PRODUCED FOR PROFESSOR AND LIBRARY STAFF OR PATRONS
Lesson plans for workshop sessions
Exercises and materials for workshops

---

3 Find out how your work will be evaluated. The fact that you must write for several audiences sometimes makes it hard to figure out whether you're doing a good job with a service-learning project. For example, what if your instructor expects you to write very detailed lesson plans for tutoring sessions in an adult literacy program, when most tutors in the program take a more relaxed approach to planning by jotting down just a sentence or two?

When you encounter different sets of expectations, you'll feel more confident if you know how your work will be evaluated: Which pieces of your writing will your instructor grade? Will he or she evaluate them according to academic criteria? Will the community members you work with judge some or all of your writing? If so, what criteria will they use, and will they determine part of your course grade? Once you know these parameters, you can make decisions to adjust your work accordingly. In the above situation, knowing that your instructor will be grading your lesson plans, you might jot down a rough draft for the program's records, then use that draft to develop a more polished plan to turn in to your professor. See Chapter 6 for more on how writing is evaluated.

9b
service

4 Be willing to learn and to collaborate. When you engage in community service, it may be tempting to adopt a "savior" mentality—that is, to feel that your job is to bestow your knowledge and skills on needy individuals. Certainly a key goal of service-learning programs is to make university students' energy and talents available to others in the community. But remember that anytime you enter a new writing situation, *you're* the novice. Be ready to learn from the people you work with and to collaborate productively with them.

When Ray McManus and his classmates began designing poetry workshops for local teenagers, he had had plenty of experience with writing poetry and had researched ways to engage teenagers in learning about it. But when it was time to craft publicity materials for the sessions, they knew little about how to reach young people likely to attend. They knew that they wanted to make the sessions sound "cool," rather than something that was too much like school. Ray came up with the title "Split P Soup," which he thought reflected that goal. But Ray and his partners needed the expertise of library staff who had advertised previous youth programs, who had contacts with local teachers and youth and educational organizations, to determine how best to attract potential attendees. They also needed the library's publication office to translate their ideas into an eye-catching format. The flyer that resulted from this collaboration is featured on page 141.

Once the workshops began, Ray and his classmates worked collaboratively with the participants. While he and his co-leaders set a basic agenda for each session, participants took charge in selecting topics for writing and discussion and in recruiting new participants. By asking the young people to take part in shaping the sessions, Ray could be sure that the workshops met their interests and needs.

Community work involves exactly that—working in a community. As Ray McManus found, if you cultivate an open mind and are willing to learn from others, you'll likely be successful in your service-learning project.

Going Public   *Collaboration and Service Learning* _____

Here's the publicity flyer that resulted from the collaborative efforts of Ray McManus and numerous library staff. Do you think the flyer is effective? Why or why not? Do you think Ray could have created it alone?

9b
service

Checklist 9.1

When You Write in a Service-Learning Course . . .

* Understand that your writing has both academic and practical goals.
* Be aware of the different audiences you will address.
* Find out how your writing will be evaluated.
* Learn from and collaborate with others.

CHAPTER **10**

How Do You Read and Think Critically?

Each day you are bombarded with messages that try to influence you—that urge you to buy a particular brand of toothpaste, to give money to a certain charitable organization, to vote for one candidate rather than another, and to see the latest blockbuster film. Dealing with these competing texts requires that you examine ideas, ask questions, challenge arguments, and decide which viewpoints are worth accepting—in other words, that you think *critically*. Much of the information you absorb in college will be obsolete ten years from now, but the critical and analytical skills you develop in school will serve you the rest of your life.

In college, a crucial element of critical thinking involves learning to read critically, because much of what you write and think about is in response to textbooks, articles, research reports, and other readings. This chapter will guide you through the basic steps of the reading process and suggest ways you can bring your critical abilities to bear on the texts you read, both inside and outside the classroom.

10a How do you read to understand complex material?

College reading assignments pose special challenges. In high school, teachers may cover a textbook chapter in a week; in college, instructors often assign several chapters in the same amount of time, along with supplementary readings from scholarly journals, literary texts, and other sources. College assignments may also address more abstract ideas and use more complicated language than you're accustomed to. Whereas you may be accomplished at reading sources that summarize and analyze issues *for* you—like high school textbooks or popular magazines do—in college you'll often have to weigh conflicting approaches to an issue or interpret research findings and data on your own.

But the classroom isn't the only place you'll encounter difficult texts. You'll also sift through competing viewpoints and complex terminology when you research campaign issues before voting, when you use the Internet to become expert on a topic, or when you draft a report at work or follow news coverage of an important local event. These challenges present complex material that you can't read in the same way you'd read a paperback mystery novel or a grocery list. You'll need to develop specialized skills that help you become an active, engaged reader.

1 Preview the text. Just as you can navigate an unfamiliar city more easily when you have a map, you'll find it easier to read an unfamiliar text if you first preview its important features.

- **Genre.** What kind of document is it? an introductory textbook? an opinion piece? a literary work? a commercial Web site? Different genres have different purposes and audiences, which you should keep in mind as you read.
- **Title.** What does the title tell you about the piece's content and purpose?
- **Organization.** If you're reading a printed text, are there headings or subheadings? If you're reading a Web site online, are major sections listed in the left-hand frame or on a home page? What do these divisions suggest about what the text will cover?
- **Sources.** Inspect the bibliography and index. What do the sources listed there tell you about the kinds of information the writer will draw on?

Before reading a piece, determine your goals: Are you skimming the piece to see if it's relevant to a paper you're writing? Are you mainly interested in major concepts and arguments, or do you need to know details? Do you want to develop your own opinions on the subject? These goals should influence how much time you spend reading and which of the strategies discussed in the following sections you decide to use.

2 Look up unfamiliar terms and concepts. It's always easier to understand difficult material if you have the relevant background knowledge. When you preview a text, circle major terms, concepts, or topics that sound unfamiliar. For instance, you'll feel completely at sea reading an article about the African diaspora if you don't know what *diaspora* means and your knowledge of the continent is limited to vague memories from eighth-grade social studies. A look at a dictionary and an encyclopedia entry on Africa will put you on more solid ground.

Even if you have some general knowledge about a topic, it's not a bad idea to keep a dictionary at hand while you read so that you can clarify confusing references as they crop up.

10a

crit

■ **3 Slow down.** The best readers usually aren't the fastest ones. When you're reading about ideas new to you, expect to read slowly and to reread two or three times before you fully grasp an argument or explanation. Some experts advise making it a habit to read everything twice: the first time just to understand what the writer is saying, the second to focus on your own reactions and opinions. But whatever your strategy, don't rush. Speed-reading may sound good on "infomercials," but it doesn't produce a thorough understanding of a text.

■ **4 Annotate the text to clarify and respond to its content.** You can often spot a skilled reader by looking at the condition of his or her books: dog-eared pages, heavily underlined or highlighted passages, and margins overflowing with notes are sure signs. Critical readers understand that reading involves more than passively absorbing words on a page. It's an active process of creating a new understanding.

If you're not accustomed to taking notes on your reading, here are some useful strategies.

- **Content notes.** Most college students highlight key passages in their texts. But if you want to get the most from your reading, don't stop there. When you arrive at an important point or get tangled in a difficult passage, translate it into your own words. Expressing a concept or argument in your own language helps you to clarify its meaning.
- **Context notes.** Notes can also help you follow a text's structure. At crucial transitions, jot down a key word or two that explains where the argument is going or how a new point fits in: "Opposing argument," "Previous theories," "Example 3," for instance.
- **Response notes.** When you're reading something difficult, don't just accept what it says; talk back. Does a proposal excite or anger you? Write "Yes!" or "Bad logic." If the text raises questions, write them down: "But what about the innocent victims?" or "Does this argument follow?" Carrying on this kind of dialogue with your reading develops your own perspective on the issues being raised.

The Highlight box on page 145 shows how one reader used these three strategies to annotate the opening passage of an opinion piece she read while researching a paper on moral education. She made response notes in the left-hand margin and content and context notes in the right-

10a
crit

? look up

these =
"civil society"

?

?

But what
about
people whose
communities
can't help?

Is she saying
all these
beliefs are
wrong? Not
sure I agree.

"Second Thoughts on Civil Society"

by Gertrude Himmelfarb

I would like to think that it is not just contrariness on my part that makes me wince, these days, on hearing talk of civil society. Liberals and conservatives, communitarians and libertarians, Democrats and Republicans, academics and politicians appeal to civil society as the remedy for our dire condition. They agree upon little else but this, that mediating structures, voluntary associations, families, communities, churches, and workplaces are the correctives to an inordinate individualism and an overweening state.

The ubiquity of the phrase is enough to make it suspect. What can it mean if people of such diverse views can invoke it so enthusiastically? I am as critical as anyone (perhaps more so than most) of an individualism that is self-absorbed and self-indulgent, obsessively concerned with the rights, liberties, and choices of the "autonomous" person. And I am no less critical of a state that has usurped the authority of those institutions in civil society which once mitigated that excessive individualism. But I am also wary of civil society used as a rhetorical panacea, as if the mere invocation of the term is a solution to all problems—an easy, painless solution, a happy compromise between two extremes.

Civil society is indeed in a sorry condition. But one reason is that some of its institutions have been complicitous in fostering the very evils that civil society is supposed to mitigate. The welfare state is a classic case of the appropriation by government of the functions traditionally performed by families and localities. Neighbors feel no obligation to help one another when they can all upon the government for assistance. Private and religious charities are often little more than conduits of the state for the distribution of public funds (and are obliged to distribute those funds in accord with the requirements fixed by government bureaucrats.)

But it is not only weakness of civil society that is at fault. Some of the institutions of civil society—private schools and universities, union and nonprofit foundations, civic and cultural organizations—are stronger and more influential than ever. The individualistic ideology of rights and the statist ideology of big government are reflected in the causes that these institutions have promoted: feminism, multiculturalism, affirmative action, political correctness.

Everyone is
saying that
civil society
can solve
the probs.
caused by
big gov't.

But she
is suspicious.

2 reasons

①Churches
charities now
rely on gov't
$

②Other
institutions
are
promoting
big gov't.'s
ideas

hand margin; notice how these notes help her follow a fairly complicated argument.

When you're working on a project that involves substantial research, it's especially important to take careful notes. Your annotations can identify ideas and information worth returning to, highlight passages you want to quote in your paper, and, more important, help you synthesize and engage in dialogue with the authors and texts you are encountering. See Chapters 48 and 49 for more on incorporating material you've read into a research paper.

10a
crit

■ **5 Adapt your reading process to online settings.** While most of the reading strategies described in the preceding sections apply to both print and online environments, electronic texts pose special challenges. Experts on reading have even coined a new term—*screen literacy*—to describe the skills readers need to navigate online texts.

Online texts are often less stable and more loosely structured than printed texts. Reading a Web site or an electronic book, for example, you may scroll through long passages without page markers, follow complicated series of links, or encounter sophisticated audio and visual elements. The text may look different on your home computer than it does in the campus computer lab, and its content or format may change periodically. These features can make it hard to find your place within a text, to return to important material, and to figure out how the pieces of a text fit together.

The boundaries that separate one online text from another are also blurred. When you follow hyperlinks, you may find it hard to distinguish where one text begins and another ends. In researching a paper for your American literature class, for example, you may wonder whether a link to biographical information on the poet Walt Whitman that's embedded in an online text of *Leaves of Grass* is a part of that text or a separate text.

These differences mean that when you go online, you have to adjust your reading process accordingly. James Sosnoski, a composition theorist, has identified several strategies you may find especially useful.

- **Filtering.** Skillful online readers are especially selective about what they choose to read, **skimming** and **pecking** to find the most relevant items.
- **Imposing.** Online readers approach reading with their own agendas rather than always following the author's preferred path through a text.

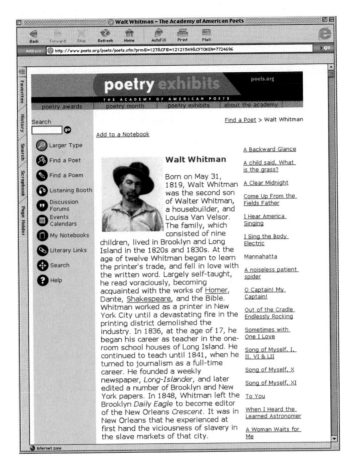

- **Filming.** Online readers pay as much attention to visual elements as they do to the words in a text. (See Section 11b for more on this topic.)

Cultivating these skills will help you navigate the vast array of materials on the Internet without feeling overwhelmed.

Once you've browsed through material online, you'll need to develop strategies for keeping track of it. The safest strategy is this: when you want to read an online text carefully or return to it later, download and print it. Having the document in hand will help you follow the arguments and see how components of the text work together. Also consider using your browser's "bookmark" feature to mark sites that you refer to frequently, so that you don't lose them. You can "bookmark" all sites or pages relevant to a project, arranging the items in folders that reflect its overall structure, one folder for each major section or theme. If a site is likely to change frequently, download and save material that you want to return to.

Finally, online texts support different methods of responding to your reading. You can use the annotation features of many word-processing programs to record your reactions to files you download onto your computer. (But be careful to clearly separate your comments from the original text.) Web pages can be marked with comments and, in some cases, annotated as part of an ongoing online discussion. It's even possible to annotate bookmarks you've created to remind yourself why a particular site or page is important. (See Section 43b for more advice on organizing research materials and Sections 49b and 50c for advice on incorporating research into a writing project.)

10a

crit

EXERCISE 10.1 Use the three note-taking strategies described in Section 10a-4 to annotate a reading assignment in one of your other courses. How do these strategies compare to your typical approach to reading? Which strategy helped you learn the most, and why?

EXERCISE 10.2 Find and read a text that is published in both print and online versions. Possibilities include magazines (like *Newsweek* and *Newsweek.MSNBC.com,* shown below and on next page), informational materials about a nonprofit organization or political candidate, and university documents. Which version do you find more difficult to read? Why? How did your reading process differ in the two settings? Discuss your answers with a group of classmates.

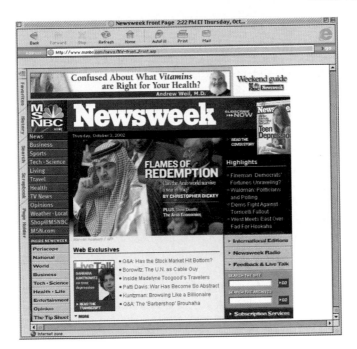

10b
crit

SUMMARY *Reading and Understanding Complex Material*

When you're reading new or difficult material . . .

- Preview the text.

- Look up unfamiliar terms and concepts.

- Take your time.

- Take notes to clarify content and target points of confusion.

- Adapt appropriately to online settings.

10b How do you think critically about your reading?

Critical thinking is only an extended and focused version of the kind of thinking we all do every day when we set out to solve problems:

we gather evidence, we examine options, we look at advantages and dis-advantages, and we weigh others' opinions for possible bias.

A voter thinks and reads critically when he or she researches can-didates' backgrounds and positions on major issues before approaching the ballot box. So does the person who reads *Consumer Reports* and does some comparative shopping before buying a cellular phone. So do you when you wade through all the information you need to consider in de-ciding whether to find a second part-time job or to take out a student loan to pay next year's tuition. All these situations demand that you cultivate an attitude of inquiry—that you *inquire* and *reflect* on com-plex material in order to arrive at the best possible judgment.

1 Read as a believer and as a doubter. You'll get the most from your reading if you approach it with an open mind—if you appre-ciate that it's possible to learn something even from perspectives con-trary to your own. An excellent way to engage with readings that pre-sent difficult or unfamiliar arguments is to play what the writing expert Peter Elbow calls the "believing and doubting game." This approach asks you to read and respond to a piece twice, each time adopting a dra-matically different attitude.

To play the "believing" half of the game, read the piece with as much generosity as you can muster. Try to see what makes the argument so compelling to the writer, and look for claims, examples, or beliefs that seem reasonable or persuasive. Even if you don't agree with the writer's overall position, you may find enough common ground to understand it better than you would have if you had rejected it out of hand. Write a paragraph exploring whatever seems most worth believing in the piece.

Then read the piece a second time as a "doubter." Scrutinize every statement for gaps, exaggerations, errors, and faulty reasoning. Ferret out any problems you can see in the writer's perspective, even if you agree with it. Again, summarize your conclusions in a paragraph. Keying in on weaknesses will guard against your accepting the argument too readily.

Here's how one writer played the "believing and doubting game" with the excerpt from the article on civil society in Section 10a-4.

> *believing* I agree with Himmelfarb that neighbors, families, churches, etc., are less likely to get involved and help others if they think that the government will step in. They think it's not their job or even that "experts" know more about how to help. This does weaken commu-nity ties and make people more isolated from each other.

doubting What about the people whose families, neighbors, and churches can't or won't help them? Isn't that why government took over welfare programs to begin with, because too many people were slipping through the cracks? That's how tragedies happen; think of children who are abused for years because their relatives and neighbors don't want to intervene.

10b
crit

2 Assess the writer's qualifications. Get into the habit of checking the author's qualifications for everything you read. Does the writer have special expertise on a subject from either personal experience or academic training? Does he or she demonstrate adequate knowledge? You might find, in reading a debate about violent lyrics in "shock rock," that some of the loudest calls for censorship come from writers who admit they have never listened to the music. Or you may find that the author of a Web site on managing your investments has neither a business degree nor a substantial stock portfolio. A lack of expert qualifications doesn't necessarily invalidate a writer's arguments, but it should make you examine them with extra care. See Section 48a-3 for more on evaluating a writer's credentials. Section 48a-2 tells how to evaluate the credibility of different kinds of publications.

3 Look carefully at the evidence presented. A strong academic argument must adequately back up its claims. When you read an argument, size up the quantity and quality of its supporting evidence.

- **How much evidence does the writer present?** Does the amount of support seem substantial enough for the claims being made, or does the writer rely on just one or two examples?
- **Where does the evidence come from?** Is it recent, or is it so old that it may no longer be accurate? Does it seem trustworthy, or does the writer rely on sources of dubious credibility?
- **Is the evidence fairly and fully presented?** Do you suspect that the writer has manipulated information in order to make his or her case look better?

Critical thinkers guard themselves against the tendency we all have to gravitate toward arguments that confirm our own beliefs and to avoid those that don't. Thus, when you're researching an issue, seek out readings that reflect different perspectives—for example, *Slate* as well as the *Wall Street Journal*, *Ms.* as well as *Esquire*. Try to find arguments written by women and men, liberals and conservatives, and supporters as well as opponents of a proposal. See Section 12b-3 for more on evaluating the evidence presented in an argument.

4 Assess whether the writer's claims go beyond what the evidence actually supports.

Closely allied to the quality of the evidence in an argument is how the writer applies that evidence. Does the writer draw conclusions that go beyond what his or her support warrants? For instance, some safety experts once made claims about the safety of air bags based on crash-test data calculated for crash dummies the size of adult men. These claims didn't hold true for children and small women. Faced with dozens of fatalities attributed to injuries caused by air bags, those experts admitted that their original claims went beyond what the data had established.

Although overstating one's claims doesn't usually result in such tragic consequences, you can and should question any argument that stretches its conclusions too far.

5 Look for what's *not* there: the unstated assumptions, beliefs, and values that underlie the argument.

Does the writer take it for granted that he or she and the audience share certain knowledge or beliefs when in fact they don't? If what someone takes for granted in an argument can reasonably be disputed, then you should challenge the author's claims.

Consider the assumptions made in this sentence, taken from an article advocating the legalization of drugs.

> The violence brought about by the black market in drugs is attributable in large part to the fact that we have chosen to make criminals out of people who have a disease.

The statement makes two assumptions: (1) People who buy and sell drugs do so primarily because they suffer from a sickness—addiction—beyond their control. (2) It's wrong to criminalize behavior that results from illness. Both assumptions may well be true, but without further explanation and support, a reader might question them on the following grounds: (1) Drug offenders may engage in illegal behavior not because they're sick but for profit, for entertainment, as a response to peer pressure, or because they can't find legal work. (2) Even if drug abuse results from illness, so do many other crimes punishable by law; we don't legalize serial murder just because most perpetrators are mentally ill or legalize drunk driving because many drunk drivers are alcoholics.

See Sections 12a-3 and 12b-4 on how to spot and evaluate hidden assumptions in an argument.

6 Note any contradictions. Look for places where pieces of an argument don't fit together. Suppose a political candidate advocates mandatory prison sentences for first-time drug offenders yet dismisses as "immature behavior" her own abuse of alcohol and other drugs as a young woman. One should question why the candidate excuses for herself behavior that she condemns in others. One might even conclude that the contradiction weakens the candidate's arguments on drug policy.

10b
crit

7 Examine the writer's word choices to identify underlying biases. Everyone has biases—it's unavoidable. We wouldn't be human if we weren't influenced by our experiences, values, and opinions. So it's only natural that writers who want to convince others use language that favors their own point of view. But critical reading requires that you be sensitive to such biases so that you aren't unwittingly swayed by them.

Here's a passage from an article arguing that governments and businesses should work as partners in urban planning. It describes one such project.

> Addison Circle is not just a group of buildings; it is a dream, a vision that has brought together a city, a major landowner, and a developer renowned for producing unique, unusual, and highly successful projects. The result is a new "city center" for Addison, where there will be housing, retail, offices, theaters, and even a park.

This kind of sentence should make your bias detector buzz—it's all good words and positive connotations. Sure enough, checking the byline reveals that the writer who made the statement works for the real-estate developer who helped to create Addison Circle. Her claims may be true, but given her built-in bias, you should withhold judgment until you get more information.

Being a critical reader doesn't mean you have to distrust everything you read. But you should be alert when writers overload their prose with what rhetoricians call "god terms" (words like *democratic, responsible, natural*) or "devil terms" (words like *destructive, immoral, selfish*). See Section 18d for a more detailed discussion of biased language.

8 Be skeptical of simple solutions to complex problems, and resist black-and-white thinking. Be wary of arguments or explanations that offer quick, easy answers to difficult problems. Critical thinkers realize that most serious problems in our society are so complex that anyone who hopes to write about them intelligently must resist casting those involved as "good guys" and "bad guys" or suggesting that the problem could be solved quickly if someone would just do the right thing. There is seldom one "right thing."

Consider the complex issue of affirmative action in college admissions and the calls from many sectors that schools judge prospective students on merit rather than taking racial, ethnic, and economic background into account. Here are a few of the questions that complicate this solution.

- What, exactly, constitutes "merit"? Test scores and grades? Special talent in a single area, like music or sports? Character? If all these factors count, how should each be weighed?
- Should students who come from educationally disadvantaged backgrounds be judged by the same standards as more privileged students?
- Do some measures of merit favor certain groups of students over others? For example, some studies indicate that standardized tests often underestimate how well women, members of ethnic and racial minorities, and students with learning disabilities will fare in college.
- Do schools have a responsibility to make up for past discrimination against particular groups? If so, how long should this responsibility last and what should it entail?

Any solution to a problem, however perfect it may seem, has consequences. As you read an argument, look for evidence that the writer has neglected to consider the long-term implications of his or her position. Don't settle for easy answers.

| SUMMARY | *Critical Reading Strategies* |

To respond critically to a text . . .

- Read both as a believer and as a doubter.
- Assess the writer's credibility.
- Scrutinize the evidence presented.
- Decide whether the writer's claims are overstated.
- Look for what's left out.
- Check for contradictions.
- Be alert to biased language.
- Be suspicious of easy answers to complex problems.

EXERCISE 10.3 Read the lead editorial in today's newspaper twice, playing the "believing and doubting game" described in Section 10b-1. Which did you find more challenging, reading as a believer or reading as a doubter? Why? Did you notice anything using this method that you might not have noticed if you had read the piece just once?

CHAPTER 11

How Do You Interpret Visual Rhetoric?

Decades ago, your grandparents learned about events mostly through words—they read books, magazines, and newspapers, and they talked with others in their community. Today, you may catch the evening news on television, follow political campaigns on C-SPAN, and choose your new school clothes from pictures on an Internet site. Literacy researchers say that over the past century or so, our society has shifted from being a "print culture," in which people got information primarily through words, to an "image culture," in which people learn just as much through visual media like film, television, and photography. Even traditional print media like newspapers and books increasingly make use of eye-catching charts, pictures, and other graphic devices.

Since images are so ingrained in our everyday lives, it's important to know how to approach them critically, how to "read" them just as

In many texts, images and words work together to convey information, as in this New York City memorial wall dedicated to the late hip-hop artist Tupac Shakur and this copy of The New York Times *front page.*

carefully as we do words. This skill is called *visual literacy.* Like any critical thinking, visual literacy means cultivating an attitude of inquiry. It means learning to ask the right questions about what you see, so that you can make informed decisions about it rather than letting what you see control *you.*

11a How do you interpret charts, graphs, and tables?

When writers present information through charts, graphs, and tables, they draw pictures for readers. These pictures help readers grasp a complex body of data that could be hard to absorb through words alone. Imagine, for example, that you want to rent an apartment and can afford to pay no more than $600 a month. If you could find a fact sheet that used a bar graph to show the price ranges for two-bedroom, two-bath apartments in four areas close to your college, you could quickly determine where you should look for an apartment.

Charts, graphs, and tables present information in different ways. This section explains how each works.

1 A pie chart shows how the parts of a whole are distributed. A pie chart is a simple graphic that shows percentages (the slices) of a total (the whole pie). The following example presents basic information about how property tax revenues are spent in Indiana. Using this chart, you could answer various questions: How much of the state's revenue goes to city and county governments? Do schools receive a substantial share? And so on.

Who Receives the Property Tax?

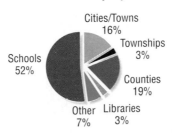

Cities/Towns 16%
Townships 3%
Schools 52%
Counties 19%
Other 7%
Libraries 3%

Source: State Board of Tax Commissions Database, Information supplied by IU Center for Urban Policy and the Environment.

Figure 11.1

But pie charts can't tell readers everything. Since pie charts generally can't include more than six or seven slices without becoming visually confusing, they can't capture fine distinctions. Writers often collapse several smaller categories into a single "slice." For example, you can't tell from Figure 11.1 on page 157 exactly which county and city services (police, water, roads) are funded by the property tax.

Sometimes writers vary the design of a basic pie chart, as shown in Figure 11.2. Don't let the three-dimensional aspect confuse you; each shaded area still represents a proportion (percentage of world market by country) of the whole (all countries who have a share of the market).

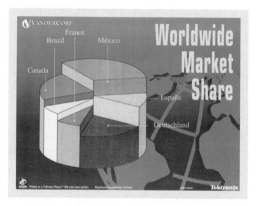

Figure 11.2

2 A bar graph shows the relationship between two variables. It does this by charting the data for one variable along a horizontal scale and the data for the other variable along a vertical scale, using vertical bars to depict data in one or more categories. In Figure 11.3 below, different parts of the world (Africa, Latin America, etc.) are shown on the horizontal axis; numerical data are represented by the vertical bars. By depicting this information visually, the graph dramatizes how reserves of natural gas compare worldwide.

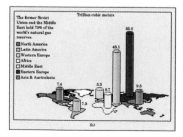

Figure 11.3

Bar graphs can give more information than pie charts. Not only can they show general trends, but they can show subtle distinctions within categories of data. For example, each bar in Figure 11.3 could be divided into two or three subcategories, perhaps using different colors for different countries in each region or for urban versus rural areas.

3 Line graphs also show relationships but depict trends more emphatically. Like bar graphs, line graphs chart the relationship between two variables, one depicted along the horizontal axis and one along the vertical axis. The sharply declining line in Figure 11.4 makes a strong impact on readers, who will immediately grasp the sense of what they're seeing.

Writers can also use the impact of a line chart to mislead readers. Figures 11.4 below and 11.5 on the next page present exactly the same data on unemployment rates in the United States, but Figure 11.4 appears to show a sharp drop in the national rate during the 1990s, while Figure 11.5 makes the decrease look insignificant by plotting it on a grid that shows the full range of rates, from 0 to 110 percent of the population. The writer who prepared Figure 11.5 has unfairly manipulated data to deceive readers by including numbers on the scale that aren't typically part of the range of this phenomenon. Even though it's theoretically possible to have 100 percent unemployment, the rate in this country has rarely been below 4 percent or above 11 percent. In this context, a drop of one percentage point is extremely significant.

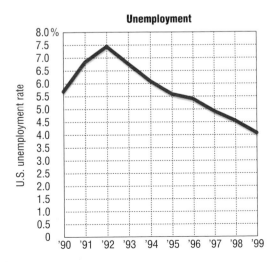

Figure 11.4

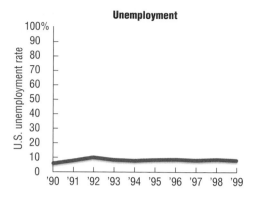

Figure 11.5

4 Tables organize categories of information into vertical columns and horizontal rows that show relationships. Tables can provide more detailed information than graphs or charts, but they're visually less appealing because readers must read more carefully, analyze data for themselves, and draw their own conclusions.

To get the most out of a table, don't just plow through it from top to bottom. First look at the heading to identify the data being given, then look at the categories to see how the data are broken down. Table 11.1 provides information about unemployment in the United States, but the table shows data for a single year; it breaks down the data by state and ranks each state according to its unemployment rate and the size of its labor force. Here you could find which regions of the United States have the greatest unemployment and use that information in an essay.

5 Assess the accuracy of charts, graphs, and tables. You should approach visual representations of data with a critical eye. Numbers *themselves* don't lie, but they can be presented in misleading ways.

Say, for example, that a writer superimposes a drawing of a tearful child onto a bar graph tracing cuts in Head Start funding. Recognize that he or she is trying to shape your views on the issue, and don't allow yourself to be distracted from the factual information. If the dates on the same graph end with 1998, ask why. Would more recent data alter the apparent downward trend? (See Section 11a-3 on the manipulation of scales to overemphasize or downplay a drop or a rise in a line graph.)

Writers will use charts, graphs, and tables just as they do other sorts of evidence: to persuade readers. It's your responsibility to read critically and carefully so that you aren't fooled into accepting weak or

Table 11.1   Unemployment in the United States, 1999

	Unemployed Persons	Unemployment Rate	Unemployment Rate Rank	Total Labor Force	Labor Force as % of Population	% of Population Rank
Alabama	87,600	4.0%	24	2,170,300	49.9%	41
Alaska	19,110	6.0	2	316,700	51.6	34
Arizona	116,900	4.4	19	2,406,110	51.5	35
Arkansas	58,500	4.7	14	1,258,000	49.6	45
California	881,700	5.3	6	16,605,300	50.8	38
Colorado	69,000	3.0	39	2,286,900	57.6	2
Connecticut	44,800	2.6	46	1,706,500	52.1	30
Delaware	13,300	3.3	36	398,200	53.6	18
Florida	286,110	3.8	26	7,468,500	50.1	39
Georgia	148,900	3.7	28	4,059,600	53.1	22
Hawaii	32,000	5.4	5	596,700	50.0	40
Idaho	33,300	5.0	8	659,900	53.7	17
Illinois	293,500	4.6	15	6,388,700	53.0	23
Indiana	73,110	2.4	50	3,081,110	52.2	27
Iowa	42,800	2.7	45	1,597,300	55.8	7
Kansas	48,600	3.4	35	1,449,700	55.1	8
Kentucky	80,200	4.1	22	1,955,000	49.7	43
Louisiana	97,110	4.7	12	2,054,500	47.0	48
Maine	27,800	4.1	21	670,000	53.8	15
Maryland	118,900	3.9	25	2,815,300	54.8	11
Massachusetts	115,500	3.2	37	3,286,700	53.5	20
Michigan	175,300	3.4	31	5,092,000	51.9	31
Minnesota	81,000	3.0	42	2,740,600	58.0	1
Mississippi	60,300	4.7	13	1,281,700	46.6	49
Missouri	113,110	3.5	29	2,911,800	53.5	19
Montana	22,600	4.8	11	475,300	54.0	14
Nebraska	22,400	2.4	49	933,400	56.1	6
Nevada	36,600	3.8	27	955,500	54.7	11
New Hampshire	16,600	2.5	48	671,300	56.6	5
New Jersey	206,000	4.8	9	4,250,900	52.4	26
New Mexico	50,000	6.0	3	832,110	47.9	47
New York	461,800	5.2	7	8,911,200	49.0	46
North Carolina	113,900	3.0	41	3,845,900	51.0	37
North Dakota	9,800	2.9	43	341,110	53.4	21
Ohio	266,400	4.6	16	5,848,600	52.2	28
Oklahoma	57,500	3.5	30	1,661,600	49.6	44
Oregon	97,200	5.5	4	1,763,000	53.7	16
Pennsylvania	255,200	4.3	20	5,979,200	49.8	42
Rhode Island	20,800	4.1	23	509,400	51.5	36
South Carolina	66,600	3.4	34	1,980,200	51.6	33
South Dakota	11,300	2.6	47	400,400	54.2	13
Tennessee	96,000	3.4	33	2,813,700	51.8	32
Texas	464,500	4.5	18	11,308,800	52.2	29
Utah	37,900	3.4	32	1,115,400	52.6	25
Vermont	11,700	3.1	38	340,000	57.5	3
Virginia	96,300	2.7	44	3,593,900	52.9	24
Washington	148,600	4.8	11	3,120,600	54.9	9
West Virginia	49,800	6.1	1	813,900	44.9	50
Wisconsin	88,200	3.0	40	2,964,110	56.7	4
Wyoming	11,800	4.5	17	261,600	54.4	12
D.C.	16,300	6.0	—	271,500	51.9	—
U.S.	5,947,200	4.3	—	139,254,000	51.5	—

Source: U.S. Bureau of Labor Statistics.

11a
visuals

inaccurate claims. It's also your responsibility to be fair and accurate when you use charts, graphs, and tables to present information.

Checklist 11.1 will help you detect problems that commonly appear in visual representations of information.

Checklist 11.1

Evaluating Charts, Graphs, and Tables

When you read a chart, a graph, or a table, ask yourself . . .

* Are the data up to date?

* What is the source of the data? Is that source credible?

* Does the writer try to argue for more than the data can actually prove?

* Does the writer use color or emotionally loaded graphics to influence readers' opinion?

* Does the writer manipulate the scale or select information in a way that distorts the data?

E-Tips

For more information on how numbers are used in charts, graphs, and tables, and for useful definitions of common statistical terms, consult Robert Niles's *Statistics Every Writer Should Know* at <www.robertniles.com/stats>.

EXERCISE 11.1 Imagine that you want to give an oral presentation that uses data on umemployment according to region. Read Table 11.1 with this focus in mind. Working with another student, decide what information from the table would be most useful for your talk. Share your findings with the class.

EXERCISE 11.2 Pick up a copy of *USA Today, Time, Newsweek,* or another popular publication that uses charts, graphs, and tables to present information. See if you can find an example that you think presents data in an inaccurate, oversimplified, or misleading way. Bring your example to class for discussion.

11b How do you interpret layout, graphics, and Images in a document?

Have you ever bought a novel just because the cover design caught your eye? Or opened by mistake a piece of junk mail formatted to look like a legitimate business letter? Graphic representations, photos, other images, and the way a document is laid out on a page often work together to shape a writer's message. Such strategies can be powerful and useful, but you need to be aware of how they're used so that you can approach them critically.

1 Recognize that writers use layout and design to influence readers. The "body language" of a document—the way a page is laid out and the choice of such graphic features as font, color, and headings—can influence readers' responses to a text. (See Chapters 21 and 22 for an extended discussion of graphics and layout.) When you look at a page that obviously has been carefully planned, ask yourself these questions.

- **What ideas or information does the writer emphasize?** Are particular items boxed or set in boldface or in a larger font size than the rest of the text?
- **What ideas or information does the writer downplay?** What information is buried in the middle of the text or set in small print?
- **What formatting devices does the writer use?** Does the writer use decorative borders, unusual fonts, or the formatting conventions of a particular genre—headlines and columns like a news article, or a business letter format, for example?

2 Evaluate images critically. Pictures trigger impressions that are stronger and more immediate than those most writers can convey with words. And because images can be so powerful, it pays to view them with caution. When you look at pictures or graphic images in a magazine or brochure, on a Web site, or in a fund-raising letter, ask yourself these questions.

- **How does the picture or graphic reinforce or add to the written information?** Is this addition helpful, or is it only decoration? For example, you've probably seen personal Web pages that make distracting use of flashy graphics—multicolored backgrounds, blinking lights, animated characters—that don't relate clearly to the content.

- **What emotions, values, or beliefs does the illustration appeal to?** Is this appeal relevant and fair? Suppose that an organization that opposes animal research includes a photograph of injured rabbits in its annual fund-raising letter without providing a clear explanation of what's depicted in the photo and how it relates to the organization's work. Such emotional appeals are unfair.

- **What does the graphic or picture reveal about the writer's opinions or biases?** If a newspaper story on successful local entrepreneurs includes only pictures of men, you might wonder whether the story slights women business owners.

- **Does the picture or image exaggerate or distort the content of the document?** This might happen if a report on a city-sponsored summer camp featured only photos showing well-attended activities, when the text of the report indicates that the camp was sparsely attended.

11c How do you critically interpret visual media?

Visual literacy means more than simply attending to the graphical features of printed or written texts. Many of the messages you encounter every day come through mass media (television and film) that consist almost entirely of images. When we watch a music video, drive by a billboard, or tune in the evening news, we take in information so quickly that we have little time to critically reflect on it. But it's important to remember that, like printed messages, the visual media are carefully constructed to appeal to readers, and we must read them as critically as we would any other text.

The mass media are so complex that trying to explain all their components would take us well beyond the scope of this book. However, the basic critical skills discussed in this chapter can generally be extended to apply to these media.

The nonprofit Center for Media Literacy suggests these additional starting points for critically approaching mass media.

- **Remember that visual media texts are purposefully constructed for a particular audience and purpose.** In a single news story, for example, a team of people filmed footage, interviewed sources, wrote an announcer's script, and combined all that raw material into a selective, carefully produced package. We never see what the film crew *didn't* shoot, what the story would have looked like with a different headline, or what portions of film the producer edited out. Because visual texts are the products of human choices, they generally reflect their creators' values, viewpoints, and biases.

11c
visuals

- **Be aware that visual texts come in many genres, each of which operates according to its own conventions.** Think how different your expectations are when you watch a daytime talk show, a late-night talk show, and a documentary film. These different formats govern how information can be presented.

- **Recognize that visual media may be interpreted differently by different viewers.** Parents often say that they can't make any sense of the music videos their teenaged children watch; it's all just noise and disconnected images, they complain. On the other hand, adults who watch the Disney cartoons they loved as kids often catch cultural references or jokes that eluded them when they were younger. Creators of visual media rely on these differences when they try to reach several audiences at once.

Being aware of these basic ways in which visual media persuade viewers will help you sharpen your visual literacy skills as you apply them to various situations.

Going Public   *Analyzing an Advertisement*

In the following excerpt from a student essay, Michael Boynton pays particular attention to an advertiser's purpose and intended audience. Notice how he analyzes the images and text separately and then examines how they work together to achieve their purpose.

One of the most visible types of advertising is for cars. These ads usually include information about durability and performance as well as flashy images to catch the attention of potential consumers. In a recent ad for the PT Cruiser, however, Chrysler markets its product based on an ideal. In this ad, from People magazine, Chrysler places the car in an urban office building at dusk. The character is a middle-aged white man who is working hard in his office, but, strangely, does so out of the back of a brand-new, platinum-colored Chrysler. The setting and the character show specifically the target audience for this ad--the average middle-aged, white businessman. The ad tries to tell these guys that the ideal man, who works diligently and often past quitting time in order to succeed, needs this ideal car.

The ad also uses text to lead consumers to believe that this car is especially useful to individuals who work hard and get things done. The text hints that the car can act as a personal assistant; it can "stow an eight-foot presentation, haul an office full of co-workers, and still look like a nuclear fusion of past and future." There are a few unwritten messages, as well. One of these is that this car is for educated, sophisticated individuals. It is not a toy, but a valuable machine for those who can afford it.

Overall, this ad successfully captures the attention of its target audience through text and images. Through its connotations, the ad tells people outside the target audience that they are not good enough to own one of these vehicles. It implies that those of us who do not own PT Cruisers need to take a long look at the character in the ad. If we ever want to own one, we need to be a little more like him.

E-Tips

Interested in learning more about visual literacy? The Center for Media Literacy provides materials and links for writers who are interested in becoming more media-savvy. Visit <http://medialit.org>.

EXERCISE 11.3 Examine the Web site of an organization, a public figure, or a government agency that interests you. How has its author used layout, graphics, and images to emphasize and de-emphasize certain information or to influence readers? Discuss your findings with a group of classmates.

EXERCISE 11.4 Keeping in mind the principles discussed in Section 11b-2, watch a television show, movie, music video, or commercial with a critical eye. What features do you notice that you hadn't noticed before? Do you enjoy the text more or less than you would have had you watched it less critically? Why or why not? Bring your answers to class for discussion.

11c
visuals

CHAPTER 12

How Can You Write Powerful Arguments?

12a What does argument involve?

Many of the writing projects you undertake will involve constructing an argument. If you write a letter to convince your instructor that your last paper merited a *B* rather than a *C,* that's an argument. So is a flyer urging fellow students to get their free flu shots at the campus clinic or an editorial that takes a position on federal income tax reform. Each of these documents tries to persuade a particular audience to accept a general claim, using *logical reasoning* supported by facts, examples, statistics, or other kinds of *evidence.* The ability to construct powerful arguments is an advantage in almost any writing situation. This chapter introduces you to the basic structures and strategies of argument.

1 Know the difference between genuine arguments and other kinds of disagreements. In everyday life, people use the term *argument* to refer to any disagreement. But rhetoricians use the term in a more specialized way. When we talk about *argument* in this chapter, we mean a discussion of an issue with two qualities:

1. People might reasonably disagree about it.
2. There are *reasonable* grounds for supporting one viewpoint over another.

This narrow definition disqualifies some kinds of exchanges. An assertion that no one would dispute is not an argument. Statements like "Pain is bad" and "If you drop that chair, it will hit the ground" can be immediately proved, so there's no need to engage in debate about whether they're true.

Disputes about subjective personal tastes aren't true arguments either. It's possible to disagree about whether vanilla ice cream is tastier than chocolate and whether Brad Pitt is more handsome than Harrison Ford, but it's impossible to come up with solid support—that is, support that most people would regard as reliable—to prove one opinion more valid than the other.

One *could* logically argue that vanilla ice cream is more popular than chocolate and that Brad Pitt has a narrower range as an actor than Harrison Ford—because there exists evidence about these assertions that most readers would consider logical and convincing. Statistics on ice cream sales and flavor preference polls could support the former argument, and examples from particular films and quotations from reviews and experts on acting could build a case for the latter.

Finally, a statement is not an argument when it seeks to persuade with threats, emotional manipulation, or trickery rather than with reasoning. An employer who persuades workers to sign up for weekend shifts by hinting that their annual raises depend on it is using threat, not argument. A campaign advertisement that depicts a candidate alongside cooing babies and proud veterans is appealing to viewers' emotions, not their intelligence. Although writers who use these techniques may present them as though they were arguments, don't be fooled. Arguments draw on different strategies entirely.

EXERCISE 12.1 Read a brochure, a flyer, or some other promotional literature from a political organization or an advocacy group (for example, College Republicans, Planned Parenthood, Campus Crusade for Christ, People for the Ethical Treatment of Animals, the American Federation of Teachers). Does the document meet the criteria for argument outlined above? Why or why not? Share the document and discuss your conclusions with a group of classmates.

2 Understand an argument as a claim supported by reasons and evidence.

British logician and philosopher Stephen Toulmin has developed a useful model for understanding how arguments are structured. (Note: We follow the Toulmin model throughout this chapter because it is a comprehensive, useful, and commonly used way of understanding argument, but your instructor or classmates may use different terminology to refer to the basic parts of an argument. Ask your instructor to clarify any confusion you may have about these terms.)

The Toulmin model says that in every argument, a writer begins by making a general assertion—a *claim*—and then produces one or more grounds for supporting that claim. Support for a claim may include *reasons* (smaller assertions that often begin with the word *because*) and *evidence* (relevant examples, facts, statistics, or experts' statements).

Here's a simple way of outlining how an argument is put together.

Argument = Claim + Reason(s) and Evidence

Suppose that you're writing an article for your campus magazine on the benefits of working during college. Using Toulmin's model, you might develop your argument as follows.

CLAIM	First-year students at large universities benefit academically from having a job.
REASON	(Because) The social contacts they make at work help them feel less isolated on campus.
EVIDENCE	**1.** A recent poll conducted by the admissions office found that working students have more friends than students who do not work.
	2. My ex-roommate developed a network of friends and study partners while working part time in a campus copy shop.

3 Recognize that arguments rest on unstated beliefs, or warrants.

Simply laying out a claim and some kind of support isn't enough to make a solid argument. For example, the argument "Mina should do well in college because she's wealthy" would convince no one. A thinking person would respond, "That's an unwarranted conclusion. Being rich has nothing to do with excelling in school." Obviously some ways of connecting claims with reasons and evidence are more persuasive than others.

Toulmin's model uses the term *warrant* to describe the justification—a general belief, rule, or principle—that links together the claim and its support in an argument. A persuasive argument must rest on warrants that readers find satisfactory, or readers will reject it.

Sometimes a warrant is so self-evidently true that it's left unstated. The writer assumes that once the claim and its support are presented, readers will supply and accept the warrant on their own. For example, one might assert, "Mina should do well in college because she made straight A's in high school." The writer doesn't really need to state and support the warrant—that making straight A's is a good indicator of success in college—because just about everybody believes this connection is true. To predict college success based on previous good grades is a "warranted," or justified, conclusion.

But sometimes an argument rests on a warrant that not all readers will agree with. Consider this statement: "Mina should do well in college because she has worked at her parents' restaurant for six years." While the connection may seem reasonable to some readers, others might need convincing. The writer needs to state the warrant and provide some explanation and support for it. Reasons and evidence used to

Parts of an Argument

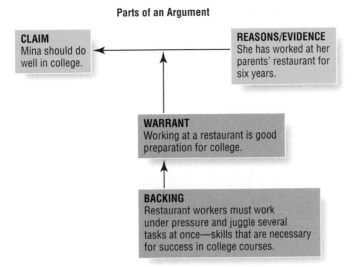

Figure 12.1

support the warrant in an argument are called *backing*. Figure 12.1 above shows how the argument would look with warrant and backing.

EXERCISE 12.2 Each argument below contains a claim and supporting reasons or evidence. Supply the unstated warrant(s) that link each claim to its data, and then evaluate the warrant. Do you find the warrant convincing? Why or why not? We've done the first one for you.

ARGUMENT   *Claim:* The federal government should spend more money on cutting-edge cancer research.

Reason/evidence: Studies show that the treatments developed in this kind of research save lives.

RESPONSE   *Warrant:* The government should fund programs that save lives.

Analysis: This warrant is fairly convincing. However, it's possible that the government doesn't have enough money to fund *every* program that might save lives. What if a program is very expensive but will save only a few lives? This argument needs some support to show that cancer research saves more lives than other kinds of programs.

1. *Claim:* The push to legislate tougher safety standards for the trucking industry is misguided.

   Reason/evidence: Federal data show that trucks are responsible for only a small percentage of highway accidents.

2. *Claim:* State governments should not approve lotteries as a way to avoid raising taxes.

   Reason/evidence: Lotteries make the state a partner in the legalized gambling business, whose tactics include airing misleading advertisements that entice citizens to play.

4 Recognize that many claims include a qualifier that clarifies the limited circumstances in which that claim holds true. Because most claims aren't true in every single case, many arguments include a limiting phrase or statement called a *qualifier—probably, in most cases, primarily in urban areas,* for example. The argument about student jobs laid out in Section 12a-2 would overstate its case if it claimed that *all* students benefit academically from holding *any* kind of job. Students who need extra time for studying and students whose work hours cut into class time are obvious exceptions. A more solid statement of this argument would add what Toulmin calls a *qualifier: "Except in cases in which work hours interfere with school,* first-year students at large universities benefit academically from having a job."

EXERCISE 12.3 Working with a group of classmates, analyze the following argument taken from a magazine article reviewing recent perspectives on women, welfare, and work. Identify the statements that come after each number as claim, reason, evidence, warrant, backing, or qualifier. You may use some terms more than once and others not at all.

There are two [. . .] big reasons why [1] the responsible choice for a low-income single mother might be welfare rather than work. [2] Welfare provides health insurance for her children, and most low-wage jobs don't. [3] And welfare, however miserly, provides security that most jobs don't—at least before [welfare reform laws passed in] 1997. [4] In the jobs available to many low-skilled or unskilled women, such as fast food or home health care, workers can never be sure of getting enough hours to make enough money while they have a job, and they are always subject to firing or layoffs. [5] When insecurity doesn't just mean a little less of something but the possibility of starvation or homelessness, the rational risk-benefit calculation counsels taking the secure but less rewarding option.

—Deborah Stone, "Work and the Moral Woman"

12b How do you construct a solid written argument?

Dissecting the logical elements of an argument is one thing; constructing an argument that interests and persuades readers is another. But you'll find that Toulmin's model offers a helpful framework for generating material to include in an argumentative paper.

Start by asking yourself, "What's my claim going to be?" You may not need to spell it out completely to begin with, but you do need to know the general position you plan to take. When you determine your claim, ask yourself

- What reasons and evidence can I gather to support my claim? Can I get them? Are they solid? (Whether or not you can develop a strong case may depend on your answers.)
- What is the warrant that will tie the evidence to the claim? Will readers accept it without question, or should I state and support it with backing?
- Do I need to qualify the claim in some way?

Once you've roughed out your answers to these preliminary questions, you'll have a good start.

1 Clarify your claim.
Figure out what you want readers to take from your piece: Do you want readers to look at some phenomenon in a new way? Do you want them to be aware of a problem they hadn't noticed before? to hold a particular position on a current issue? to take action? Your answer is your claim.

Suppose that, after reading in a child development course some studies about the influence of movies on children, you decide to write an article for the parents' newsletter of the preschool where you work. You want to argue that parents should avoid buying many of the films sold as children's classics because they are not in fact suitable for children. That assertion is your claim, the one set forth in Figure 12.2. (For more detailed advice about discovering and narrowing a topic and developing a thesis, see Sections 2a and 2b. For more on building a research project around a particular claim, see Chapter 46.)

2 Gather reasons and evidence to support your claim.
What material can you find to develop and strengthen your claim? Check the library for books, periodical articles, research reports, and government documents on the topic. Conduct a search on the Internet. For expert testimony, consider setting up an interview with a professor

or teacher who specializes in children's development, or subscribe to a listserv devoted to children's entertainment.

Depending on the audience for your newsletter article, you might also explore more personal and anecdotal kinds of support. Say your interest in writing about films for children stems from your memories of being terrified at seeing certain so-called children's classics. To use that experience, you'll need firsthand evidence from the films themselves. You might rent several films that frightened you as a child—*The Wizard of Oz, 101 Dalmatians, The Little Mermaid*—and take notes on the scariest scenes. You could also ask friends whether their children had similar responses.

As you gather evidence, cast a wide net. You may not include everything you find in the finished article, but new evidence may help you adjust claims that might have been overstated or misguided. Evidence can also suggest supporting reasons that hadn't initially occurred to you. For example, even if your planned focus is the violence in children's classics, reviewing the films may remind you that many of the stories also promote sexist stereotypes—a point you can then add to your argument.

For more information about finding sources, see Chapter 47.

3 Evaluate your evidence. A skilled arguer knows how to select the supporting materials most appropriate to his or her writing situation. If you're writing a paper for a course, you'll probably concentrate on scholarly research and theories. If you're writing for a preschool newsletter, you might balance academic sources with real-life anecdotes that will catch busy parents' interest.

No matter where your evidence comes from, be sure that it meets certain basic requirements.

- **Timeliness.** Are the statistics, information, and examples you use recent, or are they so old that they may no longer be accurate?
- **Comprehensiveness.** Do you have enough support for your claim, or are you making generalizations based on one or two examples?
- **Credibility.** Do you draw your evidence from sources that both you and your readers trust?

For detailed discussions of how to evaluate evidence, see Sections 10b and 48a.

4 Identify the warrants, or beliefs, that underlie your argument and consider whether readers will accept them. The fact that your arguments seem reasonable to you is no guarantee that readers will immediately embrace them. If you suspect that readers

A Developed Argument

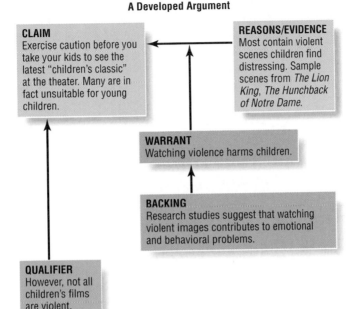

CLAIM
Exercise caution before you take your kids to see the latest "children's classic" at the theater. Many are in fact unsuitable for young children.

REASONS/EVIDENCE
Most contain violent scenes children find distressing. Sample scenes from *The Lion King*, *The Hunchback of Notre Dame*.

WARRANT
Watching violence harms children.

BACKING
Research studies suggest that watching violent images contributes to emotional and behavioral problems.

QUALIFIER
However, not all children's films are violent.

12c
arg

Figure 12.2

may doubt or disagree with any of your assumptions, be prepared to explain and support them.

This step is especially important when you're writing for a hostile or unfamiliar audience. In the newsletter article on children's movies, you'd need to consider whether some parents might question your warrant that watching frightening, violent scenes is harmful to children. Some parents might believe that such scenes do no real damage. Here's where the research studies from your child development course might fit in: since they establish a causal link between violent films and emotional harm, you can cite them as *backing* for your warrant.

Figure 12.2 above shows how the fully developed argument might look.

12c How do you write an argument that appeals to readers?

Some people see an argument as a sort of verbal war in which enemies line up on opposing sides of an issue, each with the goal of demolishing the other side. To find samples of this "take no prisoners" attitude, you need only turn on a television talk show, visit a courtroom, or attend a political debate. Certainly competitive, winner-take-all arguments have their place in settings where compromise is impossible or undesirable, but they're not appropriate for much of the writing you'll do.

When you want your readers to accept your arguments and perhaps act on them, remember that you won't persuade people by making them angry. You'll only make them stick to their positions more stubbornly. For this reason, we suggest that you think of argument not as a battle but as a dialogue. In a dialogue, both sides exchange ideas as they search for a solution. The following section explores strategies for working productively with readers who disagree with you. (See also Section 18d on inclusive language.)

■ 1 Draw on shared beliefs and values.

Even if you're addressing readers whose position is completely opposed to your own, search for common ground. Any shared belief or value, no matter how general, may serve as a warrant on which you can build an argument those readers will find reasonable. For instance, both proponents and opponents of gun-control legislation value public safety, though they have different ideas about how to achieve it, and both supporters and opponents of school vouchers are concerned about the quality of public education. An argument that begins from these common beliefs may not change anyone's mind immediately. But it probably will get a fair hearing, and it may initiate a civil exchange of ideas.

Here's how one professional writer drew on shared values to make an unpopular argument. The following passage comes from an anti-abortion editorial that Mary Meehan wrote for *The Progressive*, a liberal magazine. To appeal to a strongly pro-choice readership, she invokes the political left's traditional concern with protecting society's downtrodden.

It is out of character for the Left to neglect the weak and helpless. The traditional mark of the Left has been its protection of the underdog, the weak, and the poor. The unborn child is the most helpless form of humanity, even more in need of protection than the poor tenant farmer or the mental patient or the boat people on the high seas. The basic instinct of the Left is to aid those who cannot aid themselves—and that instinct is absolutely sound. It is what keeps the human proposition going.

—Mary Meehan, "Abortion: The Left Has Abandoned the Sanctity of Life"

Did Meehan's argument change many readers' minds? Perhaps not, but her respect for their values won readers' respect and gave them something to think about. And that's what public argument is all about. (See Section 18c for more strategies for building consensus with readers.)

2 Present opposing arguments fairly. If you're going to write about controversial issues, you can't simply pretend that your position is the only one. You'll need to acknowledge that other arguments exist, or readers will think that you haven't done your homework. It is equally important that you learn to describe other positions accurately and respectfully. In doing so you enhance your own credibility.

12c
arg

Here are two rules to follow.

- **Don't oversimplify** another position to make it look weaker than yours.

This tactic is not only uncivil, it's bad argument. Logicians use the term *straw man fallacy* to describe this kind of misleading practice, in which a writer reconstructs another position in an oversimplified way that makes it easy to knock down. The following statement, made on a talk-radio program addressing the trial of a nanny whose infant charge died in her care, slips into this tactic. The speaker derides the infant's working mother.

> It's obvious that she didn't really care about the child, or she wouldn't have allowed a stranger to raise him just so she could earn a few dollars. By putting her paycheck ahead of her children, she got what she deserved.

Parents go to work for numerous reasons, including economic necessity; to pretend that selfishness is their sole reason is inaccurate, unjustified, and ungenerous.

- **Don't use hostile language** to describe another viewpoint.

It's natural to have strong feelings about positions you disagree with, but name-calling, stereotyping, and overly emotional terminology hurt your credibility and may offend readers. This kind of language, unfortunately, is all too common—you can find many examples in the "flame wars" that frequently erupt in online discussion forums and in partisan political debates. Here are two examples, one from a Republican and one from a Democrat.

> Midnight basketball [a government-funded recreational program for inner-city youths] is based on the theory that the person who stole your car, robbed your house, and assaulted your family is no more than a would-be NBA star.
> —Lamar Smith, U.S. Representative (R–Texas), "Midnight Basketball Is Winner on Street"

Does it scare you to think that many prominent Republicans now sound like the members of an Idaho militia? It scares the hell out of me. The party has swung so far to the anarchistic right that a reasonable Republican like Dwight Eisenhower simply wouldn't be able to recognize today's GOP.

—James Carville, Democratic campaign adviser, *We're Right, They're Wrong: A Handbook for Spirited Progressives*

12c

arg

Both statements rely on negative stereotypes (that inner-city youths are all criminals, that all conservatives sympathize with the militia movement) and emotionally loaded examples and terms ("assaulted your family," "anarchistic"). Exaggerating the negative qualities of an opponent in this way commits what logicians call the *fallacy of special pleading*. This kind of language won't appeal to anyone but the most die-hard believers in your position. You'll find guidelines for using more civil kinds of language in Section 18d.

■ 3 Consider refuting an opposing argument. Once you've acknowledged other viewpoints, what do you do with them? Don't just let them sit there; readers want to know how they affect the strength of your argument.

One option is to *refute* an opposing position—that is, to disprove the argument by pointing out its weaknesses or fallacies. It's possible to critique an argument on several grounds.

- **Question the claim.** Is it overstated? Is it insufficiently supported? (See Section 10b-5 for more on how to spot a flawed claim.)
- **Question the evidence.** Does the evidence come from reliable sources? Is there enough of it? Is it recent enough to be accurate? (Sections 10b-4 and 48a contain guidelines for evaluating evidence.)
- **Question the warrants and backing.** Does the argument rest on beliefs, values, or assumptions that you think are invalid? Does the writer need to justify and support those assumptions? (See Section 10b-6 for more on critiquing warrants and backing.)

When you've identified problems in one or more of these areas, point them out and call on readers to reject the argument. But again, even if you feel strongly about your rebuttal, be fair and avoid uncivil language.

Going Public *An Argument That Addresses Opposing Views* ___

Barbara Westbrook wrote the paper excerpted below in response to a class assignment that asked her to refute opposing arguments to a position she felt strongly about. As you read, notice how she describes and discusses these arguments. Is she fair? How does she attempt to create common ground between her position and that of others? Does she support her own position adequately?

Barbara Westbrook

Professors Matalene and Friend

14 October 2003

A $20,000 Signing Bonus Won't Fill Empty Classrooms

The day that Evelyn Lasky decided to quit teaching high school wasn't her first day of teaching when she arrived to find 36 students, 22 desks, and no textbooks. And it wasn't the day when she calculated the time it would take for her to pay off her college loans. Evelyn Lasky decided to quit teaching on the day that her assistant principal required her to pass a student who had clearly failed but whose father, an influential member of the PTA, had threatened to sue her. "It's not worth it," the assistant principal told Lasky. "Just change the grade and save us all a lot of headaches."

Lasky felt like she had been dropped in a combat zone only to find that those she thought were her allies--administrators, parents, and other teachers--were fighting against her. She ultimately agreed that it wasn't worth the battle. That June, she was among the one-third of the faculty at that school who chose not to renew their contracts.

Unfortunately, Lasky is not unusual. She reflects a larger phenomenon in American education-- the mass exodus of bright new teachers from the profession. Several studies estimate that up to 50 percent of new teachers leave the profession within five years (Colbert and Wolff 193; Odell and Ferraro 200), with urban schools showing the highest attrition rate (Adams and Dial 90). As if this outlook weren't dismal enough, Richard Murnane and Randall J. Olsen's study found even more disturbing news: the higher teachers score on aptitude tests, the more likely they are to leave the profession (128). In other words, we are losing the brightest teachers at the very time when we need them most.

To address the national teacher shortage, schools across the nation have instituted aggressive recruiting strategies. Boston has begun to offer new teachers a signing bonus of $20,000. Baltimore has not only boosted teachers' starting salary by $3,000 but has also offered to pay teachers' relocation expenses and to assist them with down payments on homes (Streisand and Tote).

A low salary is certainly one of teachers' perennial complaints. It is also, according to a 2002 survey conducted by the National Education Association, the dominant reason why people interested in teaching do not enter the field (Tennessee Education Association). But higher pay is only one way--and a relatively ineffective one--to keep good teachers. According to a poll by the National Center for Education Information, 55 percent of teachers feel that they are underpaid. Yet over 90 percent say that they wouldn't quit teaching because of salary alone (Flanagan). Unfortunately, keeping good teachers won't be as simple as padding their wallets because good teachers don't go into teaching for money. They won't stay unless other things change.

As Kathleen Brady documents, many men and women who give up higher earning potential for teaching do so because they find working with students rewarding and fulfilling (36). David James, who plans to return to his middle school classroom after earning a master's in English, exemplifies this kind of teacher. He told me, "The personal interaction with students was probably the most satisfying aspect of teaching." Researcher Mary Shann has found that David James is typical; teachers consistently rank teacher-pupil relationships as the factor most important to their job satisfaction (70). (Salary ranked thirteenth out of fourteen.)

If salary is, as Dominic J. Brewer writes, "a factor [in retaining teachers] but a small one" (320), then we will have to find more effective ways to attract new teachers. I believe there is a better, cheaper way: administrators and parents need to go out of their way to support beginning teachers! It <u>is</u> that simple.

One of the best ways to keep idealistic young teachers in the classroom is to offer them plenty of administrative support. I learned just how powerfully a school administrator can affect her teachers when for an education class I wrote an ethnography of a diverse and unusually high performing urban elementary school. The principal, Thea Jacomides, had her work cut out for her when she came to the school, which was experiencing "white flight" (of students <u>and</u> teachers) as a result of recent demographic changes in the neighborhood. Nevertheless, five years after arriving at the school, Ms. Jacomides had a fiercely loyal following of students, parents, and teachers.

How did Thea Jacomides win the respect of her teachers? As she told me herself, she subscribed to an administrative philosophy based on trust and support; she hired teachers whom she would want to

12c
arg

teach <u>her</u> children, and then she did everything she could to help them do a good job. And teachers did a good job; they raised student achievement scores to the highest in the city.

In addition to having support from administrators in their schools, new teachers also need support from community members outside the school, especially parents. In fact, researcher Mary H. Shann (70) found that teachers value parent-teacher relationships even above collegial relationships. Teachers value parents because they know that when parents support them, kids behave, try harder, and succeed more often in school. Yet Shann found that although most teachers recognize the importance of parent--teacher relationships, they are dissatisfied with their contact with parents (69-70).

Probably because of the negative press that public schools receive, many Americans are skeptical and critical of teachers—especially new ones. Parents often question grades, attendance, discipline, and make-up work policies. And too often questions of policy become personal attacks on a teacher. During the time that Evelyn Lasky taught, for example, two parents threatened to sue her over the grades their children received in her courses. Parents <u>should</u> make sure that competent teachers are teaching their children, but they need to recognize that supporting a teacher who holds every student to high academic standards <u>is</u> in the best interest of their children.

If the high turnover rate of new teachers is any indication, K-12 teaching poses challenges that most new teachers aren't willing to endure alone. As we are considering ways to recruit and retain new teachers, we need to expand our strategies beyond increasing salaries to consider a few simple, inexpensive, and ultimately more effective methods. If we care deeply about our children's education, the best chance we may have of keeping classrooms filled with bright, idealistic, committed teachers is to support them.

12c
arg

¶[New Page]

Works Cited

Adams, Gerald J., and Micah Dial. "Teacher Survival: A Cox Regression Model." Education and Urban Society 26.1 (Nov. 1993): 90–99.

Brady, Kathleen. "In Search of Meaning . . . Not Money." Techniques 72.4 (Apr. 1997): 34–36.

Brewer, Dominic J. "Career Paths and Quit Decisions: Evidence from Teaching." Journal of Labor Economics 14.2 (Apr. 1996): 313–27.

Colbert, Joel A., and Diana E. Wolff. "Surviving in Urban Schools: A Collaborative Model for a Beginning Teacher Support System." Journal of Teacher Education 43.3 (May-June 1992): 193–97.

Flanagan, Anna. "Administrative Support Is Key Element in Job Satisfaction." English Journal 86.4 (Apr. 1997): 54.

Jacomides, Thea. Personal interview. 4 April 1997.

James, David. Personal interview. 13 Oct. 1999.

Lasky, Evelyn. Personal interview. 12 Oct. 2003.

Murnane, Richard J., and Randall J. Olsen. "The Effects of Salaries and Opportunity Costs on the Length of Stay in Teaching." Journal of Human Resources (Winter 1990): 106–36.

Odell S., and D. Ferraro. "Teacher Mentoring and Teacher Retention." Journal of Teacher Education 43 (May-June 1992): 200–04.

Shann, Mary H. "Professional Commitment and
     Satisfaction Among Teachers in Urban Middle
     Schools." Journal of Educational Research 92.2
     (Nov. 1998): 67–73.

Streisand, Betsy, and Thomas Tote. "Many Millions of
     Kids, and Too Few Teachers: Across America,
     Teaching Jobs Go Wanting." US News and World
     Report 14 Sept. 1998: 24.

Tennessee Education Association. "Tennessee's
     Teachers: News Center." 8 Sept. 2002.
     <http://www.teateachers.org/newsctr>.

12c
arg

4 Consider making concessions to another position.

Often you won't be able to reject an opposing argument completely; most reasoned arguments do have some merit. In such cases you'll do well to concede that some of your opponent's points are valid and then argue that under the circumstances you believe yours are stronger. When you do this, you not only seem fair-minded but you avoid backing yourself into an untenable position.

One community organizer successfully used this strategy when she convinced the city council to grant her a permit to locate a homeless shelter across the street from a popular playground.

> I agree with you that safety concerns often make it inappropriate to locate shelters in areas frequented by children. The people served by homeless shelters are often troubled and difficult for shelter staff to monitor. However, the shelter I am proposing is different, because it will serve only mothers with small children who have been recommended by churches and social service agencies as good candidates for job training. These mothers will pose little danger to the neighborhood and their children will make good use of the playground.

By admitting that the city council's concerns are valid in many situations, she established valuable common ground with her audience. In addition, she freed herself from having to argue about the safety of homeless shelters in general, allowing her to focus on the special features of her particular shelter.

> SUMMARY **Writing Arguments That Appeal to Readers**
>
> • Draw on shared beliefs and values.
>
> • Present opposing arguments fairly.
>
> • Use civil language.
>
> • Refute opposing views when appropriate.
>
> • Make concessions to other views when appropriate.

12d How can you recognize and avoid fallacies?

Critical thinkers learn to recognize *fallacies,* those shoddy imitations of well-reasoned arguments. Most fallacies are flashy shortcuts that look good at first but turn out to be based on dubious assumptions and careless generalizations. Here are 10 kinds of fallacy you're likely to encounter frequently.

1 Avoid argument to the person (in Latin, *ad hominem*).

This fallacy makes a personal attack on an opponent rather than focusing on the issue under discussion. Ad hominem arguments become smear tactics when a speaker or a writer attacks an opponent's personality or personal life. Here is an example.

> A legislator arguing for a bill that would raise taxes on alcohol to provide low-cost housing claims that those who oppose the bill are heartless people more concerned with keeping down the price of their evening cocktails than with helping others.

The speaker who resorts to such abusive rhetoric may well be avoiding the real issues, such as whether a proposal is practical.

But don't confuse the ad hominem fallacy with relevant questions about credibility. It's perfectly legitimate to question a writer whose qualifications or motives are dubious, as long as those considerations are relevant to the issues being discussed. In the example above, it might be appropriate to note that an opponent of the alcohol tax owns a brewing company whose sales might suffer if prices rise.

12d
arg

■ **2 Avoid circular reasoning.** This fallacy—also called *begging the question*—happens when instead of supporting a claim, the writer simply restates the claim in different words. Take this faulty argument: "We should not raise taxes to build the new airport because doing so would cost taxpayers more money." Because raising taxes is the same thing as costing taxpayers more money, this statement basically says, "We should not raise taxes because doing so would raise taxes." It asks us to accept the claim at face value rather than providing substantive reasons and evidence.

Here's another example: "The death penalty is wrong because the state should not have the power to end a criminal's life." But that's exactly what the death penalty is—state-sanctioned execution. Unless the writer goes on to explain *why* it's wrong to end a criminal's life and provides supporting data, this claim begs the question.

If you hope to make effective arguments, you have to guard against this fallacy. An unsubstantiated claim is just that—it's not a reasoned argument.

■ **3 Avoid hasty generalization.** This fallacy involves drawing conclusions from too little evidence.

> It's not safe to swim at the beach because there were two shark attacks at Myrtle Beach last month and another attack last week in Miami Beach. Shark attacks at two beaches do not provide sufficient evidence on which to base a broad claim about the safety of beaches all over the U.S.

Be careful about making claims that use absolute terms such as *always, never, everyone, no one, all,* and *none.* When you're talking about human events, absolutes are seldom accurate, so cover yourself by using qualifiers like *some, in most cases,* and *many.* And as a reader and a listener, you should always be skeptical about arguments that overstate their claims in this way. (See Section 12a-4 for more about using qualifiers in an argument.)

■ **4 Avoid false cause arguments (in Latin, *post hoc, ergo propter hoc,* or "after this, therefore because of this").** These arguments incorporate the faulty assumption that because one event follows another, the first event caused the second. Setting up false cause arguments is a form of oversimplification that grows out of the desire we all have to believe in easy answers rather than wrestle with complex questions about who caused what and why.

Consider how silly the following argument sounds.

> Starting in June of this year, per capita ice cream consumption increased significantly. Just one month later, the number of

drownings increased. It's clear that eating ice cream causes people to drown.

Obviously, both ice cream consumption and drownings increase during the summer months. But one doesn't cause the other—more likely, hot weather causes people both to crave ice cream and to want to go swimming. Swimming accidents cause drowning.

It's easy to see the flaws in this example, but false cause arguments about social and political issues can be harder to spot. Consider this statement.

12d
arg

> In the years since the highway speed limit was raised to 70 miles per hour, the annual number of traffic fatalities in our state has doubled. Clearly, the new speed limit is causing unnecessary deaths.

Too many factors enter into changes in traffic fatality numbers for such a conclusion to be legitimate. Increased numbers of drivers on the road, altered traffic patterns due to new construction, an increase in the number of large trucks or other dangerous vehicles on the road, changes in how law enforcement monitors and enforces speeding or reckless driving—any of these factors might have influenced the number of fatal accidents. Without evidence *directly* linking the speed limit to traffic fatalities, one cannot reasonably infer a causal relationship.

5 Avoid either/or arguments (also called *false dilemma* or the *fallacy of insufficient options*). This type of faulty reasoning states an argument in terms that imply that one must choose between only two options—right/wrong, good/bad, moral/immoral, and so forth. This is another form of simplistic reasoning that glosses over complex issues and instead attacks the opposition.

> If we allow that factory to come into our town, we are dooming ourselves and our children to a lifetime of breathing filthy air.

Many other options are available between the extremes of no factory and filthy air; one might be to require the factory to install scrubbers to clean its emissions.

The loaded rhetorical question that allows for only one acceptable answer is another form of the either/or argument.

> Are we going to increase the number of police officers in this city, or are we going to abandon it to thugs, gangs, and drug dealers?

When an arguer tries to force a false dilemma on you, your best response is to challenge your opponent's polarized thinking immediately and point out other alternatives to his or her oversimplified view. And be careful to avoid either/or statements in your own writing: at best, they make you look naive; at worst, they make you seem like a fanatic.

6 Avoid red herrings. This tactic involves diverting the audience's attention from the main issue by bringing up an irrelevant point. (The phrase refers to the practice of dragging a strong-smelling smoked herring across a trail to confuse hunting dogs and send them in the wrong direction.) Arguers who fear they have a weak case may employ a red herring by bringing in some emotionally charged but irrelevant point in the hope they can distract their audience and keep them from focusing on the real issue. For example, a mayor might complain:

> While it may be true that my press secretary submitted false expense account vouchers, my administration is just being targeted by hostile media.

The charges of press bias might be true, but the attitude of the media has no bearing on the official's misbehavior.

7 Avoid slippery slopes. This fallacy occurs when a writer assumes that taking an initial action will automatically set in motion an unstoppable chain of events. Parents of teenagers slip into this fallacy when they make dire predictions based on a single incident.

> If I allow you to stay out until 2 a.m. this weekend, you'll want to stay out until 3 a.m. next time, and pretty soon you'll be staying out all night every weekend.

This statement offers no real proof that one late night will set off a never-ending sequence of later and later curfews.

You'll encounter slippery slopes most often when writers are promoting or opposing a particular course of action. For instance, a politician who supports funding a new complex to house agencies dealing with homelessness might argue that when homeless people have easy access to services under one roof, they will be able to get the help they need, find jobs, and become productive citizens. Perhaps so, but without explanation and argument to support each link in that chain, these predictions have no real foundation, and you shouldn't readily accept them.

8 Avoid false analogies. These are comparisons that do not hold true or prove misleading. Analogies can be invaluable in helping readers understand abstract or elusive ideas and concepts—for instance, a writer might clarify how the turbocharger in an automobile works by comparing it to a windmill or a waterwheel. Sometimes, however, in trying to make an argument more attractive to readers, writers create a false analogy in which the comparison drawn simply won't hold up. For example:

> A corporation couldn't operate without the leadership of a CEO to set priorities and make the big decisions. A family operates the same way: one spouse must be the head of the household, or chaos will result.

Certainly a business and a household share superficial similarities, but the two entities have completely different functions, involve different kinds of interpersonal relationships, and operate according to different value systems (profit and efficiency vs. nurturance and loyalty). To assume that what holds true in one environment should hold true in the other is a logical leap that readers won't be willing to take.

As a critical thinker, you'll want to pay attention to the analogies you use and those you encounter. Ask yourself this: Are the similarities between the things being compared strong enough to warrant the conclusions being drawn? If they're not, reject the analogy.

9 Avoid non sequitur. Latin for "it does not follow," this fallacy occurs when writers draw on irrelevant evidence or reasons to support a claim. Non sequitur is similar to the red herring fallacy, but whereas red herrings are designed to distract a reader from the central argument, non sequitur asks readers to accept the irrelevant material as proof. Here are two examples.

> That candidate would be an excellent mayor—after all, he was a successful businessman for years.
>
> I'm sure that it can't be a top-notch university. It's in a rundown area of the city, surrounded by housing projects and abandoned warehouses.

What does past business success have to do with being mayor? About as much as being in a bad neighborhood has to do with the quality of faculty and curriculum at a university: that is to say, little.

10 Avoid bandwagon appeal. This tactic argues that an activity or a product must be worthwhile because it is popular. Youngsters who try to persuade their parents that they must have a particular brand of sneakers or a new kind of in-line skates because "everybody has them" are using bandwagon tactics. As millions of parents have pointed out, popularity doesn't necessarily guarantee merit.

12d
arg

SUMMARY *Ten Common Fallacies*

1. **Argument to the person (ad hominem):** attacking the person instead of focusing on the issues involved.

2. **Circular reasoning:** restating instead of proving a claim.

3. **Hasty generalization:** drawing conclusions from scanty evidence.

4. **False cause:** presuming that if *B* follows *A, A* caused *B.*

5. **Either/or:** suggesting that only two choices are possible when in fact there may be several.

6. **Red herring:** bringing in an irrelevant issue to deflect attention from the main point.

7. **Slippery slope:** assuming that one event will set off an unstoppable chain reaction.

8. **False analogy:** making a comparison between things that are too dissimilar for the comparison to be useful.

9. **Non sequitur:** drawing a conclusion from irrelevant data.

10. **Bandwagon:** claiming that widespread popularity makes an object or idea valuable.

EXERCISE 12.4 Work with other students in a group to spot the fallacies in these arguments. In some instances you may find more than one.

1. Two kinds of young women come into corporations at the entry level: those who just want to work for a few years before they start a family and those who take their careers seriously. A company has to be careful not to hire the first kind.

2. Everyone knows that the next decade will be a poor time to go into medicine because government regulation is ruining the profession.

3. The great peasant rebellions in the Middle Ages happened because the rulers taxed the peasants to the limit to pay for foreign wars and neglected conditions in their own country; the United States can expect similar uprisings if it doesn't drastically cut its defense budget and invest in domestic social programs.

4. As a legislator, I can't get too upset about the proposed tuition raise when every time I drive by our state university I get caught in a traffic jam of students in their new four-wheel-drive vehicles and pricey convertibles.

CHAPTER 13

How Do You Design an Oral or Multimedia Report?

Instructors often ask students to prepare oral reports in their courses as a way of preparing them for a responsibility common in jobs and professions—managing a speech, sales talk, or group session of some kind. Many people feel uncomfortable when presenting material before groups, but public speaking is a valuable skill that can be mastered with practice, particularly in the friendly environment a classroom provides. There, the audience is generally familiar, forgiving, and already well disposed to what colleagues have to offer. A class is also a hospitable place to develop group presentations, which relieve some of the anxieties of a solo performance.

Good presentations require many of the same qualities found in good writing—coherent organization, a highly developed sense of audience, an appreciation for audio and visual elements, and memorable examples and illustra-
tions. In addition, they often require attention to performance skills like voice tone, pacing, and gestures. The sections that follow offer advice on all these elements.

13a What are the basics of an oral presentation?

Technology has transformed presentations so much that speakers sometimes forget that not every oral presentation must involve *PowerPoint,* an LCD projector, and a screen. Such tools are useful, but they should serve the overall purpose of the presentation, not overwhelm it. You still have to know what your subject is, how to organize your presentation, and how to deliver it appropriately for your audience.

■ **1 Choose your topic and structure carefully.** When you have the option of choosing your topic, speak on a subject you want to learn more about yourself: you'll investigate it with enthusiasm that will carry over into the presentation. Or talk about something you already know well enough to seem like an expert. Look particularly for subjects that connect academic interests to real-world applications. In a biology class, your report might explain one link between microbial theory and the potential abuse of antibiotics in the student health center. In a class on marketing, you might present facts about a famous (or infamous) local political ad campaign. In a sociology course, you might explore the impact of a factory's relocation on particular neighborhoods. Choosing a topic that is specific and local will also enhance your opportunities for finding or creating attractive multimedia elements, including photographs, video clips, and audio clips.

Of course, your choice of topic will be driven by the purpose of your presentation and your audience. Consider the different purposes that a report on light rail in your town might serve. One report might be historical, describing earlier forms of public transportation; another might explain the fiscal pros and cons of building a new system; and a third might be an argument against building a light-rail system. Though the core subject (light rail) would be the same, the presentations would be completely different.

■ **2 Decide on an overall organization.** Your topic and purpose will influence how you structure your presentation. In most reports, you'll want to give your listeners a sense of your organization early in a presentation so that they can keep their bearings as your presentation unfolds. A historical report might follow a chronological organization; an evaluative presentation, a comparison/contrast plan; and an argument, a claim-and-evidence design (see Chapters 3 and 12). Remember that an oral presentation must give more obvious signals about its organization than an academic report because a listener doesn't have the luxury of going back over a presentation the way a reader of a printed text can. So the introduction, body, and conclusion of a presentation must be clearly marked by words or images.

In the introduction, you may need to explain who you are and what you intend to cover. Your visual materials—whether an overhead projection or a slide—might include a title screen that gives the name

Figure 13.1 *A* PowerPoint *slide can briefly outline your oral report. Each bulleted point on this slide would become a major section of the report.*

of the talk, your name or the identity of the group that prepared the talk, a date, and any relevant institutional information. You can follow that up with a slide like the one shown in Figure 13.1 to preview the structure of the entire presentation. Openings can also include some humor to loosen up an audience and to help the speaker connect with listeners, but that's an American convention that doesn't always cross cultures.

The body of the talk should be carefully planned and punctuated by divisions of some kind. You can simply number your major points ("I am going to explore three major reasons . . . ") or make your transitions very explicit ("Now that I have covered *X,* I will explain . . . "). Preparing a set of slides or overhead projections may help you to distinguish between the minor and major transitions in your report (you need slides for major points only). Visualizing your contents should also help you notice relationships that may illuminate a subject. In *PowerPoint,* for example, you can use the "Slide Sorter" feature under "View" to rearrange your slides and experiment with different approaches, as shown in Figure 13.2.

As you move through the body of your report, you should remind readers occasionally what your main point is and summarize the points you have made in each section (without being tedious about it). You should signal clearly, too, when you are moving into the final part of your report. Even a transition as bare-bones as "In conclusion . . . " works just fine. The conclusion provides an opportunity to review your major points and to remind readers of your claim. This end-of-the-presentation summary should be direct, brief, and compelling. If you are using overheads or slides, the summary for your oral report should fit on a single screen. That's because you don't want to bore listeners at

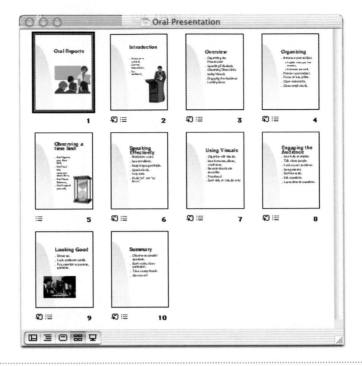

Figure 13.2   *With "Slide Sorter" selected, you can review thumbnails of all the slides you have created for a presentation and rearrange them as necessary.*

this crucial moment. Instead, give them something demanding to think about as you wrap up—one final point that draws out the implications of your report or gives your audience a specific charge or challenge.

To keep yourself and your audience on track throughout the presentation, you might speak from an outline that you share with your audience, though the version you use should be much more detailed than the one you distribute. If you are using *PowerPoint,* you can print out miniature versions of the slides you've created. (Select "Options" after you open "Print.") Or you can simply follow a set of note cards you prepare for yourself, with a single idea printed clearly on each card.

■ **3 Adapt your presentation to your audience.** When you prepare a paper, brochure, or Web project, you have to imagine people reading and reacting to it. When you present an oral report, your audience is likely sitting right in front of you—smiling, frowning, coughing, agreeing or disagreeing. So you've got to be prepared to adapt your presentation to this demanding group.

How do you make this match? First, find out as much as you can about your listeners as you prepare your talk. Naturally, you'll be at an advantage when you address classmates because you may already know them fairly well—their interests, expectations for style (formal vs. informal), their tolerance for humor, their attention spans. With other audiences, you'll have to make educated guesses about what they want to know, how formal or informal they expect the presentation to be, and what materials will interest them. For example, an audience of experts already interested in your subject will expect (and tolerate) much more technical material than a general audience would. For a general audience, you'll likely use more visual items to illustrate points and pay more attention to the performance aspects of the talk. Some groups will appreciate dynamic presentations that involve them in activities and encourage their comments throughout the session. But on other occasions, you might be expected to deliver a straight lecture without audience involvement until a question-and-audience period at the end. Do whatever you can to determine what your audience (or your instructor) wants, needs, and expects.

Of course, you'll be occupied with your audience not only as you plan your report but as you deliver it. You'll see and hear reactions immediately in smiles, furrowed brows, coughs, groans, and, maybe, applause. So you'll need to read people carefully and—as much as possible—adapt your material to the responses you are receiving. This dynamic connection with audiences is one of the pleasures of live performance, as many entertainers attest. But don't expect to master improvisation immediately. Working with audiences is a skill learned through experience.

To read an audience, pay attention to facial expressions and body language. American audiences expect and prefer eye contact with a speaker, so don't bury your nose in your notes—that's one of the biggest mistakes you can make. When you practice your presentation, try to do it with real people standing in as an audience. Keep your eyes moving, and don't be afraid to smile. And be sure you know your material well enough to feel comfortable *talking* to your audience rather than *reading* to them. (Be aware of national differences in presentation styles. Some people won't be comfortable with the directness of American address.)

Adapting to your audience may seem like common sense, but many speakers tense up and focus solely on their message. Obviously, when most of your listeners look puzzled, you should backtrack a little to clarify the point you are making. When they seem to get a point, move on; don't belabor it. Consider pausing for questions when you sense that participants have points they want to make. But don't expect to make everyone in your audience happy, especially when what you are reporting is unconventional or controversial. You want people to listen to you, but you don't have to say only what they want to hear.

Try to leave time at the end of your presentation for questions and then handle them with good humor. Occasionally, someone in your audience may ask a "hostile" question. Don't respond in kind. Your audience will respect you more if you respond to the challenge coolly and politely and then move on. Of course, you should know enough about a subject to handle basic questions. But don't be afraid to admit when you don't have an answer. If you control the length of the question-and-answer session, keep the period relatively short. If necessary, you can take questions one-on-one after the majority of the audience leaves.

E-Tips

For tips on overcoming anxiety about speaking in public and additional information about improving your oral delivery skills, visit <http://toastmasters.org>. Or check with your campus writing center to see whether they offer online tutorials or workshops on public speaking.

4 Think of your presentation as a performance. You'll need all your resources to connect with people, including your voice, gestures, and physical presence. Learn to vary the tone and intensity of your voice: raise or lower it to underscore key points; use pauses to mark punctuation or shifts in topic. Worry less about overdoing the voice effects than about droning like a fan through an entire presentation. A monotonous tone or rhythm will lull your listeners to sleep. But avoid speaking so swiftly that you garble your words. Inexperienced speakers sometimes merge all these problems. They may start out fine, but begin to speak faster and faster (and softer and softer) until they become almost unintelligible. An oral report is not a race. Take a deep breath every so often and slow down.

If you discover that you have too much material to cover in the allotted time, edit your material as you go. It is often better to skip some details or examples than to rush through the presentation or to extend it into another speaker's time. Keep a discreet eye on the clock or keep a wristwatch on the podium to monitor your time. If no length is assigned to your talk, remember the rule of any good performance: leave the audience asking for more. It takes an unusually talented speaker to keep an audience entertained for thirty or forty minutes without a break. Most academic presentations are much shorter, in the range of 10 to 20 minutes.

Don't stare relentlessly at your paper on the podium or hold your text up in front of you, blocking the audience's view. Keep your eyes moving, and convey some enthusiasm for your subject. Don't freeze up before an audience like a wax figure at Madame Tussaud's. Instead, use bodily movements deliberately. A shrug, a nod, a casual turn, a sweep of the arm, even a scratch of the head can all be used to reinforce a point. If appropriate, move away from the podium and change position during the speech a few times. Compel your listeners to refocus their attention. But don't pace—shifts of position should seem purposeful.

Above all, practice the full presentation several times aloud, complete with the equipment you intend to use, whether it involves a blackboard or a computer. Don't imagine how you'll act—speak the words just as you intend to say them; flip through your slides, overheads, or posters; and be sure to time yourself. Practice at least once in the place you will deliver the presentation. If that's not possible, at least scope out the room or auditorium so you know what to expect. A group presentation should almost be choreographed so that all participants know their jobs, whether it involves presenting materials or running machines. Leave nothing to chance. And always anticipate the failure of equipment. Be ready to deliver a professional presentation even if the bulb in the projector burns out or there's no chalk for the board.

13b How do you manage the technology of a presentation?

These days, audiences have high expectations for oral presentations because various tools—including computers, LCD projectors, and presentation software such as *PowerPoint*—have made it almost too easy to create absorbing multimedia events. But technology is seductive. Almost everyone has endured a slide presentation so full of special effects that they overwhelm the speaker's subject and even evoke giggles. The fact is that bells and whistles alone don't impress people. They want a professional presentation that uses the appropriate tools to make a memorable point.

1 Choose appropriate tools, props, and supplements for your report. Don't use more equipment than you require, and never introduce a special effect just because you know how to do it. For many presentations, all the technology you may need is a podium and your lecture notes. Good old chalkboards and flip charts can be useful when your presentation invites group participation and you want to record audience responses. But even simple tools need to be used well. If you write on a board or flip chart, do so clearly, boldly, and quickly.

Keep any materials you record brief: reduce full sentences to key words and phrases.

Plan ahead for all types of equipment you require. Know what is available in a given venue or what may be provided on the day of the presentation. And do whatever you can to practice with that equipment and, especially, to anticipate problems. The laptop computer you expected

13b

present

may turn out to be a PC that won't read your Macintosh disk. LCD projectors have notoriously unfathomable controls. Even figuring how to turn down the lights can be a problem in some situations. The more you work through ahead of time, the smoother your presentation will be.

2 Create tables, charts, graphs and other visual texts.

It's not necessary to illustrate every portion of your presentation, but charts, graphs, and other illustrations can often make a point better than words can. For instance, pie charts do an excellent job of explaining percentages while graphs plot trends nicely. (See Chapters 11 and 22 for more on interpreting and using visual texts.)

You can create professional-looking charts and graphs on your computer and then turn them into transparencies or slides. Or you can simply draw the items yourself on poster paper and display them on an easel. Just be sure whatever you present is large and clear enough to be read at a distance. Use fonts that are bold and thick. Don't clutter your illustrative materials: too much detail will make an item hard to read and interpret.

Show the same discretion with photographs. Images should be large enough to see from a distance and relatively simple. Technology makes it much easier now to download picture files from digital cameras or the Web and then manipulate them as you see fit, for example, cropping your subjects or adding titles. Be sure you credit sources for any photos, and remember to use only as many visual items as you absolutely need. An oral report that becomes a slide show will be disappointing. Most experts suggest that you should *not* display visual items continuously while you talk. Viewers will pay more attention to the photographs or pictures than to you. So display such items only briefly.

Members of your audience may also enjoy examining tangible objects when that is possible *and* when such opportunities really do contribute to your point. But don't risk delicate objects (like pottery or prints) to clumsy figures or circulate items that might be dangerous or distracting as they get passed around.

3 Use video and sound sensibly.

Some presenters like to show video clips as part of their presentations. You can, in fact, use a VCR or DVD player to show news clips, movie scenes, or even films you create yourself. But, as always, the video should not dominate the presentation or substitute for your own words and explanations. Any materials you create should be capably edited and quite brief. If you are going to rely on a video for your presentation, be sure you have access to video equipment and you know how to operate it. Turn the machine on when you need it and off when you are done. Otherwise audiences will stare at the glowing TV screen instead of looking at you.

You may also need to include audio materials in a presentation. Audiences may benefit from hearing President John F. Kennedy or Ronald Reagan at the Berlin Wall or the voice of Bessie Smith. But, again, be sure you have adequate equipment (especially speakers) and know how to operate it, and always keep the audio portions short. Such materials should serve as lively illustrations and examples, not tedious interludes.

4 Use presentation software sensibly. Presentation software such as *PowerPoint* is so popular that it has become the default method of doing an oral report in many business, professional, and academic situations. Such software is easy to use, easy to learn, and full of many tempting options, as you can see in Figure 13.3. Choose wisely and you can create a set of slides that complements your presentation perfectly.

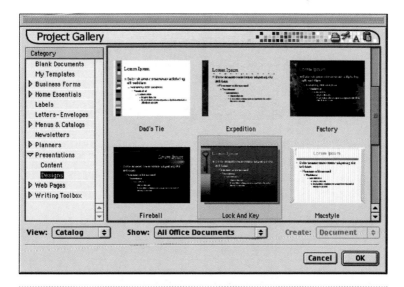

Figure 13.3 *In the* PowerPoint *"Project Gallery," you can select design templates for your presentation slides or create designs of your own.*

The best advice is to *keep it simple.* You will want all your slides to share a common style, so it makes sense to consider one of the design templates offered by the software, especially when you are a novice. But for academic presentations, you should look for the cleanest page and then select a cool palette of colors. Save the eye-dazzlers for informal situations.

Once you have established a basic style for your pages, you will have options for choosing your page layouts. Again, you can begin with the set of useful templates provided by *PowerPoint* and then modify them to suit your materials. (Just select "Slide Layout" from the "Format" menu for your options.) Or you can arrange the pages on your own. In either case, you want the slides to be simple in content and appearance, supporting your presentation and guiding your audience through the material. You don't want to read extensively from the screen or provide so much "content" that your audience finds your presence unnecessary. Figures 13.4 and 13.5 show some useful and distracting versions of slides.

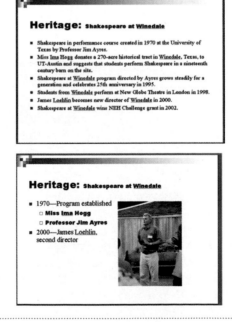

Figure 13.4   *Too many words on screen will distract and irritate audiences. The slide on the top is too wordy; the slide on the bottom works better because it supports rather than dominates the presentation.*

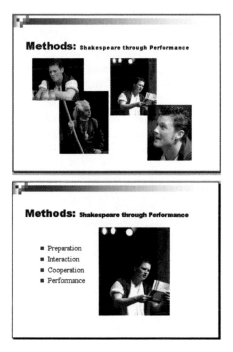

13b
present

Figure 13.5   *Too many pictures can also be distracting. The slide on top is handsome, but it doesn't make a clear point about methods for teaching Shakespeare through performance. The second slide—with a single image of actor Lawrence Kern—explains what methods the speaker intends to cover.*

As you grow familiar with the software, you'll discover many different design options and opportunities. Novices quickly discover that they can animate images to zoom in and out of their slides, with visuals accompanied by whooshes and screeches. Avoid these hysterical flourishes in your academic presentations. In some cases, a quiet dissolve or fade adds a fine touch to the transitions from slide to slide. But no special effect should draw attention to itself—unless your intention is comic (and sometimes it may be).

More sophisticated options are available as well. For instance, you can insert picture files directly into a slide and then resize them according to your needs. These files can be taken from public domain clip art files, from the Web (with appropriate permission), or from your own digital camera. Similarly, you can load sound files and video clips into a slide. But don't exercise these potentially distracting options unless you really need them. Be certain, too, that the sound and image quality reproduced will be acceptable to viewers. In particular, the audio quality of video clips can be disappointing.

Finally, be sure to edit your slides carefully. *PowerPoint* runs a spelling check as you compose your items. Be careful, especially, with the spelling of proper nouns and adjectives. Spelling *Jane Austen* as *Jean Austin* on a dozen slides will destroy your credibility. But poor spelling is the least embarrassing of the errors you can display on screen. Remember that your slide will receive the full and critical attention of your audience, so you don't want them catching gaffes in your facts, mechanics, or design.

Checklist 13.1

Preparing an Oral or Multimedia Presentation

* Choose a topic that suits your audience and purpose.

* Choose an appropriate organizational pattern.

* Adapt your material to your audience.

* Create effective audio and visual elements.

* Practice your performance.

CHAPTER 14

How Do You Write About Literature?

Writing about literature is a common assignment in most English courses, even in composition classes. But requirements and approaches vary from teacher to teacher and course to course. Instructors *do* think about literature in different ways, depending on their background, training, inclinations, and familiarity with literary theory. Critical approaches to literature today can range from close readings of individual texts to wide-ranging confrontations with issues of politics, gender, and culture. So how you write about works of literature or popular culture (movies, plays, music, television) may depend as much on how you are taught as on what you read or view.

What, then, is the point of writing about literature? It can be to heighten your appreciation for literary works, to demonstrate your ability to support a thesis about a piece of literature, to explore what it means to read, to understand how readers respond to texts, to enhance your skill at interpretation, to expand your knowledge of a particular era or literary movement, or to heighten your sensitivity to other cultures. It can also be a creative activity—a way to go public with your writing. At the very least, reading and writing about literature gives you the chance to examine and explore the best examples we have of our language in action.

In these few pages we can't give you advice for dealing with all these possibilities. What we can offer is a little practical advice for reading critically, finding a subject, and working with literary or cultural materials. Whatever your teachers' predilections, we hope that reading literature makes you wiser and gives you pleasure. Those two aims have stood the test of time.

14a How do you closely read a literary work?

There are dozens of ways to read, think about, and respond to literary works, and all of these approaches begin with a basic assumption: *the work must be read closely, often more than once.* Whether you are studying a short story, a poem, or a movie, you will have to read—or watch—that work carefully to be able to write about it authoritatively. An essay composed after one viewing of Alfred Hitchcock's *Rear Window* or a quick reading of Jamaica Kincaid's "Girl" will likely lack insight, detail, and cohesion. If your instructor expects you to make and support assertions about the works you study, the suggestions in the following sections will help you get started. (For more information on reading strategies, see Sections 10a and 12c-1.)

1 Appreciate the special challenges of reading poetry.

Many readers feel intimidated by poetry. Unfamiliar with the genre's various forms and techniques, they may feel unprepared when they tackle a poem. Or, more commonly, they may worry about "getting it"—about coming away with a poem's "right" meaning. One way to deal with these concerns is to try to see poetry as an accessible, if often challenging, form of creative communication. Beyond that, we offer two other bits of advice: slow down and listen.

You might be able to appreciate a poem after a single reading, but it is unlikely that you could absorb its beauty, complexity, and meaning. It is doubtful, too, that you could write a successful essay without rereading the poem several times. Once you accept the fact that you are going to spend some time on the poem you are reading, the pressure to "get it" should start to fade. Try to read the poem the first time without any goals or expectations—simply enjoy it for the piece of art that it is. On subsequent readings, you can start to study the work, looking carefully at its structure, imagery, or other formal features (see Section 14b for more on literary devices.) You might also keep a reading journal, a notebook in which you can jot down reactions, questions, and ideas as you read.

To fully appreciate any poem, you should read it aloud at least once (if you can, ask a friend or classmate to read the poem to you). Poetry evolved from an oral tradition of songs and chants, and there is music in the language still.

2 Read short stories, novels, and plays carefully—focusing on key patterns in longer works.

Even though works of fiction and drama are generally longer than poems, the need for careful reading remains. Some short stories are, in fact, short enough to allow multiple readings in a reasonable amount of time. But what if you have to write about a lengthy text, like Ralph Ellison's *The Invisible Man* or Shakespeare's *King Lear?* In cases such as these, you may want to focus your writing project on a single passage that you can read several times, for example, or on a particular character or theme that you can trace through portions of the work. Here again, consider keeping a reading journal; it can be a great source of raw material when you begin thinking about your papers.

■ 3 "Read" films, television, and other visual media as carefully as you do printed texts. Think about the last time you went to a movie. How much of it did you remember afterwards? If you are like most people, you probably couldn't recall much more than a few favorite scenes and pieces of dialogue; even those may have started to fade on the drive home. The point is, there's a difference between watching a film for entertainment and studying one for class. (See Section 11c for more on interpreting visual texts.)

If your instructor asks you to write about a movie, understand that, just as with written texts, you are going to have to spend some time with the work. Your professor may set up viewing times for your class or make a videotape or digital videodisc (DVD) of the film available in a media lab or the library. You also may want to rent a copy of the movie so you can study it at home.

Think about keeping a journal handy as you watch the film. If the VCR or DVD player you are using has the capability, keep track of important scenes on analog or digital counters so that you can return to them easily.

14b What elements should you look for when you read literature?

What is literature? To be honest, that question is beyond the scope of this handbook. But we can help you become familiar with a few elements that are integral to literary works. (Some of these—diction, tone, and figurative language among them—are not exclusive to literature; they matter in many kinds of writing.) Recognizing these elements and devices can help you formulate and refine a topic, develop a thesis statement, and provide evidence for a writing project.

SUMMARY	*Basic Literary Elements*	
• Diction	• Point of view	• Tone
• Character	• Setting	• Word order
• Figures of speech	• Sound and rhythm	• Visual elements
• Imagery	• Theme	
• Plot		

■ **1 Pay attention to diction (word choices).** Just as sculptors work with marble or wood and painters with oils or acrylics, writers use words to create their art. As you read, assume that every word was chosen carefully (this is especially true in poetry). If you come across words you don't understand, look them up. Dictionaries provide the primary or literal meanings of words, or their denotations; you should also be aware of possible connotations, or secondary meanings and associations. In addition, be on the lookout for ambiguity, or the possibility of two or more meanings, in the writer's diction. Deliberate ambiguity is a useful literary device, while unintended ambiguity can cause confusion.

■ **2 Look closely at the characters.** Writers create characters to populate their poems and stories and to make readers care about what is happening. Characters may also reinforce themes or symbols in the text. What would *Moby-Dick* be without Ahab, Ishmael, the whale, and all the others? It would be little more than a report on whaling.

■ **3 Find the figurative language.** In the broadest terms, a figure of speech is a deviation from the literal, a way to say or write one thing in terms of another. Instead of saying your chemistry test was hard, for example, you might call it "a bear." Figurative language takes many forms—metaphor and simile, two kinds of comparisons, are probably the most common figures of speech. Others used frequently include oxymoron, personification, hyperbole, litotes, synecdoche, and metonymy. (Explanations of these and other kinds of figurative language usually can be found in glossaries at the back of literature textbooks.) A writer might use figurative language to challenge, inspire, or connect with readers; to bring linguistic diversity and vitality to the work; or simply to stretch her creative wings.

*Maggie and Brick, shown here
as played by Frances O'Connor
and Brendan Fraser in a recent
London stage production, are
two of the most frequently
written about characters in
Tennessee Williams's play* Cat
on a Hot Tin Roof.

4 Look for imagery. One of the elements that makes good poetry so intense is its appeal to the senses through concrete images. Poets and other writers use language to make us see what they are seeing, to hear, smell, taste, and to feel. As you read, be aware of how the writer uses words to speak to your senses.

5 Follow the plot. Many readers confuse plot and theme (see below). Plot refers to the writer's arrangement of events in a story and the reasons behind that arrangement. If you read something, for example, and someone asks you to explain what happened, your answer would be a summary of the plot. Plot can be presented in a number of ways, including chronologically and by using flashbacks.

6 Notice the point of view. When you think about point of view, or perspective, focus on who is telling the story (the narrator) and how it is told. Narrators come in many types and can speak in the first, second (rarely), or third person. Some narrators are omniscient (able to tell us what is going on in the minds of characters), while others are objective (able to tell us only what the characters say and do). Some are involved in the plot, while others are mere observers.

*The etching of Charles Dickens'
young Oliver Twist asking for
more gruel in the orphanage
illustrates the novel's grim
setting. The illustration is by
George Cruickshank.*

7 Focus on setting. The setting establishes the world in which the characters live and act, including time, place, and social or cultural context.

8 Be alert to sound and rhythm. Because of the musical nature of their work, poets more often than other writers are concerned with the sound and rhythm—or meter—of words in a text. Common devices that involve sound are onomatopoeia (the sound of a word suggesting its meaning) and alliteration (the repetition of the same consonant sounds at the start of words near each other).

9 Identify symbols. It can be easy to confuse symbols with metaphors. While a metaphor is a comparison of two unlike objects or concepts, a symbol is one thing that stands for another. The dove, for example, can be a symbol for peace, just as the heart is a common symbol for love. A symbol's context will often suggest its meaning.

10 Look for important themes. The theme of a work is, to put it simply, what the work is *about* (its main concept), as opposed to what *happens* in it (see the discussion of plot above). A writer will often use the theme to pull together all the other elements of the work. Some common themes are *anger, jealousy, ambition, hypocrisy,* and *prejudice.*

11 Describe the tone. As you read a work, you should get a feeling for the mood the writer creates or his feelings about the subject matter. The mood, or tone, might be serious or comical, angry or sad, or something else. Once you get an idea about the tone of the piece, ask yourself how the writer achieves it—through imagery, descriptive details, diction, or symbols, for instance.

12 Look at word order. Just as poets choose their words carefully (see the discussion of diction above), so too do they decide where to put them. As you read, you might find it useful to ask yourself why the poet chose the order that she did. Then ask what would change if the words were in a different order.

13 Keep in mind that writing about film and television requires special considerations and terminology. While many of the elements listed in Sections 4b-1 through 4b-11 apply to the study of film and television, remember that these genres are primarily visual and, therefore, involve specialized elements—shots, scenes, camera angles, lighting, and so on. Before beginning any writing project that focuses on film, research these elements. Your instructor may explain these in class; if you're unsure, ask which elements and terms he or she expects you to be familiar with.

> **E-Tips** Two good introductory sources on writing about film are the Dartmouth University Composition Center's *Writing About Film* Web page at <http://www.dartmouth.edu/~compose/student/humanities/film.html> and the University of Pennsylvania's film studies Web page at <http://www.library.upenn.edu/resources/subject/humanities/film/film.html>.

14c What approaches can you use to write about literature?

As with any writing project, when you begin a literary analysis paper, have a general strategy in mind. Just as you wouldn't attempt to write an argument paper titled "Everything About the Crime Problem,"

As this still from The Cabinet of Dr. Caligari *(1920) illustrates, cinematographic elements like camera angles, set design, and lighting often help to establish tone, setting, and theme in a film.* (Courtesy The Museum of Modern Art/Film Stills Archive)

don't try to stuff everything you know about Zora Neale Hurston's *Their Eyes Were Watching God* into a single essay. When you write about a piece of literature or a film, or when you create a literary project (a Web site, a literary magazine), you will usually make your point by using one or two of the following approaches. (Again, we use *text* to mean written work and film.)

1 Perform a close reading. A "close reading" of a text carefully explains the meaning and possible interpretations of a selected passage, sometimes line by line (or, in the case of film, shot by shot or scene by scene). In a close reading, you ordinarily consider how the language of a work makes readers entertain specific ideas and images. If a work includes visual images, you may examine how they interact with elements of a written text. Sally Shelton's paper, which appears at the end of this chapter, offers close readings of several passages in a poem. (Also see Section 10b on how to read critically.)

2 Analyze key themes in a work. Reading a work carefully, you might discover certain key themes. In examining a theme, show how the various parts of a work convey their meanings to readers. In this introduction to an assignment for an American Literature course, the student writer identifies a central theme in Jonathan Swift's *Gulliver's Travels.*

In Gulliver's Travels, the protagonist Gulliver's sea
voyages expose him to the best and worst aspects of
human civilization. Through Gulliver's eyes, readers

```
come to share Swift's perception that no matter how
good people's intentions, their innate selfishness
corrupts the social institutions they construct. All
the societies Gulliver visits give evidence of this
theme, but we see the problem especially clearly in
his descriptions of Lilliput and Brobdignag.
```

14c
lit

3 Analyze plot or structure. You may study the way a work of literature is put together and consider why a writer chooses a particular arrangement of ideas or plot.

Here is an excerpt from a student's analysis of a subplot of Christopher Marlowe's play *Dr. Faustus,* written for a course in British drama.

```
There are two distinct plots in Dr. Faustus. The main
plot chronicles Faustus' bargain with the devil and
fall into damnation, while the subplot shows the
humorous adventures of Faustus' servant Wagner during
the same period. Although at first the two plots may
seem unrelated, the subplot serves three important
functions in the play. It serves the practical
purpose of creating a break between the main plot's
scenes, it provides comic relief from the tragic tone
of the play, and finally, by paralleling the main
plot's themes, the subplot reinforces the play's
moral message.
```

4 Analyze character and setting. You may study the behavior of characters in a novel, poem, play, or short story to understand their motivations and the ways in which different characters relate to each other. Or you can explore how a writer creates characters through description, action, reaction, and dialogue and embodies them with specific themes and ideas. See Joshua Michael French's paper excerpted on pages 213-214 for an example of a character analysis.

Similarly, you might study an artist's creation of a setting to figure out how the environment of a work (where things happen in a novel, short story, or play) affects what happens in the plot or to the characters. Settings can also be analyzed as the exterior representations of characters' inner being or as manifestations of cultural values.

5 Analyze literary archetypes. Certain recurring themes, plots, characters, and settings—such as (in Western societies) the quest, the sacrificial lamb, the harrowing of hell—can be said to represent the myths or *archetypes* of a culture. You can explore literary texts to reveal the cultural patterns they embody and the archetypes they incorporate, modify, or even parody.

6 Analyze the text as an example of a particular genre. You can study a particular work by evaluating its form—tragedy, comic novel, sonnet, detective story, epic, situation comedy, film noir, and so on. Compare the work to other literary pieces of that genre, looking for similarities and differences and perhaps comment on the relative quality of the achievement.

7 Explore an historical or cultural analysis. You can study a literary work as it reflects the society that produced it or as it was accepted or rejected by that society when it was published. Or you can study the way historical information makes a literary work from an earlier time clearer to a reader today.

You can similarly explore how a work of art embodies the culture that produced it. That is, what assumptions about the beliefs and values of a society can be found in the literary work? Such analysis may reveal how certain groups gained or maintained power through the manipulation of literary myths or symbols.

8 Analyze a work from the perspective of gender. You might examine how a literary work portrays women or men and defines their roles in society. Feminist analyses in particular have greatly influenced the reading of literary works in the last generation, though such interpretations vary as much as any other form of criticism. Many feminist critics explore the way literary works embody relationships of power between men and women. Sally Shelton's paper, which appears on pages 224–227, is an example of this kind of analysis.

9 Examine the biography of the author or the author's creative process. You might examine how a writer's life is expressed in or through a literary work. Such analyses may be related to cultural and political studies, but they may also focus on the individual psychology of a writer. Similarly, you might learn all you can about the way a particular work was created. You might examine the sources, notes, influences, manuscripts, and revised texts behind a finished book, poem, or film. Or you might compare different versions of the same work.

Kathryn Samra's paper on Langston Hughes, excerpted on page 214, is
an example of biographical analysis.

■ **10 Edit a text or produce a literary Web site.** One type of
literary work increasingly common in college settings is the production
of literary journals or, more recently, Web sites that focus on cultural
ideas and themes. Introducing new works is an important creative responsibility that requires the careful selection and editing of texts—an
important way of going public with writing. Whether in print or on
the Web, you can present and comment on new works or edit older,
neglected texts in the public domain.

14c
lit

Going Public   *Two Approaches to Literary Analysis* _____

The following selections demonstrate two approaches to
literary analysis. Both paragraphs are from papers by students at
the University of South Carolina.
    The first is from an essay by Joshua Michael French,
"Bartleby: The Lost Follower," that offers a close reading of the
central character in Herman Melville's short story "Bartleby the
Scrivener." In the essay, French has already argued that Bartleby's problems stem from the psychological process of denial. Now he uses evidence (highlighted) from the short story to explore another psychological weakness in Bartleby's character.

> By denying his responsibilities and avoiding
> conflict with the narrator of the story, Bartleby
> displays a second psychological flaw: isolation. . . .
> The narrator calls the scrivener into his office to
> ask him a few simple questions and even offers
> Bartleby his friendship, but there is no emotional
> response. Instead, Bartleby stares blankly and
> refuses the narrator's advances as usual. The
> narrator notes that Bartleby **"[keeps] his glance fixed**
> **upon [his] bust of Cicero"** (122) instead of looking
> directly at him. Even when the narrator comments, **"I**
> **feel friendly towards you"** (122), there is no
> response from Bartleby. Strangely enough, however,
> Bartleby does show a need for the narrator's

presence, meaning that he desires companionship even if he does not react to it. For instance, Bartleby **"refuses to do any copying"** (130) for anyone in the office but the narrator.

Kathryn R. Samra takes a more historical approach to a poem by Langston Hughes, a major artist of the Harlem Renaissance, in her paper "Theme for Langston Hughes." Samra draws on information 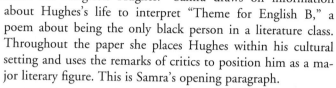 about Hughes's life to interpret "Theme for English B," a poem about being the only black person in a literature class. Throughout the paper she places Hughes within his cultural setting and uses the remarks of critics to position him as a major literary figure. This is Samra's opening paragraph.

Known for his ability to mix popular culture and radical politics with poetry and a few jazzy beats, Langston Hughes became a prominent figure of the Harlem Renaissance. Born in 1902, Hughes lived during a time when African Americans were finally able to express the types of music and literature that were a part of their cultural history. And when he died at the age of 65, it was at the pinnacle of the civil rights movement, when African Americans were beginning to be treated as equals. Most of Hughes's poetry reflects this point in his life. His poem "Theme for English B," for instance, mirrors the way he felt about his place in society. Although not written as a protest poem, it demonstrates how he felt as a black person growing up in Harlem.

14d What sources can you use in writing essays about literature?

The resources available to you as you begin a literary analysis can seem overwhelming. But many of them will in fact make your work easier, more authoritative, and more interesting.

1 Understand the primary texts you are reading. In working with literary and cultural texts, you may first need to establish certain basic facts about them. Are you reading (or viewing) a first edition of a work or a revised version, an edited version, a translation, or, in the case of a film, a later "director's cut" that differs from the version shown in theaters? Each of these considerations may have a bearing on your subsequent analysis. Evaluate any publication information you find in the prefaces or front matter of works of literature to discover when they were written, by whom they were published, how they might have been transmitted to readers, and how they may have changed over the years. In general, the older a work, the more complicated (and fascinating) its publication history might be. But even more recent texts deserve your attention. The techniques of positioning that you apply to research materials (see Section 48b-1) can be modified to work with literary and cultural texts before you analyze them.

14d
lit

2 Consult secondary sources on literary subjects. To locate secondary sources on literary topics, begin with the following indexes and bibliographies available in a library reference room.

> *Essay and General Literature Index*
> *MLA International Bibliography*
> *New Cambridge Bibliography of English Literature*
> *Year's Work in English Studies*

Many other useful reference works and Web sites are available; see Checklist 14.1.

Checklist 14.1

Reference Works for Literary Analyses

PRINTED TEXTS

Altick, Richard D., and John J. Fenstermaker. *The Art of Literary Research.* 4th ed. New York: Norton, 1993.

Beacham, Walton, ed. *Research Guide to Biography and Criticism.* Washington, DC: Research, 1990.

Bloom, Harold. *American Women Fiction Writers, 1900–1960.* 3 vols. Philadelphia: Chelsea, 1997–1999.

Crystal, David. *The Cambridge Encyclopedia of Language.* 2nd ed. New York: Cambridge UP, 1997.

(Continued)

Reference Works for Literary Analyses *(Continued)*

Drabble, Margaret, ed. *The Oxford Companion to English Literature.* Rev. ed. 2nd rev. Oxford: Oxford UP, 1998.

Encyclopedia of World Literature in the Twentieth Century. 3rd ed. Farmington Hills: St. James, 1999.

Evans, Gareth L., and Barbara Evans. *The Shakespeare Companion.* New York: Scribner's, 1978.

Gates, Henry Louis, Jr., et al. *The Norton Anthology of African American Literature.* New York: Norton, 1997.

Gibaldi, Joseph. *MLA Handbook for Writers of Research Papers.* 5th ed. New York: MLA, 1999.

Gilbert, Sandra M., and Susan Gubar. *The Norton Anthology of Literature by Women: The Traditions in English.* 2nd ed. New York: Norton, 1996.

Harmon, William, and C. Hugh Holman. *A Handbook to Literature.* 8th ed. New York: Prentice, 1999.

Harner, James L. *Literary Research Guide: A Guide to Reference Sources for the Study of Literature in English and Related Topics.* 3rd ed. New York: MLA, 1998.

Hart, James D., ed. *The Oxford Companion to American Literature.* 6th ed. New York: Oxford UP, 1995.

Howatson, M. C. *The Oxford Companion to Classical Literature.* 2nd ed. New York: Oxford UP, 1989.

Inge, M. Thomas, et al. *Black American Writers: Bibliographical Essays.* New York: St. Martin's, 1978.

Marcuse, Michael J. *A Reference Guide for English Studies.* Berkeley: U of California P, 1990.

Ousby, Ian. *The Cambridge Guide to Literature in English.* 2nd ed. New York: Cambridge UP, 1993.

Sage, Lorna. *The Cambridge Guide to Women's Writing in English.* Cambridge: Cambridge UP, 1999.

Sampson, George. *The Concise Cambridge History of English Literature.* 3rd ed. Cambridge: Cambridge UP, 1972.

WEB RESOURCES

The Complete Works of William Shakespeare. <http://the-tech.mit.edu/Shakespeare>.

The English Server. < http://eserver.org>.

Literary Resources on the Net. <http://andromeda.rutgers.edu/~jlynch/Lit>.

MLA Online. < http://www.mla.org>.

The On-Line Books Page. < http://digital.library.upenn.edu/books>.

University of Virginia Library Electronic Text Center. <http://
etext.lib. virginia.edu>.

Voice of the Shuttle. < http://vos.ucsb.edu/shuttle/english.html>

Web Resources of Interest to Literary Scholars. University of Texas at Austin.
< http://www.lib.utexas.edu/subject/english/sites.html>.

Yahoo! Arts: Humanities: Literature. < http://www.yahoo.com/Arts/Hum-
anities/Literature>.

14e How do you develop a literary project?

How you develop a literary paper or project will depend on your
course assignment and your own purpose. In some courses you'll be
asked to do a close reading of an individual poem, novel, or short story;
in others you may be expected to contribute to a Web site that places
artists or works in their historical or political contexts. Here we assume
that you are most likely to write a paper with a thesis—but the principles we discuss will apply to other projects as well. For example, if you
are participating in a Web forum or editing a literary journal, you still
need to read carefully, formulate clear ideas about your subjects, report
information accurately, and design a project that will be interesting and
enlightening to others.

1 Begin by reading carefully. The evidence you'll need to
write a thoughtful, well-organized analysis may come from within the
literary work itself and from outside readings and secondary sources.
Your initial goal is to find a point worth making, an assertion you can
prove with convincing evidence.

To find your point, begin by *positioning* the work (or works)
and then reading and *annotating* them carefully (see Sections 10a and
48b-2).

If you were assigned to read Shakespeare's *Macbeth,* you might
position the work by doing a little background reading (see Section
14b). You'd quickly learn that *Macbeth* is a tragedy written by the most
famous of English playwrights around 1605–06, though not published
until 1623. An unusually brief tragedy, *Macbeth* may have been designed expressly to please the English monarch James I, who was fascinated by witches and whose legendary ancestor appears in the work.

You can position works in many ways to enhance your initial understanding. Yet you should also read with an open mind, being certain to savor the literary experience. Do, however, annotate texts in some way to record your immediate responses. You might simply ask yourself a series of questions.

- What issues engage me immediately as I read the work?
- What puzzles or surprises me?
- What characters or literary devices seem most striking or original?
- What upsets me or seems most contrary to my own values and traditions?

Make a list of such queries as you read, and reexamine them when you have finished. While experiencing Shakespeare's *Macbeth,* you might produce annotations such as these.

- Is ambition the cause of Macbeth's defeat?
- What is the nature of the relationship between Lady Macbeth and her husband? How is Lady Macbeth inhibited by her gender?
- Is the story of Macbeth historically true?
- Why do some lines in this tragedy seem awkward or even funny?
- Can Macbeth blame the witches for his tragedy?
- What exactly makes this play a tragedy? What *is* a tragedy?

To stimulate more questions, you may want to compare and contrast the work(s) you have read with other similar works.

- Is Macbeth as ambitious as King Claudius in *Hamlet?*
- Is Lady Macbeth a more influential character in *Macbeth* than Queen Gertrude is in *Hamlet?*
- Why does Shakespeare use so much comedy in his tragedies, including *Hamlet, Romeo and Juliet,* and *Macbeth?*

At this point you might stimulate your thinking both by considering specific ways of approaching a literary text (see Section 14b–14c) and by using one of the techniques we describe for finding and focusing ideas, particularly brainstorming and idea mapping (see Sections 2a–2b).

2 Develop a thesis about the literary work(s) you are studying. Begin with questions you are eager to explore in depth, a research query or hypothesis generated perhaps by your reading of secondary sources or by your discussions with classmates and other readers. A paper on *Macbeth* might lead to research questions such as the following.

- Are some scenes missing from *Macbeth?*
- What limits on the power of women in Elizabethan England might explain the behavior of Lady Macbeth?
- Did the term *equivocation* have particular political significance to the original audience of *Macbeth?*
- Did Shakespeare tailor *Macbeth* to please England's Scottish monarch, King James?

When you've put your question into words, test its energy. Is the answer to your inquiry so obvious that it isn't likely to interest or surprise anyone?

- Is Shakespeare's *Macbeth* a great play?

If so, discard the issue. Try another. Look for a surprising, even startling question—one whose answer you don't necessarily know. Test that question on classmates or your instructor. Would they want to read a paper or examine a Web page that explores the issue you are considering?

- Could Shakespeare's *Macbeth* actually be a comedy?
- What role do the lower classes play in a dynastic struggle like the one depicted in *Macbeth?*
- Are the witches really the physical embodiment of Macbeth's own mind?

When you have found your question, turn it into an assertion—your preliminary thesis statement.

- Shakespeare's *Macbeth* is really a comedy.
- The welfare of the lower classes seems to have been ignored in dynastic struggles like those depicted in *Macbeth.*
- The witches in *Macbeth* are a physical representation of the state of Macbeth's mind.

Is this an assertion you are interested in proving? Is it a statement other readers might challenge? If so, write it down and continue. If not, modify it or explore another issue.

3 Read the work(s) again with your thesis firmly in mind.

Read even more slowly and critically this time. Look for characters, incidents, descriptions, speeches, dialogue, or images that support or refute your thesis. Take careful notes. If you are using your own text, highlight significant passages in the work.

When you are done, evaluate the evidence you have gathered from a close reading. Then modify or qualify your thesis to reflect what you have learned or discovered. In most cases, your thesis will be more specific and more limited after you have gathered and assessed your evidence.

14e
lit

- The many unexpected comic moments in *Macbeth* emphasize how disordered the world becomes for murderers like Macbeth and his wife.

If necessary, return to secondary sources or other literary works to supplement and extend your analysis. (For many papers, much of your reading will be in secondary sources and journals of literary criticism.) Play with ideas, relationships, implications, and possibilities. Don't hesitate to question conventional views of a work or to bring your own experiences to bear on the act of reading and interpreting literature.

Begin drafting your paper, drawing together your specific observations into full paragraphs. The following are two draft paragraphs analyzing lines from *Macbeth* that some readers find comic. Notice in particular how lines from the play are woven neatly into the analysis as specific evidence.

> The first such comic lines come early in Macbeth and might even pass unnoticed if actors play them with straight faces. Yet one has to laugh when Lady Macbeth boasts after drugging the grooms who guard Duncan's bedchamber: "That which hath made them drunk hath made me bold" (Mac. 2.2.1). Then, just the way a drunken person would, she apologizes gruesomely for not killing Duncan herself, almost surprised by her reluctance to murder: "Had he [King Duncan] not resembled/My father as he slept, I had done't" (12–13).
>
> Macbeth has the next comic line, this one his reaction to Lennox's description of a horrible storm that shakes Scotland while Macbeth is murdering Duncan. Deadpans Macbeth: "'Twas a rough night" (2.3.61). The audience laughs uneasily, knowing much better than Lennox how rough the night really has been for the new Thane of Cawdor. Then, when a horrified Macduff discovers that Duncan has been murdered, Lady

Macbeth screams, "Woe, alas!/What, in our house?"

(2.3.87-88). Any audience that hears those lines wants

to laugh at Lady Macbeth's self-centeredness. Even

Banquo seems to notice her callousness when he

replies, "Too cruel any where" (88).

If you consult secondary sources while writing the paper, take careful notes from the books and articles you read. Be sure also to prepare accurate bibliography cards for your Works Cited page. (See Chapter 46 on planning a research project.)

4 Use scratch outlines to guide the first draft. Try out several organization plans for the paper (see Section 3b), and then choose the one you find most solid or most challenging. Working on a Web project, you might similarly sketch out the overall site as well as individual pages (see Chapter 23). Here's how a scratch outline for a paper on comic elements in *Macbeth* might look.

Thesis: Comic moments in Macbeth emphasize how

disordered the world becomes for the Macbeths after

they murder the king.

I. Comic moments after the murder of King Duncan

II. Comedy at the feast for Banquo

III. Comedy in the sleepwalking scene

IV. Conclusion

When you have a structure, write a complete first draft. Stay open to new ideas and refinements of your original thesis, but try not to wander off into a biography of the author or a discussion of the historical period unless such material relates directly to your thesis. If you do wander, consider whether the digression in your draft might be the topic you *really* want to write about.

Avoid the draft that simply paraphrases the plot of a literary work. Equally ineffective is a paper that merely praises its author for a job well done. Avoid extremely impressionistic judgments: "I feel that Hemingway must have been a good American." And don't expect to find a moral in every literary work, or turn your analysis into a search for "hidden meanings." Respond honestly to what you are reading—not the way you think your teacher expects you to. (For full examples of literary papers, see Sally Shelton's essay on pages 224–227 and the paper demonstrating Chicago documentation style in Chapter 56.)

▌5 Follow the conventions of literary analysis. One of those conventions is to introduce most direct quotations. Don't just insert a quotation from a literary work or a critic into your paper without identifying it and explaining its significance. And be sure quotations fit into the grammar of your sentences.

14e
lit

> **When an audience hears Macbeth call his cowering servant a** "cream-fac'd loon," it begins to understand why Macbeth's men hate and distrust him.

> **The doctor in** *Macbeth* **warns the gentlewoman,** "You have known what you should not" (5.1.46–47).

> **Commenting on the play, Frank Kermode observes that** "*Macbeth* has extraordinary energy; it represents a fierce engagement between the mind and its guilt" (1311).

In shaping the paper, you may want to follow the conventions of the MLA research paper or the *Chicago Manual of Style* paper (see Chapters 53 and 56).

Checklist 14.2

Conventions in a Literary Paper

- **Use the present tense to refer to events occurring in a literary work:** Hester Prynne *wears* a scarlet letter, Hamlet *kills* Polonius. Think of a literary work as an ongoing performance.

- **Identify passages of short poems by line numbers:** (*"Journey of the Magi,"* lines 21–31). Avoid the abbreviations *l.* or *ll.* for *line* or *lines* because they are sometimes confused with Roman numerals; spell out the words. See Section 43c for advice on punctuating lines of poetry that appear within a paper.

- **Provide act and scene divisions (and line numbers as necessary) for passages from plays.** Act and scene numbers are now usually given in Arabic numbers, although Roman numbers are still common and acceptable: *Ham.* 4.5.179–85 or *Ham.* IV.v.179–86. The titles of Shakespeare's works are commonly abbreviated in citations: *Mac.* 1.2; *Oth.* 2.2. Check to see which form your instructor prefers.

- **Provide a date of publication in parentheses after your first mention of a literary work:** Before publishing *Beloved* (1987), Toni Morrison had written. . . .

- **Use technical terms accurately.** Spell the names of characters correctly. Take special care with matters of grammar and mechanics.

Going Public   *A Literary Analysis Paper*

In the following literary analysis, "Queen Jane Approximately" (a clever allusion to a song by Bob Dylan), Sally Shelton from the University of South Carolina does a close reading of a poem by Sharon Olds, "The One Girl at the Boys' Party." She approaches the work from a feminist perspective, examining the interplay of gender roles between one young girl and a group of boys. Shelton supports her analysis by carefully citing passages from the poem, which we have reprinted in its entirety. The paper was written for a course taught by Anna Moore. We have edited the paper for concision.

14e
lit

The One Girl at the Boys' Party
By Sharon Olds

When I take my girl to the swimming party	1
I set her down among the boys. They tower and	2
bristle, she stands there smooth and sleek,	3
her math scores unfolding in the air around her.	4
They will strip to their suits, her body hard and	5
indivisible as a prime number,	6
they'll plunge in the deep end, she'll subtract	7
her height from ten feet, divide it into	8
hundreds of gallons of water, the numbers	9
bouncing in her mind like molecules of chlorine	10
in the bright blue pool. When they climb out,	11
her ponytail will hang its pencil lead	12
down her back, her narrow silk suit	13
with hamburgers and french fries printed on it	14
will glisten in the brilliant air, and they will	15
see her sweet face, solemn and	16
sealed, a factor of one, and she will	17
see their eyes, two each,	18
their legs, two each, and the curves of their sexes,	19
one each, and in her head she'll be doing her	20
wild multiplying, as the drops	21
sparkle and fall to the power of a thousand from	
her body.	22

Sally Shelton

Ms. Anna Moore

21 April 2003

Queen Jane Approximately

Sharon Olds' "The One Girl at the Boys' Party"
examines the tense competition between the sexes. The
poem illustrates the innate vulnerability of men
while portraying females as winning the attention and
respect they rightfully deserve. Olds achieves these
insights by examining the isolation of a young girl
at a party of boys. She infuses the situation with
ironies, symbols, and repeated images that probe
themes of gender, sexuality, and domination.

The poem deceives the reader initially by
putting the youths in typical gender roles. The
speaker takes her daughter (1) to a party where she
"set[s] her down among the boys" (2) like a toy or
doll for their amusement. She is placed within a
situation where she must prove herself. The boys, in
turn, "tower and/bristle" (2-3) at the intrusion of
this showcase item. While she is being "set down,"
these boys move like a gang, intimidating and,
perhaps, angry. Yet suddenly, the attention of the
poem shifts from the girl to the boys as the young
woman quickly and nonchalantly asserts her dominance
over the unwitting youths.

The schism between the girl and the group of
boys begins early in the poem. While the boys "tower
and bristle," the lone girl "stands there smooth and
sleek" (3), firmly placed, establishing her ground,
unabated in her delicate sensuality, and controlling
the air about her. It is in this "brilliant air" (15)
that her "math scores" (4) begin to unfold.

References to mathematics throughout the poem illustrate how this ingenue, and perhaps the speaker of the poem, have conquered society already. They have figured the boys out through methodical and meticulous calculations.

To complete the reversal of gender roles, the boys, who were the first to dominate in the poem, assume a subordinate and effeminate role. As if to expose themselves as sensual and enticing beings, "[t]hey will strip to their suits" (5), leaving themselves vulnerable (she can count the "curves of their sexes" (19) and hoping that the girl will "strip" to her vulnerability as well. The girl, however, remains in control, "her body hard and/indivisible as a prime number" (5-6). The pool of males will forever attempt to figure her, but she has solved them. She stands before the boys in the pool, with "the numbers/bouncing in her mind" (9-10), her calculations racing. She, who was initially perceived as an outcast, a toy to be discarded, has now silently attracted the desire and curiosity of the boys.

Now that the girl's presence has consumed the scene, the boys become enchanted by her sensuality. The infinite "molecules of chlorine" (10) that comprise the girl's ricocheting intelligence intoxicate the lads, who have by now succumbed to the innocent appeal of "the bright blue pool" (11). Sexual desires come into play: her tomboyish ponytail catches their gaze. Although it "hang[s] its pencil lead" (12), a phallic symbol with piercing connotations, the boys still allow their gaze to follow the ponytail "down her back" (13). Then they notice the girl's figure, more "smooth and sleek" (3) than before, in "her narrow silk suit" (13) with the mouth-watering "hamburgers and french fries printed on it" (14) that "glisten in the brilliant air" (15). Lastly, they notice her face, "sweet," "solemn," and "sealed" (16–17). No longer an object to discard, the girl becomes for the boys an embodiment of a desire that will never be satiated.

Again, the speaker widens the schism between the girl and the youths. It began with the girl doing all the observing and calculating, but soon the boys catch on. Threatened by her magnitude and ability to strip them, they "plunge in the deep end" (7), hoping to hide their vulnerability while attempting to entice the girl. The act of plunging is risky and the boys nearly drown in their attempts to impress her. Defeated and weakened, they have to "climb out" (11), still fragile and susceptible, and, moreover, they discover how badly they are getting beaten. Then they enter the game, the observed becoming the observers. While the boys "see her sweet face . . . a factor of one" (16–17), the girl outnumbers them when she "see[s] their eyes, two each,/their legs, two each, and the curves of their sexes,/one each" (18–20). She sheds some power when she lets her "drops/sparkle and fall" (21–22), but they will never gain a hold on her because she will forever "be doing her wild multiplying" (20–21). The boys cannot enumerate her "to the power of a thousand" (22), so her "power" controls them and overwhelms them. She has reduced these once towering and bristling boys to vulnerable, starstruck, and curvy subordinates by daring them to plunge into the deep end of womanhood.

Through the girl, the speaker offers insight into how women encompass an infinite magnitude, power, and elegance that men miscalculate and misunderstand. The girl triumphs while the boys sink into her deep intelligence, stamina, and sensuality. In the game of relationships, here staged as a pool party, there are those who tower, those who plunge, and those who calculate.

14e
lit

Style

CHAPTER 15
What Makes Paragraphs Work?

Paragraphs aren't natural units of writing in the way that sentences are. People don't think in paragraphs, even though researchers believe that we do think in sentences. But paragraphs exist for an important reason: they help readers.

Imagine how you'd feel if you opened a newspaper and saw pages filled with a single, unbroken stretch of print. You'd probably think, "I'll never be able to keep this straight in my head"—and you'd be right. Readers need to process information in chunks. When writers organize material into paragraph form, treating a single idea in each paragraph and connecting the paragraphs to each other, readers can follow the material more easily. Paragraphing also makes a text look visually inviting, drawing readers in and encouraging them to read on. This chapter shows you how to write effective paragraphs.

15a How do you construct unified paragraphs?

When we say that a paragraph is *unified*, we mean that it makes a single point and develops it, without detours into irrelevant or tangential information.

1 Find a focus and stick with it. In a unified paragraph, you can follow the author's thinking because he or she concentrates on a single idea. Here's a professional example about golf:

Here, primarily, is what's wrong with Phil Mickelson, Sergio Garcia, David Duval, Justin Leonard, Jesper Parnevik, Lee Westwood, Darren Clarke, Jim Furyk and a handful of others: They were born at the wrong time. They were born too close to Tiger Woods, the same way Charles Barkley, Patrick Ewing, Karl Malone and John Stockton were born at the wrong time, too close to Michael Jordan. That's all they were guilty of, being in the wrong place at the wrong time for pretty much the duration of their careers.

—Michael Wilbon, "It's Just Tiger's Time"

Suppose, however, that this writer had written his first sentence and then gone off in another direction, jotting down sentences as they occurred to him. The paragraph might have turned out like this:

> Here, primarily, is what's wrong with Phil Mickelson, Sergio Garcia, David Duval, Justin Leonard, Jesper Parnevik, Lee Westwood, Darren Clarke, Jim Furyk and a handful of others: They were born at the wrong time. Since Tiger Woods has come along, everything in golf has changed. There are more fans watching the game on TV, and Woods is becoming one of the world's best-known people because of all his endorsement deals. Some courses are even changing their layouts to try to "Tiger-proof" them.

Now the paragraph rambles and sprawls. It lacks unity because the writer opens with a statement and then, instead of expanding on it or following through with connected examples, jumps into several new subjects.

When you begin a paragraph, first ask yourself, "What point am I trying to make?" and then check your draft periodically to be sure you haven't strayed from your purpose.

2 Anchor your paragraph with a topic sentence. One way to keep a paragraph focused is to use a **topic sentence** that states your main idea clearly and directly. The topic sentence doesn't have to be the first one in the paragraph, although it often is, particularly in academic writing. Wherever it is located, a topic sentence acts like a magnet around which related sentences cluster. Here is a paragraph from a professional writer; the topic sentence is boldfaced.

> **Sleep has become another casualty of modern life.** According to sleep researchers, studies point to a "sleep deficit" among Americans, a majority of whom are currently getting between 60 and 90 minutes less a night than they should for optimum health and performance. The number of people showing up at sleep disorder clinics with serious problems has skyrocketed in the last decade. Shift work, long working hours, the growth of a global economy (with its attendant continent-hopping and twenty-four-hour business culture), and the accelerating pace of life have all contributed to sleep deprivation. If you need an alarm clock, the experts warn, you're probably sleeping too little.

—Juliet Schor, *The Overworked American*

Schor leads into her topic with the opening sentence, going on to develop it with supporting research and evidence.

A writer can also lead up to a topic sentence, first giving readers details that build their interest and then summarizing the content in one sentence. Here is another example from a professional writer; the topic sentence is boldfaced.

15a
¶

> Felix is in his 20s and gangly. Heinrich is in his 40s, a solid block of a man who has survived three avalanches. He is one of a team of scientists at the University of Bern. With the big drills that he designed and built in the university machine shop, the Bern team brings up cylindrical cores of ice from hundreds of feet below the surface of Swiss glaciers, and from many thousands of feet down in the Antarctic and Greenland ice sheets. The ice holds an abundance of bubbles the size of seltzer fizz. **The bubbles hold a wealth of stories on themes that encompass the planet: the death of the fabled island of Atlantis; the history of the greenhouse effect; the cause of ice ages; scenarios of the Earth's climate in the next hundred years.**
>
> —Jonathan Weiner, "Glacier Bubbles"

Not all paragraphs have topic sentences, nor do they need them, since writers can unify paragraphs in a number of ways. But you may find them useful when you're searching for a way to start a paragraph. Think about a main point you want to make in a paper and construct a statement that expresses it. For example:

> If one were looking for an example of a powerful and autonomous woman from an earlier age, no one could fill the role better than Eleanor of Aquitaine, the twelfth-century queen of both France and England.

> Part of the phenomenal growth of the Internet undoubtedly comes from its appeal to a streak in the American personality that loves to circumvent authority.

Both of these topic sentences make assertions that must be elaborated and supported. As writers, we all know that once we've written such a sentence, we can't just go off and leave it. We've committed ourselves to following through.

Topic sentences work especially well to anchor and control the flow of ideas in academic writing—analyses, reports, arguments, and so forth. They help keep your writing organized and on track. By reading from one topic sentence to the next in the paragraphs that make up your paper, you can usually tell if you're developing your thesis as you have planned. For more on organizing a draft around a thesis, see Section 3b.

3 Use internal transitions to unify your paragraphs.

Even when you have a clear focus, the connections among sentences or ideas in a paragraph may not always be immediately apparent to readers. In such cases, you'll need to incorporate *internal transitions*—words and phrases that act like traffic signals to move readers from one point in an argument or explanation to another.

Consider this paragraph from a student draft. It is focused on a single issue—the rise of cheating on campus—but the first version seems choppy and disconnected because it lacks internal transitions. Notice how much clearer and more readable the revised version is.

15a
¶

WEAK TRANSITIONS

Cheating has become frighteningly common. My roommate brought her mother to campus to complain when she failed her Spanish course for copying her term paper from a Web site. My English professor reported two students in my English literature class to the dean for allowing a high school teacher to write a paper for them. The Academic Affairs office reported last week that academic misconduct is up by 30 percent over last year. What is happening on our campus? Parents and teachers once instilled in students the value of doing one's own work instead of cheating.

INTERNAL TRANSITIONS ADDED

Cheating is becoming frighteningly common **on our campus. Last week** my roommate brought her mother to campus to complain when she failed Spanish for copying her term paper from a Web site. **Earlier this semester,** my English literature professor reported two students to the dean for allowing a high school teacher to write a paper for them. **Unfortunately, these cases are not unusual, campus officials say.** The Academic Affairs office reported last week that academic dishonesty cases are up by 30 percent over last year. What is happening on our campus? Parents and teachers **used to** instill in students the value of doing their own work; **now** many are encouraging them to **cheat.**

To incorporate internal transitions into a paragraph you've written, try these strategies.

- **Use transition words** such as *first, next, however,* and *in addition* to show the relationships among sentences and ideas. Section 17b-1 lists many of these words and explains when you can use each.

- **Repeat key words or phrases** to tie related sentences together. The paragraph above that gives several examples of cheating on campus, for example, repeats terms like *dishonesty* and *cheating* to connect the examples. See Section 17b-2 for more on using repetition.

- **Use parallel phrases**—phrases that begin with the same word or that share the same grammatical structure—to emphasize connections among similar examples or related pieces of information. If you were writing a paragraph that summarized three arguments against capital punishment, you could connect them by beginning each with the phrase "Opponents believe that. . . ." For more on using parallel structure to unify a paragraph, see Section 17b-5.

15a
¶

See Chapter 17 for a detailed discussion of transitions and for advice on using them within and between paragraphs.

EXERCISE 15.1 Working with a group of classmates, identify the strategies the writer has used to unify the following paragraph: Is there a topic sentence? Do you see transition words, repetition, or parallel structures? Then discuss whether and how these devices helped you follow the writer's ideas.

Day 1 set the tone for our really heavy driving days: We stopped only for gasoline and bathroom breaks, which usually coincided after 350 to 400 miles. We averaged about 70 mph for at least 14 hours. We ate what we had in the car or what we could get from travel plazas and gas stations. We didn't run the air conditioning, though we never talked about why. We didn't listen to the radio much because we had the windows down and could barely hear. We discussed—in shouts—whatever popped into our heads: "What just hit the windshield?" "Did you see what was growing in that bathroom?" "Kansas doesn't look so flat at night." "If there is a hell, do you think I-70 is it?" We slept in cheap motels because we were too tired to pitch a tent by the time we stopped. We thought we would get farther than we did.

—Lee Bauknight, "Two for the Road"

EXERCISE 15.2 Examine critically one or two paragraphs of a draft you're currently working on: Do the paragraphs seem adequately unified? What unifying strategies have you used? Can you think of others that might be useful?

15b How can you organize paragraphs?

We don't know how many skilled writers consciously choose specific organizational patterns when they draft their essays or articles. Perhaps during the writing process certain patterns just emerge because they so closely resemble typical ways of thinking. Or perhaps some writers say to themselves, "I think I'll compare and contrast here" or "This would be a good place to use cause and effect." Whatever their origins, the paragraph patterns discussed in this section are common, and writers looking for a way to get started on a draft can profit by trying them.

SUMMARY   *Common Paragraph Patterns*

illustration	classification
question and answer	comparison and contrast
narration or process	cause and effect
definition	analogy

---

1 Illustration. A paragraph of illustration begins with a general statement or claim and develops it with supporting details, evidence, or examples. This paragraph opens an essay by the professional writer Anna Quindlen; she follows a general statement about interaction between boys and girls with vivid descriptive details.

> Perhaps we all have the same memory of the first boy-girl party we attended. The floors were waxed, the music loud, the air thick with the smell of cologne. The boys stood on one side of the room and the girls on the other, each affecting a nonchalance belied by the shuffling male loafers and the occasional high bird-like sound of a female giggle.
> —Anna Quindlen, "Between the Sexes, a Great Divide"

In an argument paper, writers often follow a general claim with one or more pieces of supporting evidence.

> The popularity of McDonald's holds true across the world except, ironically, in the United States, where sales have slumped. McDonald's now makes 59 percent of its profit outside the United States, [company spokesperson Brad] Trask said. In Moscow, where the world's busiest McDonald's opened in 1990, lines still spill out the door.
> —Lini Kadaba, "No Beef"

2 Question and answer. Asking and answering a question is another way to organize a paragraph. Here's an example from the well-known science writer Carl Sagan.

What do we actually see when we look up at the Moon with the naked eye? We make out a configuration of irregular bright and dark markings—not a close representation of any familiar object. But almost irresistibly, our eyes connect the markings, emphasizing some, ignoring others. We seek a pattern, and we find one. In world myth and folklore, many images are seen: a woman weaving, stands of laurel trees, an elephant jumping off a cliff, a girl with a basket on her back, a rabbit, . . . a woman pounding tapa cloth, a four-eyed jaguar. People of one culture have trouble understanding how such bizarre things could be seen by the people of another.

—Carl Sagan, *The Demon-Haunted World*

3 Narration or process. One popular and simple way to develop a paragraph is to relate events or the steps of a process in chronological order. This pattern is obviously appropriate for writing personal or historical accounts, but you can also use it effectively to describe a scientific or technical process. Here is a narrative written by a naturalist studying wolves.

Quite by accident I had pitched my tent within ten yards of one of the major paths used by the wolves when they were going to, or coming from, their hunting grounds to the westward; and only a few hours after I had taken up residence one of the wolves came back from a trip and discovered me and my tent. He was at the end of a hard night's work and was clearly tired and anxious to go home to bed. He came over a small rise fifty yards from me with his head down, his eyes half-closed, and a preoccupied air about him. Far from being the preternaturally alert and suspicious beast of fiction, this wolf was so self-engrossed that he came straight on to within fifteen yards of me, and might have gone right past the tent without seeing it at all, had I not banged my elbow against the teakettle, making a resounding clank. The wolf's head came up and his eyes opened wide, but he did not stop or falter in his pace. One brief, sidelong glance was all he vouchsafed to me as he continued on his way.

—Farley Mowat, *Never Cry Wolf*

4 Definition. Paragraphs of definition often work well in the first part of a report or article that explains or argues. They help to establish the meaning of important terms the author is going to use. In this example from an essay on linguistic diversity, Gloria Anzaldúa defines one of several dialects she spoke as a child.

From kids and people my own age I picked up *Pachuco*. *Pachuco* (the language of the zoot suiters) is a language of rebellion, both against Standard Spanish and Standard English. It is a secret language. Adults of the culture and outsiders cannot understand it. It is made up of slang words from both English and Spanish. *Ruca* means girl or woman, *vato* means guy or dude, *chale* means no, *simon* means yes, *churro* is sure, talk is *periquar, pignionear* means petting, *que gacho* means how nerdy, *ponte aguila* means watch out, death is called *la pelona*. Through lack of practice and not having others who can speak it, I've lost most of the *Pachuco* tongue.

—Gloria Anzaldúa, "How to Tame a Wild Tongue"

15b
¶

5 Classification. A classification paragraph that divides a subject into the categories to be discussed can work well as the opening paragraph of an essay or a section of the essay. Used this way, it helps to unify the essay by forecasting its organization. Here's the opening paragraph of an essay by a well-known conservationist.

There are, as far as I can tell, three kinds of conservation currently operating. The first is the preservation of places that are grandly wild or "scenic" or in some way spectacular. The second is what is called "the conservation of natural resources"—that is, of the things of nature that we intend to use: soil, water, timber, and minerals. The third is what you might call industrial troubleshooting: the attempt to limit or stop or remedy the most flagrant abuses of the industrial system. All three kinds of conservation are inadequate, both separately and together.

—Wendell Berry, *Sex, Economy, Freedom & Community*

6 Comparison and contrast. A paragraph can be built quite naturally on a comparison-and-contrast pattern. Here's an easy-to-follow paragraph that sets up a comparison in the first sentence, discusses each item in alternating sentences, and concludes with a sentence that again compares both objects.

Counselors and psychologists often point out that much of the conflict between men and women stems from the very different ways in which they use language. Linguistics expert Deborah Tannen supports this theory in her book *You Just Don't Understand.* She says men use language for "report talk" while women use it for "rapport talk." She believes that for women, conversation is a way of establishing connections and negotiating relationships; the emphasis is on finding similarities and matching experience. For men, talk is used to show independence and maintain status; this is done by exhibiting knowledge and skill and holding center stage by verbal performance. Thus men are usually more comfortable doing public speaking and can be taciturn at home while many women talk little in public situations but are articulate in small groups.

15b
¶

7 Cause and effect. Cause-and-effect paragraphs can proceed in two ways: they can mention the effect first and then describe the causes, or they can start by giving causes and close with the effect. We illustrate both patterns here. The first paragraph illustrates cause to effect; the second illustrates effect followed by causes.

CAUSE TO EFFECT

Problem gambling leads to other socially destructive and costly behavior. According to [Johns Hopkins University researcher Valerie C.] Lorenz, problem gamblers not only tend to have a high number of auto accidents, but they often don't have insurance to cover the costs of damages. This not only results in economic losses and physical problems to themselves, but to others involved in the accidents. "These accidents occur most often on the way home after a long day of gambling at the casino or race track," she says. "Often these accidents are not accidents; instead, they are deliberate suicide attempts." In one study, gamblers were shown to have a suicide rate ten times higher than the rest of the population.

—Robert Goodman, *The Luck Business*

EFFECT FOLLOWED BY CAUSES

One reason for the good teaching in Japan is that the profession attracts excellent people. The respect for teachers in Japan emerges in opinion polls, where teachers are awarded higher prestige than engineers or officials in city hall. Teachers are also paid very well, earning salaries that are generally higher than those of pharmacists or engineers, and so in a typical year there are five applicants for every teaching job.

—Nicholas Kristoff, "Where Children Rule"

8 Analogy. Writers who are explaining a concept they want to elaborate on or make vivid often turn to analogy. An **analogy** is an extended comparison. One especially good use of analogy is to help readers understand a concept by showing a resemblance between the known and the unknown, as the physicist John Wheeler does in this paragraph on black holes. In the preceding paragraph, he asks his readers to imagine that they are flying over a city and see a domed stadium. Then he writes:

> The domed-over stadium gives no evidence to the traveler of the crowd within. However, he sees the lines of traffic converging from all directions, becoming more and more tightly packed in traffic jams as they approach the center of attraction. A black hole whirling about, and being whirled about in orbit by, a normal star will also be the recipient of clouds of gas from this companion, with all the puffs and swirls that one can imagine from watching a factory chimney belch its clouds of smoke. This gas will not fall straight in. It will orbit the black hole in ever tighter spirals as it works its way inward, making weather on its way. It, like the traffic approaching the stadium, will be squeezed more and more.
>
> —John Wheeler, "Black Holes and New Physics"

15c
¶

EXERCISE 15.3 Use the paragraph patterns discussed and illustrated in Sections 15b-1–15b-8 to write paragraphs for two of the following situations.

1. Summarize the arguments on one side of a local controversy you feel strongly about—for example, a new city ordinance, an upcoming election, or a controversial public event or program.

2. Explain how to operate a machine you use regularly—for instance, a food processor, a jet ski, a cash register, a cellular phone.

3. Set up a classification of your relatives at a family get-together, the students in your major, or the passengers you encounter every day on a bus or subway.

15c How can you create polished paragraphs?

A paragraph that's merely focused and well organized is like a family sedan: it gets your readers where they need to go, but the ride may lack pizzazz. If you want readers to enjoy and respond strongly to your writing, you'll need to craft paragraphs that are stylish and engaging as well as clear. This section shows you how.

1 Revise for variety. Good paragraphs move readers up and down what the linguist S. I. Hayakawa calls "the abstraction ladder." That is, they offer readers a mix of general statements and vivid, specific details. This sort of variety adds texture to your paragraphs and keeps readers interested. Just as important, it helps communicate your ideas: details help to illustrate abstract concepts that readers might otherwise find difficult, and general statements tie together details that might initially seem unrelated. You may notice that the writing in textbooks, professional journals, and periodicals such as *Scientific American* can be abstract and unspecific—not incomprehensible, but difficult nonetheless. To some degree, that's inevitable since writers for these publications are often addressing complex and technical issues; they may want to use an efficient professional vocabulary familiar to many of their readers.

But writers who need to reach a broader audience—including educated nonspecialists outside their fields—find ways to include specific details, helpful analogies, anecdotes, and narration to illustrate general statements or ideas. Here is a writer clarifying a hard-to-grasp, abstract concept by helping us to picture it very specifically.

> The distinction between Newton and Einstein's ideas about gravitation has sometimes been illustrated by picturing **a little boy playing marbles in a city lot. The ground is very uneven, ridged with bumps and hollows. An observer in an office ten stories above the street would not be able to see these irregularities in the ground. Noticing that the marbles appear to avoid some sections of the ground and move toward other sections,** he might assume a "force" is operating which repels the marbles from certain spots and attracts them toward others. But **another observer on the ground would instantly perceive that the path of the marbles is simply governed by the curvature of the field.**
>
> —Lincoln Barnett, *The Universe and Dr. Einstein*

EXERCISE 15.4 Imagine that you are writing a magazine article that includes one of the following paragraphs. Revise the paragraph, incorporating specific details, examples, or other material to add variety.

1. "Reality-based television" is becoming increasingly popular in the United States. There are more shows of this type each year, and

their ratings are increasing. These shows often depict real people in physically dangerous or emotionally charged situations. This intensity level keeps viewers coming back for more.

2. College and university officials see binge drinking as a serious problem on campuses nationwide. Recent studies have documented its widespread occurrence across different demographic groups and different types of schools. The problem affects retention and graduation rates, student health, academic life, and campus safety.

2 Revise for economy. Well-crafted paragraphs don't waste words. They move readers smoothly from point to point without bogging down in unnecessary verbiage or repetition. When you revise a paragraph, you'll often have to gut whole phrases or sentences when they contribute little to your meaning. (See Section 20c for advice on streamlining sentences.)

15c
¶

In the following paragraph on bicycling in China, the writer has realized he could eliminate most of his first two sentences, which are tedious generalizations. A sentence about the number of bicycles is also expendable because it contains no information—it might have been worth keeping if it had estimated the number of cycles. A complex sentence describing people riding bikes in Beijing colorfully illustrates a key point about cycling in China, so it is worth revising. The last two sentences need to be pared back for readability and focus, but they're valuable because they introduce ideas that play a role in the next paragraph (not shown). Here's the original draft of the paragraph, with major cuts indicated, followed by a revised version.

INFLATED FIRST DRAFT

~~Bicycles are a major form of transportation in many Third World countries because they are inexpensive and easy to maintain. Asians in particular seem to depend on them heavily.~~ Nowhere are they more important than they are in China, where one can see masses of them on the streets in every city. ~~Probably no one knows how many bicycles there are in China, nor does there seem to be a way of finding~~ out. Virtually everyone seems to ride—well-dressed businessmen with their briefcases strapped to the frame; a husband with his wife riding behind him and their child on the handlebars; women of all ages, some even in long, narrow dresses; and college students carrying their books on their backs. The newly arrived American cyclist ~~in Beijing or Shanghai,~~ however, would be astonished ~~not only~~ to see ~~the great numbers of bicycles, but to see what kinds of bicycles the Chinese ride and~~ how many other uses, besides simply riding, the Chinese have been able to figure out for bicycles. ~~They're an amazingly inge-nious people when it comes to adapting the common bicycle.~~

REVISED FOR ECONOMY

   Although bicycles are a major form of transportation in all Asian countries, nowhere are they more important than in China, where one can see masses of them on the streets in every city. Virtually everyone seems to ride—well-dressed businessmen with their briefcases strapped to the frame; a husband with his wife riding behind him and their child on the handlebars; women of all ages, some even in long, narrow dresses; and college students carrying their books on their backs. The newly arrived American cyclist, however, would be astonished to see how many other uses, besides simply riding, the Chinese have been able to figure out for bicycles.

15c
¶

You'll often have to cut this deeply to make your prose work. Most good writers do. (See Chapter 5 for a detailed discussion of revising and editing.)

EXERCISE 15.5 Streamline and strengthen this paragraph from a student's first draft by cutting unnecessary generalizations or explanations and trimming in places that seem wordy. You may need to cut or revise words, phrases, or whole sentences. Compare and contrast your revised version with a classmate's version.

   There are many different scholarly views concerning Alexander the Great's ultimate goal in relation to his military pursuits. Some historians consider Alexander to have been a power-hungry tyrant without whom the world would have been better off. Others see Alexander as the great unifier of humankind, one who attempted to bring together many cultures in one coherent empire. Others view him as the ultimate pragmatist—not necessarily having any preplanned goals and aspirations of conquering the world, but merely a king who made the very best of his existing circumstances. Some believe that Alexander's accomplishments were not great at all, but that most of what was written concerning Alexander is basically just a mixture of legend and myth. Others feel his achievements stand as monuments in human history to the enormous capability of the human spirit and will.

15d How can you improve paragraph appearance?

As we point out in Chapters 21 and 22 on visual design, documents have their own body language—that's why writers need to think about how their work is going to look in print. If readers see a long stretch of text unbroken by paragraphs, white space, headings, dialogue, or images, most assume that the material will be hard to read.

That's why, no matter what kind of project you're working on, you should consider breaking up long paragraphs. Your readers are much more likely to take a friendly attitude toward a piece when they can see that your paragraphs are fairly short. How short is a "fairly short" paragraph? Probably no more than seven or eight sentences—and in many cases, even fewer.

15d
¶

1 Break up long paragraph blocks that look hard to read. You shouldn't chop up paragraphs arbitrarily just to make your paper look inviting; a paragraph is supposed to develop an idea, and it usually takes several sentences to do that. But often after you write a paragraph and reread it, you can spot places where you can divide it.

Checklist 15.1

Places to Break Up a Long Paragraph

- **Shifts in time.** Look for spots where you have written words such as *at that time, then,* or *afterward* or have given other time signals.

- **Shifts in place.** Look for spots where you have written *another place* or *on the other side* or have used words that point to places.

- **Shifts in direction.** Look for spots where you have written *on the other hand, nevertheless,* or *however* or have otherwise indicated contrast.

- **Shifts in emphasis or focus.** Look for spots where you have shifted to a new point, perhaps using words such as *another, in addition,* or *not only.*

But don't break an entire paper into one- or two-sentence paragraphs. It's true that long paragraphs intimidate readers; however, too many short ones can distract them or make them feel the material is trivial. Extremely short paragraphs are best saved for special effects, as the following section explains.

2 Use short paragraphs for effect. Sometimes one-sentence paragraphs work well, particularly when you want to give some point special emphasis. Here, in its original context, is a very brief paragraph—a single sentence fragment—from a well-regarded professional science writer.

> Ah, romance. Can any sight be as sweet as a pair of mallard ducks gliding gracefully across a pond, male by female, seemingly inseparable? Or, better yet, two trumpeter swans, the legendary symbols of eternal love, each ivory neck one half of a single heart, souls of a feather staying coupled together for life?
>
> **Coupled for life—with just a bit of adultery, cuckoldry, and gang rape on the side.**
>
> Alas for sentiment and the greeting card industry, it turns out that, in the animal kingdom, there is almost no such thing as monogamy. As a wealth of recent findings makes clear as a crocodile tear, even creatures long assumed to have faithful tendencies and to need a strong pair bond to rear their young are in fact perfidious brutes.
>
> —Natalie Angier, "Mating for Life?"

15d ¶

Don't be afraid to use one- or two-sentence paragraphs occasionally, but do so deliberately and to achieve a specific effect. Sometimes you may want to insert a very short paragraph to make a transition between two longer paragraphs. At other times you can use brevity for dramatic emphasis, as Angier has done in the passage above.

3 Adapt paragraph length to your writing situation. Finally, then, how long should a paragraph be? The answer, as you might expect, depends on your writing situation.

- **Consider your purpose.** If you're laying out a complex argument in your senior thesis project, your paragraphs might be fairly long. If you're writing an editorial for the student or local newspaper, they need to be short because the columns are narrow and newspaper readers don't expect long paragraphs. If you're writing a business report for a supervisor, you'll want to seem efficient and businesslike; keep the paragraphs short so the content can be skimmed quickly.
- **Consider your audience.** Are they experienced readers who are used to reading history or biography or technical articles? Then long paragraphs probably won't bother them. Are they casual readers who pick up a newspaper or a magazine and peruse it quickly? Then you'll do well to keep your paragraphs short.

- **Consider your medium.** Are you writing something that will be read from a computer screen? If so, it's especially important to write short paragraphs. People tire more quickly when they read material online, so content needs to be organized in compact units that can be absorbed easily. Also, if a reader misses a point while she is reading online, she has to scroll back to pick it up, and finding that point will be much harder when paragraphs are long.

Following are some guidelines for determining paragraph length.

SUMMARY   *Guidelines for Paragraph Length*

Consider long paragraphs if . . .

- You are developing complicated ideas in detail.

- Readers are experienced and skillful.

- Readers are patient and seeking information.

Choose short paragraphs if . . .

- Readers are impatient and reading for diversion.

- Readers are skimming for content.

- Readers are young or inexperienced.

- Readers are reading online.

15d
¶

CHAPTER **16**

How Do You Craft Opening and Closing Paragraphs?

16a What makes an opening paragraph effective?

Newspaper editors talk about the *lead* for a news story, the opening that has to catch the readers' attention and give them a strong signal about what to expect. The opening paragraph for whatever you write is also a lead—the introduction to your paper that gets you off to a good or a bad start with readers. Like the opening of a front-page news story, any first paragraph should do the following things.

- Get your readers' attention and interest them in reading more.
- Make a *commitment* to readers—that is, introduce your main idea in a way that promises to follow up with more information.
- Signal to readers what direction your project will take.
- Set the tone of your project.

These are important functions, and that's why first paragraphs can be difficult to write—but it's also why they're worth your time and attention.

Different kinds of writing call for different opening paragraphs. For certain kinds of writing—laboratory reports, grant proposals, business letters—readers expect specific kinds of opening paragraphs. In such cases, find out what the typical pattern is and use it. In other kinds of writing, such as newspaper articles, critical analyses, personal experience papers, and opinion pieces, you have more freedom and can try various approaches.

The following sections illustrate types of opening paragraphs that you may find useful.

1 Begin with a narrative. Many professional authors begin a piece with an attention-getting narrative or anecdote that catches their readers' attention and sparks their interest in the topic. The following opening narrative, taken from a magazine article, pulls readers into a terrifying experience and makes us want to know more about what caused it.

Like most Peace Corps volunteers, Martin Giannini embarked on his mission full of high hopes and enthusiasm. His assignment in Togo promised to be the adventure of a lifetime. It certainly was—but not the kind he expected. Giannini's African adventure ended in a padded room in a Chicago psych ward. "I was totally loony" admits Giannini. "It felt like I was in some 'X-Files' episode with instructions being planted in my brain. I tried to escape, but couldn't get past the four guards." What led Giannini, a healthy young man with no history of mental illness, to take on a battalion of guards in a psychiatric hospital? A drug, say his doctors. An antimalaria drug the Peace Corps recommended.
—Dennis Lewon, "Malaria's Not-So-Magic Bullet"

16a
¶

You may occasionally want to begin a paper with two or three short anecdotes rather than a single, longer one. This variation works well to show that your topic touches upon several issues or situations.

2 Begin with a description that establishes tone and forecasts content. Here is an example taken from an article on exotic Southern cuisine. John T. Edge's opening description creates a vivid picture of the region he's writing about and sets a tone of cautious fascination.

It's just past four on a Thursday afternoon in June at Jesse's Place, a country juke seventeen miles south of the Mississippi line and three miles west of Amite, Louisiana. The air conditioner hacks and spits forth torrents of arctic air, but the heat of summer can't be kept at bay. It seeps around the splintered doorjambs and settles in, transforming the squat particleboard-plastered roadhouse into a sauna. Slowly, the dank barroom fills with grease-smeared mechanics from the truck stop up the road and farmers straight from the fields, the soles of their brogans thick with dirt clods. A few weary souls make their way over from the nearby sawmill, the kind of place where more than one worker has muscled a log into the chipper and drawn back a nub. I sit alone at the bar, one empty bottle of Bud in front of me, a second bottle in my hand. I drain the beer, order a third, and stare down at the pink juice spreading outward from a crumpled foil pouch and onto the dull, black vinyl bar.
I'm not leaving until I eat this thing, I tell myself.
—John T. Edge, "I'm Not Leaving Until I Eat This Thing"

3 Begin with a question or a series of questions that relate to your topic. Diane Ackerman begins one of the essays in

her book *A Natural History of the Senses* with a series of provocative questions.

> What would the flutterings of courtship be without a meal? As the deliciously sensual and ribald tavern scene in Fielding's *Tom Jones* reminds us, a meal can be the perfect arena for foreplay. Why is food so sexy? Why does a woman refer to a handsome man as a real dish? Or a French girl call her lover *mon petit chou* (my little cabbage)? Or an American man call his girl cookie? Or a British man describe a sexy woman as a bit of crumpet [. . .]? Sexual hunger and physical hunger have always been allies. Rapacious needs, they have coaxed and driven us through famine and war, to bloodshed and serenity, since our earliest days.
>
> —Diane Ackerman, "Food and Sex"

16a
¶

4 Begin by quoting a key source. Have you come across in your research a statement from an expert, an interview subject, or another source that expresses a key issue more vividly than you could in your own words? If so, don't hesitate to begin your opening paragraph with a quote. Here is an example taken from an article analyzing why Y2K—the inability of many computer systems to register the year 2000—posed so many problems for U.S. businesses and government agencies.

> Seventy years ago, W. I. Thomas and Dorothy Swaine Thomas proclaimed one of sociology's most influential ideas: "If men define situations as real, they are real in their consequences." Their case in point was a prisoner who attacked people he heard mumbling absent-mindedly to themselves. To the deranged inmate, these lip movements were curses or insults. No matter that they weren't; the results were the same. The Thomas Theorem, as it is called, now has a corollary. In a microprocessor-controlled society, if machines register a disordered state, they are likely to create it. For example, if an automatic railroad switching system mistakenly detects another train stalled on the tracks ahead and halts the engine, there really will be a train stalled on the tracks.
>
> —Edward Tenner, "Chronologically Incorrect"

5 Start with your thesis. Sometimes you will do best to open your essay by simply telling your readers exactly what you are going to write about. Such openings work well for many papers you write in college courses, for reports you might have to write on the job, and for many other kinds of factual, informative prose. Here's a good example from a student essay about the film *The Princess Bride*. KC Culver announces the topic directly and forecasts the main points the paper will cover.

The Princess Bride, directed by Rob Reiner, differs from other fairy tale films in two important ways. First, the film uses live actors; this distinguishes it from the host of animated Disney films based on fairy tales and adds an element of reality. Second, the film begins and ends with a grandfather reading the story to his sick grandson, presenting a specific narrator who appears on screen and plays a role in the film itself. Thus the film alternates between images of the story itself and images of the grandfather telling the story to his grandson. This framing of the story suggests a self-awareness on the part of the film of the origins and goals of fairy tales. However, the story itself continues to perpetuate stereotypical gender assignments and aligns sex, gender, and sexuality in essentialist terms.

—KC Culver, "Patriarchal Fairy Tales and Gender Roles:
The Princess Bride"

16a

¶

See Section 3a for more on constructing a thesis statement and incorporating it into a writing project.

Going Public   *Using a Narrative to Revise an* _____
                     Opening Paragraph

When she began to write a course paper on saving local wetlands, student writer Katie Wegner started with the following thesis.

> Our neighborhood is one of many in the Myrtle
> Beach area that is built on a wetland. Burroughs and
> Chapin, the largest and most powerful developer on
> the coast, is among the companies who are building on
> these natural sponges. Wetlands are crucial to
> maintaining balance in our ecological system, but
> there is such weak legislation to prevent developers
> from building on these crucial areas that they are
> quickly disappearing.

This is a useful paragraph for getting started, but Katie knew she wanted a more vivid opening that would help readers feel a personal connection to the issue. Her final draft uses a rhetorical question and a narrative to introduce her thesis.

When a hard rain falls, do you find it relaxing to cuddle up and listen to the rhythmic drumming of raindrops on your roof? Must be nice. I can't relax because I, like many other Myrtle Beach residents, am too busy worrying about how much my neighborhood will flood after the drumming stops. This is because our neighborhood is one of many in the area built on a wetland. Burroughs and Chapin, the largest and most powerful developer on the coast, is principal among the companies who are building on these natural sponges. Wetlands are crucial to maintaining balance in our ecological system, but because there is such weak legislation to prevent developers from building on these critical areas, they are quickly disappearing. Now Burroughs and Chapin is stretching its tentacles inland toward our capital city. Something must be done before it's too late.

16b
¶

EXERCISE 16.1 Choose from the strategies discussed above and write two versions of an opening paragraph for one of the following essay titles. Then join with classmates who have chosen to write on the same title and read your paragraphs aloud. Discuss which ones seem to work well and why.

1. The American Legal System as Seen Through *Judging Amy, Law and Order,* and *The Badge*

2. What It Means to Live Below the Poverty Level: A Case Study

3. Why You Should Vote in the Next Election

4. Random Drug Testing in High Schools: Security Measure or Civil Rights Violation?

16b What makes a closing paragraph effective?

Closing paragraphs can be hard to write because it's often difficult to come to a satisfying conclusion that doesn't fall back on clichés. The only direct advice we can give is that your closing paragraph should wind up your paper in a way that makes readers feel that you have tied up the loose ends—that you have fulfilled the commitment you made in the opening paragraph. You don't want your readers asking "And so?" when they finish, or looking on the back of the page for something they may have missed.

There are no simple prescriptions for achieving that important goal. However, we suggest five general strategies you can use, alone or in combination, as seems appropriate for your rhetorical situation.

■ **1 Summarize the main points you have made.** Often you'll want to bring your paper to a close by reemphasizing your main points. (But don't repeat the very same words you have already used, or your ending may sound redundant or forced.)

16b
¶

Here is the conclusion of a paper in which the student writer has argued convincingly that spanking children is an ineffective form of discipline.

> It is unfortunate that the new spanking advocates get so much attention in the popular press, since their arguments are so poorly supported. These crusaders draw on personal anecdotes and "experts" of dubious credibility to glorify physical punishment and to blame non-spanking parents for everything from school shootings to violent rap lyrics. Yet even a cursory look at the scientific research in this area confirms that kids who are spanked are more—not less—likely to misbehave, turn to criminal behavior, or suffer from mental problems. How we choose to treat our nation's children is a serious matter. We must make these decisions based on the best information available—not on the dire predictions of a few extremists.

■ **2 Make a recommendation when one is appropriate.** Such a recommendation should grow out of the issue you have been discussing. This strategy brings a paper to a positive ending and closes the topic. Here is a conclusion from a student paper on nutrition.

> But even if you are an athlete who wants quick results, you should not go to extremes in trying to improve your overall nutrition. When you decide to change your eating habits, your motto should be "Eat better," not "Eat perfectly." By increasing carbohydrates and reducing fat in the diet—that is, by eating more fruits, vegetables, and whole grains and cutting down on whole milk and meat—you can improve your energy level rather quickly. You will also feel better, play better, and look better than you ever imagined.

■ 3 Link the end to the beginning. One excellent way to end a writing project is to tie your conclusion back to your beginning, framing and unifying your paper. Notice how skillfully the author of an editorial from *Wired* has used this strategy.

OPENING PARAGRAPH

Any significant social phenomenon creates a backlash. The Net is no exception. It is, however, odd that the loudest complaints are shouts of "Get a life!"—suggesting that online living will dehumanize us, insulate us, and create a world of people who won't smell flowers, watch sunsets, or engage in face-to-face experiences. Out of this backlash comes a warning to parents that their children will "cocoon" and metamorphose into social invalids.

CLOSING PARAGRAPH

But the current sweep of digital living is doing exactly the opposite [of isolating people]. Parents of young children find exciting self-employment from home. The "virtual corporation" is an opportunity for tiny companies (with employees spread across the world) to work together in a global market and set up base wherever they choose. If you don't like centralist thinking, big companies, or job automation, what better place to go than the Net? Work for yourself *and* get a life.

—Nicholas Negroponte, "Get a Life?"

■ 4 Place your argument in a larger context. When readers reach the end of a piece, they may want to know how what you've told them is relevant to larger issues or conversations: does your analysis of a problem have implications for the community or for others studying your topic? Concluding paragraphs that suggest these sorts of connections are especially common in academic research projects.

In this example, Jan Brunvand ends a research article documenting feminist themes in popular "spooky stories" by suggesting directions for future research.

One might not expect to find women's liberation messages embedded in the spooky stories told by teenagers, but Beverly Crane's case is plausible and well argued. [. . .] What needs to be done to analyze this finding is to collect what Alan Dundes calls "oral-literary criticism," the informants' own comments about their lore. How clearly would the girls who tell these stories perceive—or even accept—the messages extrapolated by scholars? And a related question: Have any stories with clear liberationist themes replaced older ones cautioning young women to stay home, be good, and—next best—be careful, and call a man if they need help?

    —Jan Brunvand, " 'The Hook' and Other Teenage Horrors"

■ **5 Stop when you're finished.** Probably the most important thing to remember about closing a paper or essay is not to overdo your conclusion. If you have covered all your points and are reasonably satisfied with what you've said, quit. Don't bore your reader by tacking on a needless recapitulation or adding a paragraph of platitudes.

16b
¶

EXERCISE 16.2 Read the following closing paragraphs from professional articles. What features do you find in them that give the reader a sense that the author has brought his or her essay to a satisfactory close?

1. Our new understanding of the impact of environmental challenges tends to blur some of the hard and fast distinctions between traditional definitions of security and more ambitious modern ones. Helping a Haiti or a Sierra Leone may not yield an immediately identifiable payoff in averting a particular conflict, yet it does aid the cause of peace and tranquility. In the future, a definition of security that leans exclusively on conflict and its prevention will be too cramped to accommodate the reality of a world in which renewable resources will be ever scarcer and in which it will be increasingly difficult to seal ourselves off—morally, emotionally, and physically—from poverty, disease, and environmental degradation in the less developed nations.

    —Geoffrey Dabelko, "The Environmental Factor"

2. No one could wish for a more advantageous heritage than that bequeathed to the black writer in the South: a compassion for the earth, a trust in humanity beyond our knowledge of evil, and an abiding love of justice. We inherit a great responsibility as well, for we must give voice to centuries not only of silent bitterness and hate but also of neighborly kindness and sustaining love.

    —Alice Walker, "The Black Writer and
the Southern Experience"

3. Investing in and educating all American children is an urgent moral and practical imperative. If our democracy is to remain vibrant in the dawning new century and millennium and our economy is to remain on the cutting edge in a global economy, then we must make America's promise of fair opportunities and safe

environments real right now to our children right here at home. We must take responsibility for putting into place the resources and bipartisan political support to get our priorities straight, whether we're talking about education, health care, child care, or violence prevention. There are millions of children who are depending on us.[. . .] Before one more child is lost, we must muster the necessary will to make sure all of our children receive the healthy and fair and safe start in life they require and deserve.

—Marian Wright Edelman, "A Voice for Children"

16b
¶

EXERCISE 16.3 Exchange drafts with two or three other students who are working on the same assignment. Each person should read the closing paragraphs from the other papers. Discuss what features each writer used to bring his or her paper to a conclusion. Discuss how those strategies work and which others might also be helpful.

CHAPTER **17**

How Do You Manage Transitions?

Skilled writers work hard to help their readers move easily through a piece of writing. They know that people who are reading by choice won't stick around long if they have trouble following an argument or the thread of a narrative. The best unifying device for any piece of writing is *organizational;* that is, it comes from an underlying pattern that moves the reader along smoothly. You'll find examples of such patterns in Sections 3b (for whole papers) and 15b (for paragraphs).

But even when your paper follows a clear pattern, you sometimes need to tighten your writing by using *transitions,* those words and phrases that act like hooks, links, and directional signals to keep readers moving from point to point within a paragraph, and from one paragraph to another. Section 17a helps you identify places where readers might have trouble following your writing; Section 17b offers strategies for using transitions effectively.

Without clear transitions, a document may seem disjointed—like the fragments of this ancient statue of Constantine.

17a How do you spot problems with transitions?

When you're revising, check for places where your readers might find your writing choppy or abrupt, and revise accordingly. Here are some trouble spots to look for.

1 Check for paragraphs made up of short, simple sentences that seem disconnected.

Effective paragraphs follow what writing experts call the "old-new contract"—they advance an argument or idea by linking each piece of new information to something that's gone before, so that the connections are immediately clear to readers. When a writer neglects to link old and new information, a paragraph may read more like a random series of observations than a coherent discussion. For example:

> **WEAK TRANSITIONS**
>
> Antonio Diaz is the senior sports columnist for the *Sunday Tribune.* He is an avid amateur painter. He devotes all of his spare time to his hobby. Whenever he has a free day, he sets up his easel in the Botanic Garden. His favorite subject there is the water lily pond. His work also furnishes him with subjects. He often brings a sketchbook to the games he covers. He finds his rapid sketches of the athletes useful. They help him reconstruct the excitement of a game for his column.

Here is a revised version, with some sentences combined and others connected (transitional words are boldfaced). Note how much more readable this version is.

> **BETTER**
>
> The senior sports columnist for the *Sunday Tribune,* Antonio Diaz, is **also** an avid amateur painter **who** devotes all his spare time to his hobby. Whenever he has a free day, he sets up his easel in the Botanic Garden, **where** his favorite subject is the water lily pond. Mr. Diaz's work also furnishes him with subjects, **and** he often brings a sketchbook to the games he covers. He finds his rapid sketches of the athletes useful **when** reconstructing the excitement of a game for his column.

2 Check for sentences that begin with vague references like *it is, there are,* and *there is.*

Often sentences that begin with

these phrases (called *expletives*) are poorly connected to each other because it's hard to tell who or what the subject is. For example:

WEAK TRANSITIONS

It is a truism that good manners are like skeleton keys. There are few doors they will not open. Some people think that good manners are pretentious. They are a way of condescending to people. That is a misunderstanding. The real purpose of manners is to make social situations comfortable and to put the people you are with at ease. Manners are also practical to have. There are many companies that insist that their executives have good manners. Some business schools include a course on manners in their curricula.

A reader gets little sense of the relationship between these sentences—there's no clear link between new and old information—and the repetitive patterns are boring. Here is the paragraph reworked with better sentence openings and stronger connections. Transitional terms are boldfaced.

17a
trans

BETTER

Good manners, like skeleton keys, will open almost any door. **While** some people think that good manners are pretentious and condescending, that's a misunderstanding. **On the contrary,** manners exist to make social situations comfortable by putting everyone at ease. **Moreover,** manners are a practical asset in the job market. Many companies insist on well-mannered executives, **which** has prompted some business schools to include a course on manners in their curricula.

For suggestions on revising to eliminate expletive phrases, see Section 20c-6.

3 Check for gaps between paragraphs. Sometimes major gaps appear between paragraphs, and readers get lost temporarily. Suppose that you encountered the following two paragraphs in a personal essay. You'd probably have trouble figuring out how the second paragraph relates to the first.

My daughter is tired of being a leftist. She is tired of eccentric clothes, artists, vegetarian diets, the New York subway, and living in an apartment. The culturally rich and genteel poverty in which she was raised is played out. Deep in her little African-American heart, she yearns to be Vanessa Huxtable, her age cohort in the television Cosby clan. With a perfect room, in a perfect house, with perfect parents and lots of perfectly hip clothes in the closet. She is sick of my Sixties class-suicide trip, of middle-class Mommy's vow of poverty in pursuit of the authentic Negro experience. She is tired, simply, of hanging in there with my trip.

Taking the job would not only fulfill some of her fantasies, it would provide me with a ready-made escape from New York, Ed Koch and his soul mate, subway gunman Bernhard Goetz, not to mention my life there. . . .

Here's the original passage as it appeared in Jill Nelson's memoir. Notice how Nelson successfully links the paragraphs with one short sentence that connects her own feelings and desires with her daughter's, thus making the second paragraph a logical next step. The linking sentence is boldfaced.

17b
trans

My daughter is tired of being a leftist. She is tired of eccentric clothes, artists, vegetarian diets, the New York subway, and living in an apartment. The culturally rich and genteel poverty in which she was raised is played out. Deep in her little African-American heart, she yearns to be Vanessa Huxtable, her age cohort in the television Cosby clan. With a perfect room, in a perfect house, with perfect parents and lots of perfectly hip clothes in the closet. She is sick of my Sixties class-suicide trip, of middle-class Mommy's vow of poverty in pursuit of the authentic Negro experience. She is tired, simply, of hanging in there with my trip.

She's got a point. I'm tired, too. Taking the job would not only fulfill some of her fantasies, it would provide me with a ready-made escape from New York, Ed Koch and his soul mate, subway gunman Bernhard Goetz, not to mention my life there. . . .

—Jill Nelson, *Volunteer Slavery*

Links between paragraphs can take several forms; Section 17b explains these in more detail.

17b How can you strengthen transitions?

If you want to use transitions successfully, remember the old-new contract: Each sentence or paragraph should contain a seed out of which the next sentence or paragraph can grow. Always include a hint, a reference, a hook, or a repetition that helps the reader link what you're saying with what has come before and what lies ahead. This section explains how to incorporate common kinds of transitions into your writing.

1 Use common transition words to connect ideas. You can make your paragraphs tighter and more focused by using transition words to tie sentences together.

- **Pointer words,** such as *first, second, next,* and *last,* set up a path for readers to follow by indicating shifts in time or place.

    One student, a nonsmoker, argued eloquently before the committee that there are many reasons to oppose a campus-wide ban on smoking. **First,** such a policy unduly penalizes an activity that, though obnoxious, is not illegal. **Second,** enforcement of the policy might encourage insidious intrusions on the privacy of students in their dormitory rooms and faculty in their offices. **Last,** a ban on smoking might set an unfortunate precedent, leading to the elimination of other habits and activities certain groups regard as similarly offensive or harmful: drinking alcohol, eating fatty foods, dancing, listening to rock music, or even driving a car.

17b
trans

- **Relationship words** such as *however, therefore,* and *yet* show similarity, opposition, addition, or other connections between ideas.

    Opinion at the hearing had generally favored the proposal to abolish smoking on campus. **However,** the student's arguments made some proponents waver as they considered the wider implications of their actions. What would happen, **for example,** if one group on campus, citing statistics on heart disease, demanded a campus-wide ban on fast foods? The ban on smoking would provide grounds for such a restriction.

As these examples show, transition words are not neutral; each one gives readers a different signal about where your argument is going. When you're in doubt about which term to choose, check Chart 17.1 below.

Chart 17.1
Common Transition Words and Phrases

TO SHOW SIMILARITY	TO SHOW CONSEQUENCE
likewise	hence
like	consequently
similarly	so
in the same way	therefore
just as	as a result of
	thus

(Continued)

Common Transition Words and Phrases *(Continued)*

TO SHOW CONTRAST
however
instead
nevertheless
although
in spite of
on the other hand
not only
but
rather

TO SHOW CAUSATION
because
since

TO SHOW A SEQUENCE
next
subsequently
after
finally
first, second, third

TO SHOW ACCUMULATION
moreover
in addition to
for example
and
for instance

17b
trans

■ 2 Repeat a key term throughout a paragraph to establish a central idea. Using one or two key words or phrases several times in a paragraph can tie it together effectively.

REPEATED WORDS BOLDFACED
The new black middle class came of age in the 1960s during an unprecedented American **economic boom** and in the hub of a thriving **mass culture.** The **economic boom** made luxury goods and convenient services available to large numbers of hard-working Americans for the first time. American **mass culture** presented models of the good life principally in terms of conspicuous consumption and hedonistic indulgence. It is important to note that even the intensely political struggles of the sixties presupposed a perennial **economic boom** and posited models of the good life projected by U.S. **mass culture.** Long-term financial self-denial and sexual asceticism was never at the center of a political agenda in the sixties.

—Cornel West, *Race Matters*

■ 3 Use the demonstrative pronouns *this, that, these, those,* **and** *such* **to tie ideas together.** Each boldfaced word in the following example hooks directly into the previous sentence.

DEMONSTRATIVE TERMS BOLDFACED

Making a movie is a collaborative endeavor, and scriptwriters point **this** out frequently. Occasionally a screenplay will survive the transfer from paper to film intact, but **that** is the exception rather than the rule. Typically, producers, directors, actors, and agents all have a say in the final product. Coping with **such** high-handed meddling is often difficult for young writers, and **those** who cannot compromise rarely stay in the business for long.

4 Use relative pronouns to show links between ideas.

Who, which, where, and *that* are powerful words that link a descriptive or informative statement to something that has preceded it. Relative pronouns can be especially helpful when you need to combine several short, choppy sentences into one. Notice how the boldfaced pronouns in the following paragraph serve as links to previous ideas.

17b
trans

RELATIVE PRONOUNS BOLDFACED

Miranda's first few weeks at the conservatory were exhausting but exhilarating. It was a place **that** challenged her, one **where** she could meet talented people **who** shared her passion for dance. The competition among the students was friendly but intense, **which** only increased her determination to practice and learn.

5 Use parallelism to link ideas.

You can create tightly focused paragraphs by writing a series of sentences that incorporate parallel phrases.

PARALLELL PHRASES BOLDFACED

I spent my two days at Disneyland taking rides. **I took** a bobsled through the Matterhorn and a submarine under the Polar Ice Cap and a rocket jet to the Cosmic Vapor Curtain. **I took** Peter Pan's Flight, Mr. Toad's Wild Ride, Alice's Scary Adventures, and Pinocchio's Daring Journey. **I took** a steamboat and a jungle boat. **I took** the Big Thunder Mountain Railroad to coyote country and the Splash Mountain roller coaster to Critter Country. **I took** a "Pirates of the Caribbean" ride (black cats and buried treasure) and a "Haunted Mansion" ride (creaking hinges and ghostly laughter). **I took** monorails and Skyways and Autopias and People Movers. More precisely, those rides **took** me: up and down and around sudden corners and over rooftops, and all I had to do was sit back and let whatever conveyance I was sitting in do the driving.

—William Zinsser, *American Places*

Not only does Zinsser hold the details of his paragraph together by using a parallel pattern that begins every sentence with the phrase "I took," but by repeating the phrase he captures the flavor of Disneyland as a place where the visitor travels through fantasy lands. And when he reverses the phrase to "More precisely, those rides **took** me," he wraps up his paragraph with a final unifying touch.

6 Use a semicolon to link two closely related statements. Although some writers may ignore this useful piece of punctuation, the semicolon signals a tight connection that says, "These groups of words go together." Often a semicolon can connect parts of a sentence more effectively than *and* or *also*. For more details about the semicolon, see Section 40a.

17b
trans

CONNECTING SEMICOLONS HIGHLIGHTED

The sculptor Ilya Karensky no longer has to endure his neighbors' contempt for his work; now he has to put up with their insincere and inept praise. Ilya knows perfectly well that what his neighbors admire most about his work is the amount of money for which it now sells; they like the sculptures themselves no better than they did before.

7 Consider using headings or other visual markers as transitions. In some kinds of documents, writers may use visual signals as well as—or sometimes instead of—words to help readers follow an argument.

Business and technical writers commonly use headings and subheadings to separate sections of a document so that readers can see where one idea ends and another begins. Résumés often use headings such as "Education," "Experience," "Awards," and "References" so that readers can locate relevant information. Brochures, flyers, and instructional manuals employ graphics, images, and color to mark divisions or to tie together related information. On the Web, writers create hyperlinks to connect documents.

But use common sense when you incorporate visual transitions into a writing project. Ask yourself whether the particular strategy is appropriate for the situation. Graphics and color fonts aren't always welcome in academic papers, and a flyer or short essay might not need headings. If you're not sure, look at models to see the kinds of transitions other writers have used in similar situations.

Also be sure that a particular transition gives readers the right signal. For example, a heading indicates a new topic, but it doesn't necessarily show readers how one topic relates to another. You'll often need to supplement visual devices with traditional linking words and phrases.

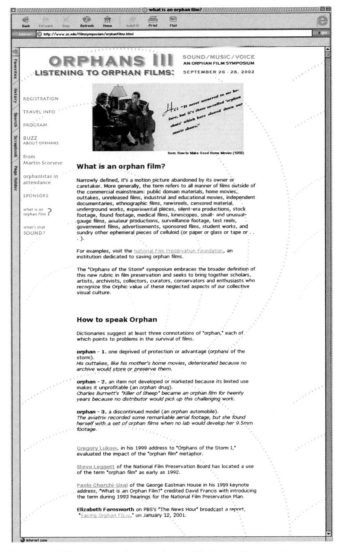

Figure 17.1   *This Web page, designed by Laura Kissel and Don Streible, uses visual devices—color, headings, hyperlinks, and a numbered list—to help readers navigate a complicated array of information about the Orphans III film symposium.*

For more information about integrating visual elements into a text, see Chapter 22. For examples of documents that incorporate visual elements, see the model documents in Chapter 24.

Going Public   *Using Transitions to Strengthen an Argument* __

In a research paper proposing that in-school health clinics might help keep at-risk students in school, student writer Jason Hatfield wanted to emphasize the problems high school dropouts face. The following paragraph, however, doesn't achieve the effect he hoped for; the choppy, disconnected sentences make it hard for readers to follow his argument.

17b
trans

> As Americans it is our duty to do whatever is
> necessary to keep our children in school. When a
> student drops out before graduation, it is a tragedy.
> He or she does not receive an education. The lack of
> a diploma will keep them out of high-paying jobs.
> They may end up poor or on the streets. Too often,
> they may go to jail. These dropouts are lost along
> with their thoughts, dreams, and creativity. They
> cannot contribute to their families and community.
> What can be done to stop this?

In his revised version, Hatfield uses parallelism and transition words to unify his argument. Note that although the content and the organization remain nearly the same, the new paragraph is much more readable and more persuasive. Parallel phrases and transition words are highlighted.

> As Americans it is our duty to do whatever is
> necessary to keep our children in school. When a
> student drops out before graduation, it is a tragedy.
> He or she will go through life without an education
> and without access to high-paying jobs. He or she may
> end up poor, on the streets, or, too often, in jail.
> Not only are our dropouts lost, but their thoughts,
> dreams, and creativity are lost. Everything that
> makes them valuable to themselves and their
> communities is lost. What can be done to stop this?

EXERCISE 17.1 Working with a small group of classmates, read the following two paragraphs and diagnose the transition problems you find between the paragraphs and within each one. Where do you have trouble following the writer's line of thought? Why? Then revise the paragraphs to improve the transitions, drawing on at least two of the strategies described in this section.

> The dangers of exercise are not only that one might injure one's back or pull a hamstring. People new to exercise need to guard against such injuries. No one wants to be a fallen weekend athlete, crippled on Monday morning from running a ten-kilometer race or biking up a mountain on Sunday. The newcomer to exercise can become a fanatic. This is in some ways encouraged by the environment at a health and fitness club. At 6:00 a.m. the hard-core weightlifters and triathlon competitors are there sweating and puffing, enjoying every minute of it. They seem to have their priorities straight— workouts come before work.
>
> Fitness can take over one's life. It is easy to use up three hours a day before you know it. What happens to earning a living or to studying if one is a student? What happens to one's social life? Exercisers have to go to bed early. When they start to preach, nonexercising friends quickly disappear.

EXERCISE 17.2 Use one or more of the transitional devices discussed in this section to strengthen connections between new and old information in a writing project you're currently working on.

17b
trans

CHAPTER 18

What Kinds of Language Can You Use?

Many people assume that *what* we say is more important than *how* we say it. "Just get to the point," we often hear. "Say what you mean." But experts know that the language choices writers make—nuances in tone, vocabulary, formality, and connotation—can powerfully affect readers. This chapter will introduce you to the repertoire of language choices at your disposal, so that you can recognize them and understand the effects they may have.

18a How formal should your writing be?

What's the difference between "a red sweater with shiny buttons" and "a 100% silk cardigan in vermilion with imported pearl fastenings"? Nothing but the language used to describe it. Language ranges from very informal (slang and casual conversation) to very formal (the language of legal documents, sermons, and expensive clothing catalogs).

Choosing the right degree of formality is an important skill for any writer. Checklist 18.1 on the next page summarizes key features of formal, informal, and casual styles and gives examples of genres that typically use each. The rest of this section discusses the levels of formality you're most likely to use when you write for college courses, in the workplace, or for community or campus groups.

1 Recognize that different writing situations call for different levels of formality. Imagine what would happen if you responded to a casual party invitation with a formal memo, or if you opened a graduation speech with a rendition of your favorite rap song. In either case, you'd be using a level of formality inappropriate to the situation—and your audience would quickly let you know it.

When you begin a writing project, you need to ask yourself, "How formal do I want this to be?" Your answer will depend on how you respond to these questions.

- What is my **purpose?** Do I hope to provide information, entertain readers, and/or persuade them to adopt a viewpoint?

Checklist 18.1

Levels of Style: What's Appropriate

FORMAL STYLE	INFORMAL STYLE	CASUAL STYLE
Often used in legal documents, scholarly articles, technical and scientific reports, and formal academic papers	Often used in newspapers, popular magazines, Web pages, memos, and less formal academic assignments	Often used in personal writing, fiction, casual conversation, and friendly email
Considerable distance between writer and readers	Moderate distance between writer and readers	Almost no distance between writer and readers
Serious topics	Mix of topics	Often personal or everyday topics
Serious tone	Conversational tone	Relaxed tone
Many long sentences	Mix of long and short sentences	Short to medium-length sentences
Abstract and specialized vocabulary	Mix of abstract and concrete vocabulary	Concrete language, slang
Few personal references	Occasional personal references	Frequent personal references
Few contractions	Occasional contractions	Many contractions
Few action verbs	Mix of active and passive verbs	Many action verbs

18a
lang

- Who is my **audience?** How well do I know them? How much distance from them do I want to establish?
- What **impression** do I hope to create? Do I want to come across as dignified and serious, straightforward and friendly, or casual and hip?
- What **kind of document** am I composing? What kinds of stylistic conventions will readers expect to see?

When you know your audience well or are writing a familiar kind of document, the answers may come intuitively. When you don't, analyze your writing situation so that you can make good language choices. (See Sections 1d to 1g for more about writing situations.)

2 Choose formal language when you don't know your audience well and want to be serious and dignified. If you are asked to give the opening address at a regional conference on environmental issues, you will probably be speaking to strangers on an important topic and will want to appear thoughtful, well informed, and dignified. Under those circumstances, you'll choose moderately formal language. Here's an excerpt from an environmental writer whose style might serve as a model for such a talk.

18a

lang

> Sustainability is a hopeful concept not only because it is a present necessity, but because it has a history. We know, for example, that some agricultural soils have been preserved in continuous use for several thousand years. We know, moreover, that it is possible to improve soil in use. And it is clear that a forest can be used in such a way that it remains a forest, with its biological community intact and its soil undamaged, while producing a yield of timber. But the methods by which exhaustible resources are extracted and used have set the pattern also for the use of sustainable resources, with the result that soils and forests are not merely being used but are being used up, exactly as coal seams are used up.
> —Wendell Berry, "Conservation Is Good Work"

Berry's writing is authoritative and his tone is serious. His image is that of a concerned and knowledgeable environmental advocate, but he maintains some distance from his audience. His choice of language reflects characteristics that are typical of formal writing.

In most college courses, instructors will expect you to write in a relatively formal style, unless the assignment designates a writing situation in which informality is appropriate—for instance, a reading-response journal or a pop quiz. When you're not sure what level of formality your instructor expects, ask.

3 Choose informal language when you feel comfortable with your audience and want a more relaxed image. Writers use an informal tone in many different writing situations. We'll give just two examples here.

The first is from an article on high school football published in the popular magazine *Texas Monthly*. It's moderately informal.

> But even if change is afoot, Texas high school football remains one of the few institutions that distinguishes us from the rest of the universe. We have more players, coaches, band members, cheerleaders, and pep squads than anyone else. We send more

of our boys to college and the pros than any other state (more than three hundred signed letters of intent to play for Division I schools last year alone). Our fans are more fanatical. Our parents are more passionate. So believe the hype: we're Number One.

—Joe Nick Patoski et al., "Three Cheers for
High School Football"

In this vividly descriptive paragraph, Patoski and his co-authors mix high-level and low-level vocabulary: *distinguishes, institution,* and *fanatical* contrast with the colloquial *our boys* and *hype.* They also mix concrete and abstract language, vary the sentence length, and maintain a moderate distance from readers.

The second example, taken from a book of personal essays, is even more informal.

**18a
lang**

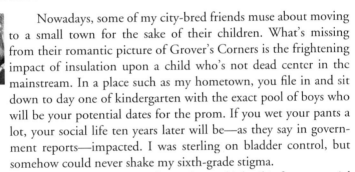

Nowadays, some of my city-bred friends muse about moving to a small town for the sake of their children. What's missing from their romantic picture of Grover's Corners is the frightening impact of insulation upon a child who's not dead center in the mainstream. In a place such as my hometown, you file in and sit down to day one of kindergarten with the exact pool of boys who will be your potential dates for the prom. If you wet your pants a lot, your social life ten years later will be—as they say in government reports—impacted. I was sterling on bladder control, but somehow could never shake my sixth-grade stigma.

At age seventeen, I was free at last to hightail it for new social pastures, and you'd better believe I did.

—Barbara Kingsolver, "In Case You Ever
Want to Go Home Again"

In this account Kingsolver is very close to her readers, writing in the first person and using personal details to make her point. The image she projects is that of someone reminiscing in conversation.

Writers who choose an informal style usually do so because, although their topics may be serious, they don't want to sound solemn or impersonal. They want their readers to feel as if they're in a conversation.

4 Choose casual language when you want to assume the persona of someone who's relaxed and open. Although it's unlikely you'd choose this style for an academic assignment, you might want to use it if you were writing something for the Web or for a small group of friends or insiders. Columnists—in print and online—often use casual language because they want their readers to feel like insiders. This

example comes from a column in the *Cleveland Free Times,* an alternative weekly published in print and online (the column is about the staff's attempts to stop swearing).

> For years we were the cussingest office it would ever be your misfortune to hear. We turned the air blue, with f-bombs exploding everywhere. Male and female workers alike swore more than a bunch of drunken sailors on shore leave (indeed, a bunch of drunken sailors on shore leave once came by the office and were absolutely appalled).
>
> —Eric Broder, *Cleveland Free Times*

18a
lang

Broder's fast-paced, conversational style—infused with sarcasm and humor—suits the *Free Times,* a publication that deliberately sets itself apart from mainstream media.

Writers also choose casual language for intensely personal writing like autobiographical essays, letters, or journals. This example comes from a published diary by a first-year teacher.

> October 5, my birthday. Terrible thing. Somebody stole the Columbus comic book. I said, "Whoever did it, just put it back," but nobody did. So after school I took the whole library down and shoved it in the closet and locked it. The kids noticed right away the next morning.
>
> "I told you if you stole from me, I'd take it all back. I'm not a liar."
>
> "That's not fair," one girl complained. "We didn't all steal the book!" [. . .] I passed out the reading textbooks. The children complained noisily. "You're getting what the rest of the school gets," I reminded them. "I don't see what's the problem."
>
> God, kid! Give me back the stupid book and let me teach you the best way I know how!
>
> —Esme Raji Codell, *Educating Esme*

Codell's choppy sentences, emotional language, and realistic dialogue create a sense of immediacy that draws readers in. While such a colloquial account wouldn't be appropriate for a research article or an academic paper, it's effective here.

EXERCISE 18.1 Working in a small group, decide how you would classify the levels of formality in these passages from two professional writers. Discuss the reasons for any differences.

1. Reading opened up the world. There I was, a skinny bookworm drawing the attention of street kids who, in any other circumstances, would have had me for breakfast. Like an epic tale-teller, I developed the stories as I went along, relying on a flexible plot line and a repository of historical events. I had a great time. I sketched out trajectories with my finger on Frank's dusty truck bed. And I stretched out each story's climax, creating cliffhangers like the ones I saw in the Saturday serials. These stories created for me a temporary community.

—Mike Rose, *Lives on the Boundary*

2. The women who assembled as delegates at Seneca Falls had demanded equality of opportunity for men and women in affairs of state, church, and family. Elizabeth Cady Stanton, the organizing force and intelligence behind this historic conclave, was an advanced and innovative thinker on women's issues, who understood the complex sources of sexual subordination and, in addition to the vote for women, advocated domestic reforms including the right of women to affirm their sexuality if they chose to do so, or contrarily, to refuse sexual relations altogether when necessary to avoid pregnancy. Stanton also supported cooperative child rearing, rights to property, child custody, and divorce. Though venerated within her own small circle, she came to be viewed by more traditional supporters as a source of potential controversy and embarrassment.

—Ellen Chesler, *Woman of Valor*

18a
lang

EXERCISE 18.2 What level of formality do you think would be appropriate for writing in these situations? In each case, consider what impression you might want to make and how much distance you would want to maintain from readers. Give reasons for your choice.

1. A letter to a representative or senator asking to be considered for a summer internship in his or her office.

2. A brochure recruiting people to work on a house being constructed by Habitat for Humanity.

3. A column in your weekly church newsletter that recounts noteworthy activities by members of the church.

4. A biographical sketch for your personal Web page.

18b How emotionally charged should your language be?

Words affect people strongly, and even subtle differences in meaning can have big effects. If they didn't, it would make no difference whether a teacher called your six-year-old "a highly imaginative child" or "a big liar." And we wouldn't see national debates over hate speech legislation and "political correctness" on college campuses.

It's simply because words are so powerful that writers must understand the kinds of emotional associations words carry and then use them appropriately. And what's appropriate will depend on your writing situation. In some situations, like academic writing and much business writing, strongly charged language may offend readers. In others, including some argumentative and political writing, you may need vehement words to get your point across. This section will help you make these kinds of decisions.

1 Understand how denotation and connotation work.

When writing experts talk about emotionally charged language, they distinguish between two kinds of meaning. **Denotation** is the literal meaning of a word, the object or concept that it refers to. For example, the denotative meaning of *puppy* is "a young dog"— nothing more.

Connotation refers to the emotional associations that go along with a word. For example, connotatively, *puppy* suggests cuteness, playfulness, innocence, and warmth. For many people, it conjures up childhood memories of a favorite pet. Contrast these associations with the ones evoked by *half-grown mongrel*. While this phrase's denotation is almost identical to that of *puppy*, its connotations are much more negative, suggesting a scruffy cur who knocks over garbage cans and probably bites.

This example shows that even when words share similar denotations, their connotations may range from strongly positive (*puppy*) to more neutral (*young dog*) to strongly negative (*little mongrel*). Here are a few more examples.

HIGHLIGHT   *Similar Denotations, Different Connotations*

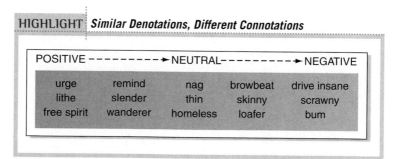

POSITIVE ---------►NEUTRAL---------►NEGATIVE

urge	remind	nag	browbeat	drive insane
lithe	slender	thin	skinny	scrawny
free spirit	wanderer	homeless	loafer	bum

Writers need to be concerned about denotation—that is, you should choose words that precisely convey the idea you're trying to express (don't use *puppy* when you really mean *wolf cub*). But for most writers, choosing words with appropriate connotations is a trickier challenge. Connotative meanings elicit stronger responses from readers. And because they have to do with the contexts in which particular words are used, they also shift more frequently and vary more from audience to audience. The following sections offer guidelines for choosing the right level of connotation in common writing situations.

2 Choose mostly neutral language for informative research, academic papers, case studies, and reports.

18b
lang

When you're writing a piece that's primarily informative, your readers usually expect you to give them a neutral report on the topic. They'll probably be put off by strongly emotional language or descriptions designed to evoke pity or outrage. In the following example, the anthropologist Michael Moffett introduces the thesis of his study examining how undergraduate students at Rutgers University chose their majors.

> The top ten majors and all the rest [. . .] fell into a gradient of status in general student opinion, one that was based on three criteria. First, how good was the occupation to which a given subject presumably led? Second, and closely related, how difficult was that subject at Rutgers? And third, much less important, how much social good did the occupation or profession in question accomplish?
>
> —Michael Moffett, "How College Students Choose Their Majors"

Although Moffett probably has opinions about what criteria students should use to pick a major, and perhaps even about which majors provide the best educational experience, his purpose here is to report what the students he interviewed for this study thought about the issue. He thus uses neutral, descriptive language, focusing not on his feelings about the topic but on communicating his data.

3 Avoid strongly connotative language when you are writing newsletters, press releases, or informative brochures.

The audience for these documents might expect a writer to put a positive spin on the information he or she is presenting, but they don't want to be showered with emotional language. They want to draw their own conclusions. Consider this paragraph from a brochure describing a student tutoring program called Helping One Student To Succeed (HOSTS).

At Zavala Elementary School, teachers select second- and third-grade students to attend the HOSTS program for four half-hour periods each week. Mentors come once a week to meet with students in a cheerful, book-lined classroom for 30 minutes. The students and their mentors read together, talk about books, learn study skills, and practice writing. They also become friends.

This is not strictly neutral language: "a cheerful, book-lined classroom" has positive overtones, as does the last sentence. But the connotation is restrained; it doesn't distract from the information or give the impression that the writer is selling something.

18b

lang

4 Use connotative language appropriately in arguments, reviews, editorials, and opinion pieces. Connotative language sometimes works well when you want to express strong feelings of approval or disapproval. Here are two examples, one that uses language with moderately strong connotations, and one that's more emotionally charged. The first example is from the conclusion of Roger Ebert's review of the movie classic *Casablanca*. It comes from his Web page, *Ebert's Great Movies,* at <www.suntimes.com/ebert/greatmovies/casablanca.html>.

Seeing the film over and over again, year after year, I find it never grows over-familiar. It plays like a favorite musical album; the more I know it, the more I like it. The black-and-white cinematography has not aged as color would. The dialogue is so spare and cynical it has not grown old-fashioned. Much of the emotional effect of *Casablanca* is achieved by indirection; as we leave the theater, we are absolutely convinced that the only thing keeping the world from going crazy is that the problems of three little people do after all amount to more than a hill of beans.

—Roger Ebert, *Casablanca*

Ebert uses connotative language effectively here. His praise is restrained but warm, and he supports his claims with details from the film. Such a review is a suitable model for an evaluative piece you might write for a class or a local paper.

Our second passage, taken from a syndicated newspaper column, uses much stronger language.

When hoopla and hype raged over the $368 billion deal with Big Tobacco [in 1997], one unasked question kept nagging. Why are we negotiating with drug pushers?

Why the haggling with an industry that lies about its product, jokes about restrictions and makes a fortune off a drug that kills 300,000 Americans a year? Why treat with kid gloves tobacco companies that sneakily aim advertising gimmicks so every day 3,000 more teenagers are hooked on coffin nails?

—Sandy Grady, "Tobacco Deal Reduced to Ashes"

One encounters this kind of heavy-handed language fairly often on the editorial pages of newspapers and in political campaign literature. Vehement language is sometimes appropriate in these settings, where writers voice strong positions on important questions. Vigorous public debate is a value our culture holds dear—democracy can't thrive without it.

Yet writers take risks when they choose such charged language. Grady's piece is so laden with extreme terms ("drug pushers," "hooked on coffin nails") that it's likely to turn many readers off. As we point out in Section 18c-4, overly sharp language can alienate readers who don't initially agree with your position. Thus, emotionally charged writing is best left for audiences you know well or for settings where readers expect it. This means that it's rarely appropriate for academic writing. (See Section 7a for detailed advice about what instructors expect in academic papers.)

18b
lang

█ 5 Be alert to the connotations in your own writing and that of others. As we point out in Section 10b-7, cultivating the ability to recognize connotation plays an important role in becoming a critical thinker. For example, if you encounter a business proposal that's full of phrases like *exciting opportunity, maximum growth potential,* and *meaningful change,* you need to make a careful analysis before you accept the claims. Whose words are these, and what specifics underlie these glowing phrases?

In your own writing, particularly in academic papers, be aware of the connotations your words evoke, both positive and negative. Highly charged words like *unparalleled, superlative, immoral,* and *stupid* are usually too extreme for reports, research papers, and oral presentations. If you do use such terms, give explicit examples that elaborate on them.

EXERCISE 18.3 Working with a group of classmates, list all the synonyms you can think of for one of the following words. Then arrange the words from those with the most positive to those with the most negative connotations. In what writing situations might each be used appropriately, and why?

large luxury car	politician	cry	disorganized
open-minded	single parent	child	strict

EXERCISE 18.4 Find a syndicated newspaper column such as those written by George Will, William Safire, Molly Ivins, or William Raspberry. Underline words and phrases with strong negative or positive connotations. Then find a news story from the same paper. Discuss the differences in how the two pieces handle connotative language.

18c How do you choose reader-friendly language?

Have you ever suffered through a lecture that went completely over your head? Or stopped reading an editorial halfway through because the writer made assumptions that insulted you? Or fallen asleep while reading a particularly dull textbook? If so, you know what it's like to try to read a text that's not reader-friendly.

Language is a powerful instrument. Writers use it to voice new ideas, to draw people together, to encourage deliberation, and to effect change. But writers who are careless about word choices or who don't think sufficiently about their audiences may find that their language alienates the readers they want to reach. This is why it's important that you choose your words carefully when you write. Draw readers into your discussion; don't shut them out.

1 Choose language familiar to your readers. When you're drafting or revising a piece of writing, ask yourself whether your readers will be comfortable with the vocabulary you're using. There are times when a difficult or technical term *is* appropriate—when it draws a subtle distinction or describes a complex phenomenon that simpler words can't capture. But writers sometimes wrongly assume that they need to impress readers by choosing formal and highly complicated language. The result is more likely to seem stuffy and difficult to read than smart and sophisticated. Here's an example from an academic paper.

UNNECESSARILY DIFFICULT LANGUAGE

Scholarly authorities hold a myriad of viewpoints with regard to the ongoing disputation involving the major prescription drug companies' ethical obligation to manufacture minimally profitable pharmaceuticals that ameliorate the world's major diseases.

REVISED

Scholars disagree on whether big drug companies have a moral obligation to manufacture low-profit drugs to treat the world's major diseases.

See how much more readable the second sentence is? Our point is that even when you're writing in a relatively formal style, you'll reach more readers by choosing familiar words when you can. Usually that's not hard to do; you can find good substitutes for most high-level words. See Section 20c for more tips on reworking inflated sentences.

2 Balance abstract and concrete language. Abstract words are general; they refer to ideas, concepts, and categories that we can't perceive directly through our five senses—words like *justice, charm, culture, life.* Concrete words do just the opposite; they name specific people and things that we can see, hear, taste, smell, or touch— *Judge Joe Brown, grin, turquoise bracelet, my pet poodle.* Of course, most words are neither wholly abstract nor concrete. They exist on a continuum between the two extremes, and writers must decide what level of specificity seems most appropriate for their purpose. For example:

18c
lang

HIGHLIGHT **From Abstract to Concrete**

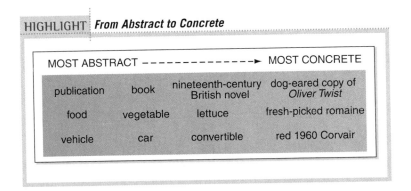

MOST ABSTRACT		----------►	MOST CONCRETE
publication	book	nineteenth-century British novel	dog-eared copy of *Oliver Twist*
food	vegetable	lettuce	fresh-picked romaine
vehicle	car	convertible	red 1960 Corvair

Passages laden with too many abstractions can be intimidating and hard to follow. Yet writing that contains nothing but specifics gives readers too little guidance; readers may not see the main point amid all the details. That's why skilled writers strive for an effective mix of both. They use abstract terms to help readers grasp big ideas and connections but provide plenty of vivid and concrete images to illustrate those ideas and to hold readers' interest. Exactly what ratio of abstract to concrete language you use in a particular text will depend on your writing situation. For more on balancing concrete and abstract language, see Sections 20b-1 (sentences) and 15c-1 (paragraphs).

3 Limit your use of jargon. Jargon comes in two forms. The specialized insider language of professional groups is one kind of jargon.

Physicians, for instance, use the terms *hypertension* and *ideopathic* among themselves; lawyers use the terms *tort* and *indemnify;* graphic artists use the terms *pixel* and *color separation.* When you're writing for a group of specialists, these technical terms are a necessary part of your vocabulary. But you'll shut out readers if you use this kind of jargon when you're writing for an audience that includes nonspecialists.

When you need to use a specialized term, define it the first time you use it and then give an example. For example, using the term *endorphin* in an article about exercise, you could explain that an endorphin is a chemical in the brain that raises an individual's pain threshold, and then you might give as an example of the chemical's effect the sense of well-being that many people claim to feel after strenuous exercise.

A second kind of jargon is abstract, impersonal writing full of long sentences and nominalizations (see Section 20c-2). Writing that contains this sort of jargon is especially common in academic and bureaucratic settings. Here is an example.

> When systems of institutional control are working without significant challenge, the authority of the knowledge embodied in the institutions seems similarly potent. When the institutions are attacked and then fragment, however, problems about knowledge and its legitimacy come to the fore.
>
> —Stephen Shapin, *The Scientific Revolution*

This isn't *bad* writing; it's clear enough to someone practiced in reading this level of language and willing to make the effort to understand it. But this kind of noun-laden, abstract writing can intimidate general readers and thus lose them. If you find you've lapsed into this style for an opinion piece, a Web page, or an important memo, you'll do well to revise, to use more concrete and readable language.

4 Use a civil, fair-minded tone for public writing.

Striking the right tone in your writing is crucial. When you want to build common ground with your readers and convince them to consider your ideas, try to come across as an open-minded person who doesn't feel she has all the answers. Treat your audience—even those whom you suspect may disagree with you—with respect.

Most readers will be put off by an author who sounds arrogant and contemptuous. Consider the following passage.

> The existence of a literature presupposes a literate and coherent public that has both the time to read and a need to take seriously the works of the literary imagination. I'm not sure whether the United States ever had such a public; certainly it hasn't had

The Fast-Food Lawsuit

On July 24, a lawsuit was filed against the fast-food industry for causing obesity and other health problems. Other recent suits:

Big Three automakers, $4.3 billion
Knowingly manufactured vehicles that take people places that aren't always fun

Magnavox, $16.5 million
Failed to produce Bud-bottle-proof TV screen

Zubaz Corp., $2.1 million
Grossly neglected to inform consumers how stupid anyone looks in Zubaz

American Cardboard Box Amalgamated, $42 billion
Maybe one of those boxes has a Dracula in it and we could all get scared

Jack Daniel's, $30 million
Failed to relate danger of losing the wife and the kids and the job the whole goddamn lot

Citibank, $167 million
Neglected to post signs clearly stating, "Do not rob this bank, or you will go to jail"

U.S. Armed Forces, $20 billion
Knowingly exposed young recruits to dangerous and even deadly working conditions

Atlantic Ocean, $33.5 billion
Contains too many sharks

18c
lang

Figure 18.1 *Humor is not always civil. Satirical items like those posted regularly on* The Onion *(<http:www.theonion.com>) push the envelope, hoping to arouse and, sometimes, even offend readers.*

one for the last thirty years. What we have instead is an opening-night crowd, astonished by celebrity and opulent spectacle, tolerating only those authors who present themselves as freaks and wonders and offer the scandal of their lives as proof of their art.
—Lewis Lapham, "Notebook"

Lapham is a longtime social critic who has been writing his grumpy column for *Harper's* for years. Undoubtedly the caustic tone—characterized by put-downs, name-calling, sarcasm, and sweeping condemnations—appeals to some people, particularly those who already agree with the author. But readers who are looking for information or enlightenment will usually feel insulted and quit reading.

If you want readers to pay attention to your concerns, begin with the assumption that your readers are intelligent and that each of you is able to understand the other's point of view. Avoid name-calling and blanket generalizations. Instead of making pronouncements, qualify your claims using words and phrases such as *One solution is . . . , in many cases, often, usually.* Such terms suggest and speculate rather than dictate. For more on constructing a credible image in your writing, see Section 1g. For advice on handling different viewpoints, consult Section 12c.

5 Build common ground by referring to experiences readers can identify with.

One of the joys of language is that it allows us to tell stories, and through stories we build community. For example, if you're writing an appeal for volunteers to work in your local Habitat for Humanity program, you can tell of the satisfaction you got from working with two young women carpenters to build a house. You could also give colorful details about the family who put in their own "sweat equity" so they could move into the house.

In an article on alcoholism, you could describe one family's struggle with it over three generations, the kind of story that former Senator George McGovern recounts in his book about his daughter, *Terry: My Daughter's Life-and-Death Struggle with Alcoholism.* The plague of alcoholism touches so many lives that such accounts strike a chord with large numbers of readers. Because McGovern based his book on excerpts from his daughter's diary, his stories are particularly effective.

18c
lang

EXERCISE 18.5 Revise one of the passages below to achieve a more effective balance between abstract and concrete language. You may need to add sentences and revise existing sentences. Discuss your revisions with a group of classmates.

1. Never buy a pet from a pet shop without first checking to see where the establishment gets its animals. Many stores buy their stock from unregulated "puppy mills," where large numbers of animals are raised in terrible conditions. Buyers may end up with a sick or mentally damaged pet.

2. During the month of February, 12 students were mugged at knifepoint in the main student parking garage. In April, a woman barricaded herself in the garage elevator to escape an assailant. In June, 2 cars parked on the top level of the garage had their windshields smashed. My roommate is even afraid to park her car on campus.

EXERCISE 18.6 Revise the following paragraph to create a more civil and appropriate tone. Assume that you're writing to readers of your campus newspaper.

Apparently the university "doesn't have the funds" this year to renovate the dorms on campus. Yeah, right. It's tough for me to believe that there's a money shortage when every time I pass by the president's house he's having another fancy party for his rich donor friends. Everyone knows that all the administrators do is go to parties, make a speech every now and then, and draw fat salaries. What a scam! They don't care about the students; they just care about lining their wallets. If they had to live in our dorms, I bet we'd see some upgrades pretty fast.

18d How do you avoid stereotyped language?

Biased language isn't always bad. Slanted but colorful writing regularly enlivens articles in popular books, humorous pieces and magazines, and the editorial pages of any newspaper. Consider this passage about Internet users.

Certain early users of the Net (bless them!) are now whining about its vulgarization, warning people of its hazards as if it were a cigarette. If only these whiners were more honest, they'd admit that it was they who didn't have much of a life and found solace on the Net, they who woke up one day in midlife crisis and discovered there was more to living than what was waiting in their e-mail boxes. So, what took you guys so long? Of course there's more to life than e-mail, but don't project your empty existence onto others and suggest "being digital" is a form of virtual leprosy for which total abstinence is the only immunization.

—Nicholas Negroponte, "Get a Life?"

The example comes from *Wired* magazine, a publication written and read by computer buffs who would freely admit they're far from objective about the Internet. And Negroponte makes no pretense to objectivity. He uses vigorous, colorful language to poke fun at attitudes held by certain members of his audience. Yet because he's written for these readers so often, and because his humor targets insiders who feel comfortable in the computer world, his exaggerated complaints entertain rather than offend his audience.

When you write papers in college, in business, or in most community settings, however, you have a different kind of audience. Now you're writing to inform or persuade readers whom you don't know well, and you don't want to offend them by lapsing into language that excludes a part of your audience or suggests that you think in stereotypes.

Thirty years ago, Americans were just beginning to see what female athletes could accomplish when given the chance. Today, women such as soccer superstar Mia Hamm garner as much attention for their athletic prowess as their male counterparts.

No matter who their audience may be, responsible writers avoid language that stigmatizes or demeans particular groups. Language that attributes to individuals negative associations based on gender, race or ethnicity, religion, profession, or class is always out of place in public writing.

■ 1 Avoid sexist language.

Over the past four decades, women's activists have made most of us more aware of how profoundly language shapes attitudes and reinforces traditional gender roles. Twenty-five years ago, when the typical writer consistently referred to doctors, scientists, inventors, and artists as "he" and to secretaries, nurses, teachers, and receptionists as "she," youngsters got strong messages about which professions they were expected to choose. You seldom see such ingrained bias today in reputable newspapers, books, and magazines—most readers find such bias offensive. To keep sexist blunders out of your writing, consider these guidelines.

- Avoid using *he* and *him* as all-purpose pronouns to refer to people in general.

WHY WRITE . . .
Every executive expects *his* bonus.

WHEN YOU COULD WRITE . . .
Every executive expects *a* bonus.
Executives expect *their* bonuses.
Every executive expects *his or her* bonus.

- **Guard against using the word *man* as a catchall term to refer to all people or all members of a group.** Instead use *people* as a general term, or refer to a specific occupation or role: *worker, parent, voter.*

WHY WRITE . . .	WHEN YOU COULD WRITE . . .
the *man* who wants to be an astronaut	*anyone* who wants to be an astronaut
men who do their own auto repairs	*car owners* who do their own repairs

- **Watch out for assumptions that professions or roles are primarily for men or for women.** Don't write "A senator will improve *his* chances of election by going back home frequently" or "A nurse usually enjoys *her* profession." Also be careful not to slip into hidden assumptions by writing "woman doctor" or "woman engineer," thereby suggesting one wouldn't expect to find women in those professions.

18d
lang

WHY WRITE . . .	WHEN YOU COULD WRITE . . .
men who hope to become scholarship athletes	*young people* who hope to become scholarship athletes
stay-home *mothers*	stay-home *parents*
police*man*	police officer
mail*man*	mail carrier/letter carrier
cleaning *woman*	custodian/janitor
business*men*	business executives

- **When possible, find out what name a married woman wants to go by and honor that choice.** Here are the possibilities.

woman's first and last names	Olga Perez
woman's first and last names + husband's last name	Olga Perez Marciano
woman's first name + hyphenated last name	Olga Perez-Marciano
woman's first name + husband's last name	Olga Marciano
title + husband's full name	Mrs. Ralph Marciano

Some traditionalists may find this array of choices complicated and unnecessary; to many women, however, the distinctions are important. Many women, single or married, prefer the title *Ms.* to *Miss* or *Mrs.* When you're not sure, *Ms.* is the best choice.

- **Watch out for between-the-lines implications that men and women behave in stereotypical ways.** Don't suggest that women are generally talkative and overly emotional or that most men are sports-minded and sloppy. Avoid sexist descriptions such as "a slim blonde" or "a petite brunette" unless you make the same kind of comments about men. Finally, the generic term *woman* (or *women*) is more appropriate than *lady* or *girl,* which many women find patronizing.

EXERCISE 18.7 Rewrite the following sentences to eliminate sexist language or implications. If necessary, refer to Chapter 32 for strategies.

1. Women in their forties and fifties who want to look their best often consider cosmetic surgery.

2. Today even a high school physics teacher should know his astrophysics, or he'll look out of date to his students.

3. The hospital's new series of nutrition workshops appeals to mothers concerned about their children's health.

4. Businesswomen often worry about leaving their children in day care while they work long hours to get ahead.

5. The lady running for Congress in my district has been a county judge for many years.

2 Avoid ethnic, racial, and religious stereotypes. In many writing situations you simply don't need to mention race or national origin—it's not relevant. In writing about general topics—business or the media or education, for example—the race or nationality of individuals is often unimportant. At other times, however, issues of race or nationality may be central to your discussion. In such cases, these guidelines may be helpful.

- **Be as accurate as possible.** For example, the term *Asian* (now widely preferred to *Oriental*) is so broad as to be almost useless. There are dozens of countries in Asia, and their cultures and the physical characteristics of their people vary greatly. You'll do much better to use *Filipino, Japanese, Chinese, Korean, Indian,* and so on. When you refer to individuals whose forebears came from one of these countries but who are themselves American-born, combine the term with *American: Japanese American, Korean American,* and so on.

  Many people of Spanish descent in the Americas no longer like the term *Hispanic*—again, it's extremely broad and suggests that all such people share similar traits and cultures. You'll do better to be specific: *Cuban, Puerto Rican, Mexican, Brazilian,* and so on. When

18d

lang

appropriate, combine the name with *American—Mexican American, Cuban American,* and so on. The term *Latino* (or *Latina*), used to refer broadly to people of Latin American descent, is widely accepted.

American Indian and *Native American* are both acceptable when you're writing about the people who originally populated North America. But many of the North American natives whom we have traditionally thought of as *Eskimos* have come to prefer the designation *Inuit,* and that term is now official with the Canadian government. *Eskimo* remains appropriate, however, in an archaeological or cultural context, such as speaking of *Eskimo carvings.*

When you're writing about individuals' religious affiliations, be similarly specific; generalizations such as *Eastern sects* and *Christian conservatives* are vague and inaccurate. It's better to specify a particular religion or denomination (*Sunni Muslims, Orthodox Jews, Southern Baptists*) or to name a particular religious group (*Promise Keepers, Campus Crusade for Christ*).

18d
lang

- **Use terminology preferred by the people you're writing about, insofar as you know their preferences.** When you're not sure, adopt the terminology you see in respected newspapers and magazines or hear on major television or radio news shows (but not call-in talk shows). Most media editors are careful about their language.

  The term currently favored by individuals whose forebears came from Africa is *African American,* although *black* is still widely used. The *New York Times,* a dependable source for up-to-date usage, shifts back and forth between the terms. The terms *Negro* and *colored people* are no longer appropriate for public writing. The term *people of color,* popular with many writers concerned about choosing unbiased language, seems too vague to be useful for identifying African Americans and probably should be reserved for broadly designating nonwhite groups.

- **Be careful not to allow ethnic, national, or religious stereotypes to seep into your writing.** Might one infer from your language that you think of Jews as rich financiers? Is there a hint that someone with an Italian surname has underworld connections? Or an innuendo suggesting that a person of Middle Eastern origin might sympathize with anti-American terrorists? Check your writing for such biases.

EXERCISE 18.8 Almost everyone has had some experience with the difficult issue of ethnic labels and names. Working with fellow students, make a list of all the ethnic groups represented in your composition class, writing on the board the terms preferred by members of each definable group. Discuss those preferences and a writer's responsibility to know and use them.

EXERCISE 18.9 Consider which of these sentences might be inappropriate in an academic paper. Which seem acceptable? Why? Write an alternative for those that aren't appropriate.

1. Jewish director-producer Steven Spielberg traces his interest in filmmaking back to his childhood, when he recorded family occasions with his parents' movie camera.

2. Negro baseball players formed their own leagues in the early 1900s.

3. Indians, Eskimos, and other primitive groups are often portrayed sympathetically in the movies.

4. Unlike most American teenagers, Asian students are typically hardworking, academically oriented, and respectful of authority figures.

18d
lang

3 Avoid stereotypes about age, physical condition, and sexual orientation.
If you were born in the United States, part of your heritage is the assertion in the Declaration of Independence that all of us are created equal. Of course, we haven't always done a good job of living up to it. Slavery, the Chinese Exclusion Act, the disenfranchisement of women and African Americans, and many other instances testify to that. But most of us still want to work toward the ideal of just treatment, and in

Astronaut John Glenn was almost 80 when he took his final space flight as a space shuttle payload specialist in 1998.

language such treatment means not demeaning or patronizing people based on traits they cannot control. These guidelines may be helpful.

- **Consider that many persons over age 60 don't like being called** *elderly, senior citizens, or old people.* Most seem to prefer *older people* or, better, a specific designation such as *people in their sixties* (or *late seventies,* and so on). Don't slip into patronizing remarks such as "For a 70-year-old, he's remarkably alert."

- **Reserve the terms** *boys, girls,* **and** *kids* **for people under age 18.** Young working adults just out of high school deserve to be called men and women. So do college students, whether they are first-year students or graduate students. The phrase *college kids,* which many people use unthinkingly, is rather patronizing. It's also inaccurate: almost half of all U.S. college students now are over 25, and a great many of them have families and major responsibilities. When you refer to people under age 18, *child* or *adolescent* is widely preferred to *kid.*

- **When referring to individuals or groups with disabilities or illnesses, be as specific as possible and avoid language that implies pity**—for example, *crippled* and *victim.* The phrases *visually handicapped* and *hearing impaired* are descriptive and objective; so are *a person with multiple sclerosis* and *a paraplegic.* In general, it works well to mention the individual first and his or her handicap or disease second— "a person with AIDS" or "my cousin who is autistic." Terms such as *disabled veteran* and *a person with*

18d
lang

Physicist Stephen Hawking, who has physical disabilities, is arguably the greatest scientific genius since Albert Einstein.

muscular disability seem generally acceptable. Once again, it's useful to know with what terms the individuals themselves feel comfortable.

- **Mention a person's sexual orientation only when it is relevant to the issue under discussion, and then use specific, nonjudgmental terminology.** Many people whose sexual orientation is toward their own gender are comfortable with the adjective *homosexual* to refer to both men and women but less comfortable with the noun, *a homosexual.* They choose the terms *gay* and *lesbian* when they want to be specific about an individual's sexual orientation. Although some groups of gay rights advocates use the word *queer* in their literature, that term is inappropriate coming from someone outside such a group. The use of the word *gay* as an all-purpose perjorative is also clearly offensive.

EXERCISE 18.10 Working in a group, decide which of these sentences have hints of offensive bias (some of them are certainly arguable). Which might be acceptable in some circumstances? How could you change those that are not?

1. The chemistry professor was impressed to see that most of the girls in his advanced course had scored high marks on the exam.

2. Barney Frank, who is almost the only open homosexual in the U.S. Congress, represents a district in Massachusetts.

3. Although Betty Friedan is over 70, she still writes extensively and travels widely.

4. The hospice is looking for volunteers to help AIDS victims with household tasks and grocery shopping.

5. Many Americans were unaware that President Franklin Delano Roosevelt was crippled, since he was rarely photographed in his wheelchair during public appearances.

4 Avoid language that reflects flippant or derisive attitudes toward some professions or implies unflattering class distinctions. When you're writing at a formal level, it's better to avoid occupational labels that carry a tinge of contempt. *Shrink* for psychiatrist is one; so is *cop* for police officer. *Prof* for professor doesn't go over well, nor does *computer nerd* or *techie* for computer technician. On the other hand, calling a medical doctor a *physician* or a lawyer an *attorney* conveys respect for those individuals, as does the word *journalist* instead of *reporter*.

Be careful, too, about using terms that may have negative class connotations. The terms *yuppie, fraternity guy,* and *soccer mom* may be literally accurate, but they have accusatory overtones that suggest shallowness and elitism. Many social work professionals have come to feel that the label *lower class* is demeaning; they prefer *low income.* The term *inner city* is preferable to *slum* or *ghetto,* which suggest squalor. Other class markers to avoid are *welfare mother* and *redneck.*

EXERCISE 18.11 Which of these sentences might alienate a reader sensitive to bias? Which ones should be changed? Why or why not? What changes would you suggest?

18d
lang

1. The cops used poor judgment about gathering evidence at the crime scene.

2. Welfare mothers have become the target of budget-conscious legislators who believe that hardworking taxpayers shouldn't have to support people who won't work.

3. That organization is known for attracting sorority girls and fraternity guys.

4. It's amazing that Jason became a successful lawyer, since he grew up in the inner-city ghetto, surrounded by poverty and despair.

5 Be careful that photos or other images you incorporate into a writing project don't suggest harmful stereotypes. Because images often affect readers more immediately than words do, select photos and other visuals as carefully as you choose your words—if not more so. Are you writing an illustrated history of jazz for your music history course? Then include photos of African American, white, and Latino musicians—otherwise your report will look uneven. Are you writing a brochure to publicize a campus organization whose members include a significant number of nontraditional students? Then be sure that your cover photo doesn't include only 18-year-olds. Both the visual elements and the text of any writing project should work together to offer readers a full and accurate account of the topic at hand.

6 Use your good judgment and keep your sense of humor. Don't sanitize your writing to the point that it becomes deadly dull. Every day we read columnists or listen to commentators who use biased language to spoof, satirize, persuade, or praise, and they do it very well. Consider this example from the syndicated columnist and humorist Dave Barry.

> If the psychology community needs further proof of the difference between genders, I invite it to attend the party held by my neighborhood each Halloween. This party is attended by several hundred children, who are experiencing stress because their bloodstreams [. . .] contain roughly the same sugar content as Cuba. Here's how the various genders respond: The females, 97 percent of whom are dressed as either a ballerina or a princess, sit in little social groups and exchange candy. The males, 97 percent of whom are dressed as either Batman or a Power Ranger, run around making martial-arts noises and bouncing violently off each other like crazed subatomic particles.
>
> —Dave Barry, "Neither Man nor Rat
> Can Properly Fold the Laundry"

Exaggerated images? Of course. Gender and age stereotypes? Definitely. Biased language? Certainly. But fun? Absolutely. Insulting to Barry's readers? Almost certainly not; they probably loved it.

It's unrealistic to say you should never use biased or exaggerated language to convey a mood, create an image, or make sardonic comments. Like a professional writer, however, you should make it your goal to be so attuned to your readers that you can write for them with respect, awareness, and good taste—and still have fun with language.

18e How do you handle language varieties?

Do you speak differently in different settings? Do you use language in different ways depending on whether you're at home with your family, hanging out with friends, working, or writing a paper for a course? If you're like most people in the United States, you know several varieties of English, each shaped by your cultural heritage, your region, and your exposure to other languages. Linguists call these varieties of English **dialects**. Dialects of English—which include southern dialect, northeastern dialect, African American Vernacular English, and many others—differ from each other in vocabulary, pronunciation, and grammar. Their features can be quite distinctive.

One dialect of English, sometimes referred to as **edited American English,** or standard English, is the language used in most academic, business, and public writing. It's the variety taught in most academic, business, and public writing. It's the variety taught in most schools and emphasized in this book. If a dialect you use in other settings differs from this "standard," you may have difficulties when some of its features appear in your writing. You can use this handbook and other resources, such as your campus writing center, to edit out those features.

Learning to use a standard dialect for certain writing situations doesn't mean that you have to abandon all others. It means only that you have to cultivate some flexibility so that you can switch back and forth among different ways of speaking as the situation demands. But all educated people need to be able to use the standard written dialect of the United States, edited American English, so they can communicate on an equal footing with the millions of others who use it.

In addition to the various dialects of English, many languages are spoken in the United States. If you speak English as your second language (ESL), you'll find information in Chapters 34 to 36 to help you with the challenges of writing in a new language.

This section offers suggestions for dealing with dialects and languages in your writing.

18e
lang

Figure 18.2   *In certain writing situations it may be effective to use a mix of different dialects or languages—as this homepage for* Urban Latino, *a magazine whose readership is mostly bilingual, illustrates.*

1 Recognize the uses and importance of dialects.

Dialects are important and useful to the groups that speak them. A dialect helps to hold a group together and to give it a sense of community and identity. Dialects thus should be appreciated and protected for private communication between individuals within a particular community. Usually such communication is spoken.

Here is how the writer James Lee Burke represents the Cajun dialect of southern Louisiana in a novel.

> She had put my three-legged raccoon, Tripod, on his chain. [. . .] She pulled him up in the air by his chain. His body danced and curled as if he were being garroted.
> "Clarise, don't do that."
> "Ask him what he done, him," she said. "Go look my wash basket. Go look your shirts. They blue yesterday. They brown now. So smell, you."
> "I'll take him down to the dock."
> "Tell Batiste not to bring him back, no. [. . .] He come in my house again, you gonna see him cooking with the sweet potato."
> —James Lee Burke, *Black Cherry Blues*

2 Acknowledge the limitations of dialect.

When dialects show up in *public writing*—and that is what most of the writing you do in college and your profession will be—they can be misunderstood and misinterpreted. Some vocabulary within a dialect may not be understood by those outside it. Certain grammatical forms that are completely natural and logical within a dialect community may be regarded as nonstandard by other users of the language.

In this passage from the novel *The Bluest Eye*, Toni Morrison represents the dialect known as African American Vernacular English.

> The onliest time I be happy seem like was when I was in the picture show. Everytime I got, I went. I'd go early, before the show started. They'd cut off the lights, and everything be black. Then the screen would light up, and I'd move right in on them pictures. [. . .] Them pictures give me a lot of pleasure, but it made coming home hard, and looking at Cholly hard.
> —Toni Morrison, *The Bluest Eye*

The passage reveals the character Pauline's most private kind of communication, inner speech to herself.

This conversation between two characters in a novel of the early West, *Zeke and Ned*, offers another example of dialect.

"Jewel's not a talker," Ned admitted. "That don't mean she's easy to live with, though."

"Why, where'd you get the notion that women are easy to live with," Tuxie asked. "Women are a passel of trouble, though I need my Dale."

"I wish Jewel would let up about my leaving," Ned said. "I need to go to town once in a while. It's boresome, getting drunk at home."

—Larry McMurtry and Dianna Ossana, *Zeke and Ned*

Here the private language of two articulate men carries the flavor of their personalities, but "passel of trouble" and "It's boresome" would sound out of place and colloquial in a written communication.

Letting a private dialect enter your writing, then, is not "wrong"— but it may be inappropriate for the writing situation. When your readers find the marks of your personal language in writing that is directed to a group of readers who don't share that dialect, they'll be jarred by the mismatch.

18e
lang

3 Use dialect when appropriate. When can you use dialect in your writing? First, you can use it in your private life among friends, family, or others who share the dialect, either in conversation or in letters or email. Second, you might use it in a first, discovery draft when you're trying to get your ideas down and don't want to slow your thinking by worrying about the conventions of standard English. (You can edit out or translate inappropriate dialect features in a future draft.) Finally, you might use dialect in an anecdote you are adding to a paper to illustrate a point, or you could incorporate it into dialogue that is an essential part of a personal narrative. Here's an example from a professional writer.

Two years ago, when I started writing this paper, trying to bring order out of chaos, my ten-year-old daughter was suffering from an acute attack of boredom. [. . .] Patiently I explained that I was working on something special and needed peace and quiet, and I suggested that she paint, read, or work with her computer. None of these interested her. Finally, she pulled up a chair to my desk and watched me, now and then heaving long, loud sighs. [. . .] I lost my patience. "Looka here, Allie," I said, "you too old for this kinda carryin' on. I done told you this is important. You wronger than dirt to be in here haggin' me like this and you know it."

—Barbara Mellix, "From Outside, In"

Except for these instances, however, spoken dialect generally doesn't fit into the kind of public writing you'll be doing in college, in business, or in community work.

4 Use languages other than English when appropriate.

If you speak a language other than English, you might use it in your writing for the same reasons that you'd use varieties of English. You might use it in your private life to communicate among friends or family or to explore and develop ideas before beginning a writing project.

You might also use another language to reproduce a speaker's exact words or to create an authentic atmosphere in a description or narrative. Finally, it's appropriate to include non-English words that can't easily be translated into English, as the essayist Judith Ortiz Cofer does in the following example.

18e
lang

> Even the home movie cannot fill in the sensory details such a gathering [a family New Year's Eve party] left imprinted in a child's brain. The thick sweetness of women's perfumes mixing with the ever-present smells of food cooking in the kitchen: meat and plantain *pasteles*, as well as the ubiquitous rice dish made special with pigeon peas—*gandules*—and seasoned with previous *sofrito* sent up from the Island by somebody's mother or smuggled in by a recent traveler.
>
> —Judith Ortiz Cofer, "Silent Dancing"

As with dialect, words and phrases from different languages should be used in public writing only to achieve a particular effect—otherwise you'll risk confusing readers. And if the meaning of a word or phrase isn't apparent from the context, it's wise to provide an English translation, as Cofer does above.

CHAPTER 19

How Do You Construct Effective Sentences?

19a How are sentences structured?

Traditional terms used to describe the architecture of sentences—*clauses, phrases, subordination, coordination, parallelism*—can make writing sentences seem complicated. But even the most complex sentences are based on a few comprehensible structures and principles. We cover these elements in this chapter.

We know, of course, that you'll rarely think about particular sentence structures when you compose. Few writers—if any—work that way. But even while dashing off a draft, you'll be more confident when you've developed a feel for the way sentences function, an instinct for how the parts fit together.

■ **1 Understand sentence patterns.** Sentences are tough to define. A **sentence** can be described as a group of words that expresses an idea and that is punctuated as an independent unit. All sentences have a **subject** (the doer of an action) and a **predicate** (the action done). Beginning with this assumption, you'll find that just five patterns can describe the framework of many sentences you write. In recognizing these patterns and their variations, you take a step toward controlling the shape of your sentences.

1. **Subject + verb (intransitive).** This is the simplest sentence pattern, the one with the fewest parts. Like all sentences, it includes a *subject,* the doer of an action; and a *verb,* the action performed. But in this pattern the verb is *intransitive*—that is, it doesn't need an object to complete its meaning.

Subject	Verb (intransitive)
The lawyer	fainted.
The floodwaters	receded.
All the children	smiled at once.

295

EXERCISE 19.1 Compose three sentences that follow the subject–intransitive verb pattern. Underline the intransitive verb in each sentence.

2. **Subject + verb (transitive) + direct object.** This sentence pattern adds a third element to the subject and verb: an *object,* which identifies to what or to whom an action has been done. Objects can be words, phrases, or clauses. The pattern requires a transitive verb that conveys its action to an object.

19a
sent

Subject	Verb (transitive)	Object
The lawyer	accepted	the case.
The heavy rains	destroyed	the levee.
Some of the children	were reading	books.

Note that the subject-verb-object pattern illustrates the *active voice,* in which the subject performs the action described by the transitive verb. But when that action is performed by the object, you have a *passive construction* (see Section 26e).

The case was accepted by the lawyer.

The levee was destroyed by heavy rains.

The books were being read by some of the children.

Only transitive verbs can be involved in passive constructions because they require an object that can become a subject. Intransitive verbs don't take objects.

It is important that a transitive verb and its object fit together logically. In the following example, the verb *intimidate* cannot logically convey its action to the object *enthusiasm. Enthusiasm* might be *undermined, dampened,* or *eroded,* but we don't usually speak of it as *intimidated.*

FAULTY	The negative attitudes of the senior staff *intimidated* the **enthusiasm** of the volunteers.
REVISED	The negative attitudes of the senior staff *dampened* the **enthusiasm** of the volunteers.

EXERCISE 19.2 Write three sentences that follow the subject-verb-object pattern. Underline the object. Be sure the verb is in the active voice.

EXERCISE 19.3 Revise any of the following sentences in which the boldfaced verb cannot logically convey its action to its object. First try to explain the problem with the original verb; then change the verb, not the object.

1. At her parents' request, Margery **interrogated** her sister Kyla's low grades at college.

2. Kyla **blasphemed** her instructor's methods of teaching history.

3. Her psychology instructor **jaded** her with long lectures about statistics and methods.

4. Her chemistry teacher **obliged** difficult lab reports every week.

5. Worst of all, her English teacher persistently **admonished** the clarity of her writing.

3. **Subject + verb (linking) + subject complement.** Linking verbs, which are often forms of *to be,* connect a subject to a subject complement, that is, to a word or phrase that extends or completes the meaning of a subject or renames it in some way. Among the common linking verbs are *to seem, to appear, to feel,* and *to become.*

Subject	Linking verb	Subject complement
The lawyer	became	a federal judge.
The storms	seemed	endless.
The children	are	happy.

A complement should be compatible with its subject. When it is not, the sentence is illogical, sometimes subtly so.

FAULTY COMPLEMENT   **Prejudice** is unacceptable **behavior** in this club.

The problem is that *prejudice* is not behavior; it's an attitude. So the sentence has to be modified to reflect this difference.

REVISED   **Prejudiced behavior** is unacceptable in this club.

For the same reason, it's wrong to use *when* as a complement.

WRONG   **Plagiarism** is **when** a writer doesn't credit her source.

When is an adverb; *plagiarism* is a noun. *Plagiarism* has to be a concept or an idea, so it cannot be *when.*

RIGHT   **Plagiarism** is the **failure** to credit a source.

EXERCISE 19.4 In the following sentences, indicate whether the bold-faced words are objects or complements.

1. Halloween may be the oddest **holiday** of the year.

2. The roots of Halloween are deeply **religious**.

3. But Halloween celebrations today seem quite **secular**.

4. Children and adults wear **costumes** and pull **pranks**.

5. For all its images of ghosts and goblins, Halloween now seems less **scary**.

EXERCISE 19.5 Write three sentences that follow the subject–verb–subject complement pattern. Underline the subject complement. Try to vary your linking verbs.

EXERCISE 19.6 Revise any of the following sentences in which the subject complement cannot work logically with its subject. First explain the problem with the original complement; then change the complement, not the subject. The complement is boldfaced.

1. Photography is an excellent **fun**.

2. Revising every paper in this class four times seems **exorbitant**.

3. Gerald felt **unconscionable** after arriving too late to say farewell.

4. Philosophy is **when** you read Plato and Aristotle.

5. Wearing baggy jeans quickly became **free and easy** among youngsters.

4. **Subject + verb (transitive) + indirect object + direct object.** An **indirect object** explains for whom or what an action is done or directed. As you can see in this pattern, indirect objects ordinarily precede direct objects.

Subject	Verb (transitive)	Indirect object	Direct object
The lawyer	found	the clerk	a job.
The storms	brought	local farmers	needed rain.
The children	told	their parents	stories.

If you have trouble understanding what an indirect object does in a sentence, turn it into the object of a prepositional phrase.

The lawyer found a job **for the clerk.**

The storms brought needed rain **to local farmers.**

The children told stories **to their parents.**

EXERCISE 19.7 In the following sentences, circle the indirect objects and underline the objects.

1. The IRS agent asked the auditor three tough questions.

2. The placement office finds students jobs after college.

3. Did you send Rosa, Peg, Lester, and Davida the same email message?

4. Give Daisy more cookies.

5. The distinguished senator gives proponents of the National Endowment for the Arts headaches.

EXERCISE 19.8 Write three sentences that follow the subject–verb–indirect object–direct object pattern. Circle the indirect object and underline the direct object.

5. **Subject + verb (transitive) + direct object + object complement.** Just as a subject complement modifies or explains a subject, an **object complement** does the same for the object of a sentence.

Subject	Verb (transitive)	Direct object	Object complement
The lawyer	called	the verdict	surprising.
The flood	caught	the town	napping.
The children	found	their spinach	vile.

EXERCISE 19.9 In the following sentences, underline the direct objects and circle the object complements.

1. Most men find football entertaining.

2. Thoroughbred horses often turn their wealthy owners poor.

3. Our careful preparation makes us lucky.

4. The mayor called the federal court decision against the city ordinance unfortunate.

5. The justices considered the mayor's appeal frivolous.

EXERCISE 19.10 Write three sentences that follow the subject–verb–direct object–object complement pattern. Underline the direct object and circle the subject complement.

2 Understand compound subjects, verbs, and objects.

You can develop sentences simply by expanding their subjects, verbs, or objects to include all the ideas you need to express. Such modifications are usually routine, but some writers do have problems punctuating the resulting sentences.

Compound subjects. Two subjects attached to the same verb are usually connected by the conjunction *and* or *or*. No comma is needed between these compound subjects.

> **Lawyers and judges** attended the seminar.
> **Storms or fires** ravage California each year.

When a third subject is added, the items are separated by commas (see Section 39c-3).

> **Storms, fires, and earthquakes** ravage California each year.

Subjects can also be expanded by expressions such as *neither . . . nor* and *either . . . or,* which are called **correlatives.**

> **Neither the judge nor the lawyer** attended the seminar.
> **Either fires or earthquakes** strike California each year.

Compound verbs. Single subjects can perform more than one action. When they do, the verbs attached to them are compound. Like nouns, verbs can be joined by *and, or,* or correlatives such as *either . . . or.* No comma should be used between two verbs that form a compound verb.

> The judge **confused and angered** the prosecutor.
> The earthquake **damaged or destroyed** many homes.
> Children **either like or hate** spinach.

When a third verb is added, the items are separated by commas.

> The judge **confused, angered, and embarrassed** the prosecutor.

Compound verbs can each take separate objects, expanding the sentence structure even more.

The judge **confused** *the jury* and **angered** *the prosecutor.*

The earthquake **damaged** *roads* and **destroyed** *homes.*

Compound objects. A verb may also have more than one object. Two objects attached to the same verb are usually connected by the conjunction *and* or *or.* No comma is needed between two objects; commas are required for three or more objects.

Lawyers attended **the seminar and the dinner.**

Forest fires ravage **California, Arizona, New Mexico, or Colorado** every year.

Objects can also be connected with correlatives.

Forest fires ravage **either California or New Mexico** every year.

19b
modif

Many variations of these elements are possible. But don't pile up more compound expressions than readers can handle easily. Sentences should always be readable.

TOO MANY COMPOUNDS
Both lawyers and judges attended the after-lunch seminars and discussion groups; broke for drinks, cocktails, and coffee in the late afternoon; returned for a film, a professional roundtable, and a business session; and then either went out to dinner or retired to their hotels.

REVISED FOR CLARITY
Both lawyers and judges attended the after-lunch seminars and discussion groups. **They** broke for drinks, cocktails, and coffee in the late afternoon **and then** returned for a film, a professional roundtable, and a business session. **Afterward,** they either went out to dinner or retired to their hotels.

19b What do modifiers do?

Modifiers are words, phrases, or clauses that expand what we know about subjects, verbs, or other sentence elements, including other modifiers and complete sentences. Although modifiers can cause problems, most writers use them routinely without difficulty (see Chapter 33). In fact, it would be hard to compose sentences without them. Even simple modifiers change the texture of sentences, while more complex modifiers increase your options for shaping sentences.

1 Use adjectives to modify nouns and pronouns. Adjectives describe and help to explain nouns and pronouns by specifying *how many, which size, what color, what condition, which one,* and so on. Single adjectives are usually placed before the terms they modify.

> The **angry** judge scowled at the **nervous** witness.

But adjectives often work in groups. Adjectives in a group are called **coordinate adjectives** when each one works on its own, describing different and unrelated aspects of a noun or pronoun.

> the undistinguished, tired-looking lawyer
> our cat, **shedding and overweight**

19b
modif

Placed before a noun or pronoun, coordinate adjectives can be linked either by conjunctions (usually *and*) or by commas. The order of the adjectives doesn't affect their meaning.

> The **angry, perspiring** judge scowled at the **balding and nervous** witness.

> The **perspiring, angry** judge scowled at the **nervous and balding** witness.

> The **tired and underpaid** jurors listened to a **tedious and awkward** interrogation.

> The **underpaid and tired** jurors listened to an **awkward and tedious** interrogation.

Coordinate adjectives may also follow the words they modify, giving variety to sentence rhythms.

> The judge, **angry and perspiring,** scowled at the witness, **balding and nervous.**

For a stylish variation, you can also move coordinate adjectives ahead of an article (*the*) at the beginning of a sentence.

> **Tired, bored, and underpaid,** the jurors listened to an endless interrogation.

Not all clusters of adjectives are coordinate. Often, groups of adjectives must follow a specific sequence to make sense. Changing their sequence produces expressions that are not *idiomatic;* that is, they don't sound right to a native English speaker.

> NOT IDIOMATIC   the wooden heavy gavel
> IDIOMATIC   the heavy wooden gavel

NOT IDIOMATIC a woolen green sweater
IDIOMATIC a green woolen sweater
NOT IDIOMATIC the American first satellite
IDIOMATIC the first American satellite

Adjectives in such groupings—which often include numbers—are not separated by commas.

The judge wielded a **heavy wooden** gavel.
The **first American** satellite was Explorer I.
The police rescued **two lucky** kayakers.

Adjectives (along with adverbs and nouns) can also form *compound* or *unit modifiers,* groups of words linked by hyphens that modify a noun (see Section 43b-5). The individual words in compound modifiers need each other; they often wouldn't make sense standing alone in front of a noun.

19b
modif

A **well-known** case would provide a **high-impact** precedent.
The **wine-dark** sea surged in the moonlight.

Finally, adjectives play an important role as subject complements and object complements (see Section 19a-1), modifying words to which they are joined by linking verbs.

The judge's decision seemed **eccentric.**
The children were **sleepy.**
The press called the jury **inept.**

EXERCISE 19.11 Rewrite each of the following sentences so that the adjectives in parentheses modify an appropriate noun or pronoun. Place the adjectives before or after the word they modify, and punctuate them correctly (for example, be sure to add hyphens to unit modifiers and to separate coordinate adjectives with commas or *and* as necessary).

1. The elm trees once common throughout North America have disappeared, victims of disease. (*towering; graceful; Dutch elm*)

2. This infection destroys the vascular system of the elm, causing trees to become husks in a few short weeks. (*fungal; relentless; mature; thriving; leafless*)

3. Few parks in the United States can match the diversity of New York's Central Park, with its zoo, gardens and fields, ponds and lakes, and museum. (*great urban; sizable; pleasant; glistening; world class*)

4. The city seems to stop at the edge of the park where New Yorkers can stroll quietly under a canopy of shade trees or strap on roller blades and buzz tourists. (*noisy; crowded; sprawling; business suited or casual; cool; green; curious; delighted*)

5. Bankers, show people, and street people alike jostle shoulders and shopping bags in this oasis. (*wealthy; glittering; down on their luck; refreshing; urban*)

2 Use adverbs to modify verbs, adjectives, and other adverbs. Adverbs in sentences explain *how, when, where,* and *to what degree* things happen.

19b
modif

ADVERBS THAT MODIFY VERBS
The prosecutor *spoke* **eloquently** to the jury.
Immediately, the defense attorney *replied.*
The jury *tried* **hard** to follow their summaries.

ADVERBS THAT MODIFY ADJECTIVES
Tornadoes seem **freakishly** *unpredictable.*
Tornado chasing remains **quite** *popular.*

ADVERBS THAT MODIFY OTHER ADVERBS
The reading program has improved **very** *considerably.*
Less *easily* appreciated is a new interest in music at the school.

Adverbs increase your options in constructing sentences because they typically can be put in more places than adjectives, enabling you to experiment with sentence structure and rhythm. All three versions of the following sentence convey the same information, but they do so in subtly different ways.

The news reporter **passionately and repeatedly** defended the integrity of her story.

Passionately and repeatedly, the news reporter defended the integrity of her story.

The news reporter defended the integrity of her story **passionately and repeatedly.**

But this very flexibility causes significant problems. Be sure to review Section 33f on the appropriate placement of adverbs, especially *only.*

EXERCISE 19.12 Rewrite the following sentences so that each adverb in parentheses modifies an appropriate verb, adjective, or adverb. Notice which adverbs work best in one position only and which can be relocated more freely in a sentence.

1. The elm trees once common throughout North America have disappeared, victims of disease. (*sadly; quite; almost; completely*)

2. This lethal infection destroys the vascular system of the elm, causing trees to become husks in a few short weeks. (*nearly; always; completely*)

3. The delicate paintings had not been packed, so they arrived damaged. (*extremely; well; severely*)

4. Annoyed, the senator replied to the reporter in an angry tone. (*visibly; unusually*)

5. We left the photo shop poorer but better equipped for difficult telephoto shots. (*considerably; much; extremely*)

19b
modif

■ **3 Understand that nouns can operate as modifiers.** In some sentences you may find words that look like nouns but act like adjectives, modifying other words. Don't be confused: nouns often work as modifiers.

> We ordered the **sausage** plate and a **vegetable** sampler.
> The **instrument** cluster glowed red at night.

Proper nouns can serve as modifiers too.

> The choir was preparing for the **Christmas** service.
> We ordered a **New York** strip steak.

EXERCISE 19.13 In the following sentences, underline any nouns that function as modifiers. Discuss disputed cases with colleagues.

1. The Atlanta Braves, Washington Redskins, and Cleveland Indians are sports teams whose names occasionally stir controversy among Native American political interest groups.

2. Car insurance is getting so expensive in urban areas that many college students have to rely on the city bus.

3. Ike signed up for the yoga class because his doctor told him that doing the cobra stretch and the sun salutation would strengthen his injured back muscles.

4. At Martha's Fourth of July party, the Vienna sausage didn't sit well with the Boston cream pie and strawberry ice cream.

5. I'm not sure which television station carries *The Drew Carey Show*.

4 Understand that verbals can operate as modifiers.

Especially common as modifiers are participles—words like *dazzling, frightening, broken*. Because participles are based on verbs, they give energy and snap to sentences.

The waiter brought a **sizzling** steak on a **steaming** bed of rice.
The margaritas arrived **frozen,** not on the rocks.
The officer, **smiling,** wrote us a $100 ticket.
Trembling, I opened the **creaking** door.

For more about participle and infinitive phrases, see Section 19c-2.

EXERCISE 19.14 In the following sentences, underline any participles that function as modifiers. Discuss disputed cases with colleagues.

1. I. M. Pei is one of America's most original and inspiring architects.

2. Born in Guangzhou, China, in 1919, Pei came to the United States in 1935 and became a naturalized citizen in 1954.

3. Pei is responsible for some of the most startling and admired buildings of our era.

4. Pei's work includes the glittering and much debated pyramid that now serves as the main entrance to the Louvre, one of the leading museums in the world.

5. Yet Pei can also count among his commissions Cleveland's Rock and Roll Hall of Fame, a daring work poised on the shores of Lake Erie.

19c
phrase

19c What are phrases?

Technically, a **phrase** is a group of related words without a subject and a finite verb, but this definition is hard to follow. It's probably more helpful to appreciate phrases in action, doing their part to give shape to sentences.

1 Understand prepositional phrases.

Among the more mundane of sentence elements, a *prepositional phrase* consists of a preposition and its object, either a noun or a pronoun. The object can be modified.

Preposition	Modifier (optional)	Object(s)
to		Jeff and me
in	your own	words
beyond	the farthest	mountain

It's easy to generate examples of prepositional phrases: *off the sofa, on the hard drive, across the miles, under the spreading chestnut tree, over the far horizon, from me, for her.* Just try writing a paragraph without using a prepositional phrase and you'll appreciate how essential they are to establishing relationships within sentences. Don't, however, mistake prepositional phrases with *to* (*to Starbucks, to Lila*) for infinitives or infinitive phrases, which include a verb form (*to see, to watch the stars, to be happy*). For more on prepositions and infinitives see Sections 31b and 27a-1.

19c
phrase

The power of prepositional phrases resides in their flexibility and simplicity. Moving a prepositional phrase into an unexpected slot gets it noticed. Consider what happens to the first sentence in this paragraph when its prepositional phrase is repositioned.

ORIGINAL — The power of prepositional phrases resides in their flexibility and simplicity.

PREPOSITIONAL PHRASE MOVED — In their flexibility and simplicity, the power of prepositional phrases resides.

The sentence sounds just different (some might say awkward) enough to cause readers to pause—which may or may not be the effect you wish to achieve. And that's the point: where you put prepositional phrases can influence readers enough to make a difference. For additional discussion, see Section 20c-7.

EXERCISE 19.15 Study the following passages and discuss the effect of relocating the boldfaced prepositional phrases within the speeches. How would the style of the passage be changed—if at all?

1. **Upon this battle** depends the survival of Christian civilization. **Upon it** depends our own British life, and the long continuity of our institutions and our Empire. The whole fury and might of the enemy must very soon be turned **on us**. Hitler knows he will have to break us in this island or lose the war.

—Winston Churchill

2. With malice toward none, with charity for all, with firmness in the right, let us strive on to finish the work we are in, to bind up the nation's wounds, to care for him who shall have borne the battle and for his widow and his orphan, to do all which may achieve and cherish a just and lasting peace among ourselves and with all nations.

—Abraham Lincoln

2 Appreciate the versatility of verbals and verbal phrases.

Verbals are verb forms that can act as nouns, adjectives, or adverbs (see Chapter 27). Verbals can stand alone, or they can form phrases by taking objects, complements, or modifiers.

19c
phrase

	Verbal	Verbal phrase
Infinitive	to serve	to serve the sick
	to prevent	to prevent forest fires
Gerund	serving	serving the sick [is]
	preventing	preventing forest fires [is]
Participle	serving	serving without complaint,
	prevented	prevented from helping,

Verbals and verb phrases that act as nouns can serve as subjects or direct objects. As modifiers, verbals can function as adverbs or adjectives. Although verbals may seem complicated, you'll recognize the roles they play in sentences.

Verbals as subjects. Both infinitives and gerunds can act as subjects in sentences. On their own, they don't look much different from other subjects.

> INFINITIVE AS SUBJECT
> **To serve** was the doctor's ambition.

> GERUND AS SUBJECT
> **Serving** was the doctor's ambition.

But when they expand into phrases, they can be harder to recognize. Yet they remain subjects and can be either simple or compound.

> INFINITIVE PHRASES AS SUBJECTS
> **To serve the sick** was the doctor's ambition.
>
> **To serve the sick and to comfort the afflicted** were the doctor's ambitions.

GERUND PHRASES AS SUBJECTS

Serving the sick was the doctor's ambition.

Serving the sick and comforting the afflicted were the doctor's ambitions.

Verbals as objects. Both infinitives and gerunds can act as objects in sentences. On their own, they don't look much different from other objects.

INFINITIVE AS DIRECT OBJECT

The lawyer loved **to object.**

GERUND AS DIRECT OBJECT

The lawyer loved **objecting.**

As phrases, verbals can seem complicated in their role as direct objects. Yet they play that role like any other noun, simple or compound.

INFINITIVE PHRASES AS DIRECT OBJECTS

The lawyer chose **to object to the motion.**

The lawyer chose **to object to the motion and to move for a mistrial.**

GERUND PHRASES AS DIRECT OBJECTS

The lawyer loved **objecting to the prosecutor's motions.**

The lawyer loved **objecting to the prosecutor's motions and winning concessions from the judge.**

Verbals as complements. Both infinitives and gerunds can act as complements in sentences.

INFINITIVE AS SUBJECT COMPLEMENT

To know Rebecca was **to love her.**

GERUND AS OBJECT COMPLEMENT

The IRS caught Elmo **cheating on his taxes.**

Verbals as adjectives. You'll frequently want to use participles and participle phrases to modify nouns and pronouns in your sentences.

PARTICIPLES AS ADJECTIVES

Frowning, the instructor stopped her lecture.

The **suspended** fraternity appealed to the dean.

PARTICIPLE PHRASES AS ADJECTIVES

Frowning at us, the instructor stopped her lecture.

The fraternity, **suspended for underage drinking,** appealed to the dean.

We kept close to the trail, **not knowing the terrain well.**

Notice the freedom you have in placing participle phrases. You do want to be certain, however, that readers can have no doubt what a particular phrase modifies.

Infinitives, too, can function as adjectives, although it can be difficult to perceive the infinitive in this role as a modifier, providing details.

INFINITIVES AS ADJECTIVES
The manager had many items **to purchase**. modifies *items*
Reasons **to stay** were few. modifies *reasons*

INFINITIVE PHRASES AS ADJECTIVES
The manager had many items **to purchase for the grand opening**.
modifies *items*

Reasons **to stay calm** were few. modifies *reasons*

Verbals as adverbs. Infinitives and infinitive phrases can act like adverbs, answering such questions as *why, how, to what degree,* and so on.

INFINITIVES AS ADVERBS
Difficult **to please**, Martha rarely enjoyed movies. modifies *difficult*
The sedan seemed built **to last**. modifies *built*

INFINITIVE PHRASES AS ADVERBS
The gardener dug a trench **to stop the spread of oak wilt**.
modifies *dug*

The Senate recessed **to give its members a summer vacation**.
modifies *recessed*

The pilot found it impossible **to see the runway in the fog**.
modifies *impossible*

EXERCISE 19.16 Underline all verbals in the following sentences and then indicate whether they function as subjects, objects, complements, adjectives, or adverbs.

1. Waving at the crowd, the winner of the marathon took a victory lap.

2. The waiter certainly seemed eager to please us.

3. The salesperson enjoyed demonstrating the self-closing door on the minivan.

4. Harriet bought an awning to reduce the light streaming through her bay windows.

5. To cherish the weak and the dying was Mother Teresa's mission in life.

6. Reasons to applaud during the candidate's speech were few.

7. Finding an appealing painting at a reasonable price was impossible.

8. The clerk caught Liza sampling the produce.

9. Surprised by the storm front's ferocity, weather forecasters revised their predictions.

10. We decided we finally had sufficient reason to object.

3 Understand absolute phrases. Absolutes are versatile phrases that modify whole sentences rather than individual words. They are constructed from participles or infinitives. When absolute phrases are based on participles, they always include a subject and may include modifiers and other elements.

> Our representatives will, **time permitting,** read the entire petition to the city council.
>
> **The supply craft having docked,** the astronauts on the *International Space Station* were ready for their space walk.
>
> Our plane arrived early, **the winds having been favorable.**

When the participle is a form of *to be,* it can often be omitted for a more economical or elegant expression.

> **The winds [being] favorable,** our plane arrived early.

Absolutes based on infinitives don't require a noun or pronoun.

> **To speak frankly,** we are facing the gravest crisis in the history of this company.
>
> Your buzz cut, **to be honest,** would look better on a coconut.

Because absolutes are not attached to particular words, you can place them exactly where they work best in a sentence. Absolutes can add sophistication to your sentences. They are worth trying.

EXERCISE 19.17 Turn the phrases in parentheses into absolutes and incorporate them into the full sentences preceding them.

> EXAMPLE   The senator's amendment to the tax bill would fund a worthless pork barrel project. (*to put it bluntly*)
>
> REVISION   The senator's amendment to the tax bill would, to put it bluntly, fund a worthless pork barrel project.

1. Many newspaper reporters don't know beans about their beats. (*to speak candidly*)

2. We should be able to take the launch to the island. (*the weather having cleared*)

3. Johnson became a viable candidate for governor again. (*the tide of public opinion having turned*)

4. Work in the electronic classrooms had to stop for the day. (*the entire network down*)

5. We hurried from exhibit to exhibit at the art museum. (*the time being late*)

19c
phrase

▮ 4 Appreciate appositive phrases.

An **appositive** is a noun or noun phrase that restates or expands the meaning of the words it modifies. Think of appositives as variations on a theme, a second way of naming nouns and giving them more texture. Appositives are placed immediately after the words they modify and are usually surrounded by commas (see Section 39b-2).

> Napoleon, the **Emperor of France,** crowned himself.

> Death Valley, **the largest national park in the continental United States,** blooms with wildflowers in the spring.

Gerund phrases can stand as appositives too.

> Alchemy, **changing base metals into more precious ones,** is discredited medieval lore.

Appositives are also routinely introduced by words or phrases such as *or, as, for example, such as,* and *in other words.*

> Dachshunds, **or wiener dogs,** are growing in popularity.

> Katharine Hepburn's best movies, **including** *The African Queen* **and** *The Philadelphia Story,* are classics of American cinema.

> The test actually measures college survival skills, **that is, the ability to pass multiple-choice examinations.**

Most appositives are interchangeable with the words they modify: delete those modified terms and the sentence still makes sense.

APPOSITIVES AS MODIFIERS
Abraham Lincoln, **the first Republican President,** presided over the Civil War.

Halloween, **All Hallows' Eve,** comes two days before All Souls' Day, **also known as the Day of the Dead.**

MODIFIED TERMS REPLACED BY APPOSITIVES

The first Republican President presided over the Civil War.

All Hallows' Eve comes two days before **the Day of the Dead.**

Some appositives—often proper nouns—can't be deleted without blurring the meaning of a sentence. These appositives are not surrounded by commas (see Section 39d-5).

Bob Dylan's masterpiece *Blonde on Blonde* is a double album.

Nixon **the diplomat** is more respected by historians than Nixon **the politician.**

Like absolutes, appositive phrases can give your prose depth and grace.

19d
clause

EXERCISE 19.18 Turn the phrase(s) in parentheses into appositives and incorporate them into the full sentences preceding them. Be sure to use the right punctuation.

EXAMPLE   Sally Ride served on the presidential commission that investigated the 1986 explosion of the space shuttle. (*America's first woman astronaut;* Challenger)

REVISION   Sally Ride, America's first woman astronaut, served on the presidential commission that investigated the explosion of the space shuttle *Challenger.*

1. Rudolph Giuliani first gained prominence as a federal prosecutor. (*107th mayor of New York City*)

2. In Anasazi architecture, a prominent feature is the kiva. (*a covered circular enclosure sunk in the ground and used for religious ceremonies and community meetings*)

3. The technique called pure fresco produces enduring images such as those on the ceiling of the Sistine Chapel. (*painting with plaster stained with pigment; Michelangelo's masterpiece*)

4. The gizzard of a bird is thick with muscles for grinding food. (*a part of the digestive system*)

5. Shakespeare's masterpiece includes three witches. (Macbeth; *the Weird Sisters*)

19d What do clauses do in sentences?

Clauses are groups of related words that have subjects and verbs. As such, they are the framework for most sentences, the parts to which other modifying words and phrases are attached. The four basic sentence types (*simple, compound, complex,* and *compound-complex*) are based on some combination of independent and dependent clauses (see Section 19e). Writers who don't understand clauses often have problems with sentence boundaries (see Sections 38a-2 and 38a-3) or with composing longer sentences.

19d

clause

■ 1 Understand independent clauses. An **independent clause** can stand alone as a complete sentence. Most independent clauses have an identifiable subject and a predicate (that is, a verb plus its auxiliaries and modifiers). Sometimes a subject is understood and is not stated in the clause.

Subject	Predicate
The house	burned.
The dreams we had	came true today.
The children	caught colds.
[You]	Come here at once.

EXERCISE 19.19 Circle the subject and underline the predicate in the following independent clauses. If the subject is understood, write the word *understood* as the subject in parentheses after the sentence.

1. The wood on the deck warped after only one summer.

2. Jeremy has been trying to reach you all day.

3. Attend the rally this afternoon.

4. Keeping focused on schoolwork is hard on weekends.

5. Be careful.

■ 2 Understand dependent clauses. A **dependent clause** is one that cannot stand alone as a complete sentence. Many dependent clauses that have identifiable subjects and predicates are introduced by subordinating conjunctions—words such as *although, because, if, until, when, whenever, while*—that place the dependent clause in relationship to another independent clause.

Subordinating conjunction	Subject	Predicate
When	the house	burned . . .
If	the dreams we had	came true today . . .
Because	the children	caught colds . . .

Dependent clauses can have various functions in a sentence. Easiest to understand are those that act as adjectives or adverbs. Slightly more intricate are dependent clauses that act as nouns (and serve as subjects, objects, or complements). Note that all dependent clauses must work with independent clauses to create complete sentences.

19d
clause

Adjective clauses. **Adjective clauses,** also known as *relative clauses,* attach themselves to nouns or pronouns using one of the relative pronouns: *who, whom, whomever, whose, that, which.*

> Actress Gwyneth Paltrow, **who was born in Los Angeles,** moved to New York when she was 11 years old.
>
> Venus is the planet **that shines brightest in the sky.**
>
> The new engine, **which is Mercedes-Benz's first V-6,** has a dozen spark plugs and three valves per cylinder.

The adverbs *when* and *where* can introduce adjective clauses when the resulting clauses modify nouns, not verbs.

> The immigrants settled in those California cities **where jobs were plentiful.** clause modifies the noun *cities*, not the verb *settled*
>
> We enjoy the winter **when the snow falls.**
> clause modifies the noun *winter*, not the verb *enjoy*

Adjective clauses are surrounded by commas when they are considered nonessential—that is, when they can be removed from a sentence without destroying its coherence. When clauses are essential to the meaning of a sentence, they are not surrounded by commas (see Section 39d-5).

One caution about adjective clauses: sentences sometimes derail when a writer mistakes an adjective clause for a main clause.

INCORRECT	Talks with North Korea **which** may create a situation favorable to the emergence of a middle class that will push for democratization.
REVISED	Talks with North Korea may create a situation favorable to the emergence of a middle class that will push for democratization.

EXERCISE 19.20 Add an adjective clause to each of the following sentences at the point indicated. Remember that adjective clauses are usually introduced by *who, whom, whomever, whose, that,* or *which.* An adjective clause may also begin with *where* or *when* if it modifies a noun, not a verb.

1. All the students in class who . . . said they supported the Democratic party's proposals.

2. But everyone in the class who . . . opposed the Democrats' policies.

3. Companies that . . . are prospering more today than firms that. . . .

4. The original *Star Wars* trilogy, which . . . , has been joined by a new series of films in the saga.

5. Teens prefer to congregate in places where. . . .

6. A person whose . . . is unlikely to find a job quickly.

7. Tom Cruise, who . . . , has been an Oscar nominee several times.

8. Tom Cruise, whom . . . , remains a top box-office draw.

9. Many youngsters dislike September when. . . .

10. The Rolling Stones remain the rock band that. . . .

19d
clause

Adverb clauses. **Adverb clauses** work just like adverbs, modifying verbs, adjectives, and other adverbs. They are easy to spot since they are introduced by one of the many subordinating conjunctions, words such as *after, although, as, before, if, since, though, until, when,* and *while.*

> Lillian left **before the hail fell.** modifies the verb *left*
>
> The bookcase was not as heavy **as we had expected.**
> modifies the adjective *heavy*
>
> Hubert spoke haltingly **whenever a girl looked him in the eye.**
> modifies the adverb *haltingly*

Sometimes an adverb or subordinate clause seems to modify an entire sentence or a group of words.

> **Although the stock market plunged,** investors had high hopes for a quick recovery.

As subordinate clauses, adverb clauses play a notable role in crafting powerful sentences. For much more about subordination, see Section 19g.

EXERCISE 19.21 Add an adverb clause to each of the following sentences at the point indicated. Remember that adverb clauses are introduced by subordinating conjunctions such as *although, before, since, unless,* and many others.

1. Even though . . . , Americans vote in record low numbers.

2. Many young people put little faith in the social security system since. . . .

3. Because . . . , many students come to college knowing how to operate computers.

4. If . . . , the polar ice caps will melt and the level of the oceans will rise.

5. Although they . . . , surprising numbers of children still smoke.

19d
clause

Noun clauses. Whole clauses that act as nouns are quite common. Such clauses act as subjects or objects, not as modifiers.

> **How a computer works** is beyond my understanding.
> noun clause as subject
>
> The FAA report did not explain **why the jets collided.**
> noun clause as direct object
>
> The employment agency found **whoever applied** a job.
> noun clause as indirect object
>
> You may speak to **whomever you wish.**
> noun clause as an object of a preposition

Because noun clauses are distinctive structures, they can work beautifully in parallel constructions (see Section 19h), as this passage from Abraham Lincoln's Gettysburg Address illustrates.

> The world will little note, nor long remember, **what we say here;** but it can never forget **what they did here.**

EXERCISE 19.22 Underline all the noun clauses in the following sentences. Then explain the function of each clause, as either a subject or an object.

1. What politicians say often matters much less than how they say it.

2. Whoever sent a letter of condolence should receive a prompt reply from us.

3. Why so many people care so much about celebrities is beyond my comprehension.

4. Someone had better explain how the dogs got loose.

5. Where you go for a vacation reveals a great deal about who you are.

19e What types of sentences can you write?

While you'll rarely revise sentences just to make a *simple* sentence *compound* or a *compound* sentence *complex,* recognizing these terms will make it easier for you to diagnose problems in your sentences and to talk about them with peer editors. The most familiar sentence types are all built from just two basic components: independent clauses and subordinate clauses (see Section 19d).

	one independent clause
SIMPLE SENTENCE	**Windows rattled.**

	independent clause + independent clause
COMPOUND SENTENCE	**Windows rattled** and **doors shook.**

	dependent clause(s) + one independent clause
COMPLEX SENTENCE	*As the storm blew,* **windows rattled.**

	dependent clause(s) + two or more independent clauses
COMPOUND-COMPLEX SENTENCE	*As the storm blew,* **windows rattled** and **doors shook.**

■ 1   Use simple sentences to express ideas clearly and directly. Simple sentences can attract the attention of readers with the power of their single independent clauses.

Jesus wept.
I come to bury Caesar, not to praise him.

But don't assume that simple sentences will necessarily be short or without ornament.

NASA, the federal agency in charge of space exploration, has no current plans for a moon base or for human missions to Mars and Venus, the planets closest to earth in both size and distance.

As you can see, simple sentences can be expanded by compounding or modifying their subjects, verbs, or objects.

ORIGINAL SENTENCE	Extreme sports worry parents.
VERB EXPANDED	Extreme sports **have captured the attention of a fascinated media but worry many parents.**

| OBJECT EXPANDED | Extreme sports worry **police, health-care workers, and many parents.** |
| EXPANDED SENTENCE | Increasingly popular among teenagers, extreme sports such as BMX biking, bungee jumping, and skateboarding have captured the attention of a fascinated media but worry police, health-care workers, and many parents. |

Despite its increased length, the final sentence still has only one independent clause and no dependent clauses, so it remains a simple sentence.

EXERCISE 19.23 Working in small groups, expand the following simple sentences by compounding subjects, objects, and verbs and adding modifying words and phrases as necessary. You may replace a general term (*aircraft*) with particular examples (*helicopters, jets, gliders*). But do not add either full independent or dependent clauses. Make sure the final versions remain simple sentences.

| EXAMPLE | Bugs scare people. |
| EXPANDED | Tiny spiders, harmless caterpillars, and frail mantises sometimes terrify or even paralyze full-grown adults, from PhDs in physics to NFL linebackers. |

1. Pets enrich our lives.

2. The sciences challenge our assumptions.

3. Many activities can damage our health.

2 Use compound and complex sentences to express relationships between clauses.
These relationships involve *coordination* when independent clauses are joined to other independent clauses.

The rain fell for days, **but** the city's reservoirs were not filled.
Our fuel pump failed, **so** we were stranded on the expressway.

They involve *subordination* when dependent clauses are joined to independent clauses.

Although the rain fell for days, the city's reservoirs were not filled.
Because our fuel pump failed, we were stranded on the expressway.

To write effective sentences, you need to handle both coordination (see Section 19f) and subordination (see Section 19g) confidently.

19f How does coordination build sentences?

When you coordinate two or more independent clauses, you connect or associate ideas. Independent clauses can stand on their own grammatically, but they grow richer when they enter into coordinate relationships. These relationships can be established in several ways: with *coordinating conjunctions;* with various *correlative constructions;* with semicolons, colons, and dashes; and with *conjunctive adverbs.*

19f
coord

1 Use coordinating conjunctions to join independent clauses. The **coordinating conjunctions** are *and, or, nor, for, but, yet,* and *so.* They express fundamental relationships between ideas: similarity, addition, or sequence (*and*); exception, difference, or contrast (*or, nor, but, yet*); and process or causality (*for, so*). Commas ordinarily precede coordinating conjunctions (see Section 39c-1).

> The solemn service ended, **and** we went home immediately.
> sequence
>
> SAT scores in math rose nationally, **but** verbal scores dropped.
> contrast
>
> I got a high score on the final examination, **so** I passed geology.
> causality

Different coordinating conjunctions give readers different signals, so select them carefully. Many writers habitually choose *and* even when another conjunction might express a relationship more precisely.

VAGUE	The statue's hair is carved in early archaic style, **and** its feet show traits of late archaic sculpture.
MORE PRECISE	The statue's hair is carved in early archaic style, **yet** its feet show traits of late archaic sculpture.
VAGUE	Michelangelo's Sistine Chapel ceiling is among the greatest works of Renaissance art, **and** conservators approached the task of cleaning it with great caution.
MORE PRECISE	Michelangelo's Sistine Chapel ceiling is among the greatest works of Renaissance art, **so** conservators approached the task of cleaning it with great caution.

Coordinating conjunctions are also useful for combining sentences that are short, choppy, or repetitive. Linking sentences this way can produce more readable and mature writing.

CHOPPY AND REPETITIVE	We liked the features of the computer. It was too expensive for our budgets. We thought it looked complicated.
COMBINED	We liked the features of the computer, **but** it was too expensive for our budgets **and** looked complicated.

Relying too much on coordinating conjunctions (especially *and*) to link ideas can be stylistically dangerous. A string of clauses linked by *and*s quickly grows tedious and should be revised, often by making some clauses subordinate (see Section 19g).

19f
coord

TOO MANY *AND*S	The French physician Nostradamus was active in fighting the plague in the sixteenth century **and** he grew so interested in astrology that he wrote a book of prophecies called *Centuries* **and** it has fascinated readers ever since.
REVISED	The French physician Nostradamus, active in fighting the plague in the sixteenth century, grew so interested in astrology that he wrote a book of prophecies called *Centuries* which has fascinated readers ever since.

EXERCISE 19.24 Use coordinating conjunctions (*and, or, nor, for, but, yet, so*) to create compound sentences by linking the following pairs of independent clauses. Be sure to punctuate the sentences correctly.

1. The stock market finally rose. Investors remained nervous.

2. Citizens' groups invest time and money on get-out-the-vote campaigns. Many voters still skip general elections.

3. Vitamin C is good for colds. Vitamin E keeps the skin in good condition.

4. Most Americans get their news from television. News anchors are powerful people.

5. Tough drunk-driving laws are fair. There is no reason to tolerate inebriated drivers on the highway.

2 Use correlative constructions to join independent clauses. Correlatives are conjunctions that work in pairs, expressions such as *if . . . then, either . . . or, just as . . . so,* and *not only . . . but also.* Like coordinating conjunctions, correlatives can be used to form compound sentences that ask readers to examine two ideas side by side.

> **Just as** Napoleon faced defeat in Russia, **so** Hitler saw his dreams of conquest evaporate at the siege of Leningrad.

> **Not only** is Captain Janeway a better leader than Kirk, **but** she is **also** a more interesting human being.

19f
coord

EXERCISE 19.25 Create compound sentences by finishing the correlative construction begun for you. Be sure that the sentence you produce is a compound sentence, one with two independent clauses. Punctuate the sentence correctly.

1. If I agree to read *War and Peace* by the end of the summer, then you . . .

2. Either the new owners of the former Soviet Union's nuclear weapons will safeguard these deadly stockpiles, or . . .

3. Just as eating too much fat contributes to poor physical health, so . . .

4. Not only does the First Amendment protect speech, but it also . . .

3 Use semicolons, colons, and dashes to link independent clauses. Semicolons usually join independent clauses roughly balanced in importance and closely associated in meaning.

> We expected chaos; we found catastrophe.

> The eyes of the nation were suddenly on the Supreme Court; the nine justices could not ignore the weight of public opinion.

Colons are more directive than semicolons. They imply that the second independent clause explains, exemplifies, or expands on the first.

> There was a lesson in the indictment: even small acts have consequences.

Like colons, dashes can function as conjunctions, connecting clauses with verve and energy. Some writers and editors, however, object to dashes used this way.

Expect George Ratliff's new film to cause controversy —the theme is bold and provocative.

The cathedral of Notre Dame was restored in the nineteenth century —its facade had suffered damage during the French Revolution.

See Chapters 40 and 43 for more on semicolons, colons, and dashes.

EXERCISE 19.26 Use a semicolon, a colon, or a dash to link the following independent clauses. Be prepared to explain why you chose each form of linkage.

1. Don't feel sorry for the spare and thorny plants you see in a desert. They don't want or need more water.

2. Barren stalks, wicked thorns, and waxy spines are their adaptations to a harsh environment. Such features conserve water or protect the plants from desert animals and birds.

3. Spring rains can create an astonishing desert spectacle. Cacti and other plants explode into colorful bloom.

4. Even the dour prickly pear bears handsome flowers. You've got to see the display to believe it.

5. Many animals call the desert home, too, from tiny lizards to scrawny coyotes. They are just as well adapted as the plants.

19f
coord

4 Use conjunctive adverbs with semicolons to join independent clauses.
Conjunctive adverbs are words such as *consequently, however, moreover, nevertheless, similarly,* and *therefore.* Like any adverb, they can appear at various places in a sentence. But often the adverb follows a semicolon, illuminating the relationship between clauses and holding our attention.

Members of the zoning board appreciated the developer's arguments; **however,** they rejected her rezoning request.

The muffler was leaking dangerous fumes; **moreover,** the brake linings were growing thin.

The comma that typically follows a conjunctive adverb in these constructions also gives weight to the word or phrase.

Note that it is the semicolon, not the adverb, that actually links the independent clauses. That connection becomes more obvious when the conjunctive adverb is moved.

Members of the zoning board appreciated the developer's arguments; they rejected her rezoning request, **however.**

The muffler was leaking dangerous fumes; the brake linings, **moreover,** were growing thin.

The punctuation surrounding conjunctive adverbs can be confusing. See Section 40a-3 for more details.

19f
coord

EXERCISE 19.27 Use a semicolon and the conjunctive adverb in parentheses to link the following independent clauses. To gain practice punctuating this tricky construction, use the form illustrated in the example—with the semicolon followed immediately by the conjunctive adverb, followed by a comma.

EXAMPLE   The aircraft lost an engine in flight. It landed safely. (*however*)

REVISED   The aircraft lost an engine in flight; however, it landed safely.

1. Ordinary books are still more convenient than most computerized texts. They employ a technology that doesn't go out of date as quickly—paper. (*moreover*)

2. Most people would save money by using public transportation. They elect to use their private automobiles for daily commuting. (*nevertheless*)

3. American colonists resented England's interference in their political and commercial lives. The 13 colonies decided to fight for independence. (*therefore*)

4. German and Japanese automakers discovered that they could build quality products cheaper in North America than at home. Foreign computer manufacturers decided to build silicon-chip plants in the United States. (*similarly*)

5. Many cities have been unable to meet air-quality standards. Tougher air-pollution measures have been imposed on their factories and drivers. (*consequently*)

EXERCISE 19.28 Build coordinate sentences by combining the following independent clauses. You may use coordinating conjunctions, correlatives, conjunctive adverbs, semicolons, or colons. Be sure to get the punctuation right.

> EXAMPLE   Pencils were invented in the sixteenth cen-
>   tury. Erasers were not added to them until
>   1858.
>
> COORDINATION Pencils were invented in the sixteenth century;
>   however, erasers were not added to them until
>   1858.

1. Today, French Impressionist paintings are favorites among art lovers. The public loudly rejected them at their debut in the nineteenth century.

2. Painters such as Renoir and Monet wanted art to depict life. They painted common scenes and ordinary people.

3. Many critics of the time were disturbed by the Impressionists' banal subjects. They thought the Impressionists' paintings themselves looked crude and unfinished.

4. The official Salon refused to hang the Impressionists' works. The painters were forced to exhibit independently.

5. The Impressionists refused to abandon their examination of modern life. They refused to change their style to please the critics.

19g
subord

19g How does subordination build sentences?

Use subordination to create complex or compound-complex sentences. Subordinating conjunctions provide the link between main ideas (independent clauses) and secondary ones (dependent or subordinate clauses). Subordination can be achieved with the aid of relative pronouns or subordinating conjunctions. The relative pronouns are *that, what, whatever, which, who, whom, whomever,* and *whose.*

Subordinating conjunctions are more numerous and suggest a wide variety of relationships; see Chart 19.1 on the next page. For more on subordinating conjunctions see Section 19d-2.

Chart 19.1

Subordinating Conjunctions		
after	in order that	unless
although	now that	until
as	once	when
as if	provided	whenever
as though	rather than	where
because	since	whereas
before	so that	wherever
even if	than	whether
even though	that	which
if	though	while
if only	till	

19g
subord

A subordinating conjunction or a relative pronoun turns an independent clause into a dependent clause that cannot stand alone as a sentence.

INDEPENDENT	I wrote the paper.
DEPENDENT	**While** I wrote the paper . . .
DEPENDENT	The paper **that** I wrote . . .

1 Use subordination to clarify relationships between clauses.

Like most tools for building sentences, subordination provides options for stating and clarifying thoughts. So it's probably misleading to regard the independent clause in a subordinate construction as always more important or more weighty than the dependent clause. In fact, the clauses work together to establish a complex relationship—of time, causality, consequence, contigency, contrast, and so on.

USING SUBORDINATION TO EXPLAIN *WHO* OR *WHAT*

VAGUE	The *Morte D'Arthur* includes stories about the knights of the Round Table. It was the work of Sir Thomas Malory.
CLEARER	The *Morte D'Arthur,* **which** was the work of Sir Thomas Malory, includes stories about the knights of the Round Table.

USING SUBORDINATION TO EXPLAIN *UNDER WHAT CONDITIONS*

VAGUE	Many people go into debt. Credit is easy to get.
CLEARER	**If** credit is easy to get, many people go into debt.

USING SUBORDINATION TO CLARIFY *CAUSALITY*

VAGUE   The film enjoyed a brisk summer box office. It won an Academy Award last March.

CLEARER   The film enjoyed a brisk summer box office **because** it won an Academy Award last March.

USING SUBORDINATION TO HIGHLIGHT *CONTRAST*

VAGUE   Members of Congress often campaign for a balanced budget. Most of them jealously protect projects in their own districts from cuts in federal spending.

CLEARER   **Although** members of Congress often campaign for a balanced budget, most of them jealously protect projects in their own districts from cuts in federal spending.

19g
subord

2 Use subordination to shift the emphasis of sentences.

Generally readers will focus on ideas in your independent clauses. Compare the following sentences, both equally good but with slightly different emphases due to changes in subordination.

> **While** the Supreme Court usually declares efforts to limit the First Amendment unconstitutional, Congress regularly acts to ban forms of speech most citizens find offensive.

> The Supreme Court usually declares efforts to limit the First Amendment unconstitutional, **even though** Congress regularly acts to ban forms of speech most people find offensive.

The first sentence directs readers to consider the efforts of Congress to rein in the First Amendment; the second sentence gives more emphasis to the Supreme Court. The differences are small but significant. Notice the same kind of shift in focus in the following pair of sentences.

> Jared had never walked a picket line, **even though** he had been a staunch union member for twenty years.

> **Even though** Jared had never walked a picket line, he had been a staunch union member for twenty years.

3 Use subordination to expand sentences.
You can often use subordination to combine simple clauses into more graceful or powerful sentences.

CHOPPY	The running back had an ankle injury. He chalked up a hundred-yard afternoon. He had been laid off for two months too.
SUBORDINATED	**Although** he had endured an ankle injury and a two-month layoff, the running back chalked up a hundred-yard afternoon.
CHOPPY	Spectators at the air show were watching in horror. An ultralight aircraft struggled down the runway. It was built of kevlar and carbon fiber. It hit a stand of trees and disintegrated in a plume of smoke and fire.
SUBORDINATED	**While** spectators at the air show watched in horror, an ultralight aircraft built of kevlar and carbon fiber struggled down the runway **until** it hit a stand of trees and disintegrated in a plume of smoke and fire.

19g
subord

4 Use subordinate clauses sensibly. If you pile more than two or three subordinate clauses into one sentence, you may confuse readers. Be sure readers can keep up with all the relationships you establish between clauses. If you suspect they can't, simplify those relationships, perhaps by breaking one long complex sentence into several simpler sentences.

TOO MUCH SUBORDINATION	**Although** their book *Chicken Soup for the Soul,* **which** spawned a hugely successful series, **which** has sold millions of copies, was turned down 33 times **while** they tried to find a publisher, Jack Canfield and Mark Victor Hansen did not quit, **which** suggests the importance of persistence.
REVISED	Persistence counts. Jack Canfield and Mark Victor Hansen never gave up, **even though** their *Chicken Soup for the Soul,* the first in a string of best-sellers, was turned down by 33 publishers.
TOO MUCH SUBORDINATION	An assumption **that** is held by many people in certain cultures, **that** people **who** have college degrees should never have to work with their hands, is often a deterrent to capable young people in those cultures **who** seek nontraditional careers.

REVISED   Many people in certain cultures assume **that** college-educated people should never work with their hands. This attitude often, however, deters capable young people from seeking nontraditional careers.

EXERCISE 19.29 Join the following pairs of sentences by making one of the independent clauses subordinate.

1. The original books of Babylonia and Assyria were collections of inscribed clay tablets stored in labeled containers too heavy for one person to move. We think of books as portable, bound volumes.

2. Clay tablets had many drawbacks. They remained the most convenient medium for recording information until the Egyptians developed papyrus around 3000 BC.

3. Egyptian books were lighter than clay tablets but still awkward to carry or read. A single papyrus book comprised several large, unwieldy scrolls.

4. The Greeks developed papyrus leaflets. They folded and bound the leaflets to produce the first modern-looking book.

5. That first book was the Greek Bible. It takes its name from Byblos, the Phoenician city that supplied Greece with papyrus.

EXERCISE 19.30 Join the following pairs of sentences by making one of the independent clauses subordinate.

1. Japan was a powerful and thriving nation early in the seventeenth century. Its leaders pursued a policy of isolation from the rest of the world.

2. This policy lasted for more than two centuries. Commodore Matthew Perry of the United States forced Japan to open itself to trade in 1854.

3. Many Japanese resented the presence of Europeans and Americans. They attacked both the foreigners and the rulers called shoguns who had yielded to foreign military pressure.

4. A rebellion in 1867 deposed the shogun. The Japanese emperor was restored to power.

5. The emperor wanted his nation to stand on an equal footing technologically and militarily with the West. He supported major reforms in government, trade, and education.

19g
subord

EXERCISE 19.31 Rewrite the following sentences to reduce any undue complexity in subordination and in other modification. If necessary, break longer sentences into shorter ones.

1. Although for many years scientists believed that there might be another planet on the fringes of the solar system whose gravitational pull influenced the orbit of Uranus, there was no concrete evidence that this additional planet existed, even though astronomers spent decades speculating about its mass, distance from Earth, and orbital mechanics.

2. Because the orbit of Uranus seemed oddly influenced by an unseen planetary body, scientists searched for other objects until they actually discovered Neptune and, later, Pluto, which, unfortunately, did not seem to have the mass necessary to explain the orbital disruptions of Uranus that prompted the explorations.

3. If a mysterious Planet X at the fringes of the solar system is an appealing notion, few scientists now take the idea seriously because *Voyager 2* provided data that suggested that the mass of Uranus is exactly what it should be if we calculate its orbit accurately.

4. Some scientists now are debating whether Pluto itself is a real planet because rather than resembling other planets it is more like a group of asteroid-like bodies at the fringe of the solar system, which are much smaller than planets, which have irregular shapes, and which do not have atmospheres.

19h How does parallelism work?

Sentences are easier to read when closely related ideas within them follow similar language patterns. Subjects, objects, verbs, modifiers, phrases, and clauses can be structured to show such a relationship, called **parallelism.**

PARALLEL WORDS	The venerable principal spoke **clearly, eloquently,** and **invariably.**
PARALLEL PHRASES	**Praised by critics, embraced by common readers,** the novel became a best-seller.
PARALLEL CLAUSES	**It was the best of times, it was the worst of times.**

The elements of this Navaho rug in the Chinle style are roughly parallel. The rug is by Irene Harvey.

19h
//

Items are parallel when they share common grammatical structures.

clearly,
eloquently,
invariably

| praised | by | critics, |
| embraced | by | common readers, |

| It | was | the | best | of | times, |
| it | was | the | worst | of | times |

The famous opening clauses from Dickens's *A Tale of Two Cities* are exactly parallel. Longer expressions generally show more variation in their parallel terms, especially in the modifiers.

1 Recognize sentence patterns that require parallel construction.

When words or phrases come in pairs or triplets, they usually need to be parallel. That is, each element must have the same form: a noun or noun phrase, an adjective or adjective phrase, an adverb or adverbial phrase.

NOUNS/NOUN PHRASES	**Optimism in outlook** and **egotism in behavior**—those are essential qualities for a leader.
ADJECTIVES	The best physicians are **patient, thorough,** and **compassionate.**
ADVERBS	The lawyers presented their case **passionately** and **persuasively.**

Items in a list should also be parallel.

LIST ITEMS   The school board's objectives are clear: **to hire** the best teachers, **to create** successful classrooms, **to serve** the needs of all families, and **to prepare** students for the twenty-first century.

2 Use parallelism in comparisons and contrasts.
Sometimes parallelism adds a stylistic touch, as in the following example. The first version, though acceptable, is not as stylish as the revised and parallel version.

NOT PARALLEL   Pope was a poet of the mind; Byron wrote for the heart.

PARALLEL   Pope was a poet of the mind, Byron a bard for the heart.

Parallelism is required in comparisons following *as* or *than*.

NOT PARALLEL   The city council is *as* likely **to adopt the measure** *as* **vetoing it.**

PARALLEL   The city council is *as* likely **to adopt the measure** *as* **to veto it.**

NOT PARALLEL   **Smiling** takes fewer muscles *than* **to frown.**

PARALLEL   **Smiling** takes fewer muscles *than* **frowning.**

3 Recognize expressions that signal the need for parallel structure.
These include the following correlative constructions: *not only . . . but also, either . . . or, neither . . . nor, both . . . and, on the one hand . . . on the other hand.*

As Franklin once remarked, *either* **we hang together** *or* **we hang separately.**

A musician's manager sees to it that the performer is *neither* **overworked onstage** *nor* **undervalued in wages.**

We spoke *not only* **to the President** *but also* **to the Speaker of the House.**

On the one hand, **interest rates might be tightened;** *on the other hand,* **prices might be increased.**

4 Use parallelism to show a progression of ideas.
You can set up parallel structures within sentences or entire paragraphs. These structures make ideas easier to follow.

19h
//

Jane Brody, the *New York Times* health writer, says, "Regular exercise comes closer to being a fountain of youth than anything modern medicine can offer." **Exercise halves** the risk of heart disease and stroke, **lowers** the chance of colon cancer, and **reduces** the likelihood of osteoporosis. **It lessens** the chances of developing diabetes and **strengthens** the immune system. **Exercise** even **helps** people overcome depression.

5 Use parallelism for emphasis. Readers really take note when patterns are repeated in longer clauses. By using parallelism of this kind, you will get their attention.

> If welfare reform works, **the genuinely needy will** be protected and assisted, **the less conscientious will** be motivated to find work, and **the average taxpayer will** see federal dollars spent more wisely.

19h
/ /

You can also use parallelism to express an idea cleverly. Parallelism offers patterns of language perfect for setting up a joke or underscoring sarcasm.

> People who serve as their own lawyers in court have *either* **a fool for a client** *or* **a judge for a brother.**

Sentences and paragraphs can be both more economical and more powerful when you set their related ideas in parallel patterns. When revising a passage, look for opportunities to use parallelism.

6 Correct faulty parallelism. It is easy for parallel constructions to go off track. When an item doesn't follow the pattern of language already established in a sentence, it lacks parallelism and disrupts the flow of the sentence. To correct faulty parallelism, first identify the items that ought to be parallel; then choose one of the items (usually the first) as the pattern; and finally revise the remaining items to fit that pattern. Review these examples to see how they have been revised to achieve parallelism.

NOT PARALLEL	Criminals are imprisoned for two reasons: **to punish them** and **for the protection of law-abiding citizens.**
PARALLEL	Criminals are imprisoned for two reasons: **to punish them** and **to protect law-abiding citizens.**

<table>
<tr><td>NOT PARALLEL</td><td>When you open a new computer program, it's easy to **feel overwhelmed by the interface, frustrated by the vague documentation**, and **not know what to do next.**</td></tr>
<tr><td>PARALLEL</td><td>When you open a new computer program, it's easy to feel
overwhelmed by the interface,
frustrated by the vague documentation, and
confused about what to do next.</td></tr>
</table>

Sometimes you'll have to decide how much of a parallel structure to repeat. You may want to reproduce a structure in its entirety for emphasis, or you might omit a repeated item for economy.

19h
//

<table>
<tr><td>EMPHASIS</td><td>We expect you **to** arrive on time, **to** bring an ID, **to** have three sharpened pencils, and **to** follow instructions.</td></tr>
<tr><td>ECONOMY</td><td>We expect you to arrive on time, present an ID, have three sharpened pencils, and follow instructions.</td></tr>
</table>

The difference can be striking. Consider what happens when we remove the artful repetition from a famous speech by Winston Churchill that is a model of parallel structure.

<table>
<tr><td>EMPHASIS</td><td>**We shall fight** on the beaches, **we shall fight** on the landing grounds, **we shall fight** in the fields and in the streets, **we shall fight** in the hills; we shall never surrender.</td></tr>
<tr><td>ECONOMY</td><td>We shall fight on the beaches and landing grounds and in the fields, streets, and hills; we shall never surrender.</td></tr>
</table>

No simple style rule can be given for structuring a parallel sentence. But you don't want to be inconsistent within a single sentence, both including and omitting an element that is part of a parallel structure.

<table>
<tr><td>WRONG</td><td>The education bill is expected **to fund** literacy programs for another year, **give** teachers more autonomy in the classroom, **to authorize** a dozen new charter schools, and **make** honors courses more widely available.</td></tr>
</table>

The words signaling the parallel structure are inconsistent. Either all the items must be expressed as infinitives (*to fund, to give, to authorize, to make*) or only the first item should include *to*.

REVISED The education bill is expected **to fund** literacy programs for another year, **to give** teachers more autonomy in the classroom, **to authorize** a dozen new charter schools, and **to make** honors courses more widely available.

EXERCISE 19.32 Write a sentence with good parallel structure that incorporates the elements given below. Here is how one example might work.

SUBJECT A football coach: three actions during a game

SAMPLE SENTENCE Keeping his temper as best he could, the coach paced the sidelines, gnashed his teeth, and tried not to cry during the 66-to-3 drubbing.

19h
//

1. A shy guy: three actions before asking for a date

2. A senator: two actions in delivering a speech

3. A teacher: three actions in calming a noisy class

4. A diver: four actions before hitting the water

5. A schnauzer: three actions to get a cookie

EXERCISE 19.33 Read these sentences and decide which ones have faulty parallel structures. Then revise those in which you find inconsistent or faulty patterns.

1. On opening night at the new Tex-Mex restaurant, the manager called the servers together to be sure they understood all the items on the menu, could pronounce *fajitas,* and that they would remember to ask, "Salt or no salt?" when customers ordered margaritas.

2. Two servers had a wager to see whose customers would order the most drinks, devour the most chips, and, of course, leaving the biggest gratuities.

3. Offering the best Southwestern cuisine and to serve the hottest salsa were the restaurant's two goals.

4. But customers soon made it clear that they also expected real barbecue on the menu, so the manager added slow-cooked beef ribs smothered in sauce, hefty racks of pork ribs dripping with fat, and

there was smoked sausage on the menu too that was juicy and hot.

5. Servers had to explain to tourists that one was supposed to eat beef ribs with one's fingers, wrap one's own fajitas, and to bite into jalapeños very carefully.

19i How do you craft balanced sentences?

19i
sent

Effective balanced sentences merge the best attributes of coordination and parallelism (see Sections 19f and 19h). In a **balanced sentence**, a coordinating conjunction links two or more independent clauses that are roughly parallel in structure. The result is a sentence so intentionally designed and rhythmic that it draws special attention to its subject. For that reason, balanced sentences are often memorable and quotable.

And so, my fellow Americans, ask not what your country can do for you; ask what you can do for your country.
—John F. Kennedy, Inaugural Address

The inherent vice of capitalism is the unequal sharing of blessings; the inherent virtue of socialism is the equal sharing of miseries.
—Winston Churchill

We live here and they live there. We black and they white. They got things and we ain't. They do things and we can't. It's just like living in jail.
—Richard Wright, *Native Son*

In your writing you might find balanced sentences effective for openings and closings, where you want readers to remember a major point. But they may seem out of place in lighter, more colloquial writing.

In crafting a balanced sentence, you'll almost always begin with two independent clauses joined to make a compound sentence (see Section 19f). Then you can sharpen the relationship between the clauses by making them reasonably parallel. You may need to revise both clauses quite heavily.

COMPOUND	New programs to end adult illiteracy may be costly, **but** the alternative is continued support of even more expensive welfare programs.
BALANCED	New adult literacy programs may be costly, **but** current welfare programs are costlier still.
COMPOUND	Most people involved in education and business take computers for granted, **yet** that doesn't mean these people really understand what computers do.
BALANCED	Most people in business and education take computers for granted; few understand what computers do.

19j
sent

EXERCISE 19.34 Complete the following sentences in ways that make them balanced.

1. If Alfred Hitchcock is the master of suspense, then . . .

2. Politics makes strange bedfellows, and . . .

3. If all the world is really a stage, then . . .

4. In theory, college seems the surest pathway to economic security; in practice, . . .

5. When the going gets tough, the tough get going, but when . . .

19j How do you craft cumulative sentences?

The intricate architecture of balanced sentences (see Section 19i) can make them seem formal and even old-fashioned. A structure perhaps better suited to contemporary writing, which tends to be informal, is the **cumulative sentence** in which an independent clause is followed by a series of modifiers, sometimes simple, sometimes quite complex.

The apprehensive mood was shot through with shafts of gaiety, **as a black sky is streaked with lightning.**
—Maya Angelou, "Champion of the World"

She [Georgia O'Keeffe] is simply hard, **a straight shooter, a woman clean of received wisdom and open to what she sees.**
—Joan Didion, "Georgia O'Keeffe"

In writing a cumulative sentence, you add on to an original thought, expanding and enriching it by attaching modifying words, phrases, and clauses. The effect is artful but also easy and natural. In our daily speech we often state an idea and then explain or embellish it; cumulative sentences can convey the same informality.

> Dusty? Of course, it's dusty—this is Utah. But it's good dust, **good red Utahn dust, rich in iron, rich in irony.**
> —Edward Abbey, *Desert Solitaire*

19j
sent

> But then they danced down the street like dingledodies, and I shambled after as I've been doing all my life after people who interest me, because the only people for me are the mad ones, **the ones who are mad to live, mad to talk, mad to be saved, desirous of everything at the same time, the ones who never yawn or say a commonplace thing, but burn, burn, burn like fabulous roman candles exploding like spiders across the stars and in the middle you see the centerlight pop and everybody goes "Awww!"**
> —Jack Kerouac, *On the Road*

Crafting effective cumulative sentences takes practice, but the habit of addition is easy to acquire and especially useful in writing descriptive and narrative passages. Almost any of the modifying phrases and clauses described in Sections 19b through 19d can be attached gracefully to the ends of clauses.

1 Attach adjectives and adverbs. Either as individual words or as complete phrases, these modifiers play an important role in shaping cumulative sentences.

> It was a handsome sedan, **black as shimmering oil, deeply chromed, and sleek as a rocket.**

> The storm pounded the coast **so relentlessly that residents wondered whether the skies would ever clear again.**

2 Attach prepositional phrases. You can place prepositional phrases (see Section 19c-1) at the ends of sentences to describe or modify nouns or pronouns within the sentence.

> The church was all white plaster and gilt, **like a wedding cake in the public square.**

When the object of a closing prepositional phrase is artfully compounded, the effect can be memorable. In the following example, dust is described as settling *upon* a rich variety of plants.

A veil of dust floats above the sneaky, snaky old road from here to the highway, drifting gently downward to settle **upon the blades of the yucca, the mustard yellow rabbitbrush, the petals of the asters and autumn sunflowers, the umbrella-shaped clumps of blooming buckwheat.**

—Edward Abbey, Desert Solitaire

3 Attach appositives and free modifiers. You can conclude cumulative sentences with modifiers that rename someone or something within the body of a sentence. These modifiers act like appositives (see Section 19c-4), but they may be separated in distance from the noun or pronoun they embellish. Here are two such *free modifiers* from Bob Costas's eulogy for baseball legend Mickey Mantle.

19j
sent

And more than that, he [Mickey Mantle] was a presence in our lives—a fragile hero to whom we had an emotional attachment so strong and lasting that it defied logic.

He got love—love for what he had been; love for what he made us feel; love for the humanity and sweetness that was always there mixed in with the flaws and all the pain that wracked his body and his soul.

—Bob Costas

Notice the way these modifiers are introduced by dashes. Notice, too, that the modifying phrase itself can be quite complex and much longer than the original independent clause.

4 Attach clauses. You can experiment with both relative and subordinate clauses (see Section 19d) at the ends of sentences, compounding them and keeping them roughly parallel.

Mother Teresa was a woman **who gave her life to the poor and gained the admiration of the world for her service.**

The astronaut argued that Americans need to return to the moon **because our scientific explorations there have only begun and because we need a training ground for more ambitious planetary expeditions.**

As the lengthy example above from Jack Kerouac demonstrates, you can combine different kinds of modifiers to extend a sentence considerably.

The Kennedys had a spark and Jack Kennedy had grown into a handsome man, **a male swan rising out of the Billy the Kid version of an Irish duckling he had been when he was a young senator.**

—Stanley Crouch, "Blues for Jackie"

EXERCISE 19.35 Combine the following short sentences into one longer cumulative sentence.

> EXAMPLE   Virginia adopted the dog. It was a friendly pup with skinny legs. It had a silly grin.
>
> COMBINED   Virginia adopted the dog, a friendly pup with skinny legs and a silly grin.

19j
sent

1. Caesar was my friend. He had been faithful to me. He had been just to me.

2. Dr. Kalinowski recommended that her patient take up racquetball. It would ease his nerves. It would quicken his reflexes. It would tone his muscles. The muscles had grown flaccid from years of easy living.

3. The members of the jury filed into the courtroom. The members of the jury looked sullen and unhappy. They looked as if they'd eaten cactus for lunch.

4. The reviewer thought the book was a disappointment. It did not summarize the current state of knowledge. It did not advance research in the field.

5. The Constitution provides for a legislative body. It is designed to be coequal with the executive branch of government. It is also designed to be coequal with the judicial branch of government.

6. Winnetka is a suburb of Chicago. It is famous for its tree-lined streets. It is known for its wealthy residents.

7. Prohibition was repealed in 1933. It had caused bootlegging. It had spurred the development of organized crime.

8. Pagodas are pyramidal structures. They are usually octagonal, hexagonal, or square. They may have many stories. Each story has a tile roof. The tile roofs turn upward.

9. Nijinsky (1890–1950) was a dancer and a choreographer. He was considered the greatest dancer of his time. He is the subject of much interest today.

10. Jim Crow laws enacted in states that practiced segregation held African Americans in bondage. They denied African Americans access to public accommodations. They limited the educational opportunities of African Americans. They restricted access to voting. They encouraged job discrimination.

CHAPTER 20

How Do You Write Stylish Sentences?

Good sentences must be carefully and grammatically constructed. But just as there's more to cooking than preparing wholesome meals, there's more to writing than crafting competent sentences. As you revise, you want to compose sentences that are varied, rhythmic, rich in detail, and sometimes even memorable. This chapter focuses on various ways to give your sentences that subtle quality called *style*.

20a What are agent/action sentences?

You can build readable sentences by using an agent/action pattern. In agent/action sentences, clear subjects (agents) perform strong actions.

agent/action
The **pilot** *ejected.*

agent/action
My **grandmother** *makes* hand-sewn quilts.

Agent/action sentences are highly readable because they answer these important questions.

- What's happening?
- Who's doing it (and to what or to whom)?

1 Whenever you can, make persons or things the subjects of your sentences and clauses. Readers will take more interest in what you're writing if people are involved. And they usually are—most issues touch on human lives, one way or another.

WITHOUT PEOPLE — Although the federally funded student loan program has made education accessible to a low-income population, the increasing default rate among that population has had a significant effect on the program.

WITH PEOPLE — Hundreds of thousands of **young people** have been able to go to college because of federally funded student loans, but **students** who have defaulted on their loans may be jeopardizing the program for **others**.

341

Starting your sentences with references to people can contribute to sentence variety too. Compare the following pairs of sentences.

> DULL **Strong trepidation** was felt by Alexa about her first college research paper.

> LIVELIER **Alexa** felt strong trepidation about her first college research paper.

> DULL **Access to a steady stream of lively and diverse cultural events** is one of the advantages of attending college in a big city.

> LIVELIER **Students attending college in a big city** can enjoy a steady stream of lively and diverse cultural events.

20a
sent

EXERCISE 20.1 Recast these sentences in agent/action patterns that show more clearly who is doing what to whom. Break the sentences into shorter ones if you like.

1. Raising $3 million to renovate the drama facilities on campus was the goal of Lincoln Brown, the new college president.

2. The experience of playing Horatio in a college production of *Hamlet* had been influential in convincing President Brown of the value of the performing arts.

3. Helping President Brown to convince wealthy donors that restoring and expanding the old theater was a good idea was a small group of actors, all of them alumni of the school.

4. An unexpected donation of $1 million made by a prominent local banker who had once played Hamlet gave the actors and President Brown reason to celebrate.

2 Don't overload the subjects of sentences. Readers will get lost if you bury subjects under abstract words and phrases. When revising, you may have to recover the central idea of a particularly difficult or murky sentence. Ask yourself, "What is its key word or concept?" If you can locate such a word, see what happens to the sentence when you make that key word the subject. In the following difficult sentence, the main idea is buried in an opening noun phrase 24 words long.

> OVERLOADED **The encouragement of total reliance on the fed-**
> SUBJECT **erally sponsored student loan program for med-**
> **ical students from low-income families to pay**

their way through school causes many young doctors to begin their careers deeply in debt.

What is this sentence about? Many readers would say "young doctors"; indeed, *doctors* is one of those human subjects we heartily recommend (see Section 20a-1). So let's see what happens when the sentence is revised to focus on them.

REVISED   **Many young doctors from low-income families** begin their careers deeply in debt because they have relied totally on federal student loans to pay their way through medical school.

Better, isn't it?

20a
sent

EXERCISE 20.2 Rewrite the following sentences to simplify their overcrowded openings.

1. Among those who are unhappy about the lack of morality and standards in the television shows coming from Hollywood today and who would like to see pressure on producers for more responsible programming are activists from remarkably different political groups.

2. The elimination of hurtful gender, racial, and ethnic stereotypes, particularly from situation comedies, where they are sometimes a key element of the humor, is a key demand of political groups on the left.

3. TV's almost complete disregard of the role religion plays in the daily lives of most ordinary people, evident in the fact that so few sitcom characters ever go to church or pray, irritates groups on the political right.

4. Raising the specter of censorship and equating every attack on Hollywood to an assault on the First Amendment has been the quick response of many television producers to criticism of their products.

3 Make sure verbs convey real actions. Strung-out verb phrases such as *give consideration to* and *make acknowledgment of* slow down your writing. To get rid of them, read your draft and focus on the action. Ask, "What's happening?" When you find out, try to express that action in a single lively verb.

DULL VERB   Some groups who **are in opposition to** the
                     death penalty **believe that there is doubt about**
                     its morality.

STRONGER VERB   Some groups who **oppose** the death penalty
                     doubt its morality.

Identifying the action may also help you spot the real agent in a sentence, as in this example.

DULL VERB   American society **has** long **had** a fascination
                     with celebrities.

STRONGER VERB   Celebrities **have** long **fascinated** Americans.

20a
sent

EXERCISE 20.3 Rewrite the following sentences to pinpoint their centers of action and to make their verbs stronger.

1. The fears of many prospective students over age 30 are understandable to college counselors.

2. Many such students are apprehensive about seeing textbooks, syllabi, and assignments for the first time in a decade or more.

3. In many schools, counselors have proceeded to establish special groups or programs for older students so that their feelings of dislocation and discomfort will be relieved.

4. The sobering realization among those responsible for demographic studies of colleges is that older students may hold the key to financial solvency for many institutions.

4 Make sure subjects can do what their verbs demand.

Verbs describe actions that subjects perform: *butter melts; scholars read.* In most cases, you know when you've written nonsense: *butter reads; scholars melt.* But as sentences grow longer, you can sometimes lose the logical connection between subjects and predicates, a problem described as **faulty predication.**

FAULTY   The narrative **structure** of Aretha Franklin's
PREDICATION   song **begins** as a child and continues through
                     her adult life.

Can *narrative structures begin as children*? Unlikely. The writer is probably thinking either of a character in the song or of Aretha Franklin, the singer. In either case, the sentence has to be revised. Here's a possible revision.

REVISED	In Aretha Franklin's song, the narrative **structure follows** the life of a character from childhood to adulthood.

Notice how heavily the sentence had to be revised to make it work. Just swapping one verb for another often won't solve the problem. Here are two more examples. In the first, an abstract concept, *pleasure,* is asked to take a human action and *yearn;* in the second, *windows* are expected to *concentrate,* an impossibility.

FAULTY PREDICATION	Ellen's **pleasure** in gardening **yearned** for a bigger yard.
REVISED	Ellen's **pleasure** in gardening **made** her yearn for a bigger yard.

20a
sent

FAULTY PREDICATION	The **windows** of the electronics store **concentrate** their attention on audiophiles.
REVISED	The **windows** full of electronic components **attract** the attention of audiophiles.

EXERCISE 20.4 Revise any of the following sentences in which the subject cannot logically perform the action described by the verb. Try to explain what is wrong with the original verb choices, which are boldfaced.

1. Hundreds of miles from any city or large airport, Big Bend National Park in Texas **endeavors** an experience of pristine isolation unlike that of busier parks such as Yellowstone.

2. The park **comprehends** mountain, desert, and riparian environments.

3. While coyotes, road runners, and javelinas are common, a few lucky visitors also **apprehend** mountain lions and bears.

4. Other national parks can **profess** more spectacular landmarks than Big Bend, but few **entertain** a more remarkable outdoor experience.

5 Replace *to be* verbs whenever possible. Though the verbs *is, are,* and their variants are often unavoidable, they're not as interesting as verbs that do things.

DULL VERBS	It **is** the tendency of adolescents **to be more concerned** about the opinion of others in their age group than they **are** about the values parents are trying to instill in them.

ACTION VERBS   Adolescents **crave** the approval of their peers and often **resist** their parents' values.

EXERCISE 20.5 Replace the *to be* forms in these sentences with active and more lively verbs. The original verbs are boldfaced. (It may help if you make the agent a person or a concrete object.)

1. There **was** an inclination to protest among restaurateurs when the city decided to increase the number of health inspectors.

2. It **had been** the determination of city officials, however, that many restaurants **were** not in a state of compliance with local health ordinances.

3. The occurrence of rodent droppings in pantries and the storage of meat at incorrect temperatures **were** also matters of concern to several TV reporters.

4. It was the hope of both politicians and restaurateurs that there **would be** a quick solution to this embarrassing problem.

20a
sent

■ **6 Reduce the number of passive verbs.** Passive verb constructions (see Section 26e) often make sentences harder to read. Readers typically have to work harder to figure out who is doing what to whom. Passive constructions also attract abstract nouns and tedious strings of prepositional phrases. So consider turning passive verbs into active ones. It's easy to spot a sentence with a passive verb: the subject doesn't perform the action, the action is *done* to the subject. In effect, the object switches to the subject position, as in the following sentences.

      subj.   action
Madison **was selected** by Representative Barton for an appointment to the Air Force Academy.

      subj.   action
The candidate **had been nominated** for the academic honor by several teachers.

Passive verbs are always constructed with some form of *be* plus the past participle. (See Section 26d for an explanation of what a past participle is.)

             be + past participle
The latest budget bill **has been vetoed** by the President.

      be + past participle
The veto **was provoked** by a stubborn House of Representatives.

Notice that not every sentence with a form of the verb *to be* is passive, especially when *be* is used as a linking verb.

The President **was** unhappy that members of the House of Representatives **had seemed** unwilling to fund new projects.

Nor is every sentence with a past participle passive. Perfect tenses, for example, also use the past participle. (See Section 26a-2 for an explanation of perfect tenses.) Here's an active verb in the past perfect tense.

Congress **had funded** such projects in previous years.

To identify a passive verb form, look for *both* the past participle and a form of *be*.

The projects **had been supported** by previous Congresses when they **had been proposed** by other presidents.

When you have identified a passive form, locate the word that actually performs the action in the sentence and make it the subject.

	subj. performer of action
ORIGINAL PASSIVE	*Madison* **was selected** by Representative Barton for an appointment to the Air Force Academy.
	subj.
REVISED ACTIVE	*Representative Barton* **selected** Madison for an appointment to the Air Force Academy.

Notice that the revised version is shorter than the original.

But not every passive verb can or should be made active. Sometimes you don't know who or what performs an action.

Hazardous road conditions **have been predicted.**

Our flight **has been canceled.**

EXERCISE 20.6 Identify the passive verbs in the following sentences and then rewrite those that might be improved by changing passive verbs to active verbs.

1. The writing of research papers is traditionally dreaded by students everywhere.

2. The negative attitudes can be changed by writers themselves if the assignments are regarded by them as opportunities to explore and improve their communities.

3. When conventional topics are chosen by researchers, apathy is likely to be experienced by them and their readers alike.

4. But if writers are encouraged to choose topics in their communities that can be explored through books, articles, fieldwork, interviews, and online investigations, a better project will be produced.

20b How can you achieve clarity?

When something is well written, a careful reader should be able to move along steadily without backtracking to puzzle over its meaning. You can work toward this goal by using a number of strategies.

20b
clear

1 Use specific details. Writing that uses a lot of abstract language is often harder to understand and less pleasurable to read than writing that states ideas more specifically. Abstract terms like *health-care provider system, positive learning environment,* and *two-wheeled vehicle* are usually harder to grasp than concrete terms like *hospital, classroom,* and *Harley.* Of course you have to use abstract words sometimes; it's impossible to discuss big ideas without them. But the more you use specific details, the clearer your sentences will be. For example, specialists might understand the following sentence from a scholarly book. But stating its ideas more concretely gives the statement broader appeal.

ABSTRACT It is also important to recognize that just as we can learn from knowledge about the efficacy of alternative bargaining structures, we can also benefit from knowledge of alternative approaches to welfare and employment policies.
—William Julius Wilson, *The Truly Disadvantaged*

REVISED We should recognize that just as it helps us to learn more about how groups bargain in other countries, it would also help us to learn more about how they handle welfare and unemployment.

An especially effective way to add texture to sentences is to *downshift*—that is, to state a general idea and then provide more and more details. The resulting sentences will be clear and interesting.

Toi Soldier was a magnificent black Arabian stallion, **a sculpture in ebony, his eyes large and dark, his graceful head held high on an arched neck.** He was a competitor in any Arabian horse show, **equally poised in equitation classes or under harness.**

Downshifting is the principle behind many cumulative sentences (see Section 19j).

EXERCISE 20.7 Working in a group, develop one of the following sentences into a brief paragraph by downshifting. Each subsequent sentence should add more detail to the original statement.

1. High schools could do more to get students involved in their communities.

2. It's not surprising that so few Americans speak a foreign language.

3. The commercialization of sports has changed more than just professional athletics.

■ **2 State ideas positively.** Negative statements can be surprisingly hard to read. When you can, turn negative statements into positive ones. Your writing will seem more confident and may be more economical.

20b
clear

DIFFICULT	Do we have the right **not to be victims** of street crime?
CLEARER	Do we have the right **to be safe** from street crime?
DIFFICULT	It is **not unlikely** that I will attend the conference.
CLEARER	**I will probably** attend the conference.

EXERCISE 20.8 Revise the following sentences to restate negative ideas more positively or clearly where such a change makes for a better sentence. Not all sentences may need revision.

1. It would not be awful if you never turn in a paper late.

2. The remark wasn't exactly the kind I would not ever repeat to my mother.

3. Would it ever not be inappropriate not to say "Hello" to an ex-spouse?

4. What do I think of your new leopardskin pillbox hat? Why, it's not unattractive.

■ **3 "Chunk" your writing.** Consider breaking lengthy sentences into more manageable pieces or creating a list to present unusually complex information. People can comprehend only so much material at one time. Chunking is the principle behind dividing telephone and social security numbers into smaller parts: the breaks make the long strings of numbers easier to recall. It's also a principle used on many Web pages, where information is constricted to fit small screens.

TOO LONG

Citing an instance in which a 16-year-old student was working 48 hours a week at Burger King in order to pay for a new car and simultaneously trying to attend high school full time, New York educators have recently proposed legislation that prohibits high school students from working more than 3 hours on a school night, limits the total time they can work in a week to 20 hours when school is in session, and fines employers who violate these regulations as much as $2,000.

In many respects this long sentence is admirable. It uses parallelism to keep a complex array of information in order. Yet most readers would probably like to see its wealth of information broken into more digestible chunks.

20b
clear

REVISED

Educators in New York have recently proposed legislation that prohibits high school students from working more than 3 hours on a school night. In support of the proposal, they cite the example of a 16-year-old student working 48 hours a week at Burger King in order to pay for a new car while simultaneously trying to attend high school full time. The proposed law would limit the total time students can work in a week to 20 hours when school is in session and would fine employers who violate these regulations as much as $2,000.

Another efficient way to cut very specific or technical information to manageable size is to create a list. Lists give readers a sense of order and direction. Which of the following passages do you find more readable?

To get started with your new computer, unpack it, saving the Styrofoam packing; position it away from sources of heat; plug the keyboard, mouse, and printer into the designated ports on the back of the machine; check that the outlet you'll use is grounded; and, finally, attach the power cord to the computer and plug it in.

To get started with your new computer:
1. **Unpack** it, saving the Styrofoam packing.
2. **Position** your computer away from sources of heat.
3. **Plug** the keyboard, mouse, and printer into the designated ports on the back of the computer.
4. **Check** that the outlet you'll use is grounded.
5. **Attach** the power cord to the computer and plug it in.

Notice that all the items in the list are parallel (see Section 19h).

EXERCISE 20.9 Make the following sentences more readable by breaking them into manageable chunks.

1. The job a young woman has in high school can play an important role in introducing her to new responsibilities, increasing her self-confidence, and getting her accustomed to the expectation that she will likely have to earn her own way through life and shouldn't anticipate that someone else, usually a man, will shoulder the burden of providing her security, shelter, or other necessities.

2. Parents are often ambivalent about having their high school–aged children work because almost inevitably it causes a conflict between the demands of schoolwork and extracurricular activities (such as sports, civic clubs, debate teams, band) and the expectations of employers, a balance many high schoolers are simply not mature enough to handle on their own, often choosing the immediate material goods furnished by a job over the less obvious benefits afforded by a good education.

3. Many parents, however, aware of the limitations of their own training in school, may believe that it is no more important to learn square roots, the capitals of Asian countries, or the metrics of Chaucer's poetry than it is to discover how tough it is to deal with customers, show up on time, manage other workers, or pay taxes, experiences that an after-school job will quickly give most teenagers, whose images of work are badly distorted by films and television.

4 Use charts and graphs to present quantitative information. Readers grasp numbers and statistics much more quickly when they see them presented visually. See Section 11a for more on how charts and graphs work and Chapter 22 for advice on incorporating them into your writing.

20c How can you write more economically?

For those who aspire to be good writers, the war against what the writer and editor William Zinsser calls "clutter" never ends. Such clutter consists of clichés, strung-out phrases, pointless repetitions, and overstuffed descriptions. But wait until you have a first draft before you

Like some contemporary architecture, the modern sentence is spare, pragmatic, and a bit playful. This is the Centre Georges Pompidou—a cultural center in Paris—designed by Richard Rogers and Renzo Piano. You can find out more about it at <http://www.greatbuildings.com/buildings/Centre_Pompidou.html>.

start trimming your prose. Many writers overstuff a first draft because they want to get all their ideas down. That's fine: it *is* easier to cut material than to create more.

1 Condense sprawling phrases. Some long-winded expressions slow a reader's way into a sentence, especially at the beginning.

WHY WRITE . . .	WHEN YOU COULD WRITE . . .
in the event that	if
in light of the fact that	since
on the grounds that	because
regardless of the fact that	although
on the occasion of	when
at this point in time	now
it is obvious that	obviously
on an everyday basis	routinely
with regard/respect to	for

We are so accustomed to these familiar but wordy expressions that we don't notice how little they convey.

WORDY   **Regardless of the fact that** Marisol graduated from the police academy just last year, she has the confidence of a seasoned officer.

REVISED   **Although** Marisol graduated from the police academy just last year, she has the confidence of a seasoned officer.

WORDY   **At this point in time,** the committee hasn't convened.

REVISED   The committee hasn't convened **yet.**

EXERCISE 20.10 Revise the following sentences to eliminate the sprawling, wordy, or clichéd opening phrase.

1. On the occasion of the newspaper's seventy-fifth anniversary, the governor visited the editorial offices.

2. Regardless of the fact that I have revised the speech three times, I still don't like my conclusion.

3. In the modern American society in which we live today, many people still attend church regularly.

4. By virtue of the fact that flood insurance rates are so high, many people go uninsured, risking their property.

20c
wordy

2 Cut nominalizations. Nominalizations are nouns made by adding endings to verbs and adjectives. The resulting words tend to be long and abstract. Worse, nominalizations are often grafted onto terms that are themselves recent coinages of dubious merit.

WORD	NOMINALIZATION
connect	connect**ivity**
customize	customiz**ation**
historicize	historiciz**ation**
knowledge	knowledge**ableness**
prioritize	prioritiz**ation**
victimize	victimiz**ation**

Unfortunately, writers in college, business, and government sometimes think that readers will be more impressed by prose laden with these grand abstractions. Here's a parody of a "bureaucratic" style.

> The **utilization** of appropriate **documentation** will achieve a **maximization** of **accountability**, assuring a **prioritization** and ultimate **finalization** of our budgetary requisitions.

Writing larded with nominalizations gives simple thoughts the appearance of complexity and vacuous thinking the cover of darkness. Avoid such sludge.

EXERCISE 20.11 Revise the following sentences to reduce nominalizations that make the prose wordy.

1. The registrar's note is a clarification of the school's admissions policy.

2. It is a matter of substantial disputation among sociologists whether the gentrification of urban neighborhoods is a beneficial process to inner-city residents.

3. The utilization of traditional phonics in more and more elementary reading classes is an indication that many teachers are feeling dissatisfaction with more contemporary approaches to language instruction.

4. The systems analyst convinced us that the connectivity and interchangeability of our equipment gave our new computer system enhanced potential.

■ 3 Condense long verb phrases to focus on the action.

To show tense and mood, verb phrases need auxiliaries and helping verbs: I *could have* gone; she *will be* writing. But many verb phrases are strung out by unnecessary clutter. Such expressions sap the energy from sentences.

20c
wordy

WHY WRITE . . .	WHEN YOU COULD WRITE . . .
give consideration to	consider
make acknowledgment of	acknowledge
have doubts about	doubt
is reflective of	reflects
has an understanding of	understands
put the emphasis on	emphasize

Similarly, don't clutter active verbs with expressions such as *start to, manage to,* and *proceed to.*

CLUTTERED VERBS	Malls and markets **always manage to irritate me** when they **start to display** Christmas paraphernalia immediately after Halloween.
REVISED	Malls and markets **irritate me** when they **display** Christmas paraphernalia immediately after Halloween.

EXERCISE 20.12 Revise the following sentences to condense long verb phrases into more active expressions.

1. Many people are of the opinion that the federal government has grown too large.

2. An almost equal number of people hold the conviction that many citizens have need of services provided by federal programs.

3. This difference in public opinion is indicative of the dilemma faced by many politicians today.

4. Their constituents often are not in favor of paying for exactly the services that they have expectations of getting.

4 Eliminate doublings and redundancies. *Doublings* are expressions in which two words say exactly the same thing. One word can usually be cut.

trim ~~and slim~~   ~~proper and~~ fitting

ready ~~and able~~   willing ~~and eager~~

Redundancies are expressions in which a concept is repeated unnecessarily. A redundancy compels a reader to encounter the same idea twice.

Our entire society has been corrupted by ~~the evil of~~ commercialism.

Mother's holiday feast on the table was surrounded by our family ~~sitting around it~~.

One might argue, in some cases, that doublings subtly expand the intended meaning. But they usually don't.

Thanksgiving fosters a sense of belonging ~~and togetherness~~.

I am of two worlds, which are forever at odds ~~with each other~~.

Many habitual expressions are in fact redundant.

WHY WRITE . . .	WHEN YOU COULD WRITE . . .
trading activity was heavy	trading was heavy
of a confidential nature	confidential
her area of specialization	her specialty
blue in color	blue

Avoid the repetition of major words in a sentence—unless there are good reasons to emphasize particular terms.

REPETITIOUS	When college **friends come** together, you'll inevitably find some **friends** who **come** from the same background.
REVISED	When college **friends come** together, you'll inevitably find some who share the same background.
REPETITIOUS	Successful diplomats act in the best interests of the nations **for** which they are responsible **for.**
REVISED	Successful diplomats act in the best interests of the nations **for** which they are responsible.

20c
wordy

EXERCISE 20.13 Rewrite the following sentences to reduce redundancy and wordiness.

1. I realized that if I were ever to reach law school, I would have to increase my competitiveness in the skill of written prose composition.

2. *Frasier* to me is a situation comedy–type show.

3. Many traits characterize a truly excellent student adviser, and one of the more important qualities, if not the most important quality of an adviser, is a lively personality.

4. I have often wondered whether everyone's taste in toothpaste is the same and which brand is the most widely used of those brands of toothpaste that are most widely advertised.

5 Eliminate surplus intensifiers. An adverb that functions as an **intensifier** should add weight or power to an expression. You waste its energy when you use it carelessly.

WHY WRITE . . .	WHEN YOU COULD WRITE . . .
We're **completely** finished.	We're finished.
It's an **awful** tragedy.	It's a tragedy.
I'm **totally** exhausted.	I'm exhausted.
That's **absolutely** pointless.	That's pointless.
The work is **basically** done.	The work is done.

EXERCISE 20.14 Review the intensifiers in the following passage and cut any words or phrases you regard as unnecessary.

The Grand Canyon is a quite unique geological treasure in northwestern Arizona, basically formed by the relentless power of the Colorado River cutting a gorge for many, many eons through solid rock. Standing at the edge of the canyon is a totally awesome experience. The canyon walls drop far into the depths, thousands of feet, a seriously deep drop, exposing very different layers of limestone, sandstone, and volcanic rock. These really magnificent canyons recede into the distance like ancient castles, an absolutely remarkable panorama of color and shadow.

6 Cut down on expletive constructions. Expletives are short expressions such as *it was, there are,* and *this is* that function like starting blocks for pushing into a sentence or clause. For example:

It **was** a dark and stormy night.
There **were** five of us huddled in the basement.
There **are** too many gopher holes on this golf course!
It **is** a proud day for Bluefield State College.

Some expletives are unavoidable. But using them habitually to open your sentences will make your prose tiresome. In many cases, sentences will be stronger without the expletives.

WITH EXPLETIVE	Even though **it is** the oldest manufacturer of automobiles, Mercedes-Benz remains innovative.
EXPLETIVE CUT	The oldest manufacturer of automobiles, Mercedes-Benz remains innovative.

WHY WRITE . . .	WHEN YOU COULD WRITE . . .
There is a desire for	We want
There are reasons for	For several reasons
There was an expectation	They expected
It is clear that	Clearly
It is to be hoped	We hope

20c
wordy

EXERCISE 20.15 Revise the following sentences to eliminate unnecessary expletive constructions.

1. There are many different ways to fulfill the science requirement at most colleges.

2. It is usually the case that liberal arts majors benefit from science courses that are geared to the history of the field.

3. Taking a course in the hard sciences is a challenge, and it should be taken seriously.

4. This is a point that many science teachers make early in a term, but it is a concept that many students don't grasp until after their first examination.

7 Cut the number of prepositional phrases. Stylistically, prepositional phrases are capable of dignity and grandeur, thanks to their clarity and simplicity.

In the beginning, God created heaven and earth.

. . . and that government **of the people, by the people, for the people,** shall not perish from the earth.

But that very simplicity can also grow tedious if you pack too many prepositional phrases of similar length and tempo into one sentence.

TOO MANY PREPOSITIONS	**In** late summer **on** the road **from** our town **into** the country, we expected to find raspberries **in** the fields **near** the highway **by** the recent construction.

REVISED   We expected to find late summer raspberries **on** the country road, **near** the recent construction.

You also want to avoid strings of prepositional phrases that congeal around abstract nouns, making sentences thick and hard to read. In the example, the abstract nouns are boldfaced and prepositional phrases are underlined.

WORDY   The current **proliferation** of credit cards among college students is the result of extensive **marketing** by banking **institutions** who see college students in terms of their future **affluence.**

20c
wordy

Revise a cluttered sentence by looking for the center of action: *who* is doing *what* to *whom*?

REVISED   Banks today are marketing credit cards to college students because they see them as affluent future customers.

For more on prepositional phrases, see Section 19c-1.

EXERCISE 20.16 Revise the following sentences to reduce the number of prepositional phrases where they make the sentences awkward or monotonous. Some sentences may require extensive revision.

1. Patrick O'Brian was the author of one of the most popular series of novels about the history of the Royal Navy of Britain during the time of the Napoleonic wars.

2. O'Brian's books focus on the lives of a genial captain by the name of Jack Aubrey and a ship's surgeon by the name of Stephen Maturin who is also in the service of the secret intelligence of England.

3. The novels cover a long period of history, focusing on a worldwide struggle for territory and for dominance in the early nineteenth century between the British people and the forces of Napoleon Bonaparte, the emperor of the French nation.

4. In his love of the sea, in his fascination with the languages of the world, and in his professional interest in the world of espionage, O'Brian resembled his much loved heroes.

8 Cut relative pronouns (*that, which, who, whom*) when you can do it without changing the meaning of a sentence. Relative pronouns introduce many modifying clauses (see Section 19d-2). You can often cut them for economy.

WORDY   The book **that I had quoted** was missing.

REVISED   The book **I had quoted** was missing.

You may also want to cut them to avoid having to recall the appropriate pronoun: *who* or *whom; which* or *that?*

Millie Liam is a woman (**who? whom?**) everyone likes.
The Cord is an automobile (**which? that?**) collectors cherish.

Cutting the pronoun solves the problem elegantly.

Millie Liam is a woman everyone likes.
The Cord is an automobile collectors cherish.

EXERCISE 20.17 Rewrite these sentences to practice eliminating relative pronouns (*who, whom, that, which*) that might be contributing to wordiness. Retain any such pronouns you regard as necessary for clarity.

1. Some of the people who might be willing to endure a little less environmental consciousness are parents of children whom environmentalists have turned into Green Police.

2. Third graders who used to read Harry Potter novels suddenly can't wait to locate "Tips to Save Our Planet" in the daily newspaper, which carries dozens of slick, unrecyclable inserts.

3. Full of moral superiority, youngsters who can barely read are circulating petitions that condemn industries that are polluting the air.

4. Shrewd are the parents who steer their children's activist impulses in productive directions by asking them to read supermarket labels and to find the items that are marked "Recyclable."

9 Condense sentences into clauses and clauses into phrases or words. Often one forceful word can do the work of several. Say more with less.

ORIGINAL   Queen Elizabeth I was a complex and sensuous woman. She seemed to love many men, yet she never came close to marrying any of her suitors.

CONDENSED   Complex and sensuous, Queen Elizabeth I seemed to love men, yet she never came close to marrying.

ORIGINAL   Thanksgiving is a time for all of us to be together for the simple purpose of enjoying each other's company.

CONDENSED   Thanksgiving is a time for us to be together, enjoying each other's company.

EXERCISE 20.18 Rewrite the following sentences to reduce clutter by substituting single words for wordy phrases. Rearrange the sentences as necessary.

20d
.varied

1. In the event that you are in proximity to Greene County this weekend, you should not miss the opportunity to visit the autumn Concours d'Elegance, an annual exhibit of classic cars.

2. There is the possibility that you may have the chance to touch and feel many quite unusual and different vehicles, from dowdy Edsels with gearshift buttons in the middle of their steering wheels to tiny Corvairs with air-cooled engines under louvered deck lids at the back.

3. However, don't expect to make an inspection of the more unique makes and the basically timeless art of such prestigious automakers as Bugatti, Duesenberg, or Hispano-Suiza.

4. Regardless of the fact that Greene County's show is a small show, you can take great satisfaction in examining quite handsome old Hudsons, Nashes, Jaguars, and Corvettes that are tended by owners who are willing and eager to talk about them at great length.

20d How can you achieve sentence variety?

Your readers will quickly be bored if all your sentences are of the same type and pattern. You'll also want to tailor sentence length to the expectations of your audience—for example, experienced readers are typically more comfortable with long sentences than are children. Audience aside, you'll simply want to write sentences that move easily and maturely, conveying readers from point to point with appropriate clarity and emphasis. You can't do this without offering some variety.

1 Vary sentence types. The familiar sentence types discussed in Section 19e offer you a range of possibilities. Simple sentences attract

Vary your sentences so that readers don't find your writing dull and predictable.

the attention of readers with their economy and punch. Compound sentences put ideas of equal weight side by side. Complex sentences give you a means to state ideas subtly and richly. Varying these sentence types will keep your readers engaged.

2 Vary sentence patterns. The five standard sentence patterns in English (see Section 19a) are reliable but dull when repeated over and over.

1. Subject + verb
2. Subject + verb + object
3. Subject + verb + complement
4. Subject + verb + indirect object + object
5. Subject + verb + object + complement

Variations can add style. Consider inverting the usual word order.

Gone is the opportunity to win this month's lottery.

Intelligent, cultured, and politically shrewd was Eleanor of Aquitaine, a twelfth-century liberated woman.

Or play with the way a sentence opens.

ORIGINAL	The punk-rock protest songs of the early 1980s were the musicians' way of expressing their criticism of the political establishment.
VARIATION 1	To express their criticism of the political establishment, punk-rock musicians of the early 1980s wrote protest songs.
VARIATION 2	In the early 1980s, punk-rock musicians wrote protest songs as a way of expressing their criticism of the political establishment.

The variations are not necessarily better than the original. They're just different, and they demonstrate the options you have in crafting sentences.

Still another way to vary the shape of sentences is to put interesting details into modifying clauses or phrases at different points in a sentence.

AT THE BEGINNING   **Convinced that he could not master rhetoric until he knew Greek,** Thomas began studying the language when he was 40.

IN THE MIDDLE   Li Po, **one of the greatest of the Chinese poets,** drowned when he fell out of a boat while trying to kiss the reflection of the moon in the water.

AT THE END   Sixteenth-century Aztec youths played a complex game called *ollamalitzli,* **which some anthropologists believe to have been the forerunner of modern basketball.**

20d
varied

EXERCISE 20.19 The following sentences all begin approximately in the same way. Rewrite them to vary the pattern. Treat the four sentences as a single paragraph; you may not need to change all the sentences.

EXAMPLE   Directors and producers have adapted Shakespeare's plays to contemporary tastes in every age and era.

REVISED   In every age and era, directors and producers have adapted Shakespeare's plays to contemporary tastes.

1. Directors and producers have learned to move Shakespeare from the stage to the screen in the twentieth century.

2. Filmmakers first had to adapt dramas to fit the new medium of film; early Shakespeare movies from the silent era looked much like stage plays presented before a camera.

3. Directors quickly realized that actors on the big screen had to restrain their traditional facial expressions and exaggerated stage gestures.

4. Directors and producers have since produced many Shakespeare films that adapt the dress, music, style, and attitudes of particular decades.

EXERCISE 20.20 To each of the following sentences, add at least one modifying phrase or clause. Vary your placement of the modifiers.

1. Three books stand out in my mind as the ones I would recommend to a friend.

2. Lucille Ball is best known for her series *I Love Lucy.*

3. The Super Bowl occurs in January.

4. Reform of the IRS rarely gets far in Congress.

3 Vary sentence length. Readers like a balance between long and short sentences. If you've produced a cluster of short sentences, your writing may seem choppy. If you write only medium-length sentences, your prose may seem monotonous. Give readers a break; vary the rhythm of your prose.

> **20d**
> **varied**

Here is a paragraph that is tedious chiefly because all the sentences are too nearly of the same moderate length.

ORIGINAL

Our impressions of people are frequently based on our interpretation of their body language. We notice whether or not someone meets our gaze, fidgets constantly, or gestures when speaking. We use our observations to deduce personality traits such as arrogance, submissiveness, or trustworthiness. Most of us are confident of our ability to judge personality by reading body language. We reason that these skills must be highly developed since we rely on them regularly. Recent research confirms that most people can read emotion and gauge social skills from nonverbal signals. However, the same research suggests that they just as consistently fumble or misinterpret cues to more subtle personality traits.

A more lively revised version not only varies the length of sentences but uses varied sentence types, including several questions.

REVISED FOR VARIETY

Our impressions of people are frequently based on our interpretation of their body language. Does someone meet our gaze or turn away? Does he fidget? Does she gesture? From nonverbal cues such as these we draw our conclusions: this person is arrogant, that one is trustworthy. Most of us are confident of our ability to judge personality from nonverbal cues—after all, we've been doing it all our lives. But how accurate are we really? Not very, it turns out. Recent research reveals that while most people can read emotion and gauge social skills correctly, they consistently fumble or misinterpret nonverbal cues to more subtle personality traits.

As the example above suggests, an occasional short sentence works well even in academic and professional writing—where the tendency is to avoid the quick jab. The fact is that short sentences catch the attention of readers. They work well to underscore key points. Mixed with longer sentences, they can mark a writer as direct and confident, able to make a bold claim or a clear statement.

20e
lang

EXERCISE 20.21 The sentences in the following paragraph are monotonously brief. Combine some of these short sentences and edit as necessary to produce a more readable passage. Compare your version to others written by classmates.

The National Air and Space Museum is in Washington, D.C. It is located on the Mall near the Hirshhorn Museum and Sculpture Garden. The Air and Space Museum is one of the capital's most popular attractions. It presents the artifacts of aviation history. It presents these artifacts in a creative manner. The museum houses a replica of the Wright brothers' first plane. Lindbergh's plane hangs from the ceiling. The plane carried him across the Atlantic to Paris in 1927. It was a solo flight. Also in the museum are planes from World War II and a full-size lunar landing module. Every manner of flying machine is represented in the museum. There are dirigibles and zeppelins. There are fighter planes, passenger planes, and space capsules. There are helicopters and balloons. There is even a remarkable movie projected onto a large screen. The screen towers six stories.

20e How do you use figurative language?

Writers who make an impact on their readers are often those with a gift for finding the image that lasts, the analogy that clarifies, the metaphor that makes a concept come alive. Probably no writer finds it easy to learn to use figurative language. It is a talent developed over time through careful reading and self-conscious experimentation. Stay alert for the way authors use figures of speech such as analogy and metaphor, and have the courage to experiment in your own writing.

1 Look for fresh images that will strike your reader's imagination. Such images can often be found by paying close attention to the world you can see and feel, as this writer did.

I went to high school at J. W. Sexton in Lansing, Michigan, a **Depression-era brick fortress that sat across the street from a Fisher Body auto assembly plant.** The plant was blocks long on each side and wrapped in **a skin of corrugated steel** painted a **shade of green somewhere between the Statue of Liberty and mold.** It loomed so near the high school that on football Fridays, when the Big Reds butted heads in Memorial Stadium, night-shift workers stood on balconies and watched the game.

—Ted Kleine, "Living the Lansing Dream"

To create such powerful images, sometimes all you have to do is turn general terms into more particular ones.

GENERAL TERMS   While striking baseball players drove off in **their fancy sports cars,** the **newly created unemployed** at ballparks struggled to **find work.**

SPECIFIC IMAGES   While striking baseball players drove off in **Porsches and Jaguars,** the **peanut vendors and grounds crews** at ballparks found themselves **in unemployment lines.**

2 Use similes and metaphors to dramatize ideas. Similes are comparisons that use *as* or *like*. Here are two examples.

As another fire season approaches, **anxiety about fires in the West is building as inexorably as piles of dead wood** on the forest floor.

—Ted Williams, "Only You Can Postpone Forest Fires"

Life in China was for millennia **like a lethal board game in which a blind destiny threw the dice, and to land on the wrong square at the wrong moment** could mean sudden ruin and repulsive death.

—Dennis Bloodworth, *The Chinese Looking Glass*

Metaphors are direct comparisons, without the use of *as* or *like*. Here are two examples.

Better watch out or **the pendulum of medical dogma** will bash your head in. **It swings back and forth** far more often than most people realize, and with far more velocity.

—Sherwin B. Nuland, "Medical Fads: Bran, Midwives, and Leeches"

20e
lang

The **geological time scale is a layer cake** of odd names, learned by generations of grumbling students with mnemonics either too insipid or too salacious for publication: Cambrian, Ordovician, Silurian, Devonian.

—Stephen Jay Gould, "The Power of Narrative"

A word of advice: don't mix metaphors. What's a mixed metaphor? It's a comparison that is either inconsistent or illogical because it begins with one image and ends with another.

Don't count your **chickens** until the **tide** comes in.

The Internet marketing **ship has sailed,** and companies that have failed to establish a presence on the Web are already **circling the wagons.**

20e
lang

EXERCISE 20.22   Complete the following clauses by creating metaphors or similes.

1. The kitchen smelled awful, like a _____ that had _____.

2. Like a _____, the mayor protested over and over that she was innocent of taking illegal campaign contributions.

3. At the end of summer break, I'm usually a _____.

4. My seat in coach for the six-hour flight felt like a _____.

Design
and Shape
of Writing

CHAPTER 21

What Is
Visual Design?

Chances are good that, the instant you see a movie, you can place it in a specific time or decade—the Depression era, World War II, the 1960s. You can do so even when you don't recognize the stars in the movie or can't guess the date from such clues as music or cars. The style of the film alone—what it looks like on screen—helps you to distinguish, for example, a real 1950s film like *Rebel Without a Cause* (1955) from a nostalgic look at the same period such as *American Graffiti* (1973). How can you tell the difference? It's likely you are picking up dozens of pointers, visual and aural, that define the fashions of a period—the colors, contours, shapes, poses, and rhythms that separate one time (and place) from another.

We find these expressions of design everywhere in our world. Whole periods in the twentieth century were defined by such styles as Art Deco or Bauhaus or even a fascination with streamlining. Objects as dissimilar as buildings, refrigerators, and fountain pens came to share common design themes. It is no different in our own era. We see style not only in clothes and fashions but in mundane objects from sprinkling cans to desktop computers. Everything seems to have a *look*.

Writing, too, has always been influenced by visual and tactile elements. Arguably, the earliest writing developed from objects or pictures that evolved into hieroglyphs and symbols. Writing communicated through varying physical surfaces (clay, papyrus, parchment, paper) and changing instruments (the stylus, quills, pens, typewriters). Early books, especially Bibles, were often so vibrantly illustrated that we describe them as *illuminated*. The era of print introduced new ways of conveying messages, both visual and verbal. In short, every era has its artful ways of conveying messages to people.

Today, computers and digital media are influencing the style of writing by providing remarkable new design opportunities to anyone with the patience to explore these tools. Even academic writers need not think solely in terms of black-and-white words on plain paper any more. Instead, they can shape the design of their documents to fit the needs of their audiences. For instance, a simple "what I saw at the Guggenheim" narrative might be enhanced by digital photographs and

The contrasts between different wars (World War II and Vietnam) in different eras are evident in the visual styles of famous posters from those periods. During World War II, Rosie the Riveter symbolized civilian support for the war effort. The Vietnam-era poster, employing very different visual elements, sends a contrary message.

21a
design

audio clips. The treasurer of a campus organization might liven up a financial report by inserting pie charts generated by database programs. Or campus activists could design a visually provocative Web site, newsletter, or brochure to spread their ideas and arguments.

It is not surprising, then, that when you want your work to reach an audience, you have to think about not just what it says, but how it looks. Readers today expect writing to be visually inviting and easy to navigate—otherwise they may not bother to read it. Web surfers may avoid a home page if its graphics load too slowly. Your employer may ignore a long report if all she needs is an executive summary. And your instructor will cringe if you submit a term paper printed in an ornate font in orange ink. In short, successful writers need to know the basics of *visual style* and *document design*.

Creating documents with visual or even multimedia effects might sound intimidating at first—in fact, it can be a sophisticated process—but it involves quite manageable decisions you'll make about a document's format and style: Should you send an email, a letter, or a memo? Would your audience prefer a printed brochure or a Web site? Should you use a playful or a serious font for the main text? Are colors and graphics appropriate? These are just a few of the questions you'll resolve as you turn working drafts into finished documents.

This chapter introduces you to elements of document format and visual style and offers tips on how to address them throughout your writing process.

21a How do documents work?

Documents are the means by which we present writing to an audience. You may think of a document as something people can hold in their hands, like a newspaper, a letter, or some other printed text. But documents also include electronic texts that readers view on computer screens. Email, Web pages, and software formats have expanded writers' options for reaching an audience. This new flexibility makes it important to understand how different kinds of documents work, so that you can choose the options that best fit your audience and purpose.

21a
design

1 Understand document format. *Document format* refers to how writers arrange material on a page or a computer screen. The format of a document tells readers—at a glance—something about its audience and purpose. We recognize a letter by its initial greeting, body

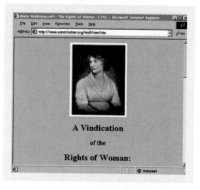

Mary Wollstonecraft, one of the first Englishwomen to try to support herself through writing, had few options for spreading her message to a mass audience. In 1792, while composing A Vindication of the Rights of Women *(at left), she could not have imagined the ease with which writers now publish their thoughts on the Internet, where her works now are available to millions of readers. (John Opie,* Mary Godwin, *née Wollstonecraft. Courtesy the National Portrait Gallery, London)*

paragraphs, and closing signature, all on an 8½-by-11-inch page. We know a newsletter by the masthead on the front page, the headlines and articles in the body, and sometimes the use of multiple columns. Chart 21.1 on page 372 lists common document formats.

By choosing the right format for your project, you set your audience at ease and help them concentrate on your main points. Here are issues to keep in mind.

- **Formats vary in the audiences they reach.** Formats like email and letters allow you to address your writing reliably to a single person or group. Flyers and Web pages, on the other hand, are posted in public spaces for anyone passing by. Whether you choose a personal format over a public one will depend on the subject you're writing about and whom you want to reach.

- **Formats vary in how they announce purpose.** Most formats use headings, titles, or subject lines to focus readers' attention on important points, but the length and style of these features differ. Book covers and pamphlets allow writers to accompany titles with images and decorative typefaces that hint at the tone of what's inside. In contrast, email and traditional memos, which are read by busy professionals, state the document's purpose in a single line of text.

- **Formats vary in how they introduce writers.** Not all formats emphasize the role of the individual writer, as personal letters and academic papers do. Formats such as brochures and pamphlets put a writer's organization first. While a single person may have composed a document, it represents the common purpose of everyone in the group.

- **Formats vary in the kinds of content they allow.** Some material just doesn't work with certain formats. For example, you wouldn't waste space by putting a large photo of yourself on a printed résumé. Often these limitations are technical: for example, some email formats don't support font styles and images.

- **Formats vary in how they guide readers through material.** Most formats allow headers, footers, page numbering, and subsections that help audience members follow a document from beginning to end. In addition, electronic formats often provide hyperlinks and keyword searches to let readers move through material nonsequentially. Which format and features you choose will depend on how you want your audience to read your document: from start to finish? as a reference source? one piece at a time?

21a
design

Chart 21.1

Document Formats

TRADITIONAL PRINT FORMATS

Letters	Résumés	Papers/Reports	Booklets
Memorandums	Articles	Flyers	Spreadsheets
Pamphlets	Brochures	Books	Newsletters

COMMON ELECTRONIC FORMATS

Email	Web pages (.htm, .html)	Message forums
Word-processing files	Graphics files	Spreadsheets
Help files	Sound files	Animation files
Program scripts	Style sheets	Databases
Rich Text Format (.rtf)	Portable Document Format (.pdf)	

OTHER PRESENTATION FORMATS

Speeches	Slide shows	Video clips
Dramatic performances	Colloquiums	Debates

21a
design

2 Consider the different requirements of print and electronic formats. Since print and electronic documents rely on different media, each has special formatting needs. When you create a print document, for instance, you may need to make decisions about paper and binding, as the photo below demonstrates. And you will face rhetorical decisions, depending on your purpose in writing. In preparing a brochure, you may need words to support your images. In an argument, the relationship might be reversed, with photographs illustrating the claims your are making.

Electronic documents have special requirements of their own, some of them quite technical. You may need particular software to convert a computer file to readable text on a screen. HTML pages require Web browsers; email messages require a mail client; text files require word processors. Figure 21.1 illustrates some of these differences and, of course, electronic documents also must reflect your rhetorical concerns of audience and purpose.

Electronic and print formats often overlap. On-screen versions of traditional kinds of writing tend to resemble their print counterparts. Web pages, for example, include section titles, running heads, and numbered figures, just like the pages of a print document. But the electronic medium also allows for additional elements like hypertext links and animation. When you convert a print document to an electronic format, try to preserve some traditional visual cues in the new medium,

Print formats don't just differ in the quality of their paper and binding; they also differ in size, shape, and color spectrum. Often the format of print documents will depend on cost, not the writer's taste. Thick paper and more colors are usually more expensive—but some projects are worth it.

so that the writing will look familiar to readers—whether or not they are computer-savvy.

3 Know when to combine formats. Long documents may use several different formats. A firm seeking investors, for example, might publish a packet containing sales statistics, product descriptions, and an introductory cover letter. Each component requires a slightly different format, but it makes sense to combine them into one coherent document. Design elements such as colors, images, or logos can provide that connection.

21a
design

Sometimes you'll want to combine print and electronic formats. Such combinations are useful when your readers have varying levels of comfort with technology, or when your material can't easily be arranged within a single medium. Suppose your readers use the Internet for locating information but don't typically read long documents on-line. Use a short, attractive Web page to get their attention; on that

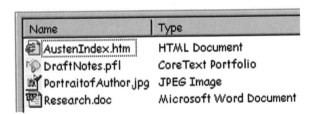

Figure 21.1   *This snapshot from a computer screen shows how icons, file suffixes, and "Type" descriptions help you determine what kind of viewing software your readers might need.*

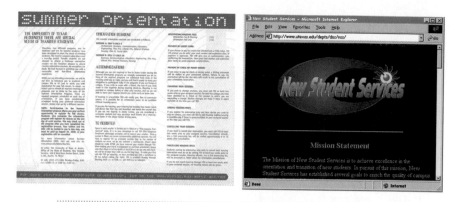

Figure 21.2 *A print brochure can't provide the same complete and up-to-date information as a Web site. But only tech-savvy readers may feel comfortable locating material online. A printed WWW address on a brochure helps low-tech readers know exactly where to go.*

21a

design

page, provide an email address to which your audience can write to request print versions of longer documents. Ideally, the print document and the Web site would share some design features.

4 Understand visual style. Unlike *writing style,* which focuses on the word choices, sentence structures, and figurative language you use in writing, *visual style* refers to the ways in which you present your writing through fonts, colors, graphics, images, and even various forms of nonvisual media. Understand that these choices are now a basic part of the composing process. You should not think of words and design as separate elements in a creative process. Thanks to new technologies, they are increasingly inseparable. The decisions you make about style will influence readers in many ways.

- **Attract readers' attention.** Sometimes a catchy title isn't enough to reel in an audience. On the Web, readers often encounter documents amid a sea of search-engine-identified links. Your page will need something special. Depending on your audience and purpose, that something might be flash, fun, or simple readability.
- **Set a tone.** Images, colors, and fonts convey moods and evoke feelings. You'll want them to set a tone that matches the purpose and audience for your document. In academic writing, you may want a low-key and serious design. For an online memorial, you might use somber colors and fonts to demonstrate respect. Infor-

mal documents, on the other hand, might use bright colors, playful fonts, and cartoon images.

- **Make content more meaningful.** Besides creating a mood, the style of your document can add meaning. Typefaces, type styles, and colors can accentuate contrasts among words, phrases, even entire paragraphs. Such effects help you emphasize, downplay, or simply group related material. Graphics, photographs, and diagrams reinforce and illustrate ideas, sometimes revealing in a single image what would take pages to explain. You can also manipulate these images to achieve a variety of effects, changing a playful color image into a sober black-and-white photograph with the click of a button.

- **Help readers follow your arguments.** Elaborate page layouts and long documents are sometimes difficult to navigate. Frames, rules, and variations in background color can provide useful visual cues, showing readers where one set of ideas ends and another begins. This book, for example, uses colored tabs in the margins and bold headings in the body of the text to keep readers on track.

21a
design

Colors clearly mark areas of the layout, accentuate text, and set a casual tone.

Fonts give text passages a consistent look and provide special emphasis.

Images attract the eyes to special sections of the page and complement explanatory text.

Lines and **boxes** group related material, making the layout easy to follow.

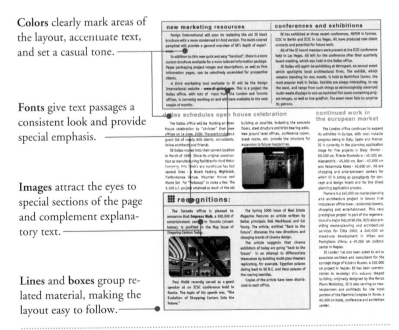

Figure 21.3 *In this newsletter page you can see the basic elements of document style at work.*

EXERCISE 21.1 Find a print or electronic document that you think is either extremely effective or extremely ineffective in communicating its message to readers. Working with a small group of classmates, identify specific features of document format and visual style that make the piece successful or unsuccessful.

21b How do you prepare and plan a design?

In the past, document format and visual style were often the last things writers worried about, but improvements in technology, from digital cameras to presentation software (see Chapter 13), have made visual elements an inseparable part of composing. Design, after all, is what audiences notice first. It has to be an integral part of your composing process.

21b
design

1 Identify suitable formats for your document. When you're planning a writing project, start by learning what kinds of formats will best reach your readers. For example, if members of your audience don't regularly check their email accounts, a printed memo may spread the word better than an email message. Choosing an appropriate format, however, is not simply a matter of going online or off. There are many print and electronic formats, and audiences expect certain kinds in certain situations. For instance, a prospective employer might skip over job applications not accompanied by a cover letter. Likewise, online readers won't download documents that are incompatible with their viewing software.

As you research the expectations of your audience, look for standard formats or *templates*—layouts that are regularly used for particular kinds of writing. Standard formats have been tested by time and across audiences, and they provide reliable guidelines for producing effective, readable documents.

When there isn't a clear format, weigh the merits of different layouts according to your purpose and message. When you need to make many separate supporting points, for example, opt for a layout that allows multiple subsections. If you have to present statistical evidence, you might look for formats with space for supplementary graphics—like tables and pie charts.

Jeanette Shelley
12003 Market Street Apt. 4
San Jose, California 95115
(408) 555-1234
jshelley@mail.provider.com

Education   UC San Jose
                   • B.B.A. with High Honors (1999)
                   • Majored in Management Information Systems
                   • Runner-up in Mock Management Contest

Computer Skills   • Languages: HTML, CSS, XBASE
                   • Software: *MS Office*, including *Access*
                     Web Modify Pro 3.0, DataOK Pro v1
                   • Macintosh and Windows Operating Systems

Work Experience   FlyByNight.com (Web Designer, 1999-Present)
                   • Maintained major portion of company Web site
                   • Designed Web-to-database applications
                   • Wrote programmer orientation manual
                   • Participated in creating company's 2-year plan

                   Byron and Associates (SA, 1997-1999)
                   • Managed all of firm's computer systems
                   • Designed database and reports as needed

                   NW Telecom (Tech Support, Sum. 1997)
                   • Formatted customer information
                   • Provided technical support to customers

The Qualifications of Jeanette Shelley

In 1999, Jeanette graduated from UC San Jose with a B.B.A. in Management Information Systems. She received High Honors in her studies, and won the university-wide Mock Management Council. These points show Jeanette's successful educational background.

Jeanette knows a variety of computer languages, such as HTML, CSS, and XBASE. She knows a variety of software programs, including *MS Office, MS Access, Web Modify Pro* version 3.0, and *DataOK Pro* version 1. She is familiar with Macintosh and Windows operating systems.

She attained these computer skills by working in a number of technical positions. The latest technical position was at FlyByNight.com, where she maintained a portion of the company's Web site and designed a number of Web-to-database applications. She also wrote the company's programmer orientation manual. And finally, she participated in developing the firm's two-year business plan.

Before working at FlyByNight.com, she held a position at Byron and Associates. There she managed the company's computer systems, created databases, and designed reports. Her first technical job was at NW Telecom, where she helped organize customer information. At this job she also provided technical support for many important customers.

To contact Jeanette, write to 12003 Market Street, Apt. 4, in San Jose, California 95115. Her telephone number there is (408) 555-1234. Finally, her e-mail is jshelley@net.provider.com

Figure 21.4   *Résumés have evolved to include a section with basic contact information followed by a series of bulleted lists showing achievements. This layout, illustrated at left, showcases the writer's vocational skills. Imagine the disadvantages you would face if you sent a résumé formatted like an academic essay, like the one on the right, to apply for a job.*

21b
design

E-Tips
Find potential formats by surfing the Web, exploring the library, or surveying your word processor's document templates. These templates adhere to traditional page layouts, so they provide a great starting place for designing a document, even if you will eventually want a customized final product.

2 Explore possible visual styles. As part of your planning, get to know your audience's expectations about style. Has your instructor requested particular fonts or graphics? Will the readers of your soccer club's newsletter expect colors and photos? If you don't know much about these expectations, aim for a style that reflects the kind of relationship you have with your readers. In a business letter, flashy graphics or colors could distract from a serious message. But a striking design might be appropriate for Web pages and brochures that must compete for attention.

Planning a document's visual style is often more challenging than choosing a format. That's because style evokes different reactions, and you may not be able to predict these effects until you've completed and tested a first draft. Still, think about the lasting impression you want your document to make. What do you want your audience to remember about your project?

Once you've thought about the impact you'd like to make, identify stylistic elements that will achieve that effect. Look at similar documents others have written: Do they have conventions for using fonts, colors, and images? Which examples do you like best? What features of these documents do you remember most?

3 Assess the design resources available to you. Producing documents usually requires more than just pen and paper. When you plan a writing project, assess what you already have available, what you might need to acquire to get the job done, and how much time and money you have for procuring new resources. Don't be discouraged if all you have are a word processor and a black-and-white printer—you can still make attractive, professional-looking documents.

Checklist 21.1

Planning a Document

- What formats will reach your audience? Will they accept electronic formats? What software will they use to view and/or print your document?

- Are there standard formats for this kind of project? Will standard formats allow you to present everything you need to include? What adjustments will you need to make to standard layouts?

- What features of visual style are conventionally used for this kind of project? What will readers expect or accept? Can you use graphics, colors, or images?

- Do you want to create a certain mood? Do you want your audience to feel comfortable? excited? informed? respected?

- How will you produce your document? Do you have the necessary computer resources? Do you need to hire a professional printer? How much time and money will new resources cost?

21c How do you polish your design?

In designing a document, you'll need to tinker with it to achieve the best combination of format and style. This experimentation can be frustrating, especially when you're working with new software programs or techniques, but it's an essential part of the design process. In this section we offer guidelines to help you keep the final product in mind, so you can reduce the trial and error required to produce a polished document.

1 Start with standard formats. Since audiences expect certain layouts for certain kinds of writing, these formats are good starting points. A standard format may even help you shape your first draft. For instance, when a layout includes a section for documenting outside sources, you can assume that you'll need to include research. When a format requires itemized lists of information (a résumé, for example), you know that you probably won't need to develop traditional paragraphs.

For some projects, however, you may want to alter a standard layout or even develop an entirely new format. Innovations like these are especially popular when print documents are converted to Web formats, which allow new kinds of content (graphics, images, sound) and new ways of navigating documents (hyperlinks, search engines). But when customized formats don't meet your goals, stick with something more traditional.

21c
design

2 Work with accessible formats. It's pointless to work with a format or a style that will never reach your audience. Why pour hours into the design of a Web page if you know your readers don't browse the Internet? Why spend money on paper and binding if your instructor has asked you to submit a course project as an email attachment? At this stage of the process you'll save time and frustration by drafting only in formats that you know will reach your readers.

3 Experiment with document style. After you've selected a workable format, tinker with sets of fonts, colors, and graphics. Consider how these features work together to create an overall tone and direct readers' attention. Here are stylistic features that you should be experimenting with at this stage.

- **The main text.** Try a variety of readable typefaces, sizes, and color schemes; supplement text with images; set aside special material with boxes or frames; emphasize phrases and words with boldface or italics. Carefully examine successful examples of design work in the format you are using. Let them inspire you.
- **Headings.** Increase size; adjust type styles; highlight with colors; separate material from main text with horizontal rules.
- **Lists.** Consider using small images instead of bullets; vary left and right indentation; frame with boxes or background colors.

- **Tables.** Adjust type size, type style, and color scheme for column and row headings; add background color or shading to groups of cells.
- **Margins.** Offset with color or shading; use vertical rules; insert explanatory images and supplementary text; use decorative images.
- **Headers and footers.** Add navigational icons; use horizontal rules; vary type; use decorative images. (Note that *headers*, which appear only at the top of each page, differ from *headings*, which appear in the body.)

See Sections 22d and 22e for more on working with fonts, type size, and graphics.

4 Revise for readability, impact, and flow.

When you've created a design draft, evaluate how well format and style work together. Can readers move through the document easily and intuitively? Do its immediate impact and lasting impressions serve your writing goals? Even if your first draft seems relatively successful, chances are you'll need to revise to enhance readability, impact, and flow.

- **Add meaningful contrasts to improve readability.** Imagine the nightmare of reading a 20-page document with no paragraphing or sentence punctuation to show where ideas begin and end. Readers might have a similar reaction—though not so drastic—to pages that contain a great deal of material in a plain format or style. Variations in color, font size, and font style help readers more clearly identify points of special interest and transitions.
- **Enhance contrasts where appropriate.** If you want to strengthen the effect your document has on readers, increase the contrast among design elements. Bright colors, extra-large fonts, and vivid images all attract readers' eyes. Keep in mind, however, that use of striking features can make it difficult for a reader to focus on the surrounding material. You'll need to weigh the importance of making a big splash versus leaving a more subtle impression.
- **Group related material to improve flow.** When readers' eyes dance around the page, they can't easily focus on a single point. Help readers navigate smoothly by grouping related material—explanatory text, graphics, images, tables. You can emphasize groupings by framing material in boxes or using a common background color.
- **Position material strategically for balance.** Too much material in one area makes it difficult for readers to focus. Too much space between material disrupts flow. Use white space strategically to show places where readers might pause as they move to-

ward a new thought—but don't create such a wide gap that they don't know which way to go.

21d How do you edit and proof your design?

Once you've decided on a good overall combination of format and style, you can turn your attention to the subtler details that mark the difference between a truly professional-looking document and one that's merely competent. This section discusses ways to add this final polish. For more technical explanations of the design techniques discussed here, see Chapter 22.

1 Fine-tune fonts, colors, and type styles. Even slight adjustments to typeface, type size, type style, and colors can add meaning and make material easier to read, as Figure 21.5 illustrates.

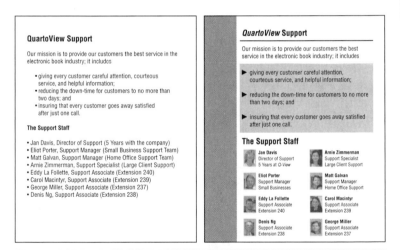

Figure 21.5   *While the formatting in the document on the left is generally effective, the revision on the right has enhanced the layout with colors, images, multiple type styles, and simple graphics. The original would be fine for an internal policy statement; the revision is more appropriate for a customer information packet. Note these changes: (1) Display text has been highlighted with color. (2) The first list uses stylized bullets and background color for contrast; the second list has portrait photos instead of bullets, is set in two columns, and uses boldface to emphasize each name. (3) The margin has been colored and widened to hem in the main content of the page.*

■ **2 Add functional graphics and images.** Don't just add graphics and images because you think a plain, black-and-white page looks dull. Make sure these striking design features serve a purpose (see the examples in Figures 21.6 and 21.7). Here are five good reasons to insert graphics and images into your document.

- To attract attention when your document competes with others
- To illustrate a point that can't be better explained with words
- To provide visual cues to the organization of a document
- To set a mood for your reader
- To enliven the discussion of a topic

Keep in mind that not all writing situations and formats allow images. If you think images would help you achieve your purpose, but you aren't using a format that supports them, consider adding supplementary documents—an attachment to an email message, for example. Be sure, though, not to *require* your audience to use a format with which they aren't comfortable.

■ **3 Adjust alignment, spacing, and positioning.** Page layouts need to balance written material and open space. (See Figure 21.8 on p. 384.) After editing your text, altering fonts, and adding images,

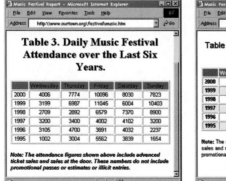 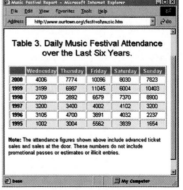

Figure 21.6 *The Web page on the right is clearer and more readable than the original on the left. (1) The heading is reduced and changed to the same typeface as the rest of the page. (2) The column headings have a lighter color to contrast with the dark background. (3) The row headings are boldfaced to distinguish them from the numbers in the body of the table. (4) Subtle background coloring added to odd-year rows makes each series of numbers easier to follow. (5) The "Note" text appears in plain style, since an extended text in italics and boldface is difficult to read.*

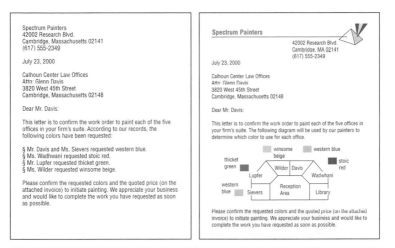

Figure 21.7 *Even a standard business letter (left) can be made more effective with the addition of images (right): (1) A horizontal rule helps distinguish the letterhead from the main content. (2) A graphic logo creates a professional persona. (3) An explanatory diagram helps to clarify written instructions.*

21d
design

you may notice that your layout has become cluttered in some areas and empty in others. Another common problem occurs when one or two lines of text are separated from the preceding or following paragraphs by a page break or a graphic. Lines left by themselves are said to be "widowed" or "orphaned." Many word processors now provide features that help you avoid widowed or orphaned lines, but you may need to tinker with the layout on your own. Take a few minutes to adjust the alignment, spacing, and positioning of paragraphs, graphics, and images to give your audience a clear path to follow.

4 Make visual style consistent. You don't want your readers to have to adjust to a new style every time they turn a page. Although the content will differ, the layout of each page should follow a shared design motif. Professional document designers use tools called *style sheets* to guarantee consistency across a number of pages. Style sheets, which are now available in many word processors and Web browsers, specify the look of pages and passages in a section or an entire document. If your composing software doesn't provide style sheets, you can check the consistency of your design by skimming the layout of each page.

5 Test a final draft in your audience's viewing environment. Before you deliver your document to an audience, proof the final

Figure 21.8   *The Web page on the right has improved the original on the left by making just a few alignment and spacing changes. (1) The page was changed from center alignment to left alignment. (2) The photograph was right-aligned so that the text could wrap around it, eliminating the need for scrolling and preventing an orphaned heading above the photo. (3) Extra space was added above and within the navigation bar, reducing the clutter of images and text.*

21e
design

draft in the same reading environment your audience will use. For print documents, verify that page numbering and section headers are accurate and that the binding of the document does not inhibit reading. For electronic documents, make sure your writing is readable with the version of viewing software your audience will use.

21e How do you copyright your work?

When you have a final product, protect your work by copyrighting it. You don't need to be a professional writer to take advantage of the copyright laws. In fact, you already have exclusive rights to the work you create in a writing class. Be aware, however, that copyrights are not always simple, nor do you always automatically own what you create. When you work for a company, your employer often owns the rights to all writing you compose on the job. And if you're a freelance author, you may be asked to give up your copyright in order to have your work published.

Currently the most complex issues related to copyright involve the Internet and computer software. Who, for example, owns the copyright to an online conversation involving many private participants? Does a software company own any rights to an electronic document created with its program? These questions will probably take many lawyers to resolve. While they wrangle, you can protect yourself and your work by following a few simple guidelines.

1 Copyright your final product. To protect your work, you need to include four elements somewhere on the document you wish to protect.

- The word *Copyright* or the universal copyright symbol: ©
- The year of publication (that is, printing, posting, or sending, depending on your document format)
- The name of the copyright holder
- A reservation-of-rights statement (optional) stipulating under what conditions you permit the copying of your document—or that you allow no copying whatsoever

Here are two examples of copyright lines.

© 2001 Dan's Alaskan Sportfishing Ventures, Inc. All rights reserved.

© 2000 by Daniel J. Kurland. All rights reserved. This Web page may be linked to other Web pages. Please inform the author.

Material you copyright is protected during your lifetime plus 50 years.

21e
design

2 Document or credit borrowed images. With rights come responsibilities. You need to acknowledge all images and graphics you borrow from another author or designer, just as you would cite works consulted or quoted in the body of your writing. Before you publish your work, give credit for images and graphics obtained from outside sources, even when they come from easy-to-access public spaces such as the WWW. Most Web sites that allow people to use their images state clearly the conditions of free use. In other cases, ask the Web developers by email for permission. If you don't have permission for an image, remove it from your design, even if—especially if—it's there simply for decorative purposes.

3 Respect software copyrights. You'll sometimes need expensive software to design intricate documents, and your audience may need special programs to view them. In both cases you must take care to avoid software pirating. There are legal ways to work around such problems: you can usually rent time with expensive design software at your local printing shop, and readers can usually download trial versions of viewing software.

EXERCISE 21.2 Imagine that you've been asked to create one of the documents described on page 386. Working on your own or with a small group of classmates, draft a plan for designing and composing the document. What format and stylistic features would you incorporate, and why? What software or other resources would you need? How would you tailor the document to suit the audience's needs?

1. A publicity package for your brother's bluegrass band.

2. A report on spending trends among teenagers for your business marketing class. Your instructor has asked you to submit a formal written report to her and to deliver to the class a short oral presentation summarizing your findings.

3. A Web site for a campus organization to which you belong.

4. A campaign flyer supporting a candidate in a local or campus election.

CHAPTER 22

How Do You Design Documents?

As Chapter 21 points out, successful writers know how to create the right combination of document format and visual style to fit a writing situation. Yet even when you know how you want a document to look, creating that look—usually with a computer these days—is a separate matter. Computers and software programs have different features and capabilities, and they don't always provide obvious instructions. Fortunately, most word-processing and design programs do share a standard language for document design. This chapter will help you build a basic design vocabulary, and it offers pointers for working with specific design elements and avoiding common pitfalls.

22a How do you design documents with a computer?

Whether the final product will be printed on paper or viewed on an electronic screen, you'll most likely use a computer when you create a document. People have become so accustomed to composing with word processors that, for most of us, typewriters have been relegated to storage closets and pen and paper serve only for taking notes. But although most writers use computers, few use them to their full advantage. By familiarizing yourself with your computer's capabilities, you can make the design process easier and improve the quality of your final product.

1 Explore the design features of your word processor. Before you decide on a design for your document, make sure you know what choices are available. Word-processing programs are much more than glorified typewriters. Most of them support a variety of print and electronic formats, and they often have sophisticated options for enhancing visual style (see Figure 22.1). In recent versions of word processors, you can save in online formats (such as HTML), insert

With a personal computer and a color printer, writers can publish on their desktops in minutes what historically has taken elaborate equipment and long hours of labor. The lithograph press illustrated here shows how many hands were once involved in producing a professionally printed document.

22a
design

pictures and graphics, add tables, use multiple columns, enhance text with colors and decorations, and do much, much more.

The only way to find out what you can accomplish with your word-processing program is to explore its features, either through the user's manual or by hands-on experimentation (see Figure 22.1).

—**Save** in different formats; view available templates; change margins, paper size and orientation; preview printed versions.

—**Add** section and page breaks; insert graphics, footnotes, tables, and other special material.

—**Use** the extra tools provided by word processors: spell checking, revision tracking, etc.

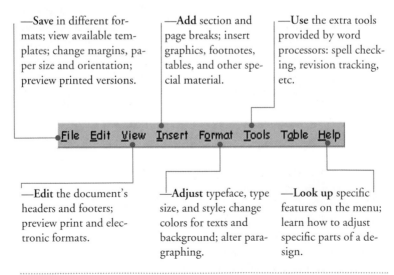

—**Edit** the document's headers and footers; preview print and electronic formats.

—**Adjust** typeface, type size, and style; change colors for texts and background; alter paragraphing.

—**Look up** specific features on the menu; learn how to adjust specific parts of a design.

Figure 22.1   *Learn the basic features of your word processor through its menu.*

2 Consider using other kinds of software. Although you can do a lot with word processors alone, other types of software, like those listed in Chart 22.1, offer additional design options. For instance, if you aren't satisfied with your word processor's clip art selection, you may need drawing software to design your own graphics or a program to import photographs you have taken with a digital camera. If you want to include a sophisticated table of numerical data, you'll need spreadsheet software.

Chart 22.1

Design Software	
SOFTWARE	WHAT IT CAN CREATE
HTML editors	Web pages of varying complexity
Spreadsheet software	Complex tables, graphs, statistical reports
Image editors	Digitized photos, complex images
Drawing software	Simple images, charts, decorated text
Presentation software	Slide shows and handouts
Sound and video editors	Digitized music and film clips
Page layout software	Posters, brochures, letterheads, pamphlets

22b
design

22b How do you organize long documents?

When you're composing a long document or one that combines several formats, you'll need to consider how your audience will digest so much information. Readers can be overwhelmed by large documents that offer little direction, confused by documents that abruptly change formats. This section offers guidelines to help you minimize confusion and manage what might otherwise be an unwieldy project.

1 Divide long documents into sections. When you compose with a word processor, you can divide a document into sections in two ways: you can insert multiple sections into one file or you can generate a new file for each section. One file is more convenient when you need to print the sections in a specific order and when you don't plan to reuse sections in another document. Multiple files, on the other

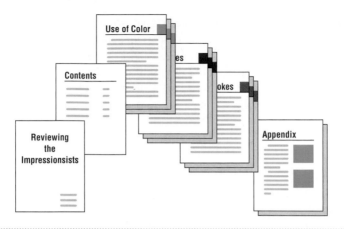

Figure 22.2   *A print essay might be divided into sections according to both topic and format. Breaks appear between the title page and the table of contents, before major changes in topic, and before supplementary material.*

hand, are often used on the WWW in order to reduce the amount of scrolling required to read a page and to allow readers to jump from page to page in a nonlinear fashion.

Where should you divide your document? Begin by creating a new section each time you change formats. Create a new section, for example, when you switch from one column to two or change the width of your margins. Also consider creating sections when you begin the discussion of a new topic. You might find it helpful to vary subtly the stylistic features of sections divided in this way, thereby providing visual cues to the document's organization, as Figure 22.2 illustrates.

2 Insert a table of contents. It's hard for readers to gauge what's inside a long document simply by looking at its cover. Provide a comprehensive list of sections early so that your audience will have an overview of what you've written.

Some formats don't allow for a standard table of contents, but there are ways to work around such limitations. Suppose you are preparing a job application that includes a cover letter, a résumé, a list of references, and a sample of your work. List the accompanying pages in the cover letter so that your readers will know they have everything. Web sites often use a *site map,* which functions like a table of contents.

3 Attach appendixes, indexes, and glossaries. If you expect your document to be used as a reference, an index can help readers locate information. Appendixes and glossaries, too, will help you streamline long, complex pieces of writing. These sections appear at the end of a document and contain detailed material (statistics, definitions, graphics, extended technical discussions) that would disrupt the flow of the text if it were included in the body of the document.

22c How do you lay out pages?

Many formats specify rules for page size, margin width, paragraphing, alignment, and so on. When the specifications are rigid, you're best served by following them to the letter. But when you have flexibility, take full advantage of it by shaping your document's layout to suit your purpose. Below you'll find a list of page features you can use to achieve specific effects. Most of these features are available in the latest word processors.

1 Choose a manageable size and orientation. The size of your pages will affect the amount of material you can put on each. Large pages give you more surface area, but they can be difficult to manipulate: for example, they don't work well for extended passages of text because readers must concentrate on a relatively small area of a wide surface. Large electronic pages may require too much scrolling.

Orientation—the direction material faces on the page—also affects readers. The most common orientation is *portfolio,* shown on the left in Figure 22.3. Portfolio orientation works well with most formats because it presents the main text in one medium-sized column. *Landscape* orientation is generally reserved for graphic material too wide for portfolio orientation.

2 Break material into units. You do this even when you aren't designing a document. Paragraphs and sentences, for example, divide

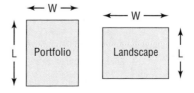

Figure 22.3 *Portfolio layouts are longer than they are wide. In landscape layouts, width is greater than length.*

text into digestible chunks. When you take advantage of visual layout techniques, you have even more options for dividing your thoughts into manageable units.

■ **3 Arrange material according to relevance.** Readers of English tend to move from the upper left corner of a page to the lower right. So put important lead-ins, such as titles and informative images, at the top of a page and less interesting but necessary material toward the bottom. Here are specific suggestions.

- Place the most important material in one or more columns spanning the body of the page (but be aware that columns wider than six or seven inches can be difficult for readers to follow).
- Move supplementary material, such as comments and brief notes, toward the side and bottom margins.
- Group related pieces of material (explanatory text and illustrations, for example) near each other.
- Distinguish special material by indenting or framing it.
- In headers, add navigational details such as current section titles (also called *running heads*), page numbers, and information about the writer.
- In footers, place routine but necessary information such as contact addresses, page numbers, organizational information, and credits (in cases where the writer's organization is emphasized more than the writer).

■ **4 Align material to direct readers' eyes down and across the page.** Left alignment is usually the most readable layout for extended passages of text, but images and graphics often work well with center or right alignment. Right-aligned images are effective when

Subsections. Subsections, groups of related paragraphs under a heading, are just a step up from plain paragraphs. By highlighting topics within a larger section, subsections help readers follow your discussion.

Reviews from Center Stage

Lame indeed.
The recent popularity of boy-band parody Wounded Duck isn't all that surprising. What is surprising is the ability of surly fans to endure the tiresome antics for an hour-long set. How many times can you watch the elaborately choreographed dancers flub their moves before it gets old?
Okay, I'll admit to guffawing through the first three songs—but once you get the gist of the show, there isn't much more to see. My advice—should the Duck fly into town opening for another band—show up ten minutes before the headliners, get a few laughs, and then listen to some real music.

How old school is too old school?
Before Friday, I thought I had an answer to this question. DJ Crusty's energetic set showed that digging up musical fossils isn't all about giving rock legends cameos in your music video. There are still treasures to be found—treasures encased in wax. Crusty's ability to synthesize diverse flavors of vinyl into addictive compounds explains why he has crossed over from the club set into the mainstream.

Lists. It's often awkward to form a series of regular, repetitive statements into a paragraph. Try a list instead. Use numbered lists when information needs to be presented in a strict order.

Festival 2003: Survivor's Guide

The spring rains and crowds can sometimes put a damper on your ability to enjoy the music. Never fear! We've provided a list of suggestions to make the best of your aural outing.

♪ Take your own water bottles. You'll have to wait in line for even the basics once inside.
♪ A waterproof mat is also a good idea. The ground gets pretty muddy, especially by the final days.
♪ Bring plenty of your own toilet tissue. Supplies in the portable facilities run low after just a few hours.
♪ If you're planning on attending more than one day, earplugs will keep your hearing from going dull.
♪ A hooded raincoat can keep you dry during the early afternoon showers.
♪ If you plan on heading for the mosh pit, ignore all of the above and just bring elbow pads.

Tables. Tables work well for presenting more structured information, especially (but not exclusively) statistical data, which can also be turned into graphs (see Section 22e-1). You can also use tables to display categories of information and complicated lists. See Section 11a for more on how tables and graphs work.

Festival 2003: Daily Venue Schedules

	Center Stage	East Stage	West Stage	Welcome Stage
Wed.	Classic Rock	World Beat	Punk	Polka
Th.	Funk and Soul	Swing	Reggae and Ska	Metal Mania
Fri.	Rock and Pop	Blues	Hip-hop and R & B	Local Grab Bag
Sat.	Rock and Pop	Jazz	Country	DJ Showcase
Sun.	International Folk	Classical	Gospel	Amateur Contest

22c pages

Frames. When you want to set material apart from the main text, place it in a *frame* or a box, which you can create with lines and/or changes in background color.

About the Festival (cont.)

The annual festival began in 1982 as a relatively small, "y'all come" event. There was only one stage in the town square at that time. Those first few years didn't attract much national attention, but the music was rich with a variety of local flavors—from rock to jazz to punk to (we're not ashamed to admit) disco.

1987: Going National
A big break came for the festival in 1987, when national, independent label Snub Pop agreed to host a second stage. Before long, other national labels were seeing the festival as an opportunity to promote otherwise unknown bands.

The menu of bands was interesting enough to attract music lovers from all over the state. Eventually, the small festival grew to include most types of American music, until, last year, we finally added a fourth venue, allowing us to accommodate more and more international genres as well.

Rules for Hiking in the Park	Rules for Hiking in the Park
Don't go off the trail. The animal habitats in the park are extremely fragile. While we encourage people to enjoy the natural benefits provided inside, in order to maintain the survival of the fauna and flora, visitors must restrict themselves to clearly marked trails.	**Don't go off the trail.** The animal habitats in the park are extremely fragile. While we encourage people to enjoy the natural benefits provided inside, in order to maintain the survival of the fauna and flora, visitors must restrict themselves to clearly marked trails.
Don't take anything out of the park. Just as we don't want visitors leaving their marks, we don't want them removing what might be necessary parts of a fragile ecology.	**Don't take anything out of the park.** Just as we don't want visitors leaving their marks, we don't want them removing what might be necessary parts of a fragile ecology.
Don't feed the animals. Wild animals can become dependent upon humans, if they expect to be fed. Once in the habit of receiving handouts they can become aggressive when refused—then they must be removed.	**Don't feed the animals.** Wild animals can become dependent upon humans, if they expect to be fed. Once in the habit of receiving handouts they can become aggressive when refused—then they must be removed.
Report violations of these rules. It's your park. When other visitors violate these rules, they are destroying public property.	**Report violations of these rules.** It's your park. When other visitors violate these rules, they are destroying public property.

Figure 22.4   *While the subsection headings are clearly emphasized in both pages, the center alignment in the page on the right makes them stand out even more. This alignment doesn't lead fluently into the main text—but maybe that's not important here.*

they are "wrapped" by left-aligned text—that is, when the lines of text appear on the same horizontal lines used by the image (see p. 393). Center alignment is better for images not wrapped by text, since left or right alignment leaves too much white space in the body of the page.

You can also use alignment to make readers pause at important points, as Figure 22.4 illustrates. Page designers will use this technique to make section openings stand out by centering or right-aligning headings within a left-aligned body of text. Use this method of emphasis carefully; too many disruptions can make pages seem choppy.

5 Format paragraphs for readability. Layouts with a significant amount of text require extra attention to paragraphing. First, decide on a paragraph format. *Block paragraphs* have no indentation on the first line but are separated by extra spacing between them. Standard *indented paragraphs,* on the other hand, need no extra spacing. Besides paragraph format, you must determine line spacing. Print formats often use indented paragraphs with more than single spacing between lines of type. Web pages and email, on the other hand, are easier to read when they are single-spaced. Not only does the type look lighter on a screen, but single spacing means that readers need not do extra scrolling to get through the document.

6 Use white space to avoid clutter. White space reduces clutter by separating material into readable units. Here are common ways of creating white space.

- Leave ample margins at the top and sides of your pages.
- Surround titles, graphics, and frames with unused space.
- Double-space between paragraphs.
- Indent special blocks of material.
- Allow adequate space between columns in multicolumn documents.

22d How do you choose type?

Typefaces (or *fonts*) and *type styles* have their own personalities; they convey mood, attitude, and tone, and they affect the readability of a document. A thick, heavy typeface like **Helvetica Black** speaks loudly and commands attention; a script font like *Coronet* conveys a delicate, artistic mood. Type styles, such as **boldface,** *italic,* and SMALL CAPS, serve more practical purposes, enhancing words and phrases to make them stand out. Finally, you can adjust *type size* (usually measured in *points*) to enhance your document's style and readability.

22d type

1 Select a suitable typeface. What typeface you choose for a project will depend on a variety of factors, from the tone you want to achieve to your document's format. Some fonts read better in print than on a computer screen. Some fonts serve decorative purposes and are not designed for extended passages of text. Fortunately, fonts have been divided into families that share certain characteristics. Knowing the general characteristics of each family will help you make appropriate choices.

- **Serif fonts.** Serifs are the little lines, or "feet," that appear at the bottom or top of the main strokes in a letter. Two common serif fonts are `Courier` and **Bookman.** Serif fonts are highly readable for print documents.
- **Sans serif fonts.** Sans serif fonts—letters without the little feet— have a clean, avant-garde look that appeals to many readers. Two common sans serif fonts are Arial and Helvetica. Sans serif fonts are generally the best choices for display type (see Section 21c-3) and material to be read on an electronic, faxed, or photocopied page.
- **Decorative or ornamental fonts.** Decorative fonts have a lot of personality—they can be elegant, jazzy, authoritative, comical. But they aren't always easy to read, which makes them poor choices for long passages of text. Save these fonts for display text

or where you want to create a special effect. When you use a decorative font, explore the options available in your word processor, from **OldTown** to *OPI Camella Handscript* to *Vivaldi*. Only a few will fit the tone you want to convey.

- **Symbol fonts.** Special characters, called *dingbats,* allow you to add simple graphic ornaments to your documents. To find out what you have available, select a font with "symbol" or "ding" in its title and start typing characters, or choose the "Insert Symbol" command in your word processor. You'll see small graphics suitable for various purposes, as shown in Chart 22.2.

Chart 22.2

Symbol Fonts ("Dingbats")	
Stylized bullets	▶ ◇ ☛ ✓ ❶
Explanatory diagrams	📁 💾 ⇒ 📄 ↑ 🖼
Business-related text	© ® ™ % ¢ £ ¥
Technical writing	θ ∠ ⊆ π √ Ω Σ ♭ ♯
Informative symbols	♂ ♀ ? –
Thematic icons	♈ ♦ ☯ ∞
Playful imagery	♣ ♥ ☺ ♆

22d type

■ 2 Use type styles strategically. Type styles that differ from plain text will draw readers' attention. But use them sparingly, or they'll lose their impact. Chart 22.3 shows common type styles and suggestions for using each.

Chart 22.3

Type Styles	
TYPE STYLE	COMMON USES
Boldface	Strong emphasis, headings
Italic	Highlights, special/foreign words, book titles
<u>Underline</u>	Emphasis, headings, book titles
Superscript and subscript	Footnotes, endnotes, technical notation
~~Strikethrough~~	Revisions in drafts
SMALL CAPS	Subtle emphasis, strong highlights, headings
Shadow, Emboss, Wave	Decorative emphasis, highlights, headings

3 Adjust type size for readability. Medium type sizes (usually 10 or 12 points) work best for the main body of text. Extended passages in large type can be difficult to process, since readers can barely digest a few words before they have to jump to a new line. Instead, use larger type to emphasize headings and titles. "Fine print," on the other hand, isn't always bad. Use smaller type to downplay less important material in margins, headers, and footers. You'd rather draw readers' eyes toward the body of a page than toward running titles, contact information, or supplementary comments—material that is useful but not essential to your main points.

Here are a few final cautions.

- Electronic documents may look strange if the fonts you use aren't installed on your readers' computers.
- Changing the font face may change the height and length of lines.
- Serif fonts can be difficult to read on computer screens.
- Certain font styles and colors (such as blue underlining) may have special meaning in Web pages and other hyperlinked documents.

22e
images

22e How do you use graphics and images?

According to the maxim, a picture is worth a thousand words. Used thoughtfully, it can be worth much more; used poorly, much less. Effective images take a good deal of planning and editing. The tips in this section will help you use images to enhance and complement the text of your document.

1 Present numerical data with graphs. Graphs help readers visualize the significance of statistical information. How better to show a trend in rising prices than a line shooting upward? What more clearly illustrates the allocation of a budget than a simple pie chart? With the help of word-processing or spreadsheet software, you can graph quantitative information clearly and quickly. Below are examples of common types of statistical graphs. For more on understanding and interpreting graphs, see Section 11a.

2 Clarify details through charts and diagrams. Statistics aren't the only kind of information you can present visually. Use a chart or a diagram to give readers details about your topic that are difficult to explain in words. Suppose you're making a presentation that

Bar graphs show comparative values.

Pie charts show portions of a whole.

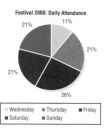

Line graphs show trends and changes across time.

Area graphs show portions of a whole as comparative trends.

22e
images

Organizational charts show hierarchical relationships.

Flow charts show procedural relationships.

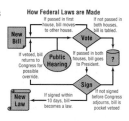

Timelines show sequential relationships.

Diagrams illustrate textual descriptions.

touches on the work groups in your organization. You could try to describe the complex intergroup relationships with words alone, or you could simply provide an organizational chart. This strategy allows you to focus your text on the discussion of important policy issues without bogging down in preliminary details.

While charts show connections among related things, diagrams supplement verbal descriptions with instructive images. Without diagrams, how-to manuals would be a nightmare: "Step 7. Connect four-prong plug A into socket B, above panel C. . . . " Such instructions are easier to follow when accompanied by a diagram of the parts involved. At left are examples of common types of charts and diagrams.

3 Enliven writing with photos and illustrations. Some ideas and emotions are difficult to express in words. Photos and illustrations (cartoons, drawings, engravings) let you show readers—at a glance—aspects of your subject that would otherwise need lengthy description. Because photos and illustrations affect readers so powerfully, you need to use them with care. Be sure that they reinforce important points and do not distract or mislead readers. Viewers of your personal home page might enjoy seeing a photo of your children, but the same photo would distract potential employers from your credentials in an online résumé.

Many options exist for acquiring photos and illustrations to use in a document. You can purchase digitized photos on the Web (some are even free) or on CDs, usually with certain copyright restrictions. You can create your own with a digital camera. You can translate existing photos or illustrations into electronic formats with a scanner.

For a minimal cost, you can buy disks or CDs that have thousands of clip art images. Clip art collections may not furnish you with sophisticated images, but they can be useful when you need graphics for posters, brochures, newsletters, and other low-cost publications.

22f
color

4 Separate material with borders and rules. Borders and rules—horizontal or vertical lines between units of material—provide visual guides to how you have divided material in a document. Create borders around frames, photographs, tables, and graphs to more clearly distinguish them from surrounding paragraphs. Select a line width and color that isn't overwhelming; if you use a thick blue border for a supplementary diagram, you'll end up distracting readers from a more important focal point.

Horizontal lines or rules often mark the beginning of new sections; they also distinguish marginal material from the central content of a page. You'll often see rules separating footnotes or running heads from the main text. You might see a vertical rule wherever marginal comments or graphics appear on the sidebar of a page.

22f How do you work with color?

Color complicates design and increases the costs of printing, but it does make documents more vivid. You'll need to match your use of color to your writing situation. Color may not be appropriate

in academic papers, but it may be necessary to attract attention to brochures, newsletters, and
Web pages. Once you've decided to use color,
there are many factors to consider. In Web pages,
you need to be aware that tones and hues will
look different on different types of screens. Such
complications can usually be worked out, especially if you test design drafts before creating
your final product.

dark blue on biege
black on orange
brick red on blue
white on blue-green
light gray on red
black on gold

1 Select a readable color scheme. Color schemes assign colors to various elements on a page (headings, rules, frames, borders,
graphics). Designers create color schemes to orchestrate the interaction
of multiple tones and hues within a layout, all to achieve specific effects, from adding emphasis to setting a mood. The most important decisions in any color scheme are what to use for background and type.
To be readable, these colors must contrast but not clash. Bright colors
must be used sparingly, since they can tire the eyes. Below you will find
a selection of readable color combinations.

2 Create a mood for your document. Different colors evoke
different emotions. Bright colors have a bold effect, even when applied
sparingly. Soft colors, on the other hand, may need to cover an entire page
to have a noticeable impact. Combinations make a difference too. Some
combinations—for example, purple and orange or yellow and black—are
bold; they shout for attention. Others—shades of blue combined with
ivory—are subtle. Some colors just seem to clash—pink and bright green,
for instance, and purple and yellow. But tastes in color vary greatly, and
one can't say flatly that certain colors should never be combined.

Bright red always gets attention, dominating other colors.

Blues, at least in the softer shades, are soothing.

Greens are often cheerful, associated with nature and good
health.

Yellow is vibrant and attention-getting.

Browns and grays seem somber and formal.

3 Use color to highlight or soften elements of your layout. Colors, because of their wide range of effects, give you more control over the impact created by other features of your layout. Once you've decided to go beyond black and white, you'll have many more options for emphasizing or downplaying text and images. A bold heading can be made less striking, for example, by changing the color from black to a softer blue or gray. Plain text in the body of a paragraph can be made more striking by changing it to red.

22f
color

CHAPTER 23

How Do You
Create Web Sites?

Web sites, perhaps more than any other documents, have made writers realize how important visual design is today. An entire design vocabulary has evolved—perhaps *exploded* is a better description—for Web sites in the past decade. Early sites were simple and text-heavy—blocks of prose with occasional images and links. Today, Web pages are as diverse as any type of document.

If you've never created a Web page (or a Web site consisting of several hyperlinked Web pages), you might find the prospect daunting. Yet college instructors and employers increasingly expect writers to be able to compose documents for this medium. Creating a Web page or site is both simple and difficult. The basic process is relatively easy and requires not much more skill than it takes to operate word-processing software—if a little more patience.

But the enhanced, flexible design possibilities of Web sites pose a peculiar challenge to designers, namely, a wealth of options. You can combine on one Web site diverse elements, including stylized text, graphics, flashing animations, sound, and video. Consequently, we cannot offer models and guidelines to suit every possible occasion. (Besides, if you have access to the Internet, you're within a few mouse clicks of any number of examples—albeit of varying quality.) What we can offer here is an outline of the basic processes involved in writing for the Web, which should be enough to get you started. We have outlined the process in Chart 23.1, but your work may take different paths, depending on your skills, materials, and work habits.

23a How do you plan a Web project?

Planning a Web project isn't that different from planning other types of documents (see the flow chart at right). You'll need to determine your audience, assess your resources, choose an effective layout, and make decisions about document style. Web projects, however, do have special demands.

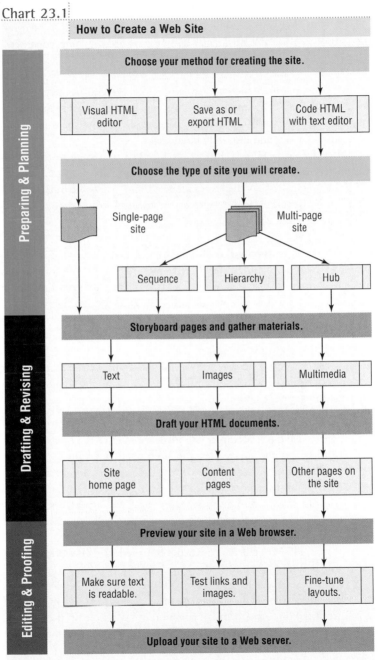

Chart 23.1

How to Create a Web Site

Preparing & Planning

Choose your method for creating the site.

| Visual HTML editor | Save as or export HTML | Code HTML with text editor |

Choose the type of site you will create.

Single-page site Multi-page site

| Sequence | Hierarchy | Hub |

23a
Web

Drafting & Revising

Storyboard pages and gather materials.

| Text | Images | Multimedia |

Draft your HTML documents.

| Site home page | Content pages | Other pages on the site |

Editing & Proofing

Preview your site in a Web browser.

| Make sure text is readable. | Test links and images. | Fine-tune layouts. |

Upload your site to a Web server.

First, Web documents use the HTML (HyperText Markup Language) electronic format. HTML tags or codes tell WWW browsers how to display words and images and how to link separate documents to each other—the feature that makes the Web what it is. (See Section 23b for more on HTML tags.) There are several methods for creating HTML documents, which we explain below. As you begin your project, think about what method you'll use to create your HTML documents, whether you'll use a single-page or a multi-page format, and how you'll lay out and link individual pages.

Besides using HTML format, you'll need to adhere to the publication requirements of the WWW. You'll eventually need to "upload" your documents to a Web server to make them accessible to the world. You can, however, create Web pages without uploading them (see Sections 23b through 23d).

23a
Web

1 Choose a method for creating HTML pages. Many programs exist to help you create HTML documents. These tools vary in their user interfaces, sophistication, and adherence to Web publishing standards. Later in this chapter we will walk you through the process of creating simple Web pages using each of three basic methods.

One method we do not cover in this chapter is creating Web pages using Web forms on a class Web site (see Section 8a). The "Web forms" method is a good way to post information in fixed formats, but it does not typically allow you to make decisions about layout and design, as these methods do.

- **HTML text editors.** These are the original tools for creating Web pages. Using a text editor, you must enter HTML codes by hand, turning text and image files into Web pages. Obviously, to do so, you have to understand the codes. Text editors don't have many user-friendly design tools, but they are extremely flexible, since you can always compose with the latest Web standards and features. Use this method if you like to see what's going on "under the hood" of your Web documents. (See Section 23b.)
- **Visual HTML editors.** Sometimes called WYSIWYG ("wizzy-wig") editors, for "What You See Is What You Get," these visual editors are especially useful for new Web writers. The design tools they offer allow you to edit materials as they'd look in WWW browsers (in other words, you don't have to edit the HTML codes). But these tools don't always support the latest standards or design features. (See Section 23c.)
- **"Save as HTML" or "Export HTML" options.** You will find these commands in word processors and other kinds of software.

They allow you to work on HTML documents as you would any other format. Once you have a finished product, you'll convert your work to HTML by selecting one of these menu options, typically under the "File" menu. This method of creating HTML documents (shown in Figure 23.1 on p. 406) is fast and easy, but the pages generated often need fine-tuning to make them appealing. (See Section 23d.)

You can also combine different methods for creating HTML pages in order to take advantage of the strengths each has to offer. For example, you might start a page by exporting an existing document to HTML and then add features with a visual editor. Or you might use a visual editor to experiment with page features you're thinking of coding yourself. Even if you begin with a visual editor, you can later tinker with the HTML tags directly.

2 Choose a single-page or a multi-page format. Decide early in your design process how you want to organize your Web page. Will you create a single, scrolling page or multiple pages connected by links? If you have a limited amount of information to present—as in a personal home page, a résumé, or a brief report—consider choosing a single, scrolling page. A single page is simple and clear: readers need only move down the page to find information. But most online readers don't like to scroll much beyond a few screens. If you have more than two or three screens of information or if your material breaks easily into sections, consider a set of pages connected by links.

A site that consists of multiple pages requires more deliberation than a single-page site. You have to decide how to arrange your information so readers can navigate the pages easily and intuitively. You'll need to create a home page as the entry into the site. But material deeper in the site may be connected to that home page in different ways—again depending on your purpose and subject. Three common patterns for linking pages are a **hierarchy**, a **sequence**, and a **hub** (see Chart 23.2).

Besides creating links on your site that reflect the structure of your content, you'll also make links directly between pages or to other sites on the Internet. As you build your site, keep these suggestions in mind.

- Make sure all your pages link to your site's home page.
- Don't create "dead ends" that require endless clicking on the "Back" button to return to your navigational menus.
- When you link to Web pages outside your site, make it clear to readers that they are being taken somewhere else.

23a
Web

- As your site grows, consider providing a *site map,* a special page that outlines the organization of your material.
- Use hypertext links to cross-reference material you discuss on a number of pages.
- Gather material you refer to often into a central resource, such as a glossary, to which other pages can easily link.

Menus and **toolbars** vary with each visual editor, but all are based on standard Web design features and vocabulary.

The **body** looks almost exactly as it would if you were viewing it in a browser. But the editor allows you to modify text, insert pictures and tables, format fonts, and change colors.

Header information, such as page title and author, does not appear in the main window of visual editors. Instead you edit this information through the menus of your program.

Menus and **toolbars** are often much simpler in text editors.

Header information appears like the rest of the document, in coded format.

The **body** includes a mix of HTML *tags* (special snippets of text enclosed by angle brackets: <>) and text. Textual styles, images, colors, hypertext links, paragraph breaks, horizontal rules—all are added through standard HTML tags, which won't appear when you look at the page in the browser.

23a
Web

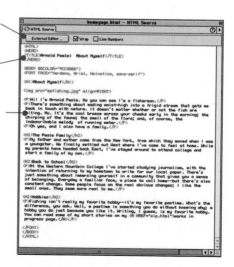

Figure 23.1 *The same personal home page in two different HTML editors. Compare the codes used in the HTML text editor (bottom) with the enhanced appearance of the same text in a visual editor (top).*

Chart 23.2

Common multi-page formats for Web sites

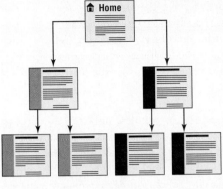

A **hierarchical** pattern organizes pages into increasingly more specific groupings. Readers find material by starting with general categories (topics, areas, units) and working their way down to more specific information. This structure is regularly used by large organizations (such as colleges and corporations), since their units and activities are already organized this way.

Sequential sites present readers with fewer options. If you are offering a proposal argument, your site might move readers step by step from problem to solution, with each stage of the argument building on material from the preceding screen. Readers are encouraged to click "Next Page" rather than select from a menu of options. Make sure to provide links back to the home page so readers won't reach a dead end.

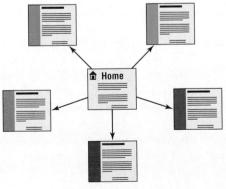

A **hub** structure encourages exploration. Here the home page links to related pages that neither require a specific order of reading nor fit into hierarchical groups. You might use a hub design to catalog items—say, all the native plants in a particular wetlands. Readers could browse each item, going back and forth from the home page. You might also provide direct links to related pages on the hub.

23a
Web

EXERCISE 23.1 Experiment with the three organizational models discussed in Chart 23.2 as part of the planning process for a Web site you're composing. What are the advantages and disadvantages of using a hierarchy, a sequence, or a hub to organize your site? Which pattern will work best for your project, and why? If you're not composing a Web site, use these questions to evaluate the structure of a Web site created by someone else.

3 Storyboard your pages. As you determine the overall structure of your site, consider also the on-screen layout of individual pages you'll create. For the sake of simplicity, new Web writers should focus on two types of pages: the *home page,* which clearly conveys the purpose of the site and how to navigate it, and *content pages,* which present, in a consistent and readable manner, the site's most important material. The "Women in Science" Web site on page 445 illustrates basic features of home pages and content pages. (If you're designing a single-page site you might want to think in terms of *areas* on the page—with *home* at the top and *content* below.)

As you prepare your page layouts, you'll no doubt have questions.

- What text is needed for the site to achieve its purpose?
- How will you break up text into different pages? (See Section 22c.)
- Will you use images or multimedia? (See Section 22e.)
- What elements of document style help you achieve your purpose? (See Section 21a-4.)
- What materials can you gather from outside sources?
- What materials can you create yourself?
- How will you gather all these materials to create your site?

4 Gather your materials. Whatever materials you add to your site, you'll need to assemble them in electronic formats accessible to those browsing the Web. Photographs from your last vacation can't go onto a Web site until they have been "digitized" by a scanner and converted to JPG or GIF files (two graphics formats that are Web-compatible). Although we don't have space here to explain how to digitize photographs, make animations, and record voices—all of which involve an understanding of specific software programs—we can give you guidelines for gathering material already (or easily) converted to Web formats.

- **Create a working folder on your disk.** Place all your materials—HTML files, graphics files, and other media files—for the project in this folder. When you're ready to publish your project, all you'll need to do is upload the entire folder to the Web server. As you're storing files here, follow the WWW naming conventions discussed in Section 23f.

- **Write the text that will appear on your site.** Web sites may contain less written matter than you'd find in printed sources. But online prose needs to be just as clear and grammatical as any other professional writing. Remember, too, that what you post on a Web page is very public. So proofread carefully and edit to eliminate wordiness (see Section 20c). Because reading on screen is more tiring than reading print, make every word count.

- **Collect images from the Web.** Section 22e provides general suggestions for using images. The same guidelines apply here. In Checklist 23.1 we explain how to collect images from the Web. These images will already be in the proper electronic format for Web publication. But you still need to ensure that you have permission, either from a posted statement on the site or through email correspondence. It's a good idea to keep a running list of images you have borrowed and from where. You'll want to cite these locations on a credits page or in the footers of pages where you use images. Sound files and other types of multimedia can sometimes be gathered from Web galleries too. When you use these sources, document them as you would a borrowed image.

- **Create other media.** You may decide to compose your own media files. For example, you may want to publish on the Web a graph you have drawn. Sometimes graphics and drawing software allow you to convert your file to Web formats, an option that often appears in the program's "File" menu. At other times you will need more advanced or specialized software to achieve the conversion. The same is true for recording voice or sound, digitizing photographs, and creating animations in Web-compatible formats. But before you buy new software, explore what you already have on your computer. You may be surprised at what you can do with software you already own.

E-Tips   As you gather and create materials, consider the size of each file you link to your Web document. Larger files take longer to download. If possible use more compressed formats, especially if your readers are on a slow network.

Checklist 23.1

Saving an Image from the Web

1. Go to an image gallery, such as <http://gallery.yahoo.com>.

2. Find an image you like.

3. Right-click (Windows) or control-click (Macintosh) to bring up the floating menu.

4. Select "Save Image As . . ." (*Netscape*) or "Save Picture As . . . " (*Internet Explorer*).

5. Choose your Web project folder from the file chooser dialog box.

6. Note the online gallery's fair use requirements. If necessary ask for permission by email.

23b
Web

EXERCISE 23.2 Storyboard a home page and content pages for a Web site you're working on, using the guidelines in Section 23a-3. Ask classmates to review your designs and offer suggestions for improvement. Once you have a design that suits your purpose, gather in a project folder all the materials you will need for a Web site you're composing, including the text you plan to use and at least one image. Refer to the guidelines in Section 23a-4 if you need help.

23b How do you create Web pages with an HTML text editor?

As we've said, creating Web pages with an HTML text editor isn't the easiest way for new Web writers to construct Web documents. We start here, however, because this method exposes the nuts and bolts of all Web pages—no matter how they're created. To see what we mean, go to any location in your Web browser and from the "View" menu choose "Source" or "Page Source" (or see Figure 23.1). You now see a document containing the HTML codes for the page you were just viewing. This document will include the readable text you see in the browser window and a number of HTML tags (or *elements*)—those cryptic letters and words that appear between angle brackets.

Depending on the page you're viewing, the HTML tags may seem daunting. In fact, composing with HTML is relatively easy—if you start with the basics. While these basics won't allow you to make flashy, elaborate sites, they will allow you to publish material on the Web in a clear and organized fashion. Once you feel comfortable with the basics, you can then increase your HTML vocabulary, learning more striking Web design techniques.

1 Choose your editing software. Most computer operating systems—whether on a desktop computer, a laptop, or even a handheld device—come with a basic text editor. Macintosh and Windows, the most popular desktop and laptop operating systems, come with *Simple Text* and *Notepad*, respectively. These programs have all you need to write HTML documents. If, however, you have access to a text editor specialized for HTML documents, such as *BBEdit* on the Macintosh, you will probably want to use it.

2 Create and preview an HTML template. All HTML documents have a basic structure, a required series of tags that tell browser programs necessary information about the organization of the page. Type the tags that are shown in Figure 23.2 into a new document

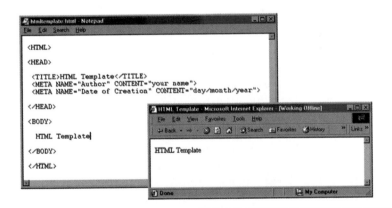

Figure 23.2   *Creating and previewing an HTML template. You can create an HTML template by typing the tags and words into your text editor exactly as shown above. The area between the <BODY> . . . </BODY> tags will contain the main content for each page. Preview your template and notice how little of what you typed appears in the final product. Browsers hide all HTML tags or convert them to special kinds of content, such as images or blank lines. You'll need to review what different tags do in order to know how they can help you achieve the layout you want. (Title bar screen shot reprinted by permission of Microsoft Corporation.)*

using your HTML text editor. Save that document in your working folder as *template.html*—you will make a copy of this document every time you start composing a new page, knowing that it will have the required structure.

After you enter the HTML tags into your editor, save your document and preview it in a Web browser. This is an action you'll repeat again and again as you draft your Web pages. By using a Web browser to open the pages you save in your working folder, you'll be able to see how they will appear once uploaded. To preview your HTML template, open your Web browser, choose "Open" from the "File" menu, and browse for the file you just saved in your working folder. You should then see something like the second window shown in Figure 23.2.

EXERCISE 23.3 Using the guidelines in Section 23b-2, create and preview an HTML template for a Web site you're composing. After you've created a template, browse the Web for examples of sites whose design you think will suit your purpose. View the HTML source (see Section 23b) of these documents and use similar HTML codes to re-create similar visual effects in your template.

23b

Web

3 Review the basic HTML tags. Making a simple Web page template is easy, but a template doesn't do much itself. To achieve the design you want, you'll need to learn more about HTML tags. First let's consider the function of the tags we just used to create the template.

Notice how tags come in pairs. The first in each pair is the *opening tag;* the second, which *always* includes a slash before the tag name, is the *closing tag.* All text between the opening and closing tags is formatted in a special manner, depending on the tag. Some tags, such as <BODY>, <HEAD>, and <HTML>, help the browser software identify parts of the document. Other tags, such as those in Chart 23.3, add stylistic features to the text they surround.

Some tags, however, don't come in pairs, among them the <META> and <HR> tags. These tags add special content or layout information to the page. The <IMG> tag, for example, tells the browser to insert an image; the <HR> tag creates a horizontal rule.

Now that you know how to create a template for your Web page and how to use basic HTML tags, the best way to learn to create a Web page using an HTML text editor is to practice. The following sections guide you step by step through the process of drafting a simple Web page that includes text, an image, a hypertext link, and a footer.

Chart 23.3

Basic HTML Tags and What They Do

`<HTML>`
 . . .
 `</HTML>`
	The first and the last tags in an HTML document. These tags tell browser programs to translate codes on the page to a readable hypertext format.

`<HEAD>`
 . . .
 `</HEAD>`
	Follows the opening `<HTML>` tag in a document. Elements between the `<HEAD>` tags provide information about the document, but this material does not appear in the browser window.

`<TITLE>`
 . . .
 `</TITLE>`
	Identifies the title that will appear in the title bar on the browser when a page opens. The words between the title tags also identify the page in search engine result lists.

`<META` `< . . . />`	Provides extra information about the document, data often used by Web search engines to index the document once it has been uploaded to a Web server.

`<BODY>`
 `< . . . />`
 `</BODY>`
	Brackets the material representing the main content of the page, including text, images, and any formatting that will appear in the browser window.

`<H1>`
 . . .
 `</H1>`
	Forms a level 1 heading—the largest HTML heading size. To vary heading size, choose <H2>,<H3>, <H4>, <H5>, or <H6>. <H6> is smallest.

`<P>` . . . `</P>`	Formats text between the tags as a simple paragraph.
`<B>` . . . `</B>`	Boldfaces text between the tags.
`<I>` . . . `</I>`	Italicizes text between the tags.
`<IMG . . . />`	Inserts an image onto the page.
`<A . . .>` `</A>`	Hyperlinks the text between the tags.
`<FONT . .` `</FONT>`	Sets the font for text between the tags.

`<UL><LI>. . .`
 `</UL>`
 `<LI>`
	Creates a bulleted list. Place the <LI> tag before each item in the list. Use <OL> . . . </OL> to create a numbered list.

` `	Inserts a line break.
`<HR>`	Inserts a horizontal line across the page.

E-TipS

For more tags, see Kevin Werbach's *The Bare Bones Guide to HTML* at <http://werbach.com/barebones/barebones.html> or *A Beginner's Guide to HTML* at <http://www.ncsa.uiuc.edu/General/Internet/WWW>.

4 Add a new page to your Web project. With an understanding of some simple HTML tags, you can draft a new Web page to suit the needs of your project. First, in your project folder make a copy of a Web page template, either one you created or one you are sharing with members of a group. Name this copy something appropriate to the page you are drafting, for example, "home.html" or "car-research.html."

You should also title your page using HTML tags. Open the new document (the copy of your template) in your HTML text editor and change the words between the opening and closing <TITLE> tags to match the content it will contain. See the top image of Figure 23.3 for an example.

5 Insert the text you have written into the body of your document. The text of Web pages always appears within the opening and closing tags of HTML elements. Different elements present the text they contain in different formats. Enter the text you've prepared for the page between the <BODY> . . . </BODY> tags in the new document. If you don't have the text written yet, make up something with which you can experiment. In Figure 23.3, the example HTML creates a page heading by entering the title between the <H1> . . . </H1> tags, just below the opening <BODY> tag. You can format paragraphs by surrounding them with <P> . . . </P> tags.

6 Modify HTML attributes to improve layout and style. Most HTML tags allow you to set *attributes,* or special features that help you better control document layout and style. All attributes appear in the opening tag followed by an equal sign and a value (always between quotation marks). The <BODY> tag provides an attribute—BGCOLOR—that lets you set the background color of the page. Change the background color for your HTML document by modifying your opening <BODY> tag: <BODY BGCOLOR= "TAN">. Check your HTML guide to learn more about attributes you can set and the values you can use to control the layout and style of your page.

```
lessons.html - Notepad
File  Edit  Search  Help

<HTML>

<HEAD>
<TITLE>Teaching Life's Lessons</TITLE>
<META NAME="Author" CONTENT="Stella Galvan">
<META NAME="Date of Creation" CONTENT="2000-12-15">
</HEAD>

<BODY BGCOLOR="TAN">

<H1>Teaching Life's Lessons</H1>

<IMG SRC="baum-bandit.jpg" ALIGN="RIGHT">

<P>A great deal of criticism is leveled at modern media based upon their influence over
children: too much violence, too much offensive language, too many adult situations.
But is this a new trend? How did past ages teach children lessons about the world
they live in, a world populated by adults and their problems? At right you'll see one
method: through fairy tales, in this case Frank Baum's <I>Father Goose, His Book</I>
(1899). Like Hans Christian Andersen, Baum accompanied illustrations with simple
fables, making children his primary audience. But notice how the "bandit" is presented
in a romanticized fashion, as "handsome." Isn't the romanticized criminal a primary
target of critics of the late 20th century?

<P>This section of the Modern Media Project takes up the question of how
entertainment media--past and present--instruct children on harsh reality. On the
group's <A HREF="conc.html">Conclusions</A> page, we'll consider more closely whether
these lessons do more harm than good, and in what way they should be presented.

<UL>
<LI><A HREF="people.html">Bad people: Learn by watching or doing?</A>
<LI><A HREF="places.html">Dangerous places: Ignorant bliss or sure knowledge?</A>
<LI><A HREF="things.html">Harmful substances: Avoiding or experimenting?</A>
<LI><A HREF="sources.html">Works Consulted and Image Credits</A>
</UL>

<CENTER>
<HR>&copy 2001 Stella Galvan<BR>
<A HREF="homepage.html"><B>Return to Modern Media Project Homepage</B></A>
</CENTER>

</BODY>

</HTML>
```

(Microsoft® Notepad and Microsoft® Explorer are trademarks of Microsoft. Title bar screen shots reprinted by permission of Microsoft Corporation.)

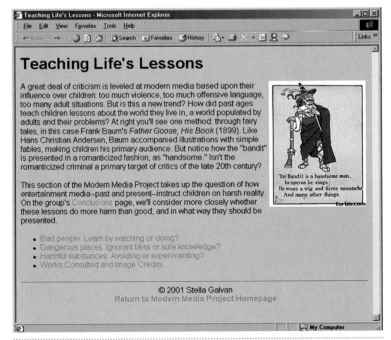

Figure 23.3 **An HTML document in a text editor and Web browser.** *By matching the text within the HTML codes in the top image with the text displayed in the Web browser, you can see how the codes enhance and modify layout and style.*

■ **7 Enhance your layout by adding an image.** Not all HTML tags present textual information. The <IMG> tag, for example, allows you to add pictures to your Web page. Add the following text to your document, setting the SRC attribute to match the name of a graphics file in your working folder: <IMG SRC= "yourimage. jpg">. When you preview your page in a browser, you'll see the image. Figure 23.3 shows an image element with its ALIGN attribute set to "RIGHT."

■ **8 Hyperlink your page to another document.** Using the <A> tag (also called the *anchor tag*), link your page to others, either within your Web project or at another location on the WWW. To link to the Internet search engine *Google,* for example, you would enter this text:

```
<A HREF= "http://www.google.com"> Search at Google</A>
```

The HREF attribute allows you to specify an Internet address to which the text between the <A> ... </A> tags will be linked. To link to another page in your project, set the HREF element to match the name of another HTML document in your working project folder. Figure 23.3 shows a number of examples of links to "internal" documents.

■ **9 Copyright your document in a page footer.** Footers on Web pages are useful places to unobtrusively credit yourself and others and to link readers to the site's home page (from content pages). Here are the HTML codes for the footer used on the sample Web page in Figure 23.3. You can create a simple footer using similar codes.

```
<HR />&copy 2002 Stella Galvan

<A HREF="homepage.html">Return to Home</A>
```

Notice that you won't find *&copy* on the list of HTML tags in Chart 23.3. This *special character code* creates a copyright symbol. Check your HTML guide for more extensive lists of special character codes.

■ **10 Fine-tune your text.** Use HTML tags to change font face and style where it's appropriate. The <FONT> tag includes three important elements: COLOR, FACE, and SIZE. In combination with the <I> (italics) and <B> (boldface) tags, you can have nearly as much control over the style of your text as you do with a word processor. For ex-

23b
Web

example, in a Web browser the text between the <I> . . . </I> tags below will be Helvetica, a size larger than normal, red, and italicized.

```
<FONT COLOR= "RED" SIZE="+1" FACE="Helvetica">

<I> This is upsized, italicized, red, Helvetica

text.</I>

</FONT>
```

To adjust the layout of text, use the list tags <UL> and <OL> and the line break tag <BR>. The <BR> tag is especially useful for presenting text that doesn't extend a full line but shouldn't be double spaced (such as lines in poems). The list tags are useful for presenting all kinds of material. You can make a hyperlinked table of contents for your site by creating a list that links each item to a separate page. For more advanced HTML tags and attributes, consult your HTML guide.

EXERCISE 23.4 To begin this exercise, you will need to have created a project folder that contains all the materials you want to include on your Web page (see Exercise 23.2) and an HTML template for your page (see Exercise 23.3). Use these materials as you follow the instructions in Sections 23b-4 through 23b-10. When you finish, you'll have a completed Web page that will look something like the example in Figure 23.3, depending on how many of the HTML elements and attributes you have used in your design.

23c
Web

23c How do you create Web pages with a visual HTML editor?

If you aren't concerned about the nuts and bolts of HTML, or if you need to produce an attractive Web document quickly, try a visual Web authoring program. The quality of the page you finally produce will depend on the software you have available—but most programs generate suitable layouts. For new Web writers, almost any visual editor will do, even an up-to-date word-processing program that has an HTML editing mode.

1 Choose your editing software. Visual editors often cost money, but some computers come with them preinstalled. *Netscape's* suite of Internet applications comes with both a Web browser (*Communicator*) and an editor (*Composer*). Other editors include *Microsoft FrontPage, Dreamweaver,* and *Claris Home Page.* Predictably, the more

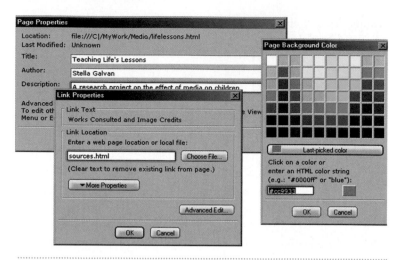

Figure 23.4   *Visual HTML editor dialog boxes. Unlike HTML text editors, visual editors allow you to use the program's menus and dialog boxes to make modifications to your document. For this reason you'll need to explore your software, learning the available options. The images above show dialog boxes from* Netscape Composer. *You'll find similar dialog boxes for editing your HTML pages in all visual editors.*

23c
Web

features offered, the more expensive the program. You'll notice, whichever program you choose, that document style and layout are modified by choosing menu options and entering information into dialog boxes. Figure 23.4 shows just a few of the dialog boxes offered.

■ **2 Add a new page to your Web project.** When you use a visual HTML editor, you won't need to create your own HTML template, as you would when coding with an HTML text editor (see Section 23b-2). In most programs, all you'll need to do is select "New" from the "File" menu, just as you would in a word processor. Save the blank page in your project folder. Note that your editing software might provide a gallery of preformatted templates. Choose a template for your new document if you find one that's appropriate. Make sure to adjust the template to suit your needs.

■ **3 Insert the text you have written into the new document.** If you have already stored the text in a word-processed document, you can cut and paste the material using your program's "Edit" menus. Otherwise type your words into the visual editor as you would into any other program. Notice, however, that you'll have less flexibility in the way you format your paragraphs, which will normally appear in single-spaced block style (this is the Web standard). You can change font and alignment by using options found in your program's formatting menus and toolbars. Follow the guidelines in Section 22c for formatting passages of text.

4 Preview your page in a Web browser. Most visual editors have a "Preview" option among their menus and toolbars. This option will display your page in a Web browser program, allowing you to see how it will appear to readers on the Web. Ideally, your page won't change much from the editor to the browser program—that is, after all, the claim of WYSIWYG software. If the page does look significantly different, try upgrading either your editor or your browser; the versions you have may not have the latest standards. Many software makers provide free updates on the Web.

5 Insert an image into your page. Most WYSIWYG editors have an "Insert" menu that allows you to add nontextual content to your page, such as pictures, tables, and horizontal rules. After moving your cursor to the location where you want the picture, select the menu option that allows you to place an image on your page. Select an image you have already saved in your Web project folder. After clicking "OK" in the dialog box, you should see the image on your page, as it will appear to browsers on the Web (see Figure 23.5).

23c
Web

6 Link your page to another. Set the cursor where you want to add a link to another page. Type the text you would like to be linked, such as "Search at Google" or "Next Page." Select the text you just typed and choose the option to insert a link from your editor's menus. In the dialog box that appears, type the Internet address. To link to a page in your working folder, simply enter the filename, as shown in Figure 23.4. Some editors allow you to edit other elements of the link, such as the target window or the color of linked text. To link to a site outside your folder, use the complete URL.

7 Change fonts, colors, and other design elements. One especially useful feature of visual editors is their ability to assign colors and fonts according to how they appear on the screen, rather than through codes or names. To change the background color of your page, choose the appropriate menu option, probably "Change Background" or "Format Page." You will then see a dialog box displaying color options, as shown in Figure 23.4. To select your color, click on

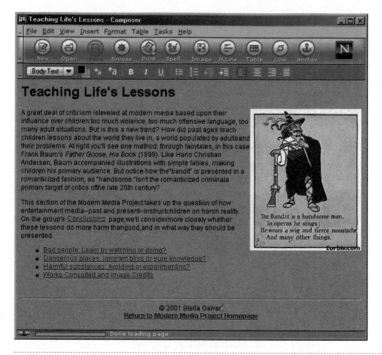

Figure 23.5   *Example page in a visual editor. A page in a visual editor looks nearly the same as it would in a Web browser. (See Figure 23.3.) The main differences here are in the menus and toolbars, which allow you to edit material rather than navigate it.*

the box with the desired hue and then select the "OK" button. When you return to the editor's main window, the background will have changed. Similar dialog boxes are often used to assist in picking fonts.

Using the knowledge you have so far, try building a footer for your page. Insert a horizontal rule, a copyright symbol followed by the year and your name, and a link to your project's home page. Finally, use your editor's alignment tools to center the footer material.

Even with a rich design, your page in a visual editor should look something like it would in a Web browser. (Compare Figures 23.3 and 23.5.) What shows up in the browser may differ from the page you created in the program, but the inconsistencies don't usually outweigh the ease of laying out pages with a visual editor. If you wanted to use the visual editor to create an exact image of what your readers will see, you could probably come close, but you might have to do some tweaking with the program's menus and dialog boxes.

23d How do you create Web pages by exporting from your word processor?

As we've discussed, this is the fastest and easiest method for creating Web documents. The latest word processors and spreadsheets allow you to open any existing document and convert it to HTML within seconds. The resulting pages may not have the layouts you expect, but they will be Web compatible (which may be all you care about).

1 Open the text you've prepared in your word processor. To make your text more readable on screen, create block paragraphs (see Section 22c-5). Feel free to use bullets and numbers for lists, and if your word processor allows, set background and font colors. Be aware that some word processors accommodate standard Web layouts, allowing you to identify different levels of headings to help organize your material.

2 Convert your page to HTML and preview it. Some word processors allow you to "Save as HTML"; others permit you to "Export" the document to HTML. After selecting the appropriate option, you'll be prompted to name the file and storage location. Create a name that is compatible with Web standards (see Section 23f) and store the document in your project folder. Note that your word processor may generate files besides the HTML document you explicitly name. This often occurs when you have images in your document. When you publish your document on the Web, you'll need to upload to the server all files and folders created by your word processor.

To see the results created by your word processor, open the new HTML document in a Web browser. If the results aren't satisfactory, return to your word processor, experiment with simpler layouts, and try again. Alternatively, edit the HTML document directly using one of the other two methods discussed earlier in this chapter.

23e How do you edit Web page drafts?

Although Web pages have many special features, the writing that appears on them requires the same care and attention that you would give to a print document. Besides editing for style and clarity, keep in mind some basic document design concerns. Will readers be able to move through the material in the manner you expect? Are the colors you have chosen readable on screen? Have you cited your images correctly? Finally, be aware of these common problems for Web pages.

- **Broken links.** These occur whenever linked text goes nowhere. Remember that the URL specified by your link must match exactly the Web address or HTML page to which you're linking.
- **Broken images.** If the images you inserted into your page don't appear correctly in Web browsers, check that you've correctly spelled their filenames and that they are in the proper Web folder.
- **Absent closing tags.** If you've entered the HTML codes using a text editor, you have an extra error to look out for. Check your codes to make sure you've provided closing tags for all headings, font styles, and lists. Otherwise your text may be unreadable.
- **Accessibility problems.** A major concern of Web developers is making sure that content on the Internet is available to readers with physical impairments. The visually impaired, for example, can now browse the Web using special programs that convert text to speech. However, these tools don't work if authors fail to provide textual alternatives to visual content. Most visual editors provide a space to enter a textual description for your image. If you edit HTML codes yourself, use the ALT attribute in your image tags to provide an informative description of the graphics you use.

23f
Web

EXERCISE 23.5 Use the guidelines in Section 23e to edit and proof the Web page you drafted in Exercise 23.4 or another Web project you're composing.

23f How do you upload to a Web server?

We are limited in the kind of instruction we can offer for this step, primarily because how you publish your pages will depend on your writing situation. If you are composing a project for class, your instructor should give you uploading instructions. If you are composing pages for yourself or your organization, you'll probably need to establish an account with an Internet service provider, which might be your college or university. In any case, prepare your pages for uploading by making sure they follow Internet filename conventions.

- Use *no* spaces or punctuation in your filenames, except periods. You can separate words with hyphens (-) or underscore marks (_) rather than spaces.
- Use the appropriate file suffix: ".html" or ".htm" for HTML documents; ".jpg" or ".gif" for graphics; ".txt" for plain text.
- Be consistent in your use of upper- and lowercase letters. Some Web servers won't acknowledge discrepancies.

Checklist 23.2

Creating a Web Site

1. **Choose a method for creating your page.** Will you use an HTML text editor, a visual HTML editor, or your word processor (Section 23a-1)?

2. **Decide on an organizational strategy.** Will you arrange your site as a hierarchy, a sequence, or a hub (Section 23a-2)?

3. **Plan page layout(s) and gather your materials in a project folder** (Sections 23a-3 and 23a-4).

4. **Draft your Web page(s)** (Sections 23b, 23c, or 23d).

5. **Edit your page(s), being sure to test all hypertext links** (Section 23e).

6. **Upload your page(s) to a Web server** (Section 23f).

23f
Web

CHAPTER 24

Model Documents

In this chapter you'll find model documents illustrating a variety of print and electronic formats. As explained in Chapter 21, many print formats have corresponding electronic formats. Where possible, we show examples of documents in both media. You may notice that electronic versions vary slightly depending on the email or Web browsing software used to display or compose them. We've tried to represent a variety of software programs in this chapter, on the assumption that you'll see at least a few that look familiar. More important, we emphasize in each example those features that regularly appear in most programs.

Each example is accompanied by a discussion of the purpose and the common uses of the format, a checklist alerting you to conventions of that format, and an explanation of the document's basic parts.

While each of the formats presented in this chapter has its own checklist, Checklists 24.1 and 24.2 provide general guidelines for presenting documents in print and on screen. And of course you should proofread every document carefully.

Checklist 24.1

Typical Print Documents

- Use standard letterhead paper (8½ " by 11").

- Use portfolio orientation unless you plan to fold the document or you need extra room for graphics and images.

- Leave at least a one-inch margin on all sides. If you plan to bind the document, add more space on the bound edge.

- Use double or single-and-a-half spacing unless otherwise specified, especially with small type. Single spacing is used in letters or sometimes in long documents to cut printing costs.

- Use headers and/or footers with running titles and page numbers for multi-page documents.

Checklist 24.2

Typical Onscreen Documents

- Make sure your audience has the right software to view the document format you're using.
- Short, single-spaced block paragraphs are most common for onscreen documents.
- Use sans serif typefaces and avoid long stretches of bold, underlined, or italicized text.
- If you have hypertext links, test them to make sure they work.

24a Email

Over the last few years, instructors and employers have come to expect students and workers to conduct business through email. In the writing class, you may be asked to submit assignments as file attachments or to collaborate with fellow students through online messages. In workplaces, email has replaced printed memos (see Section 24e) for everyday correspondence, and it has become an important means of communicating cheaply across long distances.

24a
models

Although email is used to communicate for many purposes, all email includes a few basic elements. The sample message on page 426, composed by Arnold Peale for his English composition class, illustrates basic parts of an email message. Keep in mind that the onscreen look of messages will differ according to your *email client,* the program you use to read and write messages. Take some time to explore your email client's features.

Checklist 24.3

Email

- Use short block paragraphs; long paragraphs are difficult to read on screen. Double-space between paragraphs but don't indent.
- Avoid "Reply All" when responding to messages received. Respond to everyone on an email list only when you think all will be interested in your comments.
- Make sure attached files are in a format your audience can view and that you have scanned them for viruses.
- If you use a common signature for all your messages, make sure the text of the signature is suitable for both professional and personal audiences; otherwise edit the signature when the occasion calls for it.
- Use asterisks, dashes, and capitals letters to emphasize text.
- See also the checklists for specialized types of email messages.

EMAIL MESSAGE

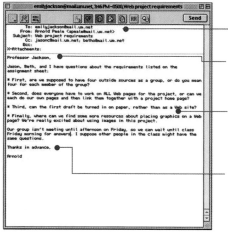

The **message header** includes all necessary delivery information. (See below.)

A **salutation** is often optional; use one when addressing an audience you don't know.

The **body** can include block paragraphs, lists, and subsections set off by dashed lines or extra spacing.

The **closing** and **signature** will depend on the formality of the message. For professional messages, include your title and organization.

EMAIL HEADER

The **To** line includes one or more email addresses for recipients. Remember that addresses must be completely accurate.

The **From** line will usually be filled out by your email program with your name and address. If you have more than one email account, you may be asked to specify which one will be used to send the message.

```
      To: emilyjackson@mail.um.net
    From: Arnold Peale <apeale@mail.um.net>
 Subject: Web project requirements
      Cc: jasonc@mail.um.net; betho@mail.um.net
     Bcc:
X-Attachments:
```

The **Attachments** line will include the file names of electronic documents you would like to send along with your message. Email clients vary in how they ask you to specify your attachments.

The **Subject** line includes a short phrase about the topic of your message—make sure it is relevant to your recipients.

Cc lines can be used to send other individuals copies of the message. (See also Section 24e.)

24b Business letters

When you write a business letter, remember that it may become part of a permanent file documenting your request or complaint. Make the letter as complete and accurate as possible so that the recipient(s) can act on it quickly. The letters on page 428 were written by a student at Bowling Green State University to the Office of the Registrar asking for action to clear up a bureaucratic mistake. The letter was successful. After receiving the complaint, the registrar sent an email message to the student, promising to watch over his loan account personally for the remainder of his stay at Bowling Green.

Checklist 24.4

Business Letters

24b
models

- Choose a *block, modified block,* or *indented* letter format.

- Single-space paragraphs and addresses in the letter; double-space between the return address, date, inside address, salutations, body paragraphs, and closing.

- Use one-inch margins on all sides.

- When using letterhead paper, you don't need to repeat the return address as long as it includes all necessary contact information.

- Make the inside address as specific as possible so that the letter will go directly to its intended audience.

- Place a colon after the salutation.

- In the body, be brief but state all pertinent facts, including names and dates. Keep your letter to one page if you can.

- Make your diction and style fairly formal, unless you already have established a casual tone with the addressee.

- Follow your closing with a comma, four blank lines, your name, and your professional title; sign in the space created by the blank lines.

- After the closing and signature, note any copies of the letter you have sent and any attached documents you have enclosed with the letter.

- Proofread your letter carefully and keep a copy for your records.

BUSINESS LETTER IN BLOCK FORMAT

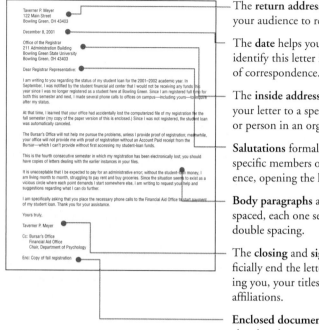

The **return address** is used by your audience to respond.

The **date** helps your audience identify this letter in a series of correspondence.

The **inside address** directs your letter to a specific office or person in an organization.

Salutations formally address specific members of the audience, opening the letter.

Body paragraphs are single spaced, each one separated by double spacing.

The **closing** and **signature** officially end the letter, identifying you, your titles, and your affiliations.

Enclosed documents are declared at the very end.

BUSINESS LETTER IN MODIFIED BLOCK FORMAT

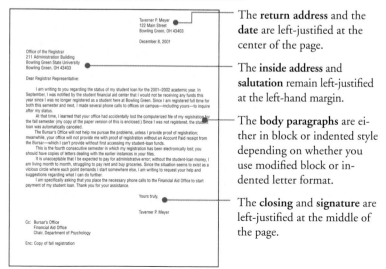

The **return address** and the **date** are left-justified at the center of the page.

The **inside address** and **salutation** remain left-justified at the left-hand margin.

The **body paragraphs** are either in block or indented style depending on whether you use modified block or indented letter format.

The **closing** and **signature** are left-justified at the middle of the page.

24c Letters of application

A letter of application is an especially important form of business communication. The same advice and guidelines apply to it as to a business letter. In a letter of application, however, you have the extra challenge of presenting yourself favorably without seeming to brag. Use the application letter to draw attention to the reasons an employer should consider you for a job or an interview.

On the next page you'll find two examples of Chad Polatty's letter of application for a Web programming position, one of them formatted as a printed document, the other as email. The salutation, the body paragraphs, and the closing are the same in both examples. The only major differences between the two are in how Chad reaches the job recruiter, how the recruiter contacts him for further information, and the formatting of attached documents, such as résumés and references.

Checklist 24.5

Letter of Application

24c
models

- Follow the basic formatting guidelines for a business letter (see Checklist 24.4) or email (see Checklist 24.3), depending on the medium you use to correspond.

- State the position for which you are applying. Follow up with a summary of your qualifications for the position. Focus on those qualifications that best suit the job in question; the résumé will cover the rest.

- Focus on how you might meet the organization's needs and on what you could accomplish *for the organization*—not on what you hope to get from the position.

- Show some knowledge about the organization or company to which you are applying, but offer praise only in order to show why you're interested in working for that employer.

- Maintain a polite and respectful—but confident—tone.

- Remember that your letter of application may have a long life. If you're hired, it will become part of your personnel record. If you're not hired, it may go into a file of applicants for later consideration.

LETTER OF APPLICATION IN BLOCK FORMAT

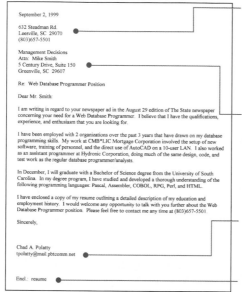

The **return address** should include a telephone number so the recruiter can contact you immediately if more information is needed or an interview is requested.

The **inside address** and **salutation** will match the contact name given in the job listing. When not responding to a listing, locate a contact name at the company's hiring office.

The **closing** and **signature** in a letter of application do not differ from those in standard business letters.

Enclosures will often include a printed résumé and a list of references.

24c
models

LETTER OF APPLICATION IN EMAIL FORMAT

Email addresses replace postal addresses in the heading of the message. Postal addresses and telephone numbers can appear in the body of the letter if needed.

The **subject line** should announce the position for which you are applying.

File attachments are used instead of enclosures. Make sure to use common or requested electronic formats.

24d Résumés

Your résumé is a concise outline of your academic and employment history, designed to give a prospective employer a quick but thorough overview of your qualifications. Take great care in preparing your résumé. Once in the hands of a recruiter, your list of achievements and skills will be used to decide whether an employer will contact you for an interview.

In your résumé you can enhance your list of qualifications by showing competency in your field. Learn the language of your profession and use the appropriate terms to describe your on-the-job training and course work. Remember, however, that you need to be comfortable with these terms—chances are you'll be expected to use them in an interview.

Consider recent trends in how employers find job candidates and store information about them. Not only do recruiters search for résumés on the Web, but they also maintain databases of digitized résumés. Most recruiters collect these résumés as electronic submissions, but some save scanned versions of print résumés. As a database entry, your résumé will receive a serious look only if it can be found through keyword searches—all the more reason for you to become fluent with the language spoken by others in your profession.

24d
models

Because résumés are so important, and because they've changed somewhat in recent years, we provide three examples. The first is a printed résumé listing the qualifications of Danny Gomez, a student at the University of Texas at Austin. The second is an email, text-only version of Danny's résumé, as is sometimes requested when recruiters want you to enter the document in a database. Finally, after Checklist 24.6, we present a Web résumé created by Jay O'Brien, a student at Shepherd College in West Virginia.

Checklist 24.6

Résumés

* At the top of your résumé give your name as you would like to be recognized in a professional setting.

* Provide up-to-date contact information so that a prospective employer can reach you for interviews.

* Before you list your skills, state your objective. This section may be omitted when your employment goals are explained in an accompanying cover letter. Some résumé guides now consider the objective line optional.

* Create a categorized list of your academic degrees and awards, professional certifications, previous jobs, technical skills, and relevant course work.

* Arrange this list according to how effective the categories and qualifications you have listed will be for attaining the desired job.

* Educational achievements usually go first. List year, degree, and institution, as well as scholastic honors won.

* If the prospective job requires specialized skills (computer skills, technical procedures), list those with which you have the most familiarity, assuming an interviewer might ask about them.

* List your work experience. Besides mentioning employers and time periods, state your responsibilities and achievements in succinct but specific terms. Account for all periods longer than a few months.

* List course work only when it explains how you attained skills outside your work experience. List nonwork, nonacademic activities and achievements only if you think an employer might consider them relevant assets.

* You cannot be required to mention age, gender, race, religious or sexual preference, political affiliation, or marital status.

* When requested, include a list of references (all of whom you have checked with beforehand) or indicate a placement service with your complete dossier. This list can usually be submitted as a separate, attached document.

24d
models

PRINT RÉSUMÉ EMPHASIZING EDUCATION AND EXPERIENCE

The **header** includes your name and contact information. Most students include a **local address** where they can be contacted at school as well as a **permanent address.**

The **body** includes a list of your qualifications divided into categories. Use different type styles to highlight information that employers might find most interesting, such as the names of companies you've worked for or your school.

The **footer** will often include the phrase "References available on request."

24d
models

RÉSUMÉ FORMATTED AS TEXT-ONLY EMAIL MESSAGE

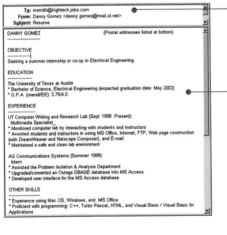

The **email header** will include the recipient's address, your return address, and a subject line indicating that the message is a résumé.

The **body** of a text-only email does not accept most types of visual formatting. Use asterisks, dashed lines, all caps, and underscores to replace the special type styles and graphics used in print or Web résumés.

ONLINE RÉSUMÉ

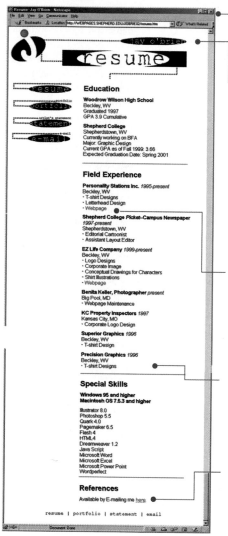

The **page title** includes your name and the word *résumé,* so that the page can be found by WWW search engines.

Jay O'Brien omits conventional **contact information** such as his postal address and current phone numbers on his Web résumé. He expects employers to reach him via an email link. However, it might be wise to offer a postal address, phone number, and full email address so employers who print out your résumé will still be able to reach you.

Links to other Web pages can help you better demonstrate your goals and qualifications. Jay O'Brien provides a link to an online portfolio of his work—something a print résumé doesn't accommodate.

The **body** can go beyond a single page—but make sure headings are easy to read, so someone browsing your résumé can quickly identify the highlights of your qualifications.

Your **list of references** should never be posted on the Web. Instead, ask interested employers to request references by email.

HIGHLIGHT *Designing Your Résumé*

Technology has upped the ante on preparing résumés. These days, even candidates for entry-level jobs are expected to present efficient, handsomely prepared documents. Although many people now use professional writing services to create their paper and electronic résumés for them, you can still design your own if you know how to use a computer and are willing to study effective models.

You can find many examples of effective résumés on the Web just by typing "resume" into a search engine such as <Google.com> and then exploring the sites of various professional writing services, most of which offer numerous sample documents. (You may even decide to hire one of these services).

You will discover that effective résumés come in many shapes and formats, but all of them make it easy for readers to find key information. You may be surprised by how much information some model résumés squeeze onto just one or two pages, especially for job candidates seeking upper-level positions. Early in your career, you won't have so many credentials to present, but do pay attention to how these résumés work. They demonstrate how to array complex information clearly by using bullets, lines, columns, white space, and type fonts and styles effectively.

Electronic résumés need to be designed with equal care. If you are posting a résumé on a Web site, remember that a reader will encounter it only one screen at a time. The opening screen therefore, might include links to other items farther down the page: Computer Skills, Work Experience, References. It is appropriate, too, to include Web links to job-related materials (such as writing samples, teaching materials, or photographs) that would not ordinarily appear on a résumé itself. Since electronic résumés are often scanned, you might even want to add a keyword section at the end of the document listing terms that an employer might be expecting in a particular job search.

Despite a move toward electronic production of résumés, most on-screen documents remain relatively simple and clean, especially for entry-level positions. You don't need brassy colors or stunning graphics if your credentials speak for themselves. Professional résumés rarely include personal photographs or headshots because they invite potential employers to make judgments about matters they should not (or legally cannot) consider: age, gender, race, appearance. So don't include a personal photograph on a résumé unless there is a very specific and legitimate reason to do so.

24d
models

24e Professional memos

Memorandums are used within organizations as a means of communication between members. As a result, memos omit some of the formalities used in business letters to be sent outside the organization: formal salutations and closings, for example, aren't usually required. But memos do maintain a professional tone, and they contain information needed for keeping records of business interactions.

Email (see Section 24a) is the online cousin of the memo. Many people have Internet email (the kind you probably have if you are at an educational institution), which can be used to communicate with people for both personal and professional reasons. Many companies, however, provide internal email systems. These systems operate like Internet email except that messages can be sent only to other members of the organization, as one would do with a memo.

Opposite you'll find, in print and electronic formats, a memo written by Ryan Starck, a student employee at the University of Texas at Austin. While the topic of the memo is one you'll rarely use—a farewell message to fellow staff members—the format and tone Starck adopts reflect the professional yet collegial nature of most work environments.

24e
models

Checklist 24.7

Memos and Professional Email

* Follow your organization's standard layout, which will usually include a date, a "To" section, a "From" section, and a subject line.

* Use block paragraphing and a one-inch margin (for print memos).

* In the subject line, enter a phrase that will make clear to your recipients the relevance and importance of your message.

* Most printed memos don't have salutations because the intended audience is named in the "To" section. An email message sent to more than one person, however, might require a group salutation.

PRINTED MEMO

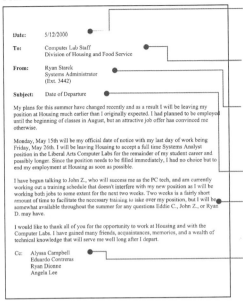

The **date** may be used to refer to the memo in future correspondence.

The **To** section names an individual or group in the organization.

The **From** section should list your name, title, department, and contact information.

The **Subject** line is brief and to the point.

The **body paragraphs** state your business clearly and succinctly.

The **Cc** section lists names of individuals who should receive copies of the memo. This list often includes co-workers who are indirectly involved in the business being discussed.

24e
models

EMAIL MEMO

Email addresses replace names and departments in the **To** and **Cc** lines.

A **salutation** is often used in email; when you email a group of people, you may need to state the name of the group, so people will know why they have been copied on the message.

An **email signature** closes the message, providing your name and title (what's in the **From** lines of print memos).

24f Messages to online forums

Besides email, other forms of online communication have recently evolved. Online forums generally consist of dated postings (messages submitted by discussion participants) and threads (lines of discussion focused on a particular topic). Web forums and newsgroups are two formats of online discussion that display threads and postings hierarchically, according to topic. The sample Web forum on the facing page shows a series of threads about an article read for a University of Texas composition class. Email lists, or listservs, are another common type of online forum. Readers and writers participate by subscribing to a listserv, which allows them to receive new postings in their email inbox, and by sending messages to the list's email address. Whichever format you use, keep in mind the common conventions for participating in online discussions—conventions often referred to as "netiquette."

24f
models

Checklist 24.8

Messages to Online Forums

- Read a number of messages in the forum before you send your own. Try to get a feel for the tone and interests of other participants.

- Avoid posting personal attacks, or *flames,* to authors of messages disagreeing with you. Flame wars make forum participants uneasy and productive discussion nearly impossible.

- Avoid starting off-topic threads—sometimes called *spamming.* Forums differ in how they treat online spam and what members believe constitutes a useless message, but expect some people to become annoyed if you regularly send messages irrelevant to them.

- Don't respond to the entire forum when you really want to respond to just one participant. Avoid this problem by making sure your "To" address doesn't match the address of the forum itself.

- When replying to a thread, remove all text from the previous message that doesn't relate to your response. Don't expect readers to scroll through screens of other people's writing to find your 10-line response.

WEB MESSAGE FORUM

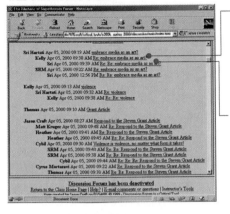

Threads appear as an initial message (starting at the left-hand margin) followed by a series of responses. Each response is attached to the message it most immediately addresses.

Responses are listed as linked text indicated by "Re:" and followed by the subject line of the initial message in the thread. Click on the link to read the message. Some forums allow respondents to create their own subject lines.

WEB FORUM RESPONSE FORM

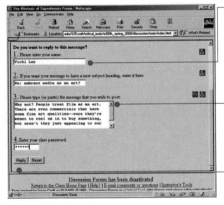

24f
models

Enter the **name** you would like to appear with your posting. Some forums allow anonymous postings; others, such as class forums, require your real name.

Enter your **message** in plain text format. Some forums allow you to use HTML codes to enhance the appearance of the message.

Click the "**Reply**" button (or "Submit") to add your message to the thread. This forum happens to require a password to participate.

24g Newsletters

A newsletter gives an organization an excellent way to keep in touch with its members. With a desktop publishing program or an up-to-date word-processing program, newsletters are relatively easy to create. The model newsletter on the facing page, created by members of an English students' honor society at the Metropolitan State College of Denver, contains six pages, of which we reproduce the first and the third. Although the newsletter includes some enhanced visual features, the students kept production costs down by limiting the layout to two colors and using black-and-white images—a modest but effective decision for print documents having wide circulation. Online newsletters can, without extra expense, include more colors and images, assuming you have the time to put into creating a more elaborate design.

Checklist 24.9

Newsletters

- Select the size of paper and the method of binding, and plan the number of pages you will use. Choose a margin width that allows for binding or folding.

- Determine whether you'll use images and how many colors you want to show. Colorful designs are more costly.

- Decide whether you'll use multi-column pages. More columns usually mean more planning, but when formatted carefully multiple columns make more efficient use of space.

- Map out each page with two goals in mind: (1) showcasing the most important articles and (2) preventing your reader from having to jump from page to page to read a single article.

- For your masthead, use a distinctive font that reflects the spirit of the organization represented by the newsletter.

- Adjust headlines according to their importance, but maintain a consistent font size and style throughout the body of the articles.

- Write short paragraphs to avoid long, unbroken stretches of print, especially when you're using narrow columns.

FRONT PAGE OF A NEWSLETTER

INTERNATIONAL ENGLISH HONOR SOCIETY

Sigma Tau Delta

2000   S P R I N G   N E W S L E T T E R

Convention Sets Records

The Savannah convention surpassed even the records set in St. Louis at our 75th anniversary celebration. A total of 609 registrants representing 125 chapters (plus 5 Sigma Kappa Delta schools) met in Savannah for a superb meeting planned by our indefatigable Eastern Regent, **Beth DeMeo** (Alvernia College) [PA]. The quality of presentations at sessions made competition for convention awards keener than ever (see *Convention Awards*, page 6), the three keynote speakers inspired us all, and tongue-in-cheek traditions continue in fine form.

Everyone would agree with Southern Regent **Lillian Schanfield** (Barry University [FL]), who said that this year's Bad Poetry was the worst she had heard in many years. Runners-up **Crystal Waters** (University of Florida), **Meredith Larson** (Northern Illinois University), and **Mary Nuxoll** (Santa Clara University [CA]) were edged out by **Shannon Roth** (Santa Clara University [CA]) with her winning bad poem, "Feminism for Breakfast." **Williams Baptist College** (AR). **Alvernia College** (PA), and the University of Idaho competed for dry T-shirt honors. Alvernia, a perennial contestant, won the T-shirt prize with the pun in "Tennyson's Tavern" and Idaho's winning skit, "Sock Monkeys," was so popular that it returned for a reprise at the Saturday banquet. "Sock Monkeys" told the tragic story of young Mary led astray by the study of poetry.

Par Conroy gave Thursday's keynote address. He denied that all Southern writing necessarily begins, "On the night the hogs ate Willy . . .", but admitted that he writes as a Southerner because "stuff happens down here." Conroy interspersed his humorous anecdotes with inspirational examples, all drawn from his own life. He described coming to books in the midst (see *Convention*, page 5, *Savannah Convention*)

Heather Frye (left) and Brandy Lynn Beteler (right) pose with innocent Mary Sock Monkey and Tim Water Monkey, a.k.a. Bad Poet Dude.

Facing Brave New Worlds

High Plains Regent **Kris Bair** is planning the 2001 international convention of Sigma Tau Delta around the theme "Facing Brave New Worlds." Join us **March 15-18, 2001**, at the Omni Bayfront Hotel in Corpus Christi, where our host chapter, explains the convention logo. "We compare our 'Island University,' Texas A&M-Corpus Christi, with the island in Shakespeare's *The Tempest*. As students, . . . we will each soon set sail, and 'Facing brave new worlds,' we will share the magic of our education: the *sincerity* of our beliefs, the *truth* of our character, and the *design* of our individual purpose."

Published by Sigma Tau Delta, Department of English, The Metropolitan State College of Denver, Denver, Colorado

---

The masthead identifies a newsletter with a specific organization, often showing logos or catchphrases members recognize immediately. Mastheads also include publication date and issue number.

Lead articles appear on the front pages of newsletters—they reflect the most important recent events appearing in the issue.

Images are "wrapped" by text so that the space on each page is used efficiently, and related material is closely grouped. **Borders** are sometimes used to frame text or decorate the margins.

24g
models

PAGE 3 OF A NEWSLETTER

Sigma Tau Delta

Web Site Awards 2000

Chapter Award: Alpha Theta Mu, Texas A&M-Corpus Christi, <www2.tamucc.edu/~xenters/sigmataudelta2/>. This easily navigable site provides a list of chapter events, awards and scholarships, and the chapter's newsletter, "The Island Scribe," **Delta Iota**, Ohio Northern U, <www.onu.edu/A+S/English/sigms>. Celebrating their 35th anniversary, this chapter's site gives their history, with many quality pictures. They also include valuable links to other Web sites from Shakespeare to theater design. Runners-up: **Eta Chi**, U of Idaho, <www.its.uidaho.edu/sigmataudelta/>. Students may read other students' writing and submit their own to "The Poet's Wall." There are details about scholarships, conferences, upcoming chapter events, and excellent links to other English Web sites. U of Alabama, <www.bama.ua.edu/~sigmatai>. Get ready to hear audio clips and view full texts of members' award-winning essays and poems. This Phi Xi chapter Web site also summarizes several conventions and the chapter's experiences at each.

Individual Service Award: **Meredith Larson** and **Jamie Hajek**, <www.onu.edu/intereses/grammar>. For the grammarians among us and for those needing a reference guide, here's useful information on the dreaded passive voice. Runner-up, **Mary Elizabeth VanLeeuwen**, <www-personal.ksu.edu~janette/installations/MaryVdilPrima.htm>. This site profiles Diane di Prima, the "most important woman writer of the Beat Movement." There are numerous pictures of the poet, a biography, bibliography, and others from her poetry.

Individual Personal Award: **Michael Peter Aiij** <www.bama.ua.edu/~zaij001>. Michael makes it easy to get to know him. He includes his résumé for prospective employers and his favorite recipes for those fellow cooks. Additionally, there are some risqué pies! Runner-up: **Gregory Paul Brown:** <home.alemnia.edu/~gprows>, and <www.alemnia.edu/confluens/>. This graduate instructor has created an overall quick resource both for his own undergraduate students and others. The site includes "basic" MLA style, other MLA resources, the *New York Times* online, and an archive of past students' work.

These awards total $6,000. Congratulations!

Student Advisor's Corner

Tammy Reed, Fort Hays State University

Savannah offered Deltans the opportunity for our first national community service project. The idea, which won Board approval last fall, grew from the belief that, through service, we could share with the citizens of Savannah our love of books.

Student Advisors and Representatives developed the project with the idea that it would become a yearly event. This year I estimate that we collected a little over 700 books and donated them to the Chatham County Public Library system. SAs and SRs plan to run a book drive next year as well. After the fall board meeting, chapters should receive information about what type of books are needed and where the beneficiary in the Corpus Christi area will be.

The **Elaine W. Hughes Outstanding Sponsor Award**, which was also developed by the SAs and SRs, honored the first annual winners at the Savannah convention. The Hughes Awards are dedicated to those sponsors who demonstrate excellence in their commitment to student members of ΣΤΔ. The awards provide one $300 prize and regional prizes of $100 each. This year's winners are **Robert Boyer, St. Norbert College** (WI), and **Kevin Stemmler, Clarion University** (PA), who both received regional awards, and **Dorothy Hatton**, **Eastern Kentucky University**, who received the Elaine W. Hughes Outstanding Sponsor Award.

A new project for next year's convention will be a high school writing competition, which the Chapter Development Committee is working on for next year's convention in Corpus Christi. Look forward to hearing more about this new outreach project.

I would like to say thank you to all of the SRs, and to Chris, my fellow SA, for helping to make my time with the board productive, interesting, and fun. I would also like to thank the Board, especially Helen, Bil, and Bob for allowing us the opportunity to jump into everything that we found interesting and for encouraging our endeavors. I learned so much from all of you, and I appreciate all that you have done to help both me and the student officer program to grow. I will miss you all and hope to see you in Corpus Christi next year.

SRs and SAs deliver books to the Savannah Public Library donated by Deltans as a part of the ReadCycle service program. They are (from left) Chris Flynn, Tammy Reed, Lesley Melecko, a library staffer, Martina Owens, and Eric Lindblad.

3

Running heads often include the same information appearing in the masthead, sometimes with page numbering.

Standard articles are introduced with enhanced headlines. This example uses a left-justified block style of paragraphing.

Regular features are columns that appear in each issue; they are often framed or otherwise distinguished from standard articles so they can be easily recognized.

Footers can include page numbering and information appearing in the masthead.

24h Brochures

Brochures can provide information about an organization and its activities easily and, depending upon the elaborateness of your design, inexpensively. Brochures generally answer a few basic questions—who? what? why? when? where?—and they share the common goal of stimulating interest. Ideally, a brochure you create will provide enough information to capture your audience's attention and show readers where to find further details.

More expensive brochures are used by organizations that want to project a high-profile image, especially for the purpose of recruiting new members. The brochure shown at right, designed by Brooke Rollins, a student employee at the University of South Carolina's College of Engineering, includes images, colors, stylized fonts, and an unusual square page layout—all features that drive up the costs of production. If your organization doesn't have a generous production budget, you might create a simple, elegant brochure that points readers to an organizational Web site—which is cheaper to develop than a printed brochure.

24h
models

Checklist 24.10

Brochures

- Decide on the purpose of the brochure. Is it to introduce your organization? to talk about events or activities? Think about how you want your audience to respond to the brochure, and choose content accordingly.

- Plan the layout of the brochure carefully, keeping in mind how it will fold and how both sides will look. If the brochure is to be mailed, leave one panel blank for the address.

- Sketch out, or storyboard, each panel to visualize how you'll lay out information in the brochure.

- If possible, make each panel of the brochure a self-contained unit so that each section will still make sense when read in its folded state.

- Limit the amount of information to what readers can absorb in a few minutes, but tell them how they can learn more.

FRONT PANEL OF BROCHURE

Use **graphics** and **colors** to attract the eyes of readers. Keep in mind that most brochures must compete for attention.

The **logo** for the organization should appear on the front panel. This logo begins building a persona that the following panels will develop.

Show **addresses** and **contact** information so that readers get a clear idea of the organization's affiliations and institutional relationships.

INSIDE PANELS OF BROCHURE

Each **panel** includes a main heading with related passages of text. Panels have consistent layouts so readers can easily see the central points.

Headings are set apart from other text using inverted background and foreground colors. Provocative, eye-catching phrases draw readers in.

Contact information and the organizational **logo** reappear on the end panel, reminding readers that further details are available if they are interested.

24h
models

Images have been carefully selected to portray themes and activities related to the organization. Here the images form a collage extending across all panels.

Paragraphs focus on the highlights of the organization, especially those that will seem most intriguing to the target audience.

24i Web pages

Web pages present a wide variety of visual layouts, often combining diverse design elements such as stylized text, graphics, animation, and sound. Consequently, it's difficult to offer models and guidelines to suit all or even a majority of occasions. There are, however, standard genres of Web pages and sites, ones you'll see regularly as you browse the Web. The model at right, for example, is an organizational Web site created by Women in Science at the University of Texas at Austin. Like all organizational Web sites, this one is designed to introduce the group to a broad audience. Not only does it include explanations of the group's mission, but it also provides contact information, listings of events, and the names of members—all useful information for people who might want to join or find out more. See Chapter 23 on composing and designing Web pages.

Checklist 24.11

Common Genres of Web Pages and Sites

* Organizational Web sites

* Personal home pages and online résumés

* Online periodicals and newsletters

* Online essays and reports

* Frequently asked questions (FAQ) pages

* Online directories and informational listings

* Search pages and database listings

24i
models

ORGANIZATIONAL HOME PAGE

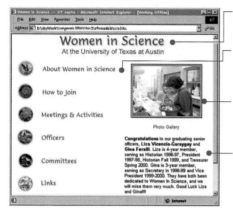

The **title** and **header** include the organization's name.

A **list of contents** links WWW browsers to the main information posted on the Web site.

Images help readers get a feel for what the organization is about.

Brief announcements give browsers the latest news and events.

CONTENT PAGES OF AN ORGANIZATIONAL WEB SITE

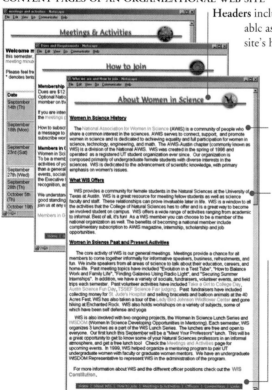

Headers include some recognizable association with the site's home page. The WIS pages are visually linked through headings, fonts, and thematic images.

The **main content** is divided into the types of details readers want to know.

The **body of each page** will be shaped by the type of content it contains.

Page footers often include contact information and a link to the site's home page.

24i
models

Chart 24.1

Model Academic Documents

Many academic writing projects, including research papers, have design requirements formulated by associations of scholars and professionals in their respective fields. These standards are described in detail in the following chapters. Ask your instructor which style you should follow.

Modern Language Association (MLA) style, used in the humanities: Chapter 53

American Psychological Association (APA) style, used in the social sciences: Chapter 54

Chicago Manual of Style (CMS) style, used in the humanities: Chapter 55

Council of Science Editors, formerly Council of Biology Editors (CBE) style, used in the sciences: Chapter 56

Columbia Online Style (COS), used to cite electronic sources: Chapter 57

For samples of different kinds of academic projects, see these examples featured elsewhere in this book.

Topic proposal	pages 27–29
Annotated bibliography	pages 105–6
Cover letter for writing portfolio	pages 94–96
Essay exam (excerpt)	pages 117–19
Literary analysis papers	pages 213–14, 223–27
Research papers—MLA style	pages 79–83, 179–83, and 821–23
Research paper—APA style	pages 852–70

24i
models

PART

V

Grammar

CHAPTER 25

Questions About Subject–Verb Agreement?

When subjects and verbs don't agree, careful readers notice. So you need to proofread carefully to be sure you've put singular verb forms with singular subjects and plural verb forms with plural subjects. An editor will use the abbreviation *agr* to indicate a problem with agreement.

A rotating wall cloud and hail *indicates* the possibility of a tornado.

  agr

25a Agreement: Is the subject singular or plural?

A verb may change its form, depending on whether its subject is singular or plural. The verb is then said to *agree in number* with its subject. Following are guidelines to help you be confident about subject-verb agreement.

1 Understand how subject-verb agreement works. With verbs in the present tense, agreement in number is relatively simple: most subjects take the base form of the verb. The base form is the word produced when *to* is placed before the verb: to *wait;* to *go.*

Subjects and verbs usually agree more readily than politicians.

First person, singular, present tense: I predict.
                                         I go.

Second person, singular, present tense: You predict.
                                         You go.

First person, plural, present tense: We predict.
                                         We go.

Second person, plural, present tense: You predict.
                                         You go.

Third person, plural, present tense: They predict.
                                         They go.

The single notable exception to this pattern occurs with third person singular subjects (for example, *he, she, it, Irene*). A regular verb in the present tense needs an *-s* or *-es* ending.

Third person, singular, present tense: She predict**s**.
                                         Irene predict**s**.
                                         He goe**s**.

So to choose a correct verb form in the third person (present tense), you must know whether the subject of a sentence is singular or plural. The choice of the verb form can be fairly easy when a subject is clearly either singular or plural.

sing. subj.
The weather channel **predicts** storms today.

plural subj.
Meteorologists **predict** storms today.

sing. subj.
He **goes** to Oklahoma City today.

plural subj.
The teachers **go** to Oklahoma City today.

25a
s-v agr

Agreement is also required with irregular verbs such as *to be* and *to have* in a variety of tenses. (See Section 26d.)

SINGULAR SUBJECTS
The weather forecast **is** clear for today.
The weather forecast **was** clear for today.
The weather forecast **has been** accurate for some time.

PLURAL SUBJECTS
The weather forecasts **are** clear for today.
The weather forecasts **were** clear for today.
The weather forecasts **have been** accurate for some time.

EXERCISE 25.1 Decide which verb in boldface is correct.

1. The most violent of all storms, tornadoes (**occur/occurs**) more often in the United States than in any other country.

2. The rotational winds sometimes (**exceed/exceeds**) 500 miles per hour in the vortex of a tornado.

3. Dust devils (**is/are**) less ferocious vortices of warm air.

4. Rising heat currents (**cause/causes**) dust devils.

5. A tornado over water (**has/have**) many of the same characteristics as one over land.

2 In most cases, treat subjects joined by *and* as plural.

Joining two subjects this way creates a *compound subject* that takes a verb without an *-s* or *-es* ending (in third person, present).

1st subj. + 2nd subj.   verb
Storm chasers and journalists alike **want** great videos of destructive storms.

subj. + subj.   verb
The press and storm chasers alike **risk** their lives in hazardous weather.

subj. + subj.   verb
Meteorologists and the Office of Public Safety **fear** that storm chasers often underestimate the magnitude of tornadoes.

However, a few subjects joined by *and* do describe a single thing or idea. Treat such expressions as singular.

subj.   verb
Peace and quiet **is** rare in tornado alley in spring.

subj.   verb
Rock and roll **is** as noisy as a thunderclap.

Similarly, when a compound subject linked by *and* is modified by *every* or *each,* the verb takes a singular form.

subj. + subj.   verb
Every wall cloud and supercell **holds** the potential for a tornado.

subj. + subj.   verb
Each spring and each fall **brings** the threat of more storms.

However, when *each* follows a compound subject, usage varies.

The meteorologist and the storm chaser each **have** their reasons for studying the weather.
The meteorologist and the storm chaser each **has** his or her story to tell.

■ **3 Understand that subjects joined to other nouns by expressions such as** *along with, as well as,* **or** *together with* **are not considered compound.** So the verb agrees only with the subject, which may be either singular or plural.

sing. subj.   plural noun

The National Weather Service, as well as many *police officers,*
verb
wishes amateurs wouldn't chase severe storms in their cars.

plural subj.   sing. noun   verb

Many *amateurs,* along with the *press,* **chase** storms in the American heartland.

When subjects linked to expressions such as *as well as, along with,* or *together with* sound awkward with a singular verb, join the subjects with *and* instead.

SLIGHTLY AWKWARD   *The National Weather Service,* as well as *local storm chasers,* **considers** tornadoes unlikely today.

BETTER   *The National Weather Service and local storm chasers* **consider** tornadoes unlikely today.

■ **4 When subjects are joined by** *or, neither . . . nor,* **or** *either . . . or,* **be sure the verb (or its auxiliary) agrees with the subject closer to it.** In these examples the arrows point to the subjects nearer the verbs.

25a
s-v agr

plural   sing.

Neither police officers nor the National Weather Service **is** able to prevent people from tracking dangerous storms.

sing.   plural

Either severe lightning or powerful bouts of hail **mark** the development of a supercell.

sing.   plural

Does *the danger or the thrills of chasing storms* attract people to the "sport"?

plural   sing.

Do *the thrills of chasing storms or the danger* attract people to the "sport"?

plural.   plural

Heavy rains or strong winds **cause** much damage.

sing.   sing.
Heavy rain or baseball-sized hail usually causes the most damage.

The rule holds when one or both of the subjects joined by *or, either . . . or,* or *neither . . . nor* are pronouns: the verb agrees with the nearer subject.

Neither *she* nor *we* admit to fear of thunder.

Neither *we* nor *she* admits to fear of thunder.

Neither *Jimail* nor *I* have any weather predictions today.

Neither *I* nor *Jimail* has any weather predictions today.

If a construction seems especially awkward, it can be revised—usually by making the verb plural or rewriting the sentence.

AWKWARD	Neither *you* nor *I* **am** bothered by lightning.
BETTER	Neither *I* nor *you* **are** bothered by lightning.
BETTER	*We* **are** not bothered by lightning.

5 When the subject of a sentence is a phrase or a clause, examine the subject closely. Many such constructions will be singular, though they may seem plural.

SINGULAR SUBJECTS
Chasing tornadoes **involves** risk.
To calculate all the forces involved in violent storms **requires** a sophisticated knowledge of physics.
That George survived the storms that tore through three Oklahoma counties **is** remarkable.

However, phrases and clauses can form compound subjects, requiring appropriate verb forms.

COMPOUND SUBJECTS
Locating a waterspout and taking photographs of it **are** his chief ambitions.
That the skies are darkening and that the wind is rising **concern** us.

EXERCISE 25.2 Decide which verb in boldface is correct.

1. Storms of all types (**continue/continues**) to intrigue people.

2. The storm chaser, like other thrill seekers, (**learn/learns**) to minimize the dangers of the hunt.

3. It's unlikely that either the dangers or the boredom of storm chasing (**is/are**) going to discourage the dedicated amateur.

4. The meteorologist and the storm chaser (**know/knows**) that neither ferocious tornadoes nor the less violent waterspout (**is/are**) predictable.

5. That the last ten years have seen an increase in the numbers of storm chasers (**is/are**) certain.

25b Agreement: Is the subject an indefinite pronoun?

Words like *each, none, everybody, everyone,* and *any* are called **indefinite pronouns** because they do not refer to a particular person, thing, or group. Sometimes it's hard to tell whether an indefinite pronoun is singular or plural, so you may have trouble choosing a verb that agrees with it in number.

1 Determine whether an indefinite pronoun is singular, plural, or variable. Consult the chart below (or a dictionary) to find out. Then select an appropriate verb form.

25b
s-v agr

Chart 25.1

Indefinite Pronouns

SINGULAR	VARIABLE (SINGULAR OR PLURAL)	PLURAL
anybody	all	few
anyone	any	many
anything	either	several
each	more	
everybody	most	
everyone	neither	
everything	none	
nobody	some	
no one		
nothing		
somebody		
someone		
something		

The most troublesome indefinite pronouns are *each* and *none*. *Each* is singular in college writing; *none* varies but is usually singular. Also needing attention are indefinites such as *either* and *neither* because, though plural in informal writing, they are singular in academic work. The following examples show the forms to use in college.

SINGULAR   *Each* **believes** decisive action needs to be taken.
SINGULAR   *Nobody* **knows** what the baseball team will do.
VARIABLE   *None* of the proposals **is** easy to finance.
VARIABLE   *None* but the owners **favor** a big bond issue.
PLURAL   *Many* in sports bars **support** a new stadium.
PLURAL   *Few* **want** to pay higher ticket prices.

2 Be careful when indefinite pronouns are modified. If a pronoun is always singular, it remains singular even if it is modified by a phrase with a plural noun in it. For example, *each* is usually singular in college usage, even when followed by a prepositional phrase (though this convention is often not observed in speech or casual usage).

subj.   verb
Each of the whales **makes** unique sounds.

subj.   verb
Each of the animals **has** a personality.

When the indefinite pronoun varies in number (words such as *all, most, none, some*), the noun in the prepositional phrase determines whether the pronoun (and consequently the verb) is singular or plural.

NOUN IN PREPOSITIONAL PHRASE IS SINGULAR
Some of the research **is** contradictory.

NOUN IN PREPOSITIONAL PHRASE IS PLURAL
Some of the younger whales **are** playful.

If the indefinite pronoun is more clearly plural, so is the verb.

indef. pron.   verb
A *few* in the scientific community **wonder** if the whale will survive.

indef. pron.   verb
Many very much **hope** so.

25b
s-v agr

EXERCISE 25.3 Decide which verb in boldface would be correct in academic writing.

1. Most of New York's immigrants (**is/are**) now non-European.

2. Everybody (**seem/seems**) to have something to contribute.

3. Nobody in the city (**run/runs**) politics anymore.

4. Everybody (**expect/expects**) a piece of the pie.

5. None of the candidates (**is/are**) qualified.

6. All of the groups in the city (**want/wants**) to be heard.

25c Agreement: Is the subject a collective noun?

Nouns that name a group are called **collective**: *team, choir, band, orchestra, jury, committee, faculty, family.* Some collective nouns may be either singular or plural, depending on how you regard them. Here is a sentence with the subject (the collective noun *family*) treated as singular.

> The *Begay family* **expects** that *its* restaurant will benefit from a recent increase in Arizona tourism.

Here's the same sentence with the subject taken as plural.

> The *Begay family* **expects** that *their* restaurant will benefit from a recent increase in Arizona tourism.

Both versions are acceptable.

To be sure verbs and collective nouns agree, decide whether a collective noun used as a subject acts as a single unit (the *jury*) or as separate individuals or parts (the twelve members of the *jury*). Then be consistent with your usage throughout a paper, making the verb and any pronouns agree in number with the subject.

SINGULAR	The *jury* **expects** its verdict to be controversial.
PLURAL	The *jury* **agree** not to discuss their verdict with the press.
SINGULAR	The *choir* **expects** to choose a variety of hymns and chants.
PLURAL	The *choir* **raise** their voices in song.

Usually your writing will be smoother if you treat collective nouns as singular subjects.

Chart 25.2 on the next page should help you manage collective subjects.

25c
s-v agr

EXERCISE 25.4 Decide whether the collective subjects in the following sentences are being treated as singular or plural. Then select the appropriate verb form for academic writing.

1. Lieutenant Data (**reports/report**) to Captain Picard that the data on Klingon encroachments of the neutral zone (**is/are**) not subject to interpretation.

2. The crew of the Federation starship (**is/are**) eager to resolve the conflict.

3. Five years (**has/have**) passed since the last intergalactic crisis.

4. A number of weapons still (**needs/need**) to be brought on line, but the chief engineer reports that the actual number of inoperative systems (**is/are**) small.

5. The jury (**is/are**) still out as to whether a committee of Federation officials (**intends/intend**) to authorize action against the Klingons.

Chart 25.2

Collective Nouns		
SUBJECT	GUIDELINE	EXAMPLES
Measurements	Singular as a unit; plural as individual components.	*Five miles* is quite a long walk. *Five more miles* are ahead of us. *Six months* is the waiting period. *Six months* have passed.
Numbers	Singular in expressions of division and subtraction. Singular or plural in expressions of multiplication and addition.	*Four* divided by *two* is two. *Four* minus *two* leaves two. *Two* times *two* is/are four. *Two* plus *two* is/are four.
Words ending in *-ics*	School subjects are usually singular. Other *-ics* words vary; check a dictionary.	*Physics* is a tough major. *Economics* is a useful minor. *Linguistics* is popular. His *tactics* are shrewd. *Athletics* are expensive. *Ethics* is a noble study.

25c
s-v agr

		Her *ethics* are questionable.
		Politics is fun.
		Francie's *politics* are radical.
data	Plural in formal writing; often singular in informal writing.	The *data* are reliable. The *data* is reliable.
number	Singular if preceded by *the;* plural if preceded by *a.*	The *number* has grown. A *number* have left.
public	Singular as a unit; plural as individual people.	The *public* is satisfied. The *public* are here in great numbers.

25d Agreement: Is the subject separated from its verb?

A verb agrees with its subject only, not with any nouns in modifying phrases or clauses that come between the subject and verb. So when editing for subject-verb agreement, first identify the subject in a sentence or clause and determine whether it is singular or plural; then choose the appropriate verb form. In the following sentence, for example, a singular subject (*power*) is modified by a prepositional phrase that contains a plural noun (*tornadoes*). But the subject remains singular, and it takes the appropriate verb form (*proves*).

25d
s–v agr

    sing. subj.   plural noun   verb
The *power* of Midwestern tornadoes often **proves** deadly.

The principle is the same for plural subjects modified by phrases or clauses with singular nouns. The subject remains plural.

    plural subj.   sing. noun verb
Storms that come late in the spring **are** sometimes unusually violent.

Be especially careful with lengthy or complicated modifiers. In the example that follows, the singular subject and verb are separated by ten words. But the plural nouns *mammals* and *humans* in the modifying phrase have no bearing on subject-verb agreement.

    subj.   modifying phrase
The *killer whale,* the most widely distributed of all mammals, except-

               verb
ing only humans, **demonstrates** highly complex social behavior.

EXERCISE 25.5 Choose the correct verb for academic writing.

1. As the twenty-first century begins, most politicians, regardless of their party or ideology, (**embrace/embraces**) the idea that every child should be able to read by the end of third grade.

2. Almost everyone (**agree/agrees**) with this laudable goal, but trained educators who understand the complex process of learning to read are suspicious of this bandwagon approach.

3. Children's ability to learn how to read (**depend/depends**) on a combination of psychological, physical, and social factors.

4. Moreover, many children from families in low-income neighborhoods, all too common in major cities today, (**need/needs**) intensive tutoring because they are not ready to learn when they arrive in kindergarten.

5. The HOSTS tutoring program, which has had great success in helping children to start reading, (**require/requires**) as many as fifty volunteers in a small elementary school, and such volunteers can be hard to find.

25e

s-v agr

25e Agreement: Is the subject hard to identify?

Occasionally you may simply lose track of a subject because the structure of a sentence is complicated or unusual. Just remember the rule: Keep your eye on the subject.

1 Don't lose track of your subject when a sentence or clause begins with *here* or *there*. In such cases, the verb still agrees with the subject—which usually trails after it.

SINGULAR SUBJECTS
Here **is** a surprising *turn* of events.
There **is** a *reason* for the commotion.

PLURAL SUBJECTS
Here **are** my *tickets*.
There **are** already *calls* for the police chief's resignation.

2 Don't be misled by linking verbs. Common linking verbs are *to be, to seem, to appear, to feel, to taste, to look,* and *to become.* They connect subjects to words that extend or complete their meaning.

> The mayor's deputy **was** a severe critic of the police chief.
> Many citizens **feel** betrayed.

A linking verb agrees with its subject even when a singular subject is linked to a plural noun.

> subj.   l. v.   plural noun
> Good *evidence* of the power of television **is** its effects on political careers.

> subj.   l. v.   plural noun
> The *key* to a candidate's success **is** television appearances.

The same is true when a linking verb connects a plural subject to a singular noun, but such sentences sound normal and don't ordinarily raise questions of agreement.

> plural subj.   l. v.   sing. noun
> The many new *patrol officers* **are** a tribute to Chief Carey's budget ingenuity.

3 Don't be misled by inverted sentence order. A sentence is considered inverted when some portion of the verb precedes the subject. Inverted sentence structures occur most often in questions.

> verb   subj.   verb
> **Was** their *motive* **to get** revenge?

>   verb
> Among those requesting Chief Carey's resignation **were**
> subj.
> many *citizens.*

A verb agrees with its subject, wherever the subject appears in the sentence.

> verb   subj.   verb
> **Have** their *fund-raising efforts* **inspired** the critics?

> verb   subj.
> Also disappointed **is** the *assistant chief.*

4 Don't mistake singular expressions for plural ones. Singular terms such as *series, segment, portion, fragment,* and *part* usually remain singular even when modified by plural words.

> A *series* of questions **is** posed by a reporter.

25e
s-v agr

A substantial *portion* of many political talk shows **is** devoted to forecasting the future.

The word *majority,* however, does not follow this guideline; it can be either singular or plural, depending on its use in a sentence. In this sentence, *majority* is treated as singular.

The *majority* **rules.**

Yet it can also function as a plural noun.

The *majority* of critics **want** Chief Carey's head on a platter.

🍎 Fine Tuning

One of the subtlest subject-verb agreement problems occurs within clauses that include the phrase *one of those who.* In college English, the verb in such a clause is plural—even though it looks as if it should be singular.

Carey is one of those people who never **seem** [not **seems**] dispirited.

The verb is plural because its subject is plural. To understand the situation more clearly, rearrange the sentence this way.

Of those people *who* never **seem** dispirited, Carey is one.

Now watch what happens if you add the word *only* to the mix.

Carey is the only one of the city officials who **seems** eternally optimistic.

Why is the verb singular here? The subject of the verb *seems* is still the pronoun *who,* but its antecedent is now the singular pronoun *one,* not the plural *officials.* Again, it helps to rearrange the sentence to see who is doing what to whom.

Of the city officials, Carey is the only one who **seems** eternally optimistic. 🍎

EXERCISE 25.6 Choose the correct verb.

1. The mayor of the town (**strides/stride**) to the microphone.

2. Among grumbles from the reporters, the crowd (**take/takes**) their seats.

3. (**Does/Do**) the mayor's decision to fire Carey surprise anyone after the last election?

4. The city council president claims that she is one of those people who (**objects/object**) most strongly to politics taking precedence over community unity.

5. But she knows she's not the only one who (**wants/want**) a nationally admired park system.

CHAPTER 26

Questions About Verb Tense, Voice, and Mood?

26a How do you choose verb tenses?

Perhaps you first discovered the complexity of verb tenses when you tried to learn a foreign language. **Tense** is that quality of a verb that expresses time. Tense is expressed through changes in verb forms and verb endings (*see, saw, seeing; work, worked*) and through the use of auxiliaries—what you may know as *helping verbs* (*had* seen, *will have* seen; *had* worked, *had been* working). Most native speakers of English handle basic past, present, and future tenses easily. But as a writer, you'll want to be confident about using all the tenses—for example, the more subtle perfect and progressive tenses.

Editors may simply write *tense* in the margin next to a sentence where some problem with tense is evident.

When she arrived, we will go. *tense?*

1 Know the tenses and what they do. Tense depends, in part, on *voice.* Verbs that take direct objects—that is, transitive verbs—can be either in **active** or in **passive voice.** They are in active voice when the subject in the sentence actually does what the verb describes.

            subj.   action
Professor Gates **invited** the press to the lecture.

Photographer Eadweard Muybridge (1830–1904) used stop-action photography to study the motion of people and animals: The horse will gallop; the horse gallops; the horse is galloping; the horse has galloped. For more Muybridge images, look for him at <http://www.masters-of-photography.com>.

They are in passive voice when the action described by the verb is done *to* the subject.

      subj.   action
The press **was invited** by Professor Gates to the lecture.

Below is a chart of English tenses—past, present, and future—in the *active voice*. (See also Section 26e on voice and the more complete Anatomy of a Verb on pp. 475–77.)

Chart 26.1

Verb Tenses in the Active Voice

WHAT IT IS CALLED	WHAT IT LOOKS LIKE	WHAT IT DOES
Past	**I answered** quickly.	Shows what happened at a particular time in the past.
Past progressive	**I was answering** when the alarm went off.	Shows something happening in the past at the same time something else happened in the past.
Present perfect	**I have answered** that question often.	Shows something that has happened one or more times in the past.
Past perfect	**I had answered** the question twice when the alarm went off.	Shows what had already happened before another event, also in a past tense, occurred.
Present	**I answer** when I must.	Shows what happens or can happen now.
Present progressive	**I am answering** now.	Shows what is happening now.
Future	**I will answer** tomorrow.	Shows what may happen in the future.
Future progressive	**I will be answering** the phones all day.	Shows something that will continue to happen in the future.
Future perfect	**I will have answered** all the charges before you see me again.	Shows what will have happened by some particular time in the future.
Future perfect progressive	**I will have been answering** the charges for three hours by the time you arrive at noon.	Shows a continuing future action that precedes some other event also in the future.

26a
tense

Verbs usually look even more complicated when they are in the passive voice, as shown in the following chart.

Chart 26.2

Verb Tenses in the Passive Voice

WHAT IT IS CALLED	WHAT IT LOOKS LIKE
Past	I **was invited** to her party last year.
Past progressive	I **was being invited** by Alicia when the phone went dead.
Present perfect	I **have been invited** to many of her parties.
Past perfect	I **had been invited** to this one too.
Present	I **am invited** to everyone's parties.
Present progressive	I **am being invited** now! That's Alicia calling, I'm sure.
Future	I **will be invited** tomorrow.
Future perfect	I **will have been invited** by this time tomorrow.

26a
tense

As you can see above, many tenses require **auxiliary verbs** such as *will, do, be,* and *have.* These auxiliary or helping verbs combine with other verbs to show relationships of tense, voice, and mood. Two important auxiliaries—*to have* and *to be*— are *irregular. Irregular* means that they show agreement in ways other than just an additional *-s* or *-es* in the third person singular. *To have* is only slightly irregular, forming its third person singular by changing *have* to *has.*

I have	we have
you have	you have
he/she/it has	they have

To be changes more often, in both the present and past tenses.

PRESENT	PAST
I am	I was
you are	you were
he/she/it is	he/she/it was
we are	we were
you are	you were
they are	they were

Other auxiliary verbs, such as *can, could, may, might, should, ought,* and *must,* help to indicate possibility, necessity, permission, desire, capability, and so on. These verbs are called **modal auxiliaries.**

> Rosalind **can** write well.
> Audrey **might** write well.
> Marco **should** write well.

2 Use perfect tenses appropriately. Some writers seem intimidated by the perfect tense because it looks complicated, so they avoid it in all its forms. But the result can be imprecise sentences.

VAGUE	Audrey could not believe that Kyle actually **asked** her to pay for his lunch. simple past
PRECISE	Audrey could not believe that Kyle **had** actually **asked** her to pay for his lunch. past perfect

Perfect tenses enable you to show exactly how one event stands in relationship to another in time. Learn to use these forms; they make a difference.

SIMPLE PAST	She already **quit** her job even before she knew that she **failed** the polygraph.
PAST PERFECT	She **had** already **quit** her job even before she knew that she **had failed** the polygraph.

26a
tense

EXERCISE 26.1 Replace the verb forms in parentheses with appropriate tenses. You may need to use a variety of verb forms (and auxiliaries), including passive and progressive forms. Treat all five sentences as part of a single paragraph. Consult the chart of irregular verbs on pages 470–72 for help with some of the verb forms.

1. Isambard Brunel (**design**) his ship the *Great Eastern* to be the largest vessel on the seas when it (**launch**) in 1857 in London.

2. Almost 700 feet long, the ship—originally named *Leviathan*—(**weigh**) more than 20,000 tons and (**power**) by a screw, paddle wheels, and sails.

3. Designed originally to be a luxurious passenger ship, the *Great Eastern* (**attain**) its greatest fame only after it (**refit**) to stretch the first transatlantic telegraph cable from England to Newfoundland.

4. In the summer of 1865, the *Great Eastern* (**lay**) cable for many difficult days when the thick line (**snap**) two-thirds of the way to

Newfoundland. Nine days (**spend**) trying to recover the cable, but it never (**find**).

5. Many people (**be**) skeptical that the *Great Eastern,* a jinxed ship, (**succeed**) in stretching a cable across the Atlantic, but it finally (**do**) so in 1866.

EXERCISE 26.2 For each verb in parentheses, furnish the tense indicated. Use active voice unless passive is specified.

1. In Shakespeare's tragedy *Macbeth,* three witches tell Macbeth that someday he (**rule**—future) Scotland.

2. Macbeth quickly explains to his wife, the ambitious Lady Macbeth, what the witches (**promise**—past perfect) him earlier that day: the Scottish crown.

3. Lady Macbeth, even more ambitious than her husband, immediately (**devise**—present) a plot to murder King Duncan that very night and then (**convince**—present) her husband to do the horrid deed.

4. But even though the plot succeeds and Macbeth becomes king, the new ruler fears that he (**challenge**—future, passive voice) by other ambitious men.

5. Macbeth is finally slain by Macduff, whose wife and children (**slaughter**—past perfect, passive voice) earlier in the play at Macbeth's orders.

26b
tense

26b Questions about tense in parallel constructions?

When verbs that go with the same subject don't share the same verb tense and form, the result is *faulty parallelism.* Parallelism is an arrangement that gives related words, clauses, and phrases a similar pattern, making it easier for readers to see relationships between the parallel expressions. For example: The college's marching band *played* out of tune, *marched* out of step, and yet *maintained* its dignity.

When a sentence has faulty parallelism, an editor will use double slashes to indicate a problem.

The lawyer **explained** the options to her client and **was recommending** a plea of guilty. //

For more on parallelism, see Section 19h.

■**1 Check to be sure that verbs are alike in form.** Don't shift the tenses or forms of parallel verbs needlessly. In the following example, the verbs describing the lawyer's action shift from past tense to past progressive tense without a good reason. The verbs lack parallelism.

LACK OF PARALLELISM

    subj.   verb   verb

The *lawyer* **explained** the options to her client and **was recommending** a plea of guilty.

The sentence reads more smoothly when the verbs are parallel in form.

REVISED FOR PARALLELISM

    subj.   verb   verb

The *lawyer* **explained** the options to her client and **recommended** a plea of guilty.

Changes in verb tense within a sentence are appropriate when they indicate obvious shifts in time.

Currently, the lawyer **is defending** an accused murderer and soon **will be defending** a bigamist.

EXERCISE 26.3 Correct any problems with parallelism that the verbs in boldface are causing. Modify the tenses as needed to achieve parallelism.

1. In the middle of the nineteenth century, young French painters **were rejecting** the stilted traditions of academic art, **found** new methods and new subjects, and **would establish** the school of art one critic derided as "Impressionism."

2. The new artists **outraged** all the establishment critics and also **were challenging** all the expectations of Paris gallery owners.

3. Traditionalists thought that painters should **work** indoors, **depict** traditional subjects, and **be using** a balanced style that hid their brushwork.

4. But the youthful Impressionists, including artists like Monet, Degas, and Renoir, soon **were taking** their easels outdoors to the streets of Paris or to public gardens, **laying** on their colors thick and self-consciously, and **had been choosing** scenes from ordinary life to depict.

5. Now these revolutionary artists and their works **are regarded** as classics on their own and **being studied** and **are collected** by an artistic establishment they **are rocking** from its foundations a century ago.

26b
tense

26c Questions about tense consistency in longer passages?

Avoid shifting from tense to tense in longer passages (for instance, from *past* to *present*) unless clarity and good sense require the switch. Choose a time frame and stick with it. The following paragraph shows what can happen when verb forms shift inappropriately.

> At the dawn of the nuclear era in the 1950s, many horror movies **featured** monsters **spawned** by atomic explosions or bizarre scientific experiments. For two decades, audiences **flock** to movies with titles like *Godzilla, Them, Tarantula,* and *The Fly.* Theater screens **come** alive with gigantic lobsters, ants, birds, and lizards, which **spent** their time attacking London, Tokyo, and Washington while scientists **look** for ways to kill them.

The passage sounds confusing because it jumps between two possible time frames. Making the tenses consistent makes the passage more readable. Here it is in the past tense.

> At the dawn of the nuclear era in the 1950s, many horror movies **featured** monsters **spawned** by atomic explosions or bizarre scientific experiments. For two decades, audiences **flocked** to movies with titles like *Godzilla, Them, Tarantula,* and *The Fly.* Theater screens **came** alive with gigantic lobsters, ants, birds, and lizards, which **spent** their time attacking London, Tokyo, and Washington while scientists **looked** for ways to kill them.

It can also be revised to feature the present tense. Notice, however, that this shift does not simply put all verb forms in the present tense. One verb (*spawned*) remains in the past tense.

> At the dawn of the nuclear era in the 1950s, many horror movies **feature** monsters **spawned** by atomic explosions or bizarre scientific experiments. For two decades, audiences **flock** to movies with titles like *Godzilla, Them, Tarantula,* and *The Fly.* Theater screens **come** alive with gigantic lobsters, ants, birds, and lizards, which **spend** their time attacking London, Tokyo, and Washington while scientists **look** for ways to kill them.

26c
tense

EXERCISE 26.4 Revise the following paragraph to make the tenses of the boldfaced verbs more consistent. You may find it helpful to emphasize the present tense throughout the passage—but not every verb ought to be in the present. (Specific events in a literary work are usually described in present tense: After Macbeth *kills* King Duncan, he *seizes* the throne.)

(1) *Macbeth,* one of Shakespeare's shortest plays, **portrays** rebellion, conspiracy, and murder most foul. (2) The smoke of battle **has** barely cleared when Macbeth **encountered** three witches who **promise** him the throne of Scotland. (3) Almost immediately, his wife **persuades** him—against his good conscience—to act, and he quickly **has murdered** King Duncan while the old man **sleeps.** (4) But Macbeth himself **will sleep** no more; his conscience **gives** him no rest for the remainder of the play. (5) Only in the fourth act **did** the pace slow, but then the action **rose** again in the fifth toward a bloody conclusion.

26d Questions about irregular verbs?

26d
irreg

Understanding irregular verbs requires a little background information. All verb tenses are built from three basic forms, which are called the *principal parts of a verb.* The three principal parts of the verb are these.

- **Infinitive** (or **present**): This is the base form of a verb, what it looks like when preceded by the word *to: to walk; to go; to choose.*
- **Past:** This is the simplest form of a verb to show action that has already occurred: *walked; went; chose.*
- **Past participle:** This is the form a verb takes when it is accompanied by an auxiliary verb to show a more complicated past tense: *had* **walked;** *will have* **gone;** *would have* **chosen;** *was* **hanged;** *might have* **broken.**

Here are the three principal parts of some regular verbs.

PRESENT	PAST	PAST PARTICIPLE
talk	talked	talked
coincide	coincided	coincided
advertise	advertised	advertised

As you can see, **regular verbs** form their past and past participle forms simply by adding *-d* or *-ed* to the infinitive. **Irregular verbs,** however, change their forms in various ways; a few even have the same form for all three principal parts.

PRESENT	PAST	PAST PARTICIPLE
burst	burst	burst
drink	drank	drunk
arise	arose	arisen
lose	lost	lost

To be sure you're using the correct verb form, consult a dictionary or check the following chart of irregular verbs. The list of troublesome irregular English verbs gives you three forms: (1) the present tense, (2) the simple past tense, and (3) the past participle. (The past participle is used with auxiliary verbs to form verb phrases: *I have ridden, I had ridden, I will have ridden.*)

When in doubt, your safest bet is to check the list, because studies show that errors in verb form irritate readers a great deal.

Chart 26.3

Irregular Verbs

26d
irreg

PRESENT	PAST	PAST PARTICIPLE
arise	arose	arisen
bear (carry)	bore	borne
bear (give birth)	bore	borne, born
become	became	become
begin	began	begun
bite	bit	bitten, bit
blow	blew	blown
break	broke	broken
bring	brought	brought
burst	burst	burst
buy	bought	bought
catch	caught	caught
choose	chose	chosen
cling	clung	clung
come	came	come
creep	crept	crept
dig	dug	dug
dive	dived, dove	dived
do	did	done
draw	drew	drawn
dream	dreamed, dreamt	dreamed, dreamt
drink	drank	drunk
drive	drove	driven
eat	ate	eaten
fall	fell	fallen

PRESENT	PAST	PAST PARTICIPLE
find	found	found
fly	flew	flown
forget	forgot	forgotten
forgive	forgave	forgiven
freeze	froze	frozen
get	got	got, gotten
give	gave	given
go	went	gone
grow	grew	grown
hang (an object)	hung	hung
hang (a person)	hanged, hung	hanged, hung
know	knew	known
lay (to place)	laid	laid
lead	led	led
leave	left	left
lend	lent	lent
lie (to recline)	lay	lain
light	lit, lighted	lit, lighted
lose	lost	lost
pay	paid	paid
plead	pleaded, pled	pleaded, pled
prove	proved	proved, proven
ride	rode	ridden
ring	rang, rung	rung
rise	rose	risen
run	ran	run
say	said	said
see	saw	seen
set	set	set
shake	shook	shaken
shine	shone, shined	shone, shined
show	showed	shown, showed
shrink	shrank, shrunk	shrunk
sing	sang, sung	sung
sink	sank, sunk	sunk
sit	sat	sat
speak	spoke	spoken
spring	sprang, sprung	sprung
stand	stood	stood
steal	stole	stolen
sting	stung	stung
swear	swore	sworn
swim	swam	swum

26d
irreg

(Continued)

Irregular Verbs (*Continued*)

PRESENT	PAST	PAST PARTICIPLE
swing	swung	swung
take	took	taken
tear	tore	torn
throw	threw	thrown
wake	woke, waked	woken, waked
wear	wore	worn
wring	wrung	wrung
write	write	written

The glossary at the end of this handbook treats in greater detail various troublesome verbs, including some listed above. Check the entries for *can/may, get/got/gotten, lie/lay, set/sit,* and so on.

EXERCISE 26.5 Choose the correct verb form from the choices in parentheses. In some cases, you may want to consult the glossary for assistance.

1. Alicia wondered whether the mayor had (**spoke/spoken**) too soon in welcoming everyone to participate in the town meeting.

2. The residents of Oakhill had not (**shown/shone**) much interest in the environmental issue until this meeting.

3. Now the Oakhill representative pulled a petition out of her purse and (**sat/set**) it before the mayor.

4. She claimed that she had (**got/gotten**) more than enough signatures to stop the proposed freeway extension.

5. Alicia had to admit that Oakhill (**chose/chosen**) well, for its representative was an effective activist.

26e Do you understand active and passive voice?

Voice is a characteristic of verbs that is easier to illustrate than to define. Verbs that take objects (called transitive verbs) can be either in **active** or in **passive voice**. They are in active voice when the subject in the sentence actually does what the verb describes.

subj.   action
Kyle **managed** the account.

26e
voice

They are in passive voice when the action described by the verb is done *to* the subject.

> subj.   action
> The *account* **was managed** by Kyle.

Passive verbs are useful constructions when *who* did an action is either unknown or less important than *to whom it was done.* A passive verb puts the *victim* (so to speak) right up front in the sentence where it gets attention. Passive verbs also work well in scientific writing when you want to focus on the process itself.

> *Serena Williams* **was featured** on ESPN.
> *Serena Williams* **was interviewed** by several reporters.
> *The beaker* **was heated** for three minutes.

The passive is also customary in many expressions where a writer or speaker chooses to be vague about assigning responsibility.

> Flight 107 **has been canceled.**
> The check **was lost** in the mail.

When you need passives, use them. But most of the time you can make your sentences livelier by changing passive constructions to active ones. In a sentence with an active verb, it is often easier to tell who is doing what to whom. For advice on revising sentences to eliminate weak passive verbs, see Section 20a-6.

26e
voice

EXERCISE 26.6 Identify all the passive verbs in the following sentences; then revise those passive verbs that might be better stated in the active voice. Some sentences may require no revision.

1. Even opponents of chemical pesticides sometimes use poisons after they have been bitten by fire ants, aggressive and vicious insects spreading throughout the southern United States.

2. These tiny creatures have been given by nature a fierce sting, and they usually attack en masse.

3. Gardeners are hampered in their work by the mounds erected by the ants.

4. By the time a careless gardener discovers a mound, a hand or foot has likely been bitten by numerous ants.

5. The injured appendage feels as if it has been attacked by a swarm of bees.

26f What is the subjunctive mood and how do you use it?

As a grammatical term, **mood** indicates how you intend a statement to be taken. Are you making a direct statement? Then the mood is **indicative** ("I enjoy reading science fiction"). Are you giving a command? If so, the mood becomes **imperative** ("Watch out for flying objects!").

When you express a wish or hope, make a suggestion, or describe a possible situation, you may need to indicate the **subjunctive** mood—which often involves no more than using *were* instead of *was*. For example:

> *If* George **were** [not **was**] in charge, we'd be in good hands.
> The minister wished there **were** [not **was**] more young people in her church.
> *If* she **were** [not **was**] to accept their terms, she could sign the contract.

1 Recognize the subjunctive form of the verb. For all verbs, the present subjunctive is simply the base form of the verb—that is, the present infinitive form without *to*.

VERB	PRESENT SUBJUNCTIVE
to be	be
to give	give
to send	send
to bless	bless

The base form is used even in the third person singular, where you might ordinarily expect a verb to take another form.

> It is essential that *Fernando* **have** [not **has**] his lines memorized by tomorrow.
> Albertina insisted that *Travis* **be** [not **is**] on time for their dinner at her mother's.

For all verbs except *be,* the past subjunctive is the same as the simple past tense.

VERB	PAST SUBJUNCTIVE
to give	gave
to send	sent
to bless	blessed

For *be,* the past subjunctive is always *were.* This is true even in the first and third person singular, where you might expect the form to be *was.*

I wish *I* **were** [not **was**] the director.
Suppose *you* **were** the director.
I wish *she* **were** [not **was**] the director.

2 Recognize additional forms of the subjunctive. The subjunctive is employed in *that* clauses following verbs that make demands, requests, recommendations, or motions. These forms can seem legalistic and formal, but they are traditional in expressions such as these.

The presiding officer asked that everyone **be** silent.
I ask only that you **be** courteous to the speaker.
The president asked that everyone **show** courage.

Some common expressions also require the subjunctive.

Be that as it may . . .
As it **were** . . .
Come what may . . .
Peace **be** with you.

EXERCISE 26.7 In the following sentences, underline any verbs in the subjunctive mood.

1. It is essential that we be at the airport at 2:00 p.m. today.

2. I wish I were less susceptible to telephone solicitors!

3. Far be it from me to criticize your writing!

4. Come what may, the show must go on.

5. If Avery were to arrive early, what would happen to our plans?

6. It is essential that you take over as the supervisor.

26f
mood

Chart 26.4

Anatomy of a Verb: *to pay*

PRINCIPAL PARTS

Infinitive:	pay
Past tense:	paid
Past participle:	paid

TENSE

Present:	I pay
Present progressive:	I am paying

(Continued)

Anatomy of a Verb: *to pay* *(Continued)*

PRINCIPAL PARTS
Present perfect: I have paid
Past: I paid
Past progressive: I was paying
Past perfect: I had paid
Future: I will pay
Future progressive: I will have been paying
Future perfect: I will have paid

PERSON/NUMBER
1st person, singular: I pay
2nd person, singular: you pay
3rd person, singular: he pays
                            she pays
                            it pays
1st person, plural: we pay
2nd person, plural: you pay
3rd person, plural: they pay

MOOD
Indicative: I pay.
Imperative: Pay!
Subjunctive: I suggested that he pay me.

VOICE
Active: I pay
                            you paid
                            he will pay
Passive: I am paid
                            you were paid
                            he will be paid

NONFINITE FORMS (VERBALS)
Infinitives: to pay present tense, active voice
                            to be paying progressive tense, active voice
                            to have paid past tense, active voice
                            to have been paying past progressive tense, active voice
                            to be paid present tense, passive voice
                            to have been paid past tense, passive voice
Participles: paying present tense, active voice
                            having paid past tense, active voice

26f
mood

PRINCIPAL PARTS

being paid present tense, passive voice

paid, having been paid past tense, passive voice

Gerunds:

paying present tense, active voice

having paid past tense, active voice

being paid present tense, passive voice

having been paid past tense, passive voice

26f
mood

CHAPTER 27

Questions About Verbals?

27a What are verbals?

Verbals lead a double life: they look like verb forms but act like other parts of speech—nouns, adjectives, adverbs. Like verbs, verbals can express time (present, past), take objects, and form phrases. Though you may not recognize the three types of verbals by their names—*infinitives, participles,* and *gerunds*—you use them all the time. (See also Section 36a.)

1 Understand infinitives. You can identify an **infinitive** by looking for the word *to* preceding the base form of a verb: *to seek, to find.* Infinitives also take other forms to show time and voice: *to be seeking, to have found, to have been found.* Infinitives sometimes act as nouns, adjectives, and adverbs.

INFINITIVE AS NOUN	**To work** in outer space is not easy. subject of the sentence
INFINITIVE AS ADJECTIVE	Astronauts have many procedures **to learn.** modifies the noun *procedures*
INFINITIVE AS ADVERB	NASA compromised **to fund** the International Space Station. modifies the verb *compromised*

An infinitive can also serve as an *absolute*—that is, a phrase, standing alone, that modifies an entire sentence.

> **To make** a long story short, the current space station is smaller than it might have been.

In some sentence constructions, the characteristic marker of the infinitive, *to,* is deleted.

> Space station crews perform exercises to help them [**to**] **deal** with the consequences of weightlessness.

2 Understand participles. A **participle** is a verb form that acts as a modifier. The present participle ends with *-ing*. For regular verbs, the past participle ends with *-ed;* for irregular verbs, the form of the past participle varies. Participles take various forms, depending on whether the verb they are derived from is regular or irregular. Following are the participle forms of two verbs.

Chart 27.1

Forms of the Participle

perform (a regular verb)	PARTICIPLES
Present, active:	performing
Present, passive:	being performed
Past, active:	performed
Past, passive:	having been performed
write (an irregular verb)	PARTICIPLES
Present, active:	writing
Present, passive:	being written
Past, active:	written
Past, passive:	having been written

(For the forms of some irregular past participles, check the list of irregular verbs on pp. 470–72.)

As modifiers, participles may be single words. In the following example, the participle *waving* modifies *astronaut*.

27a
verbal

> **Waving,** the astronaut turned a cartwheel in the space station for the television camera.

But participles often take objects, complements, and modifiers to form verbal phrases. Such phrases play an important role in structuring sentences.

> **Clutching** a camera, the astronaut moved toward a galley window.
> The designers of the station, **knowing** they had to work within budget constraints, used their ingenuity to solve many problems.

Like an infinitive, a participle can also serve as an *absolute*—that is, a phrase, standing alone, that modifies an entire sentence.

> **All things considered,** the International Space Station is a remarkable machine.

3 Understand gerunds. A gerund is a verb form that acts as a noun: *smiling, flying, walking.* Because most gerunds end in *-ing,* they look exactly like the present participle.

GERUND	**Daring** is a quality moviegoers admire in heroes.
PARTICIPLE	Almost all passengers, however, would prefer not to have a **daring** cab driver.

The important difference is that gerunds function as nouns, while participles act as modifiers. Gerunds usually appear in the present tense, but they can take other forms. In the following example, the gerund is in the past tense (and passive voice) and acts as the subject of the sentence.

>**Having been treated** unfairly by the news media has angered directors of the program.

Here the gerund is in the present tense and passive voice.

>**Being asked** to design a space station was an opportunity NASA wouldn't have missed.

Gerunds have many functions.

GERUND AS SUBJECT	**Keeping** within current budget restraints poses a problem for NASA.
GERUND AS OBJECT	Some NASA engineers prefer **flying** space missions without crews.
GERUND AS APPOSITIVE	Others argue that NASA needs to cultivate its great talent, **executing** daring missions.
GERUNDS AS SUBJECT AND COMPLEMENT	subj. comp. **Exploring** the heavens is **fulfilling** the dreams of humankind.

27a
verbal

EXERCISE 27.1 Identify the boldfaced words or phrases as infinitives, participles, or gerunds.

1. **Regretting** compromises in the original design, engineers refined the shuttle after the *Challenger* explosion.

2. At the time, the press questioned both NASA's **engineering** and its **handling** of the shuttle program.

3. **To be** fair, NASA's safety record in the **challenging** task of space exploration has been remarkable.

4. **Costing** even more than the space shuttle, the International Space Station is sure **to stimulate** new controversies over the years.

5. **To make** budget matters more interesting, NASA has recommended **exploring** the possibility of a human mission to Mars.

27b How do verbals cause sentence fragments?

A verbal phrase that stands alone can create a sentence fragment—that is, a clause without a complete subject or verb. Fragments are considered errors in academic and professional writing.

The Secretary of Homeland Security declined to be interviewed on CNN. **Having been ambushed in the recent past by an unfriendly reporter.**

Verbals alone cannot act as verbs in sentences. In fact, verbals are even described as **nonfinite** (that is, "unfinished") verbs. A complete sentence requires a **finite** verb, which is a verb that changes form to indicate person, number, and tense.

NONFINITE VERB—INFINITIVE	**To have found** success . . .
FINITE VERB	I **have found** success.
NONFINITE VERB—PARTICIPLE	The comedian **performing** the bit . . .
FINITE VERB	The comedian **performs** the bit.
NONFINITE VERB—GERUND	**Directing** a play . . .
FINITE VERB	She **directed** the play.

Verbal phrases are accepted in much informal writing. You'll see such fragments often in magazine articles and in advertising copy.

Harold loved playing comedy clubs—every bit of it. **Telling political jokes. Making satirical comments.** It made life worthwhile.

But in academic writing, fragments should usually be revised. For help on recasting such fragments, see Section 38a.

**27c
sp inf**

27c What is a split infinitive?

An infinitive interrupted by an adverb is considered split.

to **boldly** go   to **really** try   to **actually** see

Some writers believe that constructions such as these are incorrect, a point disputed by grammarians. Split infinitives are such common expressions in English that most writers use them without apology.

Here are guidelines to help you through this minor, but still touchy, matter.

1 Check whether any words separate the *to* in an infinitive from its verb.

If a sentence sounds awkward because a word or phrase splits an infinitive, move the interrupter.

SPLIT INFINITIVE	Harold's intention as a stand-up comic was **to,** as best he could, **make** people laugh at themselves.
REVISED	Harold's intention as a stand-up comic was **to make** people laugh at themselves, as best he could.

2 Revise any split infinitives that cause modification problems.

In the following sentence, for example, *only* seems to modify *mock* when it should refer to *the crudest aspects*.

CONFUSING	Harold intended **to** only **mock** the crudest aspects of human behavior.
CLEARER	Harold intended **to mock** only the crudest aspects of human behavior.

27c
sp inf

Consider, too, whether a word dividing an infinitive is needed at all. Where the interrupting word is a weak intensifier that adds nothing to a sentence (*really, actually, basically*), cut it.

WEAK INTENSIFIER	Harold found it especially easy **to** basically **demolish** the pretensions of politicians.
INTENSIFIER CUT	Harold found it especially easy **to demolish** the pretensions of politicians.

3 Consider whether a split infinitive is acceptable.

In most situations, split infinitives are neither awkward nor confusing, so revising them won't improve a sentence.

SPLIT INFINITIVE	Words fail **to** adequately **describe** the cluelessness of some public figures.
REVISED	Words fail **to describe** adequately the cluelessness of some public figures.

In academic and business writing, it's probably best to keep *to* and the verb together because some readers still object strongly to split infinitives.

EXERCISE 27.2 Find the split infinitives in the following sentences and revise them. Decide which revisions are necessary, which optional. Be prepared to defend your decisions.

1. In his comic monologue, Harold decided to candidly describe his own inept campaign for city council.

2. Harold usually didn't allow his personal life to too much color his comedy routines.

3. But to really appreciate how absurd politics could be, a person had to basically run for office himself.

4. Harold quickly discovered that it wasn't easy to persuade contributors to only support the best candidate.

5. To actually succeed in politics, Harold learned that a candidate had to really understand human nature.

27c
sp inf

CHAPTER 28

Questions About Plurals, Possessives, and Articles?

28a Questions about plurals of nouns?

Plurals can be tricky. Most plurals in English are formed by adding *-s* or *-es* to the singular forms of nouns.

demonstration → demonstrations
picture → pictures
dish → dishes

However, substantial numbers of words are simply irregular. You could not reliably predict what their plurals would be if you didn't know them.

IRREGULAR
man → men
ox → oxen
mouse → mice
goose → geese
child → children
fungus → fungi (or funguses)

Plurals may vary, too, according to how a word is used. You might find maple *leaves* on your driveway but several Toronto Maple *Leafs* on the cover of *Sports Illustrated*.

There are other complications. Some collective nouns can be understood as either singular or plural (*trout*), yet they may still have *s* forms. Compare the following sentences.

The *trout* is delicious. singular
We spotted several *trout* in the stream. plural
The *trouts* depicted in James Prosek's collection include the Mexican golden trout and the Colorado River cutthroat trout. plural

Also troublesome are the plurals of compound words and of numerals. For instance, no one has yet decided whether Sony manufactures *Walkmans* or *Walkmen*. So you need to be careful with plurals, and you should always check the latest dictionaries when you have any doubt about a standard form.

An editor may indicate a faulty plural by circling the problem and writing *pl* in the margin. Or the error may be marked as a misspelling.

We rented two (videoes.) *pl*

Two (sentrys) stood guard. *sp'*

1 Check the dictionary for the plural form of a noun.
Most up-to-date college dictionaries provide the plurals of all troublesome words. If your dictionary does not give a plural for a particular noun, assume that it forms its plural with *-s* or *-es*.

You may eliminate some trips to the dictionary by referring to the following guidelines for forming plurals. But the list is complicated and full of exceptions, so keep that dictionary handy.

2 Use *-es* when the plural adds a syllable to the pronunciation of the noun.
This is usually the case when a word ends in a soft *ch, sh, s, ss, x,* or *zz.* (If the noun already ends in *-e,* you add only *-s.*)

dish → dishes
glass → glasses
bus → buses or busses
buzz → buzzes
choice → choices

28a
plural

3 Add *-s* to form a plural when a noun ends in *-o* and a vowel precedes the *-o;* add *-es* when a noun ends in *-o* and a consonant precedes the *-o.*
This guideline has exceptions. A few words ending in *-o* have two acceptable plural forms.

VOWEL BEFORE *-O* (ADD *-S*)	CONSONANT BEFORE *-O* (ADD *-ES*)
video → videos	hero → heroes
rodeo → rodeos	tomato → tomatoes
studio → studios	veto → vetoes

4 Add *-s* to form a plural when a noun ends in *-y* and a vowel precedes the *y.*
When a consonant precedes the *y,* change the *y* to an *i* and add *-es.*

VOWEL PRECEDES *-Y* (ADD *-S*)	CONSONANT PRECEDES *-Y* (CHANGE *-Y* TO-*IES*)
attorney → attorneys	foundry → foundries
Monday → Mondays	candy → candies
boy → boys	sentry → sentries

An exception to this rule occurs with proper nouns. They usually retain the -*y* and simply add -*s*.

PROPER NAMES ENDING IN -*Y*	EXCEPTIONS TO THE EXCEPTION (ADD -*S*)
Gary → Garys	Rocky Mountains → Rockies
Nestrosky → Nestroskys	Smoky Mountains → Smokies
Germany → Germanys	

5 Check the plural of nouns ending in -*f* or -*fe*. Some form plurals by adding -*s*, some change -*f* to -*ves*, and some have two acceptable plural forms.

ADD -*S* TO FORM PLURAL	CHANGE -*F* TO -*VES* IN PLURAL
chief → chiefs	leaf → leaves
belief → beliefs	wolf → wolves
roof → roofs	knife → knives

TWO ACCEPTABLE FORMS
elf → elfs/elves
hoof → hoofs/hooves
scarf → scarfs/scarves

6 Check the plural of certain nouns that derive from other languages.

28a
plural

analysis → analyses	medium → media
criterion → criteria	phenomenon → phenomena
curriculum → curricula	syllabus → syllabi

7 Check the plural of compound words. In most compounds, pluralize the last word.

dishcloth → dishcloths
bill collector → bill collectors
housewife → housewives

But pluralize the first word in a compound when it is the important term. This is often the case in hyphenated expressions.

attorney general → attorneys general
father-in-law → fathers-in-law
hole-in-the-wall → holes-in-the-wall
man-of-war → men-of-war
passerby → passersby

Words that end with *-ful* add *-s* to the end of the whole word, not to the syllable before *-ful.*

> handfuls [not hand*s*ful]
> tablespoonfuls [not tablespoon*s*ful]
> cupfuls [not cup*s*ful]

8 Check the plural of letters, abbreviations, acronyms, and numbers. These constructions usually form their plurals by adding *-s*.

> the SAT s
> all CEO s
> the 2000 s
> four Ph.D. s

Use *-'s* only where adding *-s* without the apostrophe might cause a misreading.

> three *e*'s and two *y*'s
> several of the *I*'s in the paper

For more on apostrophes see Sections 28b and 31g.

9 Use plurals consistently within a passage. For example, if the subject of a clause is plural, be sure that words related to it are appropriately plural. In the following example, *mind* and *job* should be plural because the subject *leaders* is plural.

INCONSISTENT	**Leaders** able to make up their **mind** usually hold on to their **job.**
REVISED	**Leaders** able to make up their **minds** usually hold on to their **jobs.**

28a
plural

EXERCISE 28.1 Form the plurals of the following words. Use the guidelines above or a dictionary as necessary.

basis	gas	soliloquy
duo	loaf	zero
tooth	alkali	mongoose
alumnus	datum	heir apparent
moose	Oreo	court-martial

EXERCISE 28.2 Form the plurals of the boldfaced words in the following passage. Use the guidelines on plurals above or a dictionary as necessary.

1. The Corner Café sold typical coffeehouse beverages, including several different **espresso.**

2. On the walls of the café were **photo** of the local soccer team and their moms.

3. The decor embodied the style of the late **1990,** sleek and jazzy.

4. With its sports **trophy** and open doors, the coffeehouse also reflected the **interest** of the neighborhood.

5. No one knows how many **cupful** of coffee have been served there.

6. Many of yesterday's soccer heroes think of themselves as **alumnus** of the Corner Café.

28b Questions about possessives?

A noun or pronoun takes a possessive form to show ownership or some similar relationship: *Rita's, the students', the governor's approval, the day's labor, the city's destruction, hers, his, theirs.* Possession can also be signaled by the pronoun *of: the pride of Brooklyn, the flagship of the company, the signature of the author.*

An editor might signal problems with possessives in several ways. An error might be circled and *poss* written in the margin.

28b
poss

Al lived a dogs⌒life. *poss*

Or the editor may simply use a caret to insert an apostrophe where one is required. Omitting the apostrophe in a possessive form is a common mechanical error.

The teacher listened to his students ⌄opinions.

■ 1 Add an apostrophe + -s to most singular nouns and to plural nouns that do not end in -s.

SINGULAR NOUNS	PLURALS NOT ENDING IN -S
dog's life	geese's behavior
that man's opinion	women's attitude
the NCAA's ruling	children's imaginations

Singular nouns that end in -s or -z may take either an apostrophe + -s or the apostrophe alone. Use one form or the other consistently throughout a paper.

Ross's handball or Ross' handball
Goetz's play or Goetz' play

The apostrophe alone is used with singular words ending in *-s* when the possessive does not add a syllable to the pronunciation of the word.

Texas' first settlement
Jesus' words

Although you may occasionally see the apostrophe omitted in signs—*mens room, Macys*—in academic writing don't omit an apostrophe that shows the possessive.

2 Add an apostrophe (but not an *s*) to plural nouns that end in *-s*.

hostesses' job   senators' chambers
students' opinion   Smiths' home

3 Show possession only at the end of compound or hyphenated words.

president-elect's decision
fathers-in-law's Cadillacs
the United States Post Office's efficiency

4 Show possession only once when two nouns share ownership.

Marge and Homer's family
Smith-Fallows and Luu's project

But when ownership is separate, each noun shows possession.

Marge's and Homer's educations
Smith-Fallows' and Luu's offices

5 Use an apostrophe + *-s* to form the possessive of living things and titled works; use *of* with nonliving things.

Follow this guideline sensibly. Many common expressions violate the convention, and many writers simply ignore it.

TAKE APOSTROPHE + *-S*	TAKE *OF*
the dog's bone	the size **of** the bone
Professor Granchi's taxes	the bite **of** taxes
Time's cover	the timeliness **of** the cover

28b
poss

Use *of* whenever an apostrophe + *-s* seems awkward or ridiculous.

RIDICULOUS	The **student** sitting next to Peg's opinion was radical.
REVISED	The opinion **of the student** sitting next to Peg was radical.

In a few situations, English allows a double possessive, consisting of both *-'s* and *of.*

That idea **of** Mariah's didn't win support, although an earlier one did.

An opinion **of** Lane's soon spurred another argument.

6 Do not use an apostrophe with personal pronouns.

Personal pronouns don't take an apostrophe to show ownership: *my, your, her, his, our, their, its.* The forms *it's* and *who's* are contractions for *it is* and *who is* and shouldn't be confused with the possessive pronouns *its* and *whose* (see Section 31g).

It's an idea that has **its** opponents alarmed.
Who's to say **whose** opinion is right?

Indefinite pronouns—such as *anybody, each one, everybody*—do form their possessives regularly: *anybody's, each one's, everybody's.* For more about possessive pronouns, see Section 31f.

28b
poss

EXERCISE 28.3 Decide whether the forms boldfaced in these sentences are correct. Revise any that you believe are faulty.

1. That claim **of her's** may be right.

2. **Moufida's** belief was that the main concern **of most citizens'** was a thriving economy.

3. **Society's** problems today are not as great as they were in the **1900s**; each generation benefits from its **parent's** sacrifices while tackling **it's** own problems.

4. **Its** a shame that people forget how much they have benefited from **someone elses** labor.

5. Children are notorious for ignoring their **elders** generosity; ingratitude is even one of the major themes of *King Lear's* plot.

28c Are possessives needed before gerunds?

Gerunds (see Section 27a-3) are verb forms that function like nouns: *eating, biking, walking.* Nouns or pronouns often precede gerunds. When they do, you must decide whether the noun or pronoun will be possessive or not.

A few guidelines may help you decide when the noun or pronoun should be possessive.

Chart 28.1

Possessives Before Gerunds

ACADEMIC WRITING	INFORMAL WRITING
Possessive + gerund	*Regular* + gerund
the *student's* **arguing**	the *student* **arguing**
the *owner's* **complaining**	the *owner* **complaining**
the *baby's* **crying**	the *baby* **crying**
the *siren's* **wailing**	the *siren* **wailing**

1 Use the possessive form of the noun in formal or academic writing; use the common (nonpossessive) form in informal situations. This first guideline does not apply to proper nouns or to pronouns.

28c
poss

FORMAL

poss. noun   gerund
The woman was startled by the *shelf's* **collapsing** in the shoe store.

INFORMAL

noun   gerund
The woman was startled by the *shelf* **collapsing** in the shoe store.

2 Use the possessive form in *both* formal and informal writing when the word preceding the gerund is a proper noun or a pronoun.

proper noun   gerund
The editor had little patience with *Libertarians'* **whining** about how wonderful the good old days were in Boston.

pronoun   gerund
She ridiculed *their* **glorifying** a time in which many citizens had fewer rights.

■ **3 Use the common form of the noun even in formal writing when the subject of the gerund is modified by other words.**

The complainers admitted they had forgotten about the *Irish* **being** discriminated against in nineteenth-century Boston.

EXERCISE 28.4 Select the appropriate form for the nouns or pronouns used before gerunds in the sentences below. Gerunds are boldfaced. Assume that the passage is written for an academic audience.

1. The same discussions had been going on at the (*art commission/art commission's*) **gatherings** for the past several years.

2. The question was always this: should the commission sponsor local (*artists/artists'*) **painting** or should it seek work from nationally famous figures?

3. Unfortunately, whatever the members of the commission decided, they could count on (*someone/someone's*) **being** unhappy.

4. Mayor Casterbridge and City Councilwoman Meredith decided the (*local artists/local artists'*) **contributing** was the most important concern.

5. Both also knew the council could always count on (*them/their*) **understanding** local tastes.

28d
a(n)

28d Is it *a* or *an?*

Some writers think that they should simply use *a* before all words that begin with consonants and *an* before all words that begin with vowels. In fact, usage is just a bit more complicated, as a few examples show: *an* argument, *a* European, *a* house, *an* honorable person. (See also Section 36b.)

Use *a* when the word following it begins with a consonant *sound;* use *an* when the word following it begins with a vowel *sound.* In most cases, it works out that *a* actually comes before words beginning with consonants, *an* before words with vowels.

INITIAL CONSONANTS	INITIAL VOWELS
a boat	an aardvark
a class	an Egyptian monument

a **d**uck	an **i**gloo
a **f**inal opinion	an **o**dd event
a **h**ouse	an **O**edipus complex
a **X**erox product	an **u**tter disaster

But *an* is used before words beginning with a consonant when the consonant is silent, as is sometimes the case with *h*. It is also used when a consonant itself is pronounced with an initial vowel sound (*f* → *ef; n* → *en; s* → *es*), as often happens in acronyms.

SILENT CONSONANT	CONSONANT WITH A VOWEL SOUND
an heir	an SAT score
an honest man	an HMO
an hors d'oeuvre	an *X*-ray star
an hour	an *F* in this course

Similarly, *a* is used before words beginning with a vowel when the vowel is pronounced like a consonant. Certain vowels, for example, sound like the consonant *y*, and in a few cases, an initial *o* sounds like the consonant *w*.

VOWEL WITH A CONSONANT SOUND
a European vacation (**eu** sounds like **y**)
a unique painting (**u** sounds like **y**)
a one-sided argument (**o** sounds like **w**)
a U-joint (**u** sounds like **y**)

28d
a(n)

EXERCISE 28.5 Decide whether *a* or *an* should be used before each of the following words or phrases.

1. L-shaped room

2. hyperthyroid condition

3. zygote

4. *X*-rated movie

5. Euclidean principle

6. evasive answer

7. jalapeño pepper

8. unwritten rule

9. unit of measure

10. veneer of oak

CHAPTER **29**

Questions About Pronoun Reference?

29a Do pronouns lack antecedents?

Pronouns stand in for and act like nouns, but they don't name a specific person, place, or thing—*I, you, he, she, it, they, whom, this, that, one,* and so on. The person, place, or thing a pronoun stands in for is called the **antecedent,** the word you would have to repeat in a sentence if you couldn't use a pronoun. This connection between a pronoun and antecedent is called *pronoun reference.*

Jill demanded that the clerk speak directly to **her.**

ANTECEDENT   PRONOUN
JILL   *HER*

Number: singular   *Number:* singular
Gender: feminine   *Gender:* feminine

Workers denied that **they** intended to strike.

ANTECEDENT   PRONOUN
WORKERS   *THEY*

Number: plural   *Number:* plural
Gender: neuter   *Gender:* neuter

You have a problem with pronoun reference if readers can't find a specific word in your sentence that could logically serve as an antecedent, the word the pronoun replaces.

> VAGUE   We compared SUVs to minivans, but our budget was so tight we couldn't afford **one.**

In this example, the antecedent of *one* cannot be either *SUVs* or *minivans* because both are plural nouns. To make the sentence clearer, you could replace the pronoun with a noun.

> REVISED   We compared SUVs to minivans, but our budget was so tight we couldn't afford **any new vehicle.**

An editor will usually indicate a problem with pronoun reference by circling or underlining the troublesome pronoun and writing *ref* in the margin.

> Passengers had been searched for weapons, but(it)did not prevent the hijacking. ref?

Revise a sentence or passage to eliminate pronouns without clear antecedents. When you aren't sure that the pronoun has an antecedent, ask yourself whether another word in the sentence could substitute for the pronoun. If none can, replace the vague pronoun with a word or phrase that explains precisely what it is.

> VAGUE The pollsters chose their participants scientifically, but **it** did not prevent a faulty prediction of the mayoral election.
>
> REVISED The pollsters chose their participants scientifically, but **their random sampling** did not prevent a faulty prediction of the mayoral election.

When a word that might stand in for the pronoun is possessive, you need to study the potential antecedent carefully. In the sentence below, *they* seems to refer to *pundits'*, but that word doesn't act as a noun in the sentence.

> VAGUE As for the television **pundits'** coverage, they either mock third-party candidates or ignore them.

29a
pro ref

Pundits' is a possessive form. But since *they* can't refer to *pundits'* (or to *coverage*), the sentence has to be revised.

> REVISED As for the television **pundits, they** either mock third-party candidates or ignore them.

EXERCISE 29.1 Revise or rewrite the following sentences to eliminate vague pronouns. Treat the sentences as a continuous passage.

1. Leah read avidly about gardening, although she had never planted one herself.

2. Her fondness for the convenience of apartment living left Leah without a place for one.

3. Leah found herself buying garden tools, seeds, and catalogs, but it did not make much sense.

4. Leah's friends suggested building planters on her deck or installing a window garden, but Leah doubted that the landlord would permit it.

5. As for her parents' idea that she invest in a condominium, they overestimated her bank account.

29b Are pronoun references ambiguous?

You have a problem with pronoun reference when a pronoun could refer to more than one antecedent.

AMBIGUOUS   When Ms. Walker talked to Mrs. Mendoza that noon, **she** did not realize that **she** might be resigning before the end of the day.

AMBIGUOUS   As soon as the FDA approves the revolutionary antibiotic, the drug company will begin production in a new plant. **It** will make a major difference when **it** happens.

In the first sentence, who is resigning is not clear; in the second, *it* might be the approval of the drug or the opening of a plant. You can usually eliminate such confusion by replacing the ambiguous pronouns with more specific words or by recasting the sentence. Sometimes you have to do both.

REVISED   When **they** talked to each other at noon, **Ms. Walker** did not realize that **Mrs. Mendoza** might be resigning before the end of the day.

REVISED   As soon as the FDA approves the revolutionary antibiotic, the drug company will begin production in a new plant. **The drug** will make a major difference **as soon as it becomes available.**

29b
pro ref

EXERCISE 29.2 Revise the following sentences to eliminate ambiguous pronoun references. Treat the sentences as a continuous passage. Several versions of each sentence may be possible.

1. Amanda could hardly believe that the representatives from Habitat for Humanity would visit wintry Madison, Wisconsin, when it was so bad.

2. When she met them at their hotel, the winds were howling, the visitors were hungry, and it was predicted that they would get worse.

3. But the two women were bundled up and ready to brave the elements, so she figured this wasn't a problem.

4. Later Amanda learned that one of the visitors, Sarah Severson, had been born in Wisconsin, and she told her she knew a great deal about northern winters.

5. The three of them took off through the blizzard in Amanda's lumbering SUV, but it didn't slow them down a bit.

29c Questions about *this, that, which,* and *it?*

Readers may be confused if you use the pronouns *this, that, which,* or *it* to refer to ideas you haven't named specifically in your writing. Vague pronouns of this kind are a problem not just because readers can't locate a clear antecedent, but because writers sometimes resort to vague pronouns when they aren't sure themselves what they mean in a sentence or paragraph. So unpacking a vague *this* or *that* may at times help you get a firmer grip on your ideas.

CONFUSING   In Act III, Hamlet has a chance to avenge his dead father by stabbing his murderous uncle while the man is alone at prayer. But **it** bothers him. [What bothers him?]

REVISED   In Act III, Hamlet has a chance to avenge his dead father by stabbing his murderous uncle while the man is alone at prayer. But **killing a man in cold blood** bothers Hamlet.

29c
pro ref

1 Revise a sentence or passage to make it clear what *this, that, which,* **or** *it* **means.** Constructions such as the following can be confusing or imprecise.

CONFUSING   The minutes of the committee are usually filled with data, charts, and vivid accounts of the debate. I especially like **this.**

Readers can't tell whether you like data, charts, or debate—or all three. You can usually clear up such confusion by putting a space after the pronoun (*this* _____? or *that* _____?) and filling it in with a word or phrase that explains what *this* or *that* is.

CONFUSING   The minutes of the committee are usually filled with data, charts, and vivid accounts of the dialogue. I especially like **this** _____?

Now fill in the blank.

REVISED   I especially like **this detailed reporting of informa-tion.**

When the unclear pronoun is *which* or *it,* you ought either to revise the sentence or supply a clear and direct antecedent. Here's an example with *it* as the vague pronoun.

VAGUE   While atomic waste products are hard to dispose of safely, **it** remains a reasonable alternative to burn-ing fossil fuels to produce electricity.

What is the alternative to burning fossil fuels? Surely not *atomic waste products.* The *it* needs to be replaced by a more specific term.

REVISED   While atomic waste products are hard to dispose of safely, **nuclear power** remains a reasonable alterna-tive to burning fossil fuels to produce electricity.

Here's an example with *which* as the vague pronoun.

VAGUE   The house has a tiny kitchen and a slate roof, **which** Mario and Paula intend to remodel.

The *which* seems to refer to the roof, but it's more likely that Mario and Paula plan to remodel their tiny kitchen. Here is an obvious revision.

REVISED   The house has a slate roof and a tiny **kitchen, which** Mario and Paula intend to remodel.

29c
pro ref

2 Avoid using *they* or *it* without antecedents to de-scribe people or things in general.

VAGUE   In Houston, **they** drive worse than in Dallas.
REVISED   In Houston, **people** drive worse than in Dallas.

3 Avoid sentences in which a pronoun merely repeats the obvious subject. Such constructions are unacceptable in writing.

INCORRECT   The **mayor,** a Democrat, **he** won the election.
REVISED   The **mayor,** a Democrat, won the election.

4 Don't let a nonpossessive pronoun refer to a word that is possessive.

INACCURATE Supporting **Senator Clinton's** motion, Senator Hatch applauded **her.**

REVISED Supporting Senator Clinton's **motion,** Senator Hatch applauded **it.**

EXERCISE 29.3 Decide whether a reader might find the pronouns in boldface unclear. Revise the sentences as necessary.

1. Even tourists just visiting the building soon noticed the aging state capitol's sagging floors, unreliable plumbing, and exposed electrical conduits. **This** was embarrassing.

2. When an electrical fire in the office of the Speaker of the House was soon followed by another in the Senate chamber, it was clear **it** was a problem.

3. Old paintings and sculptures were grimy and cracked, **which** had been donated by citizens over the decades.

4. The governor's proposal for reconstructing the state capitol, the legislators endorsed **it** almost unanimously.

5. **This** was passed by a voice vote.

29c
pro ref

CHAPTER 30

Questions About
Pronoun Agreement?

30a Are pronoun antecedents lost?

Pronouns and nouns are either singular or plural. Singular pronouns (such as *she, it, this, that, her, him, my, his, her, its*) refer to something singular; plural pronouns (such as *they, these, them, their*) refer to plural nouns. This connection is called **agreement in number**.

The soccer **players** gathered **their** equipment.

ANTECEDENT	PRONOUN
players	*their*
Number: plural	*Number:* plural

The **coach** searched for **her** car.

ANTECEDENT	PRONOUN
coach	*her*
Number: singular	*Number:* singular

Problems with *pronoun agreement* occur when you use a singular pronoun to stand in for a plural noun (or its *antecedent*) or a plural pronoun to sub-

Like wax figures, pronouns stand in for the nouns they replace. This head is being prepared for the Wax Museum at Fisherman's Wharf. See <http://www.waxmuseum.com>.

stitute for a singular noun (or its *antecedent*). You're apt to make the error when words and phrases come between a pronoun and its antecedent, causing a kind of "misdirection." You lose track of the actual antecedent.

sing.
AGREEMENT ERROR   A typical **voter** today expects all sorts of
plural
government services, but **they** often don't

want to pay for them.

The plural pronoun *they* refers inconsistently to a singular noun, *voter*. The simplest way to be sure that pronouns and antecedents agree in this sentence is to make *voter* plural.

plural
REVISED   Typical **voters** today expect all sorts of gov-
plural
ernmental services, but **they** often don't

want to pay for them.

Some editors will mark an agreement error by placing *agr* in the margin next to a problem sentence.

(Everyone) believes that (they) are fair. *agr?*

1 Be sure that singular pronouns refer to singular antecedents and plural pronouns to plural antecedents.
Here's an example.

sing.
AGREEMENT ERROR   An **American** always takes it for granted
plural
that government agencies will help **them**

when trouble strikes.

Since *American* is singular and *them* is plural, revision is necessary to make pronoun and antecedent either consistently plural or consistently singular.

plural
REVISED   **Americans** always take it for granted that
plural
government agencies will help **them** when

trouble strikes.

sing.
REVISED   An **American** always takes it for granted that
sing.
government agencies will help **him or her**

when trouble strikes.

30a
pron agr

Note that words such as *student, individual,* and *person* are singular, not plural. Don't use *they* to refer to them.

AGREEMENT ERROR   If a **person** watches too much television, **they** may become a couch potato.

REVISED   If a **person** watches too much television, **he or she** may become a couch potato.

2 Keep pronouns consistent in number throughout a passage. Don't switch back and forth from singular to plural forms of pronouns and antecedents. The following paragraph—with pronouns and antecedents boldfaced—shows this common error.

One reason some **teenagers** [pl.] quit school is to work to support **their** [pl.] families. If **he or she** [sing.] is the eldest child, the **teen** [sing.] may feel an obligation to provide for the family. So **they** [pl.] look for a minimum wage job. Unfortunately, the **student** [sing.] often must work so many hours per week that **they** [pl.] cannot give much attention to schoolwork. As a result, **he or she** [sing.] grows discouraged and drops out.

To correct such a tendency, be consistent. Treat the troublesome key term—in the passage above it is *teenager*—as either singular or plural, but not both. Notice that making such a change may require adjustments throughout the passage.

One reason some **teenagers** [pl.] quit school is to work to support **their** [pl.] families. If **they** [pl.] are the eldest children, such **teens** [pl.] may feel an obligation to provide for **their** [pl.] families. So **they** [pl.] look for minimum wage jobs. Unfortunately, these **students** [pl.] often must work so many hours per week that **they** [pl.] cannot give much attention to schoolwork. As a result, **they** [pl.] grow discouraged and drop out.

30a
pron agr

EXERCISE 30.1 Revise the following sentences wherever pronouns and antecedents do not agree in number. You may change either the pronouns or the antecedents.

1. Many a college class is conducted using the Socratic method, but they aren't always successful.

2. In the Socratic method, a teacher leads a student through a series of questions to conclusions that they believe they've reached without the instructor's prompting.

3. Yet when instructors ask leading questions, the cleverer students sometimes answer it in unexpected ways.

4. However, no instructor, except perhaps for Socrates himself, can foresee all the questions and answers eager students might have for them.

5. But an instructor should be as open as students to accepting new ideas when lively debates lead them to question their beliefs.

30b Questions about agreement with indefinite pronouns?

A troublesome and common agreement problem involves references to pronouns described as indefinite. Common indefinite pronouns include *everyone, anybody, anyone, somebody, all, some, none, each, few,* and *most.* It is not always easy to tell whether one of these indefinite words is singular or plural.

Everyone should keep (**his? their?**) temper.
No one has a right to more than (**his or her? their?**) share.

Yet a decision usually has to be made before a pronoun can be selected.

30b
pron agr

1 Use the chart below or a dictionary to determine whether an indefinite pronoun or noun in your sentence is singular, variable, or plural. The chart, which is not exhaustive, reflects formal and college usage.

Chart 30.1

Indefinite Pronouns

SINGULAR	VARIABLE (SINGULAR OR PLURAL)	PLURAL
anybody	all	few
anyone	any	many
anything	either	several
each	more	
everybody	most	
everyone	neither	

(Continued)

Indefinite Pronouns (*Continued*)

SINGULAR	VARIABLE (SINGULAR OR PLURAL)	PLURAL
everything	none	
nobody	some	
no one		
nothing		
somebody		
someone		
something		

2 If the indefinite word is regarded as singular, make any pronouns that refer to it singular.

Did **anybody** misplace **her** notes?
<small>sing.   sing.</small>

Everyone should keep **his** temper.
<small>sing.   sing.</small>

No one has a right to more than **his or her** share.
<small>sing.   sing.</small>

Using singular pronouns in these cases may seem odd at times because the plural forms occur so often in speech and informal writing.

30b
pron agr

INFORMAL	**Each** of the candidates has **their** own ideas.
INFORMAL	We discovered that **everyone** had kept **their** notes.
REVISED—FORMAL	**Each** of the candidates has **his or her** own ideas.
REVISED—FORMAL	We discovered that **everyone** had kept **her** notes.

In a few situations, however, the singular indefinite pronoun does take a plural referent, even in formal and college writing.

Because **each** of the players arrived late, the coach gave **them** a stern lecture on punctuality.
<small>sing.   plural</small>

Nobody was late, were **they?**
<small>sing.   plural</small>

Everybody has plenty of money, and **they** are willing to spend it.
<small>sing.   plural</small>

🍎 *Point of Difference*

Some grammarians and linguists now support these informal constructions. They point out that, in effect, indefinite pronouns like *everyone* or expressions like *each of the legislators* describe groups, not individuals. That's why most speakers of English intuitively consider them as plurals. Moreover, treating such indefinites as plurals avoids the need to use a clumsy *his or her* to avoid sexist language.

> **Everyone** is entitled to **his or her** opinion.

Nonetheless, most editors and professional writers do not accept these forms—yet.

3 If the indefinite word is usually plural, make any pronouns that refer to it plural.

> plural   plural
> **Several** of the jet fighters had to have **their** wings stiffened.
> plural   plural
> **Few,** however, had given **their** pilots trouble.

4 If the indefinite word is variable, use your judgment to determine which pronoun suits the sentence better. In many cases, words or phrases modifying the pronoun determine its number.

> var.   plural   var.
> **All** of the portraits had yellowed in **their** frames. **Some** will be re-
>   plural
> stored to **their** original condition.
> var.   sing.   var.
> **All** of the wine is still in **its** casks. **Some** of the vintage is certain to
>   sing.
> have **its** quality evaluated.

None is considered variable because it is often accepted as a plural form. However, in formal writing, you should usually treat *none* as singular. Think of *none* as meaning *not one*.

> **None** of the women is reluctant to speak **her** mind.
> **None** of the churches has **its** doors locked.

30b
pron agr

EXERCISE 30.2 Select the word or phrase in parentheses that would be correct in formal and college writing.

1. Anybody can learn to drive an automobile with a manual transmission if (**they are/he or she is**) coordinated.

2. But not everyone will risk (**his or her/their**) (**life/lives**) trying.

3. Few today seem eager to take (**his or her/their**) driver's tests in a five-speed.

4. Everyone learning to drive a manual car expects (**his or her/their**) car to stall at the most inopportune moment.

5. Most of all, nobody wants to stop (**his or her/their**) manual-shift car on a steep hill.

30c Questions about agreement with collective nouns?

Questions about agreement occur frequently when pronouns refer to collective nouns, that is, to nouns that describe groups of things: *class, team, band, government, jury.* Collective nouns like these can be either singular or plural, depending on how they are used in a sentence.

The **chorus** sang **its** heart out.
The **chorus** arrived and took **their** seats.

The **team** looks sharp today.
The **team** lost their luggage.

A pronoun that refers to a collective noun should be consistently either singular or plural.

30c
pron agr

Identify any collective noun in a sentence to which a pronoun refers. Choose whether to treat that noun as a single body (the *jury*) or as a group of more than one person or object (the twelve members of the *jury*). Then be consistent. If you decide to treat the word as singular, be sure that pronouns referring to it are singular. If you decide it is plural, all pronoun references should be plural.

The **jury** rendered **its** decision.
The **jury** had **their** pictures taken.

In most cases, your sentences will sound more natural if you treat collective nouns as single objects. Notice how awkward the following sentence seems because the collective noun is treated as plural.

AWKWARD   The **band** are unhappy with **their** latest recordings.

EXERCISE 30.3 In the following sentences, select the appropriate words in parentheses. Be prepared to defend your answers.

1. The **class** entered the lecture hall and took (**its/their**) seats, eager to hear from the architect after (**its/their**) field trip to several of his buildings.

2. He belonged to a revitalized **school** of design that had enjoyed (its/their) best days four decades ago.

3. The aging architect was accompanied by several **members of his firm,** carrying (its/their) designs in huge portfolios.

4. Students hoped that the **board of directors** of the college might give (its/their) blessing to a commission by the architect.

5. Any **panel of experts** was likely to cast (its/their) vote in favor of such a project.

30d Questions about agreement with *or, nor, either . . . or, neither . . . nor?*

When the antecedents for a pronoun are nouns joined by *or, nor, either . . . or,* or *neither . . . nor,* the choice of a pronoun can be puzzling.

1 When two nouns joined by *or, nor, either . . . or,* or *neither . . . nor* are singular, be sure any pronoun referring to them is singular.

sing.
Neither Brazil nor Mexico will raise **its** oil prices today.

2 When two nouns joined by *and* or *or* are plural, be sure any pronoun referring to them is plural.

plural
Players or managers may file **their** grievances with the commissioner.

3 When a singular noun is joined to a plural noun by *or, nor, either . . . or,* or *neither . . . nor,* any pronoun should agree in number (and gender) with the noun nearer to it.

sing.   plural
Either poor **diet** or long, stress-filled **hours** in the office will take
plural
their toll on the business executive.

plural   sing.
Either long, stress-filled **hours** in the office or poor **diet** will take
sing.
its toll on the business executive.

Pronouns also agree in gender with the nearer antecedent when two nouns are joined by *or*.

masc.   fem.   fem.

Either a **priest** or a **nun** will escort you to **her** office.

fem.   masc.   masc.

Either a **nun** or a **priest** will escort you to **his** office.

EXERCISE 30.4 In the sentences below, select the appropriate words in parentheses.

1. Neither the tour guide nor any of his customers had bothered to confirm (**his/their**) flight from Chicago's O'Hare Airport back to Toledo.

2. Either the ticket agents or a flight attendant working the check-in desk had misread (**their/her**) computer terminal and accidentally canceled the group's reservations.

3. Either the tourists or their guide had to make up (**their/his**) (**minds/mind**) quickly about arranging transportation back to Toledo.

4. Neither the guide nor his wife relished the thought of spending (**his/her/their**) hard-earned money on yet another expensive ticket.

5. Wandering about the vast terminal, the guide located a commuter airline willing to fly either the group or its bags to (**its/their**) destination cheaply.

30d
pron agr

CHAPTER 31

Questions About Pronoun Case?

31a Do you understand case: subjective/objective/ possessive?

Some personal pronouns (and *who*) change their form according to how they are used in a sentence. These different forms are called **case.** **Subjective** (or **nominative**) **case** is the form a pronoun takes when it is the subject of a sentence or a clause: *I, you, she, he, it, we, they, who.* A pronoun is also in the subjective case when it follows a linking verb as a **predicate nominative.**

> It is **I.**
> It was **they** who cast the deciding votes.

Objective case is the form a pronoun takes when something is done to it: Elena broke *them;* Will loved *her.* This is also the form a pronoun takes after a preposition: (to) *me, her, him, us, them, whom.* The subjective and objective forms of the pronouns *you* and *it* are identical.

The **possessive case** is the form a pronoun takes when it shows ownership: *my, mine, your, yours, her, hers, his, its, our, ours, their, theirs, whose.*

In most situations, writers are able to select the appropriate form (or *case*) without thinking much about their choices.

> **Whose** book did **she** give to **him?**
> **They** were more confident of **their** position than **we** were of **ours.**

But at other times, selecting the right case is no easy matter. The correct pronoun choice may even look or sound wrong.

An editor will ordinarily circle an error in case and write *case* in the margin next to a sentence with such a problem.

> To who did you write? *case*

1 Use the appropriate case. Choose subjective forms when pronouns act as subjects, objective forms when pronouns act as objects (especially in prepositional phrases), and possessive forms when pronouns show ownership. Use the chart below to select the appropriate forms.

Chart 31.1

Pronoun Case

SUBJECTIVE FORMS	OBJECTIVE FORMS	POSSESSIVE FORMS
I	me	my, mine
we	us	our, ours
you	you	your, yours
he	him	his
she	her	her, hers
it	it	its, of it
they	them	their, theirs
who	whom	whose

You are most likely to have a problem selecting the correct case when faced with a pair of pronouns. The second pronoun is usually the troublesome one.

> **You** and (**I? me?**) need to review the grant proposal.

31a
case

The pronouns here are both part of the subject. So you should select the subjective form of the *I/me* pair—which is *I.*

But even if you didn't recognize the need for a subjective form, you could still make the right choice by imagining how the sentence would read if you dropped the first pronoun. With only one pronoun in the sentence, you can usually tell immediately what the correct form should be.

> WRONG   **Me** need to review the grant proposal.
> RIGHT   **I** need to review the grant proposal.

Given this choice, most people will select the correct pronoun: *I.*

> REVISED   **You** and **I** need to review the grant proposal.

This simple but effective technique works with many confusing pairs of pronouns or nouns and pronouns.

2 When a pronoun is followed by an appositive, the pronoun and noun share the same case. An *appositive* is a noun or noun phrase that describes or explains another noun.

SUBJECT   **We** *lucky sailors* missed the storm.
OBJECT   The storm missed **us** *lucky sailors.*

You may run into a problem when a pronoun in a prepositional phrase is followed by an appositive noun. The proper form for the pronoun is the objective case, even though it may sound odd to the ear.

For **us** engineers, the job market looks promising.

We engineers may sound more correct, but *we* is the subjective form and should not be used after the preposition *for.*

31b Questions about pronoun case in prepositional phrases?

Prepositions are words that link nouns or pronouns to the rest of sentences; they point out many basic relationships: *on, above, to, for, between, beyond,* and so on. When you join a preposition and a pronoun, you create a *prepositional phrase: above it, to him, of whom.* Pronouns in such phrases are the objects of the prepositions and are almost always in the objective case. Difficulties with case are rare when a single pronoun closely follows its preposition.

Come *with* **me** now.
Wait *for* **us**.

31b
case

You would never say *Come with I now* or *Wait for we.*
But add another pronoun or noun after the preposition, and you may suddenly have questions about the correct form.

Come *with* Josh and (**I**? **me**?) now.
Wait *for* (**he**? **him**?) and (**I**? **me**?).

Just remember to use the objective case when pronouns are the objects of prepositional phrases.

prep.   obj.   obj.
Come *with* **Josh** and (**I**? **me**?) now.
prep.   obj.   obj.
Wait *for* (**he**? **him**?) and (**I**? **me**?).
prep.   obj.   obj.
Just *between* **you** and (**I**? **me**?), the answer is "Yes."

A glance at the chart on page 510 shows that the forms needed in these sentences are the objective ones: *me* and *him.*

Come with Josh and **me** now.
Wait for him and **me**.
Just between you and **me**, the answer is "Yes."

In some cases, you can reach the same conclusion by deleting the words causing problems and considering the alternatives.

FIRST VERSION   Come *with* **I** now.
SECOND VERSION   Come *with* **me** now.

In this case, the deletion makes it clearer that the second version is correct, and so the full sentence can be restored.

REVISED   Come *with* Josh and **me** now.

EXERCISE 31.1 Select the correct pronoun from the choices offered in parentheses.

1. In the reporter's opinion, neither (**she/her**) nor her competitors had done a good job in covering the city's financial crisis.

2. It was likely that both political parties would now accuse (**she/her**) and (**they/them**) of media bias.

3. Knowing her colleagues at the competing TV stations, the reporter was convinced that both she and (**they/them**) had rushed their stories.

4. She had assumed that the city manager's staff had been honest about the financial problems, but now she wasn't sure they had been truthful with (**she/her**).

5. "You and (**I/me**) will just have to accept the criticism," the reporter told a professional colleague, who just frowned at (**she/her**).

31c
case

31c Questions about pronoun case in comparisons?

You may have questions about pronoun case when you're writing a comparison that includes *than* or *as* followed by a pronoun. You'll recognize this familiar difficulty immediately.

I am taller *than* (**him? he?**).
Politics does not interest me as much *as* (**she? her?**).

1 Expand the comparison into a complete clause. For example, you might be puzzling over a choice like this.

I am taller *than* (**him? he?**).

To expand the comparison—*than* (*him? he?*)—into a clause, you need to add a verb, in this case *is.*

I am taller *than* (**him? he?**) *is.*

2 Now choose the appropriate form of the pronoun. The correct pronoun form will usually be more obvious once a verb is in place.

REVISED   I am taller *than* **he** (is).

To work as the subject of the verb *is,* the pronoun (*him/he*) must take its subjective form (*he*). However, you don't have to write the verb *is* into the sentence; it can remain implied.

Here is another example, with *as.*

Politics does not interest me as much *as* (**she? her?**).

Notice, however, that the comparison can be expanded in two different ways.

Politics does not interest me as much *as* it interests (**she? her?**).
Politics does not interest me as much *as* (**she? her?**) does.

As a result, the pronoun you select will determine what the sentence means. Select the subjective pronoun *she,* and this is the result.

REVISED   Politics does not interest me as much *as* **she** (does).

Choose the objective pronoun *her,* and the sentence has a different meaning.

REVISED   Politics does not interest me as much *as* (it interests) **her.**

For the sake of clarity, it often makes sense to write out the implied verbs in such situations.

Here's a second example.

Sean likes Keesha better *than* (**I? me?**).

FIRST VERSION   Sean likes Keesha better *than* **I** do.
SECOND VERSION   Sean likes Keesha better *than* he likes **me.**

31c
case

EXERCISE 31.2 Select the correct pronoun from the choices offered in parentheses.

1. Although the Cowardly Lion needed the Wizard's help as much as Dorothy did, the King of the Jungle was less determined than (**she/her**) to hike to Oz.

2. Dorothy probably felt more confident than (**he/him**) that she could deal with the wonderful Wizard.

3. Perhaps Dorothy could relate more easily to (**he/him**) than a lion could.

4. Although more cautious in his appraisal of the Wizard than Dorothy, the Scarecrow was no less eager for guidance than (**she/her**).

5. Perhaps the Scarecrow even feared that Dorothy would like the Wizard more than (**he/him**).

31d Questions about pronoun case after linking verbs?

31d
case

Linking verbs, such as *to be, to seem, to appear, to feel,* and *to become,* connect a subject to a word or phrase that extends or completes its meaning—the **subject complement.** When complements are pronouns, they are in the subjective case.

    subj.   l. v.   subj. comp.
The *culprits* are obviously **they.**

         subj.   l. v. subj. comp.
The *commander in chief* will be **he.**

    subj.   l. v.   subj. comp.
The *one* who will prevail is **I.**

Yet complements can be puzzling. Many writers would have a tough time deciding which of the following pairs of sentences is correct.

It is **I.**	It is **me.**
That is **she.**	That is **her.**
This is **he.**	This is **him.**

In college English, the left-hand column is considered correct. The pronouns after the verb are all subject complements in the subjective case: *I, she, he.* But exceptions are allowed: *It is me* is acceptable too.

So in most academic writing, use the subjective case of a pronoun when it is the complement of a linking verb.

The next CEO of the corporation will be **she**.
The director was **he**.

But do use the objective case of a pronoun when it sounds more natural. You'd certainly use these forms when writing dialogue, for example.

It is **me**.
That's **her**.

Or work around the problem. Rather than write "The director was he," reverse the order and try "He was the director."

EXERCISE 31.3 Review Sections 31a through 31d. Select the correct pronoun from the choices in parentheses below.

1. That is **(he/him)** in the office there.

2. The guilty party certainly was not **(she/her)**.

3. Spying three men in uniform, we assumed that the pilots were **(they/them)**.

4. They are **(who/whom)**?

5. We were surprised that the person who had complained was **(she/her)**.

31e
who(m)

31e Is it *who* or *whom?*

In informal spoken English, the distinction between *who* and *whom* (or *whoever/whomever*) is usually ignored. In written English, however, many readers still expect the convention to be honored.

1 Choose between the subjective and objective forms of *who*.
Select the subjective form (*who*) when pronouns act as subjects, the objective form (*whom*) when pronouns act as objects. The appropriate choice is especially important in prepositional phrases.

SUBJECTIVE FORM   **Who** wrote this report?
OBJECTIVE FORM   You addressed **whom?**
OBJECTIVE FORM   To **whom** did you write?

The problem, of course, with *who/whom* is figuring out whether the word is acting as a subject or an object. Which is right?

> **Who** did you address?
> **Whom** did you address?

To select the appropriate form, you need to identify the subject and the object.

	obj.	subj.

APPROPRIATE   **Whom** did you address?

If you can locate the verb, you can usually figure out who is doing what to whom.

> (**Who? Whom?**) are you taking on the tour?

The verb is *are taking*. The doer of the action is clearly *you: you are taking*. The person receiving the action, then, is the objective form of *who/whom: whom*.

APPROPRIATE   **Whom** are you taking on the tour?

Be careful with sentences containing passive verbs, where the subject remains in the subjective case (*who*) even though it does not actually perform the action described by the verb.

APPROPRIATE   **Who** was accused of cheating?

31e
who(m)

When you can't recall all the fine points of *who/whom,* play it safe by using *who* in most situations—except immediately after a preposition. After a preposition, use *whom: to whom, for whom, with whom.* Using *who* in all other circumstances will mean you are technically incorrect whenever the word is acting as an object. But *who* misused as an object usually sounds less awkward than *whom* misused as a subject.

WHO MISUSED AS AN OBJECT	You addressed **who?**
WHOM MISUSED AS A SUBJECT	**Whom** wrote this report?

2 Take care with *who/whom* in dependent clauses.

When *who/whom* (or *whoever/whomever*) is part of a dependent clause, *who/whom* takes the form it would have in the dependent clause, not in the sentence as a whole. Constructions of this kind are quite common. The phrases underlined in the following examples are clauses within full sentences.

The system rewards <u>whoever works hard</u>. subjective

The surplus will decrease no matter <u>whom we elect president</u>. objective

<u>Whomever we nominate</u> is likely to be elected. objective

EXERCISE 31.4 Decide which of the pronoun forms in parentheses is correct in each of the following sentences.

1. Sam Donaldson looks like a man (**whom/who**) wouldn't trust a nun with a prayer.

2. (**Whom/Who**) wouldn't like to win the state lottery?

3. To (**who/whom**) would you go for sound financial advice?

4. Are these the young children (**who/whom**) you took by bus to Santa Fe?

5. Officials couldn't determine (**who/whom**) rigged the club elections.

31f Questions about possessive pronouns?

The most common way of showing ownership in English is to add an apostrophe + -*s* to a noun: *Akilah's book,* the *dog's owner.* The familiar -*'s* is not, however, used with **personal pronouns** (or *who*)—and this exception confuses some writers who are inclined to add -*'s* to personal pronouns that don't require it.

The possessive forms of **indefinite pronouns** can be troublesome as well. Some indefinite pronouns take the apostrophe + -*s* to indicate ownership, but others do not.

31f
poss

1 Remember that personal pronouns don't need apostrophes to show ownership. This is true whether the possessive pronoun comes before or after a noun.

BEFORE THE NOUN	AFTER THE NOUN
That is **my** *book.*	The *book* is **mine.**
That is **your** *book.*	The *book* is **yours.**
That is **her** *book.*	The *book* is **hers.**
That is **his** *book.*	The *book* is **his.**
That is **our** *book.*	The *book* is **ours.**
That is **their** *book.*	The *book* is **theirs.**
Whose *book* is this?	The *book* is **whose?**

2 Remember that while some indefinite pronouns can form the possessive by adding -'s, others cannot. Among the indefinite pronouns that cannot add -'s to show possession are the items in Chart 31.2.

Chart 31.2

Possessive Forms of Indefinite Pronouns	
INDEFINITE PRONOUN	FORM OF THE POSSESSIVE
all	the opinion **of all**
any	the sight **of any**
each	the price **of each**
few	the judgment **of few**
most	the dream **of most**
none	the choice **of none**
some	the expectation **of some**

Indefinite pronouns ending in *-body* or *-one* can form the possessive with *-'s* or with *of.*

INDEFINITE PRONOUN	FORMS OF THE POSSESSIVE
anybody	**anybody's** opinion
	the opinion of **anybody**
someone	**someone's** hope
	the hope of **someone**

31g
its/it's

31g Special problems: *its/it's* and *whose/who's*

Don't mistake the possessive pronoun *its* for the contraction *it's* (which means *it is* or *it has*). This error is both very common and easy to fix. A related error is mistaking *whose* for *who's*.

1 Remember that *its* is a possessive form; *it's* is a contraction of *it is.*

WRONG	The school lost **it's** charter because of low test scores.
RIGHT	The school lost **its** charter because of low test scores.

WRONG	**Its** a fact that property crimes in the neighborhood have decreased.
RIGHT	**It's** a fact that property crimes in the neighborhood have decreased.
WRONG	**Its** unlikely that the aircraft will lose **it's** way in the dark. **Its** equipped with radar.
RIGHT	**It's** unlikely that the aircraft will lose **its** way in the dark. **It's** equipped with radar.

The apostrophe makes the contracted form—*it's*—look suspiciously like a possessive. And the possessive form—*its*—sounds like a contraction. But don't be fooled. The possessive forms of a personal pronoun never take an apostrophe, while contractions always require one.

| POSSESSIVE FORM | The iron left **its** grim outline on the silk shirt. |
| CONTRACTION | **It's** a stupid proposal. |

If you consistently misuse *its/it's,* circle these words whenever they appear in your work and then check them. It may help if you always read *it's* as *it is.* Eventually you will eliminate this error.

2 Remember that the possessive of *who* is *whose*. Don't mistake *whose,* the possessive, for *who's,* which is the contraction for *who is* or *who has.*

31g
its/it's

| POSSESSIVE FORM | **Whose** teammate is on first base? |
| CONTRACTION | **Who's** on first? |

EXERCISE 31.5 Circle all occurrences of *its/it's* in the following passage and correct any errors.

1. Its been decades since Americans have felt as comfortable traveling in Eastern Europe as they do now.

2. Its likely that tourism will remain a major industry in Hungary, Poland, and the Czech Republic.

3. Each of these countries has much to attract tourists to its cities.

4. Yet its the small towns of Eastern Europe that many Americans may find most appealing.

5. In rural areas, sensitive travelers often get a better feel for a country and its people.

EXERCISE 31.6 Review Sections 31f and 31g. Identify and correct any pronoun-related errors in the sentences below.

1. There is usually not much doubt about whose responsible for enormous environmental disasters.

2. Its not hard to spot a capsized oil tanker.

3. Yet anybodys home or yard can contribute to environmental pollution.

4. The earth is our's to protect or despoil.

5. Ecology has to be everyone's responsibility.

31g
its/it's

CHAPTER 32

Questions About Pronoun Choices?

32a Questions about reflexive and intensive pronouns?

Reflexive and **intensive pronouns** are created when *-self* is added to singular personal pronouns and *-selves* to plural personal pronouns: *myself, yourself, herself, himself, itself, oneself, ourselves, yourselves, themselves.* These words are *reflexive* in sentences like the following, where both the subject and the object of an action are the same person or thing.

   subj.   obj.
They took **themselves** too seriously.

They are *intensive* when they modify a noun or another pronoun to add emphasis.

Warren **himself** admitted he was responsible.

   noun   pron.
I never vote **myself.**

Some writers use reflexive pronouns—especially *myself*—inappropriately because they think that intensive forms are more formal than simple personal pronouns. Other writers use the nonstandard forms *hisself* or *theirselves.* Both issues are addressed in this section.

There are no specific proofreading symbols for problems with reflexive and intensive pronouns. An editor is likely just to circle a doubtful form and mark *pron.* in the margin.

Jack ⟨hisself⟩ appeared at the meeting. *pron.*

1 Don't use reflexive pronouns to make sentences sound more formal. The basic pronoun form is adequate.

NONSTANDARD   The memo is for Ms. Matthews and **yourself.**
REVISED   The memo is for Ms. Matthews and **you.**

Use the pronoun reflexively only when the subject and object in a sentence refer to the same person or thing.

> subj.   obj.
> *Maggie* rediscovered **herself** in her paintings.

> subj.   obj.
> *Jones* had only **himself** to blame.

Similarly, don't use *myself* in place of a more suitable *I* or *me*.

> NONSTANDARD   *Jose and myself* wrote the **lab report.**
> REVISED   *Jose and I* wrote the **lab report.**

Compare the sentence above to a similar one using *myself* correctly as an intensive pronoun.

> *I* wrote the lab report **myself.**

2 Use intensive pronouns for emphasis.

> The gift is for *you* **yourself.**
> The *residents* did all the plumbing and wiring **themselves.**

3 Never use *hisself* or *theirselves.*

Although you may hear these expressions—especially *theirselves*—in speech, the correct forms in writing are always *himself* and *themselves.*

32a
pron

> WRONG   Lincoln wrote the letter **hisself.**
> CORRECT   Lincoln wrote the letter **himself.**

> WRONG   They saw **theirselves** on television.
> CORRECT   They saw **themselves** on television.

EXERCISE 32.1 Correct any problems with reflexive or intensive pronouns in the sentences below.

1. "God helps them who help themselves" is an adage credited to Benjamin Franklin.

2. The delegates to the Constitutional Convention in 1787 were not sure they could agree among theirselves on a new form of government.

3. George Washington hisself presided over the convention.

4. Aaron and myself wrote a paper on Madison's contribution to the Constitution.

5. You might want to read about the topic yourself.

32b Questions about *that, which, and who?*

The puzzler here is when to use the pronouns *that* and *which*. You may have learned a rule that requires *that* as the lead-in for essential or restrictive modifiers (that is, for clauses that strictly limit the meaning of the word modified).

ESSENTIAL CLAUSE   The car **that hit me** rolled into the shallow ditch.

The same rule insists that *which* be used with nonessential or nonrestrictive clauses (that is, with modifiers that add information not crucial to the meaning of a sentence).

NONESSENTIAL CLAUSE   My vehicle, **which is a sport utility,** sustained little damage.

Yet in reading you may have noticed that some writers use *which* interchangeably.

ESSENTIAL CLAUSE   The car **which hit me** rolled into the shallow ditch.

What form is correct? And when is *who* a better alternative to *which* and *that?*

32b
pron

1 Use *that* to introduce essential (restrictive) clauses. A clause introduced by *that* will almost always be essential. No commas are used around such clauses.

The concept **that** intrigued the shareholders most involved profit sharing.
Only the report **that I** wrote recommended that concept.

2 Use *which* to introduce nonessential (nonrestrictive) clauses. Such clauses are ordinarily surrounded by commas.

NONESSENTIAL CLAUSE   The Web site, **which** is not on the university's server, contains controversial advice about plagiarism.
NONESSENTIAL CLAUSE   The agency, **which** was created in 1978, helps businesses use energy more efficiently.

But understand that many writers use *which* to introduce essential clauses as well. In these clauses, context and punctuation may determine whether a *which* clause is essential or not. If the clause is essential, no commas separate it from the rest of the sentence; if nonessential, commas enclose the clause.

ESSENTIAL CLAUSE	The business plan **which** intrigued the shareholders was the simplest one.
NONESSENTIAL CLAUSE	The business plan, **which** intrigued the shareholders, was quite simple.

Some readers still prefer to distinguish between *that* and *which* even though the distinction is disappearing in general usage. For more about this issue, see Section 33i.

3 Use *who* rather than *that* or *which* when modifying a person.

INAPPROPRIATE	The woman **that** was promoted is my boss.
BETTER	The woman **who** was promoted is my boss.
INAPPROPRIATE	The delegates, **which** represented all regions of the country, met in Philadelphia for their convention.
BETTER	The delegates, **who** represented all regions of the country, met in Philadelphia for their convention.

32b
pron

EXERCISE 32.2 Decide among *that/which/who* in the following sentences. Add commas where needed.

1. Charlie Chaplin's tramp (**that/which/who**) wore a derby, baggy trousers, and a mustache may still be the most recognized character on film.

2. The popularity (**that/which/who**) Chaplin had in the early days of film may never be equaled either.

3. His graceful gestures and matchless acrobatics (**that/which/who**) some critics likened to ballet were perfectly suited to the silent screen.

4. A flaw (**that/which/who**) weakens many of Chaplin's films is sentimentality.

5. Chaplin's tramp made a last appearance in *The Great Dictator* (1940) (**that/which/who**) satirized Hitler's regime.

32c When to use *I, we, you,* or *one?*

Pronouns change the distance between writers and readers. Choosing *I* or *you* puts you closer to readers; using *one* creates distance.

1 Use *I* when you or your opinions belong in what you're writing. In general, avoid the first person *I* in scientific reports and expository essays.

WITH *I* I **learned** through a survey **I did** that students who drive a car on campus are more likely to have jobs than those who do not.

REVISED **A survey showed** that students who drive a car on campus are likely to have jobs.

However, when you find that avoiding *I* makes you resort to an awkward passive verb, use *I* instead.

WORDY **It is believed** that procedures for voting in campus elections are too complex.

REVISED **I believe** that procedures for voting in campus elections are too complex.

You can often eliminate an awkward passive without using *I.*

REVISED WITHOUT *I* Procedures for voting in campus elections are too complex.

The same advice—to use *I* sensibly—applies when you find yourself cobbling clumsy phrases just to avoid the pronoun.

WORDY **In the opinion of this writer,** federal taxes should be lowered.

REVISED **I believe** federal taxes should be lowered.

REVISED WITHOUT *I* Federal taxes should be lowered.

32c
pron

🍎 *Point of Difference*

You should know that some instructors and editors simply will not allow *I* in college, professional, or scientific prose. When writing for them, respect their rules. However, most writers today recognize that using *I* is both natural and sensible even in relatively formal work. Not using *I* or *we* (when more than one author is involved) can even lead to questions about who is taking responsibility for a statement.🍎

2 Use *we* whenever two or more writers are involved in a project or when you are writing to express the opinion of a group.

> When **we** compared our surveys, **we** discovered the conflicting evidence.
>
> **We** believe that the city council has an obligation to reconsider its zoning action.

Or use the first person *we* to indicate a general condition when it is appropriate to comment editorially.

> **We** need better control of our medical care systems in the United States.

Avoid *we* or *us* as a chummy way of addressing your reader. In most college writing, *we* used this way sounds pompous.

3 Use *you* to address readers personally or to give orders or directions. *You* sounds direct, cordial, and personal. So be sure you really want your readers included when using the second person in college writing. The following sentence, for example, may be too personal. It seems to implicate readers directly in scholastic dishonesty.

INAPPROPRIATE	A recent student government survey suggested that **you** will cheat in two courses during **your** college career.
REVISED	A recent student government survey suggested that **most students** will cheat in two courses during **their** college careers.

Because *you* is both vague and potentially personal, it is a pronoun to avoid in most academic writing, especially reports and research projects. *You* may be more appropriate in persuasive writing, however, where your goal is to move people to act.

4 Use *one* to express a general thought. *One* is often useful for conveying moral sentiments or sweeping claims.

> Consider the anxiety of not knowing where **one's** next meal is coming from.
>
> **One** learns a great deal about old Russia from reading Dostoevsky.

Notice that *one* makes the sentence more formal than it would be if *one* were replaced by *I* or *you*.

Sentences with too many *ones,* however, may seem like the butlers of British comedy—sneering and superior.

POMPOUS   **One** can never be too careful about maintaining **one's** good reputation, can **one?**

In most cases, *you* or an appropriate noun sounds less stiff than *one,* especially when giving directions.

WORDY   If **one** is uncertain about the authority of **one's** sources, **one** should consult a librarian in the reference room.

REVISED   If **you** are uncertain about the authority of **your** sources, consult a librarian in the reference room.

5 Whatever pronouns you choose, be consistent. Don't switch pronoun forms in the middle of a sentence or paragraph. Problems are most likely to occur with the indefinite pronoun *one.*

NONSTANDARD   **One** cannot know what **their** future holds.

Here the pronoun shifts incorrectly from *one* to the plural form *their.* Several revisions are possible.

REVISED   **One** cannot know what **his or her** future holds.

REVISED   **People** cannot know what **their** futures hold.

REVISED   **One** cannot know what the future holds.

You may shift between *one* and *he* or *she,* as the example above demonstrates.

32c
pron

EXERCISE 32.3 Revise the sentences below to create a passage appropriate for a college report. Pay particular attention to the words and phrases in boldface.

1. **I was amazed to learn that** the Chinese speak a variety of dialects of a language **they** describe as Han.

2. Although there are only eight major varieties of Han, **you would find them** as different from each other as one Romance language is from another.

3. **One finds,** moreover, that each of the eight versions of Han occurs in a great many dialects, adding to **your** linguistic confusion.

4. **You will be glad to know,** however, that the Chinese use only one system of writing—a set of common ideographs—for expressing all **their** dialects.

5. As **you** might expect, there have been efforts to reform the Chinese language to make it easier **for you** to communicate between one region and another in the vast and populous country.

32d Do your pronouns treat both sexes fairly?

What happens when you need to use a pronoun but don't know whether it should refer to a man or a woman?

Each of the engineers we hire will earn (**his? her?**) job.

Until just a few decades ago, most writers would use a masculine pronoun (**he, him, his**) in any such situation—on the grounds that someone talking about *man*kind is also thinking about *woman*kind.

SEXIST	Each of the engineers we hire will earn **his** job.
SEXIST	An experienced **pilot** can sense when **his** plane has a problem.

In fact, such male-only constructions can exclude women from more than just grammar. (See also Section 18d.)

Today members of either sex may belong to almost every profession or group—students, athletes, coal miners, truckers, secretaries, nurses. Let your language reflect that diversity. Obviously, you should acknowledge the inevitable exceptions.

Each of the nuns received an award for **her** service to the community.

None of the NFL quarterbacks received a payment for **his** appearance at the benefit.

But in situations where you cannot assume that members of a group will all be male or female, be sure your language accommodates both sexes. You can do that in a variety of ways.

1 Use the expressions *he or she, him or her,* or *his or her* instead of the pronoun of either sex alone.

SEXIST	Every secretary may invite **her husband.**
REVISED	Every secretary may invite **his or her partner.**

32d
pron

Unfortunately, variations of *he or she* grow tiresome when they occur more than once in a sentence. Other expressions have been created to express gender diversity, including *he/she, s/he,* and *(s)he.* But many readers and editors don't like these inventions. So when the widely accepted *he or she* seems clumsy, try another strategy to avoid sexist usage.

2 Make singular pronoun references plural.

Because plural pronouns do not have a specific gender in English, you can often avoid the choice between *he* and *she* simply by turning singular references into plural ones.

SEXIST	Every secretary may invite **her husband.**
REVISED	All secretaries may invite **their partners.**
TIRESOME	Before **he or she** leaves, **each** band member should be sure **he or she** has **his or her** music.
REVISED	Before leaving, **all** band members should be sure **they** have **their** music.

Notice that these revisions eliminate *he or she* entirely.

3 Cut any troublesome pronouns.

Here are more examples.

ORIGINAL	*Anybody* may bring **his or her** favorite CD.
REVISED	*Anybody* may bring **a** favorite CD.
ORIGINAL	*Nobody* should leave until **he or she** has signed the guest book.
REVISED	*Nobody* should leave without **signing** the guest book.
ORIGINAL	*Each* should keep a record of **his or her** losses and gains in weight.
REVISED	*Each* should keep a personal record of losses and gains in weight.

**32d
pron**

These options are useful, but they are not always available.

4 Alternate between *he* and *she.*

In most cases, you can vary the pronouns sensibly and naturally within chunks of prose—between paragraphs, for example, or between the examples in a series. Handled skillfully, the shift between masculine and feminine references need not attract a reader's attention.

The dean of students knew that any student could purchase term papers through mail-order term paper services. If **he** could afford the scam, a student might construct **his** entire college career around papers **he** had purchased.

Yet the dean also acknowledged that the typical plagiarist was rarely so grossly dishonest and calculating. **She** tended to resort to such highly unethical behavior only when **she** believed an assignment was beyond **her** capabilities or **her** workload was excessive.

Avoid varying pronoun gender within individual sentences.

EXERCISE 32.4 Revise the following sentences to make them read better and to eliminate exclusionary pronouns. Treat the sentences as part of one paragraph.

1. Earlier this century, a laborer might fear that heavy equipment would mangle his limbs or that pollutants might damage his lungs.

2. Today a worker has to be concerned with new threats to her health.

3. Anybody who faces a computer terminal eight hours a day must worry about his exposure to radiation and wonder whether his muscles and joints are being damaged by the repetitive limb motions required by his job.

4. Frankly, the typical worker is often so concerned with her job performance that she may not consider that her workplace poses risks.

5. Of course, every worker wants their job to be safe.

32d
pron

CHAPTER 33

Questions About Modifiers?

Much of the work in sentences is handled by modifiers—especially adjectives and adverbs (see Section 19b). These modifying words and phrases expand what we know about subjects, verbs, and other sentence elements. In this chapter, we examine some issues writers face when dealing with modifiers, including familiar problems such as misplaced modifiers and double negatives.

We also help you to distinguish between modifying clauses that are essential (restrictive) or nonessential (nonrestrictive), a tricky problem. If you are unsure when such clauses need to be surrounded by commas, see Section 39b. If you are unsure whether to introduce these clauses with a *that, which,* or *who,* see Section 32b.

33a Questions about misplaced or dangling modifiers?

Adjectives and adverbs can cause confusion if they become detached from the words they are supposed to modify in a sentence. Two

Modifiers, like fashion accessories, should be selected carefully.

forms of this common problem are **misplaced modifying phrases** and **dangling modifiers.** A modifier is considered misplaced when it hooks up with the wrong word or phrase, sometimes with comic effect.

MISPLACED MODIFIER	**Carved from solid oak,** the angry matriarch could not break down the door.
CORRECTED	The angry matriarch could not break down the door **carved from solid oak.**

A modifier dangles when it doesn't have a word or phrase to connect with in a sentence. As a result, it doesn't make a logical connection.

DANGLING MODIFIER	**Before sending out the invitations,** a hall for their wedding has to be found. The boldfaced phrase doesn't apply to anything in the main part of the sentence. The sentence needs people to carry out the action.
CORRECTED	**Before sending out the invitations,** the couple will have to find a hall for their wedding.

An editor who spots a dangling modifier in your work will write *dm, dang,* or *dang mod* in the margin next to the offending phrase or clause.

⟨Angered by the crowd's booing,⟩ the concert was canceled.
dang mod

■ **1 Be sure that an introductory modifying phrase is followed by the word it modifies.** Sometimes you will have to supply a word that the introductory phrase can modify. In other cases, the whole sentence may have to be rearranged.

MISPLACED MODIFIER	**Never having had children,** rising college costs do not concern Mirella. The boldfaced phrase doesn't describe *costs,* the closest noun to it; it describes *Mirella.*
REVISION	**Never having had children,** Mirella is unconcerned about rising college costs.
MISPLACED MODIFIER	**Insulting and predictable,** fewer and fewer television viewers are attracted to the comedian's monologues. The boldfaced phrase doesn't describe *viewers*; it describes *monologues.*

REVISION   **Insulting and predictable,** the comedian's monologues attracted fewer and fewer television viewers.

2 Supply a word for a dangling modifier to modify.

This often means rewriting the entire sentence, since you must usually add a word or phrase that the sentence alludes to but doesn't actually include. For example:

DANGLING
MODIFIER

On returning to the office, the furniture had been rearranged.

There is nothing in the sentence for *On returning to the office* to modify. The sentence has to be revised to include a subject to which the modifier will relate.

ONE POSSIBLE
REVISION

On returning to the office, the staff found that the furniture had been rearranged.

3 Distinguish between absolute phrases and dangling modifiers.

Some modifying phrases may look like dangling modifiers but are actually **absolute phrases;** that is, they are complete in themselves, serving only to give additional information about the sentence of which they are a part.

    absolute
Given the fiasco at dinner, the guests weren't surprised when Martha pushed her husband into the pool.

    absolute
To be quite honest, Axel is a whining nerd and we would prefer that you leave him at home.

For more on absolute phrases, see Section 19c-3.

33a
mm/dm

EXERCISE 33.1 Rewrite or rearrange these sentences, placing modifiers in appropriate positions. You may need to add a noun for the modifier to modify. Not all of the sentences need to be revised.

1. Although they are among the most famous of reptiles, biologists have only recently begun to study rattlesnakes.

2. The deadly snakes, which take their name from the two characteristic pits on their snouts, belong to the family of pit vipers.

3. After studying the habits of pit vipers, the pits, which serve as infrared sensors and enable the snakes to seek heat, evolved to detect danger rather than to hunt prey.

4. Given their lethal capabilities, it is not surprising that pit vipers are universally loathed.

5. Despite their fearful reputation, however, people are seldom bitten by the snakes unless they are provoked.

33b How do you place adjectives effectively?

Adjectives are words that modify nouns or pronouns. They explain how many, which color, which one, and so on. All the words in boldface here function as adjectives.

An **honest** audit is **rare** these days.
The **darkest** nights are **moonless.**
German beers pour slowly.
The truck, **tall** and **ungainly,** rolled down the hill.
Pale and **redheaded,** she looked **Irish.**

Most, but not all, adjectives come before the nouns or pronouns they modify: *red* Viper; *outstanding* athlete.

But you must take care to place adjectives carefully to avoid ambiguity and pileups. An adjective becomes ambiguous when readers can't tell which word it modifies. For example:

AMBIGUOUS   Adam had his **enthusiastic parents' support.**
        Enthusiastic attaches itself to parents instead of to support.

CLARIFIED   Adam had his **parents' enthusiastic support.**

Adjectives pile up when writers place one modifier after another until readers get confused or bored. For example:

TEDIOUS   **Recent, controversial, divisive** anti-gun legislation met defeat in the state legislature.

REVISED   **Recent** antigun legislation, **controversial and divisive,** met defeat in the state legislature.

▍1 Relocate adjectives that are potentially confusing or ambiguous.

You may have to read your sentences carefully to appreciate how they might be misread. Better still, ask a friend to read your work and point out where readers might get confused.

AMBIGUOUS   The **long-lost diplomats's memoirs** were revealing. *Does long-lost go with diplomat or memoirs?*

CLARIFIED	The **diplomat's long-lost memoirs** were revealing.
AMBIGUOUS	The **ingenious** Web **site's designer** resigned.
	Does *ingenious* go with *Web site* or *designer?*
CLARIFIED	The **ingenious designer** of the Web site resigned.

2 Consider placing adjectives after the words or phrases they modify. You can avoid tedious strings of adjectives this way and make sentences more graceful.

TEDIOUS	A **new, powerful, quick,** and **easy-to-use** database program was installed today.
REVISED	A new database program, **powerful, quick,** and **easy to use,** was installed today.

EXERCISE 33.2 Rearrange the adjectives to make each of these sentences clearer or more effective. Several options are possible.

1. Lisa and Julia wanted to find a politically sophisticated women's group that could help them plan their lobbying strategy.

2. Professional children's care in the workplace of employed parents was one of their goals.

3. They viewed the negative board members' attitudes as a challenge to their persuasive abilities.

4. Before explaining their plan, Lisa asked for the undivided employees' attention.

5. Obtaining an endorsement was essential if they were to overcome the stubborn management's resistance.

33c
adj

33c How do you handle predicate adjectives?

Many people have problems selecting the right term to follow linking verbs such as *seem, become, look, appear, feel, smell.* An adjective that follows a linking verb is called a **predicate adjective.**

I *feel* **bad.**
You *seem* **uneasy.**
The lawyer *became* **angry.**
The perfume *smells* **vile.**
Iris *appears* **calm.**

■ **1 Remember that only adjectives, not adverbs, can modify a noun.** So after a linking verb you need an adjective—not an adverb—to modify a noun. In the following examples, the first version of the sentence shows the incorrect *adverb* modifier; the second version shows the correct *adjective* form.

INCORRECT   The accountant feels **badly** about underestimating our quarterly taxes.

The modifier *badly* completes the linking verb *feels* and describes *accountant*, a noun, so it should be the adjective *bad*.

CORRECT   The accountant feels **bad** about underestimating our quarterly taxes.

INCORRECT   Lillian appears **pessimistically** about her chances for getting into the graduate program.

The term modifies *Lillian*, a noun, so it must be an adjective.

CORRECT   Lillian appears **pessimistic** about her chances for getting into the graduate program.

The same principle applies when you modify a noun that acts as the object in a sentence, as in the following example.

INCORRECT   The tenant kept the woodwork in his apartment **flawlessly.**

To describe *woodwork* (a noun), the writer should use the adjective form (*flawless*) rather than the adverb (*flawlessly*).

CORRECT   The tenant kept the woodwork in his apartment **flawless.**

■ **2 Learn to manage *good* and *well*.** Among the modifiers most often confused are *good* and *well*. Remember that *good* is always an adjective and that *well* is usually an adverb. But *well* can also be an adjective that describes someone's physical condition. Use *good* after a linking verb when you want to give information about the subject. For example:

Jasper Hayes looks **good.**
His scholastic record is **good.**
He feels **good** about being a father too.

But when you are referring to someone's state of health, use *well* to finish the linking verb. In this case, *well* functions as an adjective.

Most college students feel **well** in spite of their eating habits.
Despite five hours of heart surgery, Mr. Seltzer looks remarkably **well.**

33c
adj

In academic and professional writing, don't use *good* as an adverb.

> NO   The system doesn't run **good.**
>
> NO   Most jobs in child care don't pay **good.**

In such cases, use *well* to describe the action of the verb. *Well* functions as an adverb in these sentences.

> YES   The system doesn't run **well.**
>
> YES   Most jobs in child care don't pay **well.**

EXERCISE 33.3 In these sentences, replace the boldfaced modifier with a better one.

1. In the United States, most people feel **confidently** that their drinking water is safe.

2. In many parts of the world, however, even water that looks **well** can be full of bacteria and pollution.

3. Some major relief organizations, such as the International Rescue Committee, feel **optimistically** that they can bring clean water to the rural areas of Africa and India.

4. They teach villagers what must be done to keep a sanitation system running **good.**

5. Parents who know that their children's drinking water should be boiled feel **badly** because often they cannot afford the fuel to boil it.

**33d
adj**

33d Questions about absolute adjectives?

Some words called *absolute adjectives* cannot be compared or qualified—at least not logically. For example, since *equal* means "exactly the same," you shouldn't write that something is *more equal* any more than you'd say it is *more empty*. Similarly either a thing is *perfect* or it's flawed. An object is either *unique* or there are others like it.

In practice, writers and speakers do qualify absolute expressions all the time, often meaningfully. Even the preamble of the Constitution describes "a more perfect union," and the pigs in George Orwell's satire *Animal Farm* are famously *more equal* than other animals. But in most cases you should avoid using qualifiers (such as *less, more, most, least,*

very) with the following absolute words: *unique, perfect, singular, empty, equal, full, definite, complete, absolute,* and, of course, *pregnant.*
Consider these examples.

ILLOGICAL	We doubted that the new operating system was **absolutely perfect.**
REVISED	We doubted that the new operating system was **perfected yet.**
ILLOGICAL	Jack's story is **more unique** than Jane's.
REVISED	Jack's story is **unique;** Jane's is not.

EXERCISE 33.4 Working with other students in a group, read over these sentences and decide which ones have faulty modifiers. Confer to decide how any problems with modifiers might be solved.

1. Ms. Oliveras was disappointed with the grant proposals she had read—she thought the projects proposed should have been more unique.

2. She was looking for a very singular plan in which to invest the foundation's money.

3. The board of trustees had most definite opinions about what constituted "community values," a situation that made her a little nervous.

4. But because her knowledge of the community was more complete than theirs, she felt she better understood what was important.

5. When she finally came across the B'nai B'rith proposal for a preschool learning center, she decided it was the most perfect to meet the needs of the town.

33e
adv

33e Questions about adverb form?

Adverbs are words that modify verbs, adjectives, or other adverbs, explaining where, when, and how. Many adverbs end in *-ly.*

The Secretary of State spoke **angrily** to the press.
The water was **extremely** cold.
The candidate spoke **evasively.**

Some adverbs have both short and long forms.

slow/slowly	fair/fairly	rough/roughly
quick/quickly	tight/tightly	deep/deeply

The problem for many writers is that the short adverb forms look suspiciously like adjectives. Is it correct then to say "drive slow" or "tie it tight" instead of "drive slowly" and "tie it tightly"? The answer is "Yes"—but you have to consider your audience.

In most cases, the short form of the adverb sounds more casual than the long form. Consequently, in most academic and business situations, you'll do better to use the *-ly* form.

COLLOQUIAL	The computer booted **quick.**
STANDARD	The computer booted **quickly.**
COLLOQUIAL	The employees expected to be treated **fair.**
STANDARD	The employees expected to be treated **fairly.**

EXERCISE 33.5 Working with a group of other students, discuss the following sentences and decide what the problems are. Then replace nonstandard adverb forms with appropriate ones.

1. Max was real surprised when he got a response from the IRS to his initial suggestion for clearer tax forms.

2. The local IRS director seemed to take his suggestion very serious.

3. She had written back prompt to Max, and that made him think good of her.

4. Max sat down quick and designed a handsome template for IRS consideration.

5. But Max reacted bad when the IRS rejected his design.

33f
adv

33f Where do you place adverbs?

Adverbs are usually easier to work with than adjectives because they're flexible and can take various positions in a sentence. For example:

George daydreamed **endlessly** about his vacation, **thoroughly** reviewing each travel brochure.

George daydreamed about his vacation **endlessly,** reviewing **thoroughly** each travel brochure.

Endlessly George daydreamed about his vacation, reviewing each travel brochure **thoroughly.**

But because adverbs are so flexible, it's also easy to drop them in inappropriate spots, particularly when a sentence has two verbs and the adverb might modify either one of them. The result may be a confusing or ambiguous sentence.

ADVERB MISPLACED	Analyzing an argument **effectively** improves it. *Does* effectively *go with* analyzing *or* improves?

1 Place adverbs so it is clear which words they modify.

ADVERB MISPLACED	Before the Battle of Agincourt, King Henry V urged his troops to fight **eloquently**.
ADVERB REPOSITIONED	Before the Battle of Agincourt, King Henry V **eloquently** urged his troops to fight.
ADVERB MISPLACED	Hearing the guard's footsteps approach **quickly** Mark emptied the safe. *The reader doesn't know whether* quickly *goes with* footsteps *or* Mark.
ADVERB REPOSITIONED	Hearing the guard's footsteps approach Mark **quickly** emptied the safe.

33f
adv

A comma after *approach* in either sentence would also clarify the meaning.

2 Place the adverbs *almost* and *even* next to the words they modify. Notice the ambiguities these words cause in the following sentences because they are misplaced.

ADVERB MISPLACED	Much to his dismay, Hugo realized he had **almost** dated every woman at the party. *Putting* almost *next to* dated *instead of* every *confuses the meaning.*
ADVERB BETTER PLACED	Much to his dismay, Hugo realized he had dated **almost** every woman at the party.
ADVERB MISPLACED	A true workaholic, Jen **even** thought time spent driving to the office could be used productively. *Even could modify* thought *here, but it really goes with* time.

ADVERB BETTER PLACED   A true workaholic, Jen thought **even** time spent driving to the office could be used productively.

3 Place the adverb *only* directly ahead of the word you want it to modify. The word *only* means "this one and no other." In the wrong place, *only* can lead to a misreading.

CONFUSING

Verna **only** knew of one person who opposed her marriage plans.

Could be misinterpreted to mean that Verna was the only person who knew of someone opposed to her marriage.

CLEARER

Verna knew of **only** one person who opposed her marriage plans.

CONFUSING

Her parents **only** worried about how much the elaborate affair would set them back.

Could be misinterpreted to mean that Verna's parents never did anything but worry about the cost of their daughter's wedding.

CLEARER

Her parents worried **only** about how much the elaborate affair would set them back.

33f
adv

EXERCISE 33.6 Rewrite the sentences to clarify them.

1. People who attend the theater regularly complain that the manners of the average audience member are in severe decline.

2. Far from listening in respectful if not attentive silence, he broadcasts a running commentary frequently modeled, no doubt, on his behavior in front of the television at home.

3. Sitting next to a woman who spends most of the evening unwrapping cellophane-covered candies slowly can provoke even the most saintly theatergoer to violence.

4. Cellular phones, beepers, and wristwatch alarms even go off intermittently causing an evening in the theater to resemble a trip to an electronics store.

5. For their part, actors marvel at how audiences today only manage to cough during the quietest moments of a play.

33g Questions about double negatives?

Sentences that say *no* in two different ways are emphatic and usually very colloquial.

Ain't no way I'm revising this paper again!

They make their point, but you need to avoid them in academic and professional writing.

▓ 1 Check that you don't have two *no* words (a *double negative*) in the same sentence or independent clause. In addition to *no*, look for such words as *not, nothing, nobody,* and *never.* If you've doubled them, you can usually just drop or alter a single word.

DOUBLE NEGATIVE	That modem will **not** work **never**.
CORRECTED	That modem will **never** work.
DOUBLE NEGATIVE	The child does **not** want **no** help tying his shoes.
CORRECTED	The child does **not** want help tying his shoes.

▓ 2 Don't mix the adverbs *hardly, scarcely,* or *barely* with another negative word or phrase. Such pairings create double negatives, which should be edited.

DOUBLE NEGATIVE	The morning was so cool and clear that the hikers **couldn't hardly** wait to get started.
CORRECTED	The morning was so cool and clear that the hikers **could hardly** wait to get started.
DOUBLE NEGATIVE	They figured there **wouldn't be scarcely** any other groups on the trail.
CORRECTED	They figured there **would be scarcely** any other groups on the trail.

Double negatives shouldn't be confused with negative statements that express ideas indirectly—and perhaps with ironic twists. Consider the difference in tone between these simple sentences, framed negatively and positively.

NEGATIVE	The proposal was not unintelligent.
POSITIVE	The proposal was intelligent.
NEGATIVE	Sean was hardly unattractive.
POSITIVE	Sean was attractive.

EXERCISE 33.7 Rewrite sentences that contain double negatives to eliminate the problem. Not every sentence is faulty.

1. Some critics claim that in this age of videos, computers, and the Internet, young people don't hardly read anymore.

2. Yet cities like Madison, Wisconsin, which are centers of education and technology, haven't never had so many bookstores.

3. Many bookstores aren't no longer just places to buy books.

4. They serve as community centers where people can buy coffee, go to poetry seminars, and get on the Internet without never buying any books.

5. But bookstore owners know that scarcely any browsers leave the store empty-handed.

33h Questions about comparatives and superlatives?

The comparative and superlative forms of most adjectives and a few adverbs can be expressed two ways.

ugly (an adjective)
Comparative   uglier   more ugly
Superlative   ugliest   most ugly

slowly (an adverb)
Comparative   slower   more slowly
Superlative   slowest   most slowly

You can usually trust your ear when selecting the forms. As a general rule, you add *-er* and *-est* endings to one-syllable adjectives and adverbs but use the terms *more* and *most* (or *less* and *least*) before words of two or more syllables.

Curtis likes **brighter** colors than Kyle.
Kyle wears **more conservative** clothes than Curtis.
Kyle's white Oxford is the **most conspicuous** shirt he owns.
Camille talks **faster** than Susi.
Susi usually speaks **more deliberately.**

Two problems typically arise with comparatives and superlatives. The first is using a superlative form when comparing only two objects.

FAULTY COMPARISON   Jason was the **tallest** of the two men.
should be *taller*

FAULTY COMPARISON   Martina was the **most talented** of the two gymnasts. should be *more talented*

A less frequent error involves doubling the comparative and superlative forms, using both the ending *-er* or *-est* and *more* or *most.*

FAULTY COMPARISON   That was the **most ugliest** dog of all.
should be *most ugly* or *ugliest*

1 Be sure to use the comparative form, not the superlative, when comparing two items. That means using an adverb or adjective with an *-er* ending or modified by *more* or *less.*

FAULTY COMPARISON   Marta was the **smartest** of the two children.
Smartest is the superlative, not the comparative, form.

REVISED   Marta was the **smarter** of the two children.

FAULTY COMPARISON   Celeste, her twin, was the **most imaginative.**
Most imaginative is the superlative, not the comparative, form.

REVISED   Celeste, her twin, was the **more imaginative.**

33h
modif

2 Use the superlative form when comparing more than two objects or qualities. In most cases when you compare three or more things or qualities, you need to use *-est* adjectives or adverbs or preface the modifiers with *most* or *least.* For example:

Given the choice of several toys, Celeste would choose the one that was the **most** challenging.
Of all the children in her kindergarten class, Marta was the **liveliest.**

3 Avoid doubling the comparative or superlative forms.
You'll confuse your reader if you use the two comparative forms in the same phrase. For example:

CONFUSING   Jasper was **more stricter** as a parent than Janice was.

CLEAR   Jasper was **stricter** as a parent than Janice was.

CONFUSING   Of all the members of the archery team, Diana was the **most angriest** about the stolen targets.

CLEAR   Of all the members of the archery team, Diana was the **angriest** about the stolen targets.

EXERCISE 33.8 Write sentences in which you use the appropriate forms of comparison for the situation given.

1. Today community librarians are constantly trying to decide what is (**more/most**) important: expanding computer facilities or buying more books.

2. These librarians consider who among their clients has the (**greater/ greatest**) need—schoolchildren, working adults, or retired people.

3. In general, librarians enjoy the reputation of being among the (**most helpful/helpfullest**) of city employees.

4. In good libraries, librarians are also likely to be among the (**most bright/brightest**) city employees.

5. Well-trained librarians, or information specialists as they are often called today, will find their (**better/best**) job prospects in medium-sized cities with growing populations.

33i
modif

33i Questions about nonessential and essential modifiers?

Writers sometimes puzzle over how to introduce (Section 32b) or how to punctuate (Section 39b) nonessential and essential modifiers. In either case, you first have to understand and reliably identify these structures. (Although many texts use only the terms *nonrestrictive* and *restrictive* modifiers, we prefer the terms *nonessential* and *essential* because they are more descriptive.)

1 Understand nonessential modifiers. A modifier is **nonessential** when it adds information to a sentence but can be cut without a loss of sense. Observe what happens when nonessential modifiers are removed from these sentences.

WITH NONESSENTIAL MODIFIER	The police officers, **who were wearing their dress uniforms,** marched in front of the mayor's car.
MODIFIER REMOVED	The police officers marched in front of the mayor's car.
WITH NONESSENTIAL MODIFIER	The chemistry building, **which had been erected in 1928 and badly needed repairs,** was scheduled for demolition.
MODIFIER REMOVED	The chemistry building was scheduled for demolition.

Useful information is sacrificed when the nonessential modifiers are cut, but the sentences still make good sense.

2 Understand essential modifiers. When you can't remove a modifying expression from a sentence without affecting its meaning, you have an *essential modifier*—which is not surrounded by commas. Watch what happens when essential modifiers are removed from sentences.

ESSENTIAL MODIFIER	Diamonds **that are synthetically produced** are more perfect than natural diamonds.
ESSENTIAL MODIFIER REMOVED	Diamonds are more perfect than natural diamonds. The sentence now makes little sense.
ESSENTIAL MODIFIER	We missed the only speaker **whose work dealt with business ethics.**
ESSENTIAL MODIFIER REMOVED	We missed the only speaker. Removing the modifier changes the sentence significantly.
ESSENTIAL MODIFIERS	The fruit basket **that we received** was not the one **we ordered.**
ESSENTIAL MODIFIERS REMOVED	The fruit basket was not the one. The sentence makes no sense with the essential modifiers removed.

Understand, however, that context will often determine whether a modifier is essential. Remember this sentence?

NONESSENTIAL	The police officers, **who were wearing their dress uniforms,** marched in front of the mayor's car.

We can make its nonessential modifier essential just by pairing the sentence with another that affects its overall meaning.

33i
modif

| ESSENTIAL | The police officers **who were wearing their dress uniforms** marched in front of the mayor's car. The officers **who were in plain clothes** mingled with the crowd as part of a security detail. |

Notice that the punctuation changes too, with the modifiers no longer surrounded by commas.

When in doubt whether a phrase or clause is essential, imagine the sentence with the modifier in parentheses. If the sentence no longer makes sense, the modifier is essential and no commas should surround it. If the parentheses work, the modifier is nonessential and should be enclosed by commas. Of course, you should always read any sentences in context.

PARENTHESES DON'T WORK	The stocks **(we bought last year)** declined in value.
MODIFIER IS ESSENTIAL	The stocks we bought last year declined in value.
PARENTHESES WORK	The oil stocks **(which luckily are only a small part of our portfolio)** declined in value last year.
MODIFIER IS NOT ESSENTIAL	The oil stocks , **which luckily are only a small part of our portfolio** , declined in value last year.

Any clause introduced by *that* will be essential (restrictive) and should not be surrounded by commas. (See Section 32b.)

33i
modif

| WRONG | The committee, that I chair, meets every Monday. |
| RIGHT | The committee that I chair meets every Monday. |

EXERCISE 33.9 Following the model provided, first write a sentence with a nonessential modifier. Then add a second sentence that would make the modifier in the first sentence essential. Be sure your version shows the same changes in punctuation that occur in the model.

| NONESSENTIAL | The students, who had stood for hours in line, applauded when the ticket window opened. |
| ESSENTIAL | The students **who had stood for hours in line** applauded when the ticket window opened. Those **who had only just arrived** despaired at ever getting seats for the game. |

CHAPTER 34

Are You an ESL Writer?

Jocelyn Steer and Carol Rhoades

As a writer whose first language is not English, you will face some special challenges as you work to express your ideas in a new language. Writing in your own language is not always simple, and writing in a second language can be even harder. You may, for example, have questions about grammar, or you may need to learn new vocabulary or idioms in order to complete a writing project. It's easy to become discouraged as you navigate these challenges and to wonder if you will ever be able to communicate your ideas as well as you would like. When that happens, remind yourself that the language skills you have already developed have enabled you to reach college-level classes in English.

In addition, because you have studied the grammatical systems and vocabularies of at least two languages, you already have a lot of knowledge that will help you become a proficient writer in English. You already understand that the grammatical rules and idiomatic expressions in a language limit the ways in which a writer can say something. Another valuable attribute you already have is flexibility. You realize that a particular idea can be expressed in many different ways. If you can't remember the precise word for something in another language, you quickly learn to describe what you mean or to use synonyms. You probably also have learned words or expressions in another language that you can't quite express in your own language.

The next three chapters of this book are designed to help you to build on the language skills you already have and further develop your abilities to write well in English.

- This chapter, **Chapter 34,** reviews common problem areas for ESL (English as a Second Language) writers. We list common errors you need to be aware of as you proofread your own writing and identify resources to which you can turn for more help. Also look for the boxed **ESL Tips,** which feature specific advice from successful ESL writers and instructors.
- **Chapter 35** gives detailed guidelines for choosing the proper verb forms in your writing.

- **Chapter 36** offers detailed advice for using gerunds, articles, count and noncount nouns, and other grammatical elements that ESL writers often ask questions about.

Of course, even though these three chapters focus specifically on the needs of ESL writers, you will also find useful material in other chapters. See Chapters 25 to 33 for general discussions of grammar and mechanics. (Chart 34.2 on p. 555 lists the most relevant sections of these chapters.)

34a Common problem areas for ESL writers

It's always a good idea to proofread papers for grammar and punctuation errors before handing in the final copy. (See Section 5c.) Reading your work aloud can help you find errors that you may not otherwise spot. You'll find that the mistakes you notice when you are proofreading are usually mistakes you know how to correct. Many errors that instructors mark on final drafts could probably have been corrected by more thorough proofreading.

If you know what your most common errors are, check for them first and then look for other problems. Also, make sure that you haven't unconsciously typed some words or word endings in your own language rather than English. This can happen even if you are thinking in English as you write.

In this section you'll find a list of the most common problems for ESL writers—and their solutions.

**34a
ESL**

ESL Tip   **State Your Thesis Early**
Monika Shehi, Albania

When I came to America, I found writing papers to be an intimidating task. When I wrote papers in Albania, I would start with an idea and follow wherever my thoughts led, often progressing to several new ideas. My American professors found my papers very chaotic, because in U.S. universities, most papers are about establishing and developing one main point. Once I became aware of that basic structure, writing became much easier. Now I begin a draft by determining my main idea, then supplying evidence to support that idea.

1 Be sure each clause has a subject. Every clause in English must have a subject, except for imperative sentences ("Sit down").

The subject is missing.

INCORRECT	∧ Is difficult to write in English.
CORRECT	**It** is difficult to write in English.
	You must have *it* before the verb *is*.

2 Be sure a main or an auxiliary verb isn't missing.

The main verb is missing.

INCORRECT	The teacher ∧extremely helpful. *verb missing*
CORRECT	The teacher **is** extremely helpful.

The auxiliary verb is missing.

INCORRECT	Hurry! The plane∧leaving right now. *verb missing*
CORRECT	Hurry! The plane **is** leaving right now.

3 Don't forget the *-s* on verbs used with third person singular nouns and pronouns (*he, she, it*). If this is a problem for you, check all present tense verbs to make sure you haven't forgotten an *-s*.

INCORRECT	The library clos⊝ at 5:00 today. *3rd person sing. –s*
CORRECT	The library clos**es** at 5:00 today.

When you have the auxiliary *do* or *does* in a sentence, add *-s* to the auxiliary, not to the main verb.

INCORRECT	He ⌓don't⌐ know✗ the answer to the question.
	3rd person sing. –s
CORRECT	He **doesn't** know the answer to the question.

4 Don't forget *-ed* endings on past participles. Check your papers to be sure that you use the past participle (*-ed* ending) for verbs in the following cases. (See Section 26d for a list of the three parts of a verb.)

In passive voice (see Section 26e).

INCORRECT	The amenities were **provid⊝** by the hotel.
CORRECT	The amenities were **provided** by the hotel.
INCORRECT	The documents were **alter** by the thief.
CORRECT	The documents were **altered** by the thief.

34a
ESL

In the past perfect tense (see Section 35a-3).

INCORRECT	Juan had **finish** the race before Fred came.
CORRECT	Juan had **finished** the race before Fred came.

In participle adjectives (see Section 19c-2).

INCORRECT	She was **frighten** by the dark.
CORRECT	She was **frightened** by the dark.

Be sure that you *don't* add endings to infinitives.

INCORRECT	George started to **prepared** dinner.
CORRECT	George started to **prepare** dinner.

5 Don't confuse adjective pairs like *bored* and *boring*.

The following sentences are very different in meaning, although they look similar.

John is bored. This means that John is bored by *something*—maybe his class or his homework; it is a feeling he has as a result of something.

John is boring. This means that John has a personality that is not interesting; he is a boring person.

The ending of the adjective, *-ed* or *-ing,* is what creates a difference in meaning. Adjectives ending in *-ed* have a passive meaning. Adjectives ending in *-ing* have an active meaning. (See Section 26e for an explanation of passive voice.)

The English spelling system often confuses Jorge.

-ED ENDING	Jorge is **confused** by the English spelling system. passive
	The **confused** student looked up words in his spelling dictionary. passive
-ING ENDING	English spelling is **confusing.** active
	It is a **confusing** system. active

Joan's work satisfies her.

-ED ENDING	She is **satisfied** by her work. passive
	She is a **satisfied** employee. passive
-ING ENDING	Her work is **satisfying.** active
	Joan does **satisfying** work. active

Chart 34.1 shows some common pairs of adjectives that confuse students, along with the preposition that is used after the *-ed* adjectives.

34a
ESL

Chart 34.1

Adjective Pairs

amusing	amused by	exciting	excited by/about
annoying	annoyed by	frightening	frightened by
boring	bored by	interesting	interested in
confusing	confused by	irritating	irritated by
embarrassing	embarrassed by	satisfying	satisfied with

6 Avoid repeating sentence elements. You may find that you repeat unnecessary words in your sentences. Be on your guard for the three types of repetition shown in these examples.

In adjective clauses.

> The store that I told you about ~~it~~ closed down.
> *It* is not necessary because *that* replaces *it.*

> The man whom I met ~~him~~ yesterday was kind.
> *Whom* replaces *him.*

> The school where I go ~~there~~ is very expensive.
> *Where* replaces *there.*

In the subject of the sentence.

> My brother ~~he~~ is the director of the hospital.
> Because *my brother* and *he* refer to the same person, the *he* is unnecessary repetition.

Multiple connectors.

> Although the employee was diligent, ~~but~~ she was fired.
> *Although* and *but* both express contrast. You don't need two connectors in one sentence with the same meaning. You must remove one of them.

> Because she fell asleep after eating a big lunch, ~~so~~ she missed her class.
> *So* and *because* both express cause. Cut one of them.

**34a
ESL**

ESL Tip   *Don't Repeat Points; Develop Them* ——————
Mila Tasseva, Bulgaria

The academic essay model I was accustomed to before I began college in the United States is the one typically taught to students in the countries of the former Soviet bloc. Students are taught to structure their essays so that they spiral around the thesis, repeating the same statement in different words again, and again, and again without actually developing the argument. In contrast, professors in the United States will expect students to support the thesis with details and examples.

If your instructor asks you to work on developing your paper, try the following strategy. When you review a draft, look closely into the argument's development and identify the points that give you evidence in support of the claim. Now review what you just identified and see if you can find the same point repeated in the same or different words. Do you find the spiral? I bet so. It always comes as surprise; at least it did to me when I received back my first paper written in an American university with the note in the margin, "Why did you repeat this idea so many times?"

---

7 Place adverbs correctly in the sentence. Adverbs can appear in many different places in a sentence—at the beginning, in the middle, at the end. However, there are a few positions where adverbs *can't* be placed. Here are some guidelines. (For more help with adverb placement, see Section 33f.)

Don't put an adverb between the verb and its object.

<blockquote>
                verb   adverb   obj.
INCORRECT   She answered slowly the question.
</blockquote>

<blockquote>
                verb   obj.   adverb
CORRECT   She answered the question **slowly**.
</blockquote>

Don't place adverbs of frequency before the verb *be*.

<blockquote>
INCORRECT   Louise regularly is late for class.
CORRECT   Louise is **regularly** late for class.
</blockquote>

Don't place adverbs of frequency after other verbs.

<blockquote>
INCORRECT   Juan arrives often late to class.
CORRECT   Juan **often** arrives late to class.
</blockquote>

34a
ESL

EXERCISE 34.1 Review Section 34a. Then read the following paragraph and proofread it for the mistakes described in that section. In some cases you will need to add something and in others you will delete an element. (There are seven errors. For answers, see p. 556.)

> There are long lines at the cashier's office
> because students signing up for financial aid. Is
> extremely frustrating to spend the entire day in
> line. Because some students they have other jobs and

classes, so they can't wait very long. Then you very
tired when you finally arrive at the desk where you
can talk to the clerk there. The clerk usually give
you a form to fill out, and then you have to wait in
another line!

ESL Tip   *Cite Sources Carefully* ——————————
Carl Jenkinson, England

For me, one of the most significant differences in
America is the emphasis placed on full and accurate citation
using MLA style. Although citation is required in the UK,
and to a lesser extent in France, where it seems more of a
courtesy than a necessity, full and accurate citation in the
United States is imperative. The solution is straightforward: become
as familiar as possible with the MLA handbook, and if in doubt, cite
your source.

34b
ESL

34b Finding other ESL resources

You may have questions about grammar or punctuation that
aren't covered in Chapters 34 through 36, which deal specifically
with the concerns of ESL writers. This section points you to additional resources in this book and in other publications that you can
consult.

**█ 1 Consult relevant material in other chapters of this
book.** Many questions you have about grammar and mechanics are
not specific to ESL writers. Native speakers of English have many of
these questions too. Chart 34.2 lists possible questions, each with the
chapter or section in this handbook that covers that problem. If you
have several areas of difficulty with grammar, focus on one at a time.

Study the examples in this chapter and those in the other grammar chapters in this handbook, and work through the practice exercises on rules that you find especially tricky.

Chart 34.2

Where to Find More Help with ESL Grammar Questions

IF YOU HAVE A QUESTION ABOUT	EXAMPLES	GO TO THIS CHAPTER/ SECTION
Abbreviations	Dr., APA, Ms.	45a
Adjective clauses	clauses beginning with *who, which, that*	19d, 32b
Capitalization	English, Japanese	44b–44c
Comparatives/ superlatives	more interesting/the most interesting	33h
Dangling modifiers	Reading the paper, the phone rang.	33a
Irregular verbs	*sit, sat, sat*	26d
Parallelism	I like swimming and fishing	19h, 23b
Passive voice	I was hit by a car.	26e
Plural nouns	child: children	28a
Possessives	the teacher's book	28b–28c
Pronouns	his gain; their loss	29–32
Punctuation	commas, periods	37–43
SENTENCE PROBLEMS		
Run-ons	I am a student I come from Mexico	38d
Fragments	Because it is my house.	38a–38b
Subject-verb agreement		22

2 Consult reference books especially designed for ESL writers. A general writer's handbook like this one cannot cover all the ESL information you need. We suggest, therefore, that you refer regularly to ESL reference books for help with grammar and usage. ESL grammar textbooks can give you more detailed grammatical explanations. Some ESL dictionaries provide useful spelling and usage information. See the following list of ESL reference books.

HIGHLIGHT *References for ESL Students*

We suggest the following reference books and Web sites for ESL students who have questions about grammar and usage.

- Betty S. Azar. *Basic English Grammar: English as a Second Language.* 3rd ed. New York: Pearson ESL, 1996.

- Betty S. Azar. *Understanding and Using English Grammar.* 3rd ed. New York: Pearson ESL, 1998.

- *Dave's ESL Café* < http://www.eslcafe.com/>.

- ESL Resources at OWL—the Online Writing Lab at Purdue University < http://owl.english.purdue.edu/handouts/esl/eslstudent.html>.

- The *Learning English Online (LEO) Lab* at the University of Kansas < http://www.aec.ukans.edu/leo/>.

We also recommend the following dictionary written for the ESL student.

- *Longman Dictionary of American English.* 3rd ed. New York: Longman, 2000.

34b ESL

3 Look for opportunities to listen to, speak, read, and write English in your everyday activities. While books can give you thorough explanations of grammatical rules, experts agree that the best way to increase your proficiency in English is to practice, practice, practice. In addition to working conscientiously to complete homework and papers for your academic courses, look for opportunities to use English in everyday contexts: email friends and classmates in English; write letters; join a chat session on a Web site that interests you; read English novels and newspapers; and watch the news in English. When you converse with friends or colleagues who are native speakers of English, don't hesitate to ask them to explain idioms, terms, or conventions of usage that are unfamiliar to you. Activities such as these will enrich your knowledge of English and enable you to write and speak more easily and fluently.

ANSWER KEY

EXERCISE 34.1

There are long lines at the cashier's office because students **are** signing up for financial aid. **It** is extremely frustrating to spend the entire day in line. Because some students ~~they~~ have other jobs and classes, ~~so~~ they can't wait very long. Then you **are** very tired when you finally arrive at the desk where you can talk to the clerk ~~there~~. The clerk usually **gives** you a form to fill out, and then you have to wait in another line!

CHAPTER 35

ESL Questions About Verbs?

Jocelyn Steer and Carol Rhoades

English verbs are complicated. If you are a nonnative speaker, you will probably still have questions about them, even after many years of studying English. For example, do you have difficulty deciding between "I have lived in the United States for a year" and "I lived in the United States for a year"? Should you write "She is liking the class very much" or "She likes the class very much"? Are you still confused about transitive and intransitive verbs? This section addresses some common questions ESL writers have about verbs. For additional help with verbs, see Chapters 26 and 27.

35a Which verb tense should you use?

A verb's tense expresses time. Chart 35.1 shows the 12 most commonly used verb tenses, along with a list of common adverbs and expressions that accompany them. These words and phrases are the signposts that help you choose the best verb tense. A diagram illustrates the timeline for each tense; in the diagram, an *X* indicates an action, and a curved line indicates an action in progress.

The remainder of this section explains how to use these tenses appropriately. For more information on verb tenses, see Chapter 26.

Chart 35.1

Verb Tenses

WHAT IT IS CALLED	WHAT IT LOOKS LIKE	WHAT IT DESCRIBES	TIME WORDS USED WITH IT
Simple present	• I *sleep* eight hours every day.	Habits, regular activities	• every day • often • regularly • always
——X——	• Water *freezes* at 0°C.	Facts, general truths	• usually • habitually

(Continued)

Verb Tenses *(Continued)*

WHAT IT IS CALLED	WHAT IT LOOKS LIKE	WHAT IT DESCRIBES	TIME WORDS USED WITH IT
Simple past	• I *slept* only four hours yesterday. • He *went* to sleep three hours ago.	A finished action in the past	• yesterday • last year • ago
Simple future	• I *will* try to sleep more. • I *am going to sleep* early tonight.	A single action in the future A planned action in the future (use *be going to*)	• tomorrow • in *x* days • next year
Present perfect	• I *have* already *written* my paper. • I *have lived* here for three months.	A past action that occurred at an unspecified time in the past An action that started in the past and continues to the present	• already • yet • before • recently • so far • for + time period • since + date
Past perfect	• She *had* already *slept* three hours when the burglar broke into the house.	One action in the past that occurs before another action in the past	• when • after • before • by the time
Future perfect	• I *will have finished* the paper when you stop by tonight.	One action in the future that will be completed before another action in the future	• by the time • when
Present progressive	• He *is sleeping* now.	A continuous activity in progress now	• right now • at this time • this week/year

35a
ESL verb

WHAT IT IS CALLED	WHAT IT LOOKS LIKE	WHAT IT DESCRIBES	TIME WORDS USED WITH IT
Past progressive 	• While he *was sleeping*, the telephone rang. • He *was sleeping* at 10 A.M.	A continuous activity in progress in the past; often interrupted by another time or action	• while • during that time • between *x* and *y*
Future progressive 	• I *will be sleeping* all day.	A continuous activity happening in the future	• all the while • during that time • between *x* and *y*
Present perfect progressive 	• The woman *has been waiting* for many hours. • He *has been sleeping* since eight o'clock.	A continuous activity that began in the past and continues to the present; emphasis is on the duration	• for + time period • since + exact date
Past perfect progressive **1 2**	• She *had been waiting* for three hours before he arrived. • He *had been sleeping* for an hour when the train crashed.	A continuous activity in the past that is finished before another action in the past	• for • since
Future perfect progressive **1 2**	• I *will have been sleeping* for twelve hours by the time you arrive.	A continuing future activity which started before another future event	• by • when

35a
ESL verb

1 Review the difference between the simple present tense and the present progressive tense. You may be confused because the simple present tense doesn't really refer to an action going on in the present; rather, it is used to talk about repeated and habitual actions. You should use the simple present tense when you want to talk about *regular, repeated* activity.

SIMPLE PRESENT	The mail carrier usually **arrives** at 10 A.M. This is an activity that is repeated daily.
PRESENT PROGRESSIVE	Look! She **is putting** the mail in the box now. This is an activity occurring at the moment of speaking—now.
PRESENT PROGRESSIVE	She **is delivering** mail for John this month. This is an activity that is in progress over a period of time. Use the progressive tense with the expression *this + time period.*

2 Review nonaction verbs and the present tense. Some verbs in English can't be used in a progressive form because they express a state and not an activity. Nonaction verbs include verbs of existence, of thought, of emotions, and of sense perceptions. Chart 35.2 lists some of these verbs. To use one of these nonaction verbs, you must use a simple form of the verb even though the time intended is *now.*

INCORRECT	I can't study because I **am hearing** my roommate's singing.
CORRECT	I can't study because I **hear** my roommate's singing.
INCORRECT	Maria **is preferring** Carlos's apartment to her own.
CORRECT	Maria **prefers** Carlos's apartment to her own.

35a
ESL verb

Chart 35.2

Nonaction Verbs*			
appear	forget	owe	seem
be	hate	own	smell
belong	have	possess	sound
consist	hear	prefer	surprise
contain	know	recognize	taste
deserve	like	remember	think
desire	love	require	understand
dislike	mean	resemble	want
feel	need	see	wish

*There are exceptions to the nonaction rule ("I **am thinking** about getting a job"; "He **is seeing** a doctor about his insomnia"). These exceptions can usually be paraphrased using other verbs ("He **is seeing** a doctor about his insomnia" means "He **is consulting** a doctor about his insomnia"). You will need to keep a list of these exceptions as you come across them.

3 Review the difference between the simple past tense and the present perfect tense.

If an action happened in the past and is finished, you can always use the simple past tense to describe it. (See Chapter 26 on how to form the past tense and for a list of irregular verbs.) Often you will also use a time word like *ago* or *yesterday* to show the specific time of the past action.

SIMPLE PAST   My brother **saw** that movie three days ago.
We know exactly when the brother saw the movie—three days ago. You *must* use the simple past in this sentence.

Use the **past tense** to show that something is completed, and use the **present perfect tense** to indicate that the action may continue or that it still has the possibility of occurring in the future. Compare these sentences to see how the two tenses express different ideas.

SIMPLE PAST   My grandmother never **used** a computer.
This implies that the grandmother may no longer be alive.

PRESENT PERFECT   My mother **has** never **used** a computer.
This sentence indicates that the mother is still alive and may use a computer in the future.

When you don't know or you don't want to state the exact time or date of a past action, use the present perfect tense.

PRESENT PERFECT   Sarah **has seen** that movie before.
We don't know when Sarah saw the movie; she saw it at an unspecified time in the past.

35a
ESL verb

You must use the present perfect for an action that began in the past and continues up to the present moment, especially when you use the time words *for* and *since.*

PRESENT PERFECT   This theater **has shown** the same film for three months! I hope they change it soon.
The action started in the past—three months ago—and continues to the present. The film is still playing.

4 Review the difference between the present perfect tense and the present perfect progressive tense.

You can use a **present perfect progressive** tense to show that an action is still in progress.

PRESENT PERFECT   Catherine **has been writing** that letter
PROGRESSIVE   since this morning.   She hasn't finished; she's still writing.

In general, when the statement emphasizes *duration* (length of time), you need to use a present perfect progressive tense.

PRESENT PERFECT
PROGRESSIVE

My best friend **has been writing** her novel for five years.

This tells us how long the friend has been writing; the emphasis is on duration, or length of time.

However, when the statement emphasizes *quantity* (how much), you will use a **present perfect tense.**

PRESENT PERFECT

Toni Morrison **has written** several well-received novels.

This tells us how many books; it talks about quantity.

EXERCISE 35.1 Review Sections 35a-1 and 35a-2. Choose the correct tense—simple present or present progressive. (For answers, see p. 573.)

1. Many people have bizarre dreams, but I usually (**dream/am dreaming**) about something that (**happens/is happening**) during the day.

2. I often (**remember/am remembering**) my dreams right after I (**wake/am waking**) up.

3. Sometimes when I (**hear/am hearing**) a noise while I (**dream/am dreaming**), I will incorporate that into my dream.

4. I (**know/am knowing**) a lot about dreams because I (**write/am writing**) a paper about them this semester.

5. To prepare for the paper, I (**research/am researching**) many psychological explanations for various dream symbols, such as snakes, bodies of water, and people.

6. I'm not sure that I (**believe/am believing**) those explanations, but they are very interesting.

EXERCISE 35.2 Review Section 35a-3. Choose the best verb tense—simple past or present perfect. Use the present perfect whenever possible. (For answers, see p. 573.)

1. This month the newspapers (**had/have had**) many articles about a phenomenon called the glass ceiling.

2. This refers to an unofficial limitation on promotion for women who (**worked/have worked**) in a corporation for several years and who cannot advance beyond middle management.

3. Last year my mother (**applied/has applied**) for the position of vice president of the company she works for, but they (**did not promote/have not promoted**) her.

4. She (**had/has had**) the most experience of all the candidates for the job, but a man was chosen instead.

5. She (**was/has been**) with that company for ten years. Now she doesn't know how much longer she will stay there.

EXERCISE 35.3 Review Section 35a. Fill in the blanks with the most precise and appropriate tense of the verb *talk.* Pay special attention to time words. Incorporate the adverbs in parentheses into your answers. (For answers, see p. 573.)

1. They _____ about the issue since yesterday.

2. Some employees _____ about it when we arrived at work.

3. They _____ (**probably**) about the issue when they leave work.

4. We _____ about it many times in the past.

5. I never _____ about this topic last week.

6. We _____ about this problem for two hours by the time the president visited our office.

7. Workers _____ about this issue quite often these days.

8. They _____ about the subject right now.

9. After they _____ about it for many weeks, they reached a consensus.

10. They _____ (**never**) about this issue again.]

35a
ESL verb

ESL Tip   *Punctuate Sentences Carefully* ━━━━━
Humberto Castillo, Mexico

Remember that your native language may form and punctuate sentences differently than English does. For example, many sentences that are grammatically correct in Spanish become run-on sentences if they are translated literally into English. When you translate a sentence from your native language, check the punctuation carefully, and ask a friend or your instructor if you are unsure about where to place commas and periods.

35b How do you use transitive and intransitive verbs?

A **transitive verb** is a verb that has a direct object. This means that the verb has an effect on, or does something to, that object. The verb *raise* in the sentence "She raised her children" is transitive because the subject of the sentence (*she*) is acting on someone else (*her children*). Without the direct object (*her children*), this sentence would be incomplete; it would not make sense.

INCORRECT   She raised.
This thought is incomplete; we need to know *what* she raised.

CORRECT   She raised **her children** on a farm.

There are two types of transitive verbs. (See Chart 35.3 on page 565 for a list of them.) One type—verb + direct object—*must* be followed directly by a noun or pronoun.

VERB + DIRECT OBJECT (trans. v. = transitive verb)

    subj.   trans. v.   noun
This university **needs** more parking lots.

     subj.   trans. v. pronoun
The trustees **discussed** it at the last meeting.

The second type—verb + (indirect object) + direct object—*can* be followed by an indirect object (a person receiving the action) before the direct object. When you use *to* or *for* in front of the indirect object, the position changes, as you can see in these examples.

VERB + (INDIRECT OBJECT) + DIRECT OBJECT

                dir. obj.
Ron bought **a rose.**

          indir. obj.   dir. obj.
Ron bought *his wife* **a rose.**

or

          dir. obj.   + for/to + indir. obj.
Ron bought **a rose** *for his wife.*

An **intransitive verb** is complete without a direct object. In fact, you cannot put a direct object after an intransitive verb.

INCORRECT   She grew up **her children.** *Her children* cannot come after the verb *grew up* because *her children* is an object; objects cannot come after intransitive verbs.

However, other words can come after intransitive verbs.

CORRECT	She grew up **quickly**. *Quickly* is an adverb. You can put an adverb after this verb. This sentence means that she matured at a very fast rate.
CORRECT	She grew up **on a farm**. *On a farm* is a prepositional phrase, not a direct object.

There are two kinds of intransitive verbs—linking verbs and action verbs. (See Chart 35.3 below for a list of these verbs.)

subj.   l. v.   comp.

LINKING VERBS   This book **seems** very old. l. v. = linking verb

subj.   l. v.   comp.

Your professor **is** an expert in law.

subj.   a. v.

ACTION VERBS   Jacqueline **complained**. a. v. = action verb

subj.   a. v.   prep. phrase

Jacqueline **complained** to me before breakfast.

(For more information on transitive and intransitive verbs, see Section 26e.)

Chart 35.3

Transitive and Intransitive Verbs

TRANSITIVE VERBS[*]

● **Verb + direct object:** attend, bring up, choose, do, have, hit, hold, keep, lay, need, raise, say, spend, use, want, watch, wear

● **Verb + (indirect object) + direct object:** bring, buy, get, give, make, pay, send, take, tell

INTRANSITIVE VERBS[*]

● **Linking verbs:** appear, be, become, seem, look

● **Action verbs:** arrive, come, get dressed, go, grow up, laugh, lie, listen, live, rise, run, sit, sleep, walk, work

[*]These lists are not complete. You can always consult your dictionary to find out whether a verb is transitive or intransitive.

35c
ESL verb

35c How do you use two-word and three-word verbs?

Some verbs in English consist of two or three words, usually a main verb and a preposition. These verbs are idioms because you can't understand the meaning of the verb simply by knowing the separate meaning of each of the two or three words. For example, the verb *put* has a completely different meaning from the verb *put off* ("to postpone"), and the verb *put up with* ("to tolerate") has yet another distinct meaning. There are many two- and three-word verbs in English. Since it would be difficult to memorize all of them, it's best for you to learn them as you hear them and to keep a list of them for reference. Chart 35.4 below lists common two- and three-word verbs. Two-word verbs that are transitive—which means they can have a direct object—are divided into two groups: **separable** and **inseparable**. (See Section 35b for an explanation of transitive verbs.)

Chart 35.4

Common Two-Word and Three-Word Verbs

Here are some common two- and three-word verbs. Such verbs have two parts: the main verb and one (or more) prepositions. This list is not complete; there are many more such verbs. An asterisk (*) indicates an *inseparable* verb: the verb and the preposition cannot be separated by an object. A cross (+) indicates verbs that have additional meanings not given here.

VERB	DEFINITION
break down*	stop functioning
bring on	cause something to happen
call off	cancel
catch up with* +	attain the same position, place
check into*	explore, investigate
come across*	encounter unintentionally
cut down on*	reduce the amount of
do over	repeat
figure out	solve a problem, dilemma
find out	discover
get along with*	have harmonious relations
get in* +	enter a car
get off* +	exit from (a bus, a train, a plane)
get on*	enter (a bus, a train, a plane)
get over*	recover from (a sickness, a relationship)
give up	stop trying
go over*	review
grow up*	mature, become an adult
keep up with*	maintain the same level
look after*	take care of
look into*	explore, investigate

VERB	DEFINITION
make up+	invent
pass away*	die
pick out	make a selection
put off	postpone
put up with*	tolerate
run into* +	meet by chance
show up*	appear, arrive
stand up for*	defend, support
sum up	summarize, conclude
take after*	resemble, look alike
touch on*	discuss briefly

1 Separable verbs. You can place the object *before* or *after* the preposition.

CORRECT   Lee checked **the book** *out* from the library.
The object (*the book*) is placed *before* the preposition (*out*).

CORRECT   Lee checked *out* **the book** from the library.
The object comes *after* the preposition.

However, whenever the object is a *pronoun* (such as *it* in the following example), the pronoun *must* come *before* the preposition.

INCORRECT   Gary checked out **it** from the library.
CORRECT   Gary checked **it** out from the library.

35c
ESL verb

2 Inseparable verbs. You cannot separate the verb and the preposition.

INCORRECT   My sister **majored** history **in**.
CORRECT   My sister **majored in** history.

INCORRECT   The frantic student **stayed** all night **up** to study.
CORRECT   The frantic student **stayed up** all night to study.

INCORRECT   Please **after** your brother **look**.
CORRECT   Please **look after** your brother.

INCORRECT   The detective **looked** the case **into**.
CORRECT   The detective **looked into** the case.

EXERCISE 35.4 Review Sections 35a through 35c. Each of the following sentences contains errors related to verb tense, transitive/intransitive verbs, and two-word verbs. Identify the errors and correct them. (For answers, see p. 573.)

1. Before I study psychology, I thought it was an easy subject.

2. Now I am knowing that it isn't easy.

3. It has had a lot of statistics.

4. I am studying psychology since April, and I only begin to learn some of the concepts.

5. I have been tried to learn more of the concepts every day.

6. Last night I have studied from 9:00 to midnight.

7. I went my adviser last Monday.

8. She told to me to see her after class.

9. But when I went to see her after class, she already left.

10. It's January. By the middle of June, I have studied psychology for six months.

35d
ESL verb

35d Which modal should you use?

You already know that a verb's tense expresses time. A *modal,* which is an auxiliary or helping verb, expresses an attitude about a situation. For example, if you want to be polite, you can say, "Open the door, please." To be even more polite, you can add a modal auxiliary verb: "*Would* you open the door, please?" Modals are used to express necessity, obligation, regret, and formality. Modals can be used to express ideas about the past, present, or future.

PAST   I **could** speak Japanese as a child.
PRESENT   My brother **can** speak Japanese now.
FUTURE   I **might** learn another language next semester.

You probably already know the common modals, such as *should, must,* and *have to.* However, you may have questions about others, such as *had better,* or perhaps you are uncertain about the difference between, for example, *have to* and *ought to.* In this section we list the modals by their uses or functions and provide a list of common modal errors to avoid.

▨ 1 Choose the modal that best expresses your idea.

Chart 35.5 below summarizes the functions of modals. It also lists the past form of the modals. Modals in the present are followed by the base form of the verb—for example, "Kim **may** win the prize" (subject + modal + base form of the verb). The form of modals in the past varies. (See Section 35d-3 for more details.)

Chart 35.5

Modals		
WHAT IT MEANS	PRESENT OR FUTURE FORM	PAST FORM
Permission		
(Informal → Formal)		
can	**Can** I be excused?	He **could have**
could	**Could** I be excused?	**been** excused, but
may	**May** I be excused?	he didn't ask.
would you mind*	**Would you mind** if I *brought* my dog?	**Would you have minded if** I *had brought* my dog?
Ability		
can	Joe **can** drive a car.	He **couldn't** drive a car last year.
be able to	Carl **is able to** study and listen to music at the same time.	Celia **was never able to** play the Mozart concertos.
Advice		
should	You **should** quit.	He **should have**
ought to	You **ought to** quit.	quit last year.
had better	You **had better** quit.	He didn't quit; this sentence shows regret.
Necessity		
have to	He **has to** pay a fine.	He **had to** pay a fine last week.
must	She **must** pay her taxes.	No past form; use *had to.*

35d
ESL verb

Would you mind is followed by *if* + the past tense of the verb.

(Continued)

Modals *(Continued)*

WHAT IT MEANS	PRESENT OR FUTURE FORM	PAST FORM
Lack of necessity		
not have to	You **don't have to** attend school in summer.	He **didn't have to** take the final exam last year.
not need to	You **don't need to** pay in advance.	You **didn't need to** pay in advance.
Possibility *(More sure → Less sure)*		
can	It **can** get cold in May.	No past form.
may	It **may** get cold in June this year.	I'm not sure, but it **may have** just happened.
could	It **could** get cold in July this year.	It **could have** just happened.
might	It **might** get cold in July this year.	It **might have** just happened.
Conclusion		
must	Your eyes are all red; you **must have** allergies. I'm almost certain that this is true.	You got an *A* on your test. You **must have studied** hard! I'm certain that you did this in the past.
Expectation		
should/ **ought to**	Your keys **should be** on the desk where I left them. I expect them to be there.	John **should have been** elected. He didn't get elected, but I expected him to.
Polite requests *(Informal → Formal)*		
can	**Can** you give me a hand?	No past forms.
will	**Will** you give me a hand?	
could	**Could** you give me a hand?	
would you **mind +** present participle	**Would you mind giving** me a hand?	

2 Use the correct form of the modal auxiliary and the main verb that follows it. Modals that express present and future time have this form.

SUBJECT + MODAL + BASE FORM OF VERB

Clarissa **had better** register for classes soon.

Here are specific tips to help you with modal formation.

* Don't use *to* or a present participle (*-ing* form of a verb) after the modal.

INCORRECT	Jacquie **can to** play the guitar very well.
CORRECT	Jacquie **can** play the guitar very well.

INCORRECT	**Must I to** hand in this paper tomorrow?
CORRECT	**Must I** hand in this paper tomorrow?
EXCEPT	We **have to** write a 10-page paper.

INCORRECT	They **should reading** before class.
CORRECT	They **should read** before class.

* There is no *-s* on the third person singular of a modal.

INCORRECT	Kwang **mights** go to graduate school.
CORRECT	Kwang **might** go to graduate school.

* Never use two modals together.

35d
ESL verb

INCORRECT	They **might could** drive all night.
CORRECT	They **might** drive all night.

* *Do, does,* and *did* are not used in questions with modals, except for the modal *have to.*

INCORRECT	**Do I must** answer all the questions?
CORRECT	**Must I** answer all the questions?
EXCEPT	**Do I have to** answer all the questions?

* *Do, does,* and *did* are not used in negative statements with modals; use *not* instead, placed after the modal.

INCORRECT	They **do not can** enter the test room.
CORRECT	They **cannot** enter the test room.

INCORRECT	Jorge **did not could** have worked any harder.
CORRECT	Jorge **could not have** worked any harder.

3 Use the perfect form to express past time. As you can see from the chart of modals on pages 569–570, many modals have a past form. The past of modals that give advice or express possibility, expectation, and conclusion have a *perfect* verb form (modal + *have* + past participle), as you can see in the following examples.

ADVICE   Gail **should have taken** that marketing job last year. Gail didn't take the job.

POSSIBILITY   Although he chose not to, Bob **could have gone** to Mexico over spring break. Bob didn't go to Mexico.

EXPECTATION   Where is Sue? She **should have been** here by now. Sue hasn't arrived yet.

CONCLUSION   Ted finished; he **must have worked** all night.

EXERCISE 35.5 Review Section 35d-1. Fill in the blanks with a modal from the list below. More than one answer is possible for each blank. Try to use each modal only once. (For answers, see p. 573.)

would	must	have to	ought to	should have
should	can	might	had better	must have

1. Can you believe the line waiting to see the movie *Spider-Man?* That _____ be a good movie!

2. Where is my purse, Mom? It _____ be on the table where you put it last night.

3. I'm sorry, Professor Lopez, but I _____ not take the test tomorrow because I _____ go to Immigration about my visa.

4. Jason, you _____ eat your vegetables or you won't get any dessert.

EXERCISE 35.6 Review Section 35d. Each of the following sentences contains errors related to modal auxiliaries. Identify the errors and correct them. (For answers, see p. 573.)

1. Megan's boss told her, "You had better to improve your attitude, or we will have to take disciplinary action."

2. Megan was very distressed by this news; she did not could understand the basis for her boss's complaints.

3. She tried to think of things that she had done wrong. She knew that she should had been more enthusiastic at the last meeting, but she felt she couldn't be hypocritical. She simply didn't agree with her boss.

35d
ESL verb

4. Megan was really worried. Her boss mights send her a "pink slip," which would mean that she had been fired.

ANSWER KEY

EXERCISE 35.1
1. dream; happens
2. remember; wake
3. hear; am dreaming
4. know; am writing
5. am researching
6. believe

EXERCISE 35.2
1. have had
2. have worked
3. applied; did not promote
4. had
5. has been

EXERCISE 35.3
1. have been talking
2. were talking
3. will probably be talking
4. have talked
5. talked
6. had been talking
7. are talking (or talk)
8. are talking
9. had talked
10. will never talk

EXERCISE 35.4
1. Before I **studied** psychology, I (**had**) **thought** it was an easy subject.
2. Now I **know** that it isn't easy.
3. It **has** a lot of statistics.
4. I **have been studying** psychology since April, and I **have only begun** to learn some of the concepts.
5. I **have been trying** to learn more of the concepts every day.
6. Last night I **was studying** from 9:00 to midnight.
   or

Last night I **studied** from 9:00 to midnight.
7. I went **to** my adviser last Monday.
8. She told ~~to~~ me to see her after class.
9. But when I went to see her after class, she **had** already **left.**
10. It's January. By the middle of June, I **will have studied** psychology for six months.

EXERCISE 35.5
1. must; should
2. should; ought to; must; had better
3. cannot/might have to; might/should
4. had better; must; should; ought to

EXERCISE 35.6
1. Megan's boss told her, "You had better ~~to~~ improve your attitude, or we will have to take disciplinary action."
2. Megan was very distressed by this news; she **could not** (*or* **did not**) understand the basis for her boss's complaints.
3. She tried to think of things that she had done wrong. She knew that she **should have been** more enthusiastic at the last meeting, but she felt she couldn't be hypocritical. She simply didn't agree with her boss.
4. Megan was really worried. Her boss ~~mights~~ send her a "pink slip," which would mean that she had been fired.

35d
ESL verb

CHAPTER 36

ESL Questions About Gerunds, Infinitives, Articles, or Number?

Jocelyn Steer and Carol Rhoades

This chapter offers guidelines for handling grammatical concepts that many ESL writers find confusing: gerunds, infinitives, articles, and number agreement. If you have learned British English but will now be writing American English, you should pay special attention to Section 36b on articles and count/noncount nouns, for there are differences between the British and American rules.

36a How do you use gerunds and infinitives?

In English, gerunds and infinitives have several functions. (See Section 27a for definitions of *gerund* and *infinitive*.)

Gerunds can function as subject, object, complement, and object of a preposition. (See Sections 19a-1 and 31b for explanations of *complement* and *object of a preposition*.)

subj.
Finding a parking space is impossible here!

obj.
George enjoys **reading** for half an hour before bed.

comp.
His favorite hobby is **cooking**.

obj. prep.
She is afraid of **flying**.

An **infinitive** can be the subject of a sentence, and it can be the object of a verb.

subj.
To find a parking space here is impossible!

obj.
My sister hopes **to be** a marine biologist.

ESL writers often have difficulty with gerunds and infinitives that act as objects in a sentence. This section will focus on this problem.

1 Review which form—gerund or infinitive—to use.
You already know that some verbs in English are followed by gerunds
and other verbs are followed by infinitives.

INFINITIVE (*TO* + BASE FORM OF VERB)
I want **to go** with you.

GERUND (BASE FORM OF VERB + *-ING*)
He enjoys **jogging** in the park.

Other verbs, however, can have *either* a gerund or an infinitive after
them without a difference in meaning.

GERUND OR INFINITIVE (NO CHANGE IN MEANING)
gerund
The dog began **barking** at midnight.
infinitive
The dog began **to bark** at midnight.
These two sentences have exactly the same meaning.

Finally, some verbs in English (including *forget, regret, remember, stop,
try*) can be followed by *either* a gerund or an infinitive, but with a
change in meaning.

GERUND OR INFINITIVE (CHANGE IN MEANING)
Paul stopped **working** in the cafeteria.
Paul *no longer* works in the cafeteria.

36a
ESL

Paul stopped his tennis game early **to work** on his homework.
Paul stopped his game *in order to* work on his homework.
Paul forgot **to visit** his cousin while he was in Mexico.
He did *not* visit his cousin.
Paul will never forget **visiting** Mexico.
Paul visited Mexico and he will always remember the trip.

Native speakers know intuitively whether to use a gerund or an infinitive after a verb, but this is not usually true for ESL students.
   Chart 36.1 on page 576 and Chart 36.2 on pages 576–77 can
help you; be sure to keep these charts handy when you write.

**2 Review when a verb must be followed by a noun or a
pronoun.** As we've seen, some verbs in English (called *transitive
verbs*) need to have a noun or pronoun after them. For example, when
you use *tell*, you need a direct object (*What did you tell?*) or an indirect
object (*Whom did you tell?*) to complete the sentence.

Chart 36.1

Verbs Followed by Gerunds or Infinitives

VERB + INFINITIVE

These verbs are followed by **infinitives.**

afford	consent	intend	pretend
agree	decide	learn	promise
appear	deserve	manage	refuse
arrange	expect	mean	seem
ask	fail	need	threaten
beg	hesitate	offer	wait
claim	hope	plan	wish

VERB + GERUND

These verbs are followed by **gerunds.**

admit	deny	mention	recommend
anticipate	discuss	miss	resent
appreciate	dislike	postpone	resist
avoid	enjoy	practice	risk
complete	finish	quit	suggest
consider	can't help	recall	tolerate
delay	keep	recollect	understand

VERB + GERUND OR INFINITIVE

These verbs can be followed by either a **gerund** or an **infinitive**, with no change in meaning.

begin	can't stand	hate	prefer
can't bear	continue	like	start

36a

ESL

Chart 36.2

Verbs Followed by Gerunds or Infinitives with a Change in Meaning

VERB + GERUND OR INFINITIVE

These verbs can be followed by either a **gerund** or an **infinitive**, but the meaning of the sentence will change depending on which one you use.

VERB	MEANING
try (to be)	make an attempt to be
try (being)	do an experiment
regret (to be)	feel sorry about
regret (being)	feel sorry about *past* action

remember (to be)	not forget
remember (being)	recall, bring to mind
forget (to be)	not remember
(never) forget (being)	always remember
stop (to be)	stop in order to be
stop (being)	interrupt an action

ESL Tip   *Finish Your Draft Early* ———
Kalina Saraiva de Lima, Peru

I tell my students that they need to have their drafts ready to review at least one week before they are due. There may be many items that need to be corrected, edited, or rewritten, and it's important to allow enough time to work through these changes before turning in the paper.

INCORRECT   I told ∧ to write me a letter.
The object is missing; the sentence is incomplete.

CORRECT   I told **my son** to write me a letter.
My son is the indirect object; this sentence is complete.

36a
ESL

Remember that an *infinitive verb* comes after transitive verb + noun or pronoun constructions. The chart below lists the verbs that follow this pattern.

Chart 36.3
Verbs Followed by Nouns, Pronouns, or Infinitives

VERB + (NOUN OR PRONOUN) + INFINITIVE
These verbs must be followed by a **noun** or a **pronoun** + an **infinitive**.

advise	forbid	persuade
allow	force	remind
cause	hire	require
challenge	instruct	tell
convince	invite	urge
encourage	order	warn

3 Instead of being followed by an infinitive, the verbs *have, make,* and *let* are followed by a noun or pronoun and the base form of the verb. This means that you omit *to* before the verb.

HAVE   I **had** my mother *cut* my hair.
Here *had* means to cause someone to do something.

MAKE   The teacher **made** him *leave* the class.
Here *made* means to force someone to do something; it is stronger than *had.*

LET   Professor Betts **let** the class *leave* early.
Here *let* means to allow someone to do something.

4 Use a gerund after a preposition. Many verbs are followed by prepositions. Sometimes adjectives are followed by prepositions. Always remember to use a gerund, not an infinitive, after prepositions. Here are two common sentence patterns with prepositions followed by gerunds.

     verb   adj. prep. gerund
Carla has been very worried **about passing** her statistics class.

     verb prep. gerund
Mrs. Short apologized **for interrupting** our conversation.

The chart [below] lists common preposition combinations with verbs and adjectives.

36a
ESL

Chart 36.4

Common Verb (+ Adjective) + Preposition Constructions

be accustomed to	be faithful to	pray for
be afraid of	be familiar with	prevent from
approve of	be fond of	prohibit from
be aware of	be good at	protect from
believe in	be grateful to	be proud of
be capable of	be guilty of	rely on
be committed to	hope for	be responsible for
complain about	insist on	be satisfied with
be composed of	be interested in	be scared of
consist of	be jealous of	stop from
depend on	look forward to	succeed in
be disappointed in	be made of	take advantage of
be divorced from	be married to	take care of
dream of/about	object to	be tired of
be envious of	be opposed to	be worried about
be excited about	be patient with	

EXERCISE 36.1 Fill in the blanks with the infinitive, gerund, or base form of the verbs in parentheses. (For answers, see p. 585.)

1. Women who have not wanted (**work**) _____ because of health threats can now relax.

2. A recent study completed in California, shows that women who work outside the home seem (**have**) _____ fewer health problems than those who work inside the home.

3. Another federal study reports that women employed outside the home do not risk (**have**) _____ more "stress-induced" heart attacks than women working inside the home.

4. In fact, this study appears (**support**) _____ the benefits of working outside the home for women.

5. In general, working women are found (**be**) _____ physically and mentally healthier than women who stay at home.

6. Many working women will appreciate (**hear**) _____ that their chances for depression actually increase if they decide (**drop**) _____ out of the work force.

7. These studies do not pretend (**decide**) _____ for women what is best for them.

8. However, the studies might help some women (**make**) _____ a decision about (**go**) _____ back to work outside the home or about (**quit**) _____ their jobs because they have children.

36b
ESL

36b Questions about articles and number agreement?

Are you sometimes confused about which article to use—*a, an,* or *the?* Do you know when no article should be used? Are you still uncertain about whether to use *a few* or *a little* before some nouns? If so, you are certainly not alone; many ESL students ask these questions. This section gives you general guidelines about articles and expressions of quantity. For the finer points about article use that are not covered here, we suggest that you consult one of the ESL grammar references listed on page 556.

1 Decide whether the noun is count or noncount. Before you can know which article to use, you will need to determine whether

the noun in question is *count* or *noncount*. A **count noun** refers to something that you can count or that you can divide easily.

COUNT NOUNS   There are sixty **seconds** in one **minute**.
Joan bought six **books** for her class.

When there is more than one of the noun (*seconds*), the count noun must be plural. (See Section 28a for a discussion of plural nouns.) If there is only one (*one minute*), the count noun is singular.

A **noncount noun** generally refers to something that cannot usually be counted or divided. Noncount nouns include **mass nouns** such as materials (*wood, plastic, wool*), food items (*cheese, rice, meat*) and liquids (*water, milk*), and **abstract nouns** (*beauty, knowledge, glory*).

NONCOUNT NOUNS   Joe drank a lot of **milk** as a teenager.
"Give me **liberty** or give me **death!**"

Some nouns that are noncount in English may seem like things that you can count, such as *money*. Many other noncount nouns in English can confuse ESL students: *furniture, hair, traffic, information, advice*. It is always a good idea to consult an ESL dictionary or grammar book when you are unsure whether a noun is count or noncount.

Unlike count nouns, which can be singular or plural, noncount nouns have only the singular form. In addition, since you can't count these nouns, you can't use numbers or words that express number (*several, many*) to describe them. You will use other types of expressions to indicate quantity for noncount nouns; these expressions, called *quantifiers*, are discussed in Section 36b-5.

Most nouns are either count or noncount. However, some noncount nouns can change to have a count meaning. Using a noncount noun as a count noun usually limits the noncount noun in some way. For example, imagine you are at a restaurant and your English-speaking friend asks the waiter, "Can we have three waters, please?" You are confused because you learned that *water* is a noncount noun, but your friend has used it in the plural form, with a number. In this case, *three waters* means *three glasses of water,* and it is acceptable to say that. Other instances in which a noncount noun changes to a count noun include when you mean *an instance of, a serving of,* or *a type of* the noncount noun.

count noun
His grandmother started a **business.**   one instance of business
count noun
I'd like two **coffees** to go, please.   two servings of coffee
count noun
There are three new **wines** on the menu.   three kinds of wine

36b
ESL

2 Decide whether the count noun requires a definite article (*the*) or an indefinite article (*a/an*). When the count noun is singular, you'll need an article, either *a/an* or *the,* in front of it. How do you know which article to use? Generally, when you introduce the noun, without having referred to it before, then you will use the *indefinite* article, *a* or *an.* (See Section 28d for the difference between *a* and *an.*)

INDEFINITE MEANING

Bob: I just signed up for **a** literature class.

Ted: Oh, really? I didn't know you were interested in that.

This is the first time Bob has mentioned the class to Ted.

After that, when both of them know what is being discussed, Bob will use the *definite* article, *the.*

DEFINITE MEANING

Bob: Can you believe **the** class meets on Friday evenings?

Both Bob and Ted now share the same information.

Note how the same guidelines apply to written English in the following sentences on homelessness.

There are several reasons why **a** person may end up homeless. Perhaps **the** person lost his or her job and could not pay for **an** apartment. Or perhaps **the** apartment was sold to **a** new owner who raised the rent. **The** new owner may not realize how expensive the rent is for that person.

36b
ESL

Certain other situations also require the definite article, *the.*

• When there is only one of the noun.

The earth is round. There is only one earth.

• When the noun is superlative.

This is **the best** brand you can buy.

There can only be one brand that is the best.

• When the noun is limited. You will usually use *the* before a noun that has been limited in some way to show that you are referring to a *specific* example of the noun.

The book **that I read** is informative.

That I read limits the book to a specific one.

The book **on George W. Bush** is out.

On George W. Bush limits the book.

If you are making a *generalization*, however, *the* is not always used.

A book **on plants** can make a nice gift.

On plants limits the noun, but the sentence does not refer to a specific book on plants—it refers to *any or all books on plants*. The definite article, *the*, would not be correct here.

ESL Tip   *Use Familiar Words When Possible*
Ricardo Pumarejo, Jr., USA

When you write an academic paper, don't try to use vocabulary that is unfamiliar to you. Trust that your knowledge will often be sufficient to communicate your ideas— good writing is often simple writing.

3 Choose articles before general nouns carefully.

When you want to make generalizations, choosing the correct article can be tricky. As a rule, use *a/an* or *the* with most *singular count nouns* to make generalizations.

A dog can be good company for **a** lonely person.

Use *a/an* to mean any dog, one of many dogs.

The computer has changed the banking industry dramatically.

Use *the* to mean *the computer in general.*

The spotted owl is an endangered species.

The capitalist believes in free enterprise.

Use *the* to make general statements about specific species of animals (*spotted owl*) or groups of people (*capitalists*).

He was ill and went to **the** hospital.

American English uses the definite article with *hospital* even when we do not refer to a specific hospital; British English does not use the article with *hospital.*

Use a *plural count noun* to make general statements, without *the.*

Capitalists believe in free enterprise.
Computers have changed the banking industry dramatically.

Finally, *noncount nouns* in general statements do not have an article in front of them.

Sugar is a major cause of tooth decay.
Many educators question whether **intelligence** can be measured.

Consumed in moderate amounts, **red wine** is thought by some researchers to reduce chances of heart disease.

4 Be aware of two possible article problems with noncount nouns. First make sure that you don't use *a/an* with noncount nouns.

INCORRECT	I need a̶ work.
CORRECT	I need work.

Second, keep in mind that a noncount noun can never be plural.

INCORRECT	Joe needs some information̶s̶ about the class.
CORRECT	Joe needs some information about the class.

And remember that sometimes noncount nouns can change to have a count meaning (see Section 36b-1).

5 Pay careful attention to quantifiers. The words that come before nouns and tell you *how much* or *how many* are called **quantifiers**. Quantifiers are not always the same for both count and noncount nouns. See Chart 36.5 below for a list of quantifiers.

Chart 36.5

Quantifiers

36b
ESL

USE THESE WITH COUNT AND NON- COUNT NOUNS	USE THESE WITH COUNT NOUNS ONLY	USE THESE WITH NONCOUNT NOUNS ONLY
some books/money	**several** books	**a good deal of** money
a lot of books/money	**many** books	**a great deal of** money
plenty of books/money	**a couple of** books	**(not) much** money*
a lack of books/money	**a few** books	**a little** money
most of the books/money	**few** books	**little** money

Much is ordinarily used only in questions and in negative statements: "Do you have *much* milk left?" "No, there isn't *much* milk."

A few/a little and *few/little* It may not seem like a big difference, but the article *a* in front of the quantifiers *few* and *little* changes the meaning. *A few* or *a little* means "not a lot, but enough of the item."

There are **a few books** in the library on capital punishment.
Use *a few* with count nouns.

There is **a little information** in the library on capital punishment.
Use *a little* with noncount nouns.

Few or *little* (without *a*) means that there is *not enough* of something. These quantifiers have a negative meaning.

There are **few** female leaders in the world.
not enough of them

My mother has **little** hope that this will change.
not much hope

Most **and** *most of* Using *most of* can be tricky. You can use *most of* before either a count or a noncount noun, but if you do, don't forget to put *the* before the noun.

MOST OF + *THE* + SPECIFIC PLURAL NOUN
Most of the *women* in the class were married. Not: *most of women*

MOST OF + *THE* + SPECIFIC NONCOUNT NOUN
Most of the *jewelry* in the house was stolen. Not: *most of jewelry*

MOST + GENERAL PLURAL NOUN
Most *cars* have seat belts. Not: *most of cars*

EXERCISE 36.2 In the list of nouns below, write *C* after the count nouns and *NC* after the noncount nouns. If you are not sure, consult an ESL dictionary. Then make a note of the nouns you had to check. (For answers, see p. 585.)

36b
ESL

1. furniture   6. people

2. work   7. equipment

3. dollar   8. money

4. job   9. newspaper

5. advice   10. traffic

EXERCISE 36.3 Review Section 36b. Each of the following sentences has at least one error in the use of articles or quantifiers. Circle the error and correct it. (For answers, see pp. 585–86.)

1. Much people have visited the new restaurant downtown called Rock-and-Roll Hamburger Haven.

2. Most of customers are young people because music in restaurant is very loud.

3. The restaurant serves the usual food—hamburgers, pizza, and pasta. It is not expensive; in fact, most expensive item on the menu is only $8.

4. Food is not very good, but the atmosphere is very appealing to these young men and women.

5. There are much posters on the walls of famous rock star. There is even authentic motorcycle of one star on a platform.

6. Some of regular customers say they have seen some stars eating there.

7. These "regulars" give these advices to anyone who wants to spot a star there: look for dark glasses and a leather coat.

EXERCISE 36.4 Write a descriptive paragraph about ordering and eating a meal at your favorite restaurant. Refer to Chart 36.5 on page 583, which lists quantifiers used with count and noncount nouns, and use at least four words from this list in your paragraph. Underline all the nouns in your paragraph and write *C* (for count nouns) and *NC* (for noncount nouns) above them. Then check your use of articles. (For help, refer to Sections 36b-2 through 36b-4.) Make sure your subject-verb agreement is correct.

ANSWER KEY

EXERCISE 36.1
1. to work
2. to have
3. having
4. to support
5. to be
6. hearing; to drop
7. to decide
8. to make; going; quitting

EXERCISE 36.2
1. NC
2. NC
3. C
4. C
5. NC
6. C
7. NC
8. NC
9. C
10. NC

EXERCISE 36.3
1. **Many** people have visited the new restaurant downtown called Rock-and-Roll Hamburger Haven.
2. Most of **the** customers are young people because **the** music in **the** restaurant is very loud.
3. The restaurant serves the usual food—hamburgers, pizza, and pasta. It is not expensive; in fact, **the** most expensive item on the menu is only $8.
4. **The** food is not very good, but the atmosphere is very appealing to these young men and women.
5. There are **many** posters on the walls of famous rock stars. There is even **an** authentic

36b
ESL

motorcycle of one star on a platform.

6. Some of **the** regular customers say they have seen some stars eating there.

7. These "regulars" give **this advice** to anyone who wants to

spot a star there: look for dark glasses and a leather coat.

EXERCISE 36.4

Answers will vary.

Punctuation and Mechanics

CHAPTER 37

How Do You Punctuate Sentence Endings?

37a When do you use periods?

Sentences and some abbreviations end with periods. Periods say, "That's all there is." Although periods cause few problems, writers occasionally put them in the wrong place or forget them entirely.

An editor will use a caret and a circled period to show where a period has been omitted.

He told me, "Yes ᴧ" But he lied. ⊙

1 Use periods at the end of statements.

Hannibal, a Carthaginian general, was a brilliant military strategist.

2 Use periods at the end of indirect questions and mild commands.

Military theorists wonder whether any battle plan has been more tactically perfect than Hannibal's at Cannae (216 BC).

On the map, locate the Roman and Carthaginian positions.

Strong commands may also be punctuated with exclamation points.

3 Use periods to punctuate some abbreviations.

Cong.   natl.
sing., pl.   pp.

When a statement ends with an abbreviation, the period at the end of the sentence is not doubled.

We visited the Folger Library in Washington, D.C.

The period at the end of the abbreviation is retained when the sentence is a question or an exclamation.

Have you ever been to Washington, D.C.?
Our flight departs at 6 a.m.!

When an abbreviation occurs in the middle of a sentence, it retains its period. The period may even be followed by another punctuation mark.

> Though he signed his name Quentin P. Randolph, Esq., we called him Bubba.

Abbreviations for institutions, corporations, networks, or government agencies usually don't require periods; neither do words shortened by common use.

> NFL   GM   HBO   FEMA
> lab   auto   dorm   co-op

Similarly, acronyms—first-letter abbreviations pronounced as words—don't take periods.

> CARE   NATO   NOW

When in doubt about punctuating abbreviations, check a dictionary.

4 Use periods in conventional ways. Not all periods mark the ends of sentences. They are also used, for example, to indicate decimals, to mark chapter and verse in biblical citations in MLA style, and to separate parts of email addresses and URLs.

> 0.01 $189.00   75.47

> Matthew 3.1
> sugarbear@mail.utexas.edu
> < http://www.google.com>

37b
?

37b When do you use question marks?

Question marks terminate questions; they can also be used to suggest doubt or uncertainty.

An editor will use a caret and a question mark (or sometimes a question mark alone) to show where this piece of punctuation is needed. Unnecessary question marks are indicated by *No?*

> To whom did you speak⌃ ?

> I asked Sue if she were angry? *no?*

1 Use question marks to end direct questions.

Have you ever heard of the Battle of Cannae?
Who fought in the battle?
Do you know that Hannibal defeated the Roman legions?
How?

2 Use question marks to indicate that a name, date, or fact cannot be established with certainty. Such a question mark should not be used to indicate that a writer is unsure of facts that might be available with more research.

Hannibal (247?–183 BC) was a Carthaginian general and military tactician.

3 Do not use question marks to terminate indirect questions. Indirect questions are statements that seem to have questions within them. Compare these examples to see the difference.

INDIRECT QUESTION	Varro wondered whether Hannibal's strategy would succeed.
DIRECT QUESTION	Will Hannibal's strategy succeed?
QUESTION WITHIN A STATEMENT	Varro wondered, "Will Hannibal's strategy succeed?"
INDIRECT QUESTION	The reporter asked how the new agency would be funded.
DIRECT QUESTION	How will the new agency be funded?
QUESTION WITHIN A STATEMENT	"How will the new agency be funded?" the reporter asked.

37b
?

4 Punctuate as questions any compound sentences that begin with statements but end with questions.

The strategy seemed reasonable, but would it work on the battlefield?

Don't confuse these constructions with indirect questions.

5 Place question marks after direct questions that appear in the middle of sentences. Such questions will usually be surrounded by parentheses, quotation marks, or dashes.

Skeptical of their tour guide's claim—"Would Hannibal really position his cavalry here?"—the scholars in the group consulted a map.

6 Place question marks outside quotation marks except when they are part of the quoted material itself.

Was it Terence who wrote "Fortune helps the brave**"?**
The teacher asked, "Have you read any Cicero**?"**

For a more detailed explanation of quotation marks, see Section 41a.

7 Do not allow question marks to bump against other punctuation marks. For instance, you wouldn't place a comma, colon, or semicolon after a question mark.

WRONG "Where did the battle begin**?,"** the tourist asked.
RIGHT "Where did the battle begin**?"** the tourist asked.

Don't multiply question marks to add emphasis. One mark is sufficient.

WRONG Are you serious **???**
RIGHT Are you serious**?**

37c When do you use exclamation marks?

Exclamations give emphasis to statements. They are vigorous punctuation marks with the subtlety of a Lamborghini Murcielago. In academic writing, they should be about as rare too.

An editor will use a caret and an exclamation point (or sometimes an exclamation alone) to show where this piece of punctuation is needed or should be omitted.

I won the $90 million lottery. ˄

Columbus wasn't the first European in America! *no!*

1 Use exclamation marks to express strong reactions or commands.

They are retreating**!**
Our time has come at last**!**

Save exclamations for those occasions—rare in college and business writing—when your words really deserve emphasis. Too many exclamations can make a passage seem juvenile.

OVERDONE The Roman forces at the Battle of Cannae outnumbered Hannibal's forces roughly two to one**!** Yet

37c
!

Roman casualties would be ten times higher than those suffered by Hannibal's army!

TEMPERED The Roman forces at the Battle of Cannae outnumbered Hannibal's forces roughly two to one. Yet Roman casualties would be ten times higher than those suffered by Hannibal's army.

2 Do not allow exclamation marks to bump against other punctuation marks. For instance, you wouldn't place a comma, colon, or semicolon after an exclamation mark.

WRONG "Please check your records again!," the caller demanded.

RIGHT "Please check your records again!" the caller demanded.

Don't multiply exclamation marks to add emphasis. One mark is sufficient.

WRONG Don't shout!!

RIGHT Don't shout!

EXERCISE 37.1 Edit the following passage, adding, replacing, and deleting periods, question marks, exclamation points, and any other marks of punctuation that need to be changed.

1. Hannibal simply outfoxed the Roman general Varro at Cannae!!!

2. Hannibal placed his numerically smaller army where the Aufidius River would protect his flank—could the hotheaded Varro appreciate such a move—and arrayed his forces to make the Roman numbers work against themselves!

3. It must have seemed obvious to Hannibal where Varro would concentrate his forces?

4. "Advance!," Hannibal ordered!

5. Is it likely that Varro and the Romans noticed how thin the Carthaginian forces were at the center of the battle line?

6. Predictably, the Romans pressed their attack on the weakened Carthaginian center. But in the meantime, Hannibal's cavalry had destroyed its Roman counterpart!

7. You might be wondering, "Why didn't Hannibal use his cavalry to strengthen his weak center"?

37c
!

8. It was because he wanted it behind the Roman lines to attack from the rear!

9. Hannibal expected the troops at the ends of his battle line to out-flank the Romans, but would such a strategy work.

10. It did! The Romans found themselves surrounded and defeated!

37c
!

CHAPTER 38

Questions About Sentence Boundaries: Fragments, Comma Splices, and Run-ons?

Three of the most troublesome and common punctuation problems are the fragment, the comma splice, and the run-on. All three problems arise from confusion about sentence boundaries—that is, where sentences begin and end. Once you get a feel for those boundaries and the signals writers use to mark them, you are less likely to have these problems.

38a How do you repair sentence fragments?

Sentence fragments are phrases or clauses that look like complete sentences, but either they lack subjects or verbs (see Section 19a-1) or they are subordinate constructions (see Section 19g).

NO SUBJECT	Fits perfectly!
NO VERB	The gold ring.
SUBORDINATE	That I found on the subway.
COMPLETE SENTENCE	The gold ring that I found on the subway fits perfectly.

An editor or instructor will usually mark such constructions with the abbreviation for sentence fragment, *frag*.

The bill died. Because the President vetoed it. *frag*

1 Check that all sentences have complete subjects and verbs, either stated or implied. To avoid a fragment, you need a subject and verb that can stand alone; don't be fooled by subjects or verbs in subordinate clauses (see the next section). Subject and verb pairings can be as simple as *It is* or *They were*. Sometimes, too, subjects may be understood rather than stated—for example, in commands. But complete sentences always need subjects and verbs.

The sun rose. subject is *sun;* verb is *rose*

When we arrived at the canyon, the sun, hidden beneath a thick blanket of clouds, had already risen.
subject is *sun;* verb is *had risen*

It was a beautiful morning. subject is *it;* verb is *was*

Keep quiet. subject *you* is understood; verb is *keep*

2 Check that you have not allowed a dependent or subordinate clause to stand alone as a sentence. Subordinate clauses—that is, clauses that begin with words such as *although, because, if, since, unless, when, while*—won't work as sentences by themselves even though they have a subject and a verb (see Section 19d-2).

FRAGMENT	It will be a miracle. **If the mail comes on time.**
FRAGMENT	The town decided to ration water. **Since there had been no rain for months.**

Standing alone, these fragments can leave readers wondering what's missing. Usually, such fragments can be repaired by attaching them to surrounding sentences.

COMPLETE SENTENCE	If the mail comes on time, it will be a miracle.
COMPLETE SENTENCE	The town decided to ration water since there had been no rain for months.

Here is another sentence fragment resulting from a dependent clause not linked to a complete sentence.

FRAGMENT	Rainbows can be observed only in the morning or late afternoon. **When the sun is less than forty degrees above the horizon.**
FRAGMENT ELIMINATED	Rainbows can be observed only in the morning or late afternoon when the sun is less than forty degrees above the horizon.

38a
frag

3 Check that you have not allowed a relative clause or appositive to stand alone as a sentence. Words like *who, which, that,* and *where* typically signal the beginning of a relative clause that must be connected to a sentence to make a complete thought (see Section 19d-2). If the clause is left unattached, a fragment results.

> FRAGMENT   The Capitol is on Congress Avenue. **Which is the widest street in the city.**
>
> CORRECTED   The Capitol is on Congress Avenue, which is the widest street in the city.

The appositive, a group of words that gives more information about a noun, is another construction that produces fragments when allowed to stand alone (see Section 19c-4).

> FRAGMENT   Dr. Anderson resigned her professorship. **A position she had held for twenty years.**
>
> The phrase starting with *A position* is punctuated as a sentence, but it doesn't express a full idea by itself.
>
> CORRECTED   Dr. Anderson resigned her professorship, a position she had held for twenty years.

4 Check that you have not substituted a verbal for the verb in a sentence.

If you have, the result will be a fragment. Verbals (see Sections 27a and 27b) are tricky constructions because they look like verbs, but they act as nouns, adjectives, or adverbs. For instance, in the phrase "to look at something," *to look* is the infinitive of a verb, but it doesn't act as a verb. In the phrase "running for office," *running* is a gerund, not a verb. In the phrase "recognizing his weakness," *recognizing* acts as a noun, not a verb (see Section 19c-2). To eliminate fragments caused by verbals, it helps to remember the following:

- An *-ing* word by itself can never act as the verb of a sentence. To qualify as a verb, the *-ing* word must have an auxiliary such as *have been, is,* or *were.*
- An infinitive, such as *to run* or *to go,* can never act as the verb of a sentence.

Here are examples of verbals causing sentence fragments. The fragments are boldfaced.

> FRAGMENT   The reporter from Reuters asked the senator probing questions. **Suspecting a coverup.**
>
> The boldfaced portion is a verbal phrase modifying *reporter* that cannot act as a sentence.
>
> FRAGMENT   Suspecting a coverup, the reporter from Reuters
> ELIMINATED   asked the senator probing questions.
>
> FRAGMENT   **To break the story.** That was the reporter's goal.
>
> The boldfaced portion is an infinitive phrase acting as a noun and shouldn't be punctuated as a sentence.
>
> FRAGMENT   To break the story was the reporter's goal.
> ELIMINATED

38a
frag

5 Check that you have not treated a disconnected phrase as a sentence.
Turning a disconnected phrase into a full sentence usually means adding a subject or a verb (sometimes both), depending on what has been left out of the phrase. Here the disconnected phrases that are sentence fragments are boldfaced.

FRAGMENTS   David cleaned his glasses. **Absentmindedly. With the hem of his lamb's-wool sweater.**

The **prepositional** phrase—*with the hem of his lamb's-wool sweater*—can be joined to the end of the sentence. *Absentmindedly* needs to be attached to the word it modifies: *David.*

FRAGMENTS   Absentmindedly, David cleaned his glasses
ELIMINATED   with the hem of his lamb's-wool sweater.

6 Check that you have not treated a list as an independent sentence.
Sometimes a list gets detached from the sentence that introduced or explained it. The result can be a sentence fragment that needs to be revised either by connecting it to the preceding sentence or by making it stand as a sentence on its own.

FRAGMENT   Bucking a Washington tradition, some politicians have willingly left office to pursue new interests. **Pat Schroeder and J. C. Watts among them.**

FRAGMENT   Bucking a Washington tradition, some politicians
ELIMINATED   have willingly left office to pursue new interests, among them Pat Schroeder and J. C. Watts.

Lists are often introduced by words or phrases such as *especially, for example, for instance, such as,* and *namely.* If a fragment follows such an expression, be sure to correct it—usually by attaching the fragment to the preceding sentence.

FRAGMENT   People suffer from many peculiar phobias. For example, ailurophobia (fear of cats), aviophobia (fear of flying), ombrophobia (fear of rain), and vestiphobia (fear of clothes).

FRAGMENT   People suffer from many peculiar phobias—for
ELIMINATED   example, ailurophobia (fear of cats), aviophobia (fear of flying), ombrophobia (fear of rain), and vestiphobia (fear of clothes).

38a
frag

EXERCISE 38.1 Rewrite the following sentences to eliminate any sentence fragments.

1. Although most movie stars are human and created by the usual birds-and-bees process. One of the most popular movie stars

ever, the liquid-metal cyborg in *Terminator 2,* was created by a computer.

2. The technology of computer animation has developed rapidly over the past decade. Making a spectacular range of special effects possible.

3. Industrial Light and Magic was responsible for the astonishing cyborg. A special-effects company owned by director George Lucas.

4. The company was founded to create the special effects for *Star Wars.* Subsequently creating the special effects for a string of hits, including *E.T.: The Extra-Terrestrial* and *Who Framed Roger Rabbit?* Also the special effects for *Ghost.*

5. While the cyborg appears in *Terminator 2* for only about five minutes, creating the footage cost millions of dollars. Keeping thirty-five computer animators busy for ten months.

38b Do you understand intentional fragments?

Writers concerned to avoid fragments in their own work may sometimes wonder why incomplete sentences occur in newspapers, popular magazines, and fiction, as well as in much electronic communication. For example, in a passage from *Men's Journal* (January 2000) evaluating the classic film *The Big Sleep,* the first sentence is a fragment.

38b
frag

Bogart, Bacall, and Raymond Chandler rewritten by William Faulkner: hard-boiled heaven. Scene for scene, the private-eye movie doesn't get any better than this.

Are sentence fragments considered wrong at some times but not at others? The answer is "yes," depending on a writer's purpose and audience.

1 Understand what intentional fragments are. Intentional
fragments are groups of words that convey complete ideas even though they may lack subjects, verbs, or both. Presented and punctuated as sentences, such constructions enable writers to set a quick pace, present vivid images, convey information quickly, or establish a casual tone in their informal work. Fragments make writing sound like conversation, direct and personal. You can hear that tone in a

passage from a road test in *Bicycling,* in which the first and third sentences are obvious fragments.

> **Glitches?** We noticed an undercut in the weld between the top and seat tubes, which the bright yellow paint showed in stark relief when the light was right. **Too bad, as the rest of the welds were just first rate.**

2 Use intentional fragments cautiously. The problem is that intentional fragments can look just like the fragments many readers consider major errors. They should not appear regularly in any formal or academic writing, and certainly not in a research paper, report, job application letter, or literary analysis. You might use them judiciously in email, listservs, memos, narratives, journal pieces, and other informal writing. For readers conservative about grammar, avoid fragments entirely.

EXERCISE 38.2 Bring to class some advertisements that use intentional fragments or locate a Web site or listserv that routinely includes fragments. Working with other students in a small group, identify these fragments; then join forces to rewrite them and eliminate all incomplete sentences. Assess the difference between the original material and the revised versions. Why do you think the writers may have used fragments?

38c How do you avoid comma splices?

A comma splice occurs when you try to join two independent clauses with a comma only. The error is common and considered serious in academic and professional writing—but it is easy to identify and fix. Look at this example of a comma splice.

COMMA SPLICE
Local shopkeepers were concerned about a recent outbreak of graffiti, they feared that it indicated the arrival of troublesome gangs in the neighborhood.

Notice that the groups of words on each side of the comma could stand alone as complete sentences. When that happens, you ordinarily have a comma splice.

An editor or instructor will usually mark a comma splice with the abbreviation *cs.*

Yellowstone is the oldest of America's national parks, it is located in Wyoming. *cs*

38c
cs

█ 1 Remember that commas can't link complete sentences. When two independent clauses are joined, they require a linkage stronger than a comma alone to show their relationship. Using a comma where a semicolon or conjunction is needed will usually blur the meaning of a sentence: readers may not know if a writer wants to show a connection between the clauses, a subordination of ideas, or a contrast. Consider how confusing these sentences are.

> COMMA SPLICE   The report is highly critical of the media, it has received little press coverage.

> COMMA SPLICE   Shawna is an outstanding orator, she has no formal training in speech.

Although the independent clauses are obviously connected, the comma splices do not explain how. Inserting conjunctions relieves the confusion.

> COMMA SPLICE
> ELIMINATED   The report is highly critical of the media, so it has received little press coverage.

> COMMA SPLICE
> ELIMINATED   Shawna is an outstanding orator, although she has no formal training in speech.

Here are more examples of typical kinds of comma splices.

> COMMA SPLICE   A technician carefully measured the chemicals for the experiment, she made sure all weights were exact.

> COMMA SPLICE
> ELIMINATED   A technician carefully measured the chemicals for the experiment, and she made sure all weights were exact.

> COMMA SPLICE   Maria was supposed to be on stage in five minutes, however, she was still donning her costume.
>
> This example illustrates a frequent mistake: using a comma before *nevertheless* or *however* in a compound sentence. You need a semicolon.

> COMMA SPLICE
> ELIMINATED   Maria was supposed to be on stage in five minutes; however, she was still donning her costume.

Very short sentences, usually in threes, may be joined by commas. These constructions are rare.

> I came, I saw, I conquered.
> He ate, I paid, we left.

38c
cs

2 Eliminate a comma splice by replacing the faulty comma with a semicolon.

COMMA SPLICE
When David detailed his Mustang, every brush, sponge, and swab was arranged in one neat row, he laid out each towel, chamois, and duster in another.

The separation between these two closely related independent ideas gets lost among the commas that are separating items in the series.

COMMA SPLICE ELIMINATED
When David detailed his Mustang, every brush, sponge, and swab was arranged in one neat row; he laid out each towel, chamois, and duster in another.

3 Eliminate a comma splice by replacing the faulty comma with a period.

COMMA SPLICE
David polished a square inch of his car at a time, by the end of the day he had finished the hood and one fender.

These two independent clauses should have a stronger separation to emphasize their difference.

COMMA SPLICE ELIMINATED
David polished a square inch of his car at a time. By the end of the day, he had finished the hood and one fender.

4 Eliminate a comma splice by inserting a coordinating conjunction after the comma. The coordinating conjunctions are *and, or, nor, for, but, yet,* and *so.*

COMMA SPLICE
His progress was slow because he did every step by hand, it wasn't easy work.

These two independent clauses need a strong separation to stress that they are in a sequence. The comma doesn't provide that separation.

COMMA SPLICE ELIMINATED
His progress was slow because he did every step by hand, and it wasn't easy work.

38c
cs

5 Eliminate a comma splice by subordinating one of the independent clauses. You can do that by introducing one of the independent clauses with a subordinating word such as *although, because, since,* or *when.* For more on subordination, see Section 19g.

COMMA SPLICE	Detailing a vehicle requires skill, learning to do it can pay off in a profitable career.

The two clauses of the sentence are not equally important, so the first one should be changed to a subordinate clause and the comma retained.

COMMA SPLICE ELIMINATED	Although detailing a vehicle requires skill, learning to do it can pay off in a profitable career.

🍎 Point of Difference

Although comma splices are nonstandard in academic writing, alert readers will notice them in contemporary fiction. In that genre, authors often feel less bound by strict conventions. So don't be surprised if you spot a comma splice now and then in the novels of respected writers. Here are two instances.

The first is from *The Desert Rose* by the Pulitzer Prize–winning novelist Larry McMurtry.

> If she needed money she could always just steal it out of Billy's billfold, she had done that a few times and he hadn't even noticed.

The second is from *Monk's Hood,* a medieval mystery by the English historian Edith Pargeter, who wrote mysteries under the name of Ellis Peters.

> Brother Mark had done his part, the habit was there, rolled up beneath Brother Cadfael's bed. 🍎

38c
cs

EXERCISE 38.3 Identify the sentences that have comma splices and correct them.

1. At one time the walls in many Philadelphia neighborhoods were covered with graffiti, however they are covered with murals today.

2. Since 1984 a city-sponsored program has been teaming young graffiti writers with professional artists, the result is the creation of over a thousand works of public art.

3. The murals are large, they are colorful, they are 99 percent graffiti-free.

4. A forty-foot-tall mural of Julius ("Dr. J") Erving has become a local landmark, even Dr. J himself brings friends by to see it.

5. The theory behind the program is that graffiti writers, being inherently artistic, will not deface a work of art they respect, so far the theory holds.

38d Do you have questions about run-on sentences?

A *run-on* occurs when no punctuation at all separates two independent clauses (see Section 19d-1). The reader is left to figure out where one sentence ends and a second begins.

RUN-ON — We were surprised by the package quickly we tore it open.

You need to provide a boundary strong enough to separate the independent clauses clearly. You usually have several options for repairing a run-on.

RUN-ON — We were surprised by the package;
ELIMINATED — quickly, we tore it open.

RUN-ON — We were surprised by the package.
ELIMINATED — Quickly, we tore it open.

An editor or instructor will usually write *run-on* (or *r-o*) next to a sentence with such a problem.

The Taj Mahal is one of the world's most beautiful buildings it is located near Agra in India. *run-on*

1 Eliminate a run-on by separating independent clauses with a period.

RUN-ON — Politicians were once fearful of reforming the social security system now they are scrambling to prevent its bankruptcy.

The sentence needs to be punctuated after *system* so as not to confuse readers. Adding a period makes a natural separation.

RUN-ON — Politicians were once fearful of reforming
ELIMINATED — the social security system. Now they are scrambling to prevent its bankruptcy.

38d
run-on

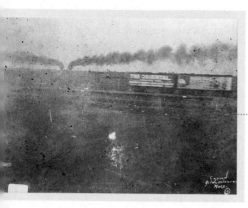

A run-on is a grammatical train wreck, two clauses colliding like these locomotives in a staged exhibition near Waco, Texas, on September 15, 1896. As many as 40,000 people witnessed this notorious run-on.

2 Eliminate a run-on by inserting a semicolon between independent clauses. A semicolon suggests that the ideas in the two sentences are closely related.

> RUN-ON   Emily's entire life revolves around ecological problems she can speak of little else.
>
> The two clauses are closely related but need to be separated to show they are separate ideas. A semicolon separates the sentences but preserves a relationship between them.

> RUN-ON
> ELIMINATED   Emily's entire life revolves around ecological problems; she can speak of little else.

For more on semicolons, see Section 40a.

3 Eliminate a run-on by joining independent clauses with a comma and a coordinating conjunction. The coordinating conjunctions are *and, or, nor, for, but, yet,* and *so.*

> RUN-ON   Poisonous giant toads were introduced to Australia in the 1930s to control beetles they have since become an ecological menace.

> RUN-ON
> ELIMINATED   Poisonous giant toads were introduced to Australia in the 1930s to control beetles, but they have since become an ecological menace.

> RUN-ON   The manager suggested a cut in our hourly wages then I walked out of the negotiations.

> RUN-ON
> ELIMINATED   The manager suggested a cut in our hourly wages, so then I walked out of the negotiations.

38d
run-on

4   Eliminate a run-on by subordinating one of the independent clauses to the other.

RUN-ON   Albert had to finish the financial report by himself his irresponsible co-author had lost interest in the cause.

RUN-ON   Albert had to finish the financial report by
ELIMINATED   himself because his irresponsible co-author had lost interest in the cause.

EXERCISE 38.4   Rewrite these sentences to eliminate punctuation problems that create run-on sentences.

1. Centuries of superstition and ignorance have given bats a bad reputation millions of the flying mammals are killed each year in a misguided effort to protect livestock, crops, and people.

2. Entire species of bats are being wiped out at an alarming rate for example, in the 1960s a new species of fruit-eating bat was discovered in the Philippines by the 1980s it was extinct.

3. In truth, bats are industrious and invaluable members of the natural order they spread the seeds of hundreds of species of plants.

4. Strange as it may sound, bats are essential to the economies of many countries the plants they pollinate or seed include such cash crops as bananas, figs, dates, vanilla beans, and avocados.

5. Many plants essential to such delicate ecosystems as the African savanna and the South American rain forest rely solely on bats for propagating should the bats disappear, the entire system could collapse.

38d
run-on

CHAPTER 39

Questions About Commas?

Commas are interrupters or signals to pause. As signals, they aren't as strong as semicolons, which typically appear at major intersections between clauses. And they are certainly not as forceful as periods, which mark the ends of sentences. Instead, commas make a reader slow down and pay attention to the words and ideas they set off. For this reason, it's just as important to omit commas where they aren't needed as it is to include them where they are.

Rules may help you manage commas, but ultimately you have to develop a *feel* for them. One way to develop good comma sense is to observe writers using the mark. So the next time you read an enjoyable article or story, notice how commas make it clearer and easier to read.

An editor will usually suggest where a comma is needed with a comma and caret.

The garden, which had been neglected for years∧now ⌐
flourished under the rabbi's care.

Where you need to delete a comma, an editor may draw a slash through the mark and write *no comma (no,)* in the margin.

The painting⁄ that I bought appreciated in value. *no,*

39a Do you understand commas that separate?

Some commas keep words, phrases, and clauses from colliding. But you may have to rely on both some rules and your instincts to place them appropriately. Use too many commas, and your writing will seem plodding and fussy; use too few, and your readers may be confused.

1 Use commas after introductory phrases of more than three or four words. Pauses at these points can make sentences easier to read.

In some situations, commas have the message of a yield sign—slow down, but don't quite stop.

To appreciate the pleasures of driving in snow, you have to live in Michigan or Wisconsin.

Over the loud objections of my passengers, I turned off the main road.

An introductory comma isn't necessary when an introductory phrase is only two or three words long and the sentence is clear without the punctuation.

For now I'll abstain from voting.
On Tuesday we'll be in New Mexico.

However, in these situations commas aren't wrong either. Use a comma whenever it helps to avoid confusion or to clarify a sentence, as it might after an introductory prepositional phrase or verbal.

In Louisiana, state laws are still influenced by the Napoleonic Code.
Stranded, the hikers headed due south.
To write better, she read the best magazines and novels carefully.

39a
ˆ
ˌ

2 Use commas after introductory subordinate clauses.
Subordinate clauses are signaled by words such as *although, if, when, because, as, after, before, since, unless, while.* (See Section 19d-2.)

Although the vote was close, we passed the motion.
While the military band played taps, the flag was lowered.
When the police officers arrived, they found the window broken.

3 Use commas before sentence elements or clauses that follow a main clause when the additional thought is incidental, explanatory, or contrasting. Such clauses may be signaled by words such as *although, though, if, when, because, as, after, before, since, unless, while, that is.*

> We will attend the judge's lecture, which is scheduled to last an hour.
>
> The orientation adviser urged us to be sensitive to our neighbors, implying that we might offend someone verbally.
>
> The restaurant was second-rate, though its prices were steep.

Commas are not used, however, when the additional clause is closely related to the main idea of the sentence.

> We drove on to Detroit **even though** the roads were crowded.
>
> The flag was lowered **while** the military band played taps.
>
> The police officers found the window broken **when** they arrived.

Deciding whether a modifying clause is closely related to a main clause is often a judgment call; writers won't agree in every case. Notice, however, that if these sentences started with the subordinate clauses, most writers would put a comma after them—for instance, "While the band played taps, the flag was lowered."

4 Use commas after conjunctive adverbs at the beginning of sentences or clauses.

Commas are needed because words of this kind—*consequently, nevertheless, however, therefore*—are interrupters that mark a shift or contrast in a sentence. For a chart of conjunctive adverbs, see page 625.

> Mr. Howard reviewed the testimony carefully. **However,** he found no evidence of perjury.
>
> Althea studied hard; **therefore,** she passed the examination easily.

Putting a comma after these words sets them off and draws attention to them (but see also Section 40a-3).

5 Use commas to set off absolute phrases.

Absolutes are phrases made up of nouns and participles. You are most likely to recognize them through examples.

> **His head shaved,** Martin was in the Marines now.
>
> The pioneers pressed forward across the desert, **their water almost gone.**

Absolutes like these are always separated from the rest of the sentence by commas. See Section 19c-3 for more about absolutes.

39a
^
i

6 Use commas to mark contrasts or transitions.

Owning a car in most cities is a necessity, not a luxury.

On the other hand, a car in a place like New York City is not practical.

Ollie had seen many celestial events, but never an eclipse.

Kelly's chief requirement in clothes is not style, but low price.

7 Use commas to separate words where verbs or predicates have been deleted to avoid repetition. Constructions of this kind are fairly common.

Appollonia is the patron saint of toothaches; Blaise, of throat infections; Vitus, of epilepsy.

Brad Pitt once worked as a giant chicken; Rod Stewart, as a gravedigger; Whoopi Goldberg, as a makeup artist in a mortuary.

8 Use commas to keep ideas clear and distinct.

The motto of some critics seems to be whatever is, is wrong.
People who must, can operate cars with hand controls only.
Those who can, do; those who can't, complain.

9 Use commas to separate conversational expressions from the main body of a sentence. Such expressions are probably more common in speech than in writing, but here's how they are punctuated.

No, I am sure the door was locked.
The dancers are full of themselves, aren't they?
"Well, I'm not sure I recall," said the former governor.

39a
^
,

EXERCISE 39.1 Insert commas in these sentences where needed.

1. When Mount St. Helens erupted in 1980 the north slope collapsed sending torrents of mud and rock down into the Toutle River valley.

2. Stripped of all vegetation for fifteen miles the valley was left virtually lifeless; whatever trees there were were dead.

3. In an effort to prevent erosion and speed the valley's recovery ecologists planted grasses and ground covers.

4. However the species they planted were not native but alien or exotic.

5. All things considered the scientists probably should have left nature to take its course since the alien plants are now inhibiting the
regrowth of native species.

39b Do you understand commas that enclose?

Enclosing some words and phrases with commas makes sentences
more readable; the commas help to chunk information into manageable segments. But it's important to place commas only around expressions that really need to be separated. Remember, too, that it usually
takes two commas to bracket material in the middle of a sentence; it's
easy to forget that second comma. Of course, only one comma is
needed before a modifier at the end of a sentence.

**1 Use commas to mark nonessential (nonrestrictive)
modifiers.** A **nonessential modifier** adds information to a sentence
that can be removed without radically altering the basic meaning of the
sentence. (For a detailed discussion of essential and nonessential modifiers, see Section 33i.)

> Authentic Navajo rugs, **which can take months to weave,** come in
> several distinctive styles.
>
> Neil Armstrong, **who was born in a small Ohio town,** was the
> first human to walk on the moon.

**2 Use commas to enclose nonessential (nonrestrictive)
appositives.** An **appositive** is a noun or noun equivalent that follows
a noun and gives additional information about it. Appositives are usually nonessential modifiers.

> Colleen O'Brien, **our neighborhood-watch coordinator,** was ar-
> rested last week for shoplifting.
>
> George Washington, **the first President of the United States,**
> served two full terms.

Some appositives are essential modifiers, giving information that
can't be removed from a sentence. Such modifiers should not be enclosed by commas. Because *the psychiatrist* and *the father* in the following example are essential to the meaning of the sentence, setting them
off with commas would confuse readers.

39b
∧
⌄

Sue Ellen reflected that Dr. Rizzo **the psychiatrist** was quite a different person from Dr. Rizzo **the father.**

Deciding whether modifiers are essential or nonessential can be especially tricky when the appositives involved are titles. Use commas around titles when they can be deleted from a sentence, no commas when they cannot. Compare the following examples.

ESSENTIAL   Shakespeare's tragedy *Hamlet* is one of his longest plays.
                 Cut *Hamlet* here and the sentence is meaningless.

NONESSENTIAL   Shakespeare's longest tragedy, *Hamlet,* lasts more than four hours.
                 The sentence would still make sense with *Hamlet* cut.

ESSENTIAL   The Beatles' song "Yesterday" remains one of the most popular tunes of all time.

NONESSENTIAL   The Beatles' final album, *Let It Be,* remains my favorite.

3 Use commas to enclose various interrupting words, phrases, and clauses. It is important to use commas in pairs when the interruptions come in the middle of sentences.

The President intends, **predictably,** to veto the bill in its current form.

The first landmark we recognized, **well before the plane landed,** was the Washington Monument.

The senators, **it seemed,** were eager for a filibuster.

Tell me, **Mr. Wellborn,** what is your opinion?

She could not, **in good conscience,** ignore the clamor for passage of the measure.

He could, **of course,** make a strong case in the media.

The student government voted to cut, **not eliminate,** the art society's grant.

Be especially careful with words such as *however, nevertheless, moreover, therefore,* and *consequently.* They should appear between commas when they fall in the middle of a sentence because they're strong interrupters.

Popular opinion, **however,** began to move toward the President's position.

39b
^
*

Point of Difference

Contemporary editors are moving toward using fewer commas around words such as *however* and *therefore*. In many newspapers and magazines—even the august *New York Times*—you will often find no commas around *of course* when it appears in the middle of a sentence. ◀

EXERCISE 39.2 Discuss the following sentences to decide which modifiers are essential and which are not; then fix the sentences that need to be changed.

1. Carter a salesclerk with a passion for Native American art urged Iona his manager at a gallery in Alpine to increase her stock of Navajo rugs.

2. On a sales trip, Carter had met with several art dealers who specialized in Native American crafts; the dealer Carter met in Tuba City had offered rugs produced by several well-known artists.

3. The rugs that he showed Carter included examples of all the classic Navajo designs produced from wool which the weavers had shorn, carded, and dyed themselves.

4. Iona who had managed the store for ten years was uncertain that her regular customers would buy the premium rugs which cost as much as $6,000.

5. But because Iona the lover of art was more speculative than Iona the businesswoman, the gallery soon featured a selection of Navajo rugs which quickly increased sales traffic.

39c

39c Do you understand commas that link?

Though commas often mark separations, they can also inform readers that certain ideas belong together. When commas come before linking words, they let readers know that the ideas will continue; the stop isn't as full as it would be if it were marked by a semicolon or period. Similarly, commas that mark off the items in a series help readers understand that those items belong together.

1 Use commas before the coordinating conjunctions *and, or, nor, for, but, yet,* and *so* when those words link independent clauses to form compound sentences. Clauses

are described as **independent** when they can stand on their own as sentences (see Section 19d-1). Joining two independent clauses with a comma and a coordinating conjunction produces a compound sentence (see Sections 19e and 19f).

> Texas is larger in land area than California, **and** its history is different too.

> Some people find California more appealing, **but** such persons often have not spent much time in Texas.

> West Texas can seem empty at times, **yet** the vastness of its deserts and high plains is part of its appeal.

> Desert plants are fully adapted to their harsh terrain, **so** they wouldn't survive in more hospitable climates.

A comma is especially important when the two clauses separated by the conjunction are lengthy. In the following example, the comma emphasizes the break between the two clauses and prevents any misreading.

> Experts have tried to explain why dogs wag their tails, but they have not come up with a satisfactory reason for this attention-grabbing behavior.

Be especially careful not to place the comma after a conjunction that joins independent clauses. This is a common error.

WRONG	My friends shared my opinion but, they were afraid to say so.
RIGHT	My friends shared my opinion, but they were afraid to say so.
WRONG	Bart's father remembers his first sports car fondly so, he knows how Bart feels behind the wheel of his Boxster S.
RIGHT	Bart's father remembers his first sports car fondly, so he knows how Bart feels behind the wheel of his Boxster S.

39c
^
î

2 Don't use commas alone to link independent clauses.

Doing so produces the error called a *comma splice*. For much more about comma splices, see Section 38c.

COMMA SPLICE	The plane to Atlanta was late, we missed our connecting flight to Indianapolis.
COMMA SPLICE ELIMINATED	The plane to Atlanta was late; we missed our connecting flight to Indianapolis.

3 Use commas to link more than two items in a series.

Commas are needed to mark pauses for readers and to keep the items in a series from colliding.

> The mapmaker had omitted the capital cities of Idaho, New York, and Delaware!

> Maggie found traces of spaghetti sauce on the floor, in the cabinets, under the rug, and on the ceiling.

> The tabloid exposé failed to explain who had seen the aliens, where exactly they had landed, or why they had decided to visit New Orleans.

Point of Difference

Most English teachers and editors of books recommend that you use a comma before the conjunction (usually *and* or *or*) that signals the end of a series.

> . . . for tax cuts, job security, and pay equity.
> . . . the Indians, White Sox, or Yankees.

But this guideline is not followed by journalists, who usually omit what they regard as an unnecessary comma.

> . . . for tax cuts, job security and pay equity.
> . . . the Indians, White Sox or Yankees.

Leaving out the final comma can occasionally cause confusion, which is why many editors think it should be used.

> . . . chicken, peas, and pork and beans.
> . . . by coach, wagon, and horse and buggy.

39c
^
ϯ

4 Use commas to link coordinate adjectives in series.

Coordinate adjectives modify the noun they precede, not each other (see Section 19b-1).

> *Everybody Loves Raymond* is a **lively, hilarious, and innovative** sitcom.
> Raymond is a **hapless, flustered, thoughtless** husband.

When adjectives are coordinate, they can be switched around without affecting the sense of a phrase much. The examples above could just as easily and accurately read like this:

Everybody Loves Raymond is an **innovative, lively, and hilarious** sitcom.
Raymond is a **flustered, thoughtless, hapless** husband.

5 Do not use commas to mark off noncoordinate modifiers in series. **Noncoordinate adjectives** or **adjectivals** work together to modify a noun or pronoun (see Section 19b-1). The order of the modifiers is either essential to their meaning or idiomatic—as a result, they cannot be switched around.

> the **best supporting** actor
> a **new Mustang** convertible
> his **customary good** humor
> a **long fly** ball
> in **large cardboard** boxes

To determine whether a series of modifiers is coordinate or noncoordinate, try inserting *and* between them. Coordinate modifiers will still make good sense separated by *and*. Noncoordinate modifiers will not.

COORDINATE	a hapless and flustered and underappreciated manager
NONCOORDINATE	a new and Mustang convertible

EXERCISE 39.3 Rewrite the following sentences, adding commas where they are needed to link ideas, moving commas that are misplaced, and correcting comma splices. Some sentences may be correct.

1. The mower cut its final swath across the deep green grass, the long golden rays of the setting sun toyed listlessly with the dancing grasshoppers in its wake.

2. Although all of the day's daylilies had already closed up shop the night-blooming flowers were starting to offer their perfumes to the hushed expectant air.

3. An orchestra of crickets tree frogs and, whippoorwills warmed up for the evening's concert; fireflies silently urgently signaled their ardor in the undergrowth.

4. Overhead, the moon's bright silver slipper held court with an audience of stars: Orion the Pleiades Pegasus Cassiopeia.

5. Wafting romantically out of the gazebo and across the lawn, Heather tripped on a lone red roller skate and pitched headlong into the pool.

39c
^
,

39d Do you put commas where they aren't needed?

A comma where none is needed disrupts the flow of meaning in a sentence. Every comma in a sentence should be placed for a reason: to mark a pause, to set off a unit, to keep words from running together. Cut those that don't serve any such purpose.

1 Eliminate commas that interrupt the flow of a sentence.

Sentences with commas inserted where they are not needed can be more confusing to a reader than those with a few commas omitted. Sometimes a comma interrupts what would otherwise be a clear statement.

UNNECESSARY COMMA   Five years into graduate school, Frida found herself, without a degree or prospects for a job.

The writer doesn't mean "Frida found herself," but "Frida found herself without. . . . " Revision is necessary.

COMMA CUT   Five years into graduate school, Frida found herself without a degree or prospects for a job.

At other times, unneeded commas seem to fit a guideline, but they really don't. In the following example, the writer may recall that commas often follow introductory words, phrases, and clauses and so places a comma after what looks like an introductory word.

UNNECESSARY COMMA   Although, Frida is 51 years old, she has decided to pursue a new career.

In this case *although* introduces a subordinate clause: *Although Frida is 51 years old*. *Although* can't be separated from the rest of the clause and still make sense. The comma must be cut.

COMMA CUT   Although Frida is 51 years old, she has decided to pursue a new career.

Here's a second example of a subordinating word incorrectly separated from the remainder of its subordinate clause.

UNNECESSARY COMMA   However, cold it gets, the train arrives on time.

COMMA CUT   However cold it gets, the train arrives on time.

2 Don't use a comma to separate a subject from a verb.

This common error usually occurs when the full subject of a sentence is more complex than usual—perhaps a noun clause or a verb phrase.

UNNECESSARY COMMA	What happened to the team since last season, isn't clear.

What happened to the team is the subject of the sentence, so it shouldn't be separated from the verb *is* with a comma. The comma must be cut.

COMMA CUT	What happened to the team since last season isn't clear.

Here are additional illustrations of the problem.

WRONG	Fighting for the championship, means playing hard.
RIGHT	Fighting for the championship means playing hard.
WRONG	To keep the team's spirit up, won't be easy.
RIGHT	To keep the team's spirit up won't be easy.

Of course, when modifiers separate subjects from verbs, commas are used to set off the modifying expressions (see Section 39b). Compare these sentences.

NO MODIFIER/ NO COMMAS	Frida is determined to complete her education.
MODIFIERS/COMMAS	Frida, who just turned 51 years old, is determined to complete her education.

In rare cases, a comma may be required between subject and verb to assure clarity.

Those who hope, thrive; those who despair, fail.

39d
^
,

3 Don't use commas to separate compound subjects, predicates, or objects.

WRONG	The Mississippi, and the Missouri are two of the United States' great rivers.
RIGHT	The Mississippi and the Missouri are two of the United States' great rivers.

WRONG   We toured the museum, and then explored the monument.

RIGHT   We toured the museum and then explored the monument.

WRONG   Alexander broke his promise to his agent, and his contract with his publisher.

RIGHT   Alexander broke his promise to his agent and his contract with his publisher.

WRONG   I tried to contact the company by posting an email to its Web site, and by sending a certified letter to its Denver office.

RIGHT   I tried to contact the company by posting an email to its Web site and by sending a certified letter to its Denver office.

Of course, commas are used to separate full independent clauses joined by conjunctions. Compare the following sentences, both punctuated correctly.

RIGHT   We toured the museum and then explored the monument.

RIGHT   We toured the museum, and then we explored the monument.

■ 4 Don't use commas to introduce a series. Usually no punctuation mark is needed. When one is called for, it will usually be a colon, not a comma.

39d
^
↑

WRONG   States with impressive national parks include, California, Utah, Arizona, and New Mexico.

RIGHT   States with impressive national parks include California, Utah, Arizona, and New Mexico.

Commas can be used to enclose lists that function as nonessential modifiers.

RIGHT   States with impressive national parks, California, Utah, and Arizona among them, benefit from tourists' dollars.

In such cases, however, all the commas can be confusing. The modifier might be better enclosed by dashes (see Section 43a).

RIGHT   States with impressive national parks—California, Utah, and Arizona among them—benefit from tourists' dollars.

5 Don't use commas around modifiers that are essential to the meaning of a sentence.

When a modifying phrase is essential, it should *not* be set off with commas (see Section 33i).

WRONG   What Asha observed, as a civic volunteer, changed her opinion of journalists.

RIGHT   What Asha observed as a civic volunteer changed her opinion of journalists.

WRONG   Journalists, who say they are dedicated to community service, often have political agendas of their own.

RIGHT   Journalists who say they are dedicated to community service often have political agendas of their own.

EXERCISE 39.4 Working in a group, analyze these sentences to see if all the commas are needed. Then work together to rewrite sentences to get rid of commas that cause awkward interruptions. Notice that some of the commas are necessary.

1. Psychologists, who have studied moods, say that such emotional states are contagious, and compare them to social viruses.

2. Moreover, some people are emotionally expressive, and likely to transmit moods; others, seem to be more inclined to "catch" moods.

3. Trying to pinpoint the exact means by which moods are transmitted, is difficult, since the process happens almost instantaneously.

4. One transmission mechanism is imitation: by unconsciously imitating facial expressions, people produce, in themselves a mood that goes with the expression.

5. People who get along well with others, generally, synchronize their moods, by making a series of changes in their body language.

39e

^
ʼ

39e Do you understand the conventional uses of commas?

Aside from the important role commas play within sentences both in linking and separating ideas, commas have many conventional uses you simply have to know to get right.

1 Use commas to introduce quotations or to follow them.
For proper placement of these commas and more about punctuating quotations, see Section 41a.

> The lawyer insisted, "He can't be held responsible."
>
> "Don't tell me he can't be held responsible," bellowed Judge Carver.
>
> Ms. Rice said, "I'm not sure about the motion on the floor."
>
> She then asked, "Would the secretary read the motion?"
>
> "Speak up," she added.

No commas are needed when a quotation fits right into a sentence without an introductory phrase or frame. Compare the following examples.

> COMMAS NEEDED
> "Experience," said Oscar Wilde, "is the name everyone gives to their mistakes."
>
> Said P. G. Wodehouse, "I always advise people never to give advice."
>
> NO COMMAS NEEDED
> Oscar Wilde defined experience as "the name everyone gives to their mistakes."
>
> P. G. Wodehouse advised people "never to give advice."

2 Use commas correctly to separate units of three within numbers.
Commas are optional in four-digit numbers.

> 4,110 or 4110
> 99,890
> 1,235,470

Do not use commas in decimals, social security numbers, street addresses, or zip codes.

3 Use commas correctly in dates.
In American usage, commas separate the day from the year. Note that a year is enclosed by commas when it appears in the middle of a sentence.

> World War II began on September 1, 1939.
>
> Germany expanded the war on June 22, 1941, when its armies invaded Russia.

39e
,

Commas aren't required when only the month and year are given.

> World War II began in September 1939.

Commas are not used when dates are given in British form, with the day preceding the month.

> World War II began on 1 September 1939.

4 Use commas correctly in addresses. Commas ordinarily separate street addresses, cities, states, and countries. When these items occur in the middle of a sentence, they are enclosed by commas.

> Miami University is in Oxford, Ohio.
>
> Though born in London, England, Denise Levertov is considered an American writer.
>
> The prime minister lives at No. 10 Downing Street, Westminster, London, England.

Commas aren't used between states and zip codes.

> Austin, Texas 78712

5 Use commas correctly to separate proper names from titles and degrees that follow.

> Tonya Galvin, Ph.D., has been chosen to replace Howard Brill, M.D.

6 Use commas to follow the salutation in personal letters.

> Dear Lee,
> Dear Aunt Sue,

39e
^
,

EXERCISE 39.5 Review the following sentences and add commas where necessary.

1. In the autumn of 1863, Abraham Lincoln President of the United States traveled to Gettysburg Pennsylvania to speak at the dedication of a cemetery there.

2. The cemetery was for the soldiers who had fallen at the Battle of Gettysburg, and Lincoln's speech—now known as the Gettysburg Address—opened with the famous words "Fourscore and seven years ago."

3. The Battle of Gettysburg had started on July 1 1863 and had raged for three days.

4. The Civil War would not end until April 1865.

5. The bloodiest battle of the war took place near Sharpsburg Maryland along the banks of Antietam Creek, where a single day of fighting produced over 23000 casualties.

CHAPTER 40

Questions About Semicolons and Colons?

40a Do you have questions about semicolons?

In a sentence, a semicolon marks a stronger pause than a comma, but a weaker pause than a period. Many writers find semicolons confusing. So they avoid them and place commas where semicolons are needed. Or they misuse them, using semicolons where commas work better. In your papers, an editor will use a caret and a semicolon to indicate where a semicolon should be inserted.

Give Matthew the book, ⋏ it belongs to him. ⁀

1 Use semicolons to separate items of equal grammatical weight. Semicolons can be used to separate one independent clause from another, one phrase from another, one item in a list from another.

independent clause; independent clause

Director John Ford released *Stagecoach* in 1939; a year later, he made *The Grapes of Wrath.*

phrase; phrase

My course in cinema taught the basics of movie production, including how to write treatments, outlines, and scripts; how to audition and cast actors; and how to edit 16-mm film.

item in a list; item in a list; item in a list

We rented cassettes of *Plains, Trains and Automobiles*; *Star Trek: Insurrection*; and *Blade Runner—The Director's Cut.*

Because semicolons work only between comparable items, it would be wrong to place a semicolon between an independent clause and a prepositional phrase. Also incorrect would be a semicolon separating a dependent clause and an independent clause. Commas are usually the correct punctuation in such cases.

independent clause, prepositional phrase

WRONG   Many young filmmakers regularly exceed their budgets; in the tradition of the finest Hollywood directors.

RIGHT   Many young filmmakers regularly exceed their budgets, in the tradition of the finest Hollywood directors.

dependent clause, independent clause

WRONG   Although director Alfred Hitchcock once said that actors should be treated like cattle; he won fine performances from many of them.

RIGHT   Although director Alfred Hitchcock once said that actors should be treated like cattle, he won fine performances from many of them.

2 Use semicolons to join independent clauses closely related in thought. Coordinating conjunctions (such as *and, or, nor, for, but, yet, so*) aren't needed when clauses are linked by semicolons.

The history of British cinema is uneven; the best British films come from the period just before and during World War II.

Italian cinema blossomed after World War II; directors like De Sica, Fellini, and Antonioni won critical acclaim.

Omitting the semicolons in the examples above would create run-on sentences (see Section 38d). Replacing the semicolons with commas would produce comma splices (see Section 38c). Both run-ons and comma splices are major sentence errors. Sometimes, however, placing semicolons between very short independent clauses can seem like punctuation overkill.

40a
;

WITH SEMICOLONS   For best director, Todd picked Alfred Hitchcock; Ryan nominated François Truffaut; and Aimee chose Agnes Varda.

When such clauses are short and closely related, they can be separated by commas.

WITH COMMAS   For best director, Todd picked Alfred Hitchcock, Ryan nominated François Truffaut, and Aimee chose Agnes Varda.

3 Use semicolons between independent clauses joined by words such as *however, therefore, nevertheless, nonetheless, moreover,* and *consequently*. These words are called *conjunctive adverbs,* but by themselves they cannot link sentences. They require a semicolon.

> Bob Hope started his career in vaudeville; **however,** he made his major mark as a film star and television comic.

> The original *Rocky* was an Oscar-winning movie; **unfortunately,** its many sequels exhausted the original idea.

> Films about British spy 007 have been in decline for years; **nevertheless,** new James Bond films continue to appear.

In sentences like those above, using a comma instead of a semicolon before the conjunctive adverb produces a comma splice. This is a common punctuation error (see Section 38c-2).

But here's an important point: when a word like *however* or *therefore* occurs in the middle of an independent clause, it *is* preceded and followed by commas. In the following pair of sentences, note carefully where the boldfaced words appear and how the shifts in their location change the punctuation required.

> *Casablanca* is now admired as a film classic; **however,** its producers and stars regarded it as an average spy thriller.

> *Casablanca* is now admired as a film classic; its producers and stars, **however,** regarded it as an average spy thriller.

Chart 40.1

Frequently Used Conjunctive Adverbs

consequently	meanwhile	rather
furthermore	moreover	then
hence	nonetheless	therefore
however	otherwise	thus

40a
;

4 Use semicolons to join independent clauses connected by words or phrases such as *indeed, in fact, at any rate, for example,* and *on the other hand*. These expressions, like conjunctive adverbs, ordinarily require a semicolon before them and a comma after.

> Box office receipts for *Spider-Man*'s opening week were spectacular; **in fact,** the film unexpectedly broke records for a summer release.

Tobey Maguire had never opened a major film before; **on the other hand,** he was perfectly cast as the boy-next-door superhero.

A period could be used instead of the semicolon in these situations.

Naturally, *Spider-Man* will spawn many imitations. **However,** few of these films will likely succeed in the market.

5 Use semicolons to separate clauses, phrases, or items in a series that might be confusing if commas alone were used to mark boundaries. Semicolons are especially helpful when complicated phrases or items in a list already contain commas or other punctuation.

The sound track for the film included the Supremes' "Stop in the Name of Love!"; Bob Dylan's "Rainy Day Women #12 & 35"; and Rodgers and Hart's "Glad to Be Unhappy."

Matt Damon's filmography includes *School Ties,* which is set in an upper-class prep school; *Saving Private Ryan,* a Steven Spielberg movie in which Damon plays the title character; and *Good Will Hunting,* a drama that earned him an Oscar for best screenplay.

6 Do not use semicolons to introduce quotations. Direct quotations can be introduced by commas or colons.

WRONG   Wasn't it Mae West who said; "When I'm good I'm very good, but when I'm bad, I'm better"?

RIGHT   Wasn't it Mae West who said, "When I'm good I'm very good, but when I'm bad, I'm better"?

40a
;

7 Do not use semicolons to introduce lists.

WRONG   Paul Robeson performed in several classic films; *Show Boat, Song of Freedom, King Solomon's Mines.*

RIGHT   Paul Robeson performed in several classic films: *Show Boat, Song of Freedom, King Solomon's Mines.*

Semicolons may separate items *within* a list (see Section 40a-1).

8 Use semicolons correctly with quotation marks. Semicolons ordinarily fall outside quotation marks (see Section 41a-6).

The first Edgar Allan Poe work filmed was "The Raven"; movies based on the poem appeared in 1912, 1915, and 1935.

EXERCISE 40.1 Revise the following sentences, adding or deleting semicolons as needed. Not all semicolons below are incorrect. You may have to substitute other punctuation marks for some semicolons.

1. For many years, biblical spectacles were a staple of the Hollywood film industry, however, in recent years, few such films have been produced.

2. Cecil B. DeMille made the grandest epics; he is quoted as saying; "Give me any couple of pages of the Bible and I'll give you a picture."

3. He made *The Ten Commandments* twice, the 1956 version starred Charlton Heston as Moses.

4. The most famous scene in *The Ten Commandments* is the parting of the Red Sea; the waters opening to enable the Israelites to escape the pursuing army of Pharaoh.

5. DeMille made many nonbiblical movies, some of them, however, were also epic productions with casts of thousands and spectacular settings.

EXERCISE 40.2 Use semicolons to arrange the following clauses, phrases, and bits of information into complete sentences. You will have to add words and ideas.

1. The action in mad-killer movies like *Scream.* A masked killer dispatches random teenagers and even an occasional high school principal. A masked killer attacks the annoying reporter, Gale Weathers. A masked killer attacks and, maybe, kills Dewey, the bumbling cop.

2. Strange titles of Bob Dylan songs from the 1960s. "Subterranean Homesick Blues" "It's Alright, Ma (I'm Only Bleeding)" "Love Minus Zero/No Limit" "Don't Think Twice, It's All Right" "I Shall Be Free—No. 10."

3. Items in E. D. Hirsch's list of everything Americans should know. Carbon-14 dating. "*Veni, vidi, vici.*" "Doctor Livingstone, I presume?" "Yes, Virginia, there is a Santa Claus."

4. Exceptionally long movie titles. *Alice Doesn't Live Here Anymore. They Shoot Horses, Don't They? Jo Jo Dancer, Your Life Is Calling. The Effect of Gamma Rays on Man-in-the-Moon Marigolds. Close Encounters of the Third Kind: The Special Edition.*

40a

;

40b Do you have questions about colons?

Colons are strong directional signals. They show movement in a sentence, pointing your reader's attention to precisely what you wish to highlight, whether it is an idea, a list, a quotation, or even another independent clause. Colons require your attention because their functions are limited and quite specific. In your papers, an editor may use a caret and a colon to indicate where a colon should be used rather than another mark of punctuation.

He spoke just one word, "Rosebud." ^

1 Use colons to direct readers to examples, explanations, or significant words and phrases.

Orson Welles's greatest problem may also have been his greatest achievement: the brilliance of his first film, *Citizen Kane.*

Citizen Kane turns on the meaning of one word uttered by a dying man: "Rosebud."

A colon that highlights an item in this way ordinarily follows a complete sentence. In fact, many readers object strongly to colons placed after linking verbs.

WRONG   America's most bankable film star is: Julia Roberts.

RIGHT   America's most bankable film star is Julia Roberts.

40b
:

2 Use colons to direct readers to lists.

Besides *Citizen Kane,* Welles directed, produced, or acted in many movies: *The Magnificent Ambersons, Journey into Fear, The Lady from Shanghai,* and *Macbeth,* to name a few.

Colons that introduce lists ordinarily follow complete sentences. Here is a pair of sentences—both correct—demonstrating your options.

VERSION 1—   The filmmakers the professor admired
WITH A COLON   most were a diverse group: Alain Robbe-Grillet, François Truffaut, Spike Lee, and Penny Marshall.

VERSION 2— WITHOUT A COLON	The filmmakers the professor admired most were Alain Robbe-Grillet, François Truffaut, Spike Lee, and Penny Marshall— a diverse group.

Colons are omitted after expressions such as *like, for example, such as,* and *that is.* In fact, colons are intended to replace these terms.

WRONG	Shoestring budgets have produced many artistically successful films, such as: *Plutonium Circus, Breaking Away,* and *Slackers.*
RIGHT	Shoestring budgets have produced many artistically successful films, such as *Plutonium Circus, Breaking Away,* and *Slackers.*

Never introduce a list with a colon that separates a preposition from its objects(s).

WRONG	Katharine Hepburn starred in: *Little Women, The Philadelphia Story,* and *The African Queen.*
RIGHT	Katharine Hepburn starred in *Little Women, The Philadelphia Story,* and *The African Queen.*

Colons are used, however, after phrases that specifically announce a list, expressions such as *including these, as follows,* and *such as the following.* Compare the following sentences to understand the difference.

VERSION 1— WITH A COLON	The producer trimmed her budget by cutting out some **frills:** special lighting, rental costumes for the cast, and crew lunches.
VERSION 2— WITHOUT A COLON	The producer trimmed her budget by cutting out **frills, such as** special lighting, rental costumes for the cast, and crew lunches.
VERSION 3— WITH A COLON	The producer trimmed her budget by cutting out **frills such as these:** special lighting, rental costumes for the cast, and crew lunches.

40b
:

3 Use colons to direct readers to quotations or dialogue.

Orson Welles commented poignantly on his own career: "I started at the top and worked down."

Don't introduce short quotations with colons. A comma or no punctuation mark at all will suffice. Compare the following sentences.

Dirty Harry said "Make my day!"
As Dirty Harry said, "Make my day!"
We recalled Dirty Harry's memorable phrase: "Make my day!"

In the last example, the colon *is* appropriate because it directs attention to a particular comment.

4 Use colons to join two complete sentences when the second sentence illustrates or explains the first.

Making a film is like writing a paper: it absorbs all the time you'll give it.

Don't use more than one colon in a sentence. A dash can usually replace one of the colons.

PROBLEM   Most critics agree on this point: Orson Welles made one of the greatest of films: *Citizen Kane.*

SOLUTION   Most critics agree on this point: Orson Welles made one of the greatest of films—*Citizen Kane.*

Colons and semicolons are not interchangeable, but you can use both marks in the same sentence. A colon, for example, might introduce a list of items separated by semicolons.

40b
:

Alfred Hitchcock's quips were often as sharp as his films: "There is no terror in a bang, only in the anticipation of it"; "Drama is life with the dull bits left out"; "Actors are cattle."

5 Use colons to separate titles from subtitles.

Nightmare on Elm Street 3: Dream Warriors
"Darkest Night: Conscience in *Macbeth*"

6 Use colons in conventional situations. Colons separate numbers when indicating time or citing Bible passages—though MLA style uses a period in biblical citations.

12:35 p.m.   Matthew 3:1 (or Matthew 3.1 in MLA style)

Colons traditionally follow salutations in business letters.

> Dear Ms. Dowd: Dear Mr. Ebert:

Colons separate place of publication from publisher and separate date from page numbers in various MLA bibliography entries.

> Glenview: Scott, 1961   14 August 1991: 154–63

Colons appear in Web addresses, with no space left after the mark.

> < http://google.com>

EXERCISE 40.3 Revise the following sentences by adding colons or making sure colons are used correctly. Don't assume that every sentence contains an error.

1. No one ever forgets the conclusion of Hitchcock's *Psycho;* the discovery of Norman's mother in the rocking chair.

2. Hitchcock liked to use memorable settings in his films, including: Mt. Rushmore in *North by Northwest,* Radio City Music Hall in *Saboteur,* and the British Museum in *Blackmail.*

3. One actor appears in every Hitchcock film Hitchcock himself.

4. *Rear Window* is a cinematic tour de force: all the action focuses on what Jimmy Stewart sees from his window.

5. Hitchcock probably summed up his own technique best; "There is no terror in a bang, only in the anticipation of it."

40b
:

CHAPTER 41

Questions About Quotation Marks and Ellipses?

41a When do you use quotation marks?

Quotation marks, which always occur in pairs, highlight whatever appears between them. Use double marks (" ") around most quoted material and around titles. Use single quotation marks (' ') to mark quotations (or titles) that fall within quotations.

An editor will use a quotation mark within an inverted caret to indicate that a quotation mark has been omitted.

> "She stole everything but the cameras, ˄ George Raft ˅ once said of Mae West.

1 Use quotation marks around material you are borrowing word for word from sources.

> Emerson reminds us that "nothing great was ever achieved without enthusiasm."

> "Next to the originator of a good sentence is the first quoter of it," writes Emerson.

2 Use quotation marks to set off dialogue. When writing a passage with several speakers, start a new paragraph each time the speaker changes.

> Mrs. Bennet deigned not to make any reply; but unable to contain herself, she began scolding one of her daughters.
>
> "Don't keep coughing so, Kitty, for heaven's sake! Have a little compassion on my nerves. You tear them to pieces."
>
> "Kitty has no discretion in her coughs," said her father; "she times them ill."
>
> "I do not cough for my own amusement," replied Kitty fretfully.
>
> —Jane Austen, *Pride and Prejudice*

When dialogue is provided not for its own sake but to make some other point, the words of several speakers may appear within a single paragraph.

> Professor Norman was confident that his colleagues would eventually see his point. "They'll come around," he predicted. "They always do." And Professor Brown, for one, was beginning to soften. "I've supported many proposals not half so intelligent."

3 Use quotation marks to cite the titles of short works.

These include titles of songs, essays, magazine and newspaper articles, TV episodes, unpublished speeches, chapters of books, and short poems. Titles of longer works appear in *italics* (see Section 44a-1).

> "Love Is Just a Four-Letter Word" song
>
> "Love Is a Fallacy" title of an essay

4 Use quotation marks to draw attention to specific words.

Italics can also be used in these situations (see Section 44a-3).

> Politicians clearly mean different things when they write about "democracy."

You might also use quotation marks to signal that you are using a word ironically, sarcastically, or derisively.

> The clerk at the desk directed the tourists to their "suites"—bare rooms crowded with cots. A bathroom down the hall would serve as the "spa."

But don't overdo it. Highlighting a tired phrase or cliché just makes it seem more fatigued.

> Working around electrical fixtures makes me more nervous than "a cat on a hot tin roof."

5 Surround quotation marks with appropriate punctuation.

A quotation introduced or followed by *said, remarked, observed,* or a similar expression takes a comma.

> Benjamin Disraeli *observed* , "is much easier to be critical than to be correct."

Commas are used, too, when a single sentence quotation is broken up by an interrupting expression such as *he asked* or *she noted.*

> "If the world were a logical place ," Rita Mae Brown *notes* . "men would ride sidesaddle."

41a
" "

When such an expression comes between two successive sentences quoted from a single source, a comma and a period are required.

> "There is no such thing as a moral or an immoral book," *says* Oscar Wilde. "Books are well written, or badly written. That is all."

No additional punctuation is required when a quotation runs smoothly into a sentence you have written.

> Abraham Lincoln observed that "in giving freedom to the slave we assure freedom to the free."

See Section 50a for guidelines on introducing and framing quotations.

■ 6 Use quotation marks correctly with other pieces of punctuation. Commas and periods ordinarily go *inside* closing quotation marks.

> "This must be what the sixties were like," I thought.

> Down a dormitory corridor lined with antiwar posters, I heard someone humming "Blowin' in the Wind."

However, when a sentence ends with a citation in parentheses, the period follows the parenthesis.

> Mike Rose argues that we hurt education if we think of it "in limited or limiting ways" (3).

In American usage, colons and semicolons go *outside* closing quotation marks.

> Riley claimed to be "a human calculator": he did quadratic equations in his head.

> The young Cassius Clay bragged about being "the greatest"; his opponents in the ring soon learned he wasn't boasting.

Question marks, exclamation points, and dashes can fall either inside or outside quotation marks. They fall *inside* when they apply only to the quotation.

> When Mrs. Rattle saw her hotel room, she muttered, "Good grief!"

> She turned to her husband and said, "Do you really expect me to stay here?"

They fall *outside* the closing quotation mark when they apply to the complete sentence.

> Who was it who said, "Truth is always the strongest argument"?

41a
" "

E-Tips

Word processors usually give you the option of choosing to print either straight quotes (" ") or smart quotes (" "). If you are preparing an HTML document for posting to a Web site, be sure to turn off smart quotes because they will be misconstrued in the HTML document. To turn them off, search for "smart quotes" in your "help" function and follow the instructions.

EXERCISE 41.1 Rework the following passage by adding or deleting quotation marks, moving punctuation as necessary, and indenting paragraphs where you think appropriate.

Much to the tourists' surprise, their "uproar" over conditions at their so-called "luxury resort" attracted the attention of a local television station. (In fact, Mrs. Rattle had read "the riot act" to a consumer advocate who worked for the station.) A reporter interviewed Mrs. Rattle, who claimed that she had been promised luxury accommodations. This place smells like old fish she fumed. Even the roaches look unwell. Didn't you check out the accommodations before paying? the reporter asked, turning to Mr. Rattle. He replied that unfortunately they had prepaid the entire vacation. But Mrs. Rattle interrupted. I knew we should have gone to Paris. You never said that! Mr. Rattle objected. As I was trying to say, Mrs. Rattle continued, I'd even rather be in Philadelphia.

EXERCISE 41.2 Write a passage extending the reporter's interview in Exercise 41.1. Or create a dialogue on a subject of your own.

41a
" "

 Point of Difference

The guidelines in this section on quotation marks apply in the United States. Conventions for marking quotations differ significantly from language to language and country to country. French quotation marks, called *guillemets,* look like this: « ». Guillemets are also employed as quotation marks in Spanish, which uses dashes to indicate dialogue. In books published in Britain, you'll find single quotation marks (' ') where American publishers use double marks (" "), and vice versa.

AMERICAN   Carla said, "I haven't read 'The Raven.' "

BRITISH   Carla said, 'I haven't read "The Raven".'

American and British practices differ, too, on the placement of punctuation marks within quotation marks. In general, British usage tends to locate more punctuation marks (commas especially) outside quotation marks than does American usage.

AMERICAN   To be proper, say "I *shall* go," not "*will*."

BRITISH   To be proper, say 'I *shall* go', not '*will*'.

In the United States, follow American practice.

E-Tips

You may be able to set your word processor to check that you have placed punctuation correctly either inside or outside quotation marks. Select and search "preferences" in your word-processing software to see whether you have this option.

41b When do you use ellipses?

In a sentence an ellipsis mark (sometimes called a "dot, dot, dot") indicates that words or even whole sentences have been cut from a passage or quotation. In MLA style, ellipses added to a quoted passage are no longer enclosed by brackets.

▌1 Place ellipses where material has been omitted from a direct quotation. This material may be a word, a phrase, a complete sentence, or more.

41b
. . .

COMPLETE PASSAGE

Abraham Lincoln closed his First Inaugural Address (March 4, 1861) with these words: "We are not enemies, but friends. We must not be enemies. Though passion may have strained it must not break our bonds of affection. The mystic chords of memory, stretching from every battlefield and patriot grave to every living heart and hearthstone all over this broad land, will yet swell the chorus of the Union, when again touched, as surely they will be, by the better angels of our nature."

PASSAGE WITH ELLIPSES

Abraham Lincoln closed his First Inaugural Address (March 4, 1861) with these words: "We are not enemies, but friends. ... The mystic chords of memory ... will yet swell the chorus of the

Union, when again touched, as surely they will be, by the better angels of our nature."

2 Use ellipses to indicate pauses of any kind or to suggest that an action is incomplete or continuing.

We were certain we would finish the report on time ... until the computer crashed and wouldn't reboot.

The rocket rumbled on its launch pad as the countdown ended, "four, three, two, one. ... "

3 Use the correct spacing and punctuation before and after ellipsis marks. An ellipsis is typed as three spaced periods (. . . not ...). When an ellipsis mark appears in the middle of a quoted sentence, leave a space before the first and after the last period.

```
mystic chords of memory ... will yet swell
```

If punctuation occurs before the ellipsis, include the mark when it makes your sentence easier to read. The punctuation mark is followed by a space, then the ellipsis mark or (in MLA style) the brackets.

```
The mystic chords of memory, ... all over this broad

land, will yet swell the chorus of the Union.
```

When an ellipsis occurs at the end of a complete sentence from a quoted passage or when you cut a full sentence or more, place a period at the end of the sentence, followed by a space and then the ellipsis.

```
We must not be enemies. ... The mystic chords
```

When a parenthetical citation follows a sentence that ends with an ellipsis, leave a space between the last word in the sentence and the ellipsis. Then provide the parenthetical reference, followed by the closing punctuation mark.

41b
. . .

```
passion may have strained it ... " (2001).
```

4 Keep ellipses to a minimum at the beginning and end of sentences. You don't need ellipses every time you break into a sentence. If your quoted material begins with a capital letter, readers will know you are quoting a complete sentence.

```
According to Richard Bernstein, "The plain and

inescapable fact is that the derived Western European
```

```
culture of American life [has] produced the highest

degree of prosperity in the conditions of the

greatest freedom ever known on planet Earth" (11).
```

If the quoted material begins with a small letter, readers can assume introductory words have been cut, so no ellipses are needed.

```
According to Richard Bernstein, the United States has

"produced the highest degree of prosperity in the

conditions of the greatest freedom ever known on

planet Earth" (11).
```

Similarly, if your quoted material begins with a capital letter in brackets, readers should understand that you've added that capital because the quoted material is not from the beginning of a sentence. No ellipses are required.

```
"[T]he derived Western European culture of American

life," according to Richard Bernstein, has "produced

the highest degree of prosperity" (11).
```

You need ellipses at the beginning of a quotation only when a capital letter in a proper noun (or the pronoun *I*) might lead readers to believe that you're quoting a complete sentence when, in fact, you are not.

```
According to Richard Bernstein, ". . . American life

[has] produced the highest degree of prosperity in

the conditions of the greatest freedom ever known on

planet Earth" (11).
```

41b
. . .
Whenever you use an ellipsis, be sure your shortened quotation accurately reflects the meaning of the uncut passage.

5 Use a full line of spaced dots when you delete more than a line of verse.

```
For Mercy has a human heart,

Pity a human face,

. . . . . . . . . . . . . . . . . . . . . . . . . . . . .

And Peace, the human dress.
```

—William Blake, "The Divine Image" (1789)

EXERCISE 41.3 Abridge the following passage, using at least three ellipses. Be sure the passage is still readable after you have made your cuts.

Within a week, the neglected Victorian-style house being repaired by volunteers began to look livable again, its gables repaired, its gutters rehung, its roof reshingled. Even the grand staircase, rickety and worm-eaten, had been rebuilt. The amateur artisans made numerous mistakes during the project, including painting several windows shut, papering over a heating register, and hanging a door upside down, but no one doubted their commitment to restoring the historic structure. Some spent hours sanding away layers of varnish accumulated over almost six decades to reveal beautiful hardwood floors. Others contributed their organizational talents—many were managers or paper-pushers in their day jobs— to keep other workers supplied with raw materials, equipment, and inspiration. The volunteers worked from seven in the morning to seven at night, occasionally pausing to talk with neighbors from the area who stopped by with snacks and lunches, but laboring like mules until there was too little light to continue. They all felt the effort was worth it every time they saw the great house standing on the corner in all its former glory.

41b
. . .

CHAPTER 42

Questions About Parentheses and Brackets?

42a When do you use parentheses?

Parentheses are enclosures for comments, asides, or extra information added to sentences; the marks also enclose in-text notes for MLA and APA documentation (see Chapters 53–54). Parentheses are much more common than brackets, which are used in a few specific situations (see Section 42b). An editor will indicate a need for parentheses with carets and symbols in the margin.

During his first term ∧1969–1973∧as President, Richard (/)
Nixon visited both Moscow and Beijing.

▨ 1 Use parentheses to separate material from the main body of a sentence or paragraph. This material may be a word, a phrase, a list, even a complete sentence.

The airplane flight to Colorado was quicks **(only about ninety minutes)** and uneventful.

Don't use parentheses to explain what will be obvious to most readers.

The emergency kit contained all the expected items (**jumper cables, tire inflator, roadside flares**).

The buses arrived early, and by noon the stagehands were working at the stadium. (**One of the vans carried a portable stage.**) Preparations for the concert were on schedule.

2 Use parentheses to insert examples, directions, or other details into a sentence.

The call to the police included an address (**107 West St.**).

If the children get lost, have them call the school (**346-1317**) or the church office (**471-6109**).

3 Use parentheses to highlight numbers or letters used in listing items.

The labor negotiators realized they could (**1**) concede on all issues immediately, (**2**) stonewall until the public demanded a settlement, or (**3**) hammer out a compromise.

4 Use the correct punctuation with or around parentheses. When a complete sentence standing alone is surrounded by parentheses, place its end punctuation inside the parentheses.

The neighborhood was run-down and littered. (Some houses looked as if they hadn't been painted in decades.)

However, when a sentence concludes with a parenthesis, the end punctuation for the complete sentence falls outside the final parenthesis mark.

On the corner was a small church (actually a converted store).

42a
( )

When parentheses enclose a very short sentence within another sentence, the enclosed sentence ordinarily begins without capitalization and ends without punctuation.

The editor pointed out a misplaced modifier (**the writer glared at her**), crossed out three paragraphs (**the writer grumbled**), and then demanded a complete rewrite.

Punctuation may be used, however, when an enclosed sentence is a question or exclamation.

The coup ended (**who would have guessed it?**) almost as quickly as it began.

▪ **5 Don't use punctuation before a parenthesis in the middle of sentences.** A comma before a parenthesis is incorrect; if necessary, a parenthesis may be followed by a comma.

WRONG   Although the Crusades failed in their announced objective, (Jerusalem still remained in Muslim hands afterward) the expeditions changed the West dramatically.

RIGHT   Although the Crusades failed in their announced objective (Jerusalem still remained in Muslim hands afterward), the expeditions changed the West dramatically.

EXERCISE 42.1 Add parentheses as needed to the following sentences.

1. Native Americans inhabited almost every region of North America, from the peoples farthest north the Inuit to those in the Southwest the Hopi, the Zuni.

2. In parts of what are now New Mexico and Colorado, during the thirteenth century, some ancient tribes moved off the mesas no one knows exactly why to live in cliff dwellings.

3. One cliff dwelling at Mesa Verde covers an area of 66 meters 217 feet by 27 meters 89 feet.

4. Spectacular as they are, the cliff dwellings served the tribes known as the Anasazi for only a short time.

5. The Anasazi left their cliff dwellings, possibly because of a prolonged drought AD 1276–1299 in the entire region.

42b
[ ]

42b When do you use brackets?

Like parentheses, brackets are enclosures. But brackets have fewer and more specialized uses. Brackets and parentheses are usually *not* interchangeable.

An editor will indicate a need for brackets with carets and symbols in the margin.

"She∧ Aretha Franklin∧ is almost as gifted a pianist as she is a ⌊/⌋ singer," the reviewer commented.

▪ **1 Use brackets to insert comments or explanations into direct quotations.** Although you cannot change the words of a direct quotation, you can add information between brackets.

"He [**George Lucas**] reminded me a little of Walt Disney's version of a mad scientist."

—Steven Spielberg

In other cases, you can insert bracketed material to make the grammar of a quotation fit smoothly into your own syntax. But use this strategy sparingly, taking care not to change the meaning of the original.

Any change you make in an original text, even if only from an uppercase to a lowercase letter or vice versa, should be signaled with brackets.

In *The Dinosaur Heresies*, Robert T. Bakker rejects " [o]rthodox theory."

Dinosaurs, he argues, are not just big reptiles with a "metabolism [**that is**] pitifully low compared to mammals'.'"

Brackets around the letter *o* indicate that you have changed Bakker's original capital letter to lowercase.

2 Use brackets to avoid one set of parentheses falling within another Turn the inner pair of parentheses into brackets.

The Web site included a full text of the resolution (expressing the sense of Congress on the calculation of the consumer price index [**H.RES.99**]).

3 Use brackets to acknowledge or highlight errors that originate in quoted materials In such cases the Latin word *sic* ("thus") is enclosed in brackets immediately after the error. See Section 50c-1 for details.

The sign over the cash register read "We don't except [**sic**] personal checks for payment."

42b
[ ]

CHAPTER 43

Questions About Dashes, Hyphens, and Slashes?

43a When do you use dashes?

Dashes can either link or separate ideas in sentences. They are bold marks of punctuation to be used with care and a little flair.

Professional editors will use a caret and the symbol $\frac{|}{M}$ to indicate where a dash is needed.

They were brave soldiers‸ men and women the country $\frac{|}{M}$ could cheer for.

1 Use dashes to add illustrations, examples, or summaries to the ends of sentences. A dash gives emphasis to any addition.

Dvorak's *New World* Symphony reflects musical themes the composer heard in the United States—including Native American melodies and black spirituals.

Beethoven's Ninth Symphony was a great accomplishment for an artist in bad health—and completely deaf.

2 Use pairs of dashes to insert information into the middle of a sentence. Information between dashes gets noticed.

The giants of nineteenth-century Italian opera—Rossini, Donizetti, Bellini, Verdi—worked for demanding and sensitive audiences.

Many regard Verdi's *Otello*—based on Shakespeare's story of a marriage ruined by jealousy—as the greatest of Italian tragic operas.

3 Use dashes to highlight interruptions, especially in dialogue. The interruption can even be punctuated.

Candice sputtered, "The opera lasted—I can hardly believe it— five hours!"

"When—perhaps I should say if?—I ever sit through Wagner's *Ring,* I expect to be paid for it," Joshua remarked.

4 Use dashes to set off items, phrases, or credit lines.

Charles Ives, William Grant Still, Aaron Copland, George Gershwin—these composers sought to create an American musical idiom.

Members of the audience are asked
—to withhold applause between movements
—to stifle all coughing and sneezing
—to refrain from popping gum.

"Music is the universal language." —Henry Wadsworth Longfellow

5 Don't use a hyphen when a dash is required.
Keyboarded dashes are made up of two unspaced hyphens:--. No space is left before or after a dash.

WRONG	Beethoven's music-unlike Mozart's-uses emphatic rhythms.
RIGHT	Beethoven's music --unlike Mozart's --uses emphatic rhythms.

You should also be able to create an actual long dash ("em dash") on your word processor by selecting an option that automatically turns - into—. Or you may be able to create the em dash with a key command.

6 Don't use too many dashes. They can clutter a passage.
One pair per sentence is the limit.

WRONG	Mozart—recognized as a genius while still a child— produced more than six hundred compositions during his life—including symphonies, operas, and concertos.
RIGHT	Mozart, recognized as a genius while still a child, produced more than six hundred compositions during his life—including symphonies, operas, and concertos.

43a

EXERCISE 43.1 Add and delete dashes as necessary to improve the sentences below.

1. Legend has it that Beethoven's Third Symphony was dedicated to Napoleon Bonaparte the champion of French revolutionary ideals until he declared himself emperor.

2. Scholars believe—though they can't be sure—that the symphony was initially called *Bonaparte*—testimony to just how much the idealistic Beethoven admired the French leader.

3. The Third Symphony a revolutionary work itself is now known by the title *Eroica*.

4. The Third, the Fifth, the Sixth, the Seventh, the Ninth Symphonies, they all contain musical passages that most people recognize immediately.

5. The opening four notes of Beethoven's Fifth, da, da, da, dum, may be the most famous in all of music.

43b When do you use hyphens?

Hyphens either join words or divide them between syllables. They should not be confused with dashes, which have an entirely different function (see the preceding section). An editor will usually place carets within the line to indicate missing hyphens.

My mother‸in‸law will retire in June. ‒

■1 Learn common hyphenation patterns. Hyphenate words beginning with the prefixes *all-*, *self-*, and *ex-* or ending with the suffix *-elect*.

all‑encompassing	**ex**‑hockey player
self‑contained	mayor‑elect

Hyphenate most words beginning with *well-*, *ill-*, and *heavy-*.

well‑dressed	**ill**‑suited	**heavy**‑handed

Most common nouns beginning with *un-*, *non-*, *anti-*, *pro-*, *co-*, and *pre-* are not hyphenated.

uncertain	**anti**slavery	**co**ordinate
nonviolent	**pro**democracy	**pre**recorded

Unabridged dictionaries provide extensive lists of combinations formed with these troublesome prefixes.

■2 Follow the conventional uses of hyphens. Use hyphens to write out numbers from twenty-one to ninety-nine. Fractions also take hyphens, but use only one hyphen per fraction.

twenty‑nine	one forty‑seventh of a mile
one‑quarter inch	two hundred forty‑six

43b
‑

Use hyphens to indicate double titles, elements, functions, or attributes.

the secretary-treasurer of our club

members of the AFL-CIO

a city-state such as Sparta

in the space-time continuum

Use hyphens in some technical expressions:

uranium-235   A-bomb

Use hyphens to link prefixes to proper nouns and their corresponding adjectives.

pre-Columbian   **anti**-American
mid-Victorian   **neo**-Darwinism

Use hyphens to prevent words from being misread.

a recreation area   the re-creation of an event
a chicken coop   a student co-op

3 Use hyphens to link some compound nouns and verbs.
The conventions for hyphenating words are complicated and inconsistent. Here are some expressions that do take hyphens.

brother-in-law   great-grandmother
two-step   walkie-talkie
water-skier   hit-and-run
hocus-pocus   president-elect
cold-shoulder   double-talk
strong-arm   off-Broadway

Here are some compounds that aren't hyphenated. Some can be written as either single words or separate words.

cabdriver   best man   sea dog
cab owner   blockhouse

When in doubt whether to hyphenate, check a dictionary or a reference tool such as the Government Printing Office's *Manual of Style*.

4 Use hyphens to create compound phrases and expressions.

Some classmates resented her **holier-than-thou** attitude.

Product innovation suffered because of a **not-invented-here** bias.

43b

5 Use hyphens to link compound modifiers before a noun. The hyphen makes the modification easier to read and understand.

> an **up-or-down** vote
> an **English-speaking** country
> a **sharp-looking** suit
> a **stop-motion** sequence
> a **seventeenth-century** vase

How can you tell when you are dealing with a compound modifier? Try removing one of the modifiers, placing a comma between them, or inserting *and*. If the expression changes in meaning or becomes difficult to understand, it may require a hyphen (but see also Sections 39c-4 and 39c-5).

> a stop, action camera?→ a **stop-action** camera
> a well, known artist?→ a **well-known** artist
> a bone and chilling scream?→ a **bone-chilling** scream

Do not use hyphens with adverbs that end in *-ly*. Nor should you use hyphens with *very*.

> a **sharply honed** knife   a **quickly written** note
> a **bitterly cold** morning   a **very hot** day

When compound modifiers follow a noun, omit the hyphen.

> The artist was **well known.**
> The scream was **bone chilling.**

6 Handle suspended modifiers correctly. Sometimes a word or phrase may have more than a single hyphenated modifier. These **suspended modifiers** should look like the following.

> Anne planned her vacation wardrobe to accommodate **cold-, cool-,** and **wet-**weather days.

> Whether the math class should be a **first-** or **second-**semester course was the one thing we couldn't determine.

7 Do not hyphenate words at the end of lines. Most style manuals advise against such divisions when typing. On a computer, word wrap automatically eliminates end-of-line divisions.

If you must divide a word, break it only at a syllable. Check a dictionary for accurate syllable breaks. Don't guess.

> fu/se/lage   vin/e/gary
> lo/qua/cious   cam/ou/flage

43b
-

Never hyphenate contractions, numbers, abbreviations, acronyms, or one-syllable words at the end of lines. The following divisions would be inappropriate.

would- n't	250,- 000,000
NA- TO	U.S.- M.C.
Ph.- D.	ES- PN

EXERCISE 43.2 In the following sentences, indicate which form of the words in parentheses is preferable. Use a dictionary if you are not familiar with the terms.

1. Local citizens have a (**once in a lifetime/once-in-a-lifetime**) opportunity to preserve an (**old-growth/oldgrowth**) forest.

2. A large, wooded parcel of land is about to be turned into a shopping mall by (**real-estate/realestate**) speculators and (**pinstripe suited/pinstripe-suited**) investors.

3. The forest provides a haven for (**wild-life/wildlife**) of all varieties, from (**great horned owls/great-horned owls**) to (**ruby throated/ruby-throated**) hummingbirds.

4. Does any community need (**video stores/video-stores**), (**T shirt/T-shirt**) shops, and (**over priced/overpriced**) boutiques more than acres of natural habitat?

5. This (**recently-proposed/recently proposed**) development can be stopped by petitioning the (**city-council/city council**).

43c When do you use slashes?

Slashes are used to indicate divisions. They are rare pieces of punctuation with a few specific functions. About the only problem slashes pose concerns the spacing before and after the mark. That spacing depends on how the slash is being used.

1 Use slashes to separate expressions that indicate a choice. In these cases, no space is left before or after the slash.

either / or	he / she	yes / no	pass / fail
win / lose	up / down	on / off	right / wrong

Some readers object to these expressions, preferring *he or she,* for example, to *he/she* (sometimes even written as *s/he*).

2 Use slashes to indicate fractions.

2/3   2 2/3   5 3/8

3 Use slashes in typing World Wide Web addresses.

<http://www.nps.gov/parks.html>

Note that no spaces precede or follow slashes in World Wide Web addresses.

4 Use slashes to divide lines of poetry quoted within sentences. When used in this way, a space is left on either side of the slash.

```
Only then does Lear understand that he has been a
failure as a king: "O, I have taken / Too little care
of this!"
```

If you cite more than three lines of verse, set the passage as a block quotation and break the lines as they occur in the poem itself. No slashes are required.

```
Poor naked wretches, wheresoever you are,
That bide the pelting of this pitiless storm,
How shall your houseless heads and unfed sides,
Your looped and windowed raggedness, defend you
From seasons such as these?
```

43c
/

CHAPTER 44

Questions About Italics and Capitalization?

44a When do you use italics?

Italics, like quotation marks, draw attention to a title, word, or phrase. In a printed text, italics are *slanted letters*. In typed or handwritten papers, italics are signaled by <u>underlining the appropriate words</u>. In email systems that don't yet transmit underscoring or italic letters, italics can be signaled by typing before and after the emphasized word or expression: _Newsweek_.

If you are using a computer that can print italicized words, ask your instructor or editor whether you should print actual italics in a paper. (They may still prefer that you use an underscore.)

An editor will underline a word that needs to be italicized and mark *ital* in the margin.

I was reading Stephen King's <u>Christine</u>. *ital*

1 Use italics to set off some titles. Some titles and names are italicized; others appear between quotation marks. Chart 44.1 on page 652 provides guidance.

Neither italics nor quotation marks are used for the names of *types* of trains, ships, aircraft, or spacecraft.

DC-10	Trident submarine
B-1	Boeing 757

Neither italics nor quotation marks are used with titles of major religious texts, books of the Bible, or classic legal documents.

the Bible	the Qur'an
1 Romans	the Magna Carta
the Constitution	the Declaration of Independence

2 Use italics to set off foreign words or phrases. Italics emphasize scientific names and foreign terms that haven't become accepted into the English vocabulary.

Pierre often described his co-workers as *les bêtes humaines*.

Chart 44.1

Titles *Italicized* or "In Quotes"

TITLES *ITALICIZED*

books	*Twelve* or Twelve
magazines	*Time* or Time
journals	*JAMA* or JAMA
newspapers	*USA Today* or USA Today
films	*Casablanca* or Casablanca
TV shows	*Smallville* or Smallville
radio programs	*All Things Considered* or All Things Considered
plays	*Macbeth* or Macbeth
long poems	*Beowulf* or Beowulf
long musical pieces	*The Mikado* or The Mikado
albums	Wilco's *Yankee Hotel Foxtrot* or Yankee Hotel Foxtrot
paintings	Schnabel's *Adieu* or Adieu
sculptures	Christo's *Running Fence* or Running Fence
dances	Antonio's *Goya* or Goya
ships	*Titanic* or Titanic
	U.S.S. *Saratoga* or U.S.S. Saratoga
trains	the *Orient Express* or the Orient Express
aircraft	*Enola Gay* or Enola Gay
spacecraft	*Apollo 11* or Apollo 11
software programs	*Microsoft Word* or Microsoft Word

TITLES "IN QUOTES"

chapters of books	"Lessons from the Pros"
articles in magazines	"Is the Stock Market Too High?"
articles in journals	"Vai Script and Literacy"
articles in newspapers	"Inflation Heats Up"
sections in newspapers	"Living in Style"
TV episodes	"Drew's New Car"
radio episodes	"McGee Goes Crackers"
short stories	"Araby"
short poems	"The Red Wheelbarrow"
songs	"God Bless America"

44a
italic

Foreign words absorbed by English over the centuries should not be italicized. To be certain, look them up in a recent dictionary.

crèche   gumbo   gestalt   arroyo

Common abbreviations from Latin appear without italics or underscoring.

etc.   et al.   i.e.   viz.

3 Use italics (or quotation marks) to emphasize or clarify a letter, a word, or a phrase.

Does that word begin with an *f* or a *ph?*

"That may be how you define *fascist*," she replied.

When some people talk about *school spirit,* they really mean "Let's party."

EXERCISE 44.1 Indicate whether the following titles or names in boldface should be italicized, in quotation marks, or unmarked. If you don't recognize a name below, consult an encyclopedia or another reference work.

1. launching a **Titan III** at Cape Kennedy

2. **My Fair Lady** playing at the **Paramount Theater**

3. watching **I Love Lucy**

4. sunk on the passenger ship **Andrea Doria**

5. returning **A Farewell to Arms** to the public library

6. watching **Casablanca** again on a **Panasonic** DVD player

7. discussing the colors of Picasso's **The Old Guitarist**

8. reading Jackson's **The Lottery** one more time

9. picking up a copy of the **Los Angeles Times**

10. whistling **Here Comes the Sun** from the Beatles' **Abbey Road**

11. The White House Web site is at < **http://www.whitehouse.gov/**>.

12. You can write the senator at < **senator@hutchison.senate.gov**>.

44a
italic

44b How do you capitalize sentences, titles, and poems?

Capital letters can cause problems simply because you have to remember the conventions guiding their use. Fortunately, you can observe the guidelines for capital letters in almost every sentence you read. In your papers, an editor may write *cap* in the margin next to a small letter that needs to be changed to uppercase.

I wrote a letter to ₚresident Bush. *cap*

An editor will write *lc* (for "lowercase") in the margin indicating a capital letter that needs to be changed to a small letter.

We spoke to the Ḻibrarian today. *lc*

1 Capitalize the first word in a sentence. You can set most
word processors to capitalize sentence beginnings automatically.

Naomi picked up the tourists at their hotel.

What a remarkable city Washington is!

2 Capitalize the first word in a direct quotation that is a full sentence.

Ira asked, "Where's the National Air and Space Museum?"

"Good idea!" Naomi agreed. "Let's go there."

Use lowercase for quotations that continue after an interruption.

"It's on the Mall," Naomi explained, "near the Hirschhorn gallery."

3 Don't capitalize the first word of a phrase or clause that follows a colon unless you want to emphasize the word.
You may also capitalize the first word after a colon if it is part of a title.

NO CAPS AFTER COLON	They ignored one item while parking the car: a no-parking sign.
CAPS FOR EMPHASIS	The phrase haunted her: Your car has been towed!
CAPS FOR TITLE	*Marilyn: The Untold Story*

44b
cap

4 Don't capitalize the first word of a phrase or sentence enclosed by dashes.

Audrey's first screenplay—a thriller about industrial espionage—had been picked up by an agent.

Her work—she couldn't believe it—was now in the hands of a studio executive.

5 Capitalize the titles of papers, books, articles, poems, and so on. In MLA style, capitalize the first and last word of the title. Capitalize all other words *except* articles (*a, an, the*), prepositions, the *to* in infinitives, and coordinating conjunctions—unless they are the first or last words.

Nonfiction book: *Amusing Ourselves to Death*
Novel: *With Fire and Sword*
Magazine article: "Confessions of a Sports Car Bolshevik"
Title of a term paper: "Can Quality Survive the Standardized Test?"

Articles and prepositions are capitalized when they follow a colon, usually as part of a subtitle.

A Dream Deferred: The Second Betrayal of Black Freedom in America

Checklist 44.1

Capitalizing Titles

TO CAPITALIZE A TITLE, FOLLOW THESE THREE STEPS.

• Capitalize the first word.

• Capitalize the last word.

• Capitalize all other words *except*

—articles (*a, an, the*)

—the *to* in infinitives

—prepositions

—coordinating conjunctions

44b
cap

6 Capitalize the first word in lines of quoted poetry unless the poet has used lowercase letters.

Sumer is ycomen in,
Loude sing cuckoo!
Groweth reed and bloweth meed,
And springth the wode now.
Sing cuckoo!
—"The Cuckoo Song"

Ida,
ho, and Oh,
Io!
spaces
with places
tween 'em
—T. Beckwith, "Travels"

EXERCISE 44.2 Correct the problems in capitalization in the following sentences.

1. The passenger next to me asked, "do you remember when air travel used to be a pleasure?"

2. I couldn't reply immediately: My tray table had just flopped open and hit me on the knees.

3. The plane we were on—A jumbo jet that seated nine or ten across—had been circling Dulles International for hours.

4. "We'll be landing momentarily," the flight attendant mumbled, "If we are lucky."

5. I had seen the film version of this flight: *airplane!*

44c When do you capitalize persons, places, and things?

When you are unsure whether a particular word needs to be capitalized, check a dictionary. Don't guess, especially when you are dealing with proper nouns (nouns that name a particular person, place, or thing—*Geoffrey Chaucer, Ohio, Lincoln Memorial*) or proper adjectives (adjectives formed from proper nouns—*Chaucerian*). The guidelines below move from persons to places to things.

1 Capitalize the names and initials of people and characters.

W. C. Fields
Cher
I. M. Pei

Anzia Yezierska
Minnie Mouse
J. Hector St. Jean Crèvecoeur

A few people prefer that their names not be capitalized. Respect that choice. Similarly, you should follow the capitalization people use in their email addresses—where lowercase letters dominate.

> e. e. cummings   bell hooks
> sugarbear@mail.utexas.edu

2 Capitalize titles that precede names.

> Commissioner Angela Brown
> Vice President Mondale
> Justice Sandra Day O'Connor
> Auntie Mame

3 Capitalize titles after names when the title describes a specific person. But don't capitalize such a title when the title is more general. Compare:

> Robert King, the Dean of Liberal Arts
> Robert King, a dean at the university

Don't capitalize the titles of relatives that follow names. Compare:

> Anthony Pancioli, Cathy's uncle
> Cathy's Uncle Anthony

Exception. Capitalize academic titles that follow a name.

> Iris Miller, **Ph.D.**
> Enrique Lopez, Master of Arts

4 Don't capitalize minor titles when they stand alone without names.

> a commissioner in Cuyahoga County
> a lieutenant in the Air Force
> the first president of our club

44c
cap

Exceptions. Prestigious titles are regularly capitalized even when they stand alone. Lesser titles may be capitalized when they clearly refer to a particular individual or when they describe a position formally.

> President of the United States
> the President
> Secretary of State
> the Chair of the Classics Department argued . . .

 Point of Difference

Style manuals don't always agree about capitalizing titles. Some recommend, for example, that you not capitalize expressions such as *the president* or *the secretary of state* unless they are followed by a name: *President Carter, former Secretary of State Henry Kissinger.* You should follow whatever manual of style is recommended in your course, field, or office.

5 Capitalize the names of national, political, and ethnic groups.

Kenyans	Australians	African Americans
Chinese	Chicanos	Croatians
Libertarians	Democrats	Republicans

Exception. The names of racial groups, economic groups, and social classes are usually not capitalized.

blacks	whites
the proletariat	the knowledge class

6 Capitalize the names of businesses, corporations, organizations, unions, clubs, schools, and trademarked items.

Time, Inc.

Oklahoma State University

National Rifle Association

Chemical Workers Union

Kleenex

Xerox copy

44c
cap

Note that some companies and institutions capitalize more than just an initial letter in their names or logos.

DaimlerChrysler

FedEx

AOL

7 Capitalize the names of religious figures, religious groups, and sacred books.

God	the Savior	Buddha
Buddhism	Catholics	Judaism
the Bible	the Qur'an	Talmudic tradition

Exceptions. The terms *god* and *goddess* are not capitalized when used generally. When *God* is capitalized, pronouns referring to God are also capitalized.

> The Greeks had a pantheon of gods and goddesses.
>
> The Goddess of Liberty appears on our currency.
>
> The cardinal praised God and all His works.

8 Do not routinely capitalize academic ranks. Such ranks include the terms *freshman, first-year, sophomore, junior, senior, graduate, postgrad.*

> The college had many fifth-year seniors.
>
> The freshman dormitory was a dump.
>
> The teacher was a graduate student.

Exception. Capitalize academic ranks when these groups are referred to as organized bodies or institutions.

> a representative of the Senior Class
>
> the Freshman Cotillion

9 Capitalize academic degrees when they are abbreviated. Abbreviated degrees include *Ph.D., LL.D., M.A., M.S., B.A., B.S.* Do not capitalize those degrees when they are spelled out. (Note that MLA style omits the periods in these abbreviations.)

> Maria earned her **Ph.D.** the same day Mark received his **LL.D.**
>
> Leon Railsback, **M.A.**
>
> Leon has a master of arts degree.
>
> Who conferred the bachelor of science degrees?

Exception. Academic degrees spelled out in full are capitalized when they follow a name.

> Leon Railsback, Master of Arts
>
> Maria Ramos, Doctor of Philosophy

44c
cap

10 Capitalize the names of places. Also capitalize words based on place names and the names of specific geographic features such as lakes, rivers, and oceans.

Asia	Old Faithful
Asian	the Amazon

the Bronx	the Gulf of Mexico
Lake Erie	Deaf Smith County
Washington	the Atlantic Ocean

Exception. Don't capitalize compass directions unless they name a specific place or are part of a place name.

north	North America
south	the South
eastern Ohio	the Middle East

Many writers forget to capitalize words that identify nationalities or countries—words such as *English, French,* or *Mexican.*

WRONG   Kyle has three english courses.

RIGHT   Kyle has three English courses.

WRONG   Janet drives only american cars.

RIGHT   Janet drives only American cars.

When proofreading, be sure to capitalize most words derived from the names of countries.

11 Capitalize abstractions when you want to give them special emphasis. Terms such as *love, truth, mercy,* and *patriotism* (which ordinarily appear in small letters) may be capitalized when you discuss them as concepts or when you wish to give them special emphasis, perhaps as the subject of a paper.

What is this thing called Love?

The conflict was between Truth and Falsehood.

There is no need to capitalize abstractions used without special emphasis.

Byron had fallen in love again.

Either tell the truth or abandon hope of rescue.

44c
cap

12 Capitalize the names of buildings, structures, or monuments.

Yankee Stadium	Hoover Dam
the Alamo	the Golden Gate Bridge
Trump Tower	Indianapolis Speedway

13 Capitalize the names of particular objects. They might include ships, planes, automobiles, brand-name products, events, documents, and musical groups.

SS *Titanic*
Ford Focus
Super Bowl XXX
Rolling Stones

Boeing 777
Eskimo Pie
the Constitution
Fifth Amendment

14 Capitalize most periods of time. Periods of time include days, months, holidays, historical epochs, and historical events. You can set most word processors to capitalize days of the week automatically.

Monday
May
Middle Ages
Fourth of July

the Reformation
World War II
Bastille Day
Pax Romana

Exception. Seasons of the year are usually not capitalized.

winter   spring   summer   fall

15 Capitalize terms ending in *-ism* when they name specific literary, artistic, religious, or cultural movements. When in doubt, check a dictionary.

Impressionism
Judaism
Buddhism

Vorticism
Catholicism
Romanticism

Exception. Many terms ending in *-ism* are not capitalized.

socialism   capitalism   monetarism

16 Capitalize school subjects and classes only when the subjects themselves are proper nouns.

biology
English
French

chemistry
Russian history
physics

44c
cap

Exception. Titles of specific courses (such as you might find in a college catalog) are capitalized.

Biology 101   Chemistry Lab 200   English 346K

17 Capitalize all the letters in acronyms and initialisms. (See Section 45a for more detail.)

NATO
DNA

OPEC
GMC

SALT
MCAT

Exception. Don't capitalize familiar acronyms that seem like ordinary words. When in doubt, check a dictionary.

radar   sonar   laser

EXERCISE 44.3 Capitalize in the following sentences as necessary.

1. The east asian students visiting the district of columbia were mostly juniors pursuing b.a.'s while the african-american students were predominantly graduate students seeking master's degrees.

2. The constitution and the declaration of independence are on view at the national archives.

3. I heard the doorkeeper at the hilton speaking spanish to the general secretary of the united nations.

4. Visitors to washington, d.c., include people from around the world: russians from moscow, egyptians from cairo, aggies from texas, buckeyes from ohio.

5. At the white house, the president will host a conference on democracy and free enterprise in the spring, probably in april.

44c
cap

CHAPTER **45**

Questions About Abbreviations and Numbers?

45a How do you handle abbreviations?

Using abbreviations, acronyms (*NATO, radar*), and initialisms (*HBO, IRS*) can make some writing simpler. Many conventional abbreviations are acceptable in all kinds of papers.

a.m.	p.m.
Mrs.	Mr.
B.C.	A.D.
Ph.D.	M.D.

Other abbreviations are appropriate on forms, reports, and statistics sheets, but not in more formal writing.

Jan.—January
ft.—foot
no.—number
mo.—month

An editor will usually indicate a problem with an abbreviation by circling a word or expression and marking *abbr* in the margin.

The house has more than 2,400 (sq. ft.) *abbr*

An abbreviation is the Mini-Me for a complete word or expression.

1 Be consistent in punctuating abbreviations and acronyms. Abbreviations of single words usually take periods.

vols.   Jan.   Mr.

Initialisms are usually written without periods. You may still use periods with these terms, but be consistent.

HBO   IRS   AFL-CIO   URL

Acronyms ordinarily do not require periods.

CARE   NATO   NOW

Acronyms that have become accepted words never need periods.

sonar   radar   laser   scuba

Periods are usually omitted after abbreviations in technical writing unless a measurement or other item might be misread without a period—for example, *in.*

Consistently use three periods or none at all in terms such as the following. Current usage generally omits the periods.

m.p.g. *or* mpg   r.p.m. *or* rpm   m.p.h. *or* mph

2 Be consistent in capitalizing abbreviations, acronyms, and initialisms. Capitalize the abbreviations of words that are capitalized when written out in full.

General Motors—GM   University of Toledo—UT
U.S. Navy—USN   98° Fahrenheit—98° F.

Don't capitalize the abbreviations of words not capitalized when written out in full.

pound—lb.   minutes—min.

Capitalize most initialisms.

IRS   CRT   UCLA   NBC

Always capitalize *B.C.E.* and *C.E.* or *B.C.* and *A.D.* Printers may set these items in small caps: *B.C.E.* and *A.D.*

You may capitalize *A.M.* and *P.M.*, but they often appear in small letters: *a.m.* and *p.m.* Printers may set them as small caps: *A.M.* and *P.M.*

Don't capitalize acronyms that have become accepted words: *sonar, radar, laser, scuba.*

3 Use the appropriate abbreviations for titles, degrees, and names. Some titles are almost always abbreviated (*Mr., Ms.,*

45a
abbr

Mrs., Jr.). Other titles are normally written out in full, though they may be abbreviated when they precede a first name or initial.

President	President Bush	Pres. George W. Bush
Senator	Senator Clinton	Sen. Hillary Clinton
Professor	Professor Davis	Prof. Diane Davis
Reverend	Reverend Call	Rev. Ann Call
	the Reverend Dr. Call	Rev. Dr. Call
Secretary of State	Secretary Powell	Sec. Colin Powell

Never let abbreviated titles of this kind appear alone in a sentence.

> WRONG   The **gov.** urged the **sen.** to support the bill.
>
> RIGHT   The **governor** urged the **senator** to support the bill.

Give credit for academic degrees either before a name or after—not both. Don't, for example, use both *Dr.* and *Ph.D.* in the same name.

> WRONG   **Dr.** Katherine Martinich, **Ph.D.**
>
> RIGHT   **Dr.** Katherine Martinich
>   Katherine Martinich, **Ph.D.**

Abbreviations for academic titles often stand by themselves, without names attached.

> Professor Kim received her **Ph.D.** from Penn State and her **B.S.** from St. Vincent College.

4 **Use the appropriate technical abbreviations.** Abbreviations are often used in professional, governmental, scientific, military, and technical writing.

| DNA | UHF | EKG | START |
| SALT | GNP | LEM | kW |

When writing for nontechnical audiences, spell out technical terms in full the first time you use them. Then in parentheses give the specialized abbreviation you will use in the rest of the paper.

> The two congressional candidates debated the effects a tax increase might have on the gross national product (GNP).

5 **Use the appropriate abbreviations for agencies and organizations.** In some cases, the abbreviation or acronym regularly replaces the full name of a company, agency, or organization.

FBI	IBM	MCI	AT&T
AFL-CIO	GOP	PPG	MGM
A&P	BBC	NCAA	MTV

45a
abbr

6 Use the appropriate abbreviations for dates. Dates are not abbreviated in most writing. Write out in full the days of the week and months of the year.

> WRONG They arrived in Washington on a **Wed.** in **Apr.**
>
> RIGHT They arrived in Washington on a **Wednesday** in **April.**

Abbreviations of months and days are used primarily in notes, lists, forms, and reference works.

7 Use the appropriate abbreviations for time and temperatures. Abbreviations that accompany time and temperatures are acceptable in all kinds of writing.

43 B.C.	A.D. 144	1:00 a.m.	98° F
143 B.C.E.	1066 C.E.	4:36 p.m.	13° C

Notice that the abbreviation *B.C.* appears after a date, *A.D.* usually before one. Both expressions are always capitalized. You may also see *B.C.E.* (*Before the Common Era*) used in place of *B.C.* and *C.E.* (*Common Era*) substituted for *A.D.* Both follow the date. MLA style deletes the periods in these items: BC, BCE, AD, CE.

8 Use the appropriate abbreviations for weights, measures, and times. Technical terms or measurements are commonly abbreviated when used with numbers, but they are written out in full when they stand alone in sentences. Even when accompanied by numbers, the terms usually look better in sentences when spelled out completely.

28 mpg	1 tsp.	40 km.	450 lbs.
50 min.	30 kg.	2 hrs.	40 mph

Ella didn't really care how many **miles per gallon** her Escalade got in the city.

The abbreviation for number—*No.* or *no.*—is appropriate in technical writing, but only when immediately followed by a number.

> NOT The **no.** on the contaminated dish was **073.**
>
> BUT The contaminated dish was **no. 073.**

No. also appears in footnotes, endnotes, and citations.

9 Use the appropriate abbreviations for places. In most writing, place names are not abbreviated except in addresses and in ref-

45a
abbr

erence tools and lists. However, certain abbreviations are accepted in academic and business writing.

USA   USSR   UK   Washington, D.C.

In addresses (but not in written text), use the standard postal abbreviations, without periods, for the states.

Alabama	AL	Montana	MT
Alaska	AK	Nebraska	NE
Arizona	AZ	Nevada	NV
Arkansas	AR	New Hampshire	NH
California	CA	New Jersey	NJ
Colorado	CO	New Mexico	NM
Connecticut	CT	New York	NY
Delaware	DE	North Carolina	NC
Florida	FL	North Dakota	ND
Georgia	GA	Ohio	OH
Hawaii	HI	Oklahoma	OK
Idaho	ID	Oregon	OR
Illinois	IL	Pennsylvania	PA
Indiana	IN	Rhode Island	RI
Iowa	IA	South Carolina	SC
Kansas	KS	South Dakota	SD
Kentucky	KY	Tennessee	TN
Louisiana	LA	Texas	TX
Maine	ME	Utah	UT
Maryland	MD	Vermont	VT
Massachusetts	MA	Virginia	VA
Michigan	MI	Washington	WA
Minnesota	MN	West Virginia	WV
Mississippi	MS	Wisconsin	WI
Missouri	MO	Wyoming	WY

45a
abbr

All the various terms for *street* are written out in full, except in addresses.

boulevard	road	avenue	parkway
highway	alley	place	circle

But *Mt.* (for *mount*) and *St.* (for *saint*) are acceptable abbreviations in place names when they precede a proper name.

Mt. Vesuvius   **St.** Charles Street

10 Use the correct abbreviations for certain expressions preserved from Latin.

i.e. (*id est*—that is)
e.g. (*exempli gratia*—for example)
et al. (*et alii*—and others)
etc. (*et cetera*—and so on)

In most writing, it is better to use English versions of these and other Latin abbreviations. Avoid using the abbreviation *etc.* in formal or academic writing. Never write *and etc.*

11 Use the appropriate abbreviations for divisions of books.

The many abbreviations for books and manuscripts (*p., pp., vols., ch., chpts., bk., sect.*) are fine in footnotes or parenthetical citations, but don't use them alone in sentences.

WRONG   Richard stuck the **bk.** in his pocket after reading **ch.** 5.

RIGHT   Richard stuck the **book** in his pocket after reading **chapter** 5.

12 Use symbols as abbreviations carefully.

Symbols such as %, +, =, ≠, <, > make sense in technical and scientific writing, but in other academic papers, spell out the full words. Most likely to cause a problem is % for *percent*.

ACCEPTABLE   Mariah was shocked to learn that **80%** of the cars towed belong to tourists.

PREFERRED   Mariah was shocked to learn that **80 percent** of the cars towed belong to tourists.

45a
abbr

You can use a dollar sign—$—in any writing as long as it is followed by an amount. Don't use both the dollar sign and the word *dollar.*

WRONG   The fine for parking in a towing zone is **$**125 dollars.

RIGHT   The fine for parking in a towing zone is **$125**.

RIGHT   The fine for parking in a towing zone is **one hundred twenty-five dollars.**

The ampersand (&) is an abbreviation for *and*. Do not use it in formal writing except when it appears in a title or name: *Road & Track.*

EXERCISE 45.1 Correct the sentences below, abbreviating where appropriate or expanding abbreviations that would be incorrect in college or professional writing. Check the punctuation for accuracy and consistency. If you insist on periods with acronyms and initialisms, use them throughout the passage.

1. There's a better than 70% chance of rain today.

2. Irene sent angry ltrs. to a dozen networks, including NBC, A.B.C., ESPN, and CNN.

3. The Emperor Claudius was born in 10 b.c. and died in 54 A.D.

4. Dr. Kovatch, M.D., works for the Federal Department of Agriculture (FDA).

5. I owe the company only $175 dollars, & expect to pay the full amount before the end of the mo.

45b How do you handle numbers?

You can express numbers in writing either through numerals or through words.

1	one
25	twenty-five
100	one hundred
1/4	one-fourth
0.05%	five hundredths of a percent *or*
	five one-hundredths of a percent

You'll likely use numerals in technical, scientific, and business writing. In other kinds of documents, you may combine words and numerals. (For guidelines on using hyphens with numbers that are spelled out, see Section 43b-2.)

45b
num

1 Write out numbers from one to nine; use numerals for numbers larger than nine.

10	15	39
101	115	220
1001	1021	59,000
101,000	10,000,101	50,306,673,432

In most cases, spell out ordinal numbers (that is, numbers that express a sequence): *first, second, third, fourth,* and so on. Spell out numbers that identify centuries.

in the fifteenth century
twentieth-century philosophers

🍎 *Point of Difference*

These guidelines have variations and exceptions. The MLA style manual, for example, recommends spelling out any number that can be expressed in one or two words.

thirteen   twenty-one
three hundred   fifteen thousand

The APA style manual suggests using figures for most numbers above ten unless they appear at the beginning of a sentence.

Thirty-three workers were rescued from an oil platform.

Check the style manual in your field to confirm how numbers ought to be presented in your writing.🍎

2 Combine words and figures when you need to express large round numbers.

100 billion $32 million   103 trillion

Avoid shifting between words and figures. When you need numerals to express some numbers in a sentence, use numbers throughout.

There were over **125,000** people at the protest and **950** police officers, but only **9** arrests.

When one number follows another, alternate words and figures for clarity.

33 fifth graders   12 first-term representatives
2 four-wheel-drive vehicles   five 5-gallon buckets

45b
num

3 Use numerals when comparing numbers or suggesting a range. Numerals are easier to spot and compare than words.

A blackboard at the traffic office listed a **$50** fine for jaywalking, **$100** for speeding, and **$125** for parking in a towing zone.

4 Don't begin sentences with numerals. Either spell out the number or rephrase the sentence so that the numeral is not the first word.

WRONG   32 people were standing in line at the parking violation center.

RIGHT   Thirty-two people were standing in line at the parking violation center.

5 Use numerals for dates, street numbers, page numbers, sums of money, and various ID and call numbers.

July 4, 1776	1860–1864
6708 Beauford Dr.	1900 East Blvd.
p. 352	pp. 23–24
$2,749.00	43£
Channel 8	103.5 FM
PR 105.5 R8	SSN 111-00-1111

Don't use an ordinal form in dates.

WRONG   May 2nd, 1991

RIGHT   May 2, 1991 *or* 2 May 1991

6 Use numerals for measurements, percentages, statistics, and scores.

35 mph	13° C	Austin, TX 78750
75 percent	0.2 liters	5.5 pupils per teacher
2½ miles	15%	Browns 42—Steelers 7

Use numerals for time with *a.m.* and *p.m.;* use words with *o'clock.*

2:15 p.m.   **6:00 a.m.**   **six** o'clock

7 Form the plural of numbers by adding -s or -'s.

five 6s in a row   five 98's

See Section 25a for more on plurals.

EXERCISE 45.2 Decide whether numbers used in the following sentences are handled appropriately. Where necessary, change numerals to words and words to numerals. Some expressions may not need revision.

45b
num

1. 4 people will be honored at the ceremony beginning at nine p.m.

2. The culture contained more than 500,000,000,000 cells.

3. We forgot who won the Nobel Peace Prize in nineteen ninety-one.

4. The examination will include a question about the 1st, the 4th, or the Tenth Amendment.

5. We paid $79.80 for the hotel room and twenty dollars for admission to the park.

Research and Writing

CHAPTER 46

How Do You Design a Research Project?

Until recently, most instructors assigned research projects to introduce students to academic standards for research—that is, to the procedures for gathering, evaluating, and reporting information that apply in higher education. The resulting research papers were—and remain—important exercises in handling information responsibly. Not many students, however, wrote such research papers expecting to publish them or share them with anyone except teachers and classmates. Few undergraduates had the time, resources, or incentive to dig deep into scholarly archives or to develop ground-breaking projects on their own. What's more, there was no audience for such work, and there was no easy way for a writer to reach a public interested by the questions a college student might ask.

But times have changed. Students in college courses can now find tools, media, and audiences to support their serious academic writing and research. At some schools, college writers can get funding for their projects and then present their findings at conferences that focus on undergraduate research. One university even offers a $20,000 annual prize for such work. Thanks to the Internet, students and instructors anywhere in the world can explore each other's online courses and Web

The Library of Congress in Washington, D.C., is one of the world's greatest storehouses of knowledge. Visit its Web site at <http://lcweb.loc.gov> to tour its online collections. You'll have to visit in person to study the main reading room, depicted here.

sites. And anyone with modest computer skills can do things with technology that skilled technicians couldn't imagine a decade ago, including earning a degree from an online university.

So where just a few years ago, a research paper was typically a 10-page effort with a dozen sources—six books and six articles—a research project today can be that very same paper, or that paper moved to a Web site, or a Web site itself, or a hypertext, a multimedia presentation, a service-learning project, a CD-ROM, or any combination of these forms. College researchers, often working collaboratively, now can reach beyond the walls of their classrooms, "publishing" their work themselves and finding audiences potentially larger than those claimed by most printed journals.

Of course, the electronic tools that make all this possible do not supplant the need for clear, powerful, and responsible writing. Though you may be entering a brave, new electronically mediated world of learning and writing, you'll still need to know how to find a topic for a project, how to use research tools, and how to evaluate, organize, and document information. Even if we can't anticipate the kinds of work you'll do in college, we can offer reliable methods for managing research, whether you are preparing a traditional paper, an electronic project, or something in between. But don't let our advice restrict your creativity: the point of research is not to limit horizons, but to expand them.

E-Tips For more about research opportunities, see the Council on Undergraduate Research at <http://www.cur.org>. For undergraduate funding opportunities in the sciences, explore the Community of Science database at <http://fundingopps2.cos.com> or the list of research sponsors maintained at the University of Virginia <http://www.cs.virginia.edu/research/sponsors.html>. In the arts, check out the National Endowment for the Humanities at <http://www.neh.gov/grants/index.html>. For general advice about grants, see the Foundation Center at <http://www.fdncenter.org>.

46a
res

46a How do you claim a topic?

If you think of research as an active process of creating knowledge rather than a passive one of reporting information, you'll be more comfortable with the notion that almost every college project should be

supported by research. College projects can start intellectual conversations that last a lifetime; many students find themselves changing their majors and redirecting their careers as a result of work they began in a paper or a service project. That's normal and wonderful.

1 Size up an assignment carefully. In most cases, you'll receive a sheet of instructions when you are assigned a major college research project. Go over the sheet carefully, as if it were a contract, highlighting its key features. Consider issues such as the following.

- **Scope.** An instructor may give you options for presenting a project—as a conventional paper, an oral report, a Web project, a community service project. Be sure you understand what you must do and at what length. Look for word, page, or time limits at both ends (*no less than, no more than*).
- **Due dates.** There may be separate due dates for different stages of the project: topic proposal, annotated bibliography, outline, first draft or prototype, final version.
- **Presentation.** Note exactly what you must eventually turn in. The instructor may require items such as a research journal, transcripts of interviews, cover sheet, abstract, appendixes, bibliographies, illustrations, charts, links, and so on. Gather these important materials into a folder or portfolio from the start of the project or into an appropriate electronic storage device.
- **Format.** Note any specific requirements for margins, placement of page numbers, line spacing, titles, headings, illustrations, graphics, and so on. If an instructor doesn't give specific format instructions for a paper, model it on one of the professional styles explained in this book: MLA—for papers in English and the humanities; APA—for papers in psychology and the social sciences; CMS—for work in the humanities and other fields; CBE—for papers in the natural sciences; COS—for projects using many electronic sources. The formats for electronic projects may vary just as widely. An instructor may specify a particular platform, medium (video, audio, text), or software program.

46a

res

- **Documentation.** Follow your instructor's directions for documenting a project. Some may ask for MLA, APA, or COS documentation; others may let you choose any system, so long as you handle it consistently.
- **Collaboration.** Instructors may encourage or require collaboration on research projects. If that's the case with your project, read the ground rules carefully to see how the work may be divided and what reports and self-assessments may be required from project participants. Pay attention, especially, to how the group project itself will be evaluated.
- **Key words.** Take notice of key words in the assignment. Are you being asked to analyze, classify, define, discuss, evaluate, review, explain, compare, contrast, prove, disprove, persuade, survey? Each of these words means something different. (For a discussion of such terms, see pp. 115–16.)

2 Browse your topic area. When you can pick your own topic for a project, look for a subject, cause, or concern about which you can honestly say, "I'd love to learn much more about it" or "I want to do something about it." You'll do a better job if you have an investment in your project.

Avoid stale and general controversies that students have been writing about for decades. Don't be one of a half dozen students turning in projects on gun control, capital punishment, abortion, or legalization of marijuana. You'll find plenty of material on such subjects, but it's unlikely you'll add much to the debate.

Checklist 46.1

Your Browsing and Background Reading Should . . .

- Confirm whether you are, in fact, interested in your topic.
- Survey your subject so you can identify key issues and begin narrowing the scope of your project, as appropriate.
- Determine whether enough resources exist to support your project in the time available.

46a
res

Get closer to your subject by spending a few hours browsing, first in your library and then on the Web. One shrewd way to begin exploring an academic topic is to read a specialized encyclopedia, one that deals specifically with your subject. You'll learn enough about your topic to decide whether you really want to stay with it. Library reference rooms have dozens of specialized encyclopedias covering many fields, most of which are not yet available online. See the checklist below and ask reference librarians for their help.

Checklist 46.2

Specialized Encyclopedias

DOING A PAPER ON . . . ?	BEGIN BY CHECKING . . .
American history	*Encyclopedia of American History*
Anthropology, economics, sociology	*International Encyclopedia of the Social Sciences*
Art	*Encyclopedia of World Art*
Astronomy	*Encyclopedia of Astronomy*
Communications, mass media	*International Encyclopedia of Communication*
Computers	*Encyclopedia of Computer Science*
Crime	*Encyclopedia of Crime and Justice*
Economics	*Encyclopedia of American Economic History*
Ethical issues in life sciences	*Encyclopedia of Bioethics*
Environment	*Encyclopedia of the Environment*
Film	*International Encyclopedia of Film*
Health/medicine	*Health and Medicine Horizons*
History	*Dictionary of American History; Guide to Historical Literature*
Law	*The Guide to American Law*
Literature	*Cassell's Encyclopedia of World Literature*
Multiculturalism	*Encyclopedia of Multiculturalism*
Music	*The New Grove Dictionary of American Music*
Philosophy	*Dictionary of the History of Ideas; Encyclopedia of Philosophy*
Political science	*Encyclopedia of American Political History; Oxford Companion to Politics of the World*
Psychology, psychiatry	*International Encyclopedia of Psychiatry, Psychology, Psychoanalysis and Neurology*

46a
res

Religion	*The Encyclopedia of Religion; Encyclopedia Judaica; New Catholic Encyclopedia*
Rhetoric	*Encyclopedia of Rhetoric*
Science	*McGraw-Hill Encyclopedia of Science and Technology*
Social sciences	*International Encyclopedia of the Social Sciences*
Sociology	*Encyclopedia of Sociology*

To get a feel for your topic area, examine books or journals in the field. What are the major issues? Who is affected by them? Who is writing on the topic? Find two or three books on the subject you are researching and compare their bibliographies. Books that appear in more than one bibliography are likely to be key sources on the subject.

Check out your subject on the Internet too, exploring both newsgroups and Web sites. For example, if your subject is related to religion in the United States, you will find dozens of newsgroups under <alt.religion>, < soc.religion>, or < talk.religion>. Not all such sources are equally helpful, but remember that at this point you're simply deciding whether an issue warrants your attention; you aren't seeking research material.

E-Tips You can usually access newsgroups from your Web browser and explore them with a search engine. To search Usenet groups, try <http://groups.google.com>.

46b How do you plan a project?

You shouldn't wait to organize your project. From the start, you'll need a plan to deal with the complexities of a research project that may draw on many different kinds of sources and technologies.

46b
res

■ **1 Write a research proposal.** For some research assignments, you may be asked to prepare a proposal that outlines your project. A proposal enables an instructor to give you the help and direction you may need. Such topic proposals will vary in scope. The prospectus for a short project might fit on a single page; that for a senior thesis might run many pages. Any proposal, however, will likely include some of the following elements, all worth considering even if you do not have to prepare a formal document.

- **Identification of a topic or topic area.** Explain your topic area and, if required, provide a reason for selecting this subject. See Chapter 2 for detailed advice.

- **A hypothesis, research question, or thesis.** State your hypothesis or question clearly. If required, discuss the hypothesis in some detail and defend its significance, relevance, or appropriateness. Be prepared to explain any premises or assumptions that support your basic claim(s). See Chapter 3 for help in formulating a thesis.

- **Background information or review of literature.** Identify the books, articles, and other materials you expect to read to gain background information on your subject. For major projects, you may need to do a thorough literature review, surveying all major work done in your research area.

- **A review of research resources.** Identify the types of materials you'll need for your project and determine their availability: books, articles, newspapers, documents, manuscripts, recordings, videos, artworks, databases, online sources, and so on. You might list these items in a preliminary bibliography. See Chapter 47 for much more about research resources.

- **A description of your research methodology.** Outline the procedures you will follow in your research, and justify your choice of methodology.

- **An assessment of the ethics of your project if it involves experiments on people or animals.** Most universities have institutional review boards that govern research with human or animal subjects. Your instructor will likely tell you about these rules, especially in fields where such research is common, such as psychology and the social sciences.

- **A schedule or timeline.** For more information about scheduling a project, see Section 46c.

46b
res

E-Tips

For detailed advice about writing a serious proposal in pursuit of a research grant, see Sea Coast Web Design's grant writing guide at <http://www.npguides.org>.

2 Decide how you will handle your research materials. If you'll rely chiefly on printed sources, you can still use a system of photocopies, note cards, and bibliography cards to manage much of the project (see Section 46b-4). But most writers now routinely use both printed and electronic sources and rely on their word processors or database research programs (such as *TakeNote!* or *ProCite*) to organize their work. Many projects today also require charts, graphs, and illustrations, some of them created on software, some downloaded from electronic sources. To store all this data, you'll want to rely both on the hard disk in your computer and a computer disk, Zip disk, or CD-R for backup.

Consider other kinds of resources you may need for your project, including any software or electronic equipment such as tape recorders, digital cameras, and printers. Consider, too, where to keep all the stuff you accumulate. A rugged portfolio with ample pockets and safe storage for printouts, notebooks and disks is a good investment. Be sure it bears appropriate contact information in case you lose it. And put such information on all your computer disks; sooner or later, you'll forget an important disk in a machine at a computer facility.

3 Prepare a working bibliography. It doesn't matter whether you are using print or electronic sources or whether your project will culminate in a paper, a Web site, a slide show, or a brochure— you need to know where your information came from. The best way to keep track of all your various resources is to develop a working or annotated bibliography as you move your way through your numerous sources (see pp. 105–6).

Keep track of every one of the sources either with your word processor, an electronic database program, or a stack of 3-by-5-inch bibliography cards, one source per card. Typical bibliography cards look like those on the next page.

46b
res

```
1034
C67
1991
PCL Stacks

Corbett, H. Dickson, and Bruce L. Wilson.

     Testing, Reform, and Rebellion. Norwood: Ablex,

     1991.
```

```
Sierra Club. "Earth Day 2002." 22 April 2002. 23

     April 2002 < http://www.sierraclub.org/

     earthday2002>.
```

Eventually you will need the bibliographical information you have gathered to generate the Works Cited or References pages required of every standard academic paper. No matter how you record it, each bibliographical record should contain all the information necessary to find a source again later.

The bibliographical information you need will vary considerably for books, articles, newspapers, and electronic sources. For the exact information required, check the MLA, APA, CMS, CBE, and COS Models in Chapters 53 through 57. When using a Web page, always record the full electronic address and write down the date you viewed the site.

In some cases, writers will not record their sources because they can print out a list of potential items from online library catalogs, electronic databases, and Web search engines. This strategy can be risky because the information on a printout is usually insufficient for preparing a Works Cited or References list. Printouts can also be misplaced easily among the stack of papers a research project typically generates. So if you rely on such printouts for bibliographical information, keep the lists in one place and know what's on them.

4 Make photocopies and note cards for printed sources.

Photocopy or print out passages from sources that you expect to quote from directly and extensively. While a case can be made for taking all notes on cards, the fact is that most researchers—both faculty members and students—now routinely either photocopy or download their major sources when they can. In such cases, be sure your copies are complete and legible (especially any page numbers). When you are copying from a book or magazine, take a moment to duplicate the title page and publication/editorial staff information. You'll be glad you did later.

In all cases, attach basic bibliographical information directly to photocopies and printouts so that you know their source, making sure each document is keyed somehow to a full bibliography card or record. That way, you'll later be able to connect information and source easily. Use highlighter pens to mark passages in photocopies and printouts that you expect to refer to later, and keep all these materials in a folder. Never highlight material or write comments in margins of library books.

Even when you rely heavily on copied material, you may still need to record information on index cards. While 3-by-5-inch cards are fine for bibliographic entries, larger ones work better for notes. Be sure each note card for a source includes the author's last name or a short title so that you can connect the notes with the right bibliography card. For example, a note card recording information from Corbett and Wilson's *Testing, Reform, and Rebellion* might be headed simply "Corbett, *Testing*," since you have a bibliography card with fuller information on the book (see p. 682).

Don't crowd too much information on a single note card; it's more efficient to record only one major point, quotation, or statistic on each. That way, later, you will be able to arrange cards into an outline of your work, with data exactly where you need it. For the same reason, write on only one side of a note card. Information on the flip side of a card is easily ignored.

Double-check bibliographical information, especially the spelling of names, as they may be difficult to recall or guess. Accuracy in transcribing names will help you and your reader.

Electronic programs are also available to help you keep notes. These programs often include helpful features for finding and sorting information.

46b
res

Checklist 46.3

Information for Note Cards

• Author's last name and a shortened version of the source's title (for accurate reference to the corresponding bibliography card)

• A heading to identify the nature of the information on the card

• The actual data or information, correctly summarized, paraphrased, or quoted

• Page numbers or correct World Wide Web address for locating the source

5 Print or download electronic sources. How you record data from an electronic source will depend on how you expect to use it. If you're simply looking for facts, you may want to treat it like a printed source, recording the data on note cards or printing out the source itself. Printouts may be essential from sources whose content changes from day to day—such as Web sites, newsgroups, sessions on Interchange, or online conversations. Some of this material may be archived electronically, but it is always safe to print out material you will cite, carefully recording all necessary bibliographical information on the sheets. Also be sure to record when you made the printout, since most documentation for electronic material requires a date of access.

It is possible to copy many electronic sources directly to disk. The finder on your computer may already have folders where you can store text files, movies, pictures, music files, and Web sites. Label any folders you create carefully so that you or a co-worker on the project can find information easily. Do back up all such materials, keeping them, for example, on both a disk or CD and your hard drive. Be especially careful that you know where all downloaded images come from and who owns their copyrights. As you do with printed sources, you will have to document and credit all copyrighted pictures, photographs, and images borrowed from the Web, whether you use the image in a paper or in an electronic project. To use copyrighted material in your own electronic publications, you must get permission from the holder of the copyright.

46b
res

A particularly efficient way to organize information gathered mainly from the Web is to use your browser's "bookmarks" or "favorites" feature. Bookmarking a site simply adds it to a menu list available on the browser so that you can return to the item easily. Web browsers also enable you to sort bookmarked items in various ways and even to annotate them briefly.

6 Consider collaborative research. You may be expected or invited to work as part of a team for some college projects. If so, use the occasion to learn how to work productively to achieve a common goal.

You'll quickly discover that careful management is an important part of any collaborative effort. In a group you may want to discuss questions such as the following. See Section 4c for more on collaborative writing.

- What research and writing skills might your project require?
- What qualities and skills should you look for in your colleagues?
- How will you organize your team?
- How will decisions be made?
- Who—if anyone—will be in charge?
- How will you communicate and coordinate your efforts?
- How will you schedule the work, and how will you deal with deviations from the schedule?
- How will you assess your work and share the credit?

46c How do you schedule a project?

Few projects follow a simple sequence from start to finish, and most projects have to meet tight deadlines. Because projects have to move forward, you may need to schedule your work carefully.

1 Determine the hard points of your project. *Hard points* are those features of a project you can't change; they are usually described on the assignment sheet. For instance, when an instructor asks for a 10-page APA-style paper on genetic engineering, due in two weeks, you have four hard points.

1. Format: 10-page paper
2. Topic: genetic engineering
3. Documentation style: APA
4. Due date: two weeks from today

All four points will shape your planning, but perhaps none more so than the due date. You know that 10 pages in two weeks is a lot of work.

Many college assignments will have only one due date: the day the project must be turned in. When that's the case, you'll have to schedule the rest of the project yourself. But take that final due date seriously; instructors rarely tolerate late work.

However, some instructors may give you a series of due dates for a major project, asking that you submit items such as the following at specific times.

- Project proposal, prospectus, or thesis
- Annotated working bibliography
- Storyboards (for projects with graphics)

46c
res

- First draft
- Web site design specifications
- Responses to peer editing

When you are given several due dates, they can be arranged in sequence to form a preliminary timeline into which the remaining hard points of your project can be fitted.

PROJECT PROPOSAL		ANNOTATED BIBLIOGRAPHY		FIRST DRAFT		FINAL DRAFT
Oct. 2	→	Oct. 16	→	Oct. 23	→	Nov. 6

2 Create a calendar. Once you have outlined your writing process and established the hard points of your project, you are ready to sketch out a calendar for your work.

To create a calendar, mark down the due dates of a project, leaving enough space between them to list the activities necessary to meet those deadlines. Then estimate the time available for each step in the project. Here's a calendar for a paper with four major due dates and a variety of support activities. You would have to determine an appropriate completion date for each activity.

CALENDAR: RESEARCH PAPER
_____ Choosing a topic and defining the project
_____ Determining campus resources
_____ Drafting the proposal
Topic proposal: Due October 2

_____ Generating a working bibliography
_____ Gathering and evaluating materials
Annotated bibliography: Due October 16

_____ Summarizing and paraphrasing sources
_____ Organizing/designing the paper
_____ Drafting the project
First draft: Due October 23

_____ Getting/responding to feedback on the draft
_____ Refining/rewriting the project
_____ Documenting the project
_____ Preparing the final materials
Final draft: Due November 6

Your calendar should not be much more detailed; you'll waste time if you try to account for every movement in an unpredictable process.

You can also mark off your research project on an actual calendar—the kind that provides a box for listing each day's appointments and activities. Or record your due dates on a PDA device, using its alarm function to remind you of due dates several days before they arrive. Whatever type of calendar you create, allow some slack toward the end to make up for the time you'll likely lose early in the project.

E-Tips You can find software programs now to help you design and organize your research projects. These database products typically have a number of integrated features. They help you to outline a project; they keep track of your notes; they format your bibliography items in proper MLA, APA, or other documentation form; they help you upload your notes either to a word-processing program or to an HTML file you can use in building a Web site. Fortunately, these programs (such as *TakeNote!*) are easy to learn and to use. You might look into one at the outset of a major project.

A screen from a software program designed to support research might look like this "Card Editor" from *TakeNote!*

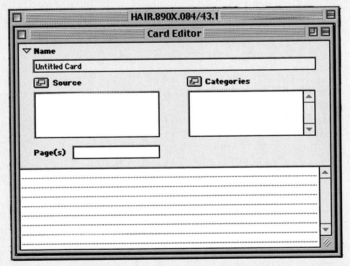

Notice that the software enables you to assign categories to the information you record on the card—a useful way of keeping track of the information in any number of related sources.

Electronic note-taking programs overcome some of the limitations of cards. They will prompt you to provide the information essential to track a source, and they may help you find and rearrange information more ingeniously and quickly. A disadvantage of an electronic database is that it resides on a machine. Unless you have a laptop computer, you may not be able to take the program with you to a library.

46c
res

CHAPTER 47

How Do You Find Information?

As you begin a research paper or project, your goal is to find potential sources and to prepare a *working bibliography,* that is, a preliminary list of materials related to your topic (see pp. 105–6 for an example). Today, you can tap in to more information than ever before. By the same token, the enormous range of possibilities can be intimidating. In this section we outline strategies to use in finding information.

We urge you to be organized and persistent in your research. Don't quit an investigation just because you haven't located materials you want. And don't be satisfied, either, if your initial research produces more sources or data than you expect. That first pass is liable to be superficial; always push deeper into the archives, libraries, and networks. Be curious and take risks.

47a How do you use a library?

A first priority for any college student is to learn the physical arrangement of campus libraries and research facilities. Don't be intimidated. Take a tour of these buildings, study the collections, and, above all, get to know the research librarians.

1 Explore your library. Be sure you can locate the following places, features, and services important to your research.

- **Online catalog.** Learn how to use these terminals, which are the pathway into your library's collection of books, journals, and other materials. In addition, many libraries have comprehensive Web sites with links to powerful indexes, databases, and online reference tools. Explore the site supported by your own campus library or examine those posted by other colleges and universities. Ask your librarian to direct you to sites helpful to your own research.
- **Card catalog.** Most libraries now have electronic catalogs. But online terminals sometimes may not cover older library materials or

special collections. They may still be listed only in a card catalog. Find out if that is the case. And know where the card catalog is located.

- **Reference room.** Study this useful collection carefully. Notice how its materials are arranged and where heavily used items (encyclopedias, almanacs, phone books, databases) are located. Find out, too, where the reference librarian is stationed.
- **Databases and bibliographies.** Ask your librarian to point out the location of databases and important print bibliographies in the library reference room. Research databases will be arrayed around terminals, with information either online or accessed via CD-ROM disks. Older print bibliographies in various fields will often be large multi-volume collections.
- **Microforms collections.** Many important materials including documents, newspapers, and periodicals are collected on rolls of film called *microfilm* or rectangular sheets of film called *microfiche.* Know where these collections are, how they are arranged, and how you can gain access to them.
- **Periodical collections.** You'll need to know both where current journals and periodicals are located and where older bound or microfilmed copies of these materials are kept.
- **Newspapers.** As with periodicals, current newspapers are usually available in a reading room. Older newspapers will often be available chiefly on microfilm, and then you are likely to have access to only a limited number of major papers, depending on the size of your library collection. Online archives of newspapers are a recent innovation: you won't be able to search back more than a few years.
- **Special collections.** Libraries will often have rooms or sections that contain rare or special items such as pictures and photographs, maps, government documents, and so on. Learn the location of any important collections in your library.
- **Audio/video collections.** Many libraries now have extensive holdings of audio/video materials as well as facilities for listening to or viewing CDs, DVDs, tapes, and video disks. Learn where these

47a
library

collections are located, where and how they are cataloged, and how to use the playback equipment.

- **Circulation desk/library services.** Learn what circulation desk services are available to a researcher. For instance, you can usually recall materials already on loan if you need them for your project. Most libraries participate in interlibrary loan programs that enable you to acquire materials your library may not own. (These orders take time, so don't wait until the last minute to make such a request.)
- **Directories.** Large libraries can be complicated. Look for directories or pamphlets to help you locate collections. Note how the collections are organized, where library call numbers are displayed, how the shelves themselves are arranged, and any other aspects of the physical arrangement.
- **Photocopiers/computers/study areas.** Find out where in the library you can reliably copy information. It's smart to track down two or three copying locations since copiers get heavy use. Also check to see whether computer terminals or ports are available in the library and whether certain areas are reserved for study and research.
- **Study carrels.** Many colleges and university libraries provide carrels in the library for people pursuing serious research. Find out whether you are eligible for such a carrel.

2　Use traditional and online library catalogs efficiently.

Almost all libraries now provide access to their resources via computer terminals or the World Wide Web. But electronic catalogs sometimes cover only a library's more recent acquisitions. To do a thorough job, be prepared to move back and forth from computer terminal to card file during your research.

47a
library

In traditional card catalogs, books and other materials can usually be located by author, title, and key word. Electronic catalogs can be searched by similar categories, but more quickly and with more powerful options. Electronic catalogs can indicate whether books have been checked out, lost, or recalled. If your library has an electronic catalog, study its screens and learn its basic search techniques and commands.

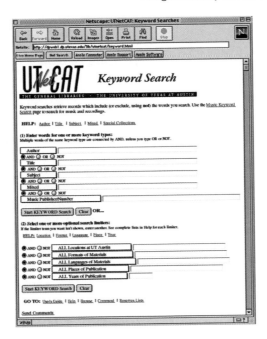

The search menu screen for the online library catalog at the University of Texas at Austin, shown above, can be viewed at <http://utdirect.utexas.edu/lib/utnetcat/kword.html>.

Notice that the screen supports a variety of keyword search combinations and permits a user to pick the location, format, and language of the research material. Librarians find that most people use online catalogs by using keyword searches. For much more about keyword searches, see Section 47d.

E-Tips

For a list of online library catalogs, examine the LIBCAT Web site at <http://www.metronet.lib.mn.us/lc/lca.cfm>.

47a
library

An online catalog offers detailed information about most library holdings. On screen, you'll often be given a short entry first—typically the author, title, publishing information, date, and call number—with an option to select a fuller listing. The full listing describes additional features of the item—whether it is illustrated or has an index or a bibliography.

Most card and online catalog use subject headings determined by the Library of Congress and compiled in the multi-volume *Library of Congress Subject Headings,* commonly known by its abbreviation *LCSH.* Be sure to consult this volume (or its electronic equivalent) in the reference room of your library at the start of your research: it will tell you how your topic is described and treated in the library catalog. On any given subject card or screen, pay attention, too, to any additional subject headings offered because these may be keywords to use for additional searches. For instance, if you were exploring "hieroglyphics," a listing on that topic might offer the keywords "Egyptian language—grammar" and "Egyptian language—writing." You might not have considered using those terms in a keyword search of your own.

SUMMARY   *Online Catalogs*

For a book, online catalogs typically list

• Call number and library location

• Author, title, publisher, and date of publication

• The number of pages and the book's physical size

• Whether the book is illustrated

• Whether it contains a bibliography and an index

• The subject headings under which it is listed

47b How do you find research materials?

47b
info

Not long ago, writers often worried about finding enough sources for a research project. Today, resources on almost any topic can seem overwhelming—and that is why it helps to know exactly what kinds of materials provide what types of information. In this section we survey the basic search tools and strategies you might use on a project.

1 Locate suitable bibliographies. You will save time if you can locate an existing bibliography—preferably an annotated bibliography—

on your subject. Bibliographies are lists of books, articles, and other documentary materials that deal with particular subjects or subject areas. Ask a reference room librarian whether a bibliography on your specific subject has been compiled. If not, consult one of the more general bibliographies available in almost every field.

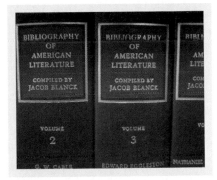

Chart 47.1
Types of Printed Bibliographies

- **Selective bibliographies** usually list the best-known or most respected books and articles in a subject area.

- **Annotated bibliographies** briefly describe the works they list and may evaluate them.

- **Annual bibliographies** catalog the works produced within a field or discipline in a given year.

Although printed bibliographies are losing ground to electronic indexes and databases, they are still available on many subjects. Also be sure to look for bibliographies at the back of scholarly books, articles, and dissertations you examine in your research. Usually compiled by researchers themselves, such bibliographies offer a focused look at a specific topic.

Only a few of the hundreds of bibliographic resources in specific disciplines are listed below.

Checklist 47.1
Bibliographies

DOING A PAPER ON . . . ?	CHECK THIS BIBLIOGRAPHY . . .
American history	*Bibliographies in American History*
Anthropology	*Anthropological Bibliographies: A Selected Guide*
Art	*Guide to the Literature of Art History*
	(Continued)

47b
info

Bibliographies *(Continued)*

DOING A PAPER ON . . . ?	CHECK THIS BIBLIOGRAPHY . . .
Astronomy	*A Guide to the Literature of Astronomy; Astronomy and Astrophysics: A Bibliographic Guide*
Classics	*Greek and Roman Authors: A Checklist of Criticism*
Communications	*Communication: A Guide to Information Sources*
Engineering	*Science and Engineering Literature*
Literature	*MLA International Bibliography*
Mathematics	*Using the Mathematical Literature*
Music	*Music Reference and Research Materials*
Philosophy	*A Bibliography of Philosophical Bibliographies*
Physics	*Use of Physics Literature*
Psychology	*Harvard List of Books in Psychology*
Social work	*Social Work Education: A Bibliography*

For general subjects, electronic subject guides offered by major public libraries can offer useful lists of print and electronic resources on a vast number of subjects and disciplines, from art and architecture to women's studies. You may find the following Web sites especially helpful.

- New York Public Library Resource Guides
  <http://www.nypl.org/admin/genweb/guides.html>
- Columbia University Library Web "Selected Subject Guides and Resources"
  <http://www.columbia.edu/cu/lweb/eguides>
- The University of California at Berkeley Libraries
  <http://www.lib.berkeley.edu>
- The University of Chicago "Libraries, Collections, and Subjects"
  <http://www.lib.uchicago.edu/e/lcs.html>
- The University of Texas at Austin
  <http://www.lib.utexas.edu/subject>
- The University of Virginia Subject Guides
  <http://www.lib.virginia.edu/resguide.html>

47b
info

2 Locate suitable indexes to search the periodical literature. Indexes list important items that cannot be recorded in a library catalog: journal articles, magazine pieces, and stories from newspapers, for instance. Such material is called the *periodical literature* on a subject.

You shouldn't undertake any college-level research paper without surveying this extensive body of information. For example, to explore the subject of school vouchers, you'd likely want information from magazines such as *Newsweek* and *U.S. News & World Report* and newspapers such as the *New York Times* and *Washington Post*. To find such information, you would go to indexes, not traditional library catalogs.

In the past, all periodical indexes were printed works, and you may still have to use these helpful volumes to find older sources. For more recent materials, however, you'll likely use electronic indexes. Many indexes now offer not only the basic bibliographical information on an article— who published it, where, and when—but an abstract of the piece or even the full text. Depending on copyright rules, you can print out the text, download it to your computer, or have it sent to you via email.

You may want to begin periodical searches with general and multidisciplinary indexes such as the following.

Readers' Guide to Periodical Literature (print)

Readers' Guide Abstracts (electronic)

ArticleFirst (electronic)

Ethnic NewsWatch (electronic)

Expanded Academic ASAP (electronic)

LEXIS-NEXIS Academic Universe (electronic)

All major academic fields and majors have individual indexes for their periodical literature, most of them computerized. Because new indexes may be added to a library's collection at any time, check with your reference librarian or your library's Web site about the best sources available for any given subject.

Checklist 47.2
Indexes and Databases

DOING A PAPER ON . . . ?	CHECK THIS INDEX . . .
Anthropology	*Anthropological Literature*
Architecture	*Avery Index*
Art	*Art Abstracts*
Biography	*Biography Index*
Biology	*Biological and Agricultural Abstracts; BIOSIS Previews*
Business	*Business Periodicals Index; ABI/Inform*

(Continued)

47b
info

Indexes and Databases *(Continued)*

DOING A PAPER ON . . . ?	CHECK THIS INDEX . . .
Chemistry	*CAS*
Computer science	*Computer Literature Index*
Current affairs	*LEXIS-NEXIS*
Economics	*PAIS (Public Affairs Information Service); EconLit*
Education	*Education Index; ERIC (Educational Resources Information Center)*
Engineering	*INSPEC*
Film	*Film Index International; Art Index*
History	*Historical Abstracts; America: History and Life*
Humanities	*FRANCIS; Humanities Abstracts; Humanities Index*
Law	*LegalTrac*
Literature	*Essay and General Literature Index; MLA Bibliography; Contemporary Authors*
Mathematics	*MathSciNet*
Medicine	*MEDLINE*
Music	*Music Index; RILM Abstracts of Music Literature*
Philosophy	*Philosopher's Index*
Psychology	*Psychological Abstracts; PsycINFO*
Public affairs	*PAIS*
Physics	*INSPEC*
Religion	*ATLA Religion Database*
Science	*General Science Index; General Science Abstracts*
Social sciences	*Social Science & Humanities Index; Social Sciences Index; Social Sciences Abstracts*
Technology	*Applied Science & Technology Abstracts*
Women	*Contemporary Women's Issues*

47b
info

Ordinarily you can get access to indexes in your library reference room. Electronic tools may also be available via online library catalogs or Web sites. Most indexes, printed or electronic, are relatively easy to use—if you read the guides that come with them.

Electronic indexes usually support title, author, or keyword searches (see Section 47d), but they may also permit searching by other "fields"— that is, categories by which data is entered. For example, a database may be searchable not only by author and title but also by publisher, place of publication, subject heading, accession number, or government document number. Powerful indexes and databases such as *LEXIS-NEXIS* may require special commands and search techniques.

Checklist 47.3

Searching an Electronic Index or Database

- Be sure you are logged onto the right index. A library terminal may provide access to several different databases or indexes. Find the one appropriate for your subject.

- Read the description of the index to find out how to access its information. Not all databases and indexes work the same way.

- When searching by keyword, check whether a list of subject headings is available. To save time, match your search terms to those on the list before you begin.

- Try synonyms if an initial keyword search turns up too few items.

Expect some frustrations with any index. Printed volumes can be clumsy to handle, incorrectly shelved, dusty, and poorly printed. With electronic sources, you may have trouble logging on, finding the right keyword, or narrowing your search. Good research still takes patience.

3 Consult biographical resources. Quite often in preparing a research project, you'll need information about famous people, living and dead. Powerful sources are available to help you in the reference room. Good places to start are the *Biography Index: A Cumulative Index to Biographic Material in Books and Magazines, Bio-Base, LEXIS-NEXIS, Current Biography,* and *The McGraw-Hill Encyclopedia of World Biography.*

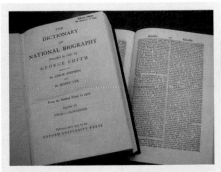

There are also *Who's Who* volumes for living British, American, and world notables, as well as volumes for African Americans and women. Deceased figures

47b
info

may appear in *Who Was Who*. Probably the two most famous dictionaries of biography are the *Dictionary of National Biography* (British) and the *Dictionary of American Biography*.

On the World Wide Web, you might look at the database maintained by the Arts and Entertainment Network program *Biography* at <http://www.biography.com>. For information about writers and authors, check the Internet Public Library's "Authors" page at <http://www.ipl.org/ref/RR/static/hum60.10.00.html>. For the wisdom of famous people, check out the Web version of the 1919 version of *Bartlett's Familiar Quotations* at <http://www.bartleby.com/100> or, for more recent remarks, *The Quotation Page* at <http://www.quotationspage.com>. To search for private individuals, you can use features such as *Yahoo!*'s "people search" on the World Wide Web. It provides addresses and phone numbers with almost frightening ease.

Checklist 47.4

Biographical Information

YOUR SUBJECT IS IN . . .?	CHECK THIS SOURCE . . .
Art	*Index to Artistic Biography*
Education	*Biographical Dictionary of American Educators*
Music	*The New Grove Dictionary of Music and Musicians*
Politics	*Politics in America; Almanac of American Politics*
Psychology	*Biographical Dictionary of Psychology*
Religion	*Dictionary of American Religious Biography*
Science	*Dictionary of Scientific Biography*

YOUR SUBJECT IS . . .?	CHECK THIS SOURCE . . .
African	*Dictionary of African Biography*
African American	*Dictionary of American Negro Biography*
Asian	*Encyclopedia of Asian History*
Australian	*Australian Dictionary of Biography*
Canadian	*Dictionary of Canadian Biography*
Female	*Index to Women; Notable American Women*
Mexican American	*Mexican American Biographies; Chicano Scholars and Writers: A Bibliographic Directory*

47b
info

4 Locate statistics. Statistics about every imaginable topic are available in library reference rooms and online. Be sure to find up-to-date and reliable figures.

Checklist 47.5

Statistics

TO FIND . . .	CHECK THIS SOURCE . . .
General statistics	*World Almanac; Current Index to Statistics* (electronic)
Statistics about the United States	*Historical Statistics of the United States; Statistical Abstract of the United States; STAT-USA* (electronic); *GPO Access* (electronic)
World information	*The Statesman's Yearbook; National Intelligence Factbook; UN Demographic Yearbook; UNESCO Statistical Yearbook*
Business facts	*Handbook of Basic Economic Statistics; Survey of Current Business; Dow Jones–Irwin Business Almanac*
Public opinion polls	*Gallup Poll*
Population data	*Population Index* (electronic)

Also consult resources such as *The Internet Public Library* at <http://ipl.sils.umich.edu/div/subject>. Even *The Old Farmer's Almanac,* chock full of information, is on the Web at <http://www.almanac.com>.

 E-TipS

When you are seeking factual information, check out <iTools.com>. It offers a dictionary, a thesaurus, a translator, a people search, maps, and much more—including an email discussion group search tool. For statistics from more than 70 agencies of the federal government, explore FedStats at <**http://www.fedstats.gov**>. The scope of information available at this site is staggering.

**47b
info**

5 Check news sources. Sometimes you'll need information from newspapers, particularly when your subject is current and your aim argumentative or persuasive. For information earlier than the mid-1990s

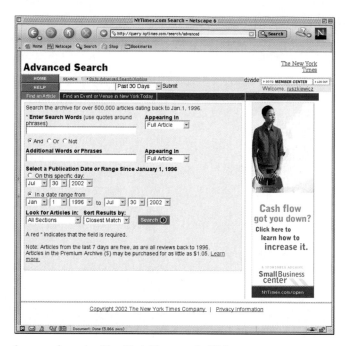

Search screen from the *New York Times on the Web.*

you'll have to rely on printed papers or microfilm copies since electronic newspapers and news services are a recent phenomenon. When you know the date of a particular event, however, you can usually locate the information you want. If your subject isn't an event, you may have to trace it through an index or online archive. Only a few printed papers are fully indexed. The one newspaper you are most likely to encounter in most American libraries is the *New York Times,* usually available on microfilm. The *New York Times Index* provides chronological summaries of articles on a given subject. A reference librarian can guide you to other news indexes available in your library—products such as *Newsbank* or *InfoTrac.*

For very current events, you can search the hundreds of newspapers and news services currently online. (The search page from one such newspaper—the *New York Times on the Web*—appears above.) Online news sources differ significantly from their print or video counterparts both in coverage and interactivity. What they offer is immediate information from a wide range of sources. You can consult online news resources from around the globe and with many points of view. As with any source, you must exercise caution when reporting information you find on the Web, making sure that the source is rep-

47b

info

utable (see Section 48a). The following online news resources are worth consulting.

NEWS RESOURCE	ADDRESS
CNN Interactive	<http://www.cnn.com>
C-SPAN Online	<http://c-span.org>
Fox News	<http://foxnews.com>
London Times	<http://www.thetimes.co.uk>
MSNBC	<http://msnbc.com/news>
New York Times	<http://www.nytimes.com>
Reuters	<http://reuters.com>
Time.com	<http://www.time.com/time>
USA Today News	<http://usatoday.com>
Washington Times	<http://washtimes.com>

A directory such as *Yahoo!* at <http://www.yahoo.com> can point you to hundreds of online newspapers of every sort. Check under its "News & Media" category. You may have to register to use some online newspapers and pay to download archived materials.

6 Check book and film reviews. To locate reviews of books, see *Book Review Digest* (1905), *Book Review Index* (1965), or *Current Book Review Citations* (1976). *Book Review Digest* lists fewer reviews than the other two collections, but it summarizes those it does include—a useful feature. Many electronic periodical indexes also catalog book reviews. Enter "book reviews" on a search engine or directory, and you will turn up many sites, such as the *New York Times Sunday Book Review* at <http://www.nytimes.com/books/yr/mo/day/home/contents.html> and *The New York Review of Books* at <http://www.nybooks.com>.

For film reviews and criticism, see the printed volumes *Film Review Index* (1986) and *Film Criticism: An Index to Critics' Anthologies* (1975) as well as the electronic index *Film Index International.* Numerous Web sites are devoted to films and film reviews; *Yahoo!* alone lists more than 500 sites (of greatly varying quality) under "movie reviews."

7 Write or email professional organizations. Almost every subject, cause, concept, or idea is represented by a professional organization, society, bureau, office, or lobby. It makes good sense to write or email an appropriate organization for information on your topic; ask for pamphlets, leaflets, reports, and so on. Many such groups offer detailed information on their Web sites. For mailing addresses of organizations,

47b info

consult the *Encyclopedia of Associations*, published by Gale Research. Use a search engine to find Web sites.

Also remember that the U.S. government publishes huge amounts of information on just about every subject of public interest. Check the *Index to U.S. Government Periodicals* or the *Monthly Catalog of United States Government Publications* for listings. Or use a Web site such as *Fedworld Information Network* at <http://www.fedworld.gov> to look for the material you need.

■ 8 Consult collections of images. Online resources make it possible to locate images you may need for your research projects. Some search engines—such as *AltaVista, Google,* and *Excite*—look for images (as well as audio and video clips). Among the numerous collections of images and clip art on the Web are the following.

IMAGE SITE	ADDRESS
About.com	<http://webclipart.about.com>

Surveys clip art and graphic sites on the Web.

GraphicMaps.com	<http://www.graphicmaps.com>

Provides information about maps on the Web.

Image Finder	<http://sunsite.berkeley.edu/ ImageFinder>

Searches various collections of images.

The Picture Collection	<http://www.thepicturecollection.com/>

Presents images from the Time, Inc. collection.

Note that you may have to pay to acquire or use some images. You'll also need to document any borrowed images you include in your finished project, just as you cite and document other research sources. See Section 21e-2 for more details.

47c
online

47c How do you choose electronic resources?

In the past decade, the number of electronic sources has exploded, but many of these items were not designed with researchers and scholars in mind. For example, the very strength of the World Wide Web— its robust connection of millions of computers, files, and databases—is also its scholarly weakness. It presents a jumble of information, leaving users to screen nuggets of gold from mountains of slag. So it's essential that your searches be efficient and critical.

In this section we explain the basic tools and resources you should use when sorting through screens of electronic information.

■ **1 Check the World Wide Web.** The World Wide Web is a hypertext pathway into the vast resources of the Internet. Web browser software such as *Netscape Navigator* or *Microsoft Internet Explorer* presents information via "pages" that can contain text, graphics, and sound as well as hypertext links. Browsers also support email, Usenet groups, and other forms of electronic communication. The Web can distribute just about any information that fits on a screen, including photo archives, artwork, maps, audio clips, charts, magazines—and even film clips.

Understand, however, that the Web is not a library designed to support research. Online information is not (like library resources) systematically cataloged, edited, or reviewed. So you can't treat the Web like a library or assume that information you find there is always reliable. Apply your best critical reading skills to any site you visit. (See Section 48a for advice about evaluating all types of sources.)

You'll usually locate information on the Internet using search engines and directories—tools that help you cull information from the hundreds of millions of Web pages now online. Such guides, constantly being refined and upgraded, are readily available; just click the "search" button on your Web browser. But you have to use them properly. Among the best known are the following.

SEARCH TOOLS	ADDRESS
About.com	<http://about.com>
AltaVista	<http://altavista.com>
AOL Anywhere	<http://www.aol.com>
Ask Jeeves	<http://askjeeves.com>
Dogpile	<http://www.dogpile.com>
Excite	<http://excite.com>
Go	<http://go.com>
Google	<http://www.google.com>
HotBot	<http://hotbot.lycos.com>
Lycos	<http://www.lycos.com>
ProFusion	<http://profusion.com>
WebCrawler	<http://www.webcrawler.com>
Yahoo!	<http://www.yahoo.com>

47c
online

The basic tool of many search engines and databases is the keyword search. For keyword search strategies, see Section 47d. However, many

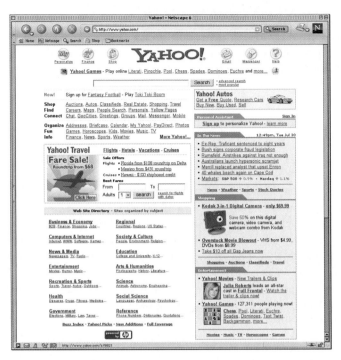

Opening screen for *Yahoo!* (Reproduced with permission of Yahoo! Inc. ©1998 by Yahoo! Inc. *Yahoo!* and the *Yahoo!* logo are trademarks of Yahoo! Inc.)

Web directories such as *Yahoo!* also enable you to search the Web by categories. The *Yahoo!* opening screen, shown above, presents a series of general categories that may narrow the topic you hope to explore.

Commercial Web search engines aren't the only resource for finding information on the Web. Libraries, universities, and government agencies have created hundreds of reference tools with more scholarly goals. Here are just a few places to look. (Be warned that Web addresses change frequently.)

47c
online

REFERENCE SITE	ADDRESS
Books on the Internet	<http://www.lib.utexas.edu/Libs/PCL/Etext.html>
EServer	<http://eserver.org>
Infomine	<http://infomine.ucr.edu>
The Internet Public Library	<http://www.ipl.org>
Librarians' Index to the Internet	<http://lii.org>
Library of Congress Research Centers	<http://lcweb.loc.gov/rr/research-centers.html>

Note that some search engine sites include online guides to both basic and advanced search techniques. Take a few minutes to read such "help" files to discover the remarkable and changing features of these highly competitive tools.

Two points to consider: (1) Web engines and directories all work a little differently and have different strengths. (2) No single search engine covers everything on the Internet. So always use several search engines to explore a subject to be sure you get adequate coverage. Don't be satisfied with your initial searches, even when they supply lots of information. Another combination of keywords or a different search path might provide still better material. If you get an unexpected response from a search, ask why. Look for clues in the results you receive (or don't receive). Check spellings and try synonyms. Don't give up.

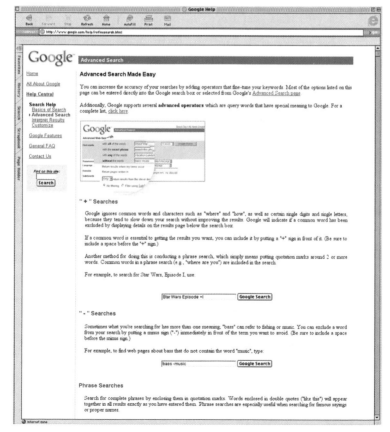

47c
online

Help screen for searching on *Google*

For advice on evaluating Web search engines (and more tips on Web searching techniques), see "Search Engine Watch" at <http://searchenginewatch.internet.com> or click "reviews" at <http://www.zdnet.com>.

2 Enter electronic conversations. Some online resources make it possible for you to read or participate in actual discussions on a huge variety of topics. You will find such resources on the Internet's Usenet newsgroups and listserv discussion groups. You may also participate in other types of electronic meeting places. In MOOs, for example, you can interact within imaginary environments, and with local networking software you can become part of class discussions held online.

Chart 47.2

Listservs and Usenet Newsgroups

LISTSERVS

A listserv is a type of email program that maintains lists of subscribers interested in discussing a specific topic. Users must subscribe to the listserv in order to read or post messages on it.

Major characteristics: Lists are run on large computers; subscribers tend to be active experts working in fields related to the list topic. Lists are often moderated to screen out irrelevant material or "noise." Old text may be archived.

Use for: Excellent window on current issues. Good for listening in on practitioners' conversations, discovering opinions, noting solutions to common problems.

Searching: When you subscribe, check the welcome message for instructions for searching the archives.

USENET NEWSGROUPS

A Usenet newsgroup works like a listserv except that you need not subscribe to the list either to read its messages or to participate in the discussion.

Major characteristics: Thousands of groups focus on a wide range of topics. There is great variation in the expertise of contributors. Anyone may read or post messages.

Use for: Conversations about popular topics and about little-known, obscure subjects. Almost every political group, social interest, religion, activity, hobby, and fantasy has a Usenet group. Just browsing the list of Usenet groups can suggest topic ideas.

Searching: Check the welcome messages and the FAQs (frequently asked questions) for information on how to search. Many lists have archives of older discussions.

47c
online

These tools can furnish you with up-to-the-second information on a topic offered from many points of view. You have an opportunity to meet experts and amateurs from all over the world who have an interest about your subject. You may be able to question people who are actually doing the research or living the experiences you are writing about. But you must be very careful when you take information from such environments: make it a habit to confirm any statistic, fact, or claim from such a source with information from a second and different type of authority—a published book, an article, a reference work. Interactive sources can provide a close-up view of your subject. But you need to keep the bigger picture in mind, too. Rely on more traditional resources—journals, books, encyclopedias—to keep the full subject in perspective and to balance other individual and idiosyncratic points of view you may find online.

Some Web search engines cover Usenet newsgroups so that you can find and even join online conversations on your topic. To find older, archived newsgroup materials, check out *Google Groups* at <http://groups.google.com>.

47d How do you search by keywords?

To explore many basic electronic resources such as online catalogs, electronic indexes and the Internet, you need to know how to do efficient keyword searches. A *keyword search* is simply a scan of an electronic text or database that finds each occurrence of a given word or phrase. When you use the "find" feature of a word processor, you are performing a simple keyword search. Increase the power of this technique and apply it to much larger databases and you have a *search engine,* one of the most useful of contemporary research tools. Such engines can find not only the word(s) you've specified but related terms and phrases as well.

Perhaps the best advice we can give you when performing a keyword search is to read the instructions for the tool you are using, whether it is an electronic catalog, a search engine, or a directory. Your ability to focus a search and get the best results depends on knowing how to direct that search. While keyword searches are similar in many respects, you'll discover that the rules and "filters" controlling any given tool may differ. You may also be surprised by the sophistication of some search engines, particularly those on the World Wide Web (see Section 47c-1) which seem, at times, to anticipate your needs. But you can waste gobs of time just because you ignored the information waiting beneath "help," "simple search" or "advanced search" buttons on the screen.

47d
online

Be sure to type keywords carefully, especially proper nouns. A misspelled search term can prevent you from finding available information.

1 Understand how a simple keyword search works. A keyword search finds the titles in a catalog or database that contain the keyword(s) you have typed into a box or line on the screen. You might get keyword ideas from the *Library of Congress Subject Headings* (*LCSH*) in the reference room of your library. A librarian or instructor may be similarly helpful in guiding you toward appropriate keywords for your searches.

Or you can use the research tools themselves creatively to find powerful keywords. When searching a library catalog, always look for cross-listings for your particular subject—that is, other terms under which your subject is entered—and follow up on those suggestions. For example, if your project on Civil War ironclad ships leads you to search with the term *Monitor* (the name of a famous Union ship), a particular catalog entry might include the cross-listings *Civil War; Merrimac; U.S. Navy, history; Ericsson, John.* You could then probe the catalog using each of these new terms.

You will have to be ingenious and dogged at times in choosing keywords for Web searches. If you need to know whether alcohol is legally considered a drug, for example, you could begin with general keywords such as "alcohol" or "drugs." But you'd be swamped by the number of responses, and you might never find the particular information you need. Here is where a little preliminary reading should pay off (see Section 46a-2). Once you learn that drugs are regulated by the Federal Drug Administration, you can try searching that term or, even better, its familiar acronym: FDA. When you locate the FDA's official site on the Web, you can then search it for "alcohol" to find the information you seek. "FDA" might not have been the first term to come to mind when you began your exploration, but it is a logical keyword, given the information you are seeking.

47d
online

So the keywords you choose—whether names, places, titles, concepts, or people—will shape your search. A comparatively small database, such as an online library catalog, may ask you to indicate whether a word you are searching is a title (t), author (a), subject (s), or some other term the system recognizes. In such cases, typing the name of an author (Stephen Carter), a title (*Integrity*), or a narrow subject keyword (ethics) will often produce manageable numbers of items to examine and read.

SEARCH . . .	KEYWORD . . .	FINDS . . .
A (author)	Stephen Carter	40 items
T (title)	*Integrity*	25 items
S (subject)	ethics	50 items

You could easily look at all the items found in this simple search. And a simple search may be adequate when the database you are exploring is relatively small or the keyword you are using is distinctive.

However, a simple search using similar terms on the World Wide Web, a huge database, might initially produce useless results (although improvements in search logic are occurring all the time).

KEYWORD . . .	FINDS . . .
Stephen Carter	2,291,000 items
Integrity	173,000 items
Ethics in America	2,902,000 items

Similarly, typing a general subject keyword into a local online library catalog may provide a substantial number of items.

KEYWORD . . .	FINDS . . .
Ethics	13,400 items

In these situations, more sophisticated search techniques are obviously required. One such technique is called Boolean searching.

2 Understand the principles of Boolean searching. A Boolean search uses specific terms (or symbols) to give you more control over what you are seeking. Most search engines in online catalogs, databases, or Web sites use some form of Boolean search.

In a Boolean search, by linking keywords with the term AND, you can search for more than one term at a time, identifying only those items in which the individual terms intersect. It may help to visualize these items in terms of sets.

You initiate a Boolean search in different ways. One way is to insert AND between terms you wish to search.

Stephen AND Carter

miniature AND schnauzer AND training

Washington AND Jefferson AND Constitution

47d
online

Another way to initiate a Boolean search is to select an appropriate command from a search engine menu, such as an "all the words" option. Narrowing your search to look for only those items in which occur *all* the words you specify usually reduces the information glut.

Other Boolean operators allow you to direct database searches in different ways.

OR   Using OR between keywords directs the search engine to find any examples of either keyword. Using OR might widen a search, but it would also allow you to locate all documents that cover related concepts.

       dog OR puppy
       Congress OR Senate

NOT   Using NOT between terms permits you to search for sites that include one term but not another. This may be useful when you want to exclude certain meanings of a term irrelevant to your search.

       Indians NOT Cleveland
       apple NOT computer
       republican NOT party

( )   Putting items in parentheses allows for additional fine tuning of a search. In the first example below, you could locate documents that mention either Senator Clinton or Senator Hutchison but not Senator Kennedy or Senator Hatch.

       Senator AND (Clinton OR Hutchison)
       church NOT (Mormon OR Catholic)
       pickup NOT (Ford OR Dodge)

Some search engines use + and − signs to select the same functions.

+   Putting + (a plus sign) immediately before an item, without a space, indicates that the word following it *must* be in the document being sought. Let's say, for example, you are looking on the Web for definitions of certain terms. You might format the request this way:

       +wetlands+definition
       +"sports car"+"definition of"

−   Putting − (minus sign) immediately before an item, without a space, indicates that the word following it *must not* be in the document being sought. Let's say you want to search for documents about Richard Nixon that don't discuss Watergate or China. You could format the request like this:

       +Nixon−Watergate−China

3 Search by exact phrase. To narrow a search even more, you can search for a specific and distinctive phrase either by placing it between quotation marks or selecting the "exact phrase" option on a search screen. This technique is essential for Web research and can produce dramatically different results. For example, placing quotation marks around "ethics in America" produces just 2,000 hits on *AltaVista* instead of the 224,000 hits produced without the exact-phrase specification. Similarly, an *AltaVista* search of the exact phrase "*Integrity* by Stephen L. Carter" produces just 14 items, most of them useful, including reviews of the book.

You can use exact-phrase searches creatively in many ways. When you can't recall who is responsible for a particular expression or quotation—for example, "defining deviancy down"— you can make it the subject of an exact phrase search. Do so on a Web search engine and you may find the expression attributed to former Senator Daniel Patrick Moynihan.

You can also combine exact phrase searches with various Boolean commands to find precisely what you need if you identify appropriate keywords.

"Ten Commandments" AND ("Charlton Heston" OR "Yul Brynner")

"pickup truck" NOT (Ford OR Dodge)

The potential of such searches is limited only by your cleverness.

4 Focus your search. Search tools ordinarily give you considerable flexibility in selecting how to search information and how to report it.

Where to search. Many search engines allow you to limit a keyword search to a specific place or type of information on the Internet. For example, the search engine *Google* allows you to make any of the following choices under its "Advanced Search" option.

- Language (for example, any language—Arabic, Bulgarian, etc.)
- News search
- Page-specific search
- Topic-specific search

Be sure to look at the results of your search to see if the search engine has returned suggestions for additional searches. You may see links marked "More like this."

When to search. Many keyword searches can be limited to specific periods of time, ranging from years to just one day. Clearly, you can reduce the number of "hits" for a given search this way, making your work more efficient.

You can also use searches limited by time to discover who was thinking what, when. How often were the terms *multiculturalism* and *partial birth abortion* being used ten years ago? How often are they being used today? You could find out on a database such as *LEXIS-NEXIS*.

How to report information. With online library catalogs and electronic indexes, you can usually print out the information you see on screen. Sometimes you have to select individual items to get full bibliographic data.

On the World Wide Web, you can usually see how many "hits" a search has found, and you can decide how many of them to view. It often makes sense to look at the abstracts for the sites first; then you can get full listings for sites that interest you.

To learn more about using Web search engines, see Ellen Chamberlain's "Bare Bones 101," a site that includes detailed descriptions of important search engines, at <http://sc.edu/beaufort/library/bones.html>.

47e How do you do field research?

While much college research occurs in the library or online, some of your work—especially in service-learning projects—may lead you to seek information on your own through interviews, surveys, and close observation. Such *fieldwork* is particularly common in disciplines such as psychology, anthropology, and education; if you are pursuing degrees in these areas, you'll likely learn formal techniques for field research. But informal fieldwork can be useful in other, less formal research situations provided that you describe your procedures accurately and properly qualify your conclusions. Here we'll look briefly at conducting interviews, using questionnaires, and making observations.

47e
research

1 Conduct interviews. Sometimes people are the best sources of authoritative or firsthand information. When you can discuss your subject with experts or learn from people in a community, you add credibility, authenticity, and immediacy to a research report or service project. If you are writing a paper about an aspect of medical care, talk to a medical professional or patients affected by a problem. If you're exploring the financial dilemmas of community theaters, try to interview a local producer or theater manager. If you're writing about problems in the building industry, find a builder or banker with thirty minutes to spare.

It is often possible to consult with knowledgeable people via email, newsgroups, or listservs. Although online communications tend to be less formal than face-to-face conversations, they still require appropriate preparation and courtesy. For a directory of experts willing to consult via email, see *Pitsco's Ask an Expert* at <http://askanexpert.com>.

Consider, too, how technology might enhance the information gained from an interview. For instance, you might photograph or videotape the people you interview and make those images part of a *PowerPoint* or Web presentation (see Chapter 13). Current digital imaging tools make such enhancements not only possible but relatively easy, depending on the technology available to you.

Checklist 47.6

Conducting a One-on-One Interview

- Write or telephone your subject for an appointment, and make it clear why you want the interview.

- Confirm your meeting the day before, and be on time for your appointment.

- Be prepared for the meeting. If possible, learn all you can about your subject's professional background, education, work history, and publications.

- Have a list of questions and possible follow-ups ready in your notebook. Establish the basic facts: Who? What? Where? When? How? Why? Then, when appropriate, pose questions that require more than one-word answers.

- Focus your queries on your research question: don't wander from the subject.

- Take careful notes, especially if you intend to quote your source.

- Double-check direct quotations, and be sure your source is willing to be cited "on the record."

- If you plan to audiotape or videotape the interview, get your subject's approval before turning the machine on.

- Promise to send your subject a copy of your completed project.

- Send a thank-you note to an authority who has been especially helpful.

47e
research

2 Conduct surveys. Research projects that focus on your local community may require surveys of public opinion and attitudes not available from other sources. So you may have to supply the information yourself by preparing questionnaires and conducting studies. Yet polling is demanding, and even the creating of a useful questionnaire requires ingenuity. You'll have to work hard to produce research results that readers will respect. Still, the principles behind effective polls and surveys are not inscrutable.

To begin with, you should have a clear idea about the information you are seeking. You distribute questionnaires not to see what turns up, but to obtain answers to specific research questions you have formulated: *Do people on my dormitory floor feel personally secure in their rooms? Would people in my neighborhood support the presence of a halfway house for juvenile offenders? Are people willing to pay additional taxes for improved public transportation?*

You have to formulate good questions, whether you are gathering factual information or sampling public opinion. Asking the right question isn't easy. You don't want to skew the answers you get by posing vague, leading, or biased questions.

VAGUE	What do you think about dorm security?
REVISED	Do you have any concerns about personal security in Aurelius Hall?
LEADING	Are you in favor of the city's building a halfway house for juvenile criminals right in the middle of our peaceful Enfield neighborhood?
REVISED	Do you favor the city's plan to build a halfway house for juvenile offenders in the Enfield neighborhood?
BIASED	Would you support yet another tax increase to fund a scheme for light rail in the city?
REVISED	Would you support a one-cent increase in the current sales tax to fund a light rail system for the city?

To make responses easy to tabulate, you will often want to provide readers with a range of options for answering your questions.

47e
research

How do you feel about the following statements? Respond using the appropriate number:
1. I disagree totally.
2. I disagree somewhat.
3. I neither agree nor disagree.
4. I agree somewhat.
5. I agree totally.

Our bus system serves the whole community.   _____

Our bus system operates efficiently.

Our bus system runs on time.   _____

Bus fares are too high.   _____

A sales tax increase for buses makes sense.   _____

In addition to exploring your specific issues, you may want to gather demographic data on the people you are surveying; this information may be useful later in interpreting your findings. You must be able to protect the privacy of the people you survey and offer reasonable assurances that any information they volunteer will not be used against them in any way. But personal data can reveal surprising patterns, particularly when you are asking questions on political and social topics, for example.

About you. Knowing a little about respondents to this survey will make interpretation of the data more significant. Please answer the following questions as best you can. Leave off any information you would rather not offer.

1. What is your gender?

_____M _____F

2. What is your marital status?

_____Married

_____Single, divorced/separated/widowed

_____Single, never married

3. What is your age? _____

4. What is your race? ethnicity?

_____Asian

_____Black/African American

_____Hispanic

_____White

_____Other

5. What is the highest level of your education?

_____elementary school or less

_____high school graduate

_____some college

_____college graduate

_____postgraduate or professional school

_____other

47e
research

Try to anticipate the questions your queries might raise in a respondent's mind. For example, the list of educational achievement might be puzzling to someone who went to a technical or trade school out of high school. The category "other" often helps in doubtful cases.

Be sure you survey enough people from your target group so that readers will find your sample adequate. You ordinarily need to choose people at random for your survey, yet those polled should represent a cross-section of the whole population. Surveying just your friends, just people who agree with you, or only people like yourself will almost certainly produce inadequate research. You may have to provide an incentive to get people to cooperate with your survey. In most cases, this may mean suggesting that their responses may help to solve a problem or serve others in some way. J. D. Powers, the company famous for surveying new car owners, sends a crisp dollar bill with its surveys to thank potential respondents. You may not be able to go that far, but you do need to consider whether you can offer some incentive for a response, particularly when your survey is lengthy (as the J. D. Powers survey is).

Finally, you'll have to tabulate your findings accurately, present the results in a fashion that makes sense to readers, let readers know the techniques you used to gather your information, and, most important, report the limits of your study. Those limits provide the qualifications for any conclusions you draw. Don't overstate the results.

Checklist 47.7

Conducting a Survey

- Understand the purpose of your survey or questionnaire before you create it. What information do you want to gather?

- Prepare clear, fair, and unbiased questions. Test your questions on others to be sure participants in your actual survey will understand them.

- Consider the type of responses you need from respondents. Should they respond to a scale? To a list of options you provide? Should they fill in blanks?

- Consider how much space might be adequate for responses and how much space might be too much.

- Create questionnaires that are easy to read, easy to fill out, and easy to tabulate.

47e
research

- Create questionnaires that are convenient to return. If necessary, provide properly addressed envelopes and return postage.

- Give respondents appropriate assurances about the confidentiality of their responses, and then abide by your commitment.

- Keep track of all your sampling procedures so you can report them accurately in your research paper.

3 Make systematic observations. Some of the best field research you can do may come simply from the careful study of a phenomenon. The techniques of observation you use for a college research or service project may not be so rigorous as those of professional ethnographers who make a science of such studies, but you do need to take the process seriously. On their own, people are notoriously unreliable in recounting what they have seen; their observations are often colored by their prior expectations, experiences, and assumptions. (Not surprisingly, the sworn testimonies of eyewitnesses to events are often conflicting.) So in making research observations—whether about the behavior of sports fans at a football game or the interactions between infants and staff at a day-care center—you want to employ techniques that counteract your biases and ensure the reliability of your claims.

In recording your observations, you could do worse than to begin with a double-column spiral notebook to separate actual observations of a phenomenon from your immediate reactions to it. Your written notes should be quite detailed about matters such as time, place, duration of the study, conditions of the observation, and so on. You may have to summarize such information later.

Of course, you need not rely on notebooks alone for your records. To assure an accurate account of what you are studying, use any appropriate recording methods: photography, tape or video recordings, transcriptions of online conversations, and so on. If you make multiple observations over a period of time, follow the same procedures each time and note any changes that might affect your results. For example, a group of students conducting a traffic count of the patrons entering a major campus facility would want to perform the counts on typical days, not during spring break or on days when the weather is unusually bad.

47e
research

Checklist 47.8

Making Observations

• Understand the purpose of your observation. What information do you hope to gather? In what forms can that data be gathered and reported?

• Study any literature on your subject and become familiar with the issues/subjects you are studying. What background information do you need to have on your subject(s) to make informed and perceptive observations?

• Plan the method of your observation. How can you gather the information you need? How can you minimize your own impact on the situation you are observing?

• Practice techniques of observation. Determine what methods work best.

• Work with others to confirm the reliability of your observations. Cross-check your field notes with those of fellow researchers.

CHAPTER 48

How Do You Evaluate Sources?

Finding research materials, as described in Chapter 47, doesn't come to a halt when you begin developing a project. Throughout the research process you'll find yourself gathering additional information to address new questions or plug gaps in what you've learned. At the same time, you'll be working with the sources you've gathered—first positioning them to understand their purpose and genre and then evaluating their quality to decide how they can best support the claims you wish to make.

48a How do you position research sources?

Before you begin annotating (see Section 49a), summarizing, or paraphrasing a source (see Section 49b), you may need to set it into an appropriate context to be sure you understand it—what we call *positioning a source*. This technique will encourage you to approach all research materials actively and somewhat skeptically, thinking deeply about who developed them and for what reasons. You position a source by identifying its point of view, biases, strengths, and limitations.

Of course, you will use sources in all sorts of different ways. Sometimes you'll cite materials because they offer the most balanced or authoritative treatment of a subject. At other times you'll choose sources that exemplify specific points of view—a leftist view, a right-wing perspective, a Catholic outlook. And at still other times you might select sources you know are "off the wall" but which nonetheless make revealing points about culture and society. Positioning a source helps you make such decisions with your eyes open. When you position a source, you simply identify such perspectives so that you do not misrepresent information when you report it.

Sources do reflect different political, social, economic, even generational biases. Differences of religion, gender, or worldview may similarly shape the materials you gather in ways that bear on your research. Even the methods used in creating the source materials may influence how you present them: Was a survey scientific? Was a study sponsored by a group with a stake in its outcome? Does a document you cite represent a person's carefully considered judgment, or is it a paid endorsement, a political screed, even a parody? You need to know before you go public with it.

The answers to such questions do not automatically disqualify sources; instead, they help you to determine how to work with them responsibly. You owe it to readers to be honest and forthright with information and to share what you learn about your sources when that information affects your conclusions. Occasionally you might even have to research your sources to be sure they are reliable. If a source providing statistics in support of nationalized health care is a liberal think tank, you and readers should know; when a columnist you quote in supporting a flat tax proposal is wealthy enough to benefit significantly from the policy change, that's relevant information.

Checklist 48.1

Positioning a Source

- What are the background and interests of the author(s)?
- What are the interests and biases of the publisher?
- How much authority does the source claim?
- Are the assertions of authority justified?
- Does the source purport to be objective and/or scientific?
- Does the source present itself as subjective and/or personal?
- Whose interests does the source represent?
- Whose interests does the source seem to ignore?
- To what audience(s) is the source directed?
- What do readers need to know about the source?
- Where do links in the source lead? Who advertises in the source?
- What role should the source play in my project: Authority? Opinion? Illustration?

48a

position

Utne Reader *at <http://utne.com>
appeals to a predominantly left-of-
center readership concerned with
issues of culture, earth, body, spirit,
and politics. You might discover its
point of view most readily by studying
its links to other sources.*

48a
position

The titles of articles in The Weekly Standard *at
<http://www.weeklystandard.com> might suggest its right-of-center
politics. Or you might recognize the names of some of its authors. Better
yet, check the revealing "About Us" link.*

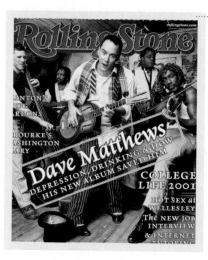

The perspectives of a magazine like Rolling Stone, *which focuses on popular culture, may not be as self-evident or consistent as those of a political journal. But the magazine will still reflect the interests and biases of its writers and publishers. To position such a source, you might examine the titles of its articles, the tone of its editorials (if any), the character of its illustrations and graphics, and even the types of ads it attracts. View its Web site at* <www. rollingstone.com>.

E-Tips   Two points on the political spectrum offer thought-provoking online assessments of media bias. See FAIR at <http://fair.org> for a left-wing take on issues of balance and fairness in the news. See the Media Research Center at <http://mediaresearch.org> for a conservative perspective.

48b How do you evaluate research sources?

48b
evaluate

Writers have always had to be careful about the sources they cited in research projects, but at least they could be confident that the library materials they used had been reviewed by publishers, editors, and librarians. Today, however, some materials—for example, pages from the Web and messages from listservs—may come to you almost directly from their authors, unreviewed and unrefereed. It falls to you, then, to judge their authority, quality, and credibility. You can learn to make sound judgments if you remember a few basic principles. (For detailed advice on reading critically, see Chapter 10.)

1 Consider the purpose of a source. Sources aren't simply *good* or *bad*. Their value will depend, in part, on how you intend to use them. For example, if you were writing a report on the positions taken by a candidate in a long-past presidential campaign, you'd probably depend on scholarly works published by reputable writers or you'd look up newspaper accounts on microfilm in the library. But if you were developing a project about a political campaign today, you might use less scholarly materials, such as campaign literature, recent articles in newspapers and popular magazines, and even Web sites. These sources might lack the authority and perspective of more scholarly works, but they could still provide a valid snapshot of current political attitudes.

Even if sources can't be described as simply good or bad without considering their purposes, they do have strengths and weaknesses to weigh. We've summarized some of those qualities in the table on pages 726–27, but our guidelines should be taken with caution. Any single source might differ from our characterizations.

In researching a subject, the best sources for you are likely to be those just a step or two above your current level of knowledge. Push yourself to learn more without exceeding your depth.

2 Consider the authority and reputation of a source. As you accumulate materials for a project, you may find that certain books, articles, and reference tools are cited more often than others. These are likely to be essential materials that people in the field assume most other researchers know. If you haven't already consulted these materials in your own collection of data, go to the library and review them. Don't hesitate to ask librarians or instructors about the authority of books, articles, or other sources that you expect to use. They will often be able to direct you to reliable materials.

Do the same with electronic sources: track down the best items so far as you can determine. Inevitably, the most valuable sites will appear on many "favorites" lists. Sometimes the Web address (URL) can also help you identify the authority of a source. Checking the domain in the address will give you some sense of who is sponsoring the site.

.edu—an educational institution

.org—a nonprofit organization

.gov—a government-sponsored site

.com—a commercial site

.net—a network site

48b

evaluate

E-Tips
> There are a growing number of guides to online materials. You might begin with the "Searching the Internet" link on the home page of the *Librarians' Index to the Internet* at <http://lii.org>. See also *ICYouSee: T Is for Thinking* at <http://www.ithaca.edu/library/Training/hott.html>, a site aimed specifically at college researchers.

3 Consider the credentials of authors and sponsoring agencies. This advice might not seem practical when you are exploring a subject new to you. But you'll quickly pick up the names of people mentioned frequently as experts or authorities—people whose work has had lasting or significant influence. (You may also hear your instructors mention writers who deal with your topic.) When scanning a lengthy printout of potential sources, look for these familiar authors. But don't be drawn in by celebrity alone, particularly when the names of famous people are attached to subjects about which they may have no special expertise.

With Web sites, listservs, and other online sources, you may find yourself clueless about the credentials of your "authors." All you might know about participants in a discussion group is a name and an email address. When you report factual information from such sources, confirm it when possible through second, more familiar sources. (Reporting opinion is a different matter.) On personal Web sites, check to see what expertise the authors claim for themselves, then try to verify their credentials. If they offer email addresses, write them and ask about the sources they used to support the claims on their pages. Be both open-minded and skeptical.

You can be more confident about electronic information when the sponsoring agency of the source is one you would trust in a print environment. Acquiring information online from *Reuters News Service* or *USA Today* is equivalent to seeing the same information in print. But don't hesitate even in these cases to raise questions about fairness, bias, and completeness.

48b
evaluate

4 Consider the timeliness and stability of a source. Timeliness is relative. For some projects, you might need sources that are both immediate and interactive like the conversations in chat rooms and MOOs. For other projects, you may turn to the more professional discussion of current issues you'll find in newspapers, magazines, and popular journals. For still other academic work, you'll want sources that offer the kind of thoughtful commentary or observation that requires time, research, and study.

With books and articles, then, the date of publication is crucial. In general, you want to support your projects with the most current and reputable information in a field. But your instructors and librarians may refer you to classic pieces, too, writings that have shaped thinking in your topic area. For many college papers, you should have a mix of sources, some from the past, some quite recent. While books and articles may sometimes be difficult to acquire, important books and printed articles don't disappear the way electronic sources sometimes do.

Timeliness is a different matter in newer electronic environments where you may not always be able to determine how current a given source is. Few conventions govern the millions of Web pages, so not every site you visit will provide a date for its original posting or its most recent update. You'll want to check for both since the Web is full of sites posted and largely forgotten by their authors. Currency is less a factor in listservs, Usenet newsgroups, and Web log postings, since the turnover of material is very rapid, changing from day to day. But this also means that something you read today may be gone tomorrow—or sooner. Obviously, you need to print out or download relevant postings from such sources. You can also check whether the source you are using archives its materials.

Web sites pose similar problems. Some sponsored sites allow you to search their archives for past stories or postings. But those archives may not be complete, and they may not go back many years. Electronic sources are not yet as stable, comprehensive, and dependable over the long run as printed books and articles—though the situation is improving. Scholarly e-journals are increasing in number and prestige, and the archives of significant newspapers and periodicals are growing. Still, the instability of electronic sources is a matter to consider, especially when you are planning a long-term research project.

48b
evaluate

5 Consider how well a source presents key information.

The design of a source is probably of greater concern with Web sites

Assessing Sources

Source	Purpose	Authors	Audience/ Language
Scholarly books	Advance or report new knowledge	Experts	Academic/ Technical
Scholarly articles	Advance or report new knowledge	Experts	Academic/ Technical
Serious books & articles	Report or summarize information	Experts or professional writers	Educated public/ Formal
Popular magazines	Report or summarize information	Professional writers or journalists	General public/ Informal
Newspapers, news services	Report current information	Journalists	Popular/ Informal
Sponsored Web sites	Varies from report information to advertise	Varies, usually Web expert	Varies/ Usually informal
Individual Web sites/ Web logs	Varies	Expert to novice	Varies/ Casual to slang
Interviews	Consult with experts	Experts	Varies/Technical to colloquial
Listservs	Discuss specific subjects	Experts to interested amateurs	Varies/Technical to colloquial
Usenet newsgroups	Discuss specific subjects	Open to everyone	Varies/Technical to colloquial

Publisher or Medium	Reviewed/ Documented?	Current/ Stable?	Dialogic/ Interactive?
University Press	Yes/Yes	No/Yes	No/No
Scholarly or professional journal	Yes/Yes	Usually no/Yes	No/ No (unless online)
Commercial publishers	Yes/No	Depends on subject/Yes	No/ No (unless online)
Commercial publishers	Yes/No	Yes/Yes	No/ No (unless online)
Commercial press or online	Yes/No	Yes/Yes	No/ No (unless online)
Online WWW	Sometimes/ Links to other sites	Regularly updated/ sometimes	Sometimes/ Often
Online WWW	Usually no/ Links to other sites	Varies/Varies	Sometimes/ Sometimes
Notes, recordings, email	No/No	Yes/No	Yes/Yes
Online email	No/No	Yes/Sometimes	Yes/Yes
Online email	No/No	Yes/No	Yes/Yes

than with printed books and articles, for which the conventions were established years ago. Still evolving as an information tool, Web sites bring together the complex resources of print, visual, and audio media, sometimes brilliantly, sometimes garishly. A successful Web site identifies its purpose clearly, arranges information logically, gives access to its materials without exhausting the capacity of its users' technology, furnishes relevant and selective links to other responsible resources, and provides basic bibliographical information: identity and email of author/sponsor, date of posting, date of most recent update, and so on. You may not wish to rely on a site that does not meet these standards.

E-Tips

For an amusing discussion of bad Web design, take a look at Vincent Flanders's *Web Pages That Suck.com* at <http://webpagesthatsuck.com>. Jakob Nielsen has a fascinating archive of his columns on Web design at <http://www.useit.com/alertbox>.

6 Consider commercial intrusions into a source. Books today rarely have advertising, and we often just ignore ads in printed magazines. But commercial intrusions into Web sites are persistent enough to warrant concern. Sponsored Web sites—especially search engines—are often so thick with commercial appeals that they can be difficult to use. Moreover, your search itself may bring up specific advertising messages in an effort to direct you to a sponsor's material. No library catalog ever exerted this kind of pressure.

Sponsored sites may also reflect the commercial connections of their owners, especially when news organizations are in fact owned by larger companies with entertainment or other commercial interests. What appears—or doesn't appear—on a site may be determined by who is supporting the message. Be aware of attempts to influence your judgment, and make it a point to visit many different sites when exploring a subject. Use a variety of search engines, too, to find your materials.

48b
evaluate

Checklist 48.2

Evaluating a World Wide Web Site

- Is the site sponsored by a reputable group you can identify?
- Do the authors of the site give evidence of their credentials?
- Is the site conveniently searchable?

- Is information in the site logically arranged?
- Is the site easy to navigate?
- Does the site provide an email address where you might send questions?
- Is the site updated regularly or properly maintained?
- Does the site archive older information?
- Is the content of the site affected by commercial sponsorship?

E-Tips   For additional advice on evaluating Web sites, see <http://www.library.cornell.edu/okuref/research/webeval.html> and <http://www.library.ucla.edu/libraries/college/help/critical/index.htm>. For an exercise on evaluating a Web site, see <http://www.lib.vt.edu/research/evaluate/evaluating.html>.

48b
evaluate

CHAPTER 49

How Do You Use Sources Responsibly?

Once you have found the best sources for your project, you must make use of the information in them. How you handle these research materials will vary, but certain techniques make sense for getting the most out of them: annotating, and summarizing and paraphrasing. Confident of what your sources offer, you can then bring them together in a coherent argument or lively conversation.

So that readers can have confidence in your research, you'll also need to know how to document your sources and how to avoid questions about plagiarism and collusion. This chapter offers you guidelines for managing sources successfully.

49a How do you annotate research materials?

Once you have positioned and evaluated a source (see Chapter 48), you can begin mining it for information. One way to do that is to annotate the material you've gathered—that is, to attach comments, questions, and reactions to it directly. The point of annotation is to identify ideas and information worth returning to and, more important, to engage in a dialogue with the authors and sources you are encountering.

Annotation is not an easy option when you are reading library books and materials; in these cases, you'll have to record your reactions in notes, summaries, and paraphrases (see Section 49b). But much research material today is photocopied, downloaded, or read online—and these media support different forms of annotation.

Many researchers working with photocopied materials will use highlighting pens to tag important passages. But marking material in this way is only part of an effective annotation process. Each section you highlight should be accompanied by a marginal comment that explains the importance of the passage or states your reaction to it. Be sure to highlight any passages worthy of direct quotation.

You can use the annotation features of word-processing programs to record your reactions to files you download from your computer. But once again your comments are the essential element. These annotations can later be incorporated into the paper or project itself if they are thoughtful and entirely in your own words.

For a detailed online guide to *Microsoft Word*'s commenting features, see <http://wwwnt.cwrl.utexas.edu/web/teaching.cfm?page=commenting>. The tutorial explains how to either edit or comment on any document you can download in *Word*.

Even pages from the World Wide Web can be marked with comments and, in some cases, annotated as part of an ongoing online discussion. For instance, you can use a browser's "bookmark" feature to gather together all Web sites or pages relevant to your project, arranging the items in folders that reflect its overall structure, one folder for each major section or theme. It is even possible to annotate each bookmark to remind yourself why the site or page is important.

You can and probably should take conventional notes on all your important sources, online or off. (See Section 10a-4 for advice about preparing *content, context,* and *response* notes.)

On pages 732–33 is an example of a source that has been annotated in its margins. This same article is both summarized and paraphrased in Section 49b.

49b Should you summarize or paraphrase research materials?

Summarizing and paraphrasing represent different ways of responding to materials you read.

A *summary* captures the gist of a source or some portion of it, boiling it down to a few words or sentences. Summaries tend to be short, taking only what is immediately relevant from a source. Summarize those materials that support your thesis but do not provide an extended argument or idea that you need to share in detail with readers.

49b
sources

When summarizing a source, identify its key facts or ideas and put them in your own words. When an article is quite long, you might look for topic ideas in each major section. If you have a photocopy of the source, highlight any sentences that state or emphasize its key themes. Then assemble these ideas into a short, coherent statement about the

An Annotated Essay

"Educational Insensitivity"

Diane Ravitch

An enterprising parent of a high school senior recently discovered that the literary texts on the New York Regents examinations had been expurgated. Excerpts from the writings of many prominent authors were doctored, without their knowledge or permission, to delete references to religion, profanity, sex, alcohol or other potentially troublesome topics.

The story was a huge embarrassment to the New York State Education Department, which prepares the examinations, and yesterday Richard P. Mills, the state education commissioner, ordered the practice stopped. From now on, all literary passages used on state tests will be unchanged except for length.

Mr. Mills is to be commended for this new policy. But the dimensions of this absurd practice reach far beyond the borders of New York, and there are many culprits. Censorship of tests and textbooks is not merely widespread: across the nation, it has become institutionalized.

For decades, American publishers have quietly trimmed sexual and religious allusions from their textbooks and tests. When publishers assemble reading books, they keep a wary eye on states like California, Texas and Florida, where textbooks are adopted for the entire state and any hint of controversy can prevent a book's placement on the state's list. In Texas, Florida and other southern states, the religious right objects to any stories that introduce fantasy, witchcraft, the occult, sex or religious practices different from its own. In California, no textbook can win adoption unless it meets the state's strict demands for gender balance and multicultural representation and avoids mention of unhealthy foods, drugs or alcohol.

Over the past several decades, the nation's testing industry has embraced censorship. In almost every state, tests are closely scrutinized in an official process known as a bias and sensitivity review. This procedure was created in the late 1960's and early 1970's to scrutinize questions for any hint of racial or gender bias. Over the years, every test development company in the nation has established a bias and sensitivity review process to ensure that test questions do not contain anything that might upset students and prevent them from showing their true abilities on a test. Now these reviews routinely expurgate references to social problems, politics, disobedient children or any other potentially controversial topic.

Original audience was readers of the New York Times, America's paper of record. Find out more about NY Regents exams.

What's the issue now if the policy has been changed? Ravitch's claim.

Can both right and left be responsible for censorship?

Looks like good intentions gone haywire. Shouldn't good literature challenge students?

This is the rationale now used within the testing industry to delete references to any topic that someone might find objectionable. As a top official in one of the major testing companies told me: "If anyone objects to a test question, we delete it. Period."

This self-censorship is hardly a secret. Every major publisher of educational materials uses "bias guidelines," which list hundreds of words and images that are banned or avoided. Words like "brotherhood" and "mankind" have been banished. A story about mountain climbing may be excluded because it favors test-takers who live near mountains over those who don't. Older people may not be portrayed walking with canes or sitting in rocking chairs.

Is Ravitch being sarcastic in this ¶ or are her examples real?

I serve on the board of a federal testing agency, the National Assessment Governing Board, which is directly responsible for reviewing all test questions on the National Assessment of Educational Progress. We have learned that bias and sensitivity rules are subject to expansive interpretations. Once reviewers proposed to eliminate a reading passage about Mount Rushmore because the monument offends Lakota Indians, who consider the Black Hills of South Dakota a sacred site.

This censorship is now standard practice in the testing industry and in educational publishing. One way to end it is to expose the practice to public scrutiny, forcing officials like Mr. Mills to abandon it. Another way, adopted by the National Assessment Governing Board, is to review every deletion proposed by those applying bias and sensitivity standards to determine whether it passes the test of common sense. I would also recommend that whenever material is deleted from a literary passage in a test, the omission should be indicated with ellipses.

Proposals to solve censorship in schools and textbooks.

The bias and sensitivity review process, as it has recently evolved, is an embarrassment to the educational publishing industry. It may satisfy the demands of the religious right (in censoring topics) and of the politically correct left (in censoring language). But it robs our children of their cultural heritage and their right to read—free of censorship.

Ravitch's actual claim—and a possible quotation.

Diane Ravitch, a historian of education at New York University, is writing a book about censorship in the educational publishing industry.

What else has she written? What are her politics?

whole piece, one detailed enough to stand on its own and make sense several weeks after you examine the material. The summary should be entirely in your own words.

A *paraphrase* usually reviews a complete source in much greater detail than does a summary. When paraphrasing a work, you report its key information or restate its core arguments point by point *in your own words*. You will typically want to paraphrase any materials that provide detailed facts or ideas your readers will need. Predictably, paraphrases run much longer than summaries.

Prepare a paraphrase by working through the original source more systematically than you would with a summary. An effective paraphrase will meet the following conditions.

- The paraphrase reflects the structure of the original piece.
- The paraphrase reflects the ideas of the original author, not your reflections on them.
- Each important fact or direct quotation is accompanied by a specific page number from the source when possible.
- The material you record is relevant to your theme. (Don't waste time paraphrasing parts of the source that are of no use to your project.)
- The material is entirely in your own words—except for clearly marked quotations.

Practically speaking, the distinction between summaries and paraphrases is often less important than that you simply take the notes you need for a project. In gathering information, you'll often find yourself switching between summary and paraphrase, depending on what you are reading.

Now let's look at a source first summarized and then paraphrased. We will use the article "Educational Insensitivity" by Diane Ravitch annotated in Section 49a (see pp. 732–33). This op-ed piece originally appeared in the *New York Times* on June 5, 2002, shortly after the New York State Department of Education admitted that, to avoid offending students, it had been censoring works of literature included in a standard examination.

49b
sources

To prepare a summary, assemble the key claim and supporting elements into a concise restatement of the overall argument. The summary should make sense on its own, forming a complete statement you might use later in the project itself. But don't be surprised if you go through several versions of that sentence before you come up with one that satisfies you.

EFFECTIVE
SUMMARY #1

Diane Ravitch, a professor at New York University, argues in the <u>New York Times</u> (5 June 2002) that educators and textbook authors should not cave in to the demands of the political right or left to censor the topics and the language of literary works because such editing robs students of their cultural heritage.

EFFECTIVE
SUMMARY #2

Diane Ravitch, a professor at New York University, argues in the <u>New York Times</u> (5 June 2002) that attempts by educators and textbook publishers to avoid objectionable topics or language are depriving students of their right to read uncensored literature.

How can something as simple as a summary go wrong? There are a number of ways. You might, for example, make the summary too succinct and leave out crucial details. Such a summary scribbled on a note card might be useless when, days later, you try to make sense of it.

INEFFECTIVE
SUMMARY

She argues that it's wrong to censor literature. Both the left and right want it.

Or your summary might fail because it misses the central point of a piece by focusing on details that are not relevant to the argument. Useful in a different context, these facts are misleading if they don't capture the essence of what the author wrote.

INACCURATE
SUMMARY

Diane Ravitch, a professor at New York University, knows about censorship in education because she serves on the National Assessment Governing Board, which reviews questions on tests.

49b
sources

Yet another danger lies in using the actual words of the original author in your summary. If these unacknowledged borrowings make their way into your project itself without both quotation marks and documentation, you are guilty of plagiarism (see Section 49d). In the example following, language taken directly and inappropriately from Ravitch's op-ed piece is underlined.

> PLAGIARIZED   Diane Ravitch, a professor at New York
> SUMMARY   University, argues in the <u>New York</u>
>   <u>Times</u> (5 June 2002) that the expurga-
>   tion of literary works by educators and
>   textbook publishers <u>robs our children</u>
>   <u>of their cultural heritage and their</u>
>   <u>right to read—free of censorship.</u>

From this "plagiarized summary" you can appreciate how tempting it might be to slip these words into the body of a paper, forgetting that you didn't write them yourself. To avoid plagiarism, the safest practice is *always* to use your own words in summaries.

A paraphrase of "Educational Insensitivity" would be appreciably longer than a summary because a researcher would expect to use the information differently, probably referring to the source in much greater detail. Here's one possible paraphrase of Ravitch's op-ed article.

> EFFECTIVE   Responding to criticism that it had
> PARAPHRASE   edited sensitive and controversial pas-
>   sages from literary works on its
>   Regents examinations, the New York
>   State Education Department announced
>   that it would abandon the practice. But
>   Diane Ravitch argues in a New York
>   Times op-ed piece (5 June 2002) that
>   the practice of trimming controversial
>   materials from educational materials is
>   so common that it is institutionalized.
>   Those on the political right demand
>   that morally offensive topics and ideas
>   be cut from exams and textbooks; those

on the political left demand gender and
ethnic balance. Standardized tests are
now routinely subject to reviews for
bias and insensitivity, as are other
educational materials. Ravitch argues
that this embarrassing practice should
be ended by letting the public know
what is happening and by carefully reviewing any standards applied to educational materials. Censorship robs students of their cultural right to read
literature as it was written.

You'll notice that this paraphrase covers all the major points in the editorial in the same order as the original. It also borrows none of the author's
language. With proper documentation, any part of the paraphrase could
become part of a final research project without a need for quotation marks.

How can paraphrases go wrong? Various problems can make the
paraphrase inaccurate or unusable. A paraphrase should accurately reflect the thinking of the original author. Reserve your comments and
asides for annotations or other, separate notes so that you don't confuse
your ideas with those of your sources. Consider how the following
paraphrase might misreport the views of Diane Ravitch if the researcher
later forgets that the underlined comments in the example should have
been personal notes or annotations.

INACCURATE   Responding to criticism that it had
PARAPHRASE   edited sensitive and controversial pas-
                  sages from literary works on its
                  Regents examinations, the New York
                  State Education Department announced
                  that it would abandon the practice <u>even</u>
                  <u>though one could argue that many stu-</u>
                  <u>dents benefited from the censorship.</u> But
                  Diane Ravitch argues in a <u>New York</u>
                  <u>Times</u> op-ed piece (5 June 2002) that
                  trimming controversial materials from
                  educational materials is so common that

49b
sources

> it is institutionalized. Those on the political right, <u>who probably don't want their children exposed to any challenging ideas,</u> demand that morally offensive topics be cut from exams and textbooks; those on the political left demand gender and ethnic balance, <u>which Ravitch should admit is often lacking in so-called classical works of literature.</u> Standardized tests are now routinely subject to reviews for bias and insensitivity, as are other educational materials. Ravitch argues that this embarrassing practice should be ended by letting the public know what is happening and by carefully reviewing any standards applied to educational materials. Censorship robs students of their cultural right to read literature as it was written.

You get the point. The reactions to the op-ed column might be genuine, but they don't represent an accurate paraphrase of the original article.

A paraphrase also should not reorganize or improve on the structure or argument of the original piece. For example, the following paraphrase doesn't actually add material to Ravitch's editorial, but it rearranges its information radically.

INACCURATE
PARAPHRASE

> Children in school should not be robbed of their cultural heritage by educators and publishers worried that reading what literary authors actually wrote might harm their tender sensitivities. But that's what is happening all across the country according to Diane Ravitch, a member of the National Assessment

49b
sources

Governing Board, a group that reviews
questions posed on the National
Assessment of Educational Progress.
Maybe if Ms. Ravitch served in the New
York State Education Department, it
would not have gotten into the business
of censoring the literary works that
appeared on its Regents examinations--
sparking a controversy about how much
censorship is occurring in education
today as a result of pressure from both
the right and the left to advance their
political agendas in our nation's
schools.

The most dangerous and academically dishonest sort of paraphrase is one in which a researcher borrows the ideas, structure, and details of a source wholesale, changing a few words here and there in order to claim originality. This sort of paraphrase is plagiarism even if the material is documented in the research project; writers can't just change a few words in their sources and claim the resulting material as their own work. (See Section 49d-1.)

PLAGIARIZED
PARAPHRASE

An inquisitive parent of a high school
student figured out recently that the
works of literature used on the New
York Regents examinations had been cut
and edited. Passages from the novels
and poems of many famous writers were
changed, without their permission or
knowledge, to remove all mention of religion, drugs, sexuality, and other
such offensive subjects.

The story embarrassed the New York
State Education department, which creates the tests, and so the state education commissioner ordered a stop to the

49b
sources

```
practice. Henceforth, all literary pas-
sages used on New York tests will be
unchanged except for length. . . .
```

You'll see the fault very readily if you compare these plagiarized paragraphs with the opening paragraphs in Ravitch's original editorial.

E-Tips

Be especially careful to paraphrase or summarize accurately when you record your notes in a research program such as *TakeNote*. Because you can export these notes directly from the program into your word processor or onto a Web site, you want to be certain that the words are your own and that quoted material is in quotation marks. Otherwise, you may find yourself inadvertently plagiarizing your sources when you transfer notes into your project itself.

1 Connect your research materials. Once you have taken notes from a variety of sources, you'll want to consider what you have learned. At this point, it may help to think of your project as a conversation among authors. The sources should *talk* to and with each other in your mind.

Sometimes you'll want to locate sources that reinforce each other, especially when you're trying to build an argument (see Chapter 12). In other situations, you'll want to highlight the differences between your sources. When sources have pronounced biases (political or otherwise), try reading them "against" pieces with different views to keep your own perspectives broad. And when you borrow material from online discussion groups, always find other, more conventional sources to confirm specific facts, figures, or claims you find there. Examine the sources you have selected, reading them as both believer and doubter (see Section 10b-1) and posing these practical questions.

- What information represents "fact" and what "opinion"?
- What have I actually learned from my sources?
- What do I still have to discover?
- What conflicts in the evidence do I need to address?
- What position(s) will I take?

49b
sources

When you actually begin to write, build your project from a variety of materials, drawing on different voices to create a coherent whole. Don't allow whole paragraphs or pages to depend on just one or two sources. If you do, your research project may begin to sound like a report that merely parrots what others have already written, a patchwork of quotations or borrowings held together by a few words or sentences of your own. Your responsibility as a writer is (ideally) to take a discussion farther than it has progressed so far. To do that, you must combine what you learn from many different sources into a coherent argument of your own.

Going Public   *Using Sources*

Following is an exemplary paragraph from a research paper by first-year composition student Andres Romay on the rising homicide rate among juveniles. It makes its case by synthesizing five different sources—as indicated by the parenthetical notes highlighted in orange. The sources furnish the information, but Andres Romay provides the logic that leads from data to conclusion.

A second factor contributing to the increasing rate of homicides committed by juveniles is easier access to firearms among adolescents. According to the Justice Information Center, between 1984 and 1994, guns became much more available to teens than in earlier decades ("Partnership"). Additionally, there was a 156 percent increase in weapons offenses for juveniles within the same decade (Butts). Approximately one in every eight suburban youth and two in every five inner-city youth carried a gun at some time (Osofsky 3-4). Since juveniles have had this increased access to guns, juvenile killings with firearms have quadrupled (Gest 36). Instead of teens settling their disputes by fist-fighting or stabbing, they now resort to shooting. Since gunshots are more likely to be fatal than other kinds of injuries, it is easy to see why the rate of homicides would increase as guns become more available. A pilot program in Boston launched in 1984 to reduce the availability of guns to adolescents through stiffer penalties and advanced systems of gun tracing has, predictably, reduced the number of juvenile killings

49b
sources

```
in the city (Kennedy). Clearly, the availability of
guns has a causal relationship to the juvenile
homicide rate.
```

49c How do you document a research project?

In your research project you will create a dialogue among the sources you have assembled. But your voice—and that of any colleagues working on the paper or project—will ultimately shape the final product. So readers will want to know which ideas and claims are your own and which should be credited to your sources. For that reason, you need to acknowledge your sources in academic or professional projects conscientiously, honestly, and gracefully.

Your notes and bibliography tell readers *who* wrote or discovered *what* and *when*. Documentation typically leads readers to printed sources of information: books, articles, volumes of statistics and research. But documentation may also point to Web pages, interviews, software, films, television programs, databases, images, audio files, and online conversations. Various systems for managing sources and documentation have been devised (see Chapter 52). Presented in this handbook are systems of the Modern Language Association (MLA), the American Psychological Association (APA), the *Chicago Manual of Style* (CMS), the Council of Science Editors (CSE—formerly Council of Biology Editors or CBE), and the *Columbia Guide to Online Style* (COS). Specific guidelines for formal documentation appear in Chapters 53 through 57. This section examines the general principles for acknowledging and using sources.

1 Provide a source for every direct quotation. A *direct quotation* is any material repeated word for word from a source. Direct quotations in college papers typically require some form of parenthetical documentation—that is, a citation of author and page number (MLA) or author, date, and page number (APA).

MLA   It is possible to define literature as simply
       "that text which the community insists on
       having repeated from time to time intact"
       (Joos 51-52).

APA   `Hashimoto (1986)` questions the value of attention-getting essay openings that "presuppose passive, uninterested (probably uninteresting) readers" `(p. 126)`.

You are similarly expected to identify the sources for any diagrams, statistics, charts, or pictures in your paper. You need not document famous sayings, proverbs, or biblical citations.

In less formal writing, you should still identify the author, speaker, or work from which you borrow any passage and indicate why the words you are quoting are significant. Many phrases of introduction or attribution are available (see Section 50a). Here are just a few.

One noted astronomer **reported** that. . .

Condoleezza Rice **asserts** that. . .

According to the GAO, the figures . . .

2 Document all ideas, opinions, facts, and information that cannot be considered common knowledge. *Common knowledge* includes the facts, dates, events, information, and concepts that an educated person can be assumed to know. You may need to check an encyclopedia to find out that the Battle of Waterloo was fought on June 18, 1815, but that fact belongs to common knowledge, and for that reason you don't have to document it.

You may also make assumptions about common knowledge within a field. When you find that a given piece of information or an idea is shared among several of the sources you are using, you need not document it. (For example, if in writing a paper on anorexia nervosa you discover that most authorities define it in the same way, you probably don't have to document that definition.) What experts know collectively constitutes the common knowledge within a field; what they claim individually—their opinions, studies, theories, research projects, hypotheses—is the material you *must* document in a paper.

3 Document materials that readers might question or wish to explore further. If your subject is controversial, you may want to document even those facts or ideas considered common knowledge. When in doubt, document. Suppose that in writing about witchcraft you make a historical assertion well known by scholars within a field but liable to surprise nonspecialists. Writing for nonspecialists, you should certainly document the assertion. Writing for experts, you would probably skip the note.

49c
research

4 Furnish dates, credentials, and other information to assist readers. Provide dates for important events, major figures, and works of literature and art. Identify any person readers might not recognize.

> After the great fire of London (**1666**), the city was . . .
>
> Henry Highland Garnet (**1815–82**), American abolitionist and radical, . . .
>
> *Pearl* (**c. 1400**), an elegy about . . .

In the last example, the *c.* before the date stands for *circa*, which means "about."

When quoting from literary works, help readers locate the passages you are citing. For novels, identify page numbers; for plays, give act/scene/line information; for long poems, provide line numbers and, when appropriate, division numbers (book, canto, or other divisions).

5 Use links to document electronic sources. Links in hypertexts (such as Web pages) can function as a type of documentation: they can take readers directly to supporting material or sources. But it's important that readers of hypertexts understand where a highlighted passage is leading them. Hyperlinks should be used judiciously to provide real information. Don't overwhelm a Web page with links; they can seem as fussy as a page with too many footnotes. And make sure the links work because Web addresses change with distressing frequency.

6 Use computer programs to document your project. Many software programs are available to help you document a paper or create a bibliography. Even most word processors have automatic footnote or endnote features. If you choose to use such a feature, be sure it supports the documentation style—for example, MLA, APA, CBE—required for your project. Also be certain that the program is up to date. The latest software, for example, can properly format footnotes or endnotes for material found on CD-ROMs and Web pages or in email communications. Typically, a bibliography entry will be generated from information you provide—usually in a box or table such as that found on the following page. Be sure to read the instructions for such software carefully and to proofread the output to be sure you have entered your data accurately.

49c
research

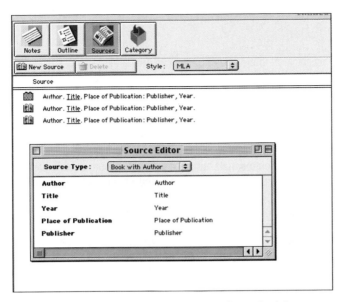

Here is a source screen from the program TakeNote! *designed to help writers organize notes and information. After providing author, title, year, and publication information, you will get a properly formatted entry for a Works Cited or References page.*

49d Do you understand academic responsibility?

Most students understand that it is wrong to buy or download a paper, to let someone heavily edit a paper for them, or to submit someone else's work as their own. This kind of activity is dishonest, and most institutions have procedures for handling scholastic dishonesty when it occurs.

But many students do not realize that taking notes carelessly or documenting sources inadequately may also raise doubts about the integrity of a paper. Representing as your own the words or ideas you found in a source constitutes *plagiarism*. Instructors take this seriously and assume their legitimate right to discipline students who do not. Plagiarism is easily avoided if you take good notes (see Section 49b) and follow the guidelines discussed in this section.

49d
plag

1 For conventional sources, acknowledge all direct uses of anyone else's work. Suppose, for example, that in preparing a

106

In fact, access and right-of-way are the two intangibles in trail cycling these days. The sport is getting too popular too fast, and in defense, or out of fear, authorities have banned cyclists from many potentially suitable areas.

You will probably use forest service or fire roads and trails intended for hikers most of the time. Don't stray off these trails, since this may cause damage, both to the environment and to our reputation. As long as you stay on the trails and do it with a modicum of consideration for others, you have nothing to fear and should not risk being banned from them by public agencies.

In many areas a distinction is made between single-track trails and wider ones. Single tracks are often considered off-limits to mountain bikers, although in most cases they are perfectly suitable and there are not enough hikers and other trail users to worry about potential conflicts. In fact, single trails naturally limit the biker's speed to an acceptable level.

research paper on mountain biking, you come across the above passage from *The Mountain Bike Book* by Rob van der Plas.

If you decide to quote all or part of the selection above in your essay, you must use quotation marks (or indention) to indicate that you are borrowing the writer's exact words. You must also identify the author, work, publisher, date, and location of the passage through documentation. If you are using MLA documentation (see Chapter 53), the parenthetical note and corresponding Works Cited entry would look like this.

As Rob van der Plas reminds bikers, they need only use common sense in riding public trails: "As long as you stay on the trails and do it with a modicum of consideration for others, you have nothing to fear and should not risk being banned from them by public agencies" (106).

49d
plag

Works Cited

van der Plas, Rob. The Mountain Bike Book: Choosing, Riding and Maintaining the Off-Road Bicycle. 3rd ed. San Francisco: Bicycle, 1993.

You must use *both* quotation marks and the parenthetical note when you quote directly. Quotation marks alone would not tell your readers what your source was. A note alone would acknowledge that you are using a source, but it would not explain that the words in a specific portion of your paper are not entirely your own. (By the way, the author in this case spells his last name exactly as shown, so *van der* is not capitalized in the Works Cited entry—though most last names, of course, are capitalized.)

2 Summarize and paraphrase carefully. When you summarize or paraphrase a source (see Section 49b), be certain that your notes are entirely in your own words. Some writers mistakenly believe that they can avoid a charge of plagiarism just by rearranging the elements or changing a few words in a source they are using. They are flat wrong.

For example, you may want to discuss the ideas raised in the selection from *The Mountain Bike Book* on page 746, borrowing the information in van der Plas's paragraphs but not his words. Here are two acceptable summaries of the passage on mountain biking that report its facts appropriately and honestly. Notice that both versions include a parenthetical note acknowledging van der Plas's *The Mountain Bike Book* as the source of information.

```
Rob van der Plas asserts that mountain bikers need

not fear limitation of their right-of-ways if they

ride trails responsibly (106).

Though using so-called single-track trails might put

mountain bikers in conflict with the hikers, such

tracks are often empty and underutilized (van der

Plas 106).
```

Without those parenthetical notes, both versions above might be considered plagiarized even though only van der Plas's ideas—not his actual words—are borrowed. That's because you *must give credit even for ideas* you take from your sources unless you are dealing with common knowledge (see Section 49c-2). Review Section 49b for detailed advice on how to write effective summaries and paraphrases and how to avoid plagiarizing in the process.

49d
plag

3 Appreciate the unique features of electronic discourse. The authorship and source problems of collaborative projects done on paper pale when compared with the intellectual property rights issues raised by electronic documents. To create a hypertext or Web site, for example, writers might link words and images from dozens of authors and artists and various sources and media. Every part of the resulting collage might be borrowed, but the arrangement of the hypertext itself will be unique. Who then deserves credit as the *author* of the project? Similar problems can arise with listserv and Usenet conversations. Such sources cannot be documented in conventional ways.

Over the next decade, as hypertexts and online materials become more common, standards for documenting electronic sources will evolve. For ways to cite Web pages, email, MUDs, MOOs, and other electronic forms, consult Chapter 57, which explains a documentation style—Columbia Online Style or COS—designed expressly for such material.

That said, you must also understand that the basic rules of scholastic honesty still apply in electronic environments. Tempting as it may be, you may *not* copy and paste information from a Web site, listserv, newsgroup, or other electronic source to your own project without fully documenting that material. Nor may you call it your own just because you have altered it in some minor way—changed a few words, reordered the ideas, or reshaped an image.

Going Public   *Copying and Pasting* _____

It can be tempting to copy and paste sentences directly from online sources into a project. Here, for example, are two paragraphs from a research essay by student Chad Briggs and faculty advisor Fred Ribich, both of Wartburg College, titled "The Relationship Between Test Anxiety, Sleep Habits, and Self-perceived Academic Competency." It was originally published in the online journal *Psych-E: An Electronic Psychology Journal for Undergraduates* at <http://truth.boisestate.edu/psyche/archives/vol1/briggs.html> and appears as the sample APA paper in Chapter 54.

49d
plag

ORIGINAL SOURCE

Quality of sleep habits was found to be a factor in self-perceived academic competence. If college students do experience REM sleep deprivation more than the average population, then the findings of this study need to be passed on to college students. The findings in this study suggest that college students with poor sleep habits may perceive themselves as having lower academic competency. The study also showed that self-perceived academic competency was positively correlated to academic performance. Thus, according to Hobson (1989), Webb & Bonnet (1979), and this study, those college students who do have poor sleep habits will negatively affect their academic performance.

It was also found that test anxiety and GPA are negatively correlated and that quality of sleep and GPA are positively correlated. This, and the fact that quality of sleep and test anxiety are negatively related, suggests interrelationships among the variables test anxiety, sleep habits, self-perceived academic competency, and academic performance. This result highlights the fact that professors need to instruct their students on how to manage test anxiety. Students also need to be aware of the effects that poor sleep and low self-perceived academic competency have on academic performance. Thus, the phrase "I think I can, I think I can. . . " may be beneficial only if students reduce their test anxiety and develop better sleep habits. More research needs to be done to find other variables that affect self-perceived academic competence.

Following are two paragraphs based much too closely on material from Chad Briggs's essay, now archived on the Web. This reformulation of the material amounts to plagiarism, even though the author of the plagiarized paragraphs credits Briggs as the source. The boldfaced material looks like it was copied and pasted directly from the online original.

PLAGIARIZED PARAGRAPHS

Getting a good night's sleep before an examination makes sense psychologically. According to Briggs (1999), **quality of sleep habits was found to be a factor in self-perceived academic competence.** That is to say that college students with poor sleep habits may perceive themselves as having lower academic competency. **Those college students who do have poor sleep habits will negatively affect their academic performance.**

There also seems to be a connection between self-perceived academic competency and academic performance. **This highlights the fact that professors need to instruct their students on how to manage test anxiety. Students also need to be aware of the effects that poor sleep and low self-perceived**

49d
plag

`academic competency have on academic performance.`
`Thus, the phrase, "I think I can, I think I can . . ."`
`may be beneficial only if students reduce their test`
`anxiety and develop better sleep habits.` So a student
really can improve performance in college courses by
making more time for sleep.

---

4 Understand the special nature of collaborative projects. Whether working with writers in your own classroom or with students in other locations across a network, you'll find that in truly collaborative projects it can be tough to remember who wrote what. And that's good. So long as everyone understands the ground rules an instructor sets for a project, joint authorship ought not to be a problem. But legitimate questions do arise.

- Must we write the whole project together?
- Can we break the project into separately authored sections?
- Can one person research a section, another write it, a third edit and proofread?
- What do we do if someone is not pulling his or her weight?
- Do we all get the same grade?

The time to ask such questions is at the beginning of a collaborative effort. First, determine what your instructor's guidelines are. Then sit down with the members of your group and hammer out the rules.

E-Tips   The Web offers a great deal of information on *plagiarism, collusion,* and *cheating.* Use keywords in a search engine and you will discover many academic sites (they end in *.edu*) that discuss the definition and terms of scholastic dishonesty. Or you might use the search engine at the Center for Academic Integrity at <http://academicintegrity.org> to explore more than 7,000 Web pages dealing with these issues. The University of Texas at Austin maintains an unusually comprehensive site on scholastic integrity at <http://www.utexas.edu/depts/dos/sjs/academicintegrity.html>.

49d
plag

CHAPTER 50

How Do You Handle Quotations?

No stylistic touch makes a research project work quite so well as quotations deftly handled. But using quotations skillfully is not simply a matter of style. The quotations you choose reveal much about the quality of your research and your understanding of a subject. They indicate, too, how well you appreciate the needs of your audience for accurate and convincing evidence as well as for lively discussion. So you have to select quotations strategically and then fit them seamlessly into the paper or project.

Every quotation in an article should contribute something your own words cannot. Use quotations for various reasons.

- To focus on a particularly well stated key idea in a source
- To show what others think about a subject—either experts, people involved with the issue, or the general public
- To give credence to important facts or concepts
- To add color, power, or character to your argument or report
- To show a range of opinion
- To clarify a difficult or contested point
- To demonstrate the complexity of an issue
- To emphasize a point

Never use quotations to avoid putting ideas in your own words or to pad your work.

50a Introduce all direct and indirect borrowings in some way

Short introductions, attributions, or commentaries are needed to introduce readers to materials you've gathered from sources. To be sure readers pay attention, give all borrowed words and ideas a context or *frame*. Such frames can be relatively simple, and they can *precede, follow,* or *interrupt* the borrowed words or ideas. The frame need not even be in the same sentence as the quotation; it may be part of the surrounding paragraph. Here are examples of ways that material can be introduced.

- *Frame precedes borrowed material:*
  In 1896, Woodrow Wilson, who would become Princeton's president in 1902, declared, "It is not learning but the spirit of service that will give a college a place in the public annals of the nation."

  —Ernest L. Boyer

- *Frame follows borrowed material:*
  "One reason you may have more colds if you hold back tears is that, when you're under stress, your body puts out steroids which affect your immune system and reduce your resistance to disease," **Dr. Broomfield comments.**

  —Barbara Lang Stern

- *Frame interrupts borrowed material:*
  "Whatever happens," **he [Karl Marx] wrote grimly to Engels,** "I hope the bourgeoisie as long as they exist will have cause to remember my carbuncles."

  —Paul Johnson

- *Surrounding sentences frame borrowed material:*
  In the meantime, [Luis] Jimenez was experimenting with three-dimensional form. "Perhaps because of the experience of working in the sign shop, I realized early on that I wanted to do it all— paint, draw, work with wood, metal, clay." **His images were those of 1960s pop culture, chosen for their familiarity and shock value.**

  —Chiori Santiago

- *Borrowed material integrated with passage:*
  The study concludes that a faulty work ethic is not responsible for the decline in our productivity; quite the contrary, the study identifies "a widespread commitment among U.S. workers to im-

50a
quotes

prove productivity" **and suggests that** "there are large reservoirs of potential upon which management can draw to improve performance and increase productivity."

—Daniel Yankelovich

Most borrowings in your research paper should be attributed in similar fashion. Either name (directly or indirectly) the author, the speaker, or the work the passage is from, or explain why the words you are quoting are significant. Many phrases of introduction or attribution are available. Note that the verb of attribution you choose can shape the way readers perceive the quotation that follows. Compare your reactions to the following statements that differ only in their verb of attribution.

Benson **reports** that "high school test scores have dropped again."

Benson **laments** that "high school test scores have dropped again."

Benson **complains** that "high school test scores have dropped again."

President Bush **claimed** that ". . .

One expert **stated** that ". . .

The members of the board **declared** that ". . .

Representatives of the airline industry **contend** that ". . .

Senator Clinton **was quoted** as saying that ". . .

Chart 50.1

Verbs of Attribution				
accept	allege	deny	mention	say
add	argue	disagree	posit	state
admit	believe	emphasize	propose	think
affirm	confirm	insist	reveal	verify

50b Modify quotations carefully to fit your needs

You must always quote accurately and fairly. You cannot leave out a word or phrase to make a source seem to agree with you or support your thesis. Such a modification would be intellectually dishonest and would undermine the credibility of your entire research project. But you can use a variety of techniques to make quotations flow naturally into the argument of your paper. All these techniques preserve the integrity of quotations while giving you some flexibility in their use.

1 Tailor your language so that direct quotations fit into the grammar of your sentences.
You want your own words to flow effortlessly into the phrases or sentences you are creating. To accomplish that seamless introduction, you may have to tinker with the words you use to frame the quotation or modify the quotation itself by careful selections, ellipses (see Section 50b-2), or additions made within brackets (see Section 50b-3).

> CLUMSY   The chemical capsaicin that makes chili hot:
> "it is so hot it is used to make antidog and
> antimugger sprays" (Bork 184).

> REVISED   Capsaicin, the chemical that makes chili
> hot, is so strong "it is used to make anti-
> dog and antimugger sprays" (Bork 184).

> CLUMSY   Computers have not succeeded as translators
> of language because, says Douglas Hofstadter,
> "nor is the difficulty caused by a lack of
> knowledge of idiomatic phrases. The fact is
> that translation involves having a mental
> model of the world being discussed, and ma-
> nipulating symbols in the model" (603).

> REVISED   "A lack of knowledge of idiomatic phrases"
> is not the reason computers have failed as
> translators of languages. "The fact is,"
> says Douglas Hofstadter, "that translation
> involves having a mental model of the world
> being discussed, and manipulating symbols in
> the model" (603).

50b
quotes

2 Use ellipses (three *spaced* periods . . .) to indicate where you have cut material from direct quotations.
For example, ellipses might be used to trim the lengthy passage following to focus on the oldest portions of the biblical text. The ellipses will tell readers where words, phrases, and even whole sentences have been cut.

ORIGINAL PASSAGE

The text of the Old Testament is in places the stuff of scholarly nightmares. Whereas the entire New Testament was written within fifty to a hundred years, the books of the Old Testament were composed and edited over a period of about a thousand. The youngest book is Daniel, from the second century B.C. The oldest portions of the Old Testament (if we limit ourselves to the present form of the literature and exclude from consideration the streams of oral tradition that fed it) are probably a group of poems that appear, on the basis of linguistic features and historical allusions contained in them, to date from roughly the twelfth and eleventh centuries B.C. . . .

—Barry Hoberman, "Translating the Bible"

PASSAGE AS CUT FOR USE IN AN ESSAY

> Although working with any part of an original
> scripture text is difficult, Hoberman describes the
> text of the Old Testament as "the stuff of scholarly
> nightmares." He explains in "Translating the Bible"
> that while "the entire New Testament was written
> within fifty to a hundred years, the books of the Old
> Testament were composed and edited over a period of
> about a thousand. . . . The oldest portions of the Old
> Testament . . . are probably a group of poems that
> appear . . . to date from roughly the twelfth and
> eleventh centuries B.C."

3 Use square brackets [ ] to add necessary information
to a quotation. You may want to explain who or what a pronoun refers to, or you may have to provide a short explanation, furnish a date, and explain or translate a puzzling word.

> Some critics clearly prefer Wagner's Tannhäuser to
> Lohengrin: "The well-written choruses **[of**
> **Tannhäuser]** are combined with solo singing and
> orchestral background into long, unified musical
> scenes" (Grout 629).

50b
quotes

But don't overdo it. Readers will resent the explanation of obvious details.

50c Observe the conventions of quotation

Following are some specific conventions that apply to direct quotations. Quotation marks themselves (" ") do more than set off direct quotations, so you may want to review Section 41a to appreciate all their uses. In that section, you'll also find guidelines that explain where to place quotation marks when they meet up with other punctuation marks in sentences.

1 Use [sic] to indicate an obvious error copied faithfully from a source. Quotations must be copied accurately, word by word, from your source—errors and all. To show that you have copied a passage faithfully, place the expression *sic* (the Latin word for "thus" or "so") in brackets one space after any mistake.

> Mr. Vincent's letter went on: "I would have preferred
> a younger bride, but I decided to marry the old
> window [sic] anyway."

If *sic* can be placed outside the quotation itself, it appears between parentheses, not brackets.

> Molly's paper was titled "King Leer" (sic).

2 Place prose quotations shorter than four typed lines (MLA) or forty words (APA) between quotation marks.

> In Utilitarianism (1863), John Stuart Mill declares,
> "It is better to be Socrates dissatisfied than a pig
> satisfied."

3 Indent more than three lines of poetry (MLA). Up to three lines of poetry may be handled just like a prose passage, with slashes marking the separate lines. Quotation marks are used.

> As death approaches, Cleopatra grows in grandeur and
> dignity: "Husband, I come! / Now to that name my
> courage prove my title! / I am fire and air"
> (5.2.287-89).

More than three lines of poetry are indented 10 spaces and quotation marks are not used. (If the lines of poetry are unusually long, you may

50c
quotes

indent fewer than 10 spaces.) Be sure to copy the poetry accurately, right down to the punctuation.

> Among the most famous lines in English literature
> are those that open William Blake's "The Tyger":
>> Tyger tyger, burning bright,
>>
>> In the forests of the night;
>>
>> What immortal hand or eye,
>>
>> Could frame thy fearful symmetry? (1-4)

4 Indent any prose quotation longer than four typed lines (MLA) or forty words (APA).

MLA form recommends an indention of one inch, or 10 spaces if you are using a typewriter; APA form requires 5 spaces. Quotation marks are *not* used around the indented material. If the quotation extends beyond a single paragraph, the first lines of subsequent paragraphs are indented an additional quarter inch, or 3 typed spaces (MLA) or 5 spaces (APA). In typed papers, the indented material—like the rest of the essay—is double spaced.

You may indent passages of fewer than four lines when you want them to have special emphasis. But don't do this with every short quotation or your paper will look choppy.

5 Refer to events in works of fiction, poems, plays, movies, and television shows in the present tense.

When quoting passages from novels or describing scenes from a movie or events in a play, think about the actions as performances that occur over and over again.

> In his last speech, Othello **orders** those around him
> to "Speak of me as I am. Nothing extenuate, / Nor set
> down aught in malice" (V.ii.338-39). Then he **stabs**
> himself and **dies**, falling on the bed of the innocent
> wife he has murdered only moments before: "I kissed
> thee ere I killed thee. No way but this, / Killing
> myself, to die upon a kiss" (354-55).

50c
quotes

CHAPTER 51

How Do You Complete a Project?

Since academic research projects represent a first level of serious professional work, they must usually meet exacting standards as you bring them to completion. These requirements vary from discipline to discipline, but the principles examined in this section apply to most papers and projects. (See also Chapter 5.)

51a Is the organization solid?

In many cases, you'll want to narrow the scope of your project during the writing process and give it a design that reinforces clear, though not necessarily simple, points. Some projects will support specific thesis statements or arguments. Others, including much service-learning work, may examine alternatives to the status quo or offer proposals to solve problems. Still other projects might invite readers to join in a conversation.

Your role is to create a framework that will make your project an effective response to the original assignment. This shaping must be deliberate and strategic. In a research project, you usually can't rely on chance to bring all the parts together.

E-Tips You can find more information about research reports at the Purdue University Writing Center at <http://owl.english. purdue.edu>. Just click the appropriate link or do a search for "research report."

1 Narrow or qualify your claim. The more you learn about a subject or problem, the more careful you'll be in making claims or offering solutions. That's why a final thesis statement will almost certainly be more specific, restrictive, and informative than an initial research question or hypothesis. If nothing else, the thesis should address questions such as *Who? What? When? Where? Under what conditions?*

With what limits? With what scope? And the topic sentences of paragraphs throughout the project (or other guideposts, such as the headings of Web pages) should relate clearly to this claim and be equally specific.

The shape you give your project will depend on what your thesis promises. One way to understand that commitment is to recall the purpose of your research study. For example, does the project ultimately make a claim of *fact,* a claim of *definition,* a claim of *value,* or a claim of *policy* or *proposal?* You'll want to refine your thesis to make a distinct and limited claim, then follow through with the appropriate support and evidence.

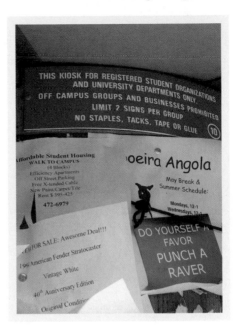

ORIGINAL CLAIM OF *FACT*
AIDS is the greatest killer of the young.

CLAIM SPECIFIED AND LIMITED BY RESEARCH
In the United States, AIDS has replaced automobile accidents as the leading cause of death among teenagers.

COMMITMENTS
- Examine American teenagers as a demographic group.
- Present figures on mortality rates among young people.
- Find figures on deaths from auto accidents.
- Find figures on deaths from AIDS.
- Ponder the mortality rate trends.
- Draw out the implications of the study for AIDS prevention.

ORIGINAL CLAIM OF *DEFINITION*
Zoos promote cruelty to animals.

CLAIM SPECIFIED AND LIMITED BY RESEARCH
Confining large marine mammals in sea parks for public amusement is, arguably, a form of cruelty to animals.

51a
research

COMMITMENTS
- Find legal/popular definitions for "cruelty to animals."
- Define specific criteria for "cruelty."
- Examine what experts say about the condition of animals in marine parks. Or do fieldwork in such a park.
- Find statistics on animal health in marine parks.
- Find expert opinion on both sides of the issue.
- Show that conditions in marine parks meet (or do not meet) criteria for "cruelty to animals."

ORIGINAL CLAIM OF *VALUE*
The EPA is ruining America.

CLAIM SPECIFIED AND LIMITED BY RESEARCH
Air-quality standards first proposed by the U.S. Environmental Protection Agency (EPA) in 1997 may damage the industrial economies of many northern and western states that depend heavily on coal.

COMMITMENTS
- Acquire the actual EPA standards.
- Determine what states may have to do in order to comply with the standards. Interview experts in local/state government.
- Explain the possible consequences of compliance.
- Present arguments of experts who favor the standards.
- Present arguments of those who oppose the standards.

ORIGINAL CLAIM OF *POLICY*
Increases in student fees on campus should be prohibited.

CLAIM SPECIFIED AND LIMITED BY RESEARCH
Additional increases in student fees on campus should be capped at a level not to exceed the national rate of inflation unless students vote in a public referendum to approve higher fees.

51a
research

COMMITMENTS
- Explain how/why fees are increasing on campus.
- Use interviews to show that students want change.
- Examine the procedure by which fees are raised.
- Detail the problems with the current procedure.
- Offer an alternative proposal.
- Defend the advantages and feasibility of the proposal.

■ **2 Test your organization.** Organizing a sizable paper or project is rarely an easy job. For the draft of a long paper, you may want to check the structure using a method such as the following.

- **Underline the topic idea, or thesis, in your draft.** It should be clearly stated somewhere in the first few paragraphs.
- **Underline just the first sentence in each subsequent paragraph.** If the first sentence is very short or closely tied to the second, underline the first two sentences.
- **Read the underlined sentences straight through as if they formed an essay in themselves.** Ask whether each sentence advances or explains the main point or thesis statement. If the sentences—taken together—read coherently, chances are good that the paper is well organized.
- **If the underlined sentences don't make sense, reexamine those paragraphs not clearly related to the topic idea.** If the ideas really are not related, delete the whole paragraph. If the ideas are related, consider how to revise the paragraph to make the connection clearer. A new lead sentence for the paragraph will often solve the problem of incoherence. Pay attention to transitions, too—those places in a paper where you can give readers helpful directions: *first of all, on the other hand, to summarize.* (See Section 17b.)
- **Test your conclusion against your introduction.** Sometimes the conclusions of essays contradict their openings because of changes that occurred as the paper developed. When you've completed a draft, set it aside for a time and then reread the entire piece. Does it hang together? If not, revise it.

Test the structure of other projects similarly. For example, if you've prepared a brochure, make sure the headings are in the right order, the various sections follow in correct sequence when the brochure is folded, and the panels contain all pertinent information, especially phone numbers and addresses.

In a Web site, try to imagine how a reader encountering it for the first time might search for information: will users find what they are seeking by following only a short sequence of links? Check that all the links work in both directions. Make sure there are no dead ends and that every page on your site provides a way to return to your home page or another helpful location in the site. (See Chapter 23 for more on composing a Web site.)

51a
research

51b Is the format correct?

Whether you are reporting your research in a conventional paper, on a Web site, or through some other less traditional vehicle, you want the presentation to be effective. Here we focus chiefly on research papers, but you can find advice about crafting other types of projects in Part IV, Design and Shape of Writing.

1 Pay attention to the format of work you submit. Be sure a paper is submitted on good-quality white paper. Print on only one side of the pages, double-spacing the body of your essay and the notes. Keep fonts simple and use boldface rarely, perhaps to highlight important headings.

Specifications for MLA and APA papers are given in Sections 53e and 54d, respectively. These guidelines, which explain where page numbers go, the width of margins, and the placement of headings, can be applied even to papers that don't need to follow a specific professional style.

In distance learning courses, you may be asked to submit your work as an email attachment or as an html document readable on the Web. In either case, be sure you understand your instructor's requirements for submitting the work. For example, if you are expected to send written work as word-processing files, be sure you use software compatible with your instructor's. Take care with any visual items in your documents (including charts and tables)—be sure they will transfer accurately. Follow your instructor's directions for naming files. Consider that an instructor may receive a great many files in a distance learning course, and you don't want your work to get lost.

2 Insert tables and figures as needed. Use graphics whenever they help readers understand your ideas better than words alone can. Pie charts, graphs, and tables (see Chapter 11) can make information easier to interpret. So learn to use the graphics tools available in word-processing or data management programs. In the latter, you can usually choose how you want your information presented (tables, bar graphs, pie charts); the program itself produces the actual image, which you can modify to suit your needs.

51b
research

If you have access to the World Wide Web, you can download pictures and other visual items for your projects, but you must document the borrowings and you must get permission to use them from the authors/owners of the material. Be careful, too, not to clutter your work with what one design expert calls "chartjunk." Just because you have easy access to graphics doesn't mean you must illustrate every page. Develop an eye for clean and attractive presentations on paper or on screen. (See Chapter 21 on document design.)

MLA form requires that you label tables (columns of data) and figures (pictures or illustrations), number them, and briefly identify what they illustrate. Spell out the word *Table*, and position the heading above the table, aligned with the left margin.

Table 1
First-Year Student Applications by Region

	Fall 1995	Fall 1994	Difference	Percent Change
Texas	12,022	11,590	432	+4
Out of state	2,121	2,058	63	+3
Foreign	756	673	83	+11

Figure, which is usually abbreviated in the caption as *Fig.,* appears below the illustration, flush left.

Fig. 7   Mountain bike.

When preparing an APA paper, you may want to check the detailed coverage of figures and tables in the *Publication Manual of the American Psychological Association.* For APA-style student papers, figures (including graphs, illustrations, and photos) and tables may appear in the body of the essay itself, placed on separate pages, immediately following their mention in the text.

51b
research

    Chromosomes consist of four different nucleotides or

    bases—adenine, guanine, thymine, and cytosine—which,

    working together, provide the code for different

    genes (see Figure 1).

Short tables may even appear on the same page as text material.

Figures and tables are numbered consecutively. Captions for figures appear below the item. If the illustration is borrowed from a source, you must get permission to reproduce it and acknowledge the borrowing as shown.

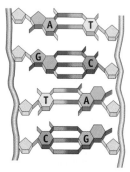

Figure 1. The four bases of the genetic code: adenine (A), guanine (G), thymine (T), and cytosine (C). From *Your Genes, Your Choice,* by. C. Baker, 1997. Copyright 1997 by the American Association for the Advancement of Science. Reprinted with permission.

Titles for tables appear above the item.

Table 2

Errors by Levels of Difficulty

■ 3 Be consistent with headings. You can use headings to give shape to any project. A short research paper (five to six pages) ordinarily needs only a title. In longer papers, however, readers will appreciate headings that explain the content of major sections. All such heads should be brief, parallel in phrasing, and consistent in format like the items in a formal outline (see Section 3c-3). For most academic papers, you probably won't use more than one level of heading after the title.

MLA style (described in detail in Chapter 53) provides fairly loose standards for headings. Titles of MLA papers are ordinarily centered on the first page of an essay while headings appear in the text, flush with the left-hand margin. If you descend to a second level, you'll have to distinguish second-level heads by numbering or lettering them or by setting them off typographically (usually by variations in capitalization or underlining). MLA style leaves you to decide how you will handle such choices, but in all cases, you must keep the headings clean and un-

51b
research

obtrusive. Here are two ways of handling headings as they might appear in a moderately long MLA-style paper on mountain biking.

Mountain Biking and the Environment	Title
The Mountain Bike	1st level
History of Mountain Biking	1st level
Mountain Bikes and the Environment	1st level
<u>Trail Damage</u>	2nd level
<u>Conflicts with Hikers</u>	2nd level
Mountain Bikes and Responsible Riding	1st level
Mountain Biking and the Environment	Title
1. The Mountain Bike	1st level
2. History of Mountain Biking	1st level
3. Mountain Bikes and the Environment	1st level
3.1 Trail Damage	2nd level
3.2 Conflicts with Hikers	2nd level
4. Mountain Bikes and Responsible Riding	1st level

APA style (described in detail in Chapter 54) defines five levels of headings for professional articles—more than you'll probably use in a college paper. Here's how to handle two levels of headings.

- First-level heads are centered, using both uppercase and lowercase letters as shown below.
- Second-level heads are capitalized like titles, but also underlined and placed flush with the left-hand margin.

Here's how those APA guidelines look in operation.

Differences in Reading Habits of College Sophomores	Title
Abstract	1st level
Method	1st level
Participants	2nd level
Materials	2nd level
Design and Procedure	2nd level
Results	1st level
Discussion	1st level

51b
research

Any Web pages you create also need accurate, well-focused headings and titles so readers quickly grasp the point of your projects. Succinct and descriptive titles are important, too, if your pages are to be located by Web search engines and directories. Finally, you want titles that will still make sense if they get shortened when added to a Web browser's list of bookmarks or favorites: the first few words of the title should include all important keywords. A heading such as "The Beauty and Mystery of Anasazi Cliff Dwellings" might be clipped back to the not very helpful "The Beauty and Mystery." Instead, title the Web page "Anasazi Cliff Dwellings: Beauty and Mystery" so that a shortened title will highlight pertinent information.

51c Are the details correct?

Give the final version of your project a careful review. By this point in your work, you've been close to the project for a long time, so you may need to put some distance between it and you before you do the final check. Even a few days, if you can afford them, can be enough to help you see features that need to be polished. Don't skip this step.

1 Include all the components your project requires.
Before you submit a project, reread the specifications of either the instructor or the professional society whose guidelines you are following. Must you, for instance, include an abstract or an outline? Check to see what leeway (if any) you have in arranging the title page, notes, bibliography, and other features. A research paper typically follows a specific order.

- Title page (not recommended in MLA; required in APA)
- Outline (optional; begins on its own page; requires separate title page)
- Abstract (optional, but common in APA; usually on its own page)
- Body of the essay (in MLA, Arabic pagination begins with the body of the essay in MLA; in APA, with the title page)
- Content or bibliographic notes
- Works Cited/References (begins on its own page separate from the body of the essay and any content or bibliographic notes)

51c
research

The sample research essay on pages 821–22 illustrates MLA style, and the essay on pages 852–53 illustrates APA style. For a more complex paper such as a master's thesis or a doctoral dissertation, follow the order recommended in a volume such as *The MLA Style Manual* (MLA) or the *Publication Manual of the American Psychological Association* (APA). Many schools publish their own guidelines for submitting graduate-level theses.

2 Follow the rules for documentation right down to the punctuation and spacing. Accurate documentation is a part of professional research. Instructors and editors notice even minor variations in documentation form. Perhaps the two most common errors in handling the MLA format, for example, are forgetting to put a period at the end of entries in the Works Cited list and placing a comma where none is needed in parenthetical documentation.

| WRONG | Pluto, Terry. The Curse of Rocky Colavito. New York: Simon, 1994 |
| RIGHT | Pluto, Terry. The Curse of Rocky Colavito. New York: Simon, 1994. |

| WRONG | (Pluto, 132-36) |
| RIGHT | (Pluto 132-36) |

You will survive both errors, but they are easy to avoid.

3 Submit your project professionally. Whether you've written a paper, designed a brochure, or created a Web site, be sure the work meets appropriate standards. Examine what you've produced to see that everything looks "detailed": the writing is sharp and correct, the images are crisp and labeled, the pagination is right, the links are operative, the documentation is solid.

Don't overdo it. For an electronic project, keep the bells and whistles (and gaudy colors) to a functional minimum. For a paper, bind the pages modestly with a paper clip. Nothing more elaborate is needed, unless an instructor asks you to place the essay (still clipped) in a folder along with all materials you used in developing it.

When you submit an article for publication, be sure to follow all instructions for submission provided by the editors. Note in particular how many clean copies they require of your work, to whom those copies should be sent, and whether they expect you to furnish a self-addressed, stamped envelope for return of your work. For more on doing research, be sure to see the Web site for this handbook at <www.prenhall.com/hairston>.

51c
research

Checklist 51.1

Research Project Requirements

• Have you placed your name, your instructor's name, the date, and the course name on the first or title page?

• Is the title centered? Are only the major words capitalized? (Your title should not be underlined or appear between quotation marks.)

• Did you number the pages? Are they in the right order?

• Have you used quotation marks and parentheses correctly and in pairs? (The closing quotation mark and parenthesis are often forgotten.)

• Have you placed quotation marks around all direct quotations that are shorter than four lines?

• Have you indented all direct quotations of more than four typed lines (MLA) or of forty words or more (APA)?

• Have you remembered that indented quotations are not placed between quotation marks?

• Did you introduce all direct quotations with some identification of their author, source, or significance?

• Did you use the correct form for parenthetical notes?

• Have you handled titles correctly, italicizing books and putting the titles of articles between quotation marks?

• Did you include a Works Cited or References list? Is your list of works cited alphabetized? Did you indent the entries correctly?

51c
research

Documentation

CHAPTER 52

What Is Documentation?

Imagine what baseball would be like if every major league club decided the fine points of the complex game on its own. Play would be chaotic and arguments even more difficult to settle than they are now. Fortunately, to resolve disputes both big and small, umpires and fans alike can consult the Official Baseball Rules at <www.mlb.com>. You can find similar rulebooks directing the play of just about every sports league, both professional and amateur.

Writers do the same thing when they agree to use a particular form of documentation and style in their own professions. In effect, they are setting down ground rules for their work that everyone agrees to follow.

Documentation refers to the forms devised to keep track of sources used in a project—typically some type of notes (endnotes, footnotes, parenthetical notes) and a full bibliography. Systems of documentation typically offer detailed models for handling a wide variety of sources, from traditional books and articles to less familiar electronic media.

Style here refers to guidelines for handling the myriad details of printed or online texts. Major newspapers and publishers, for example, will often have in-house "style sheets" describing the forms to be used by writers working for that institution. Such style sheets are designed to answer questions such as the following: Which words in a title are capitalized? How are words hyphenated or spelled? How are dates expressed? How are figures and illustrations treated? A published example of such a style sheet is *The New York Times Manual of Style and Usage,* advertised as "the Official Style Guide Used by the Writers and Editors of the World's Most Authoritative Newspaper."

52a Who sets the rules?

In high school and college, most student writers learn the documentation procedures established by the Modern Language Association (MLA). That's because writing is usually taught by English teachers who belong to this professional association. The complete *MLA Style Manual and Guide to Scholarly Publishing* (2nd edition, 1998) covers topics from copyright issues to punctuation. Almost half of this volume written for scholars explains how to format parenthetical notes, footnotes, and works cited pages. Available for students is the briefer *MLA Handbook for Writers of Research Papers* (6th edition, 2003). (For MLA guidelines and a sample paper using MLA documentation, see Chapter 53.)

Scholars in fields other than literature, especially people working in the humanities and liberal arts, use MLA guidelines because they are well adapted to research that deals with authors and their texts. But a system of style and documentation that works for people who deal with words (such as English teachers, historians, and philosophers) might not suit professionals whose occupation involves numbers, equations, and experiments and for whom a date of publication for research articles is crucial information. So different rules about documentation and style have evolved in the sciences, the most familiar to college students likely to be those recommended by the American Psychological Association (APA). Their recommendations are summarized in the *Publication Manual of the American Psychological Association* (5th edition, 2001), a volume widely consulted in the social sciences. Also influential is the newly named Council of Science Editors (CSE), which publishes *Scientific Style and Format* (6th edition, 1994), a style guide oriented to the needs of scholars in the natural sciences. (For APA guidelines and a sample paper, see Chapter 54; for CSE style, see Chapter 56.)

And there are many more professions and groups that establish committees or groups who determine and publish the rules used by writers in their worlds. For more than a hundred years, the Government Printing Office (GPO) has offered a style manual to assist writers preparing federal documents. Even more famous and almost as old is the widely cited *Chicago Manual of Style,* a compilation of guidelines that has been adopted by many publishers, journals, and writers. So-called Chicago style offers one of the most elegant systems for using footnotes, a form of documentation no longer favored by the committees responsible for MLA and APA style. (For more on Chicago style and a sample paper, see Chapter 55.)

The point is that there are many different systems of documentation and style, and each serves the needs of different professions, audiences, and purposes. The more serious your own academic work becomes, the more you'll need to know what your field expects from a writer. So you should become familiar with the professional organizations in your major and find out what stylebooks they follow.

52a
docu

Chart 52.1

Style Guides in Various Fields

- **Biology:** *Scientific Style and Format: The CBE Manual for Authors, Editors, and Publishers* (6th ed., 1994) by the Council of Science Editors

- **Chemistry:** *The ACS Style Guide: A Manual for Authors and Editors* (2nd ed., 1997) by the American Chemical Society and Janet S. Dodd

- **Earth science:** *Geowriting: A Guide to Writing, Editing, and Printing in Earth Science* (5th ed., 1995) by Robert Bates

- **English language and literature/humanities:** *MLA Handbook for Writers of Term Papers* (6th ed., 2003) by Joseph Gibaldi; student version of *MLA Style Manual*

- **Federal government:** *United States Government Printing Office Manual* (2000) by the United States Government Printing Office (GPO)

- **Journalism:** *The Associated Press Stylebook and Libel Manual* (1998) by Norm Goldstein

- **Law:** *Uniform System of Citation: The Bluebook* (16th ed., 1996) by the Harvard Law Review Association

- **Mathematics:** *A Manual for Writers of Mathematical Papers* (8th ed., 1990) by the American Mathematical Society

- **Music:** *Writing About Music: An Introductory Guide* (3rd ed., 2001) by Richard J. Wingell

- **Nursing:** *Writing for Nursing Publications* (1981) by Andrea B. O'Connor

- **Political science:** *Style Manual for Political Science* (rev ed., 2002) by the American Political Science Association and Michael K. Lane

- **Psychology and social sciences:** *Publication Manual of the American Psychological Association* (5th ed., 2001)

- **Physics:** *AIP Style Manual* (4th ed., 1990) by the American Institute of Physics.

52b Why do rules of documentation seem so complicated and arbitrary?

52b

docu

Getting the notes or bibliography page in a project exactly right can seem like an impossible task, especially the first few times you use a system of documentation. There seem to be picky rules for everything, from capitalizing titles to setting margins. (MLA even recommends that you use a paper clip to hold a research paper together.) And why does citing a Web site or labeling a chart have to be so complicated? Don't the people who offer this kind of advice have anything better to do with their time?

The fact is that there *is* a method in this madness. But the state of affairs may be even more complicated than you realize. The guidelines for style and documentation you find in a general writer's handbook like this one represent only the tip of an iceberg. The complete *MLA Style Manual* runs 343 pages, *The MLA Handbook for Writers of Research Papers* contains 332 pages, the APA *Publication Manual* is 439 pages, and the 14th edition of *The Chicago Manual of Style* fills 921 closely printed pages. In each case, the authors of these professional style guides are trying to provide bullet-proof answers to the thousands of questions that can arise when someone seeks to publish an article or book in a field. They do so to avoid the chaos that would follow if every author, editor, and publisher had to decide basic issues on their own. For the sake of clarity and consistency, groups like the MLA, APA, and CSE design their reference volumes to guide writers through even the most obscure issues and choices. These books are designed for easy reference, with rich indexes, precisely because users are not expected to memorize all the details. But they do need to know where to find help.

Of course, the rules and guidelines do evolve and change. The introduction of Web and electronic sources has caused almost every system of documentation to rethink its principles and amend its style. Committees have had to decide matters as simple as whether to use the spelling *e-mail* or *email* in professional documents. Much more troublesome has been figuring out how to handle electronic sources that lack rudimentary bibliographical features such as authors, titles, page numbers, and dates. If it is any comfort, the last decade hasn't been kind to the people who serve on editorial committees for documentation manuals. An entire system of documentation—Columbia Online Style (COS)—has been devised just to deal with electronic sources.

You may not enjoy working with documentation systems and professional manuals of style, but you should respect what they represent. In the long run, they provide a sensible and even helpful way of reporting information. They reduce the number of petty choices you have to make, leaving you time to worry about bigger research issues. And they give your work a professional character. If your research project meets MLA or APA standards of style and citation, you've learned to respect your sources and pay attention to the details. Serious readers will appreciate your efforts.

52b
docu

52c Why don't all writers document their works?

Most of the books, magazines, and newspapers we read don't come with notes and bibliographies. Even the most serious investigative reports in serious magazines or newspapers credit their sources informally—*according to a well-placed official in the State Department* or *so-and-so claims*. They certainly don't provide the detailed documentation required in a typical college research paper. Are professional writers, then, held to lower standards than the typical college student?

In one sense they are, because the college research report—with full documentation—is designed to introduce students to scholarly standards of writing in the arts and sciences. The labor of trained scholars is expected to be more careful, deliberate, and verifiable than the routine work of journalists and professional writers producing material for the general public. Although you may never aspire to be a serious scholar, working firsthand with a system of documentation teaches you what serious research involves.

That's not to suggest that professional writers don't adhere to high standards. Rather, they typically apply different kinds of rules to their reporting. Newspaper and magazine journalists, for example, don't use footnotes or other kinds of documentation to support their routine work because they are relying, quite often, on oral sources—people willing to talk to them, on or off the record. Or they may be reporting their own experiences or drawing heavily from secondary sources, which they acknowledge in the body of their work. As a result, newspapers have a different kind of authority than do scientific or scholarly articles. Readers are relying on the general reputation of the paper or the reporter because they often cannot verify the accuracy of the stories themselves. Most magazines and newspapers have professional standards for their stories: for example, a journalist may not publish someone's claim unless it can be independently verified by a second source. But be aware that journalistic ethics can be strained in the race to be first to report important stories.

The lesson for you is to pay attention to the way authors credit their sources, whether they are scholars, professional writers, or journalists. Attribution will come in many forms, the most reliable being traditional systems of documentation. But don't be surprised to see claims supported in different ways. And don't be surprised if some instructors ignore documentation in the papers they assign; not every college assignment is designed to teach research methods.

52c
docu

52d Where do I find information to document a source?

When working with research materials, you'll likely encounter many unfamiliar terms and concepts. An instructor may assume, for example, that you already know what an *edition* is, where the publication information for a book can be found, or why some magazines have volume numbers and others do not. But knowing how to document sources isn't intuitive, so be willing to ask questions—even "dumb" ones. We'll cover some basics of documenting books, articles, and electronic sources here, but you'll likely figure out more on your own as you develop a project.

1 Check the title and copyright pages on books for documentation information. For books published in English, you'll find the title page just a page or two inside the front cover. Most title pages will include a full title (including any subtitle); the names of the author(s), editors, or translators; the number of the edition; and the publisher. For the year and place of publication, check the copyright page, which follows immediately. The copyright page may also offer details about previous editions of the book, as well as its Library of Congress call number and its International Standard Book Number (ISBN). You aren't likely to need all this information for your citations, but it might be useful in locating the book later or in ordering it. If information you need is not in the book—a place of publication, a date,

Title and subtitle

Author

Publisher

52d
docu

or even an author's name—just omit that information from your citation. Don't guess or make it up.

Don't be confused, either, by the terms *reprint* and *revision*. A reprint is just more copies of a particular edition. A book might be published initially in a run of 10,000 copies; if it is successful, it might then be reprinted in a second run of 25,000 copies, and then another of 50,000, and so on. But it does not become a new edition until it is revised in some major way. You'll need to know what edition of a book you are using, but don't worry about what printing it is in.

Large books may appear in several *volumes* because a single volume would be too large or because the book was produced over a long period of time, with different volumes appearing in different years. A book in a *series* is a separate work that is part of a collection of books by different authors on a common theme. Series are typically published by institutions or professional organizations with long-term interests in a subject. If a book is published in several volumes or is part of a series, you'll need to mention the fact in your citation.

■ **2 Check the cover or contents page of scholarly journals for documentation information.** Most of the information you need in order to cite an article in a scholarly journal will be easy to find. Some key information—the title of the journal, the volume number, and the date—may even be on the cover of the periodical. Any additional information will be in its table of contents, though you'll need to check the article itself to get its closing page number.

To many people, the most mysterious aspect of scholarly journals is their use of *volume* numbers to identify the work produced in a particular year. Few scholarly journals come out monthly or on a particular date. Instead, issues appear several times during a year, sometimes irreg-

Volume number

Date

Title of journal

ularly. For easy and unambiguous reference, all the issues produced during that single year constitute one *continuously paginated* volume. (For example, the "winter" issue of a journal may begin on page 389.) When citing a journal article, you will always need the volume number, the year of publication, and the page numbers of the article you are using. You may also want to take note of the season or month the issue appeared, when such information is provided. Only rarely will you need to provide the issue number as well as the volume.

3 Check the contents and credits pages of magazines for documentation information. Most of the information you need to cite an article in a magazine will appear on its contents page, including the name of the periodical, the date of the issue, the author(s), and the title of article. Be careful with titles. To get them right, copy them from the articles themselves, especially if the title page is cluttered with descriptive blurbs or call-outs from the magazine.

Page numbers can be tricky too. While articles in scholarly journals run uninterrupted from beginning to end, those in magazines are often broken up. You can't report that an article runs from page 60 to page 99 if

Magazine title   Table of contents   Date of publication

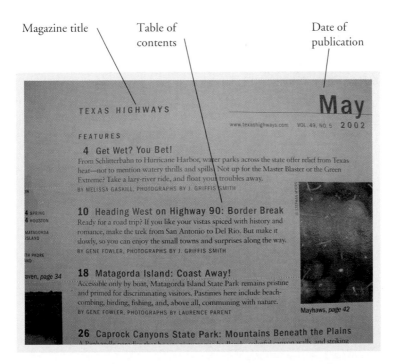

TEXAS HIGHWAYS

May

www.texashighways.com   VOL. 49, NO. 5   2002

FEATURES

4 Get Wet? You Bet!
From Schlitterbahn to Hurricane Harbor, water parks across the state offer relief from Texas heat—not to mention watery thrills and spills. Not up for the Master Blaster or the Green Extreme? Take a lazy-river ride, and float your troubles away.
BY MELISSA GASKILL. PHOTOGRAPHS BY J. GRIFFIS SMITH

10 Heading West on Highway 90: Border Break
Ready for a road trip? If you like your vistas spiced with history and romance, make the trek from San Antonio to Del Rio. But make it slowly, so you can enjoy the small towns and surprises along the way.
BY GENE FOWLER. PHOTOGRAPHS BY J. GRIFFIS SMITH

18 Matagorda Island: Coast Away!
Accessible only by boat, Matagorda Island State Park remains pristine and primed for discriminating visitors. Pastimes here include beachcombing, birding, fishing, and, above all, communing with nature.
BY GENE FOWLER. PHOTOGRAPHS BY LAURENCE PARENT

Mayhaws, page 42

26 Caprock Canyons State Park: Mountains Beneath the Plains

52d
docu

three other stories and two dozen ads also appear within those same pages. In MLA style (see Chapter 53), you would simply give the first page of the story followed by a plus sign: *60+*. In APA style (see Chapter 54), you would list all the pages on which the story appears: *60–65, 96, 98–99*.

After the title page, most magazines provide a full column or page of credits, listing just about everyone associated with the periodical, from the editor in chief on down. You will also find important contact and circulation information. You usually won't need this page to complete your documentation, but you might find it useful if you need to query a writer or an editor about a story (or even to submit an article to the magazine for publication yourself).

4 Check the masthead and credits column of newspapers for documentation information. It is hard to miss the name and date of a newspaper. You'll find that information right on the masthead—the distinctive banner that runs across the front page identifying the paper. If the masthead indicates that you are using a particular edition of the paper—*morning, evening, suburban*—be sure to note it. Copy the headline of any article you cite from the first page of the story; the continuation of a story on a later page might have an altered title. When stories appear across a series of pages, follow the same procedure for newspapers as for magazines. But note that newspapers are paginated by sections as well as numbers. In MLA style, you simply give the first section and page of the story, followed by a plus sign: *B60+*. In APA style, list all the pages on which the story appears: *B60–65, B96, B98–99*.

Newspaper masthead   Date and section

52d
docu

5 Expect full documentation from the Web sites you use. When you start documenting Web sites and other electronic media for a research paper, you'll quickly discover that they operate by different standards than printed works. Much of the online material you use may not have conventional authors, titles, or publication information. Yet the home page for a site should give you enough information to provide a reader with adequate documentation—the name of the site, an institutional sponsor, and a date for the most recent updates. For online books, articles, and newspapers, look for the same information you would gather for printed versions of these materials, with the possible exception of page numbers.

When a Web site provides virtually no documentation information, aside from the title of the page and the URL, you should question its worth as a source for your project. If you don't know who is responsible for the information you are reading, who posted it, or how old it is, don't use it.

CHAPTER 53

How Do You Use MLA Documentation?

MLA (Modern Language Association) documentation usually involves just two steps: creating a note at the point where you use a source in a paper or project (Section 53a) and then creating an entry on a Works Cited page for that source (Section 53b). That's all there is to it.

Some instructors still prefer footnotes at the bottom of a page or endnotes gathered in a single list at the end of the paper to the in-text notes we demonstrate here. We provide examples of these footnote forms in Section 53d. If you run into documentation problems not dis-

Step 1

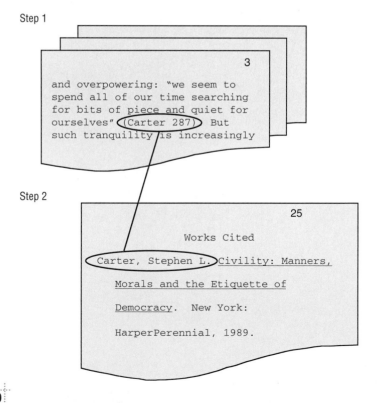

3

and overpowering: "we seem to spend all of our time searching for bits of piece and quiet for ourselves" (Carter 287). But such tranquility is increasingly

Step 2

25

Works Cited

Carter, Stephen L. Civility: Manners, Morals and the Etiquette of Democracy. New York: HarperPerennial, 1989.

cussed here, refer to the *MLA Handbook for Writers of Research Papers,* sixth edition (2003), by Joseph Gibaldi. Style updates are also available at the MLA Web site at < http://www.mla.org>.

53a Step 1: In the body of your paper, create a note for each source you use.

In MLA style, the connection between a note in the body of the paper and the item it points to on the Works Cited page is the key to successful documentation. The connection is usually made via an author's last name or, when there is no author, the name or title of the source. A note should lead readers directly to a single item on the Works Cited page. The MLA models in Section 53c will help guide you: each model includes both a note and its corresponding Works Cited entry.

IN-TEXT NOTE: (Prosek 246-47)

                    Works Cited

Prosek, James. The Complete Angler: A Connecticut

    Yankee Follows in the Footsteps of Walton. New

    York: Harper, 1999.

IN-TEXT NOTE: More information on National Parks in the
United States can be found at Parknet

                    Works Cited

Parknet. National Park Service. 12 Dec. 1999

    <http://www.nps.gov/>.

To create notes for conventional sources with authors and page numbers, enclose the author's last name and the relevant page number(s) within parentheses. Here's how you would cite a passage from *Civility* by Stephen L. Carter.

Many find modern society hectic and overpowering: "we

seem to spend all of our time searching for bits of

peace and quiet for ourselves" (Carter 287).

The note in parentheses tells readers to look for a work by Carter on the Works Cited page of the project; they will find the quoted sentence on

53a
MLA

page 287 of Carter's book. Notice that a single typed space separates the author's name and the page number, that the note itself falls *outside* the quotation marks, and that it is *followed* by the punctuation mark. In MLA documentation, page numbers are *not* preceded by *p.* or *pp.* or by a comma.

```
(Carter 287)

(Bly 253-54)
```

You can shorten a parenthetical note by naming the author of the source in the body of the essay; then the parenthetical note consists of a page number only.

Stephen L. Carter, professor of law at Yale, notes
that "we seem to spend all of our time searching for
bits of peace and quiet for ourselves" (287).

This is a common and readable form, one you should use regularly, especially when you build an entire paragraph from material in a single source. As a general rule, make all parenthetical notes as brief and inconspicuous as possible.

For sources without conventional authors or page numbers such as some Web sites and many other electronic items, the note will vary. Ordinarily, you cite such a source just by naming it or describing it within the paper or project itself.

Included in the "When Nixon Met Elvis" exhibit at the
National Archives Online Exhibit Hall is . . .

The Arkansas State Highway Map indicates . . .

Software such as Microsoft's PowerPoint . . .

You would also use this form when citing a complete book, article, or Web site rather than just a specific chapter, section, or passage.

The Media Research Center Web site offers . . .

In an article titled "Hamlet's Encounter with the
Pirates," Wentersdorf argues . . .

Under "Northwest Passage" in Collier's Encyclopedia
. . .

53a
MLA
One principle remains the same: readers must be able to connect any source you cite in the paper to a corresponding item on the Works Cited page. That means that the name you use to identify a source in

the paper or project has to be the same name by which you list the item on the Works Cited page—where readers can find more information about the source (for instance, its electronic address).

On the rare occasions when an electronic source has paragraph numbers, screen numbers, or titles for the Web pages you are citing, you can put this helpful information in parentheses.

Most MLA notes are simple, but some special situations may come up, such as the following:

- **When you cite a work without an author** (but with conventional page numbers)—an unsigned article in a magazine or newspaper, for example—list the title, shortened if necessary, and the page number. Shortened titles must always begin with the words used to alphabetize the item on the Works Cited page.

  ("In the Thicket" 18)

  ("Students Rally" A6)

  Works Cited

  "In the Thicket of Things." Texas Monthly Apr.

  1994: 18.

  "Students Rally for Academic Freedom." The Chronicle

  of Higher Education 28 Sept. 1994: A6.

- **If you need to cite more than a one book or article in single note,** separate the citations with a semicolon.

  (Polukord 13-16; Ryan and Weber 126)

- **When you cite two or more sources within a single sentence,** place the parenthetical notes right after the specific statements they support.

  While the budget cuts might go deeper than originally

  reported (Kinsley 42), there is no reason to believe

  that "throwing more taxpayers' dollars into a

  bottomless pit" (Doggett 62) will do much to reform

  "one of the least productive job training programs

  ever devised by the federal government" (Will 28).

Notice that a parenthetical note is always placed outside any quotation marks but before the period that ends the sentence.

53a
MLA

● **With a quotation long enough to require indention** (more than four typed lines), place any parenthetical note outside the final punctuation mark. Compare the following examples.

SHORT QUOTATION (NOT INDENTED)

```
Ralph Bunche never wavered in his belief that the
races in America had to learn to live together: "In
all of his experience of racial discrimination
Bunche never allowed himself to become bitter or to
feel racial hatred" (Urquhart 435). He continued to
work . . .
```

The note is placed inside the final punctuation mark.

LONG QUOTATION (INDENTED TEN SPACES)

```
Winner of the Nobel Peace Prize in 1950, Ralph
Bunche, who died in 1971, left an enduring legacy:

        His memory lives on, especially in the long
        struggle for human dignity and against racial
        discrimination and bigotry, and in the growing
        effectiveness of the United Nations in
        resolving conflicts and keeping the peace.
        (Urquhart 458)
```

The note is placed outside the final punctuation mark.

● **When you cite more than one work by a single author in a paper,** a parenthetical note listing only the author's last name could refer to more than one book or article on the Works Cited page. To avoid confusion, place a comma after the author's name and identify the particular work being cited, using a shortened title. For example, a Works Cited page (see Section 53b) might list the following four works by Richard D. Altick.

Works Cited

```
Altick, Richard D. The Art of Literary Research. New
        York: Norton, 1963.

---. The Shows of London. Cambridge: Belknap-
        Harvard, 1978.
```

53a
MLA

---. <u>Victorian People and Ideas</u>. New York: Norton,

1973.

--- <u>Victorian Studies in Scarlet</u>. New York:

Norton, 1977.

The first time—and every subsequent time—you refer to a work by Richard Altick, you need to identify it by a shortened title in the parenthetical note.

(Altick, <u>Shows</u> 345)

(Altick, <u>Victorian People</u> 190-202)

(Altick, <u>Victorian Studies</u> 59)

53b Step 2: On a separate page at the end of your project, list alphabetically every source you have cited.

This list of sources is titled "Works Cited." It should include only sources you actually mention in the body of the project itself, not all that you might have examined in preparing the work. A typical MLA Works Cited entry includes the following basic information with many variations.

- Author(s), last name first, followed by a period.
- Title of the work, followed by a period. Book titles and Web sites are underlined (or italicized), while titles of articles or individual Web pages are placed between quotation marks.
- Publication information. For books, provide place of publication (followed by a colon), the name of publisher (followed by a comma), and year of publication (followed by a period). For articles, give the title of the journal (underlined or italicized), the volume number, the date of publication in parentheses followed by a colon and the page numbers followed by a period. For Web sites, the publication information includes a date of publication, the date you looked at the information, and a Web address between angle brackets < >, followed by a period.

A Works Cited entry for Stephen Carter's book mentioned above would look like the following:

Carter, Stephen L. <u>Civility: Manners, Morals, and</u>

    <u>the Etiquette of Democracy.</u> New York:

    HarperPerennial, 1998.

Appropriate forms for dozens of Works Cited items appear in the list of MLA models in Section 53c.

The Works Cited page is placed after the body of the essay (and the endnotes, if there are any). For a sample Works Cited list, see pages 832–33. A checklist for setting up your own Works Cited list appears on page 833. The first entries on a Works Cited page might look like this.

Subsequent lines indented one-half inch or five spaces   "Works Cited" centered   All items double spaced

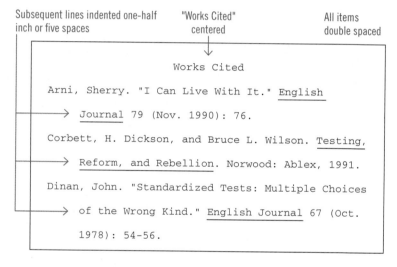

Works Cited

Arni, Sherry. "I Can Live With It." <u>English</u>

    <u>Journal</u> 79 (Nov. 1990): 76.

Corbett, H. Dickson, and Bruce L. Wilson. <u>Testing,</u>

    <u>Reform, and Rebellion.</u> Norwood: Ablex, 1991.

Dinan, John. "Standardized Tests: Multiple Choices

    of the Wrong Kind." <u>English Journal</u> 67 (Oct.

    1978): 54-56.

Works published since 1900 include a publisher's name. Publishers' names should be shortened whenever possible. Drop words such as *Company, Inc., LTD, Bro.,* and *Books.* Abbreviate *University* to *U* and *University Press* to *UP.* When possible, shorten a publisher's name to one word.

Chart 53.1

Abbreviations for Publishers in MLA Style

Addison Wesley Longman	Longman
Barnes and Noble Books	Barnes
Charles Scribner's Sons	Scribner's
Columbia University Press	Columbia UP
Doubleday and Co., Inc.	Doubleday
Gale Research	Gale

53b
MLA

Harper & Row	Harper
HarperCollins	HarperCollins
Harvard University Press	Harvard UP
Houghton Mifflin	Houghton
W.W. Norton and Co.	Norton
Random House	Random
Simon and Schuster	Simon
University of Chicago Press	U of Chicago P
The Viking Press	Viking

 Should you underline or italicize the title of a book, play, movie, or other major work? Writers working with typewriters did not have a choice; they could only underscore titles that would be italicized in printed works. Now, however, word processors and printers make it possible for writers to produce italics. However, MLA style still favors underlining the titles in material that will be graded or printed. That's because italics can sometimes be hard to read. See the "MLA Style" section at <http://www.mla.org/www_mla_org> for MLA's rationale for the policy.

53c MLA models

Below you will find MLA models to follow in creating notes and the corresponding Works Cited entries for more than sixty kinds of sources. Simply locate the type of source you need to cite in either the Models Index or the Alphabetical Index and then locate that item by number in the list that follows.

MLA Models Index

Books/Dissertations

1. Book, generic
2. Book, two or three authors or editors
3. Book, four or more authors or editors
4. Book, revised by a second author

5. Book, edited—focus on the original author
6. Book, edited—focus on the editor
7. Book, edited—focus on the editor, more than one editor
8. Book, written by a group
9. Book with no author

53c
MLA

10. Book, focus on a foreword, introduction, preface, or afterword
11. Work of more than one volume
12. Book, translation—focus on the original author
13. Book, translation—focus on the translator
14. Book in a foreign language
15. Book, republished
16. Book, part of a series
17. Book, a reader or anthology
18. Book, a second, third, or later edition
19. Book, Chapter in a
20. Book published before 1900
21. Book, issued by a division of a publisher—a special imprint
22. Dissertation or thesis—published
23. Dissertation or thesis—unpublished
24. Book review, movie review

Articles and Magazine Pieces
25. Article in a scholarly journal, generic
26. Article in a popular magazine, generic
27. Article in a weekly or biweekly magazine
28. Article in a monthly magazine—author named
29. Article or selection from a reader or anthology

Newspapers
30. Article in a newspaper
31. Editorial in a newspaper
32. Letter to the editor
33. Cartoon

Reference Works
34. Reference work or encyclopedia (familiar or online)
35. Reference work (specialized or less familiar)
36. Bulletin, brochure, or pamphlet
37. Government document

Electronic Sources
38. Computer software
39. WWW page, generic
40. WWW page, online book
41. WWW page, online scholarly journal
42. WWW page, online popular magazine
43. WWW page, online news source or newspaper
44. WWW page, personal home page
45. Listserv/newsgroup/Usenet newsgroup
46. Synchronous communication (MOOs, MUDs)
47. Email
48. CD-ROM/diskette database or publication

Miscellaneous Entries
49. Microfilm or microfiche
50. Biblical citation
51. Videotape/DVD
52. Movie
53. Television program
54. Radio program
55. Personal interview
56. Musical composition
57. Recording/audio clip
58. Speech
59. Lecture
60. Advertisement

61. Letter—published
62. Letter—unpublished
63. Artwork/photograph
64. Drama or play

MLA Alphabetical Index

1 MLA: Books checklist

Basic information	Example (see model 1)
❑ Name of author(s) or editors(s)	Prosek, James.
❑ Title of the book (underscored)	The Complete Angler . . .
❑ Publisher's location	New York:
❑ Publisher (brief name)	Harper,
❑ Year of publication	1999.

Other information
❑ Edition number
❑ Volume number
❑ Translator's name
❑ Series name

1. **Book, Generic—MLA** Provide author, title, place of publication, publisher, and year of publication. For an online book, see model 40.

IN-TEXT NOTE: (Prosek 246-47)

Works Cited

Prosek, James. The Complete Angler: A Connecticut

Yankee Follows in the Footsteps of Walton. New

York: Harper, 1999.

E-Tips

How do you document an electronic book? The technology for these products is still evolving (more slowly than expected), but since e-books are designed to emulate print volumes, treat them as books—with authors, titles, and so on. However, if the publishing information does not make it clear that you are reading an e-book edition of a work, you might describe the medium right after the title: *E-book.*

53c
MLA

2. Book, Two or Three Authors or Editors—MLA

IN-TEXT NOTE: (Collier and Horowitz 24)

Works Cited

Collier, Peter, and David Horowitz. <u>Destructive</u>

<u>Generation: Second Thoughts About the '60s</u>. New

York: Summit, 1989.

Note that the names of second and third authors are given in their normal order, first names first.

3. Book, Four or More Authors or Editors—MLA You have two options. You can name all the authors in both the note and the Works Cited entry.

IN-TEXT NOTE: (Guth, Rico, Ruszkiewicz, and Bridges 95)

Works Cited

Guth, Hans P., Gabriele L. Rico, John Ruszkiewicz,

and Bill Bridges. <u>The Rhetoric of Laughter: The</u>

<u>Best and Worst of Humor Night</u>. Fort Worth:

Harcourt, 1996.

Alternatively, you can name just the first author given on the title page and use the Latin abbreviation *et al.,* which means "and others."

IN-TEXT NOTE: (Guth et al. 95)

Works Cited

Guth, Hans P., et al. <u>The Rhetoric of Laughter: The</u>

<u>Best and Worst of Humor Night</u>. Fort Worth:

Harcourt, 1996.

4. Book, Revised by a Second Author—MLA Sometimes you may need to cite a book by its original author, even when it has been revised. In such a case, place the editor's name after the title of the book.

53c
MLA

IN-TEXT NOTE: (Guerber 20)

Works Cited

Guerber, Hélène Adeline. The Myths of Greece and

Rome. Ed. Dorothy Margaret Stuart. 3rd ed.

London: Harrap, 1965.

5. **Book, Edited—Focus on the Original Author—MLA**

IN-TEXT NOTE: (Cor. 3.3.119-35)

Works Cited

Shakespeare, William. The Tragedy of Coriolanus. Ed.

Reuben Brower. New York: Signet, 1966.

Coriolanus is a play by Shakespeare, so the note provides act, scene, and line numbers—not author and page numbers. It must be clear in the paper that the note refers to the Shakespeare play.

6. **Book, Edited—Focus on the Editor—MLA**

IN-TEXT NOTE: (Brower xxiii-1)

Works Cited

Brower, Reuben, ed. The Tragedy of Coriolanus. By

William Shakespeare. New York: Signet, 1966.

7. **Book, Edited—Focus on the Editor, More than One Editor—MLA**

IN-TEXT NOTE: (Kittredge and Smith xvi-xvii)

Works Cited

Kittredge, William, and Annick Smith, eds. The Last

Best Place: A Montana Anthology. Seattle: U of

Washington P, 1988.

8. **Book, Written by a Group—MLA** Treat the group as the author of the work. But to avoid an awkward note, identify the group

53c
MLA

author in the body of your paper and place only the relevant page
numbers in parentheses.

IN-TEXT NOTE: The Reader's Digest Fix-It-Yourself

Manual explains the importance of a UL label (123).

Works Cited

Reader's Digest. Fix-It-Yourself Manual.

    Pleasantville: Reader's Digest, 1977.

9. **Book with No Author—MLA** Cite the book by its title, alphabetized by the first major word (excluding *The, A,* or *An*). Use a
shortened title in any note.

IN-TEXT NOTE: (Kodak 56-58)

Works Cited

Kodak Guide to 35 mm Photography. 6th ed. Rochester:

    Eastman, 1989.

10. **Book, Focus on a Foreword, Introduction, Preface, or Afterword—
MLA** The note below refers to information in O'Rourke's introduction, not to material in the anthology itself.

IN-TEXT NOTE: (O'Rourke 5)

Works Cited

O'Rourke, P. J. Introduction. Road Trips, Head

    Trips, and Other Car-Crazed Writings. Ed. Jean

    Lindamood. New York: Atlantic, 1996. 1-8.

11. **Work of More than One Volume—MLA** When you use only
one volume of a multivolume set, identify both the volume you
have used and the total number of volumes in the set.

IN-TEXT NOTE: (Spindler 17-18)

Works Cited

Spindler, Karlheinz. Abstract Algebra with

    Applications. Vol. 1. New York: Dekker, 1994. 2

    vols.

53c
MLA

When you use more than one volume of a set, identify the specific volumes in the notes as you cite them. Then, in the Works Cited entry, list the total number of volumes in that set.

IN-TEXT NOTES: (Spindler 1: 17-18); (Spindler 2: 369)

Works Cited

Spindler, Karlheinz. Abstract Algebra with

Applications. 2 vols. New York: Dekker, 1994.

12. Book, Translation—Focus on the Original Author—MLA

IN-TEXT NOTE: (Freire 137-38)

Works Cited

Freire, Paulo. Learning to Question: A Pedagogy of

Liberation. Trans. Tony Coates. New York:

Continuum, 1989.

13. Book, Translation—Focus on the Translator—MLA

IN-TEXT NOTE: (Swanton 17-18)

Works Cited

Swanton, Michael, trans. Beowulf. New York: Barnes,

1978.

14. Book in a Foreign Language—MLA
Copy the title of the foreign work exactly as it appears on the title page, paying special attention to both accent marks and capitalization.

IN-TEXT NOTE: (Bablet and Jacquot 59)

Works Cited

Bablet, Denis, and Jean Jacquot. Les Voies de la

création théâtrale. Paris: Editions du Centre

National de la Recherche Scientifique, 1977.

15. Book, Republished—MLA
Give original publication dates for works of fiction that have been through many editions and reprints.

IN-TEXT NOTE: (Herbert 146)

Works Cited

Herbert, Frank. <u>Dune</u>. 1965. New York: Berkeley, 1977.

16. **Book, Part of a Series—MLA** Give the series name just before the publishing information. Do not underline or italicize a series name.

IN-TEXT NOTE: (Pemberton xii)

Works Cited

Pemberton, Michael, ed. <u>The Ethics of Writing</u>

<u>Instruction: Issues in Theory and Practice</u>.

Perspectives on Writing: Theory, Research,

Practice 4. Stamford: Ablex, 2000.

17. **Book, a Reader or Anthology—MLA** When you quote from the front matter of the collection, the page numbers for a note may sometimes be Roman numerals. (To cite a selection from within an anthology, see model 29.)

IN-TEXT NOTE: (Lunsford and Ruszkiewicz xxi-xxvi)

Works Cited

Lunsford, Andrea A., and John J. Ruszkiewicz, eds.

<u>The Presence of Others: Voices and Images That</u>

<u>Call for Response</u>. 3rd ed. New York: Bedford,

2000.

18. **Book, a Second, Third, or Later Edition—MLA**

IN-TEXT NOTE: (Rombauer 480-81)

Works Cited

Rombauer, Marjorie Dick. <u>Legal Problem Solving:</u>

<u>Analysis, Research, and Writing</u>. 5th ed. St.

Paul: West, 1991.

19. Chapter in a Book—MLA

   IN-TEXT NOTE: (Shalit 144-60)

   Works Cited

   Shalit, Wendy. "Male Character." A Return to

   Modesty: Discovering the Lost Virtue. New York:

   Free, 1999: 144-60.

20. **Book Published Before 1900—MLA** Omit the name of the publisher in citations of works published prior to 1900.

   IN-TEXT NOTE: (Bowdler 2: 47)

   Works Cited

   Bowdler, Thomas, ed. The Family Shakespeare. 10

   vols. London, 1818.

21. **Book Issued by a Division of a Publisher—a Special Imprint—MLA** Attach the special imprint (Vintage in this case) to the publisher's name with a hyphen.

   IN-TEXT NOTE: (Hofstader 192-93)

   Works Cited

   Hofstader, Douglas. Gödel, Escher, Bach: An Eternal

   Golden Braid. New York: Vintage-Random, 1980.

22. **Dissertation or Thesis—Published (Including Publication by UMI)—MLA** If the dissertation you are citing is published by University Microfilms International (UMI), be sure to provide the order number as the last item in the Works Cited entry.

   IN-TEXT NOTE: (Rifkin 234)

   Works Cited

   Rifkin, Myra Lee. Burial, Funeral and Mourning

   Customs in England, 1558-1662. Diss. Bryn Mawr,

   1977. Ann Arbor: UMI, 1977. DDJ78-01385.

53c
MLA

23. **Dissertation or Thesis—Unpublished—MLA** The titles of unpublished dissertations appear between quotation marks. *Diss.* indicates that the source is a dissertation.

IN-TEXT NOTE: (Altman 150)

Works Cited

Altman, Jack, Jr. "The Politics of Health Planning

and Regulation." Diss. Massachusetts Institute

of Technology, 1983.

24. **Book Review/Movie Review—Titled or Untitled—MLA** Not
all book, film, and arts reviews have titles, so the Works Cited
form for a review may vary slightly.

IN-TEXT NOTE: (Keen 39)

Works Cited

Keen, Maurice. "The Knight of Knights." Rev. of

William Marshall: The Flower of Chivalry, by

Georges Duby. New York Review of Books 16 Jan.

1986: 39-40.

A book title (*Uncle Tom's Cabin*) within a book title is not under-
scored or italicized (Uncle Tom's Cabin *and American Culture*).

IN-TEXT NOTE: (Baym 691-92)

Works Cited

Baym, Nina. Rev. of Uncle Tom's Cabin and American

Culture, by Thomas F. Gossett. Journal of

American History 72 (1985): 691-92.

Here's the form for a film review found online, in this case in the
e-zine *Slate.* The citation includes both the date of the review itself and the date it was accessed online.

IN-TEXT NOTE: David Edelstein finds Ben Affleck an

unlikely convict in Reindeer Games . . .

53c
MLA

Works Cited

```
Edelstein, David. "Parlor Games." Rev. of Reindeer

    Games, dir. John Frankenheimer. Slate 25 Feb.

    2000. 8 Mar. 2000 <http://slate.msn.com/

    MovieReview/00-02-25/MovieReview.asp>.
```

2 MLA: Scholarly journals checklist

Basic information	Example (see model 25)
❑ Name of author(s) or editors(s)	`Smith, Laurajane.`
❑ Title of article (between " ")	`"Heritage Management . . ."`
❑ Name of journal (underscored)	`Antiquity`
❑ Volume number	`64`
❑ Year/date of publication	`(1994):`
❑ Pages	`300-09.`

25. **Article in a Scholarly Journal—MLA** Scholarly journals are usually identified by volume number or season (rather than day, week, or month of publication). Such journals are usually paginated year by year, with a year's work treated as one volume. Provide author, title of article, title of journal, volume number, year of publication, and page numbers. For an online journal article, see model 41.

IN-TEXT NOTE: (Smith 301)

Works Cited

```
Smith, Laurajane. "Heritage Management as

    Postprocessual Archaeology?" Antiquity 64

    (1994): 300-09.
```

When a scholarly journal is paginated issue by issue, place a period and an issue number after the volume number.

53c
MLA

IN-TEXT NOTE: (Morgenroth 91-92)

Works Cited

Morgenroth, Joyce. "Dressing for the Dance." <u>Wilson</u>

　　　<u>Quarterly</u> 22.2 (1998): 88-95.

3 MLA: Magazine/Newspaper checklist

Basic information	Example (see model 26)
❏ Name of author(s) or editors(s)	Murray, Spencer.
❏ Title of article between " "	"Roaming Wyoming."
❏ Name of publication (underscored)	Open Road
❏ Date of publication	Spring 1999:
❏ Pages/sections	60-65.

26. **Article in a Popular Magazine—MLA** Magazines are paginated
issue by issue and identified by the seasonal, monthly, or weekly
date of publication (not by volume number). Provide author, title
of article, title of magazine, date of publication, and page numbers. Months are abbreviated in MLA style.

IN-TEXT NOTE: (Murray 63)

Works Cited

Murray, Spencer. "Roaming Wyoming." <u>Open Road</u> Spring

　　　1999: 60-65.

Articles in magazines often don't appear on consecutive pages.
When that's the case, list the relevant page number(s) in the note.
In the Works Cited entry give the first page on which the article
appears, followed by a plus sign.

IN-TEXT NOTE: (Mackay 170)

Works Cited

Mackay, Jordan. "A Murder on Campus." <u>Texas Monthly</u>

　　　Jan. 2000: 112+.

53c

MLA

27. **Article in a Weekly or Biweekly Magazine—MLA** Give both the day and the month of publication as listed on the issue. Note that in MLA form the day precedes the month and no comma is used: *18 July 1994.* Months are abbreviated in MLA style.

IN-TEXT NOTE: (Smolowe 20)

Works Cited

Smolowe, Jill. "When Violence Hits Home." Time 18

July 1994: 18-25.

28. **Article in a Monthly Magazine—MLA** Months are abbreviated in MLA style.

IN-TEXT NOTE: (Bond 90)

Works Cited

Bond, Constance. "If You Can't Bear to Part with It,

Open a New Museum." Smithsonian Apr. 1995:

90-97.

29. **Article or Selection from a Reader or Anthology—MLA** List the item on the Works Cited page by the author of the piece you are actually citing, not the editor(s) of the collection. Then provide the title of the particular selection, the title of the overall collection, the editor(s) of the collection, and publication information. Conclude with the page numbers of the selection.

IN-TEXT NOTE: (King 417-20)

Works Cited

King, Robert. "Should English Be the Law?" The

Presence of Others: Voices and Images That

Call for Response. Ed. Andrea Lunsford and

John Ruszkiewicz. 3rd ed. New York: Bedford,

2000. 409-21.

When you cite two or more selections from a reader or an anthology, list that collection fully on the Works Cited page.

53c
MLA

Works Cited

Lunsford, Andrea, and John Ruszkiewicz, eds. The

Presence of Others: Voices and Images That Call

for Response. 3rd ed. New York: Bedford, 2000.

Then, still in the Works Cited list, identify the authors and titles of all articles you cite from that reader or anthology, followed by the names of the editors and the page numbers of your selections.

IN-TEXT NOTES: (King 417-20); (Turkle 453)

Works Cited

King, Robert. "Should English Be the Law?" Lunsford

and Ruszkiewicz 409-21.

Turkle, Shirley. "Who Am We?" Lunsford and

Ruszkiewicz 442-58.

For a scholarly article reprinted in a collection, you should usually give more detail about its original place of publication (when known) and then give the facts about the collection.

IN-TEXT NOTE: (Hartman 101)

Works Cited

Hartman, Geoffrey. "Milton's Counterplot." ELH 25

(1958): 1-12. Rpt. in Milton: A Collection of

Critical Essays. Ed. Louis L. Martz. Twentieth

Century Views. Englewood Cliffs: Prentice-

Spectrum, 1966: 100-08.

30. **Article in a Newspaper—MLA** Provide author, title of article, name of newspaper, date of article, and page numbers. For page numbers, use the form in the newspaper you are citing; many papers are paginated according to sections. For an online newspaper, see model 43.

IN-TEXT NOTE: (Rorty E15)

Works Cited

Rorty, Richard. "The Unpatriotic Academy." New York

Times 13 Feb. 1994: E15.

A plus sign following the page number (for example, 7+) indicates that an article continues beyond the designated page, but not necessarily on consecutive pages.

IN-TEXT NOTE: (Peterson 2A)

Works Cited

Peterson, Karen S. "Turns Out We Are 'Sexually

Conventional.'" USA Today 7 Oct. 1994: 1A+.

31. Editorial in a Newspaper—Author Not Named—MLA A shortened title is used in the note. For accurate reference, the first few words of the shortened title must match the initial words of the title listed on the Works Cited page.

IN-TEXT NOTE: ("Negro College" 28)

Works Cited

"Negro College Fund: Mission Is Still Important on

50th Anniversary." Editorial. Dallas Morning

News 8 Oct. 1994: A28.

32. Letter to the Editor—MLA

IN-TEXT NOTE: (Cantu 4)

Works Cited

Cantu, Tony. Letter. San Antonio Light 14 Jan. 1986,

southwest ed.: C4.

33. Cartoon—MLA To avoid a confusing note, describe a cartoon in the text of your essay.

53c
MLA

IN-TEXT NOTE: In the cartoon "Squib" by Miles
Mathis . . .

Works Cited

Mathis, Miles. "Squib." Cartoon. Daily Texan 15 Jan.

1986: 19.

34. **Reference Work or Encyclopedia (Familiar or Online)—MLA**
    With familiar reference works, especially those revised regularly,
    identify the edition you are using by its date. You may omit the
    names of editors and most publishing information. No page
    number is given in the parenthetical note when a work is arranged
    alphabetically.

IN-TEXT NOTE: (Benedict)

Works Cited

Benedict, Roger William. "Northwest Passage."

Encyclopaedia Britannica: Macropaedia. 1974 ed.

A citation for an online encyclopedia article would include a date
of access and electronic address. However, the online version
might not list an author.

Works Cited

"Northwest Passage." Britannica Online.

Encyclopaedia Britannica. 8 Feb. 2000 <http://

search.eb.com/bol/topic?eu=57696&sctn=1>.

35. **Reference Work (Specialized or Less Familiar)—MLA** With less
    familiar reference tools, a full entry is required. (See model 34 for
    a comparison with familiar reference works.)

IN-TEXT NOTE: (Kovesi)

Works Cited

Kovesi, Julius. "Hungarian Philosophy." The

Encyclopedia of Philosophy. Ed. Paul Edwards. 8

vols. New York: Macmillan, 1967.

53c
MLA

36. **Bulletin, Brochure, or Pamphlet—MLA** Treat these items as if they were books.

IN-TEXT NOTE: (Morgan 8-9)

Works Cited

Morgan, Martha G., ed. Campus Guide to Computer and

Web Services. Austin: U of Texas, 1999.

37. **Government Document—MLA** Give the name of the government (national, state, or local) and the agency issuing the report, the title of the document, and publishing information. If it is a congressional document other than the *Congressional Record,* identify the Congress and, when important, the session (for example, *99th Cong., 1st sess.*) after the title of the document. Avoid a lengthy note by naming the document in the body of your essay and placing only the relevant page numbers between parentheses.

IN-TEXT NOTE: This information is from the 1985-86

Official Congressional Directory (182-84).

Works Cited

United States. Cong. Joint Committee on Printing.

1985-86 Official Congressional Directory. 99th

Cong., 1st sess. Washington: GPO, 1985.

To cite the *Congressional Record,* give only the date and page number.

Cong. Rec. 8 Feb. 1974: 3942-43.

38. **Computer Software—MLA** Give the author if known, the version number if any (for example: *Microsoft Word.* Vers. 7.0), the manufacturer, the date, and (optionally) the system needed to run it. Name the software in your text rather than use a parenthetical note.

IN-TEXT NOTE: With software such as Connectix's

Virtual PC . . .

Works Cited

Virtual PC. Vers. 3.0. San Mateo: Connectix, 1999.

53c
MLA

4 MLA: Web Page checklist

Basic information	Example (see model 39)
❏ Creator or author of the site	
❏ Title of the page (between " ")	"A New Lease on Life . . ."
❏ Title of site (underscored)	<u>Parknet</u>.
❏ Date of electronic publication	7 Dec. 1999.
❏ Date you examined the site	10 Feb. 2000
❏ Web address (between < >)	<http://www.cr.nps.gov>.
Other information	
❏ Sponsor of the site	National Park Service.
❏ Editor of the site	

39. **WWW Page—Generic—MLA** The variety among Web pages is staggering, so you will have to adapt your documentation to particular sources. Quite often you will be citing Web pages without authors or creators named. Here, for example, is a citation to an entire Web site.

IN-TEXT NOTE: More information on National Parks in the United States can be found at <u>Parknet</u> . . .

Works Cited

<u>Parknet</u>. National Park Service. 12 Dec. 1999

    <http://www.nps.gov/>.

A citation to a particular page on that Web site would look like the following.

IN-TEXT NOTE: ("New Lease")

Works Cited

"A New Lease on Life: Museum Conservation in the

  National Park Service." <u>Parknet</u>. 7 Dec. 1999.

  National Park Service. 10 Feb. 2000 <http://

  www.cr.nps.gov/csd/exhibits/conservation/>.

E-Tips   For any Web site you document, MLA suggests that you provide the full Web location or uniform resource locator (URL), the familiar address beginning <http://www>. But you may find that the URLs for some Web pages, especially for materials stored in archives, may be too long to offer as a reference. In such cases, give readers the URL to the home page of the Web site where the material is located: the home page will typically have a shorter Web address. Then offer readers the keyword, links, or directions they can use to locate the particular document(s) on that site. Similarly, if you search for information on metasearch engines such as *Ask Jeeves* that search other search engines, the sites you locate will have URLs you won't be able to use in a paper. In such cases, try to track the material to its original Web locations and offer those much shorter URLs.

Don't give readers a URL they can't access themselves. For example, an index or Web search tool at your school might bring up information within its own local network, but readers without that service or tool may not be able to access that information. When possible, try to track the information down to a URL available to readers from outside the network. (Ask a librarian for assistance.)

40. **WWW—Online Book—MLA** Since most online books do not have page numbers, avoid parenthetical notes by identifying the site in your paper itself. If available, give an original date of publication, the date of the electronic source, and the date you accessed the information.

IN-TEXT NOTE: In an online version of <u>The Education of</u>
<u>Henry Adams</u> by Henry Adams . . .

53c
MLA

Works Cited

Adams, Henry. The Education of Henry Adams: An

Autobiography. Boston: Houghton, 1918. The

American Studies Group at UVA Hypertext. 1996.

University of Virginia. 6 Mar. 1998 <http://

xroads.virginia.edu/~HYPER/hadams/hahome.html>.

41. WWW—Online Scholarly Journal—MLA Since most online articles do not have page numbers, avoid parenthetical notes by identifying the site in your paper itself.

IN-TEXT NOTE: In "Tenure and Technology," Katz, Walker, and Cross argue . . .

Works Cited

Katz, Seth, Janice Walker, and Janet Cross. "Tenure

and Technology: New Values, New Guidelines."

Kairos 2.1 (1997). 20 July 1997 <http://english.

ttu.edu/kairos/2.1/coverweb/bridge.html>.

42. WWW—Online Popular Magazine—MLA Since most online articles do not have page numbers, avoid parenthetical notes by identifying the site in your paper itself.

IN-TEXT NOTE: Shafer claims in "The New Walter Cronkite" that . . .

Works Cited

Shafer, Jack. "The New Walter Cronkite." Slate 18

Oct. 1996. 12 July 1997 <http://slate.msn.com/

Assessment/96-10-18/Assessment.asp>.

43. WWW—Online News Source or Newspaper—MLA Since most online newspaper stories or editorials do not have page numbers, avoid parenthetical notes by identifying the site in your paper itself.

IN-TEXT NOTE: Sue Ann Pressley suggests that the movement to teach manners in school is . . .

Works Cited

Pressley, Sue Ann. "Louisiana's Courtesy Call." The

Washington Post Online 5 Mar. 2000. 6 Mar. 2000

<http://www.washingtonpost.com/wp-dyn/articles/

A11177-2000Mar4.html>.

Here's how to cite an online editorial; in this example the date of the editorial and the date of access to it are the same.

IN-TEXT NOTE: In an editorial titled "The Proved and the Unproved," the New York Times . . .

Works Cited

"The Proved and the Unproved." Editorial. New York

Times on the Web 13 July 1997. 13 July 1997

<http://www.nytimes.com/yr/mo/day/editorial/

13sun1.html>.

> **E-Tips** The URL you offer for an article or editorial in an online newspaper may not take readers directly to the article. Many newspapers—such as the *New York Times*—charge for access to their archived stories and other materials. So researchers may be directed to the paper's archives for the article you are citing, and then they may have to pay a fee to view the material.

44. **WWW—Personal Home Page—MLA** Since most personal Web sites do not have page numbers, avoid parenthetical notes by identifying the site in your paper itself.

IN-TEXT NOTE: For an example of a digitally enhanced photograph, see the home page of Brett R. Elliott . . .

Works Cited

Elliott, Brett R. Home page. 4 Nov. 1998. 5 Mar.

2000 <http://www.cwrl.utexas.edu/wcb/students/

belliot5/belliot5.html>.

45. Listserv/Newsgroup/Usenet Newsgroup—MLA When citing material from a listserv, identify the author of the document or posting; put the subject line of the posting between quotation marks, followed by the date on which the item was originally posted and the words *Online posting;* give the name of the listserv, followed by the date you accessed the item and the electronic address in angle brackets. Because there will be no page number to cite, avoid a parenthetical note by naming the author in the text of your project.

IN-TEXT NOTE: Cook argues for . . .

Works Cited

Cook, Janice. "Re: What New Day Is Dawning?" 19

June 1997. Online posting. Alliance for

Computers and Writing Listserv. 4 Feb 1998

<acw-l@ttacs6.ttu.edu>.

IN-TEXT NOTE: Christy Heady recommends . . .

Works Cited

Heady, Christy. "Buy or Lease? Depends on How Long

You'll Keep the Car." 7 July 1997. Online post-

ing. ClariNet. 14 July 1997 <news:clari.biz.

industry.automotive>.

Sometimes the name on a listserv may be incomplete or unconventional, but reproduce it just as it appears.

IN-TEXT NOTE: With a high-paying job right out of
college, Knight wonders . . .

Works Cited

Knight. "Will BMW Let Me Test Drive?" 4 Mar. 2000.

Online posting. Bimmer.org Forums:E46. 6 Mar.

2000 <http://www.bimmer.org/3series/messages/>.

53c
MLA

46. Synchronous Communication (MOOs, MUDs)—MLA Provide the speaker and/or site, the title of the session or event, the date of the session, the forum for the communication (if specified), the date of access, and the electronic address.

IN-TEXT NOTE: In LinguaMOO, Inept_Guest observes . . .

Works Cited

Inept_Guest. Discussion of disciplinary politics in

rhet/comp. 12 Mar. 1998. LinguaMOO. 12 Mar.

1998 <telnet:lingua.utdallas.edu 8888>.

47. Email—MLA Identifying the communication in the essay itself is preferable to using a parenthetical note. Observe the hyphen in *e-mail.*

IN-TEXT NOTE: Pacheco makes the case that Al Gore . . .

Works Cited

Pacheco, Miguel. "Re: Gore or Bush?" E-mail to the

author. 1 Nov. 2000.

48. CD-ROM/Diskette Database or Publication—MLA To cite a CD-ROM or similar electronic database, provide basic information about the source itself—author, title, and publication information. Identify the publication medium (*CD-ROM; Diskette; Magnetic tape*) and the name of the vendor if available. (The vendor is the company publishing or distributing the database.) Conclude with the date of electronic publication.

IN-TEXT NOTE: (Bevington 98)

Works Cited

Bevington, David. "Castles in the Air: The Morality

Plays." The Theater of Medieval Europe: New

Research in Early Drama. Ed. Simon Eckchard.

Cambridge: Cambridge UP, 1993. MLA

Bibliography. CD-ROM. SilverPlatter. Feb. 1995.

For a CD-ROM database that is often updated (*ProQuest,* for example), you must provide publication dates for the item you are examining and for the data disk itself.

53c
MLA

IN-TEXT NOTE: (Alva 407-10)

Works Cited

Alva, Sylvia Alatore. "Differential Patterns of

    Achievement Among Asian-American Adolescents."

    <u>Journal of Youth and Adolescence</u> 22 (1993):

    407-23. <u>ProQuest General Periodicals</u>. CD-ROM.

    UMI-ProQuest. June 1994.

Cite a book, encyclopedia, play, or other item published on CD-ROM or diskette just as if it were a printed source, adding the medium of publication (*Diskette* or *CD-ROM*, for example). When page numbers aren't available, use the author's name in the text of the paper to avoid a parenthetical note.

IN-TEXT NOTE: Bolter argues . . .

Works Cited

Bolter, Jay David. <u>Writing Space: A Hypertext</u>.

    Diskette. Hillsdale: Erlbaum, 1990.

49. Microfilm or Microfiche—MLA Treat material on microfilm exactly as if you had seen its original hard-copy version.

IN-TEXT NOTE: ("How Long?" 434)

Works Cited

"How Long Will the Chemise Last?" <u>Consumer Reports</u>.

    Aug. 1958: 434-37.

50. Biblical Citation—MLA Titles of sacred works, including all versions of the Bible, are not underlined.

IN-TEXT NOTE: (John 18:37-38)

Works Cited

The Jerusalem Bible. Ed. Alexander Jones. Garden

    City: Doubleday, 1966.

51. **Videotape/DVD—MLA** Cite a video entry by title in most cases. You may include information about the producer, designer, performers, and so on. Identify the distributor, and provide a date. Avoid parenthetical notes for items on videocassette or digital videodisc (DVD) by naming the work in the body of your project.

IN-TEXT NOTE: Tae-Bo Workout offers . . .

Works Cited

Tae-Bo Workout: Instructional and Basic. Perf. Billy

Blanks. Videocassette. Ventura, 1998.

IN-TEXT NOTE: The Matrix DVD includes production notes

that . . .

Works Cited

The Matrix. Perf. Keanu Reeves and Laurence

Fishburne. Widescreen ed. DVD. Warner, 1999.

52. **Movie—MLA** In most cases, list a movie by its title unless your emphasis is on the director, producer, or screenwriter. Provide information about actors, producers, cinematographers, set designers, and so on, to suit your readers. Identify the distributor, and give a date of production. Avoid parenthetical notes for films by naming the works in the body of your paper.

IN-TEXT NOTE: In Lucas's film American Graffiti . . .

Works Cited

American Graffiti. Dir. George Lucas. Perf. Richard

Dreyfuss and Ronny Howard. Universal, 1973.

53. **Television Program—MLA** List the TV program by episode or name of program. Avoid parenthetical notes for television shows by naming the programs in the body of your paper.

IN-TEXT NOTE: In the episode "No Surrender, No

Retreat" . . .

53c
MLA

Works Cited

"No Surrender, No Retreat." Dir. Mike Vejar. Writ.

　　　Michael Straczynski. Perf. Bruce Boxleitner,

　　　Claudia Christian, and Mira Furlan. Babylon 5.

　　　KEYE-42, Austin. 28 July 1997.

54. **Radio Program—MLA** Avoid parenthetical notes for radio shows by naming the programs in the body of your paper.

IN-TEXT NOTE: Early episodes of Death Valley Days . . .

Works Cited

Death Valley Days. Created by Ruth Cornwall Woodman.

　　　NBC Radio. WNBC, New York. 30 Sept. 1930.

55. **Personal Interview—MLA** Refer to the interview in the body of your essay rather than in a parenthetical note.

IN-TEXT NOTE: In an interview, Pete Gomes explains . . .

Works Cited

Gomes, Rev. Peter. Personal interview. 23 Apr. 1997.

56. **Musical Composition—MLA** List the work on the Works Cited page by the name of the composer. If you have sheet music or a score, give complete publication information. If you don't have a score or sheet music, provide a simpler entry. In either case, naming the music in the project itself is preferable to using a parenthetical note.

IN-TEXT NOTE: Scott Joplin published "The Strenuous Life" at a time . . .

Works Cited

Joplin, Scott. "The Strenuous Life: A Ragtime Two

　　　Step." St. Louis: Stark, 1902.

IN-TEXT NOTE: Another Cole Porter song, "Too Darn Hot" . . .

53c
MLA

Works Cited

Porter, Cole. "Too Darn Hot." 1949.

57. **Recording/Audio Clip—MLA** Naming the recording in the essay itself is preferable to using a parenthetical note.

IN-TEXT NOTE: An album such as One Endless Night by Jimmie Dale Gilmore is a good example of . . .

Works Cited

Gilmore, Jimmie Dale. One Endless Night.

Windchanger/Rounder, 2000.

Here is how to cite an audio clip from a Web site.

IN-TEXT NOTE: The theme for NPR's Car Talk, "Dawgy Mountain Breakdown" by David Grisman, is . . .

Works Cited

Grisman, David. "Dawgy Mountain Breakdown." CarTalk

at Cars.com. Natl. Public Radio. 1990. 28 Feb.

2000 <http://cartalk.cars.com/Radio/Misc/

Audio/RA/theme2.ram>.

58. **Speech—MLA** When you have no printed text of the speech, give the location and date of the address. Naming the work in the essay itself is preferable to using a parenthetical note.

IN-TEXT NOTE: Reagan explained his position in an address to . . .

Works Cited

Reagan, Ronald. "The Geneva Summit Meeting: A

Measure of Progress." U.S. Congress.

Washington. 21 Nov. 1985.

With a printed text, give the speaker, title of the speech, where it was delivered, date, and publication information.

53c
MLA

IN-TEXT NOTE: (O'Rourke 20)

Works Cited

O'Rourke, P. J. "Brickbats and Broomsticks." Capital

Hilton. Washington. 2 Dec. 1992. Rpt. American

Spectator Feb. 1993: 20-21.

59. Lecture—MLA Naming the lecture in the essay itself is preferable to having a parenthetical note.

IN-TEXT NOTE: Addressing a conference of educators in Cincinnati, William W. Cook . . .

Works Cited

Cook, William W. "Writing in the Spaces Left."

Chair's Address. Conf. on Coll. Composition and

Communication. Cincinnati. 19 Mar. 1992.

60. Advertisement—MLA Provide the name of the product or company sponsoring the item, identify it as an advertisement, and give publication information. Naming the advertisement in the project itself is preferable to having a parenthetical note.

IN-TEXT NOTE: An advertisement for Austin's Wooten Barber Shop depicts . . .

Works Cited

Wooten Barber Shop. Advertisement. Texas Travesty

Apr./May 2002: 5.

List an online advertisement similarly. Provide a date of access and an electronic address.

IN-TEXT NOTE: A Polytechnic University ad includes information about . . .

Works Cited

Polytechnic University. Advertisement. 9 July 2002.

<http://www.nytimes.com/college>.

53c
MLA

61. Letter—Published—MLA

IN-TEXT NOTE: (Eliot 427)

Works Cited

Eliot, George. "To Thomas Clifford Allbutt." 1 Nov.

1873. In Selections from George Eliot's

Letters. Ed. Gordon S. Haight. New Haven: Yale

UP, 1985: 427.

62. Letter—Unpublished—MLA Identifying the letter communication in the essay itself is preferable to having a parenthetical note.

IN-TEXT NOTE: In a letter to Agnes Weinstein dated 23 May 1917, Albert Newton complains . . .

Works Cited

Newton, Albert. Letter to Agnes Weinstein. 23 May

1917. Albert Newton Papers. Woodhill Lib.,

Cleveland.

63. Artwork/Photograph—MLA Naming the artwork or image in the essay itself is preferable to having a parenthetical note.

IN-TEXT NOTE: The work resembles both the painting Ariel by Fuseli at the Folger and . . .

Works Cited

Fuseli, Henry. Ariel. Folger Shakespeare Lib.,

Washington, D.C.

64. Drama or Play—MLA Citing a printed text of a play, whether individual or collected, differs from citing a performance. For printed texts, provide the usual Works Cited information, taking special care when citing a collection in which various editors handle different plays. In parenthetical notes, give the act, scene, and line numbers when the work is so divided; give page numbers when it is not.

53c
MLA

IN-TEXT NOTE: (Ham. 5.2.219-24)

Works Cited

Shakespeare, William. The Tragedy of Hamlet, Prince

of Denmark. Ed. Frank Kermode. The Riverside

Shakespeare. 2nd ed. Ed. G. Blakemore Evans and

J. J. M. Tobin. Boston: Houghton, 1997.

1183-1245.

IN-TEXT NOTE: (Stoppard 11-15)

Works Cited

Stoppard, Tom. Rosencrantz and Guildenstern Are

Dead. New York: Grove, 1967.

For performances of plays, give the title of the work, the author, and then any specific information that seems relevant—director, performers, producers, set designer, theater company, and so on. Conclude the entry with a theater, location, and date. Refer to the production directly in the body of your essay to avoid a parenthetical note.

IN-TEXT NOTE: In a rare and memorable performance of
Shakespeare's Timon of Athens . . .

Works Cited

Timon of Athens. By William Shakespeare. Dir.

Michael Benthall. Perf. Ralph Richardson, Paul

Curran, and Margaret Whiting. Old Vic, London.

5 Sept. 1956.

53d How to use footnotes or endnotes

In some fields and majors, an instructor may ask for MLA-style endnotes or footnotes to document sources, rather than the in-text notes explained in Sections 53a through 53c. When that's the case, use the following models as examples for your notes. For endnotes and footnotes, place a raised number in your text after every sentence or passage you wish to document. This number is keyed to a specific endnote or footnote. Both endnotes and footnotes in MLA style are numbered consecutively throughout a project. On a computer you can create the raised numbers for notes by selecting *superscript* as the font type.

If you use endnotes, list them all on a separate, numbered page at the end of your project. Center the title *Notes* one inch from the top of this page. The notes are double spaced, with the first lines indented half an inch or five spaces.

If you use footnotes, place them two double spaces (that is, four lines) below the text on the same page where the citation occurs. Footnotes are single spaced, but leave a double space between notes when you have more than one on a page.

Notice that endnotes and footnotes differ in indention, arrangement, and punctuation from the style of items on a Works Cited page.

- **Book—MLA endnote/footnote**

    [1]James Prosek, The Complete Angler: A Connecticut Yankee Follows in the Footsteps of Walton (New York: Harper, 1999) 246-47.

- **Book, Edited—MLA endnote/footnote**

    [2]Reuben Brower, ed., The Tragedy of Coriolanus, by William Shakespeare (New York: Signet, 1966).

- **Article in a Scholarly Journal—MLA endnote/footnote**

    [3]Laurajane Smith, "Heritage Management as Postprocessual Archaeology?" Antiquity 64 (1994): 300-09.

- **Article in a Popular Magazine—MLA endnote/footnote**

    [4]Jordan Mackay, "A Murder on Campus," Texas Monthly Jan. 2000: 112.

- **Article in a Newspaper—MLA endnote/footnote**

    [5]Richard Rorty, "The Unpatriotic Academy," New York Times 13 Feb. 1994: E15.

53d
MLA

- **Electronic Source—MLA endnote/footnote**

> [6]Bob Sandberg, <u>Jackie Robinson in Dodgers</u>
>
> <u>Uniform</u>, 1954, <u>American Memory</u>, Lib. of Congress,
>
> Washington, 30 Jan. 2000 <http://rs6.loc.gov/pnp/
>
> ppmsc/00000/00047r.jpg>.

HIGHLIGHT *Documenting Visual and Multimedia Sources*

Because new technologies make it easier to find and use visual and multimedia sources, you'll likely use them more frequently in future projects. You'll also need to acknowledge and cite them just as you would any other kind of source that contributes to your research.

The MLA models in Section 53d cover all the following visual and audio sources:

Cartoon	Item 33
Pamphlet/brochure	Item 36
Videotape/DVD	Item 51
Television program	Item 53
Radio program	Item 54
Audio clip	Item 57
Advertisement	Item 60
Photograph	Item 63

These items are almost always easier to cite by naming them in the text of your paper rather than trying to identify them through a parenthetical note.

> In an episode of the WB Network's <u>Smallville</u> airing on 11 December 2002 . . .
>
> In an ad for the Nissan's new 350Z that appeared in <u>Newsweek</u> on . . .

Take special care with graphs, charts, and photographs, particularly any that you download from the Web. You will need permission to use most such items in any project—such as a Web site or pamphlet—that reaches beyond your classroom. See Section 51b-2 for advice.

To cite a visual or audio source you borrow from online, be sure to record the name of the Web site, the Web address, and the date you examined or downloaded the item. For example, here's what the Works Cited entry would look like for a photograph of baseball hall-of-famer Jackie Robinson taken by Bob Sandberg and available on the *American Memory* Web site.

> Sandberg, Bob. <u>Jackie Robinson in Dodgers Uniform</u>.
>
>   <u>American Memory</u>. 12 March 2000 <http://
>
>   memory.loc.gov/ammem/jrhtml/jrabout.html>.

53e Sample MLA paper

The sample paper that follows is accompanied by checklists designed to help you set up a paper correctly in MLA style. When your work meets the specifications on the checklists, it should be in proper form.

Ben Brenneman, a senior English major at the University of Texas at Austin, wrote "Can Quality Survive the Standardized Test?" in spring 2000 while a student in John Ruszkiewicz's course "Grammar and Style for Writers"—a writing class designed for students thinking about careers in teaching English. Brenneman's classmates, however, came from fields ranging from computer science to journalism, and most of them did not expect to become English teachers.

The paper appears here substantially as Brenneman wrote it. But it has been modified in several ways to enhance its value as a model. For example, a table has been added to demonstrate how such an item should be formatted, and a quotation has been extended to provide an example of an indented quotation. It is also worth noting that Brenneman chose to write the paper in APA style—the form he encountered most often in educational research. The paper has been reworked to fit MLA conventions. Note that we have numbered the paragraphs in "Can Quality Survive the Standardized Test?" for easy reference in classroom discussions; do *not* number the paragraphs in a paper unless an instructor or editor instructs you to do so.

53e
MLA

Ben H. Brenneman

Professor Ruszkiewicz

English 379

2 March 2000

          Can Quality Survive the Standardized Test?

¶1   In <u>Seeking Diversity</u> (1992), a book on teaching middle school language arts, author and teacher Linda Rief says, "I expect good reading and writing, in which process and product are woven tightly into literate tapestries of wonder and awe" (10). Rief thus describes the Holy Grail of writing instruction: a classroom in which students learn to write because they care about the final product and want to do excellent work. Such an environment would give students the ability to write by turning them into writers. Unfortunately, the American education system today is failing to teach many students even the basic skills they will need to survive. Statements by teachers that "the greater number of the young people we teach . . . do not know how to read, spell, write, use correct grammar, do simple math, remember, use logic" are supported by statistics showing "that only 55% of the nation's 17-year-olds and 49% of out-of-school adults are able to write an acceptable letter ordering a product by mail" (Neill 18). Yet the dominant response to this problem--competency testing in our public schools--may be destroying any regard students may have for language by turning writing into a formulaic exercise.

¶2   Many states, in fact, have already responded to problems in their educational systems by passing laws mandating the skills that students must learn by a specified grade. The students' ability to reach the objectives and the faculty's ability to teach this

Checklist 53.1

Title Page—MLA

MLA does not require a separate cover sheet or title page. If your instructor expects one, center the title of your paper and your name in the upper third of the paper. Center the course title, your instructor's name, and the date of submission on the lower third of the sheet, double-spacing between the elements.

The first page of a paper without a separate title page will look like the previous page. Be sure to check all the items in this list.

* Place your name, your instructor's name, the course title, and the date in the upper left-hand corner, beginning one inch from the top of the page. These items are double spaced.

* Identify your instructor by an appropriate title. When uncertain about academic rank, use *Mr.* or *Ms.*

  Dr. James Duban   Professor Melinda Turnley
  Ms. Jodi Sherman   Mr. John Kinkade

* Center the title a double space under the date. Capitalize the first and last word of the title. Capitalize all other words *except* articles (*a, an, the*), prepositions, the *to* in infinitives, and coordinating conjunctions—unless they are the first or last words.

  RIGHT   Can Quality Survive the Standardized Test?

  Do not underline or boldface the title of your paper. Do not use all-caps, place it between quotation marks, or end it with a period. Titles may, however, end with question marks or include words or phrases that are italicized, underlined, or between quotation marks.

  RIGHT   Violence in Shakespeare's Macbeth

  RIGHT   Dylan's "Like a Rolling Stone" Revisited

* Begin the body of the essay two lines (a double space) below the title. Double-space the entire essay, including quotations.

* Use one-inch margins at the sides and bottom of this page.

* Number this first page in the upper right-hand corner, one-half inch from the top, one inch from the right margin. Precede the page number with your last name.

53e
MLA

Brenneman 2

"standards-based curriculum" are then measured by
statewide standardized tests. Students and schools that
fall short of the mark can then be identified for
improvement. As Neill explains, "the strongest argument
in support of competency requirements is the potential
for motivating students, schools, and districts" (8). The
results of testing are carefully monitored and publicized
to show continuing improvement in the performance of
public schools (see Table 1).

Table 1

Percentage of Students Passing All Texas Assessment of
Academic Skills Exams (TAAS)

	1994	1995	1996	1997	1998	4-Yr. Gain
Grade 3	58	66	70	74	76	18
Grade 4	54	64	67	72	78	24
Grade 5	58	66	73	79	83	25
Grade 6	56	60	69	77	79	23
Grade 7	55	58	67	75	78	23
Grade 8	49	50	59	67	72	23
Grade 10	52	54	60	68	72	20

Source: Texas Business and Education Coalition, School
    Gains. 1999. 27 Feb. 2000. <http://www.tbec.org/gains.
    HTML>.

¶3   In many states this progress has been motivated by
attaching increasingly serious consequences to the
results of these tests. Students who fail the state
aptitude test may be held back a grade, or they may even
be denied a high school diploma. Teachers are also under
increasing pressure to get test scores up. Jack Kaufhold,
a professor of educational psychology, notes that
principals have been warned, "If your test scores don't
go up, you may lose your job." He adds, "Teachers also
know that if their students' achievement test scores

Checklist 53.2

Body of the Essay—MLA

The body of an MLA research paper continues uninterrupted until the separate Notes page (if any) and the Works Cited page. Be sure to type or handwrite the essay on good-quality paper.

• Use margins of at least one inch all around. Try to keep the right-hand margin reasonably straight. Do not hyphenate words at the end of lines.

• Place page numbers in the upper right-hand corner, one inch from the right edge of the page and one-half inch from the top. Precede the page number with your last name.

• Indent the first line of each paragraph one-half inch, or five spaces if you use a typewriter.

• Indent long quotations one inch, or 10 spaces if you use a typewriter. In MLA documentation, long quotations are any that exceed four typed lines in the body of your essay. Double-space these indented quotations. For an example, see page 828.

53e
MLA

fluctuate too much from year to year, they too could be demoted or dismissed" (14).

¶4   State officials justify these types of high-stakes assessments on the grounds that the skills the tests focus on are those students will need to function in society. They argue, moreover, that students who receive a quality education should have little trouble fulfilling the minimum requirements. For instance, the standards for writing set in Texas, called the "Texas Essential Knowledge and Skills" or TEKS, state that students who graduate from high school must "write in a variety of forms using effective word choice, structure, and sentences with an emphasis on organizing logical arguments . . .; write in a voice and style appropriate to audience and purpose; and organize in writing to ensure coherence" (Texas Education Agency). In other words, everyone who receives a high school diploma should be able to communicate effectively in writing. Students demonstrate their skill during the Texas Assessment of Academic Skills (TAAS) by composing an essay. As Mary argues on a WWW forum sponsored by Teachers.Net, "The TEKS based TAAS are a reflection of the specific standards the children of our state should meet. That's precisely what we should be teaching." Many teachers, however, find that their curriculums are already adequate. Their response to these requirements is like Sheri Arni's: "My answer has been to leave unchanged most of what happens in my classroom" (76). Rief, for example, gives her students "a two-day crash course . . . just before they take the state-mandated achievement tests. . . . Two days is all I allow" (180).

¶5   Unfortunately some schools fall short of the mark. The administrators in these institutions are then forced

Brenneman 4

to make changes to the curriculum in order to raise
scores quickly. In Maryland, teachers responded to a
writing test that they felt was too difficult by creating
writing labs, increasing the amount of writing done in
regular English, and cooperating between departments to
focus on writing in all disciplines (Corbett and Wilson).
This is the type of reform the tests were intended to
produce. The instructors at this school improved their
curriculum by finding innovative ways to teach their
students how to write. Anne Shaughnessy, when preparing
her students for the Florida assessment, had them discuss
their responses to a sample prompt. She showed them that
the qualities they felt made an essay successful were the
same criteria that would be used to score their tests.
She then had them use the actual rubric to score their
essays in class. In this way Shaughnessy gave her
students some insight into the logic behind the test,
making it more than simply an arbitrary exercise. She
writes, "Clearly I was teaching to the test, but I was
also introducing activities that extended rather than
displaced the writing curriculum" (56).

¶6   These improvements are certainly commendable. They
occur when schools are blessed with creative teachers who
are willing to take risks. However, many educators, when
faced with the possibility of unemployment, turn to the
tried-and-true method the army uses to train new recruits:
drill, drill, drill. In the Maryland case, for example,
Corbett and Wilson note that "teachers would stop what
they were doing with students . . . and inject an intense
period of . . . 'drill and review' specifically related to
the test" (124). When preparing for a writing exam,
students spend this period responding to practice prompts,
often from previous tests that have been released by the

53e
MLA

Brenneman 5

state. A teacher in Texas reported that she "had to give a
writing test AND a reading test every six weeks"
(Melissa). In teaching circles this strategy is known as
the "drill-and-kill" approach. In other words, students
are drilled until all genuine interest in the subject is
killed by weeks of prompt writing.

¶7   Teachers are alarmed by the drill-and-kill
approach to test preparation. They fear that the focus of
their instruction has shifted from producing excellent
writing for a general audience to producing adequate
writing in order to avoid the wrath of the state. This
attitude is communicated to the students simply by the
time spent in practice. As one Texas teacher laments,
"from mid-January through April we are not teachers, we
are masters of how to take a test" (Linda/tx). In this
environment students begin to believe that mastery of the
test is the goal of their education. They often create,
or are even taught, ways to improve their scores by
manipulating the test. According to Donna Garner, any
student who got a high score on the essay portion of the
TAAS could miss most of the questions on the grammar-
oriented part of the test and still pass. She says that,
when students understand this,

> it's rather hard to get them to see the serious-
> ness of correct grammar, spelling, punctuation,
> capitalization, and sentence structure. Once the
> students learn to "play the TAAS game" by
> scripting their essays to a set pattern, the ac-
> curacy of the content is of little importance to
> them.

These students see writing as a task they will have to
perform once in order to graduate, not as a skill they
will need to communicate effectively in the real world.

¶8   Kaufhold describes this mindset as "convergent thinking." He says that these types of tests emphasize "the need to search for <u>one right</u> answer. Creative ideas or divergent thinking is discouraged as students narrow the scope of their thinking toward what will be on the test" (14). Ironically, such narrowing is actually endorsed by A. D. Rison in his 1990 book designed to help students pass the language arts portion of the TAAS. He supports the use of a "Rison Design," basically the typical hourglass shape long used to teach the five-paragraph theme. He believes that students should use this design so that "many competing functions, thinking, writing, vision, and other unnecessary movements are lessened" (136). And yet for years, many teachers of composition have complained that such a standard form "almost inevitably encourages dull, formulaic writing" (Irmscher 97) and that, when these forms were taught, "all of the students seemed to write exactly alike" (104). By focusing on formulaic essays, teachers encourage convergent thinking by giving students the impression that there is only one correct way to write. In a 1990 article in the <u>English Journal</u>, John Dinan says that students "believe that barren, formulaic writing is what we want from them. Standardized tests of English cultivate this belief . . . because they implicitly define the writing process as mechanistic and impersonal" (54). The concept of writing as a mechanical process is very different from that advocated in Rief's ideal classroom.

¶9   As dull as these exercises are for teachers to grade, they are even duller for students to write. Rief makes the comment, "I cannot immerse my students in literature I don't like, anymore than any of us can write

53e
MLA

Brenneman 7

effectively on topics in which we have little interest"
(19). One of the sample prompts Rison gives for fourth
graders consists of a picture of a man sitting in a hole
eating a sandwich. Beside him lie a pick and a lunchbox.
The caption says, "This is a picture of a construction
worker. Look at this picture and describe what you see on
two sheets" (143). Is this topic supposed to produce a
student's best writing? Are there aspects of a
construction worker's life to which fourth graders can
relate their own experiences? Why should they care about
the construction worker at all? Nothing in this exercise
has any application beyond preparation for answering
similarly bland test prompts in the future. When
confronted with one such prompt, Rief cut it out of the
test books for her class and replaced it with "Write
about anything you care deeply about. Try to convince the
reader how much you care" (121).

¶10   The prompts Rison gives for tenth graders are not
much better: "Your school wants to add a new course. Your
principal has asked for suggestions. Write a letter to
your principal telling what courses you would add and
give convincing reasons for your choice" (180). The work
can seem mindless. Imagine, day after day of tedious
prompt writing for no purpose whatsoever. No wonder Dinan
complains,

>   To take such a test is to become bored, to become
>   a machine--that is, to take on the characteris-
>   tics of a dull, lifeless writer. . . . Most
>   students simply don't <u>like</u> writing very much,
>   they are apprehensive about it, beleaguered by
>   it, inclined to do it only on demand. (55)

Drilling students for these tests undermines the writing
teacher's attempts to create an environment in which

students are interested in and feel comfortable with
their writing.

¶11   Under these conditions students learn to hate
writing. They see it as a boring chore, a task they must
complete in order to please a higher authority rather
than a process intended to produce something they
themselves can take pride in. As soon as they learn to
write the type of dry, five-paragraph essay that puts
professors to sleep, their growth as writers ends. The
type of idyllic writing classroom Rief describes is still
possible under the pressure of a high-stakes test, but it
requires creative faculty willing to bet their jobs that
students can pass these tests without drills.
Unfortunately, when superintendents are receiving calls
from angry parents whose children aren't going to
graduate, what is good can take a backseat to what is
expedient. In the rush to raise the scores of those who
can't meet the state objectives, creativity is crushed in
those who can.

Brenneman 9

Works Cited

Arni, Sherry. "I Can Live with It." English Journal 79
    (Nov. 1990): 76.

Corbett, H. Dickson, and Bruce L. Wilson. Testing,
    Reform, and Rebellion. Norwood: Ablex, 1991.

Dinan, John. "Standardized Tests: Multiple Choices of the
    Wrong Kind." English Journal 67 (Oct. 1990): 54–56.

Garner, Donna. "RE: A Special Note on the TAAS Series."
    29 Jan. 2000. Online posting. EducationNews.org
    Bulletin Board. 13 Feb. 2000 <http://
    www.educationnews.org/cgi/webbbs/article/
    article_list.pl>.

Irmscher, William F. Teaching Expository Writing. New
    York: Holt, 1979.

Kaufhold, Jack. "What's Wrong with Teaching for the Test?"
    The School Administrator 55 (Dec. 1998): 14–16.

Linda/tx. "RE: Teaching to the TAAS Criticism Getting To
    Me." 4 Feb. 2000. Online posting. Texas Teachers
    Chatboard. 13 Feb. 2000 <http://texas.teachers.net/
    chatboard/>.

Mary. "RE: Teaching to the TAAS Criticism Getting To Me."
    4 Feb. 2000. Online posting. Texas Teachers
    Chatboard. 13 Feb. 2000 <http://texas.teachers.net/
    chatboard/>.

Melissa. "RE: Does Your School Give a Released TAAS
    Test?" 14 Jan. 2000. Online posting. Texas Teachers
    Chatboard. 13 Feb. 2000 <http://texas.teachers.net/
    chatboard/>.

Neill, Shirley Boes. The Competency Movement: Problems
    and Solutions. Sacramento: Educational News
    Service, 1978.

Rief, Linda. Seeking Diversity. Portsmouth: Heinemann,
    1992.

Rison, A. D. A. D. Rison's Teachers' and Parents' Guide
  to Pass the TAAS Test. Language Arts, Reading and
  Writing. Austin: Sunbelt, 1990.

Shaughnessy, Anne. "Teaching to the Test: Sometimes a Good
  Practice." English Journal 83 (Apr. 1994): 54-56.

Texas Education Agency. "Chapter 110. Texas Essential
  Knowledge and Skills for English Language Arts and
  Reading and Chapter 128. Texas Essential Knowledge
  and Skills for Spanish Language Arts and English as
  a Second Language. Subchapter C. High School." Texas
  Education Agency Administrative Rules. 1 Sept. 1998.
  6 Mar. 2000 <http://www.tea.state.tx.us/rules/tac/
  ch110_128c.html>.

Checklist 53.3
The Works Cited Page—MLA

The Works Cited list, which begins on a new page, contains full biblio-graphical information on all the books, articles, and other resources used in composing the paper. For more information about the purpose and form of this list, see Section 53b.

* Center the title "Works Cited" at the top of the page.

* Include in the Works Cited list all the sources actually mentioned in the paper. Do not include materials you examined but did not cite in the body of the paper itself.

* Arrange the items in the Works Cited list alphabetically by the last name of the author. If no author is given for a work, list it according to the first word of its title, excluding articles (*The, A, An*).

* Be sure the first line of each entry touches the left-hand margin. Subsequent lines are indented five spaces.

* Double-space the entire list. Do not quadruple-space between entries unless that is the form your instructor prefers.

* Punctuate items in the list carefully. Don't forget the period at the end of each entry.

53e
MLA

CHAPTER 54

How Do You Use APA Documentation?

APA (American Psychological Association) documentation involves just two basic steps: inserting an in-text note at each point where a paper or project needs documentation (Section 54a) and then recording all sources used in these notes in a References list (Section 54b).

Step 1

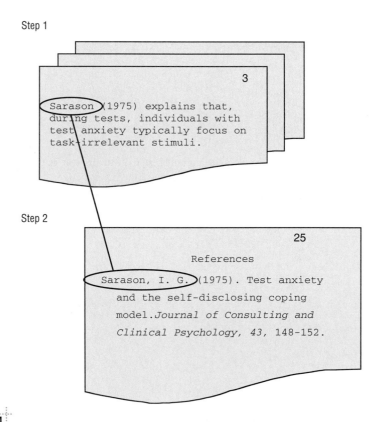

```
                              3

    Sarason (1975) explains that,
    during tests, individuals with
    test anxiety typically focus on
    task-irrelevant stimuli.
```

Step 2

```
                                25

              References

    Sarason, I. G. (1975). Test anxiety
        and the self-disclosing coping
        model. Journal of Consulting and
        Clinical Psychology, 43, 148-152.
```

54a Step 1: In the body of your paper, create a note for each source you use.

In its most common form, an APA note consists of the last name of the source's author, followed immediately by the year the material was published, in parentheses. For example, here is a sentence derived from information in an article by I. G. Sarason titled "Test Anxiety and the Self-Disclosing Coping Model," published in 1975.

> Sarason (1975) observes that a student's performance on a test can be influenced by physical distractions such as sweating and muscular tension.

Another basic form of the APA in-text note places both the author's last name and a date between parentheses. This form is used when the author's name is not mentioned in the sentence itself. Notice that a comma follows the author's name within the parentheses.

> A student's performance on a test can be influenced by physical distractions such as sweating and muscular tension (Sarason, 1975).

A page number may be given for indirect citations and *must* be given for direct quotations. A comma follows the date when page numbers are given. Page numbers are preceded by *p.* or *pp.*

> Students may also be influenced by thoughts about their test performance such as "I'm stupid, I won't pass" (Sarason,1975, p. 3).

When appropriate, the documentation may be distributed throughout a passage.

> Sarason (1975) observes that students may also be influenced by thoughts about their test performance such as "I'm stupid, I won't pass" (p. 3).

In all cases, APA parenthetical notes should be as brief and inconspicuous as possible. Most notes are simple, but some special situations may come up, such as the following:

- **If you need to cite more than one article or book written by an author in a single year,** assign a small letter after the date to distinguish between the author's two works.

```
(Rosner, 1991a)

(Rosner, 1991b)

The point is raised by Rosner (1991a), quickly
answered by Anderson (1991), and then raised again by
Rosner (1991b).
```

- **If you need to cite more than a single work in a single note,** separate the citations with a semicolon and list them in alphabetical order.

```
(Searle, 1993; Yamibe, 1995)
```

- **When you are referring to a Web site** (but not a particular Web document), you can give the electronic address directly in the paper. The site does not need to be added to the References list.

```
More information about psychology as a profession is
available on the American Psychological Association's
Web site: http://www.apa.org.
```

54b Step 2: On a separate page at the end of your project, list alphabetically every source you have cited.

This list of sources, titled "References," provides readers with bibliographical information on all the materials you used in composing an article or project. A typical APA References entry includes the following basic information, with many variations.

- Author(s), last name first, followed by a period. Use initials instead of first and middle names.
- Date of the work in parentheses, followed by a period. For books and journal articles, provide just the year of publication.
- Title of the work, followed by a period. Capitalize only the first word of the title, the first word of a subtitle (if any), and all proper nouns (e.g., *Italy*) or proper adjectives (e.g., *Italian*). Book titles are italicized, but titles of articles are neither italicized nor placed between quotation marks.
- Publication information. For books, provide place of publication (followed by a colon) and publisher (followed by a period). For articles, give the title of the journal and the volume number (italicizing both items), followed by relevant page numbers and a pe-

riod. For electronic sources, provide the date of retrieval and a Web address (URL) or electronic path. Do not add a period at the end of an entry that concludes with a URL.

```
Retrieved July 27, 2001, from

http://www.drc.utexas.edu
```

A References page entry for an article about test anxiety by I. G. Sarason would look like the following:

```
Sarason, I. G. (1975). Test anxiety and the self-

    disclosing coping model. Journal of Consulting

    and Clinical Psychology, 43, 148-152.
```

The References page itself appears on its own page following the body of the essay (and an endnotes page if there is one). For a full sample References list, see page 868. See page 869 for a checklist on setting up a References page. The first entries on a typical References page might look like this.

Subsequent lines indented five spaces   "References" centered   All items double spaced

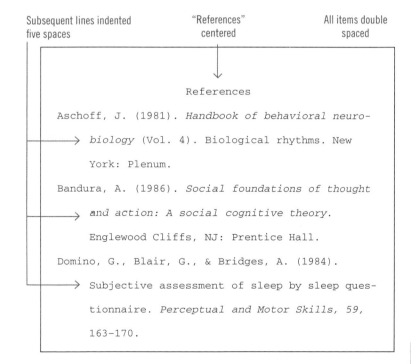

```
                    References

Aschoff, J. (1981). Handbook of behavioral neuro-

    biology (Vol. 4). Biological rhythms. New

    York: Plenum.

Bandura, A. (1986). Social foundations of thought

    and action: A social cognitive theory.

    Englewood Cliffs, NJ: Prentice Hall.

Domino, G., Blair, G., & Bridges, A. (1984).

    Subjective assessment of sleep by sleep ques-

    tionnaire. Perceptual and Motor Skills, 59,

    163-170.
```

54b
APA

54c APA models

In this section you will find the APA References page and in-text note forms for a variety of sources. Locate the type of source you need to cite in either the Models Index or the Alphabetical Index and then locate the item by number in the list that follows.

1 APA: Books checklist

Basic information	Example (see model 65)
❏ Name of author(s) or editors(s)	Pearson, G.
❏ Year of publication	(1949).
❏ Title (italicized)	*Emotional disorders of children.*
❏ Publisher's location	Annapolis, MD:
❏ Publisher	Naval Institute Press.

Other information:
❏ Edition number
❏ Volume number
❏ Translator's name
❏ Series name

54c
APA

65. Book, One Author—APA Cite books by providing author, date, title of book, place of publication, and publisher.

IN-TEXT NOTES:

Pearson (1949) found . . .

(Pearson, 1949)

(Pearson, 1949, p. 49)

References

Pearson, G. (1949). *Emotional disorders of children.*

Annapolis, MD: Naval Institute Press.

66. Book, Two Authors—APA Notice the ampersand (*&*) between authors' names in the References list and in parenthetical notes. Note, however, that *and* is used when the authors are identified in the text itself.

IN-TEXT NOTES:

Lasswell and Kaplan (1950) found . . .

(Lasswell & Kaplan, 1950)

(Lasswell & Kaplan, 1950, pp. 210-213)

References

Lasswell, H. D., & Kaplan, A. (1950). *Power and so-*

ciety: A framework for political inquiry. New

York: Yale University Press.

67. Book, Three or More Authors—APA

IN-TEXT NOTES:

FIRST NOTE. Rosenberg, Gerver, and Howton (1971)

found . . .

SUBSEQUENT NOTES. Rosenberg et al. (1971) found . . .

FIRST NOTE. (Rosenberg, Gerver, & Howton, 1971)

SUBSEQUENT NOTES. (Rosenberg et al., 1971)

References

Rosenberg, B., Gerver, I., & Howton, F. W. (1971).

Mass society in crisis: Social problems and so-

cial pathology (2nd ed.). New York: Macmillan.

If a work has six or more authors, use the first author's name followed by *et al.* for all in-text references, including the first. In the References list, however, identify all the authors.

68. Book, Revised or New Edition—APA

IN-TEXT NOTES:

Edelmann (1969) found . . .

(Edelmann, 1969)

(Edelmann, 1969, p. 62)

References

Edelmann, A. T. (1969). Latin American government

and politics (Rev. ed.). Homewood, IL: Dorsey.

IN-TEXT NOTES:

Corey (1996) explains . . .

(Corey, 1996)

(Corey, 1996, p. 14)

References

Corey, G. (2000). Theory and practice of counseling

and psychotherapy. (6th ed.). Belmont, CA:

Wadsworth.

69. Book, Edited—APA
Notice that APA uses an ampersand (&) to join the names of two editors or authors except when the names are mentioned in the body of a paper.

IN-TEXT NOTES:

Journet and Kling (1984) observe . . .

(Journet & Kling, 1984)

54c
APA

References

Journet, D., & Kling, J. (Eds.). (1984). *Readings for technical writers*. Glenview, IL: Scott, Foresman.

70. Book, No Author—APA

IN-TEXT NOTES:

In *Illustrated Atlas* (1985) . . .

(*Illustrated Atlas,* 1985, pp. 88–89)

References

Illustrated atlas of the world. (1985). Chicago: Rand McNally.

When the author of a work is actually listed as "Anonymous," cite the work that way in the References list and parenthetical note.

(Anonymous, 1995)

71. Book, a Collection or Anthology—APA

IN-TEXT NOTES:

Landers (1972) compiles . . .

(Landers, 1972)

References

Landers, D. M. (Ed.). (1972). *Psychology of sport and motor behavior, Vol. 11* (Penn State HPER Series No. 10). University Park: Pennsylvania State University Press.

72. Work Within a Collection, Anthology, or Reader—APA

List the item on the References page by the author of the piece you are actually citing, not the editor(s) of the collection. Then provide the title of the particular selection, its date, the editor(s) of the collection, the title of the collection, the pages on which the selection appears, and publication information.

IN-TEXT NOTES:

Fenz (1972) found . . .

(Fenz, 1972)

54c
APA

References

Fenz, W. D. (1972). Coping mechanisms and performance under stress. In D. M. Landers (Ed.), *Psychology of sport and motor behavior, Vol. 11* (Penn State HPER Series No. 10, pp. 3-24). University Park: Pennsylvania State University Press.

73. Chapter in a Book—APA

IN-TEXT NOTES:

Williams and Krane (1998) observe . . .
(Williams & Krane, 1998)

References

Williams, J. M., & Krane, V. (1998). Psychological characteristics of peak performance. In J. M. Williams (Ed.), *Applied sport psychology: Personal growth to peak performance* (3rd ed., pp. 158-170). Palo Alto, CA: Mayfield.

74. Book Review—APA Brackets surround the description of the item reviewed.

IN-TEXT NOTES:

Max (1999) claims . . .
(Max, 1999)

References

Max, D. T. (1999, December 27). All the world's an I.P.O.: Shakespeare the profiteer [Review of the book *Shakespeare's 21st-century economics: The morality of love and money*]. *The New York Observer,* p. 35.

54c
APA

If a review is untitled, identify the author and date and describe the item in brackets.

IN-TEXT NOTES:

Farquhar (1987) observes . . .

(Farquhar, 1987)

References

Farquhar, J. (1987). [Review of the book *Medical*

power and social knowledge]. *American Journal*

of Psychology, 94, 256.

2 APA: Scholarly Journals checklist

Basic information	Example (see model 75)
❏ Name of author(s) or editors(s)	Tebeaux, E.
❏ Year of publication	(1991).
❏ Title (no " " or underscore)	Ramus, visual rhetoric, and . . .
❏ Name of journal (italicized)	*Written Communication,*
❏ Volume number (italicized)	*8,*
❏ Pages	411-445.

75. Article in a Scholarly Journal—APA

Cite articles from such scholarly journals by providing author, date, title of article, journal, volume, and page numbers.

IN-TEXT NOTES:

Tebeaux (1991) observes . . .

(Tebeaux, 1991, p. 411)

References

Tebeaux, E. (1991). Ramus, visual rhetoric, and the

emergence of page design in medical writing of

54c

APA

the English Renaissance. *Written Communication,*

8, 411-445.

3 APA: Magazine/Newspaper checklist

Basic information	Example (see model 76)
❑ Name of author(s) or editors(s)	Morton, O.
❑ Date of publication	(2002, August).
❑ Title of article (no " " or italics)	The new air war in Europe.
❑ Name of publication (italicize)	*Wired,*
❑ Pages/sections	76-78.

76. Article in a Monthly Periodical—APA To cite a magazine published monthly, give the author's name, the date (including the month, which is not abbreviated), the title of the article, the name of the magazine and volume number if available (italicized), and the page numbers.

IN-TEXT NOTES:

Morton (2002) notes . . .

(Morton, 2002)

References

Morton, O. (2002, August). The new air war in

Europe. *Wired,* 76-78.

77. Article in a Weekly or Biweekly Periodical—APA To cite a weekly or biweekly periodical or magazine, give the author's name, the date (including month and day), the title of the article, the name of the magazine, the volume number if available (italicized), and page numbers.

IN-TEXT NOTES:

Lasch-Quinn 2000) observes . . .

(Lasch-Quinn, 2000)

(Lasch-Quinn, 2000, p. 37)

54c
APA

References

Lasch-Quinn, E. (2000, March 6). Mothers and mar-

kets. *The New Republic, 222,* 37-44.

78. **Article in a Brochure, Pamphlet or Newsletter—APA** Information will vary. For example, the author may be a person, government agency, or company. When that author is also the publisher, the publisher is identified as "Author," as in the following example.

IN-TEXT NOTES:

U.S. Dept. of Education (1996) provides . . .

(U.S. Dept. of Education, 1996)

References

U.S. Department of Education (1996). *Attention*

deficit disorder: What teachers should know.

[Brochure]. Washington, DC: Author.

For articles in newsletters, give volume and page numbers.

IN-TEXT NOTES:

Piedmont-Marton (1997) argues . . .

(Piedmont-Marton, 1997)

References

Piedmont-Marton, E. (1997, July 20). Schoolmarms or

language paramedics? *The Writer's Block, 4,* 6.

79. **Lecture or Conference Paper—APA**

IN-TEXT NOTES:

Martel(1999)examines . . .

(Martel, 1999)

References

Martel, C. (1999, February). *Emergency measures:*

Psychosocial intervention. Paper presented at

54c
APA

the Disaster Mental Health Conference,

Laramie, WY.

80. **Newspaper Article, Author Named—APA** If the article does not appear on consecutive pages in the newspaper, give all the page numbers, separated by a comma. Note that abbreviations for *page* (*p.*) and *pages* (*pp.*) are used with newspaper entries.

IN-TEXT NOTES:

Bragg (1994) reports . . .

(Bragg, 1994, p. 7A)

References

Bragg, R. (1994, October 15). Weather gurus going

high-tech. *San Antonio Express-News,* pp. 1A, 7A.

81. **Newspaper Article, No Author Named—APA**

IN-TEXT NOTES:

In the article "Scientists find" (1994) . . .

("Scientists find," 1994)

References

Scientists find new dinosaur species in Africa.

(1994, October 14). *The Daily Texan,* p. 3.

82. **Computer Software—APA** You don't need to identify common software programs (e.g., *Word, PowerPoint, Excel*) in the References list; name only specialized programs or software that is not widely known or distributed. Do not italicize or underline the titles of software. List authors only when they own the product.

IN-TEXT NOTE:

In CoreText Online (1996) . . .

References

CoreText Online [Computer software]. (1996). New

York, NY: Longman.

54c
APA

83. **Online Source/Database, Archived Listserv, or Usenet News-group—APA** For electronic sources such as newsgroups or class listservs, provide the author's real or screen name (if any), the date of the message, the thread or subject line for the message, and the address of the group or the archive in which the message is stored. If it clarifies the entry, you can put explanatory information in brackets after the subject line.

IN-TEXT NOTES:

Stewart (2001) argues . . .

(Stewart, 2001)

References

Stewart, M. (2001, October 23). Re: In God we trust.

    Message posted to http://courses.utexas.edu:80/

    bin/common/course.pl?course_id=_33295_1&frame=

    top

For databases, give the basic information followed by the date of retrieval of the material and the identity of the source, followed by the name of the database and, if an online source, the Web address for the source.

IN-TEXT NOTES:

Russell (2000) reports . . .

(Russell, 2000)

References

Russell, T. D. (2000). The shape of the Michigan

    River as viewed from the land of Sweatt v.

    Painter and Hopwood. *Law and Social Inquiry,*

    25, 507-519. Retrieved April 15, 2001, from IN-

    FOTRAC database (LegalTrac):

    http://infotrac.galegroup.com

54c
APA

4 APA: Web Page checklist

Basic information:	Example (see model 84)
❑ Creator or author of the site	Johnson, C.W., Jr.
❑ Date of publication in parentheses	(2000, January 31).
❑ Title of page (no " " or italics)	How our laws are made.
❑ Title of site (italicize)	*Thomas*.
❑ Date you examined the site	July 8, 2002.
❑ Web address (no period at end)	Retrieved from http://thomas.loc . . .

84. WWW Page—Generic—APA

IN-TEXT NOTES:

Johnson (1997) explains . . .

(Johnson, 1997)

References

Johnson, C. W., Jr. (2000, January 31). How our

   laws are made. *Thomas*. Retrieved July 8, 2002,

   from http://thomas.loc.gov/home/

   lawsmade.toc.html

85. WWW Page—Online Scholarly Article—APA

IN-TEXT NOTES:

Fine and Kurdek (1993) report . . .

(Fine & Kurdek, 1993)

54c
APA

References

Fine, M. A., & Kurdek, L. A. (1993). Reflections on determining authorship credit and authorship order on faculty-student collaborations. *American Psychologist, 48,* 1141-1147. Retrieved July 17, 2002, from http://www.apa.org/ journals/amp/kurdek.html

86. WWW Page—Online Newspaper Article—APA

IN-TEXT NOTES:

Cohen (1997) asks . . .

(Cohen, 1997)

References

Cohen, E. (1997, January 17). Shrinks aplenty on-line but are they credible? *The New York Times.* Retrieved May 5, 2001, from http:// search.nytimes.com/

87. WWW Page—Online Abstract—APA

IN-TEXT NOTES:

Shilkret and Nigrosh (1997) report . . .

(Shilkret & Nigrosh, 1997)

References

Shilkret, R., & Nigrosh, E. (1997). Assessing students' plans for college. *Journal of Counseling Psychology, 44,* 222-231. Abstract retrieved July 1, 2002, from http//www.apa.org/ journals/cou/497ab.html#10

54c
APA

88. **Email—APA** Electronic communications that are not stored or archived have limited use for researchers. APA style treats such information (as well as email) like personal communication. Because personal communications are not available to other researchers, make no mention of them in the References list. Personal communications should, however, be acknowledged in the body of the essay in parenthetical notes.

IN-TEXT NOTES:

According to Rice (personal communication, October
14, 1994), . . .

89. **Movie/Videotape/DVD—APA** This is the basic form for citing films, DVDs, audiotapes, slides, charts, and other nonprint sources. The specific medium is described between brackets, as shown here for a film. In most cases, APA references are listed by identifying the screenwriter.

IN-TEXT NOTES:

McCanlies (1998) features . . .

(McCanlies, 1998)

References

McCanlies, T. (Screenwriter). (1998). *Dancer, Texas*

[Motion Picture]. Culver City, CA: TriStar.

90. **Musical Recording—APA** Ordinarily, music is listed by the composer.

IN-TEXT NOTE:

In the song "What Was It You Wanted?" (Dylan, 1989,

track 10) . . .

References

Dylan, B. (1989). What was it you wanted? [Recorded

by Willie Nelson]. On *Across the borderline*

[CD]. New York: Columbia.

54c
APA

54d Sample APA paper

In the social sciences, articles published in professional journals often follow a form designed to connect new findings to previous research. Your instructor will usually indicate whether you should follow this structure for your paper or report.

Checklist 54.1

The Components of a Social Science Report

• **An abstract:** a concise summary of the research article.

• **A review of literature:** a survey of published research that has a bearing on the hypothesis advanced in the research report. The review establishes the context for the research essay.

• **A hypothesis:** an introduction to the paper that identifies the assumption to be tested and provides a rationale for studying it.

• **An explanation of method:** a detailed description of the procedures used in the research. Since the validity of the research depends on how the data were gathered, this is a critical section for readers assessing the report.

• **Results:** a section reporting the data often given through figures, charts, graphs, and so on. The reliability of the data is explained here, but little comment is made on its implications.

• **Discussion/conclusions:** a section in which the research results are interpreted and analyzed.

• **References:** an alphabetical list of research materials and articles cited in the report.

• **Appendixes:** a section of materials germane to the report but too lengthy to include in the body of the paper.

The following APA-style research report by Chadd Briggs and faculty adviser Fred Ribich originally appeared in volume 1 of *Psych-E,* an on-line journal of psychology for undergraduates. We have modified the essay to show how it would look as a paper a student might turn in for a college course. Because of space limitations, we've also shortened the article slightly. But we have not altered its basic style, which reflects conventions of the social sciences, particularly a heavier use of passive voice than might appear in an MLA- or Chicago-style article.

For easier reference, we've numbered the paragraphs, but these numbers would *not* appear in an actual APA paper. You can view the original, uncut and online version by searching the *Psych-E* archives at <http://www.siu.edu/departments/cola/psycho/journal>. The same site provides additional examples of undergraduate research essays in APA style.

54d
APA

Test Anxiety 1

The Relationship Between Test Anxiety, Sleep Habits, and
Self-perceived Academic Competency

Chad S. Briggs and Fred Ribich

Wartburg College

Checklist 54.2

Title Page for a Paper—APA

APA style requires a separate title page; use the facing page as a model and review the following checklist.

• Type your paper on white bond paper. Preferred typefaces (when you have a choice) include Times Roman, American Typewriter, and Courier.

• Arrange and center the title of your paper, your name, and the name of your school. Give your first name, middle initial, and last name.

• Use the correct form of the title, capitalizing all important words and all words of four letters or more. Articles, conjunctions, and prepositions are not capitalized unless they are four letters or more. Do not underline the title or use all-capitals.

• Number the title page and all subsequent pages on the same line, as shown; the short title consists of the first two or three significant words of the title.

54d
APA

Abstract

One hundred fifty-eight college students completed questionnaires and tests that measure test anxiety, sleep habits, and self-perceived academic competency. It was hypothesized that test anxiety and irregular sleep patterns will lower college students' self-perceived academic competency. The results showed that high test anxiety and poor sleep habits negatively affected students' self-perceived academic competency. It was also found that high self-perceived academic competency was positively correlated with GPA (a measure of performance). This study shows the need for further research that deals with the relationship between self-perceived academic competency and academic performance. This will enable professionals to look at another variable that affects academic performance in more detail.

Checklist 54.3

Abstract for a Paper—APA

Abstracts are common in papers using APA style.

* Place the abstract on a separate page, after the title page.

* Center the word *Abstract* at the top of the page.

* Include the short title of the essay and the page number (*2*) in the upper right-hand corner.

* Double-space the abstract.

* Do not indent the first line of the abstract. Type it in block form. Strict APA form limits abstracts to 960 characters or fewer.

54d
APA

The Relationship Between Test Anxiety, Sleep Habits, and

Self-perceived Academic Competency

Introduction

¶1   Self-perceived academic competency has been shown
to be a significant contributor to the academic success of
college students. Bandura (1986) defines self-perceived
competency as "people's judgements of their capabilities
to organize and execute courses of action required to
attain designated types of performances" (p. 10). It has
been found by Lee and Babko (1994) that when in a
difficult situation such as a college-type test, a person
with a strong sense of self-perceived academic competency
will devote more attention and effort to the task at
hand, therefore trying harder and persisting longer, than
will those who have lower levels of self-perceived
competency.

¶2   Self-perceived academic competency can be affected
by a plethora of variables. In this study, the variables
of test anxiety and sleep habits will be examined in
relationship to college students' self-perceived academic
competency.

¶3   Lewis (1970) defines anxiety as "an unpleasant
emotion experienced as dread, scare, alarm, fright,
trepidation, horror or panic" (p. 63). Test anxiety,
then, is the debilitating experience of anxiety, as
described by Lewis, during the preparation for a test or
during the test itself. Although anxiety is often
detrimental, it may be beneficial if it is not extreme.
Simpson, Parker, and Harrison (1995) convey this through
two well-known principles of anxiety: "A minimal amount
of anxiety" (an optimal amount is more accurate) "can
mobilize human beings to respond rapidly and efficiently,"
while "excessive amounts of anxiety may foster poor

54d
APA

Checklist 54.4

The Body of a Research Paper—APA

The body of the APA paper runs uninterrupted until the separate References page. Be sure to type the essay on good-quality bond paper. The first page of an APA paper will look like the facing page.

- Repeat the title of your paper, exactly as it appears on the title page, on the first page of the research essay itself.

- Be sure the title is centered and properly capitalized.

- Begin the body of the essay two lines (a double space) below the title.

- Double-space the body of the essay.

- Use at least one-inch margins at the sides, top, and bottom of this and all subsequent pages.

- Indent the first line of each paragraph five to seven spaces.

- Indent long quotations (more than 40 words) in a block five to seven spaces from the left margin. In student papers, APA permits long quotations to be single spaced.

- Include the short title of the essay and the page number (3) in the upper right-hand corner. Number all subsequent pages the same way.

- Do not hyphenate words at the right-hand margin. Do not justify the right-hand margin.

- Label figures and tables correctly. Be sure to mention them in the body of your text: (*see Figure 1*).

- Provide copyright and permission data for figures or tables borrowed from other sources.

54d
APA

Test Anxiety 4

response and sometimes inhibit response" (p. 700). Knox,
Schacht, and Turner (1993) state that test anxiety can
include performance anxiety and content (e.g., math)
anxiety. Both of these make it hard for students to
concentrate and perform adequately on tests. Knox et al.
(1993) also recognize the consequences of poorly managed
test anxiety. "Failure to manage test anxiety can result
in failing courses, dropping out of school, a negative
self-concept and a low earning potential" (p. 295).

¶4   Research on test anxiety has identified three
models that explain the origin of test anxiety: (1) The
problem lies not in taking the test, but in preparing for
the test. Kleijn, Van der Ploeg, and Topman (1994) have
identified this as the learning-deficit model. According to
this model, the student with high test anxiety tends to
have or use inadequate learning or study skills while in
the preparation stage of exam taking. (2) The second
model is termed the interference model (Kleijn et al.,
1994). The problem for people in this model is that
during tests, individuals with test anxiety focus on
task-irrelevant stimuli which negatively affect their
performance (Sarason, 1975). The attention diverted from
the task at hand can be categorized into two types,
according to Sarason. The first type of distraction can be
classified as physical and includes an increase in
awareness of heightened autonomic activity (e.g., sweaty
palms, muscle tension). The second type of distraction
includes inappropriate cognitions, such as saying to
oneself, "Others are finishing before me, I must not know
the material," or "I'm stupid, I won't pass." The
presence of either of these two task-irrelevant
cognitions will affect the quality of a student's
performance. (3) The third model of test anxiety includes

54d

APA

people who think they have prepared adequately for a
test, but in reality, did not. These people question
their abilities after the test, which creates anxiousness
during the next test.

¶5   Sleep patterns are believed to be more irregular
among college students, and irregular sleep patterns are
believed to affect both self-perceived academic
competency and academic performance. Sleep, therefore,
seems to be an important factor in a college student's
success and self-perceived ability. An optimal sleep
pattern, as defined here, is one in which an individual
goes to bed and wakes up at about the same time every day
while allowing an adequate amount of time in each of the
five stages of the sleep cycle. The function of the body
that keeps our sleep patterns in this constant waking and
sleeping cycle is called the circadian rhythm. During the
night a person enters into and out of five different
stages of sleep, the most important being rapid eye
movement (REM) sleep. When the circadian rhythm of a
person's sleep is thrown off, less time is spent in REM
sleep (Lahey, 1995). People deprived of REM sleep are
likely to experience irritability, inefficiency and
fatigue (Hobson, 1989; Webb & Bonnet, 1979). Furthermore,
they are more likely to experience irritability and
fatigue when switched from the day shift to the night
shift rather than from the night shift to the day shift
(Wilkinson, Allison, Feeney, & Kaminska, 1989). This
phenomenon is consistent with our natural tendency to
lengthen our circadian rhythms. For example, one
experiment demonstrated that participants' circadian
rhythms continued even when they were isolated in
constantly lighted chambers. However, their rhythms
quickly changed to a twenty-five-hour cycle (Aschoff,

54d
APA

1981; Horne, 1988). This phenomenon suggests that college students are particularly prone to sleep deprivation because college students are notorious for "cramming" information into their memories the night before a test. To do this, they stay up longer and wake up earlier than they usually would. The impact of sleep deprivation on academic performance is negative; consequently, it is hypothesized that students with poor sleep habits will have a lower level of self-perceived academic competency since each test is taken in a state marked by inefficient, irritable, or fatigued thinking.

¶6   While there have been numerous studies on self-perceived competency and academic performance, on test anxiety and performance, and on sleep and performance, little direct information exists on the relationship among these variables taken together. It is believed that in our findings it will be shown that test anxiety and irregular sleep patterns will lower college students' self-perceived academic competency.

Methods

Participants

¶7   One hundred fifty-eight college students participated in the study. There were 91 first- and second-year students and 67 third- and fourth-year students. Among the participants, there were 69 males and 89 females. Demographic data obtained from the participants included gender, age, year in school, major, and their estimated current grade point average (GPA).

Instruments

¶8   The Test Attitude Inventory (TAI), created by Spielberger (1980), was used to measure test anxiety. The TAI subscales measure self-reported worry and emotionality. The TAI contains 20 items that are

54d
APA

situation-specific to academically related test situations and environments. A five-point Likert scale (5 represented *usually* and 1 represented *never*) was used to obtain the participants' responses.

¶9   To measure sleep habits, the Sleep Questionnaire constructed by Domino, Blair, and Bridges (1984) was used. The questionnaire contains 54 questions pertaining to various sleep and related behaviors. The same five-point Likert scale that was used for the TAI was used by this instrument as well. In addition, 3 closed-ended questions help reveal the approximate time of sleep onset, the approximate time of awakening, and whether or not the participants take naps during the day.

¶10   The College Academic Self-Efficacy Scale (CASES), created by Owen and Froman (1988), was administered to determine the degree of confidence participants believe they have in various academic settings (e.g., note-taking during class or using the library). A five-point Likert scale was also used here, where 5 represented *a lot of confidence* and 1 represented *little confidence.* This scale consists of 33 questions covering a wide variety of academic settings and situations that are pertinent to the students' overall academic self-competency rating. Owen and Froman (1988) found the alpha internal consistency of the CASES, in two different trials, to be 0.9 and 0.92.

Procedure

¶11   Packets were prepared which contained a demographic data sheet, consent form, test anxiety inventory, CASES, and sleep habits questionnaire, in that order. Next, professors in the selected classes were given information on the purpose of the study, shown the survey instruments, and told approximately how long it

54d
APA

Test Anxiety 8

would take for students to complete the entire packet
(20-30 minutes). We were invited to six different class
meetings. The students were informed verbally that the
purpose of the study was to examine the relationships
between test anxiety, sleep habits, and self-perceived
academic competency. The students were also informed that
participation in the experiment was completely voluntary
and that their responses would be kept anonymous. The
students who agreed to participate in the study signed a
consent form. These students then filled out the
demographic data and then the four surveys. The
participants were then thanked for their willingness to
participate in the study.

Results

¶12   The mean score for test anxiety was 52.67 (out of
a possible 100), with a high score of 95 and a low score
of 24. In order to see if differences existed between
people with high test anxiety and low test anxiety, the
participants' test anxiety scores were divided into three
levels (low, moderate, and high) and compared to the
CASES using an ANOVA. Those people in the low test
anxiety group scored 124.50 (a higher score indicates
greater self-perceived academic competency) on the CASES.
Those people in the moderate test anxiety group scored
113.75 on the CASES. Those people in the high test
anxiety group scored 106.21 on the CASES. The p-value was
found to be .001. This finding is represented in Figure 1.

¶13   It was also found that there were significant
differences between test anxiety groups and GPA (a
measure of performance). The low test anxiety group
reported having a 3.29 GPA. The group that reported
moderate anxiety had a 3.13 GPA. And the group with high
test anxiety reported having a 3.02 GPA. The p-value was
found to be .05.

54d
APA

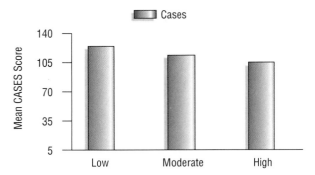

Figure 1. Levels of test anxiety.

Figure 2. Quality of sleep.

¶14   Similarly, the sleep scores were also divided into three groups (bad sleep, moderate sleep, and good sleep) for the purpose of comparing mean differences. The mean sleep score was 130.28 (out of 200), with a high score of 163 and a low score of 90. The lower sleep scores represent better sleep habits. The people in the bad sleep group scored 110.42 on the CASES. The moderate sleepers scored 114.98 on the CASES. And the people in the good sleep group scored 119.33. This is represented in Figure 2.

¶15   Furthermore, GPAs were significantly different depending on which sleep group the student was associated

with. Students in the bad sleep group reported having a
3.02 GPA, while students in the moderate sleep group
reported having a 3.11 GPA. Also, those students who fell
into the good sleep group reported having a 3.31 GPA. The
p-value was found to be .03.

¶ 16   Correlations were also figured for the following
variables (also shown in Table 1): quality of sleep
habits, test anxiety, self-perceived academic competency,
and GPA. It was found that the quality of sleep habits
and test anxiety were negatively correlated at the -.26
level (p-value of .001). The quality of sleep habits was
also found to be positively correlated with self-
perceived academic competency at the .19 level (p-value
of .016). Additionally, it was found that the quality of
sleep habits was positively correlated with GPA at the
.18 level (p-value of .024). Test anxiety and self-
perceived academic competency were negatively correlated
at the -.41 level (p-value of .001). GPA and test anxiety
were negatively correlated at the -.21 level (p-value of
.01). Lastly, self-perceived academic competency and GPA
were positively correlated at the .47 level (p-value of
.001). This can be seen in Table 1.

Table 1

Correlations between test anxiety, sleep habits, self-
perceived academic competency, and GPA

	GPA	TA	CASES	Sleep
GPA	1.0			
TA	$-.21^{**}$	1.0		
CASES	$.47^{***}$	$-.41^{***}$	1.0	
SLEEP	$-.18^{*}$	$.26^{***}$	$-.19^{*}$	1.0

TA = test anxiety

* $p < 0.05$

** $p < 0.01$

*** $p < 0.001$

Discussion

¶ 17   The findings presented indicate that bad sleep habits and high test anxiety negatively affect self-perceived academic competency, as was hypothesized. Additionally, it was found that low self-perceived academic competency negatively affected students' GPA.

¶ 18   Quality of sleep habits was found to be a factor in self-perceived academic competence. If college students do experience REM sleep deprivation more than the average population, then the findings of this study need to be passed on to college students. The findings in this study suggest that college students with poor sleep habits may perceive themselves as having lower academic competency. The study also showed that self-perceived academic competency was positively correlated to academic performance. Thus, according to Hobson (1989), Webb & Bonnet (1979), and this study, those college students who do have poor sleep habits will negatively affect their academic performance.

¶ 19   It was also found that test anxiety and GPA are negatively correlated and that quality of sleep and GPA are positively correlated. This, and the fact that quality of sleep and test anxiety are negatively related, suggests interrelationships among the variables test anxiety, sleep habits, self-perceived academic competency, and academic performance. This result highlights the fact that professors need to instruct their students on how to manage test anxiety. Students also need to be aware of the effects that poor sleep and low self-perceived academic competency have on academic performance. Thus, the phrase "I think I can, I think I can . . . " may be beneficial only if students reduce their test anxiety and develop better sleep habits. More research needs to be done to find other variables that affect self-perceived academic competence.

54d
APA

Test Anxiety 12

References

Aschoff, J. (1981). *Handbook of behavioral neurobiology: Vol. 4. Biological rhythms.* New York: Plenum.

Bandura, A. (1986). *Social foundations of thought and action: A social cognitive theory.* Englewood Cliffs, NJ: Prentice Hall.

Domino, G., Blair, G., & Bridges, A. (1984). Subjective assessment of sleep by sleep questionnaire. *Perceptual and Motor Skills, 59,* 163–170.

Hobson, J. A. (1989). *Sleep.* New York: Scientific American Library.

Horne, J. (1988). *Why we sleep: The functions of sleep in humans and other mammals.* New York: Oxford University Press.

Kleijn, W. C., Van der Ploeg, H. M., & Topman, R. M. (1994). Cognition, study habits, test anxiety, and academic performance. *Psychological Reports, 75,* 1219–1226.

Knox, D., Schacht, C., & Turner, J. (1993). Virtual reality: A proposal for treating test anxiety in college students. *College Student Journal, 27,* 294–296.

Lahey, B. B. (1995). In M. Lange, S. Connors, A. Fuerste, K. M. Huinker-Timp, & L. Fuller (Eds.), *Psychology: An Introduction.* Dubuque, IA: Brown & Benchmark.

Lee, C., & Babko, P. (1994). Self-efficacy beliefs: Comparison of five measures. *Journal of Applied Psychology, 79,* 364–369.

Lewis, A. (1970). The ambiguous word "anxiety." *International Journal of Psychiatry, 9,* 62–79.

Owen, S. V., & Froman, R. D. (1988). *Development of an academic self-efficacy scale.* Paper presented at the

Checklist 54.5

References Pages—APA

Sources contributing directly to the paper are listed alphabetically on a separate sheet immediately after the body of the essay. For more information about the purpose and form of this list, see pages 838 through 851.

- Center the title "References" at the top of the page.

- All sources mentioned in the text of the paper must appear in the References list, except personal communications; similarly, every source listed in the References list must be mentioned in the paper.

- Arrange the items in the References list alphabetically by the last name of the author. Give only initials for first names. If no author is given for a work, list and alphabetize it by the first word in the title, excluding articles (*A, An,* and *The*).

- The first line of each entry is flush with the left-hand margin. Subsequent lines in an entry are indented five spaces.

- The list is ordinarily double spaced. In student papers, APA style does permit single spacing of individual entries; double spacing is preserved between the single-spaced items.

- Punctuate items in the list carefully. Do not forget the period at the end of each entry, except those entries that terminate with an electronic address.

- In the References list, capitalize only the first word and any proper names in the title of a book or article. Within a title, capitalize the first word after a colon.

- If you have two or more entries by the same author, list them by year of publication, from earliest to latest. If an author publishes two works in the same year, list them alphabetically by title and place a lowercase letter immediately after the year: *(1998a).*

54d
APA

Test Anxiety 13

annual meeting of the National Council on
Measurement in Education, New Orleans, LA.

Sarason, I. G. (1975). Test anxiety and the self-
disclosing coping model. *Journal of Consulting and
Clinical Psychology, 43,* 148-152.

Simpson, M. L., Parker, P. W., & Harrison, A. W. (1995).
Differential performance on Taylor's Manifest
Anxiety Scale in black private college freshmen.
Perceptual and Motor Skills, 80, 699-702.

Spielberger, C. D. (1980). *Preliminary professional
manual for the Test Attitude Inventory.* Palo Alto,
CA: Consulting Psychologists Press.

Webb, W. B., & Bonnet, M. H. (1979). Sleep and dreams. In
M. E. Meyer (Ed.), *Foundations of contemporary
psychology.* New York: Oxford University Press.

Wilkinson, R., Allison, S., Feeney, M., & Kaminska, Z.
(1989). Alertness of night nurses: Two shift systems
compared. *Ergonomics, 32,* 281-292.

CHAPTER 55

How Do You Use
CMS Documentation?

Writers who prefer full footnotes or endnotes rather than in-text notes often use the "humanities style" of documentation recommended in *The Chicago Manual of Style,* fourteenth edition (1993). Basic procedures for this CMS documentary-note system are spelled out in the following sections. If you encounter documentation problems not discussed below or prefer the author-date style of CMS documentation, refer to the full manual or to *A Manual for Writers of Term Papers, Theses, and Dissertations,* sixth edition (1996), by Kate L. Turabian.

Because notes in CMS humanities style include full publishing information, separate bibliographies are optional in CMS-style papers. However, both notes and bibliographies are covered below.

Do you have specific questions about Chicago style or more general queries about editing? Check out the lively FAQ page supported by the manuscript editing department at the University of Chicago Press. It is at <http://www.press.uchicago.edu/Misc/Chicago/cmosfaq.html>.

55a CMS notes

1 In the text of your paper, place a raised number after any sentence or clause you need to document. These note numbers follow any punctuation mark except dashes, and they run consecutively throughout a paper. A direct quotation from Brian Urquhart's *Ralph Bunche: An American Life* is followed here by a raised note number.

> Ralph Bunche never wavered in his belief that the races in America had to learn to live together: "In all of his experience of racial discrimination Bunche

```
never allowed himself to become bitter or to feel
racial hatred."¹
```

The number is keyed to the first note (see Section 55a-2). To create such a raised, or *superscript*, number, select "superscript" from your word-processing font options.

2 Link every note number to a footnote or endnote.

The basic CMS note itself consists of a note number, the author's name (in normal order), the title of the work, full publication information within parentheses, and appropriate page numbers. The first line of the note is indented like a paragraph.

```
    1. Brian Urquhart, Ralph Bunche: An American
Life (New York: Norton, 1993), 435.
```

To document particular types of sources, including books, articles, magazines, and electronic sources, see the CMS models in Section 55c.

CMS style allows you to choose whether to place your notes at the bottom of each page (footnotes) or in a single list titled "Notes" at the end of your paper (endnotes). Endnotes are more common now than footnotes and easier to manage—though some word processors can arrange footnotes at the bottom of pages automatically. Individual footnotes are single spaced, with double spaces between them.

When you cite a work several times in a paper, the first note gives full information about author(s), title, and publication.

```
    1. Helen Wilkinson, "It's Just a Matter of
Time," Utne Reader, May/June 1995, 66-67.
```

Then, in shorter papers, any subsequent citations require only the last name of the author(s) and page number(s).

```
    3. Wilkinson, 66.
```

In longer papers, the entry may also include a shortened title to make references from page to page clearer.

```
    3. Wilkinson, "Matter of Time," 66.
```

If you cite the same work again immediately after a full note, you may use the Latin abbreviation *Ibid.* (meaning "in the same place"), followed by the page number(s) of the citation.

```
    4. James Morgan, "Blue Highways," in The
Distance to the Moon (New York, Riverhead, 1999), 93.

    5. Ibid., 55.
```

55a
CMS

55b CMS bibliographies

At the end of your paper, list alphabetically every source cited or used in the paper. This list is usually titled "Works Cited" when it includes only works actually mentioned in the essay; it is titled "Bibliography" if it also includes works consulted in preparing the paper but not actually cited. Because CMS notes are quite thorough, a Works Cited or Bibliography page may be optional, depending on the assignment: check with your instructor or editor about including such a page. Individual items on a Works Cited or Bibliography page are single spaced, with a double space between each item (see sample CMS paper, pp. 880–83).

When an author has more than one work on the list, those works are listed alphabetically under the author's name using this form.

```
Altick, Richard D. The Shows of London. Cambridge:

     Belknap-Harvard University Press, 1978.

---. Victorian People and Ideas. New York: Norton,

     1973.

---. Victorian Studies in Scarlet. New York:

     Norton, 1977.
```

55c CMS models

In this section you will find the CMS notes and bibliography forms for a variety of sources. The numbered items in the list are the sample note forms, often showing specific page numbers as would be the case when you were preparing actual notes; the matching bibliography entries appear immediately after.

CMS Models Index

91. Book, one author
92. Book, two or three authors or editors
93. Book, four or more authors or editors
94. Book, edited—focus on the editor
95. Book, edited—focus on the original author
96. Book written by a group
97. Book with no author
98. Work of more than one volume

55c
CMS

99. Work in a series
100. Chapter in a book
101. Article in a scholarly journal
102. Article in a popular magazine
103. Article or selection from a reader or anthology
104. Article in a newspaper
105. Encyclopedia
106. Biblical citation
107. Computer software
108. Electronic sources
109. WWW—book online
110. WWW—article online
111. Email

91. Book, One Author—CMS Provide author(s), title of the work (underlined or italicized), place of publication, publisher, and date of publication.

> 1. Steven Weinberg, *Dreams of a Final Theory* (New York: Pantheon Books, 1992), 38.

> Weinberg, Steven. *Dreams of a Final Theory*. New York: Pantheon Books, 1992.

92. Book, Two or Three Authors or Editors—CMS

> 2. Peter Collier and David Horowitz, *Destructive Generation: Second Thoughts about the '60s* (New York: Summit, 1989), 24.

> Collier, Peter, and David Horowitz. *Destructive Generation: Second Thoughts about the '60s*. New York: Summit, 1989.

93. Book, Four or More Authors or Editors—CMS Use *et al.* or *and others* after naming the first author in the notes, but list all authors in the bibliography when that is convenient.

> 3. Philip Curtin and others, eds., *African History* (Boston: Little, Brown, 1978), 77.

> Curtin, Philip, Steve Feierman, Leonard Thompson, and Jan Vansina, eds. *African History*. Boston: Little, Brown, 1978.

55c
CMS

94. Book, Edited—Focus on the Editor—CMS If you cite an edited work by the editor's name, identify the original author after the title of the work.

4. Scott Elledge, ed., *Paradise Lost,* by John
Milton (New York: Norton, 1975).

Elledge, Scott, ed. *Paradise Lost,* by John Milton.
New York: Norton, 1975.

95. Book, Edited—Focus on the Original Author—CMS

5. William Shakespeare, *The Complete Works of
Shakespeare,* 4th ed., ed. David Bevington (New York:
Longman, 1997).

Shakespeare, William. *The Complete Works of
Shakespeare.* 4th ed. Edited by David Bevington.
New York: Longman, 1997.

96. Book Written by a Group—CMS

6. Council of Biology Editors, *Scientific Style
and Format: The CBE Manual for Authors, Editors, and
Publishers,* 6th ed. (Cambridge: Cambridge University
Press, 1994).

Council of Biology Editors. *Scientific Style and
Format: The CBE Manual for Authors, Editors,
and Publishers.* 6th ed. Cambridge: Cambridge
University Press, 1994.

97. Book with No Author—CMS List it by its title, alphabetized by the first major word (excluding *The, A,* or *An*).

7. *Webster's Collegiate Thesaurus* (Springfield:
Merriam, 1976).

Webster's Collegiate Thesaurus. Springfield:
Merriam, 1976.

98. Work of More Than One Volume—CMS

8. Karlheinz Spindler, *Abstract Algebra with
Applications* (New York: Dekker, 1994), 1:17-18.

Spindler, Karlheinz. *Abstract Algebra with
Applications.* Vol. 1. New York: Dekker, 1994.

99. Work in a Series—CMS Do not underline or italicize a series name.

9. Grayson Kirk and Nils H. Wessell, eds., *The
Soviet Threat: Myths and Realities,* Proceedings of
the Academy of Political Science, no. 33 (New York:
Academy of Political Science, 1978), 62.

55c
CMS

> Kirk, Grayson, and Nils H. Wessell, eds. *The Soviet Threat: Myths and Realities.* Proceedings of the Academy of Political Science, no. 33. New York: Academy of Political Science, 1978.

100. Chapter in a Book—CMS

> 10. Delia Owens and Mark Owens, "Home to the Dunes," in *The Eye of the Elephant: An Epic Adventure in the African Wilderness* (Boston: Houghton Mifflin, 1992), 11-27.

> Owens, Delia, and Mark Owens. "Home to the Dunes." In *The Eye of the Elephant: An Epic Adventure in the African Wilderness.* Boston: Houghton Mifflin, 1992.

101. Article in a Scholarly Journal—CMS Provide author(s), title of the work (between quotation marks), name of periodical (underlined or italicized), volume number, date of publication, and page numbers.

> 11. Karl P. Wentersdorf, "Hamlet's Encounter with the Pirates," *Shakespeare Quarterly* 34 (1983): 434-40.

> Wentersdorf, Karl P. "Hamlet's Encounter with the Pirates." *Shakespeare Quarterly* 34 (1983): 434-40.

102. Article in a Popular Magazine—CMS Provide author(s), title of the work (between quotation marks), name of magazine (underlined or italicized), date of publication, and page numbers. When an article does not appear on consecutive pages (as in the example below), omit page numbers in the bibliography entry.

> 12. Don Graham, "Wayne's World," *Texas Monthly,* March 2000, 110-11.

> Graham, Don. "Wayne's World." *Texas Monthly,* March 2000.

103. Article or Selection from a Reader or Anthology—CMS

> 13. Pamela Samuelson, "The Digital Rights War," in *The Presence of Others,* 3d ed., ed. Andrea Lunsford and John Ruszkiewicz (New York: St. Martin's Press, 2000), 315-20.

> Samuelson, Pamela. "The Digital Rights War." In *The Presence of Others.* 3d ed. Edited by Andrea Lunsford and John Ruszkiewicz. New York: St. Martin's Press, 2000, 315-20.

55c
CMS

104. Article in a Newspaper—CMS Identify the edition of the paper cited (*final edition, home edition, Western edition*), except when citing editorials or features that appear in all editions. Since an individual story may move in location from edition to edition, page numbers are not ordinarily provided. Section numbers are given for papers so divided. Individual news stories are usually not listed in a bibliography.

```
     14. Celestine Bohlen, "A Stunned Venice Surveys
the Ruins of a Beloved Hall," New York Times, 31
January 1995, national edition, sec. B.
```

105. Encyclopedia—CMS When a reference work is familiar (encyclopedias, dictionaries, thesauruses), omit the names of authors and editors and most publishing information. No page number is given when a work is arranged alphabetically; instead the item referenced is named, following the abbreviation *s.v.* (*sub verbo,* meaning "under the word"). Familiar reference works are not listed in the bibliography.

```
     15. The Oxford Companion to English Literature,
4th ed., s.v. "Locke, John."
```

106. Biblical Citation—CMS Biblical citations appear in notes but not in the bibliography. If important, you may mention the version of the Bible cited.

```
     16. John 18.37-38 Jerusalem Bible.
```

107. Computer Software—CMS

```
     17. FoxPro Ver. 2.5, Microsoft, Seattle, Wash.

FoxPro Ver. 2.5. Microsoft, Seattle, Wash.
```

108. Electronic Sources—CMS
In *The Chicago Manual of Style,* fourteenth edition, the examples of notes for electronic sources generally include three features: a description of the computer source in brackets, such as [*electronic bulletin board*] or [*Web site*]; the date the material was accessed, updated, or cited [*cited 28 May 1996*]; and an electronic address, following the words *available from.* Models 108 through 111 follow these recommendations as modified in Kate L. Turabian's *A Manual for Writers of Term Papers, Theses, and Dissertations,* sixth edition (1996). The resulting citations are quite complex. Some simplification may be in order, or you may wish to consult the chapter on Columbia style for online sources (see pp. 896–901).

55c
CMS

18. Sylvia Atore Alva, "Differential Patterns of Achievement Among Asian-American Adolescents," *Journal of Youth and Adolescence* 22 (1993): 407-23, *ProQuest General Periodicals* [CD-ROM], UMI-ProQuest, June 1994.

Alva, Sylvia Atore. "Differential Patterns of Achievement Among Asian-American Adolescents." *Journal of Youth and Adolescence* 22 (1993): 407-23. *ProQuest General Periodicals.* CD-ROM UMI-ProQuest, June 1994.

109. WWW—Book Online—CMS

19. Amelia E. Barr, *Remember the Alamo* [book online] (New York: Dodd, Mead, 1888); available from http://site17585.dellhost.com/lsj/olbooks/barr/alamo.htm; Internet; cited 9 July 2002.

Barr, Amelia E. *Remember the Alamo.* Book online. New York: Dodd, Mead, 1888. Available from http://site17585.dellhost.com/lsj/olbooks/barr/alamo.htm; Internet; cited 9 July 2002.

110. WWW—Article Online—CMS

20. Paul Skowronek, "Left and Right for Rights," *Trincoll Journal,* 13 March 1997 [journal online]; available from http://www.trincoll.edu/zines/tj/tj03.13.97/articles/comm2.html; Internet; accessed 23 July 1997.

Skowronek, Paul. "Left and Right for Rights." *Trincoll Journal,* 13 March 1997. Journal on-line. Available from http://www.trincoll.edu/zines/tj/tj03.13.97/articles/comm2.html; Internet; accessed 23 July 1997.

111. Email—CMS

21. Scott Blackwood, "Re: Yosemite?" Email to author, 6 July 2002.

Blackwood, Scott. "Re: Yosemite?" Email to author, 6 July 2002

55d Sample CMS paper

The sample CMS pages are taken from "Diomedes as Hero of *The Iliad,*" a paper written by Jeremy A. Corley, a student in Joi Chevalier's course "The Rhetoric of Epic Narratives."

The sample pages demonstrate how to use both endnotes and a Works Cited page. However, the Works Cited page is optional in CMS style because the endnotes themselves include full bibliographical information. We also provide a single page reformatted to demonstrate how to use CMS-style footnotes. If you choose to use footnotes, do not also include endnotes. You may, however, present a Works Cited or Bibliography page.

The sample paper shows all titles italicized. You may either italicize or underline titles in CMS style, but be consistent. In numbering the pages of CMS papers, count the title page as part of the front matter, but do not actually number it. Any front matter, such as a preface or table of contents, is numbered in lowercase Roman numerals centered at the bottom of the page (*i, ii, iii*). The first regular page of the text is numbered in the upper right-hand corner using Arabic numerals beginning with *1*. Note that footnotes are single spaced. Any indented quotations are also single spaced. (For more on presenting student papers in CMS style, see Kate L. Turabian, *A Manual for Writers of Term Papers, Theses, and Dissertations,* 6th ed., 1996.)

55d
CMS

[New Page]

THE UNIVERSITY OF TEXAS AT AUSTIN

DIOMEDES AS HERO OF *THE ILIAD*

E 309K--TOPICS IN WRITING

DIVISION OF RHETORIC AND COMPOSITION

BY

JEREMY A. CORLEY

28 FEBRUARY 1996

[New Page]

DIOMEDES AS HERO OF *THE ILIAD*

¶1   Achilles is the central character of *The Iliad*, but is his prominence alone enough to make him the story's hero? There are many examples that would say otherwise. One of the most interesting aspects of the epic is its use of a lesser character, rather than the technical protagonist, as the tale's benchmark for heroism. This lesser character is Diomedes, and his leadership skills and maturity prove to be far superior to those of Achilles. Book V of *The Iliad* is devoted almost entirely to Diomedes' feats, and there are many scenes in which he is presented as a leader and hero throughout the rest of the text. While Diomedes is singled out for his gallantry, Achilles is, by contrast, noted for his immaturity and selfishness. Homer depicts Diomedes in a much more positive light than Achilles, despite the latter's obvious natural superiority as a soldier. It seems evident that Homer is emphasizing the total use of one's abilities, rather than just the presence of those abilities, as the basis of heroism. Diomedes, therefore, is the actual hero of *The Iliad*.

1

55d
CMS

¶2   Achilles is immediately placed at the focal point
of the story, and his pride and immaturity surface almost
instantaneously. In Book I, Agamemnon embarrasses
Achilles publicly with an outward display of his power as
the Achaians' commander: "Since Apollo robs me of
Chryseis . . . I will take your beautiful Briseis . . . to
show you how much stronger I am than you are."[1] Achilles
can hardly be faulted for taking offense at this
incident, as it "threatened to invalidate . . . the whole
meaning of his life."[2] Achilles' refusal to fight
afterward must be looked at from more than one
perspective. This is the first example of Achilles' acting
according to his pride, as proved by his regard for
himself as "the best man of all."[3] While it is
understandable for a soldier such as Achilles, who
"towers above all the other characters of The Iliad," to
be hesitant to fight for and under the man who embarrassed
him, Agamemnon, it is also folly for a soldier to stop
fighting because of anything as relatively unimportant as
an insult, even a public one.[4] A soldier's duty is to
defend his homeland and fight in its wars, and Achilles
misses this greater duty for his own selfishness. This
refusal to fight is compounded by his request to his
mother, Thetis, to "see if he [Zeus] will help the
Trojans and drive the Achaians back to their ships with
slaughter!"[5] This is wholly selfish. Achilles is willing
to put the fate of the entire Greek army in peril to feed
his own wounded ego. Achilles is acting nothing like the
leader that his divine gifts give him the power to be.
Homer clearly leaves his central character open for some
significant character development.

55d
CMS

3

¶3   In contrast to Achilles' infantile behavior, which
is consistent throughout most of the story, Diomedes is
cast in a different light. Athena gives Diomedes "courage
and boldness, to make him come to the front and cover
himself with glory."[6] While not Achilles' equal as a
soldier, "Diomedes was extremely fierce" and proved to be
a terrific leader for the Achaians.[7] Diomedes kills off
many Trojan warriors in Book V, acting as many hoped
Achilles would, and even fighting through an injury
suffered from the bow of Pandaros.[8] Rather than back
down, Diomedes prayed to Athena for aid and joined the
battle even more fiercely than before, slaying even more
Trojan soldiers.[9] It is clear at this point that Diomedes
is "obviously a paradigm of heroic behavior in Achilles'
absence."[10]

[New Page]

NOTES

1. Homer, *The Iliad,* trans. Robert Fitzgerald (New
York: Anchor Press, 1974), 14.

2. R. M. Frazer, *A Reading of "The Iliad"* (Lanham,
Md.: University Press of America, 1993), 12.

3. Homer, 15.

4. Frazer, 11.

5. Homer, 18.

6. Ibid., 58.

7. Scott Richardson, *The Homeric Narrator*
(Nashville: Vanderbilt University Press, 1990), 159.

8. Homer, 59.

9. Ibid., 60-61.

10. W. Thomas MacCary, *Childlike Achilles:
Ontogeny and Philogeny in "The Iliad"* (New York: Columbia
University Press, 1982), 95.

4

55d
CMS

[New Page]

WORKS CITED

Frazer, R. M. *A Reading of "The Iliad."* Lanham, Md.:
University Press of America, 1993.

Homer. *The Iliad.* Translated by Robert Fitzgerald. New
York: Anchor Press, 1974.

Kirk, G. S. *"The Iliad": A Commentary.* Vol. 2. New York:
Cambridge University Press, 1990.

MacCary, W. Thomas. *Childlike Achilles: Ontogeny and
Philogeny in "The Iliad."* New York: Columbia
University Press, 1982.

Richardson, Scott. *The Homeric Narrator.* Nashville:
Vanderbilt University Press, 1990.

Interested in classical Greek and Roman culture? You can find out more about Homer, *The Iliad,* and related topics at *The Perseus Project* at <http://www.perseus.tufts.edu/>.

Sample CMS page with footnotes. In CMS style, you have the option of placing all your notes on pages following the body of a paper (see the sample CMS pages above), or you may locate them at the bottom of each page as demonstrated below.

3

Book I, Agamemnon embarrasses Achilles publicly with an outward display of his power as the Achaians' commander: "Since Apollo robs me of Chryseis . . . I will take your beautiful Briseis . . . to show you how much stronger I am than you are."[1] Achilles can hardly be faulted for taking offense at this incident, as it "threatened to invalidate . . . the whole meaning of his life."[2] Achilles' refusal to fight afterward must be looked at from more than one perspective. This is the first example of Achilles' acting according to his pride, as proved by his regard for himself as "the best man of all."[3] While it is understandable for a soldier such as Achilles, who "towers above all the other characters of *The Iliad*," to be hesitant to fight for and under the man who embarrassed him, Agamemnon, it is also folly for a soldier to stop fighting because of anything as relatively unimportant as an insult, even a public one.[4] A soldier's duty is to defend his homeland and fight in its wars, and Achilles

    1. Homer, *The Iliad*, trans. Robert
Fitzgerald (New York: Anchor Press, 1974), 14.
    2. R. M. Frazer, *A Reading of "The Iliad"*
(Lanham, Md.: University Press of America,
1993), 12.
    3. Homer, 15.
    4. Frazer, 11.

55d
CMS

CHAPTER 56

How Do You Use
CSE Documentation?

Disciplines that study the physical world—physics, chemistry, biology—are called the natural sciences; disciplines that examine (and produce) technologies are described as the applied sciences. Writing in these fields is specialized; for a list of documentation guides in some of these scientific fields see Chart 52.1 on p. 772.

The Council of Science Editors (CSE), formerly the Council of Biology Editors, publishes an especially influential manual for scientific writing called *Scientific Style and Format: The CBE Manual for Authors, Editors, and Publishers* (6th ed., 1994). The manual is currently undergoing a major revision, reflecting the CSE's interest in creating a common style for international science.

The current CSE style includes the choice of two major methods of documenting sources used in research: a *name-year* system that resembles APA style and a *citation-sequence* system that lists sources in the order of their use. In this chapter, we briefly describe this second system.

56a Step 1: Where a citation is needed, insert either a raised number (preferred) or a number in parentheses.

Citations should appear immediately after the word or phrase to which they are related, and they are numbered in the order you use them.

```
Oncologists[1] are aware of trends in cancer

mortality[2].

Oncologists (1) are aware of trends in cancer

mortality (2).
```

Source 1 thus becomes the first item listed on the References page, source 2 the second item, and so on.

1. Devesa SS, Silverman DT. Cancer incidence and mortality trends in the United States: 1935-74. J Natl Cancer Inst 1978; 60:545-71.

2. Goodfield J. The siege of cancer. New York: Dell; 1978. 240 p.

You can refer to more than one source in a single note, with the numbers separated by a dash if they are in sequence and by commas if out of sequence.

IN SEQUENCE

Cancer treatment[2-3] has changed over the decades. But Rettig[4] shows that the politics of cancer research remains constant.

OUT OF SEQUENCE

Cancer treatment[2,5] has changed over the decades. But Rettig[4] shows that the politics of cancer research remains constant.

If you cite a source again later in the paper, you refer to it by its original number.

Great strides have occurred in epidemiological methods[5] despite the political problems in maintaining research support and funding described by Rettig[4].

56b Step 2: On a separate page at the end of the paper, list the sources you used in the order they occurred.

The sheet is titled "References" and the sources listed are numbered: source 1 in the paper would be the first source on the References page, source 2 the second item, and so on. Notice, then, that this References list—unlike those in MLA, APA, or Chicago styles—is *not* alphabetical. The first few entries on a CSE list might look like this.

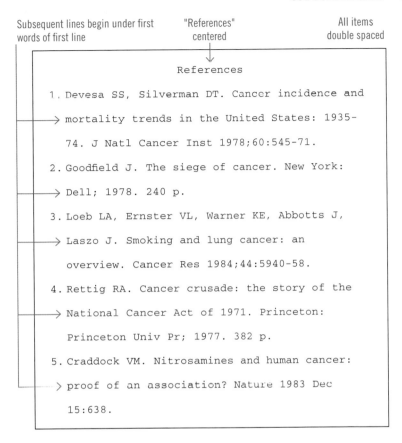

Subsequent lines begin under first words of first line   "References" centered   All items double spaced

```
                        References

 1. Devesa SS, Silverman DT. Cancer incidence and

   → mortality trends in the United States: 1935-

     74. J Natl Cancer Inst 1978;60:545-71.

 2. Goodfield J. The siege of cancer. New York:

   → Dell; 1978. 240 p.

 3. Loeb LA, Ernster VL, Warner KE, Abbotts J,

   → Laszo J. Smoking and lung cancer: an

     overview. Cancer Res 1984;44:5940-58.

 4. Rettig RA. Cancer crusade: the story of the

   → National Cancer Act of 1971. Princeton:

     Princeton Univ Pr; 1977. 382 p.

 5. Craddock VM. Nitrosamines and human cancer:

   → proof of an association? Nature 1983 Dec

     15:638.
```

A typical **CSE citation-sequence style References entry for a book** includes the following basic information.

- Number assigned to the source.
- Name of author(s), last name first, followed by a period. Initials are used in place of full first or middle names. Commas ordinarily separate the names of multiple authors.
- Title of work, followed by a period. Only the first word and any proper nouns in a title are capitalized. The title is not underlined.
- Place of publication, followed by a colon.
- Publisher, followed by a semicolon. Titles of presses can be abbreviated.
- Date, followed by a period.
- Number of pages, followed by a period.

56b
CSE

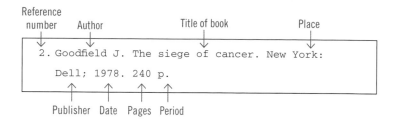

A typical **CSE citation-sequence style References entry for an article in a scholarly journal** (where the pagination is continuous through a year) includes the following basic information.

- Number assigned to the source.
- Name of author(s), last name first, followed by a period. Initials are used in place of full first or middle names. Commas ordinarily separate the names of multiple authors.
- Title of article, followed by a period. Only the first word and any proper nouns in a title are capitalized. The title does not appear between quotation marks.
- Name of the journal. All major words are capitalized, but the journal title is not italicized or underlined. A space (but no punctuation) separates the journal title from the date. Journal titles of more than one word can be abbreviated following the recommendations in *American National Standard Z39.5-1985: Abbreviations of Titles of Publications.*
- Year (and month for journals not continuously paginated; date for weekly journals), followed immediately by a semicolon.
- Volume number, followed by a colon, and the page numbers of the article. No spaces separate these items. A period follows the page numbers.

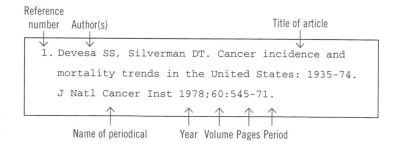

A typical **CSE citation-sequence style References entry for an article in a popular magazine** includes the following basic information.

- Number assigned to the source.
- Name of author(s), last name first, followed by a period. Initials are substituted for first names unless two authors mentioned in the paper have identical last names and first initials.
- Title of article, followed by a period. Only the first word and any proper nouns in a title are capitalized. The title does not appear between quotation marks. (Where quotation marks are needed, CBE recommends British style. See *CBE Manual,* pp. 180–81.)
- Name of magazine, abbreviated. All major words are capitalized, but the journal title is not underlined. A space (but no punctuation) separates the magazine title from the year and month.
- Year, month (abbreviated), and day (for a weekly magazine). The year is separated from the month by a space. A colon follows immediately after the date, followed by page number(s). The entry ends with a period.

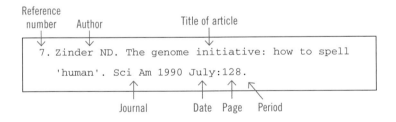

A typical **CSE citation-sequence style References entry for an electronic item** includes the basic information provided for a print document (author, title, publication information, page numbers) with the following additions.

- Electronic medium, identified between brackets. For books and monographs, this information comes after the title: [*Internet*] or [*monograph on the Internet*]. For periodicals, it follows the name of the journal: [*Internet*] or [*serial on the Internet*].
- Date of access in brackets, following date of publication.
- Availability statement, following the publication information. The electronic address is *not* followed by a period.

56b
CSE

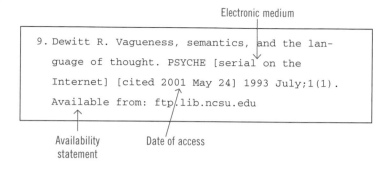

A citation to a Web site would look like the following:

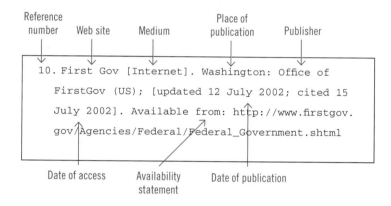

There are so many variations to these basic entries, however, that you will certainly want to check the *CBE Manual* when you do a major CBE-style paper. Also check the CBE Web site for more information about proper electronic citation forms at <http://www.councilscience editors.org>.

Checklist 56.1

CSE Style

- CSE style normally requires a separate title page. The title of the essay can be centered about a third of the way from the top of the page, followed by *by* on a separate line and the writer's name, also on a separate line. Other information such as instructor's name, course title, and date can be included on the bottom third of the page.

- CSE style normally requires an abstract of about 250 words on a separate sheet immediately following the title page. The title "Abstract" is centered on the page.

- Double-space the body of a CSE paper. Avoid hyphenating words at the end of the line.

- Number pages consecutively in the upper right-hand corner, counting the title page as the first page.

- Take special care with figures and tables. They should be numbered in separate sequences. The *CBE Manual* includes an entire chapter on handling illustrative material.

- The References page follows the text of the CSE essay on a new page. Remember that the items on this page are *not* listed alphabetically. References pages can also be titled "Literature Cited" or "References Cited."

- All works listed on the References page should be cited at least once in the body of your paper.

- Entries on the References page are single spaced, with a space left between the entries.

CHAPTER 57

How Do You Use
COS Documentation?

Columbia Online Style (COS) is a system of documentation designed expressly for electronic environments. It is the work of Janice R. Walker and Todd Taylor as presented in *The Columbia Guide to Online Style* (1998). COS style recognizes that online and computer sources differ from printed ones and yet have a logic of their own that makes reliable citation possible.

Fortunately, you don't have to forget what you have learned about other documentation systems to use COS—it doesn't replace MLA, APA, CMS, or CSE style. Instead, COS is designed to work with all of them so that writers can document electronic sources consistently and appropriately *within* the style they are expected to use in school or at work. To use COS style, simply follow it consistently for all the electronic sources in a project, choosing the COS form best suited to the documentation style you are using for printed sources. To make this adaptation simple, COS offers forms for both major types of documentation, the author–page number form favored in humanities systems (MLA, CMS) and the author-date style preferred in the sciences (APA, CSE). In this chapter, we provide separate COS Form Directories for humanities-style citations (Section 57c) and science-style citations (Section 57d).

Like the MLA and APA systems, COS documentation itself involves just two basic steps: inserting a note at each point where a paper or project needs documentation (Section 57a) and then recording all sources used in these notes in a Works Cited or References list (Section 57b).

57a Step 1: In the body of your paper, create a note for each source you use.

For a humanities paper in MLA style, the in-text note will usually be an author's last name and a page number in parentheses.

(Weinberg 38)

But for electronic sources without page numbers or other consistent divisions, simply place the author's last name in parentheses after a passage that requires documentation.

```
Jim Lehrer may be America's most trusted newsperson,
its new Walter Cronkite (Shafer).
```

If a Web site or Web page has no conventional author (a common occurrence), identify the source by placing a shortened version of its title within parentheses.

```
USA Today was among those to editorialize against the
tobacco industry's continuing influence on Congress
("Tobacco").
```

When citing a message from email, listservs, or other electronic forums, you may have to cite an author's alias or nickname.

```
In a recent posting to the newsgroup
alt.sport.paintball, jireem argued . . .
```

Note that you do not include the electronic address of a source in the note you place in the text.

For scientific papers, the in-text note will include an author's last name followed by a date of "publication" in parentheses. Give only the year even if the source furnishes day and date.

```
Jim Lehrer may be America's most trusted newsperson,
its new Walter Cronkite (Shafer, 1996).
```

You can also simply name the author in the body of your text, following the name with year of publication in parentheses.

```
Shafer (1996) claims in a Slate column that PBS's Jim
Lehrer is the new Walter Cronkite, America's most
trusted newsperson.
```

Some electronic sources such as email or Usenet messages will not have dates of publication or any dates at all. In such cases for science-style references, record the date you accessed the source, giving date, month, and year.

```
Slipstream (21 May 1997) argues that the research
design is flawed, but ksmith (22 May 1997) rejects
that claim.
```

57a
COS

57b Step 2: On a separate page at the end of your project, list alphabetically every source you have cited.

This alphabetical list of sources is usually titled "Works Cited" in humanities papers and "References" in scientific papers. You must have a Works Cited/References page for MLA and APA papers; in Chicago style, such a page is optional.

Like citations in other systems, COS items are assembled from a few basic components.

- **Author.** List an "author" when you can clearly identify someone as responsible for a source, text, or message. List an alias if you don't know the actual name of the person sending an online message. When no author can be identified, list the source on a Works Cited/References page by its title.
- **Title.** Depending on whether you are adapting COS to MLA or APA documentation, titles of electronic works might be italicized, placed between quotation marks, or left without any special marking. But in COS style, titles are never underlined.
- **Publication information.** For many online sources, the electronic address or pathway is the essential publication information.
- **Date of publication and/or access.** When an online or electronic source is based on a printed source or appears in a dated format (such as the online version of a newspaper or magazine), give the original publication date of the material. For Web sites, check the home page for information about original dates of posting and updates.

  For most electronic sources, provide a date of access—the day, month, and year you actually examined the material. When the date of publication of a source is the same as the date of your access to it (as it might be when you're reading an online news source), you need to give only the date of access.
- **Electronic address.** The electronic address will often be a World Wide Web uniform resource locator (URL), that is, the familiar Web address beginning *http://*.

57c COS models—Humanities (MLA)

Use these COS Humanities forms when you are writing a paper in which you use an author–page number citation system (such as MLA) for nonelectronic sources.

**57c
COS**

To find the form you need, simply look in the Models Index for the type of source you need to document and then locate that item by number in the list that follows.

COS Models Index— Humanities (MLA)

World Wide Web Citations

112. Web sites—various—COS/ MLA
113. Web site—books—COS/ MLA
114. Web site—online article— COS/MLA
115. Web site—article from a news service—COS/MLA
116. Web site—article from an archive—COS/MLA
117. Web site—graphic or audio file—COS/MLA

Email, Listservs, Newsgroups

118. Personal email—COS/MLA

119. Listserv—COS/MLA
120. Newsgroup—COS/MLA

Gopher, FTP, and Telnet Sites

121. Material from a Gopher or FTP site—COS/MLA
122. Material from a telnet site—COS/MLA
123. Synchronous communications (MOOs, MUDs)— COS/MLA

Databases and Software

124. Material from a CD-ROM—COS/MLA
125. Material from an online database—COS/MLA
126. Software—COS/MLA

1 COS: Web Page checklist (humanities)

Basic information	Example (see model 112)
❏ Creator or author of the site	Prosek, James.
❏ Title of the page (between " ")	"Fishing."
❏ Title of site (italicized)	*Troutsite.*
❏ Date of electronic publication	1999.
❏ Web address	http://www.troutsite.com/ fishing/index.html
❏ Date you examined the site	(28 Mar. 2002).

57c
COS

112. **Web Sites—COS/Humanities (MLA)** The title of a particular Web page appears in quotation marks while the title of the entire site is italicized. Provide author (if any), title of the page, publication information and date, electronic address, and date of access in parentheses. The documentation will vary slightly for sites with individual authors or with government institutional, or corporate sponsorship, as the following examples show.

Works Cited

Cedar Point, Inc. "Cedar Point Nears Completion of
World-Record-Breaking Roller Coaster." 15 Feb.
2002. http://www.cedarpoint.com/public/
news/story.cfm?id= 92 (29 Feb. 2002).

The Navajo Nation Web Site. Rev. Feb. 2002.
http://www.navajo.org (14 May 2002).

Prosek, James. "Fishing." *Troutsite.* 1999.
http://www.troutsite.com/fishing/index.html (28
Mar. 2002).

Texas Department of Economic Development. "Rio
Grande Float Trips." *TravelTexas.* 1998.
http://www.traveltex.com/regionviewer.
asp?region_id= 271 (19 May 2000).

United States Congress. "Floor Activity in Congress
This Week." *Thomas: Legislative Information on
the Internet.* http://thomas.loc.gov/home/
hot-week.html (28 July 1997).

113. **Web Site—Books, Available Online—COS/Humanities (MLA)** Give the name of the author, the title of the work, and the publication information for the printed version if known.

Works Cited

Austen, Jane. *Pride and Prejudice*. 1813. *Pride and*

  Prejudice Hypertext. Ed. H. Churchyard. 1994.

  http://www.pemberley.com/janeinfo/pridprej.html

  (3 Mar. 2000).

For books available only online, the entry is simpler.

Works Cited

Baker, Catherine. *Your Genes, Your Choices*. American

  Association for the Advancement of Science.

  1997. http://ehrweb.aaas.org/ehr/books/

  (15 Mar. 2000).

114. Web Site—Online Article—COS/Humanities (MLA)

The volume number of the periodical is given, followed by a colon and an issue number (if available) and date of publication.

Works Cited

Williamson, Iain. "Internalized Homophobia and

  Health Issues Affecting Lesbians and Gay Men."

  Health Education Research 15:1 (Feb. 2000).

  http://her.oupjournals.org/cgi/content/full/

  15/1/97 (1 Mar. 2000).

115. Web Site—Article from a News Service or Online Newspaper—COS/Humanities (MLA)

Provide author, title of the article, the name of the news service or online newspaper, the date of the article (if different from the date accessed), the electronic address, and the date accessed.

Works Cited

Brooke, James. "Japan Carves Out Major Role in

  China's Auto Future." *New York Times on the Web*

57c
COS

```
10 July 2002. http://www.nytimes.com/

2002/07/11/business/worldbusiness/11CARS.html

(14 July 2002).
```

```
Matthews, Karen. "Demand Outstrips Server Capacity

    in King Story's Online Debut." FoxNews.com.

    http://www.foxnews.com/entertainment/031500/

    king.sml (15 Mar. 2000).
```

If no author's name is given, list the name of the news source (such as *Reuters* or *Associated Press*).

116. **Web Site—Article from an Archive—COS/Humanities (MLA)**
Provide author, title, journal, and date as you would for a printed article, followed by the name of the archive site, the electronic address, and the date of access. In the example below, "The Compost Pile" is the name *Slate* gives to its archive of previously published articles.

Works Cited

```
Achenbach, Joel. "The Unexamined Game Is Not Worth

    Watching." Slate 9 May 1997. "The Compost

    Pile." http://www.slate.com/goodsport/

    97-05-09/goodsport.asp (1 June 1999).
```

117. **Web Site—Graphic or Audio File—COS/Humanities (MLA)**
To cite the graphic (illustration, image, photo, film clip) or audio file alone, identify the author, photographer, or artist (if known); and give its title (italicized as a work of art) or its file name without italics. Then furnish an electronic address and the date of access.

Works Cited

```
Sandberg, Bob. Jackie Robinson in Dodgers Uniform.

    http://rs6.loc.gov/pnp/ppmsc/00000/00047r.jpg

    (12 Mar. 2000).
```

To cite the graphic as it appears on a particular page, once again identify the artist and the title. Then name the site on which the graphic appears and give the electronic address for the page.

Works Cited

Sandberg, Bob. *Jackie Robinson in Dodgers Uniform.*

"Baseball, the Color Line, and Jackie Robinson—

About the Collection." *American Memory.*

http://memory.loc.gov/ammem/jrhtml/jrabout.html

(12 Mar. 2000).

118. Personal Email—COS/Humanities (MLA) COS style calls for a hyphen in *e-mail.*

Works Cited

Sherman, Lee. "Coffee Shops." Personal e-mail

(5 Mar. 1997).

119. Listserv—COS/Humanities (MLA) Give the subject line of the message as the title, followed by a date (if different from the date of access), the address of the listserv, and the date of access.

Works Cited

Cook, Janice. "Re: What New Day Is Dawning?" 19 June

1997. acw-1@ttacs6.ttu.edu (21 June 1997).

120. Newsgroup—COS/Humanities (MLA)

Works Cited

Krieger, C. R. "Re: Using BMW Emblem." 6 June 2002.

alt.autos.bmw. http://groups.google.com/

groups?q=bmw&start=40&hl=en&lr=&ie=UTF-8&selm=

3d19ecd0%240%244185%2439cecf19%40nnrp1.

twtelecom.net&rnum=46 (14 July 2002).

57c
COS

121. Material from a Gopher or FTP Site—COS/Humanities (MLA)

Works Cited

Harnad, Stevan. "Minds, Machines and Searle."

Journal of Experimental and Theoretical

Artificial Intelligence 1 (1989).

gopher://gopher.liv.ac.uk:70/00/phil/

philos-l-files/searle.harnad (30 July 1997).

The electronic address can be written to indicate the links that lead to a particular document.

gopher://gopher.liv.ac.uk, phil/philos-l-files/

searle.harnad (30 July 1997).

122. Material from a Telnet Site—COS/Humanities (MLA)

Works Cited

"Manners." Connections. telnet://connections.

sensemedia.net:3333, help manners (1 Mar. 1997).

123. Synchronous Communications (MOOs, MUDs)—COS/ Humanities (MLA)

Works Cited

Inept_Guest. Personal interview. The Sprawl.

telnet://sensemedia.net:7777/ (21 May 1997).

124. Material from a CD-ROM/DVD—COS/Humanities (MLA)

Works Cited

"Read Me." Quicken 2002 Deluxe. Intuit, 2001.

125. Material from an Online Database—COS/Humanities (MLA)
Identify the database or information service, and furnish retrieval data and a date of access.

Works Cited

```
Vlasic, Bill. "In Alabama: The Soul of a New

    Mercedes?" Business Week 31 Mar. 1997: 70.

    InfoTrac SearchBank File #A19254659. (27 July

    1997).
```

126. **Software—COS/Humanities (MLA)** If no author is given or if the corporate author is the same as the publisher, list the software by its title. Then identify the version of the software unless the version number is part of its name (*Windows 95, Word 6.0*). Give place of publication (if known), publisher, and date of release.

Works Cited

```
Virtual PC. Vers. 3.0. San Mateo: Connectix, 1999.
```

57d COS models—Sciences (APA)

Use the COS forms when you are writing a paper in which you use an author-date citation system (such as APA) for nonelectronic sources. The items in this section adhere to APA style for the names of authors and the titles of works but follow COS guidelines for the electronic portion of the citation.

To find the form you need, simply look in the Models Index for the type of source you must document and then locate that item by number in the list that follows. To handle more complex electronic sources and to learn more about developing standards for online style, consult *The Columbia Guide to Online Style* by Janice R. Walker and Todd Taylor (New York: Columbia University Press, 1998).

57d
COS

132. Web site—graphic or audio file—COS/APA

Email, Listservs, Newsgroups
133. Personal email—COS/APA
134. Listserv—COS/APA
135. Newsgroup—COS/APA

Gopher, FTP, and Telnet Sites
136. Material from a Gopher or FTP site—COS/APA

137. Material from a telnet site—COS/APA
138. Synchronous communications (MOOs, MUDs)—COS/APA

Databases and Software
139. Material from a CD-ROM/DVD—COS/APA
140. Material from an online database—COS/APA
141. Software—COS/APA

2 COS: Web page checklist (sciences)

Basic information	Example (see model 127)
❏ Creator or author of the site	Prosek, J.
❏ Date of electronic publication	(1999).
❏ Title of the page	Fishing.
❏ Title of site (italicize)	*Troutsite.*
❏ Web address	http://www.troutsite.com/ fishing/index.html
❏ Date you examined the site	(28 Mar. 2002).

127. Web Sites—COS/Sciences (APA)   As the following examples show, the documentation will vary slightly for sites with individual authors or with government, institutional, or corporate sponsorship.

References

Cedar Point, Inc. (2002, February 15). Cedar Point

nears completion of world-record-breaking roller

coaster. http://www.cedarpoint.com/

public/news/story.cfm?id= 92 (29 February 2002).

The British monarchy: The official Web site. (2000,

    March 14). (Rev. ed.). http://www.royal.gov.uk/

    (15 March 2000).

Prosek, J. (1999). Fishing. *Troutsite.*

    http://www.troutsite.com/fishing/index.html (28

    March 2002).

Texas Department of Economic Development. (1998).

    Rio Grande float trips. *TravelTexas.*

    http://www.traveltex.com/regionviewer.asp?regio

    n_id= 271 (19 May 2000).

U.S. Congress. Floor activity in Congress this week.

    Thomas: Legislative information on the

    Internet. http://thomas.loc.gov/home/hot-

    week.html (28 July 1997).

128. Web Site—Books, Available Online—COS/Sciences (APA)

Give the name of the author, the title of the work, and the publication information for the printed version if known.

References

Austen, J. (1813). *Pride and prejudice. Pride and*

    prejudice hypertext. H. Churchyard (Ed.). 1994.

    http://www.pemberley.com/janeinfo/

    pridprej.html (3 March 2000).

For books available only online, the entry is simpler.

References

Baker, C. (1997). *Your genes, your choices.*

    American Association for the Advancement of

    Science. http://ehrweb.aaas.org/ehr/books/ (15

    March 2000).

57d
COS

129. **Web Site—Online Article—COS/Sciences (APA)**
Provide an issue number (if available) in parentheses after the volume number. The issue number is not italicized.

References

Williamson, I. (2000, February). Internalized homo-

phobia and health issues affecting lesbians and

gay men. *Health Education Research, 15*(1).

http://her.oupjournals.org/cgi/content/full/15/

1/97 (1 March 2000).

130. **Web Site—Article from a News Service or Online Newspaper—COS/Sciences (APA)**

References

Brooke, J. (2002, July 10). Japan carves out major

role in China's auto future. *New York Times on*

the Web. http://www.nytimes.com/2002/07/11/

business/worldbusiness/11CARS.html (14 July

2002).

131. **Web Site—Article from an Archive—COS/Sciences (APA)**

References

Achenbach, J. (1997, May 9). The unexamined game is

not worth watching. *Slate.* The Compost Pile.

http://www.slate.com/goodsport/97-05-09/

goodsport.asp (1 June 1997).

132. **Web Site—Graphic or Audio File—COS/Sciences (APA)**
Cite a graphic file in one of two ways: either by its own URL or by the Web page on which the image appears. The first citation is for the photograph itself. The second citation is to the page on which the graphic appears. APA style permits a description of the source in brackets, useful in this case.

57d
COS

References

Savoia, S. (1997). William F. Weld [Photograph].

http://www.washtimes.com/news/images/

news2.gif (29 July 1997).

Savoia, S. (1997). William F. Weld [Photograph]. *The*

Washington Times. http://www.washtimes.com/

index.html (29 July 1997).

Audio or video files can be treated the same way as graphics, either as separate documents or as files set in the context of particular Web pages.

133. Personal Email—COS/Sciences (APA)

In APA style, you do not include personal email messages in the References list.

134. Listserv—COS/Sciences (APA)

References

Cook, J. (1997, June 19). Re: What new day is dawn-

ing? acw-l@ttacs6.ttu.edu (21 June 1997).

135. Newsgroup—COS/Sciences (APA)

References

Krieger, C. R. (2002, June 6). Re: Using BMW emblem.

alt.autos.bmw. http://groups.google.com/

groups?q=bmw&start=40&hl=en&lr=&ie=UTF-8&selm=

3d19ecd0%240%244185%2439cecf19%40nnrp1.

twtelecom.net&rnum=46 (14 July 2002).

136. Material from a Gopher or FTP Site—COS/Sciences (APA)

References

Harnad, S. (1989). Minds, machines and Searle.

Journal of Experimental and Theoretical

57d
COS

                   Artificial Intelligence 1. gopher://

                   gopher.liv.ac.uk:70/00/phil/philos-1-files/

                   searle.harnad (30 July 1997).

The electronic address can be written to indicate the links that lead to a particular document.

                   gopher://gopher.liv.ac.uk, phil/philos-1-files/

                   searle.harnad (30 July 1997).

137. Material from a Telnet Site—COS/Sciences (APA)

References

            Manners. *Connections.* telnet://connections.

               sensemedia.net:3333, help manners (1 March

               1997).

138. Synchronous Communications (MOOs, MUDs)— COS/Sciences (APA)

Identify the speaker, the type of communication and/or the title of the session, and the title of the site (if available).

References

            Inept_Guest. Personal interview. *The sprawl.*

               telnet://sensemedia.net:7777/ (21 May 1997).

139. Material from a CD-ROM/DVD—COS/Sciences (APA)

References

            Bruckheim, A. H. (1993). Basic first aid. *The family*

               doctor (Version 3). Portland, OR: Creative

               Multimedia.

57d
COS

140. Material from an Online Database—COS/Sciences (APA)

References

Vlasic, B. (1997, March 31). In Alabama: The soul of

a new Mercedes? *Business Week, 70. InfoTrac*

SearchBank. File #A19254659. (27 July 1997).

141. Software—COS/Sciences (APA)

References

Norton utilities for Macintosh (Version 6.0.3)

[Computer software]. (2001). Cupertino, CA:

Symantec.

57d
COS

Glossary of Terms and Usage

This glossary covers grammatical terms, rhetorical terms, and items of usage. Whether you require the definition of a key term (*verbals, proper noun*), an explanation of a rhetorical concept (*cliché, idiom*), or some advice about correct usage (What's the difference between *eminent* and *imminent?*), you'll find the information in this single, comprehensive list. For convenient review, key grammatical terms are marked by the symbol *.

a, an. Indefinite articles. **A** and **an** are **indefinite articles** because they point to objects in a general way (**a** book, **a** church), while the **definite article the** refers to specific things (**the** book, **the** church). **A** is used when the word following it begins with a consonant sound: **a** *house,* **a** *year,* **a** *boat,* **a** *unique* experience. **An** is used when the word following it begins with a vowel sound: **an** *hour,* **an** *interest,* **an** *annoyance,* **an** *illusory* image.

Notice that you choose the article by the *sound* of the word following it. Not all words that begin with vowels actually begin with vowel sounds, and not all words that begin with consonants have initial consonant sounds.

* **absolute.** A phrase that modifies an entire sentence. Absolutes are often infinitive or participial phrases. Unlike other modifying phrases, absolutes do not necessarily modify a word or phrase standing near them.

> **To put it politely,** Connie is irritating.
>
> She will publish the entire story, **space permitting.**
>
> **Scripts discarded, props disassembled, costumes locked away in trunks,** the annual Shakespeare festival concluded.

See **misplaced modifier** and **dangling modifier;** see Section 33a.

* **absolute adjective.** A word such as *unique, dead,* or *equal* that ought not to be qualified to suggest some degree. Logically speaking, something cannot be *more* unique, *less* equal, or *very* dead.

* **abstract noun.** A noun that names ideas, concepts, and qualities without physical properties: *softness, Mother Nature, democracy, humanism.* Abstract nouns exist in the mind as ideas. They are defined in contrast to **concrete nouns.**

accept/except. Very commonly confused. **Accept** means "to take, receive, or approve of something." **Except** means "to exclude, or not including."

> I **accepted** all the apologies **except** George's.

accidently/accidentally. **Accidently** is a misspelling. The correct spelling is **accidentally.**

acronym. A single term created by joining the first letters of the words that make up the full name or description. Acronyms are pronounced as single words and are ordinarily capitalized.

> NATO—North Atlantic Treaty Organization
> NASA—National Aeronautics and Space Administration

Some common acronyms are written as ordinary words without capitalization: *laser, radar.* See also **initialism.**

gloss

* **active verb/voice.** See **voice.**

ad/advertisement. In academic and formal writing, you should use the full word: **advertisement.**

* **adjectival.** A word, phrase, or clause that modifies a noun or pronoun.

> noun   adjectival
> the *engagement* **of Ike and Bernice**
> adjectival   noun   adjectival
> the **never-ending** *battle* **between the sexes**
> noun   adjectival
> the *ceremony* **they would have preferred**

* **adjective.** A word that modifies a noun or pronoun. Some adjectives describe the words they modify, explaining how many, which color, which one, and so on.

> an **unsuccessful** coach   a **green** motel
> the **lucky** one   a **sacred** icon

Such adjectives frequently have comparative and superlative forms.

> the **blacker** cat   the **happiest** people

Other adjectives limit or specify the words they modify.

> **this** adventure   **every** penny
> **each** participant   **neither** video

Proper nouns can also serve as adjectives.

> **Texan** wildlife   **Eisenhower** era

See also **coordinate adjective, demonstrative adjective, noncoordinate adjective,** and **predicate adjective.**

* **adjective clause.** A dependent (or subordinate) clause that functions as an adjective, modifying a noun or pronoun. See **clause** for definition of a dependent clause; see Section 19d-2.

> Margery Hutton, the woman **who writes mystery stories,** lives in the mansion **that Dr. Horace Elcott built.**
>
> Her gardens were tended by Bud Smith, **who learned to garden from his father.**

* **adverb.** A word that modifies a verb, an adjective, or another adverb. Adverbs explain where, when, and how.

> adverb verb
> Bud **immediately** *suspected* foul play at the Hutton mansion.
> adverb adjective
> It seemed **extremely** *odd* to him that Mrs. Hutton should load a large burlap sack into the trunk of her Mercedes.
> adverb adverb
> Mrs. Hutton replied **rather** *evasively* when Bud questioned her about what she was up to.

Some adverbs modify complete sentences.

> adverb
> **Obviously,** Mr. Hutton had been murdered!

* **adverb clause.** A subordinate clause that functions as an adverb. See Section 19b-2; see also **clause.**

> **After Mrs. Hutton left,** Bud slipped into the Hutton mansion.
> Bud was startled **when Mr. Hutton greeted him in the living room.**

* **adverbial.** An expression that functions like an adverb but is not actually an adverb. Adverbials can be nouns, clauses, and phrases.

> NOUN AS ADVERBIAL
> They are going **home.** Explains *where.*
> CLAUSE AS ADVERBIAL
> They go jogging **whenever they can.** Explains *when.*
> PHRASE AS ADVERBIAL
> They go jogging **in the morning.** Explains *when.*

adverse/averse. Often confused. Adverse describes something hostile, unfavorable, or difficult. Averse indicates the opposition someone has to something; it is ordinarily followed by *to.*

> Travis was **averse** to playing soccer under **adverse** field conditions.

advice/advise. These words aren't interchangeable. **Advice** is a noun meaning "an opinion" or "counsel." **Advise** is a verb meaning "to give counsel or advice."

> I'd **advise** you not to give Maggie **advice** about running her business.

affect/effect. A troublesome pair! Each word can be either a noun or a verb, although **affect** is ordinarily a verb and **effect** a noun. In its usual sense, **affect** is a verb meaning "to influence" or "to give the appearance of."

> How will the stormy weather **affect** the plans for the outdoor concert?
> The meteorologist **affected** ignorance when we asked her for a forecast.

Only rarely is **affect** a noun—as a term in psychology meaning "feeling" or "emotion." On the other hand, **effect** is usually a noun, meaning "consequence" or "result."

The **effect** of the weather may be serious.

Effect may, however, also be a verb, meaning "to cause" or "to bring about."

The funnel cloud **effected** a change in our plans.
Compare with: The funnel cloud **affected** our plans.

African American. A term now preferred by many Americans of African ancestry, although it has not displaced *black*. *Negro* is used very rarely and then for specific historical reasons. **African American** is usually not hyphenated as a noun; usage is divided when it is an adjective. You will see both **African American literature** and **African-American literature**. Whichever form you prefer, use it consistently throughout a project.

gloss

aggravate/irritate. Many people use both of these verbs to mean "to annoy" or "to make angry." But formal English preserves a fine—and useful—distinction between them. **Irritate** means "to annoy" while **aggravate** means "to make something worse."

It **irritated** Greta when her husband **aggravated** his allergies by smoking.

* **agreement, pronoun and antecedent.** A grammatical principle which requires that singular pronouns stand in for singular nouns (*his* surfboard = *Richard's* surfboard) and plural pronouns stand in for plural nouns (*their* surfboard = *George and Martha's* surfboard; *everyone's* place = *his or her* place). When they do, the pronoun and its antecedent agree in **number;** when they don't, you have an agreement problem. See Chapter 30.

Pronouns and their antecedents also must agree in **gender.** That is, a masculine pronoun (*he, him, his*) must refer to a masculine antecedent, and a feminine pronoun (*she, her, hers*) must refer to a feminine antecedent.

Finally, pronouns and antecedents must agree in **case**, whether objective, subjective, or possessive. For example, an antecedent in the possessive case (*Lawrence's* gym) can be replaced only by a pronoun also in the possessive case (*his* gym). See Section 31a.

* **agreement, subject and verb.** Verbs and nouns are said to agree in number. This means that with a singular subject in the third person (for example, *he, she, it*), a verb in the present tense ordinarily adds an -s ending to its base form. With subjects not in the third person singular, the base form of the verb is used.

Third person, singular, present tense:	Barney sits.
	He sits.
	She sits.
First person, singular, present tense:	I sit.
Second person, singular, present tense:	You sit.
First person, plural, present tense:	We sit.
Second person, plural, present tense:	You sit.
Third person, plural, present tense:	They sit.

Most **verbs**—with the notable exception of *to be*—change their form to show agreement only in third person singular forms (*he, she, it*). See Chapter 25.

ain't.   The word isn't appropriate in academic or professional writing.

all ready/already.   Tricky, but not difficult. **All ready**, an adjective phrase, means "prepared and set to go."

> Rita signaled that the camera was **all ready** for shooting.

Already, an adverb, means "before" or "previously."

> Rita had **already** loaded the film.

all right.   **All right** is the only acceptable spelling. **Alright** is not acceptable in standard English.

allude/elude.   Commonly confused. **Allude** means "to refer to." **Elude** means "to escape."

> Kyle's joke **alluded** to the fact that it was easy to **elude** the portly security guard.

allude/refer.   To **allude** is to mention something indirectly; to **refer** is to mention something directly.

> Carter **alluded** to rituals the new students didn't understand.
> Carter did, however, **refer** to ancient undergraduate traditions and the honor of the college.

allusion/illusion.   These terms are often misused. An **allusion** is an indirect reference to something. An **illusion** is a false impression or a misleading appearance.

> The entire class missed Professor Sweno's **allusion** to the ghost in *Hamlet*.
> Professor Sweno entertained the **illusion** that everyone read Shakespeare as often as he did.

a lot.   Often misspelled as one word. It is two. Many readers consider **a lot** inappropriate in academic writing, preferring **many, much,** or some comparable expression.

already.   See **all ready/already.**

alright.   See **all right.**

American.   Though often used to describe citizens of the United States of America, the term can also refer to any citizen of the Americas, North or South. Be careful how you use this term when writing to audiences that may include Americans not from the United States.

among/between.   Use **between** with two objects, **among** with three or more.

> Francie had to choose **between** Richard and Kyle.
> Francie had to choose from **among** a dozen actors.

amount/number.   Use **amount** for quantities that can be measured but not counted. Use **number** for things that can be counted, not measured: the

amount of water in the ocean; the **number** of fish in the sea. The distinction between these words is being lost, but it is worth preserving. Remember that **amount of** is followed by a singular noun, while **number of** is followed by a plural noun.

amount of money	**number of** dimes
amount of paint	**number of** colors
amount of support	**number of** voters

an.   See **a, an.**

analogy.   An extended comparison between something familiar and something less well known. The analogy helps a reader visualize what might be difficult to understand. For example:

> analogy
> A transitional word in a paper serves **as a road sign, giving readers directions to the next major idea.**

and etc.   A redundant expression. Use **etc.** alone or **and so on.** See **etc.**

and/or.   A useful form in some situations, especially in business and technical writing, but some readers regard it as clumsy. Work around it if you can, especially in academic writing. **And/or** is typed with no space before or after the slash.

Anglo.   A common term in some areas of North America for designating white or nonminority people. The term is inaccurate in that many people considered white are not, in fact, *Anglo-Saxon* in origin.

angry/mad.   The distinction between these words is rarely observed, but strictly speaking, one should use **angry** to describe displeasure, **mad** to describe insanity.

* **antecedent.**   The person, place, or thing a pronoun replaces in a sentence. The antecedent is the word you would have to repeat if you couldn't use a pronoun. In the following sentence, *Marissa* is the antecedent of *she* and *radio* is the antecedent of *it.*

> **Marissa** turned off the **radio** because *she* was tired of listening to *it.*

See Chapter 29 for more details.

antonyms.   Words with opposite meanings: *bright/dull; apex/nadir; concave/convex.*

anyone/any one.   These expressions have different meanings. Notice the difference highlighted in these sentences.

> **Any one** of those problems could develop into a crisis.

> I doubt that **anyone** will be able to find a solution to **any one** of the equations.

anyways.   A nonstandard form. Use **anyway.**

WRONG	It didn't matter **anyways.**
RIGHT	It didn't matter **anyway.**

* **appositive.** A word or phrase that stands next to a noun and modifies it by restating or expanding its meaning. Note that appositives ordinarily are surrounded by commas.

> Connie Lim, **editor of the paper and a liberal,** was furious when ex-President Clinton gave his only campus interview to Sue Wesley, **chair of the Young Republicans.**

See Section 19c-4.

* **articles.** The words **the, a,** and **an** used before a noun. **The** is called a **definite article** because it points to something specific: **the** book, **the** church, **the** criminal. **A** and **an** are **indefinite articles** because they refer more generally: **a** book, **a** church, **a** criminal. See Sections 28d and 36b.

as being. A wordy expression. You can usually cut **being.**

> In most cases, telephone solicitors are regarded **as (being)** a nuisance.

Asian American. The term now preferred by many Americans of Asian ancestry, replacing *Oriental.*

* **auxiliary verbs.** Verbs, usually some form of *be, do,* or *have,* that combine with other verbs to show various relations of tense, voice, mood, and so on. All the words in boldface are auxiliary verbs: **has** seen, **will be** talking, **would have been** going, **are** investigating, **did** mention, **should** prefer. Auxiliary verbs are also known as *helping verbs.* See Chapter 26.

averse/adverse. See **adverse/averse.**

awful. **Awful** is inappropriate as a synonym for **very.**

> INAPPROPRIATE   The findings of the two research teams were **awful** close.
>
> BETTER   The findings of the two research teams were **very** close.

awhile/a while. The expressions are not interchangeable. **Awhile** is an adverb; **a while** is a noun phrase. After prepositions, always use **a while.**

> Bud stood **awhile** looking at the grass.
> Bud decided that the lawn would not have to be cut for **a while.**

bad/badly. These words are troublesome. Remember that **bad** is an adjective describing what something is like; **badly** is an adverb explaining how something is done.

> Stanley's taste in music wasn't **bad.**
> Unfortunately, he treated his musicians **badly.**

Problems usually crop up with verbs that explain how something feels, tastes, smells, or looks. In such cases, use **bad.**

> The physicists felt **bad** about the disappearance of their satellite.
> The situation looked **bad.**

balanced sentence.   A sentence containing two or more independent clauses that have parallel structure and are joined by a conjunction or a semicolon. See Section 19i.

Chapman arrived in a cloud of glory; he departed in a mist of shame.

because of/due to.   Careful writers usually prefer **because of** to **due to** in many situations.

CONSIDERED AWKWARD	The investigation into Bud's sudden disappearance stalled **due to** Officer Bricker's concern for correct procedure.
REVISED	The investigation into Bud's sudden disappearance stalled **because of** Officer Bricker's concern for correct procedure.

However, **due to** is often the better choice when it serves as a **subject complement** after a **linking verb**. The examples illustrate the point.

       subj.   l. v.   subj. comp.
Bricker's discretion seemed **due to** <u>cowardice.</u>
     subj.   l. v.   subj. comp.
His discretion was **due to** <u>the political and social prominence of the Huttons.</u>

being as/being that.   Both of these expressions sound wordy and awkward when used in place of **because** or **since**. Use **because** and **since** in formal and academic writing.

INAPPROPRIATE	**Being that** her major was astronomy, Jenny was looking forward to the eclipse.
BETTER	**Since** her major was astronomy, Jenny was looking forward to the eclipse.

beside/besides.   **Beside** is a preposition meaning "next to" or "alongside"; **besides** is a preposition meaning "in addition to" or "other than."

Besides a sworn confession, the detectives also had the suspect's fingerprints on a gun found **beside** the body.

Besides can also be an adverb meaning "in addition" or "moreover."

Professor Bellona didn't mind assisting the athletic department, and **besides,** she actually liked coaching volleyball.

between.   See **among/between.**

black.   A term that has fallen somewhat out of favor as a term to describe people of African descent. Many American blacks now prefer the term **African American.** The terms *black* and *white* are ordinarily not capitalized, though some writers do prefer to capitalize *Black.*

British.   The term refers to the people of Scotland and Wales in addition to those of England. *English* refers chiefly to those people of the British Isles who come from within the borders of England itself.

can/may. Understand the difference between the auxiliary verbs **can** and **may.** (See also **modal auxiliary.**) Use **can** to express an ability to do something.

Charnelle **can** work differential equations.

According to the *Handbook of College Policies,* Dean Rack **can** lift the suspension.

Use **may** to express either permission or possibility.

You **may** want to compare my solution to the problem to Charnelle's.

Dean Rack **may** lift the suspension, but I wouldn't count on that happening.

cannot. **Cannot** is ordinarily written as one word, not two.

can't. Writers sometimes forget the apostrophe in this contraction and others like it: **don't, won't.**

can't hardly. A colloquial expression that is, technically, a double negative. Use **can hardly** instead when you write.

DOUBLE NEGATIVE I **can't hardly** see the road.

REVISED I **can hardly** see the road.

* **cardinal numbers.** Numbers that express an amount: *one, two, three.* In contrast, **ordinal numbers** show a sequence: *first, second, third.*

* **case.** The form a noun or pronoun takes to indicate its function in a sentence. Nouns have only two cases: the **possessive** form, to show ownership (*girl's, Greta's, swimmers'*), and the **common** form, to serve all other uses (*girl, Greta, swimmers*). See Section 28b.

Pronouns have three forms: **subjective, objective,** and **possessive.** (See Chapter 31.) The **subjective** (or **nominative**) **case** is the form a pronoun takes when it is the subject of a sentence or a clause. Pronouns in this case are the doers of actions: *I, you, she, he, it, we, they, who.*

A pronoun is in the **objective case** when something is done to it. This is also the form a pronoun has after a preposition: (*to*) *me, her, him, us, them, whom.* For the pronouns *you* and *it,* the subjective and objective forms are identical.

A pronoun is in the **possessive case** when it shows ownership: *my, mine, your, yours, her, his, its, our, ours, their, theirs, whose.*

censor/censure. These words have different meanings. As verbs, **censor** means "to cut," "to repress," or "to remove"; **censure** means "to disapprove" and "to condemn."

The student editorial board voted to **censor** the four-letter words from Connie Lim's editorial and to **censure** her for attempting to publish the controversial piece.

* **clause.** A group of related words that has a subject and verb. Clauses can be independent or dependent.

Whenever it could, **the Astronomy Club scheduled meetings at an isolated hilltop observatory.**

An **independent clause** can stand alone as a complete sentence.

The Astronomy Club scheduled meetings at an isolated hilltop observatory.

A **dependent** (or **subordinate**) **clause** is a group of words that cannot stand alone as a sentence even though it contains a subject and a verb.

gloss

Whenever it could, the Astronomy Club scheduled meetings at an isolated hilltop observatory.

See Section 19d.

cliché. A tired expression or conventional way of expressing something: *guilty as sin, hungry enough to eat a horse, sleep like a log, dumb as a rock.*

coherence. Unity in a paragraph or longer piece of writing. See Section 15a.

* **collective noun.** A noun that names a group: *team, orchestra, jury, committee.* Collective nouns can be either singular or plural, depending on how they are used in a sentence.

* **comma splice.** The mistaken use of a comma to join two groups of words, each of which could be a sentence by itself. Also called a comma fault. See Section 38c.

COMMA SPLICE   David liked Corvettes, they were fast cars.

CORRECTED   David liked Corvettes because they were fast cars.

common knowledge. Facts, dates, events, information, and concepts that belong generally to an educated public.

* **common noun.** A noun that names some general object, not a specific person, place, or thing: *singer, continent, car.* Common nouns are not capitalized.

* **comparative and superlative.** Adjectives and adverbs can express three different levels or degrees of intensity—the positive, the comparative, and the superlative. The positive level describes a single condition; the comparative ranks two conditions; the superlative ranks three or more.

POSITIVE	COMPARATIVE	SUPERLATIVE
cold	colder	coldest
bad	worse	worst
angry	more angry	most angry
angrily	more angrily	most angrily

* **complement.** A word or phrase that completes the meaning of a verb, a subject, or an object. A **verb complement** is a **direct** or **indirect object.** A **subject complement** is a noun, pronoun, or adjective (or a comparable phrase) that follows a linking verb (a verb such as *to be, to seem, to appear, to feel,* and *to become*) and modifies or explains the subject, as in these examples.

Eleanor is Bruce's **cat.**
Eleanor is grossly **overweight.**
Eleanor is the **one** on the sagging couch.

Object complements are nouns or adjectives (or comparable phrases) that follow direct objects and modify them.

A pet food company named Eleanor **"Fat Cat of the Year."**
Mackerel makes Eleanor **happy.**

complement/complementary, compliment/complimentary.
The words are not synonyms. **Complement** and **complementary** describe things completed or compatible. **Compliment** and **complimentary** refer to things praised or given away free.

Travis's sweater **complemented** his green eyes.

The two parts of Greta's essay were **complementary,** examining the same subject from differing perspectives.

Travis **complimented** Greta on her successful paper.

Greta found his **compliment** sincere.

She rewarded him with a **complimentary** sack of rice cakes from her health food store.

* **complex sentence.** A sentence that combines an independent clause and one or more dependent (subordinate) clauses. See also **clause.**

dependent clause + independent clause
When Rita Ruiz first saw the announcements for the job fair, she began to get nervous.

* **compound sentence.** A sentence that combines two or more independent clauses, usually joined by a coordinating conjunction (*and, or, nor, for, but, yet, so*) or a semicolon.

independent clause + independent clause
Recruiters from industry have set up booths on campus, *and* several corporations are sending recruiters to interview students.

* **compound-complex sentence.** A sentence that combines two or more independent clauses and at least one dependent (subordinate) clause. See also **clause.**

dependent clause + independent clause + independent clause
Although business is slow, recruiters from industry have set up booths on campus, *and* several corporations are sending recruiters to interview students.

* **concrete noun.** A noun that names objects or events with physical properties or existences: *butter, trees, asteroid, people.* Concrete nouns are defined in contrast to **abstract nouns.**

* **conjugation.** The forms of a given verb as it appears in all numbers, tenses, voices, and moods. See Anatomy of a Verb, pages 475–77.

* **conjunctions, coordinating.** The words *and, or, nor, for, but, yet,* and *so* used to link words, phrases, and clauses that serve equivalent functions in a sentence. A coordinating conjunction is used to join two independent clauses or two dependent clauses; it would not link a subordinate clause to an independent clause. See also **conjunctions, subordinating.**

> Oscar **and** Marie directed the play.
> Oscar liked the story, **but** Marie did not.

* **conjunctions, subordinating.** Words or expressions such as *although, because, if, since, before, after, when, even though, in order that,* and *while* that relate dependent (that is, subordinate) clauses to independent ones. Subordinating conjunctions introduce subordinate clauses.

> subordinate clause
> **Although** Oscar and Marie both directed parts of the show, Marie got most of the blame for its failure.
> subordinate clause
> Oscar liked the story **even though** no one else did.
> subordinate clause
> **When** the show opened, audiences stayed away.

See Section 19d-2.

* **conjunctive adverbs.** Words such as *however, therefore, nevertheless,* and *moreover,* used to link one independent clause to another. Conjunctive adverbs are weaker links than **coordinating conjunctions** (such as *and, but, or,* and *yet*) and must be preceded by a semicolon when used to join independent clauses.

> Darwin apologized; **nevertheless,** Rita considered suing him.

See Sections 19f-4 and 40a-3.

connotation. Connotation is what a word suggests beyond its basic dictionary meaning—that is, the word with all its particular emotional, political, or ethical associations. While any number of words may describe a *fight,* for example, and so share the same **denotation** (generic meaning), such words as *scrap, brawl, battle, fisticuffs, altercation,* and *set-to* differ significantly in what they imply—in their **connotations.** When using a list or collection of synonyms—such as you would find in a thesaurus—be sure you understand the connotation of any words you decide to use. See Section 18b.

conscience/conscious. Don't confuse these words. **Conscience** is a noun referring to an inner ethical sense; **conscious** is an adjective describing a state of awareness or wakefulness.

> The linebacker felt a twinge of **conscience** after knocking the quarterback **unconscious.**

consensus. This expression is redundant when followed by **of opinion**; **consensus** by itself implies an opinion. Use **consensus** alone.

> REDUNDANT   The student senate reached a **consensus of opinion** on the issue of censorship.
>
> REVISED   The student senate reached a **consensus** on the issue of censorship.

gloss

* **contraction.**   A word shortened by the omission of a letter or letters. In most cases, an apostrophe is used to indicate the deleted letters or sounds: *it is* = **it's**; *you are* = **you're**; *who is* = **who's**.

* **coordinate adjective.**   Coordinate adjectives are adjectives that modify the nouns they precede, not each other.

> Mali is a **bright, creative,** and **productive** artist.

See **noncoordinate adjective** and Sections 19b-1 and 39c-4.

* **coordinating conjunction.**   See **conjunctions, coordinating.**

* **correlatives.**   Words that work together as conjunctions: *either . . . or, neither . . . nor, whether . . . or, both . . . and, not only . . . but also.*

> **Whether** Darwin **or** Travis plays makes little difference.
>
> Brian attributed the failure of the play **not only** to a bad script **but also** to incompetent direction.

could of/would of/should of.   Nonstandard forms when used instead of **could have, would have,** or **should have.**

WRONG	Coach Rhoades imagined that his team **could of** been a contender.
RIGHT	Coach Rhoades imagined that his team **could have** been a contender.

* **count noun.**   A noun that names any object that exists as an individual item: *car, child, rose, cat.*

couple of.   Casual. Avoid it in formal or academic writing.

INFORMAL	The article accused the admissions office of a **couple of** major blunders.
REVISED	The article accused the admissions office of **several** major blunders.

credible/credulous.   **Credible** means "believable"; **credulous** means "willing to believe on slim evidence." See also **incredible/incredulous.**

> Officer Bricker found Mr. Hutton's excuse for his speeding **credible.** However, Bricker was known to be a **credulous** police officer, liable to believe any story.

criteria, criterion.   **Criteria,** the plural form, is more familiar, but the word does have a singular form—**criterion.**

> John Maynard, age sixty-four, complained that he was often judged according to a single **criterion,** his age.
>
> Other **criteria** ought to matter in hiring.

cumulative sentence.   A sentence in which an independent clause is followed by a series of modifiers.

Dr. Coles praised the volunteers as an outstanding group of young people, energetic, knowledgeable, and dependable.

See Section 19j.

curriculum, curricula. **Curriculum** is the singular form; **curricula** is the plural.

Dean Perez believed that the **curriculum** in history had to be strengthened.

Indeed, she believed that the **curricula** in all the liberal arts departments needed rethinking.

* **dangling modifier.** A modifying phrase that doesn't seem connected to any word or phrase in a sentence. Dangling modifiers are usually corrected by rewriting a sentence to provide a better link between the modifier and what it modifies. See Section 33a. See also **absolute.**

DANGLING **After finding the courage to ask Richard out,** the evening was a disaster.

IMPROVED After finding the courage to ask Richard out, Francie had a disastrous evening.

data/datum. **Data** is the plural form of *datum.* But in informal writing and speech, you will typically see *data* treated as if it were singular.

INFORMAL The *data* **is** not convincing.

In academic writing use **datum** when a singular form is expected. If **datum** seems awkward, rewrite the sentence to avoid the singular.

SINGULAR The most intriguing **datum** in the study was the rate of population decline.

PLURAL In all the **data,** no figure was more intriguing than the rate of population decline.

* **demonstrative adjective.** An adjective that points to a specific object: *this* house, not *that* one; *those* rowdies who disrupted *these* proceedings last month.

* **demonstrative pronoun.** A pronoun that points something out: *this, that, these, those.*

denotation. The specific meaning of a term. Sometimes called the dictionary meaning, the denotation of a word attempts to explain what the word is or does, stripped of particular emotional, political, cultural, or ethical associations. See **connotation.**

* **dependent clause.** See **clause.**

* **determiner.** A word indicating that a noun must follow. Determiners in English include articles (*a, an, the*) and certain possessive pronouns (*my, your*).

dialect. A spoken variation of a language. See Section 18e.

diction. See **word choice.**

different from/different than. In formal writing, **different from** is usually preferred to **different than.**

> INFORMAL   Ike's account of his marriage proposal was **different than** Bernice's.
>
> FORMAL   Ike's account of his marriage proposal was **different from** Bernice's.

* **direct discourse.** The actual words of a speaker or writer. Direct discourse is enclosed within quotation marks. See **indirect discourse.**

> DIRECT   As she approached the altar, Bernice yelled, "I won't marry you!"
>
> INDIRECT   As she approached the altar, Bernice declared that she would not marry Ike.

discreet/discrete. **Discreet** means "tactful" or "sensitive to appearances" (*discreet* behavior); **discrete** means "individual" or "separate" (*discrete* objects).

> Joel was **discreet** about the money spent on his project.
> He had several **discrete** funds at his disposal.

disinterested/uninterested. These words don't mean the same thing. **Disinterested** means "neutral" or "uninvolved"; **uninterested** means "not interested" or "bored."

> Alyce and Richard sought a **disinterested** party to arbitrate their dispute.
> Stanley was **uninterested** in the club's management.

don't. Writers sometimes forget the apostrophe in this contraction and others like it: **can't, won't.**

* **double negative.** Two negatives in a sentence that emphasize a negative idea. Such expressions are considered nonstandard in English.

> INCORRECT   **Don't never** use a double negative.
> Ike **won't** say **nothing** about his wedding plans.

To correct a double negative, eliminate one of the negatives in the sentence.

> CORRECT   **Never** use a double negative.
> **Don't** use a double negative.
>
> CORRECT   Ike will say **nothing** about his wedding plans.
> Ike **won't** say anything about his wedding plans.

* **double possessive.** A form such as *a friend of Ruth's,* which includes two indications of possession—an *of* and an *'s,* generally considered inappropriate in academic and formal writing.

due to/because of. See **because of/due to.**

due to the fact that. Wordy. Replace it with **because** whenever you can.

WORDY	Coach Meyer was fired **due to the fact that** he won no games.
REVISED	Coach Meyer was fired **because** he won no games.

effect/affect.   See **affect/effect.**

elicit/illicit.   These words have vastly different meanings. **Elicit** means to "draw out" or "bring forth"; **illicit** describes something illegal or prohibited.

gloss

The detective tried to **elicit** an admission of **illicit** behavior from Bud.

* **elliptical construction.**   A phrase or sentence from which words have been deleted without obscuring the meaning. Elliptical constructions are common.

When [she is] asked about Rodney, Sue Ellen groans.
She likes reading books better than [she likes] writing them.
Curtis is a tough guy at heart, but [he is] a softie on the surface.
He senses [that] he was wrong.

elude/allude.   See **allude/elude.**

eminent/imminent.   These words are sometimes confused. **Eminent** means "distinguished" and "prominent"; **imminent** describes something about to happen.

The arrival of the **eminent** scholar is **imminent.**

enthused.   A colloquial expression that should not appear in academic or professional writing. Use **enthusiastic** instead.

INFORMAL	Francie was **enthused** about Wilco's latest album.
BETTER	Francie was **enthusiastic** about Wilco's latest album.

Never use **enthused** as a verb.

equally as.   Redundant. Use either **equally** or **as** to express a comparison—whichever works in a particular sentence.

REDUNDANT	Sue Ellen is **equally as** concerned as Hector about bilingual education.
REVISED	Sue Ellen is **as** concerned as Hector about bilingual education.
REVISED	Sue Ellen and Hector are **equally** concerned about bilingual education.

Eskimo.   Falling out of favor as a term to describe the native peoples of Northern Canada and Alaska. Many now prefer *Inuit.*

* **essential modifier.**   See **restrictive element.**

etc.   This common abbreviation for *et cetera* should be avoided in most academic and formal writing. Instead, use **and so on** or **and so forth.** Never use **and etc.**

even though.   **Even though** is two words, not one.

everyone/every one.   These similar expressions mean different things. **Everyone** describes a group collectively. **Every one** focuses on the individual elements within a group or collective term. Notice the difference highlighted in these sentences.

> **Every one** of those problems could develop into an international crisis **everyone** would regret.

> I doubt that **everyone** will be able to attend **every one** of the sessions.

except/accept.   See **accept/except.**

* **expletive construction.**   The words **there** and **it** used as sentence lead-ins.

> <u>It is</u> going to be a day to remember.

> <u>There were</u> hundreds of spectators watching the demonstrators.

Expletive constructions often contribute to wordiness. Cut them whenever you can.

> REVISED   Hundreds of spectators were watching the demonstrators.

fact that, the.   Wordy. You can usually replace the entire expression with **that.**

> WORDY   Bud was aware of **the fact that** he was in a strange room.
>
> REVISED   Bud was aware **that** he was in a strange room.

faith/fate.   A surprising number of writers confuse these words and their variations: **faithful, fateful, faithless. Faith** is confidence, trust, or a religious belief; **fate** means "destiny" or "outcome."

farther/further.   Although the distinction between these words is not always observed, it is useful. Use **farther** to refer to distances that can be measured.

> It is **farther** from El Paso to Houston than from New York to Detroit.

Use **further,** meaning "more" or "additional," when physical distance or separation is not involved.

> The detective decided that the crime warranted **further** investigation.

fate/faith.   See **faith/fate.**

* **faulty predication.**   A term used to describe verbs that don't fit their subjects. In faulty predication, a subject could not logically perform the action specified by the verb.

> POSSIBLE PROBLEM   The purpose of radar detectors **is banned** in a few
>   states. What is forbidden—radar detectors or their purpose?
>
> POSSIBLE REVISION   Radar detectors **are banned** in a few states.

At other times a linking verb is used incorrectly to connect words that aren't really equivalent. In the following example, the noun *problem* cannot be linked to the adverb *when.*

PROBLEM	A common problem with some foreign bikes **is** *when* you have them serviced.
REVISED	A common problem with foreign bikes **is** getting them serviced.

fewer than/less than.   Use **fewer than** with things you can count; use **less than** with quantities that must be measured or can be considered as a whole.

gloss

The express lane was reserved for customers buying **fewer than** ten items.

Matthew had **less than** half a gallon of gasoline.

He also had **less than** ten dollars.

figurative language.   Language that includes analogies, metaphors, and similes that create images for the readers or listeners. See Section 20e.

* **finite verb.**   A verb that changes form to indicate person, number, and tense. A complete sentence requires a finite verb. Finite verbs stand in contrast to **nonfinite verb** forms such as **infinitives, participles,** and **gerunds,** which do not change form and which cannot stand as the only verb in a sentence. (See Section 27b.) Compare the following finite and nonfinite forms.

FINITE VERBS	He **ensures** freshness.
	The baker **kneads** the dough.
NONFINITE VERBS	**To ensure** freshness, Jean-Pierre buys eggs from local farms.
	The baker **kneading** the dough sneezed.

flaunt/flout.   These words are confused surprisingly often. **Flaunt** means "to show off"; **flout** means "to disregard" or "to show contempt for."

To **flaunt** his wealth, Mr. Lin bought a Van Gogh landscape.

Flouting a gag order, the newspaper published its exposé of corruption in the city council.

* **fragment.**   A group of words that does not fully express an idea even though it is punctuated as a sentence. A fragment may also be called a broken sentence. See Section 38a.

FRAGMENT	Despite the fact that Professor Chase had an impressive portfolio of investments.
COMPLETE SENTENCE	Despite the fact that Professor Chase had an impressive portfolio of investments, she was still careful with her money.
FRAGMENTS	Bonds. A safe investment most of the time.
COMPLETE SENTENCE	Bonds are a safe investment most of the time.

fun, funner, funnest.   Used as an adjective, **fun** is not appropriate in academic writing; replace it with a more formal expression.

INFORMAL	Skiing is a **fun** sport.
FORMAL	Skiing is an **enjoyable** sport.

The comparative and superlative forms, **funner** and **funnest**, while increasingly common in spoken English, are inappropriate in writing. In writing, use **more fun** or **most fun**.

INFORMAL	Albert found tennis **funner** than squash.
FORMAL	Albert found tennis **more fun** than squash.
SPOKEN	He thought racquetball the **funnest** of the three sports.
WRITTEN	He thought racquetball the **most fun** of the three sports.

* **fused sentence.**   See **run-on sentence.**

gay.   A term now widely used to mean "homosexual." Less formal than *homosexual,* **gay** is still appropriate in most writing when used as an adjective. (As a noun— *a gay* or *the gays*—the term is inappropriate and should be avoided.) While **gay** is often used without regard to gender, some prefer it as a term that refers mainly to homosexual men, with **lesbian** the appropriate term for homosexual women.

* **gender.**   A classification of nouns and pronouns as masculine (*actor, muscleman, he*), feminine (*actress, midwife, she*), or neuter (*tree, it*).

* **gerund.**   A verb form used as a noun: *smiling, biking, walking.* (See Section 27a-3.) Most gerunds end in **-ing** and, consequently, look identical to the present participle.

GERUND	**Smiling** is good for the health.
PARTICIPLE	A **smiling** critic is dangerous.

The difference is that gerunds function as nouns while participles act as modifiers. Gerunds usually appear in the present tense, but they can take other forms.

Having been criticized made Brian angry.
gerund in past tense, passive voice, acting as subject of the sentence

Being asked to play an encore was a compliment Otto enjoyed.
gerund in present tense, passive voice, as subject of sentence

get/got/gotten.   The principal parts of this verb are:

PRESENT	PAST	PAST PARTICIPLE
get	got	got, gotten

Gotten usually sounds more polished than **got** as the past participle in American English, but both forms are acceptable.

Aretha **has gotten** an *A* average in microbiology.
Aretha **has got** an *A* average in microbiology.

Many expressions, formal and informal, rely on **get**. Use the less formal ones only with appropriate audiences.

get it together
get straight
get real

good and. Informal. Avoid it in academic writing.

> INFORMAL   The lake was **good and** cold when the sailors threw Sean in.
>
> BETTER   The lake was **icy** cold when the sailors threw Sean in.

good/well. These words cause many problems. (See Section 33c-2.) As a modifier, **good** is an adjective only; **well** can be either an adjective or an adverb. Consider the difference between these sentences, where each word functions as an adjective.

> Katy is **good.**
> Katy is **well.**

Good is often mistakenly used as an adverb.

> WRONG   Juin conducts the orchestra **good.**
> RIGHT   Juin conducts the orchestra **well.**
>
> WRONG   The bureaucracy at NASA runs **good.**
> RIGHT   The bureaucracy at NASA runs **well.**

Complications occur when writers and speakers—eager to avoid using **good** incorrectly—substitute **well** as an adjective where **good** used as an adjective may be more accurate.

> WRONG   After a shower, Coach Rhoades smells **well.**
> RIGHT   After a shower, Coach Rhoades smells **good.**
>
> RIGHT   I feel **good.**
> ALSO RIGHT   I feel **well.**

handicapped. Falling out of favor as a term to describe people with physical disabilities. However, euphemistic alternatives such as *differently abled* and *physically challenged* have been roundly criticized. (See Section 18d.)

hanged, hung. **Hanged** has been the past participle conventionally reserved for executions; **hung** is used on other occasions. The distinction is a nice one, probably worth observing.

> Connie was miffed when her disgruntled editorial staff decided she should be **hanged** in effigy.
>
> Portraits of the faculty were **hung** in the student union.

* **helping verbs.** See **auxiliary verbs.**

he/she. Using **he/she** (or *his/her* or *s/he*) is a way to avoid a sexist pronoun reference. Many readers find expressions with slashes clumsy and prefer *he or she* and *his or her.*

Hispanic. A term falling somewhat out of favor among some groups, in part because of its imprecision. Groups that have fallen under the Hispanic label now often prefer to be identified more precisely: *Chicano/Chicana, Cuban American, Latin American, Mexican American, Puerto Rican.*

hisself. A nonstandard form. Don't use it.

homonyms. Words of different meanings and spellings pronounced alike: *straight/strait, peace/piece, their/there.*

gloss

hopefully. Some readers object to using the adverb *hopefully* as a sentence modifier. They would consider the following sentences ambiguous and incorrect.

> **Hopefully,** the stock market will grow.
> The government, **hopefully,** will not impose price controls.

Hopefully, they argue, should be used to mean only "with hope."

> Traders watched **hopefully** as stock prices approached yet another record.

However, English includes many adverbs like *hopefully* that function as sentence modifiers, including words such as *understandably, mercifully, predictably,* and *honestly,* By precedent and general usage, *hopefully* seems entrenched as a sentence modifier.

idiom. A widely accepted expression that does not seem to make literal sense. Idioms often mean more than the sum of their parts.

> The jet fighter **bit the big one** over Montana.
> Let's **get cracking.** We're late.
> Alyce hoped Richard would **cough up** the money.

Idiom can also describe a vocabulary and language style shared within certain groups or professions: the *idiom* of medical personnel, the *idiom* of computer specialists, the *idiom* of literary critics.

illicit/elicit. See **elicit/illicit.**

illusion/allusion. See **allusion/illusion.**

imminent/eminent. See **eminent/imminent.**

* **imperative mood.** The form of a verb that expresses a command (see **mood**).

> **Go! Find** that missing canister of film. **Bring** it back to the lab.

imply/infer. Think of these words as opposite sides of the same coin. **Imply** means "to suggest" or "to convey an idea without stating it." **Infer** is what you might do to figure out what someone else has implied: you examine evidence and draw conclusions from it.

> By joking calmly, the pilot sought to **imply** that the aircraft was out of danger. But from the crack that had opened in the wing, the passengers **inferred** that the landing would be harrowing.

incredible/incredulous. **Incredible** means "unbelievable"; **incredulous** means "unwilling to believe" and "doubting." See also **credible/credulous.**

> The press found the governor's explanation for his wealth **incredible.** You could hardly blame them for being **incredulous** when he attributed his vast holdings to coupon savings.

* **indefinite pronoun.** A pronoun that does not refer to a particular person, thing, or group: *all, any, each, everybody, everyone, one, none, somebody, someone,* and so on. See Section 30b.

* **independent clause.** See **clause.**

* **indicative mood.** The form of a verb that states facts or asks questions (see **mood**).

  Did he **find** the canister of film? It **was** in the lab yesterday.

gloss

indirect discourse. The substance of what a speaker or writer has said, but not the exact words. Indirect discourse is not surrounded by quotation marks. See **direct discourse.**

| DIRECT | At the altar Ike told Bernice, "If you don't marry me, I'll sue." |
| INDIRECT | At the altar Ike told Bernice he would sue her if she didn't marry him. |

infer/imply. See **imply/infer.**

* **infinitive.** A verbal that can usually be identified by the word **to** preceding the base form of a verb: *to strive, to seek, to find, to endure.* Infinitives do take other forms to show various tenses and voices: *to be seeking, to have found, to have been found.* Infinitives can act as nouns, adjectives, adverbs, and absolutes (see Section 27a).

INFINITIVE AS NOUN	**To capture** a market is not easy. subject of the sentence
INFINITIVE AS ADJECTIVE	Greta had many posters **to redesign.** modifies the noun *posters*
INFINITIVE AS ADVERB	Mr. Stavros laughed **to forget** his troubles. modifies the verb *laughed*
INFINITIVE AS ABSOLUTE	**To be blunt,** the paper is plagiarized.

* **inflection.** A change a word undergoes to specify its meaning or to reflect a relationship to other words or phrases in a sentence. For instance, verbs change to reflect shifts in tense, person, and number (*walk, walks, walked*). Nouns change to indicate number and possession (*antenna, antennae; Pearl, Pearl's*). Adverbs and adjectives show degrees of comparison (*cold, colder, coldest; happily, more happily, most happily*).

initialism. A single term created by joining the first letters of the words that make up the full name or description. Unlike acronyms, however, initialisms are pronounced letter by letter.

> **IRS**—Internal Revenue Service
> **CIA**—Central Intelligence Agency
> **HBO**—Home Box Office

See **acronym** and Section 45a-2.

* **intensifier.**   A modifier that adds emphasis: *so, very, extremely, intensely, really, certainly.*

    so cold   **very** bold   **extremely** complex

* **intensive pronoun.**   A pronoun form, created when -**self** or -**selves** is added to personal pronouns (*myself, yourself, herself, itself, oneself, ourselves, yourselves, themselves*), that modifies a noun to add emphasis. See Section 32a.

    Otto **himself** admitted he was the winner.
    The managers did all the printing **themselves.**

* **intentional fragment.**   A group of words that does not have all the usual parts of a sentence but can act as a sentence because it expresses an idea fully. See Section 38b.

    INTENTIONAL FRAGMENTS   So what?   Big deal!

* **interjection.**   A word that expresses emotion or feeling, but that is not grammatically a part of a sentence. Interjections can be punctuated as exclamations (!) or attached to a sentence with a comma. Interjections include *oh, hey, wow,* and *well.*

* **interrogative pronoun.**   A pronoun used to pose a question: *who, which, what, whose.*

* **intransitive verb.**   A verb that does not take a direct object. This means that the action of an intransitive verb does not pass on to someone or something; the sentence is complete without an object.

    INTRANSITIVE   I **slept** well.
                          Lawrence **wept.**

    Linking verbs are intransitive.

    INTRANSITIVE   I **am** happy.
                          You **have been** absent.

    Compare intransitive verbs to **transitive** verbs, which require an object to complete the action of a sentence.

    TRANSITIVE   Travis accidentally **pushed** *Kyle.*
                          Sister Anne **bit** her *lip.*

* **inversion.**   A reversal in the normal subject-verb-object order of a sentence.

    Off came the wheel.
    Our lives we hold less dear than our honor.

irregardless.   A nonstandard form. Use **regardless** instead.

* **irregular verb.**   A verb that does not form its past and past participle forms by adding -*d* or -*ed* to the infinitive (see **principal parts of a verb**). Irregular verbs are both numerous and important (see the full chart in Section 26d). They change their forms in various ways; a few even use the same form for all three principal parts.

INFINITIVE	PAST	PAST PARTICIPLE
burst	burst	burst
drink	drank	drunk
arise	arose	arisen
go	went	gone

irritate/aggravate. See **aggravate/irritate.**

its/it's. Don't confuse these terms. **It's** is a contraction for *it is.* **Its** is a possessive pronoun meaning "belonging to it." See Section 31g for a discussion of this problem.

jargon. The term has two meanings: (1) the specialized language of a profession or craft, and (2) wordy, impersonal writing full of abstract terms and long sentences. See Section 18c-3.

judgment/judgement. The British spell this word with two *e*'s. Americans spell it with just one: **judgment.**

kind of. This expression is colloquial when used to mean "rather." Avoid *kind of* in formal writing.

> COLLOQUIAL   The college trustees were **kind of** upset by the bad
> publicity.

> MORE FORMAL   The college trustees were **rather** upset by the bad
> publicity.

less than. See **fewer than/less than.**

lie/lay. These two verbs cause much trouble and confusion. Here are their parts.

| | | PRESENT | PAST |
PRESENT	PAST	PARTICIPLE	PARTICIPLE
lie (to recline)	lay	lying	lain
lay (to place)	laid	laying	laid

Notice that the past tense of **lie** is the same as the present tense of **lay.** It may help you to remember that **to lie** (meaning "to recline") is *intransitive*—that is, it doesn't take an object. You can't lie *something.*

> Travis **lies** under the cottonwood tree.
> He **lay** there all afternoon.
> He was **lying** in the hammock yesterday.
> He had **lain** there for weeks.

To lay (meaning "to place" or "to put") is *transitive*—it takes an object.

> Jenny **lays** a *book* on Travis's desk.
> Yesterday, she **laid** a *memo* on his desk.
> Jenny was **laying** the *memo* on Travis's desk when he returned.
> Travis had **laid** almost three *yards* of concrete that afternoon.

like/as. Many readers object to **like** used to introduce clauses of comparison. **As, as if,** or **as though** are preferred in situations where a comparison involves a subject and verb.

gloss

NOT   Mr. Butcher is self-disciplined, **like** you would expect a champion weightlifter to be.

BUT   Mr. Butcher is self-disciplined, **as** you would expect a champion weightlifter to be.

NOT   It looks **like** he will win the local competition again this year.

BUT   It looks **as if** he will win the local competition again this year.

Like is acceptable when it introduces a prepositional phrase, not a clause.

Yvonne looks **like** her mother.
The sculpture on the mall looks **like** a rusted Edsel.

* **linking verb.**   A verb, often a form of *to be,* that connects a subject to a word or phrase that extends or completes its meaning. Other common linking verbs are *to seem, to appear, to feel,* and *to become.*

Bob King **is** Dean of Humanities.
She **seems** tired.

See Section 19a-3.

literally.   When you write that something is **literally** true, you mean that it is exactly as you have stated. The following sentence means that Bernice emitted heated water vapor, an unlikely event no matter how angry she was.

Bernice **literally** steamed when Ike ordered her to marry him.

If you want to keep the image (*steamed*), omit **literally.**

Bernice steamed when Ike ordered her to marry him.

lose/loose.   Be careful not to confuse these words. **Lose** is a verb, meaning "to misplace," "to be deprived of," or "to be defeated." **Loose** can be either an adjective or a verb. As an adjective, **loose** means "not tight"; as a verb, **loose** means "to let go" or "to untighten."

Without Martin as quarterback, the team might **lose** its first game of the season.

The strap on Martin's helmet had worked **loose.**

It **loosened** so much that Martin **lost** his helmet.

mad, angry.   See **angry/mad.**

majority/plurality.   There is a useful difference in meaning between these two words. A **majority** is more than half of a group; a **plurality** is the largest part of a group when there is *less than* a *majority.* In an election, for example, a candidate who wins 50.1 percent of the vote can claim a **majority.** One who wins a race with 40 percent of the vote may claim a **plurality,** but not a majority.

man, mankind.   These terms are considered sexist by many readers since they implicitly exclude women from the human family.

Man has begun to conquer space.

Look for alternatives, such as *humanity, men and women, the human race,* or *humankind.*

> **Men and women** have begun to conquer space.

many times. Wordy. Use **often** instead.

may/can. See **can/may.**

media/medium. **Medium** is the singular of **media.**

> Connie believed that the press could be as powerful a **medium** as television.
>
> The visual **media** are discussed in the textbook.

The term **media** is commonly used to refer to newspapers and magazines, as well as television and radio.

> President Xiony declined to speak to the **media** about the fiscal problems facing the college.

metaphor. A comparison that does not use the word *like* or *as.*

> All the world's a stage.
> I'm a little teacup, short and stout.

See also **mixed metaphor.**

Mexican American. A preferred term for describing Americans of Mexican ancestry.

might of. A nonstandard form. Use **might have** instead.

> NOT   Ms. Rajala **might of** never admitted the truth.
>
> BUT   Ms. Rajala **might have** never admitted the truth.

* **misplaced modifier.** A modifying word or phrase that is ambiguous because it could modify more than one thing. See Section 33a. See also **absolute.**

> MISPLACED MODIFIER   Some of the actors won roles **without talent.**
>
> IMPROVED   Some of the actors **without talent** won roles.

mixed metaphor. A metaphor in which the terms of the comparison are inconsistent, incongruent, or unintentionally comic.

> Unless we tighten our belts, we'll sink like a stone.
>
> The fullback was a bulldozer, running up and down the field on winged feet.

See Section 20e-2.

* **modal auxiliary.** An auxiliary verb that indicates possibility, necessity, permission, desire, capability, and so on. Modal auxiliaries include *can, could, may, might, will, shall, should, ought,* and *must.* See Section 35d.

> Hector **can** write.
> Hector **might** write.
> Hector **must** write.

* **modifier.** A word, phrase, or clause that gives information about another word, phrase, or clause. Writers use modifiers, mainly adjectives, adverbs, and modifying phrases, to make important qualifications in their writing, to make it more accurate, and sometimes to give it color and depth. See Chapter 33.

* **mood.** A term used to describe how a writer regards a statement: either as a fact (the **indicative** mood), as a command (the **imperative** mood), or as a wish, desire, supposition, or improbability (the **subjunctive** mood). Verbs change their form to show mood. See Section 26f.

INDICATIVE	The engineer **was** careful.
IMPERATIVE	**Be** careful!
SUBJUNCTIVE	If the engineer **were** careful . . .

moral, morale. Don't confuse these words. As a noun, **moral** is a lesson. **Morale** is a state of mind.

The **moral** of the fable was to avoid temptation.

The **morale** of the team was destroyed by the accident.

must of. Nonstandard. Use **must have** instead.

NOT	Someone **must of** read the book.
BUT	Someone **must have** read the book.

Native American. The term now preferred by many people formerly described as American Indian.

nice. This adjective has little impact when used to mean "pleasant": **It was a nice day; Sally is a nice person.** In many cases, **nice** is damning with faint praise. Find a more specific word or expression. **Nice** can be used effectively to mean "precise" or "fine."

There was a **nice** distinction between the two positions.

* **nominal.** A word, phrase, or entire clause that acts like a noun in a sentence. **Pronouns** and **gerunds** often function as nominals.

The wild applause only encouraged **them.**   Pronoun *them* acts as an object.
Keeping a straight face wasn't easy.   Gerund phrase acts as a subject.

* **nominalizations.** Nouns created by adding endings to verbs and adjectives: *acceptability, demystification, prioritization,* and so on. Clumsy nominalizations of several syllables can usually be replaced by clearer terms. See Section 20c-2.

* **noncoordinate adjective.** Noncoordinate adjectives are adjectives or adjectivals that work together to modify a noun or pronoun. As a result, they cannot be sensibly rearranged.

her six completed chapters
a shiny blue Mustang convertible
our natural good humor

See **coordinate adjective** and Section 39c-5.

* **noncount noun.** A noun that names something that does not exist as a separable or individual unit: *blood, money, work, time.*

* **nonessential modifier.** See **nonrestrictive element.**

* **nonrestrictive (or nonessential) element.** A modifier, often a phrase, not essential to the meaning of a sentence. If the nonrestrictive element is removed, the basic meaning of the sentence is not altered.

> The senator, **who often voted with the other party,** had few loyal friends and a weak constituency.

> The agent, **a tall fellow from the FBI,** looked a bit self-conscious when he introduced himself.

Nonrestrictive phrases are ordinarily set off by commas. See **restrictive element** and Sections 39b-1 and 39b-2.

* **noun.** A word that names a person, place, thing, idea, or quality. In sentences, nouns can serve as subjects, objects, complements, appositives, and even modifiers. There are many classes of nouns: **common, proper, concrete, abstract, collective, noncount,** and **count.** See individual entries for details of each type.

nowheres. Nonstandard version of **nowhere** or **anywhere.**

> COLLOQUIAL The chemist couldn't locate the test tube **nowheres.** It was **nowheres** to be found.

> REVISED The chemist couldn't locate the test tube **anywhere.** It was **nowhere** to be found.

* **number.** The form a word takes to indicate whether it is singular or plural. See Section 28a.

> SINGULAR boy his this
> PLURAL boys their these

number/amount. See **amount/number.**

* **object, direct/indirect.** A word or phrase that receives the action of a verb. An object is **direct** when it states to whom or what an action was done.

> direct obj.
> Kim gave us **the signal.**

An object is **indirect** when it explains for whom or what an action is done or directed. It usually precedes the direct object.

> indirect obj.
> Kim gave **us** the signal.

* **objective case.** The form a noun or pronoun takes when it serves as a direct or an indirect object in a sentence or as the object of a preposition. See **case.**

off of. A wordy expression. **Off** is enough.

> Arthur drove his Jeep **off** the road.

gloss

O.K., OK, okay. Not the best choice for formal writing. But give the expression respect. It's an internationally recognized expression of approval. OK?

* **ordinal numbers.** Numbers that express a sequence: *first, second, third.* In contrast, **cardinal numbers** express an amount: *one, two, three.*

Oriental. A term falling out of favor as a description of the people or cultures of East Asia. Terms preferred are *Asian* or *East Asian.*

paragraph. A cluster of sentences working together for some purpose: to develop a single idea, to show relationships between separate ideas, to move readers from one point to another, to introduce a subject, to conclude a discussion, and so on. Paragraphs are marked by separations (indentions or open spaces). Paragraphs vary greatly in length but may be as short as a single sentence. See Chapters 15 and 16.

The symbol ¶, meaning "paragraph," is sometimes inserted by editors and instructors where a new paragraph is needed in a paper. *No* ¶ indicates that an existing paragraph should be combined with another.

* **parallelism/parallel structure.** Ideas or items expressed in matching grammatical forms or structural patterns. Words, phrases, sentences, and even paragraphs can demonstrate parallelism. See Section 19h.

PARALLEL VERBS	The child was **waving, smiling, jumping,** and **laughing**—all at the same time.
PARALLEL PHRASES	**On the sea, in the air, on the ground,** the forces of the Axis powers were steadily driven back.
PARALLEL CLAUSES	He was **the best of clowns;** he was **the worst of clowns.**
PARALLEL SENTENCES	The child was **waving, smiling, and laughing**—all at the same time. Her mother was **screaming, berating, and threatening— all to no avail.**

* **parenthetical element.** A word or phrase that contributes to a sentence but is not an essential part of it. Parenthetical items are usually separated from sentences by commas, dashes, or parentheses. When the element occurs in the middle of a sentence, it is set off by punctuation.

Orlando, **a wiry fellow,** climbed the sycamore tree easily.

Francie decided to climb an elm and—**still clutching her purse and camera**—soon waved from its topmost branches.

All the while, Richard (**the most vocal advocate of tree climbing**) remained on *terra firma.*

* **participle.** A verb form that is used as a modifier (see Section 27a-2). The present participle ends with **-ing.** For regular verbs, the past participle ends with **-ed;** for irregular verbs, the form of the past participle will vary. Participles have the following forms.

TO PERFORM (A REGULAR VERB)
Present, active: performing
Present, passive: being performed
Past, active: performed
Past, passive: having been performed

Participles can serve as simple modifiers.

Smiling, Officer Bricker wrote the traffic ticket.   Modifies *Officer Bricker.*

But they often take objects, complements, and modifiers of their own to form verbal phrases, which play an important role in shaping sentences.

gloss

> **Writing** the ticket for speeding, Bricker laughed at his own cleverness in catching Arthur.
>
> **Having been ridiculed** often in the past by Arthur, Bricker now had his chance for revenge.
>
> Arthur, **knowing** what his friends were doing to Officer Bricker's patrol car, smiled as he took the ticket.

Like an infinitive, a participle can also serve as an **absolute**—that is, a phrase that modifies an entire sentence.

> **All things considered,** the prank was worth the ticket.

* **parts of speech.**   The eight common categories by which words in a sentence are identified according to what they do, how they are formed, where they are placed, and what they mean. Those basic categories are **nouns, pronouns, adjectives, verbs, adverbs, prepositions, conjunctions,** and **interjections.**

passed/past.   Be careful not to confuse these words. **Passed** is a verb form; **past** can function as a noun, adjective, adverb, or preposition. The words are not interchangeable. Study the differences in the following sentences.

> *PASSED* AS VERB, PAST TENSE
> Tina **passed** her economics examination.
>
> *PASSED* AS VERB, PAST PARTICIPLE
> Earlier in the day she had **passed** an English quiz.
>
> *PAST* AS NOUN
> In the **past,** she did well.
>
> *PAST* AS ADJECTIVE
> In the **past** semester, she got straight *A*'s.
>
> *PAST* AS ADVERB
> Smiling, Tina walked **past** the teacher.
>
> *PAST* AS PREPOSITION
> **Past** midnight, Tina was still celebrating.

* **passive verb/voice.**   See **voice.**

persecute/prosecute. **Persecute** means "to oppress" or "to torment"; **prosecute** is a legal term meaning "to bring charges or legal proceedings" against someone or something.

Connie felt **persecuted** by criticisms of her political activism.

She threatened to **prosecute** anyone who interfered with her First Amendment rights.

* **person.** A way of classifying personal pronouns in sentences.

1st person:	the speaker—*I, we*
2nd person:	spoken to—*you*
3rd person:	spoken about—*he, she, it, they* + all nouns

Verbs also change to indicate a shift in person.

1st person:	I **see.**
3rd person:	She **sees.**

personal/personnel. Notice the difference between these words. **Personal** refers to what is private, belonging to an individual. **Personnel** are the people staffing an office or institution.

Drug testing all airline **personnel** might infringe on **personal** freedom.

* **personal pronoun.** A pronoun that refers to particular individuals, things, or groups: *I, you, he, she, it, we, you, they.*

phenomena/phenomenon. You can win friends and influence people by spelling these words correctly and using **phenomenon** as the singular form.

The astral **phenomenon** of meteor showers is common in August.
Many other astral **phenomena** are linked to particular seasons.

* **phrase.** A group of related words that does not include both a subject and a finite verb. Among the types of phrases are **noun phrases, verb phrases, verbal phrases** (infinitive, gerund, and participial), **absolute phrases,** and **prepositional phrases.** See Section 19c.

NOUN PHRASE	**The members of the Astronomy Club** will be going to the observatory in a van.
VERB PHRASE	The members of the Astronomy Club **will be going** to the observatory in a van.
VERBAL PHRASE— INFINITIVE	Their intention is **to observe the planet Mars.**
VERBAL PHRASE— GERUND	**Driving to the observatory** will be half the fun.
VERBAL PHRASE— PARTICIPIAL	The instructor **sponsoring the trip** will drive the van.
ABSOLUTE PHRASE	**All things considered,** the trip was time well spent.
PREPOSITIONAL PHRASE	Whenever it could, the Astronomy Club scheduled its meetings **at the hilltop observatory.**

plurality/majority.   See **majority/plurality.**

plus.   Don't use **plus** as a conjunction or conjunctive adverb meaning "and," "moreover," "besides," or "in addition to."

NOT   Mr. Burton admitted to cheating on his income taxes this year. **Plus** he acknowledged that he had filed false returns for the last three years.

BUT   Mr. Burton admitted to cheating on his income taxes this year. **Moreover,** he acknowledged that he had filed false returns for the last three years.

gloss

possess.   Don't forget the final *s* in *possess.*

* **possessive case.**   The form a noun or pronoun takes to show ownership: *Barney's, Jean-Pierre's, mine, yours, hers, theirs.* See Sections 28b (nouns) and 31f (pronouns).

* **possessive pronoun.**   The form a pronoun takes when it shows ownership: *my, mine, your, yours, her, his, its, our, ours, their, whose, anyone's, somebody's.* See Section 31f.

* **predicate.**   A verb and all its auxiliaries, modifiers, and complements.

The pregnant cat, enormous and fierce, **kittened in the back seat of Officer Bricker's car, where she planned to set up housekeeping.**

* **predicate adjective.**   An adjective that follows a linking verb and describes the subject.

Coach Rhoades is **inept.**
It was **cold.**

* **predicate nominative.**   A noun or pronoun that follows a linking verb and tells what the subject is.

Rhoades is the **coach.**
It was **she.**

prejudice/prejudiced.   Many writers and speakers use **prejudice** where they need **prejudiced. Prejudice** is a noun; **prejudiced** is a verb form.

WRONG   Joe Kamakura is **prejudice** against liberals.
RIGHT   Joe Kamakura is **prejudiced** against liberals.

WRONG   **Prejudice** people are found in every walk of life.
RIGHT   **Prejudiced** people are found in every walk of life.

COMPARE   **Prejudice** is found in every walk of life.

* **preposition.**   A word that links a noun or pronoun to the rest of a sentence. Prepositions point out many kinds of basic relationships: *on, above, to, for, in, out, through, by,* and so on.

* **prepositional phrase.**   The combination of a preposition and a noun or pronoun. The following are prepositional phrases: *on our house, above it, to him, in love, through them, by the garden gate.* See Section 19c-1.

* **principal parts of a verb.** The three basic forms of a verb from which all tenses are built. See Section 26d.

Infinitive (present). This is the base form of a verb, the shape it takes when preceded by **to: to walk, to go, to choose.**

Past. This is the simplest form a verb has to show action that has already occurred: **walked, went, chose.**

Past participle. This is the form a verb takes when it is accompanied by an **auxiliary verb** to show a more complicated past tense: **had walked, might have gone, would have been chosen.**

principal/principle. Two terms commonly confused because of their multiple meanings. **Principal** means "chief" or "most important." It also names the head of an elementary or secondary school (remember "The **principal** is your pal"?). Finally, it can be a sum of money lent or borrowed.

Ike intended to be the **principal** breadwinner of the household.

Bernice accused Ike of acting like a power-mad high school **principal.**

She argued that they would need two incomes just to meet their mortgage payments—both interest and **principal.**

A **principle,** on the other hand, is a guiding rule or fundamental truth.

Ike declared it was against his **principles** to have his wife work.

Bernice said he would just have to be a little less **principled** on that issue.

prioritize. Some readers object to this word, regarding it as less appropriate than its equivalents: **rank** or **list in order of priority.**

proceed to. A wordy and redundant construction when it merely delays the real action of a sentence.

WORDY	We **proceeded to** open the strongbox.
TIGHTER	We **opened** the strongbox.

* **progressive verb.** A verb form that shows continuing action. Progressive tenses are formed by the auxiliary verb *to be* + the present participle. See Sections 26a and 35a.

to be + present participle
Nelda **is conducting** her string orchestra.
to be + present participle
Nelda **had been conducting** the orchestra for many years.
to be + present participle
Nelda **will be conducting** the orchestra for many years to come.

* **pronoun.** A word that acts like a noun but doesn't name a specific person, place, or thing—*I, you, he, she, it, they, whom, who, what, myself, oneself, this, these, that, all, both, anybody,* and so on. There are many varieties of pronouns: **personal, relative, interrogative, intensive, reflexive, demonstrative, indefinite,** and **reciprocal.** See Chapters 29–32 and individual entries for details about each type.

* **proper adjective.**   An adjective based on the name of a person, place, or thing. Proper adjectives are capitalized.

> **British** cuisine
> **Machiavellian** politics
> **Cubist** art

* **proper noun.**   A noun that names some particular person, place, or thing: *Bryan Adams, Australia, Ford.* The first letter in proper nouns is capitalized.

* **qualifier.**   A modifier. Sometimes the word refers to particular classes of modifiers: **intensifiers** (*so, too, surely, certainly*), **restrictive expressions** (*many, most, both, some, almost*), or **conjunctive adverbs** (*however, nevertheless*).

* **quantifier.**   A word that precedes nouns and tells *how much* or *how many:* **some, several, a little.**

quote.   Some people do not accept **quote** used as a noun. To be safe, use **quotation** in formal writing.

real.   Often used as a colloquial version of **very:** "I was **real** scared." This usage is inappropriate in academic writing.

really.   An adverb too vague to make much of an impression in many sentences: **It was really hot; I am really sorry.** Replace **really** with a more precise expression or delete it.

reason is . . . because.   The expression is redundant. Use one half of the expression or the other—not both.

> REDUNDANT   The **reason** the cat is ferocious is **because** she is protecting her kittens.
>
> REVISED   The **reason** the cat is ferocious is **that** she is protecting her kittens.
>
> REVISED   The cat is ferocious **because** she is protecting her kittens.

* **reciprocal pronoun.**   A compound pronoun that shows a mutual action: *one another, each other.*

> The members of the jury whispered to **one another.**

redundancy.   Unnecessary repetition in writing.

refer/allude.   See **allude/refer.**

* **reference.**   The connection between a pronoun and the noun it stands in for (its **antecedent**). This connection should be clear and unambiguous. When a reader can't figure out who *he* is in a sentence you have written, or what exactly *this* or *it* may mean, you have a problem with unclear reference.

> UNCLEAR REFERENCES
> The sun broke through the mists as Jim and Jack, fully recovered from their accident, arrived with news about the award and the ceremony. **This** pleased us because **he** hadn't mentioned anything about **it.**

gloss

REFERENCES CLARIFIED
The sun broke through the mists as Jim and Jack, fully recovered from their accident, arrived with news about the award and the ceremony. **The news** pleased us because **Jim** hadn't mentioned anything about **a ceremony.**

See Chapter 29.

* **reflexive pronoun.**   A pronoun form created when **-self** or **-selves** is added to personal pronouns (*myself, yourself, herself, himself, itself, oneself, ourselves, yourselves, themselves*). Use the reflexive form when both the subject and the object of an action are the same (see Section 32a).

subj.   obj.
Chunyang had only *himself* to rely on.
subj.   obj.
They took *themselves* too seriously.

* **regular verb.**   A verb that forms its past and past participle forms (see **principal parts of a verb**) simply by adding **-d** or **-ed** to the infinitive. See Section 26a.

INFINITIVE	PAST	PAST PARTICIPLE
talk	talked	talked
coincide	coincided	coincided
advertise	advertised	advertised

* **relative clause.**   See **adjective clauses** and **relative pronoun.**

* **relative pronoun.**   A pronoun such as *that, which, whichever, who, who-ever, whom, whomever, whose,* and *of which* that introduces subordinate clauses. In the following example, the relative pronoun *whichever* introduces a noun clause that forms the subject of the sentence.

subordinate clause
Whichever car you buy will cost a small fortune.

In this second example, the relative pronoun *which* introduces an adjective clause modifying *club.*

subordinate clause
Mr. Rao sold the club, **which** he had owned for twenty years.

A clause introduced by a relative pronoun is called a **relative clause.**

* **restrictive (or essential) element.**   A modifier, usually a phrase, essential to the meaning of the subject or noun it modifies. If the restrictive element is removed, the sentence no longer makes sense.

Only the senator **who voted "nay"** remained in the chamber.
The agent **from the CIA** was the one who called.

Restrictive phrases are *not* set off by commas. See **nonrestrictive element** and Sections 39b-1 and 39b-2.

* **run-on sentence.**   A faulty sentence in which two independent clauses (groups of words that could stand alone as sentences) are joined without appropriate punctuation marks or conjunctions. It may also be called a **fused sentence**. See Section 38d.

> RUN-ON   Reading *Ulysses* is one thing understanding it is another.
> CORRECTED   Reading *Ulysses* is one thing; understanding it is another.

* **sentence.**   A group of words that expresses an idea and is punctuated as an independent unit.

> Whenever it could, the Astronomy Club scheduled meetings in an isolated hilltop observatory.
>
> Is that true?
>
> Explain the situation to me.

* **sentence fragment.**   See **fragment.**

* **sentence structure.**   The way a sentence is put together—its organization or arrangement of phrases and clauses. Sentences can be described in many ways—for example, as *simple, complex, compound,* or *compound-complex; periodic* or *cumulative;* or *direct, complicated, tangled,* and so on. See Chapters 19 and 20.

* **sequence of tenses.**   The way the tense of one verb in a sentence limits or determines the tense of other verbs.

set/sit.   These two verbs can cause problems. Here are their parts.

PRESENT	PAST	PRESENT PARTICIPLE	PAST PARTICIPLE
set (put down)	set	setting	set
sit (take a seat)	sat	sitting	sat

It may help you to remember that **to sit** (meaning "to take a seat") is *intransitive*—that is, it doesn't take an object. You can't sit *something*.

> Haskell **sits** under the cottonwood tree.
> He **sat** there all afternoon.
> He was **sitting** in the hammock yesterday.
> He had **sat** there for several weeks.

To set (meaning "to place" or "to put") is *transitive*—it takes an object.

> Jenny **set** a *plate* on the table.
> At Christmas, we **set** a *star* atop the tree.
> Alex was **setting** the *music* on the stand when it collapsed.
> Connie discovered that Travis **had set** a *subpoena* on her desk.

sexist language.   Language that reflects prejudiced attitudes and stereotypical thinking about the sex roles and traits of both sexes. See Sections 18d and 32d.

s/he.   Most readers object to this construction which, like *he/she* and *she/he,* is an alternative to the nonsexist but clumsy *he or she.* Avoid **s/he.**

should of.   Mistaken form of **should have.** Also incorrect are **could of** and **would of.**

simile. An explicit comparison between two things. In a simile, a word such as *like* or *as* underscores the comparison.

Driving a Porsche 911 is **like** riding the surf at Waikiki.
Graziella is **as** flaky **as** Wheaties.

simple sentence. A sentence that has only one clause.

independent clause
Mardi Gras is celebrated just before Ash Wednesday.

sit/set. See **set/sit.**

slang. Casual, aggressively informal language.

The punk wanted to bum a cigarette off us, but we told him to get lost.

Slang expressions are out of place in most academic and business writing. See Sections 18a-3 and 18a-4.

so. Vague when used as an intensifier, especially when no explanation follows **so**: *Sue Ellen was so sad.* **So** used this way can sound trite (how sad is **so** sad?) or juvenile: *Professor Sweno's play was so bad.* If you use **so**, complete your statement.

Sue Ellen was **so** sad she cried for an hour.

Professor Sweno's play was **so** bad that the audience cheered for the villains.

* **split infinitive.** An infinitive interrupted by an adverb: *to **boldly** go; to **really** try.* Though correct, split infinitives offend some readers. To alter a split infinitive, simply place the adverb somewhere else in your sentence: *to go **boldly**.* See Section 27c.

stationary/stationery. **Stationary,** an adjective, means "immovable, fixed in place." **Stationery** is a noun meaning "writing material." The words are not interchangeable.

* **subject.** A word or phrase that names what a sentence is about. The **simple subject** of a sentence is a single word; the **complete subject** is the simple subject and all its modifiers.

SIMPLE SUBJECT
    subj.   verb
The **captain** of the new team quit.

COMPLETE SUBJECT
    subj.   verb
The captain of the new team *quit.*

* **subject complement.** A word or phrase that follows a **linking verb,** completing its meaning. Subject complements can be nouns, pronouns, or adjectives.

    subj.   l.v.   subj. comp.
Sanjay Sacomdri is **student representative.**

subj.   l.v. subj. comp.
The director is she.
subj.   l.v.   subj. comp.
Kelly McKay seems **mysterious.**

* **subjunctive mood.**   The form of a verb that expresses a wish, desire, supposition, or improbability (see **mood** and Section 26f).

If he **were to find** the canister of film, we would be delighted.

It is necessary that the film **be** locked in the vault.

* **subordinate clause.**   See **clause.**

* **subordinating conjunctions.**   See **conjunctions, subordinating.**

such.   Vague when used as an intensifier, especially when no explanation follows **such:** *Shakespeare achieves* **such** *dramatic heights in his tragedies.* If you use **such,** complete your statement.

Shakespeare achieves **such** dramatic heights in his tragedies that he is regarded as the finest playwright in English.

* **superlative.**   The highest degree in a comparison of at least three things.

The **worst** play in thirty-seven years . . .

The **most vicious** of three published reviews . . .

supposed to.   Many writers forget the *d* at the end of **suppose** when the word is used with auxiliary verbs.

INCORRECT Calina was **suppose to** check her inventory.

CORRECT   Calina was **supposed to** check her inventory.

* **synonyms.**   Words of approximately the same meaning: *street/road, home/domicile.* While synonyms may share their **denotation,** or basic meaning, they often differ in **connotation**—that is, what the words imply. Both *skinny* and *svelte* denote thinness, but the terms differ significantly in how they would be used. In most situations, *skinny* sounds disparaging, while *svelte* is a positive, even glamorous description.

* **syntax.**   The arrangement and relationship of clauses, phrases, and words in a sentence.

* **tense.**   That quality of a verb which expresses time and existence. Tense is expressed through changes in verb forms and endings (*see, seeing, saw; work, worked*) and the use of auxiliaries (*had seen, will have seen; had worked, had been working*). Tense enables verbs to state complicated relationships between time and action—or relatively simple ones. See Sections 26a and 35a.

than/then.   These words are occasionally confused. **Than** is a conjunction expressing difference or comparison; **then** is an adverb expressing time.

If the film is playing tomorrow, Shannon would rather go **then than** today.

theirselves.   A nonstandard form. Use **themselves** instead.

INCORRECT All the strikers placed **theirselves** in jeopardy.

CORRECT   All the strikers placed **themselves** in jeopardy.

then/than.   See **than/then.**

this.   As a pronoun, **this** is sometimes vague and in need of clarification (see Section 29c-1).

VAGUE	We could fix the car if you had more time or I owned the proper tools. Of course, **this** is always a problem.
CLEARER	We could fix the car if you had more time or I owned the proper tools. Of course, **my lack of proper tools** is always a problem.

This (and **these**) may be inappropriate when used informally as demonstrative adjectives that refer to objects not previously mentioned.

INAPPROPRIATE *THIS*   Jim owns **this** huge Harley motorcycle.

INAPPROPRIATE *THESE* After she moved out, we found **these** really ugly roaches in her apartment.

Such forms are common in speech but should not appear in writing.

BETTER	Jim owns **a** huge Harley motorcycle.
BETTER	After she moved out, we found ugly roaches in her apartment.

throne/thrown.   A surprising number of writers use **thrown** when they mean **throne.**

Charles I was **thrown** from his **throne** by an angry army of Puritans.

thusly.   A fussy, nonstandard form. Don't use it. **Thus** is stuffy enough without the *-ly.*

till/until.   **Until** is used more often in school and business writing, though the words are usually interchangeable. No apostrophe is used with **till.** You may occasionally see the poetic form 'til, but don't use it in academic or business writing.

to/too.   Most people know the difference between these words. But a writer in a hurry can easily put down the preposition **to** when the adverb **too** is intended. If you make this error often, check for it when you edit.

INCORRECT	Coach Rhoades was **to** surprised to speak after his team won its first game in four years.
REVISED	Coach Rhoades was **too** surprised to speak after his team won its first game in four years.

topic sentence.   A sentence that states the main idea of a paragraph. See Section 15a-2.

toward/towards.   **Toward** is preferred, though either form is fine.

transitions. Connecting words, phrases, and other devices (repetitions, headings) that help readers move from one unit to the next in your writing. Transitions help to hold a piece of writing together, bridging gaps and linking sentences and paragraphs. **Transitional words** are individual terms used to link ideas: *therefore, moreover, nevertheless, nonetheless, consequently,* and so on. See Chapter 17.

* **transitive verb.** A verb that takes an object. The action of a transitive verb passes on to someone or something; the sentence would be incomplete without an object.

TRANSITIVE	Travis accidentally **pushed** *Kyle.* You can **push** someone.
	Sister Anne **wrecked** the *van.* You can **wreck** something.

Transitive verbs (unlike intransitives) can usually be changed from the active to passive voice.

ACTIVE	Travis accidentally **pushed** *Kyle.*
PASSIVE	*Kyle* **was** accidentally **pushed** by Travis.

Compare transitive verbs to **intransitive** ones, which do not require an object to complete the action of a sentence.

INTRANSITIVE	I **slept** well. You cannot **sleep** something.
	Lawrence **sat** down. You cannot **sit** something.

try and. An informal expression. In writing, use **try to** instead.

INCORRECT	After its defeat, the soccer team decided to **try and** drown its sorrows.
REVISED	After its defeat, the soccer team decided to **try to** drown its sorrows.

TV. This abbreviation for *television* is common, but in most writing it is still preferable to write out the entire word. The abbreviation is usually capitalized.

type. You can usually delete this word.

WORDY	Hector was a polite **type** of guy.
REVISED	Hector was polite.

uninterested/disinterested. See **disinterested/uninterested.**

unique. Something **unique** is one of a kind. It can't be compared with anything else, so expressions such as *most unique, more unique,* or *very unique* don't make sense. The word **unique,** when used properly, should stand alone.

INCORRECT	Joe Rhoades's coaching methods were **very unique.**
REVISED	Joe Rhoades's coaching methods were **unique.**

Quite often **unique** appears where another, more specific adjective is appropriate.

INCORRECT	The **most unique** merchant on the block was Tong-chai.
IMPROVED	The **most inventive** merchant on the block was Tong-chai.

until/till. See **till/until.**

used to. Many writers forget the *d* at the end of **use.**

INCORRECT	Leroy was use to studying after soccer practice.
CORRECT	Leroy was **used to** studying after soccer practice.

utilize. Many readers prefer the simpler term **use.**

INFLATED	Mr. Ringling **utilized** his gavel to regain the crowd's attention.
BETTER	Mr. Ringling **used** his gavel to regain the crowd's attention.

* **verb.** The word or phrase that establishes the action of a sentence or expresses a state of being (see Chapters 25–26).

verb
The music **played** on.

verb
Turning the volume down **proved** to be difficult.

A verb and all its auxiliaries, modifiers, and complements is called the **predicate** of a sentence.

complete subj.　　　　predicate
David's band **would have played throughout the night.**

complete subj.　　　　predicate
Turning the volume down on the band **proved to be much more difficult than the neighbors had anticipated it might be.**

* **verbals.** Verb forms that act like nouns, adjectives, or adverbs (see Chapter 27). The three kinds of verbals are **infinitives, participles,** and **gerunds.** Like verbs, verbals can take objects to form phrases. But verbals are described as nonfinite (that is, "unfinished") verbs because they cannot alone make complete sentences. A complete sentence requires a **finite** verb—that is, a verb that changes form to indicate person, number, and tense.

NONFINITE VERB—INFINITIVE	**To have found** security . . .
FINITE VERB	I **have found** security.
NONFINITE VERB—PARTICIPLE	The actor **performing** the scene . . .
FINITE VERB	The actor **performs** the scene.

very. Many teachers and editors will cut **very** almost every time it appears. Overuse has deadened the impact of the word. Whenever possible, use a more specific term or expression.

WEAK   I was **very angry.**
STRONGER   I was **furious.**

* **voice.** Transitive verbs can be either in the active voice or in the passive voice. They are in the **active voice** when the subject in the sentence actually performs the action described by the verb.

> subj.   action
> *Professor Chase* **donated** the video camera.

They are in the **passive voice** when the action described by the verb is done to the subject.

> subj.   action
> *The video camera* **was donated** by Professor Chase.

gloss

See Section 26e.

well/good. See **good/well.**

who/whom. Use **who** when the pronoun is a subject; use **whom** when it is an object.

> **Who** wrote the ticket?
> **To whom** was the ticket given?

See Section 31e.

-wise. Don't add **-wise** to the end of a word to mean "with respect to." Many people object to word coinages such as *sportswise, weatherwise,* and *healthwise.* However, a number of common and acceptable English expressions do end in -wise: *clockwise, lengthwise, otherwise.* When in doubt about an expression, check the dictionary.

with regards to. Drop the **s** in regards. The correct expression is **with regard to.**

won't. Writers sometimes forget the apostrophe in this contraction and in others like it: **can't, don't.**

word choice. A marginal annotation used by many instructors to suggest that the writer could find a more appropriate or effective word or phrase.

would of. Mistaken form of **would have.** Also incorrect are **could of** and **should of.**

you all. Southern expression for *you,* usually plural. Not used in academic writing.

your/you're. Homonyms that often get switched. **You're** is the contraction for *you are;* **your** is a possessive form.

> **You're** certain Maxine has been to Iran?
> **Your** certainty on this matter may be important.

Credits

TEXT CREDITS

Abbey, Edward. *Desert Solitaire.* New York: McGraw-Hill, 1968.

Ackerman, Diane. *A Natural History of the Senses.* New York: Random House, 1990.

AltaVista. "AltaVista-help-Search" at American Psychological Association. *Publication Manual of the American Psychological Association,* Fourth Ed., 1994.

Angelou, Maya. *I Know Why the Caged Bird Sings.* New York: Random House, 1969.

Angier, Natalie. "Mating for Life?" in *The Beauty and the Beastly.* New York: Houghton Mifflin Company, 1995.

Anzaldúa, Gloria. From "How to Tame a Wild Heart" in *Borderlands/La Frontera: The New Mestiza.* Copyright © 1987, 1999 by Gloria Anzaldúa. Reprinted by permission of Aunt Lute Books.

Austen, Jane. "Pride and Prejudice," 1813.

Baker, Catherine. Illustration from *Your Genes, Your Choices,* a publication of Science & Literacy for Health, a project of the AAAS Directorate for Education and Human Resources. Copyright © 1997 by the American Association for the Advancement of Science. Reprinted by permission.

Barnett, Lincoln. *The Universe and Dr. Einstein.* New York: William Morrow and Co., 1968.

Barry, Dave. From "Neither Man Nor Rat Can Properly Fold the Laundry" as appeared in *The Miami Herald,* July 2, 2000. Reprinted by permission of the author.

Bernstein, Richard. *Dictatorship of Virtue.* New York: Alfred A. Knopf, 1994, p. 11.

Berry, Wendell. *Sex, Economy, Freedom & Community.* New York: Pantheon Books, 1993.

Blackboard Web page. <http://blackboard.com>.

Blake, William. "The Divine Image," 1789.

Bloodworth, Dennis. *The Chinese Looking Glass.* New York: Farrar, Straus & Giroux, 1980, p. 155.

Bork, Robert H. "Give Me a Bowl of Texas," *Forbes,* September 1985, p. 184.

Boyer, Ernest L. "Creating the New American College," *The Chronicle of Higher Education,* 1994.

Briggs, Chad, and Fred Ribich. From "The Relationship Between Test Anxiety, Sleep Habits, and Self-perceived Academic Competency." *Psych-E,* Vol. 1, 12/1/98. Reprinted by permission of Chad Briggs.

Brunvard, Jan. *The Vanishing Hitchhiker: American Urban Legends and Their Meaning.* New York: W. W. Norton, 1982.

Burke, James Lee. *Black Cherry Blues.* Boston: Little, Brown and Company, 1989.

Carville, James. *We're Right, They're Wrong: A Handbook for Spirited Progressives.* New York: Random House, 1996.

Chesler, Ellen. *Women of Valor.* New York: Simon & Schuster, 1992.

Churchill, Winston. From a speech to the House of Commons, January, 1952.

Codell, Esmé Raji. *From Educating Esmé: Diary of a Teacher's First Year.* Copyright © 1999. Reprinted by permission of Algonquin Books of Chapel Hill and by permission of the author.

Cofer, Judith Ortiz. *Silent Dancing: A Partial Remembrance of a Puerto Rican Childhood.* Houston: Arte Publico Press-University of Houston, 1990.

Costas, Bob. "Eulogy for Mickey Mantle," August 15, 1995.

Council of Science Editors. *Scientific Style and Format: The CBE Manual for Authors, Editors, and Publishers,* Sixth Edition. Copyright © 1994 by the Council of Science Editors. Reprinted by permission.

Crouch, Stanley. "Blues for Jackie," *All American Skin Game, or the Decoy of Race: The Long and the Short of It, 1990–1994.* New York: Pantheon Books, 1995.

Culver, KC. Patriarchal Fairy Tales and Gender Roles: *The Princess Bride.* Reprinted by permission.

Dabelko, Geoffrey. From "The Environmental Factor," *The Wilson Quarterly,* Autumn 1999. Reprinted by permission.

DI: Communicator. From newsletter *DI: Communicator,* Issue No. 1, May 2000. Reprinted by permission of Design International, Dallas, TX.

Didion, Joan. "Georgia O'Keeffe," *The White Album.* New York: Simon & Schuster, 1979.

Ebert, Roger. *The Great Movies: Casablanca.*

Edelman, Marian Wright. "It's Time for America to Protect and Put Children First," *CDF Reports* June/July 1999. © Children's Defense Fund. Reprinted with permission.

Edge, John T. From "I'm Not Leaving Until I Eat This Thing," *Oxford American Magazine,* September/October 1999. Reprinted by permission of the author.

Epstein, Daniel Mark. "The Case of Harry Houdini" in *Star of Wonder.* Woodstock, NY: Overlook Press, 1986.

Goodman, Robert. *The Luck Business.* New York: Free Press, 1995.

Google Web page. Reprinted by permission.

Gould, Stephen Jay. "The Power of Narrative" in *The Urchin in the Storm.* New York: W. W. Norton, 1987, p. 77.

Grady, Sandy. "Tobacco Deal Reduced to Ashes," *Austin-American Statesman,* September 22, 1997.

Hart, Joseph. From "Chimps Are People Too," *Utne Reader,* August 16, 2000. Reprinted with permission of the author and Utne Reader.

Himmelfarb, Gertrude. "Second Thoughts on a Civil Society," *The Weekly Standard,* September 6, 1996. Reprinted by permission of the author.

Hoberman, Barry. "Translating the Bible," as originally published in the February 1985 issue of *The Atlantic Monthly,* Vol. 255, No. 2. Copyright © 1985. Reprinted by permission.

Hofstadter, Douglas. *Gödel, Escher, Bach: An Eternal Golden Braid.* New York: Vintage Books/Random House, 1979, p. 603.

Johnson, Paul. *Intellectuals.* New York: Harper & Row, Inc., 1988, p. 73.

Kadaba, Lini. "No Beef," *Philadelphia Inquirer,* February 8, 1998.

Kennedy, John F. *Inaugural Address,* January 20, 1961.

Kerouac, Jack. *On the Road.* New York: Penguin Books, 1968, p. 8.

Kingsolver, Barbara. *High Tide in Tucson.* New York: HarperCollins Publishers, 1995.

Kleine, Ted. "Living the Lansing Dream," *NEXT: Young American Writers on the New Generation,* Eric Liu, ed. New York, W. W. Norton, 1994, p. 95.

Kristoff, Nicholas. "Where Children Rule," *The New York Times Magazine,* August 17, 1997.

Lapham, Lewis. "Notebook," *Harper's,* October 1997.

Lewon, Dennis. From "Malaria's Not So Magic Bullet," *Escape,* July 1999. Reprinted by permission of the author.

McCullough, David. *Truman.* New York: Simon & Schuster, 1992, p. 324.

McManus, Ray. "Split P Soup Flyer." Reprinted by permission.

McMurtry, Larry, and Diana Ossana. *Zeke and Ned.* New York: Simon & Schuster, 1997.

Meehan, Mary. "The Left Has Betrayed the Sanctity of Life" from *The Progressive,* September 1980. Reprinted by permission.

Mellix, Barbara. "From Outside, In" originally appeared in *The Georgia Review,* Volume XLI, No. 2 (Summer 1987), © 1987 by The University of Georgia / © 1987 by Barbara Mellix. Reprinted by permission of Barbara Mellix and *The Georgia Review.*

The Modern Language Association Style Manual. "Rules." Reprinted by permission. Thanks to the *MLA Style Manual and Guide to Scholarly Publishing,* Second Edition. Copyright © 1998 Modern Language Association of America.

Moffatt, Michael. *Coming of Age in New Jersey.* New Brunswick, NJ: Rutgers University Press, 1989.

Morrison, Toni. *The Bluest Eye.* New York: Simon & Schuster, 1970, p. 97.

Mowat, Farley. *Never Cry Wolf.* Boston: Little, Brown and Company, 1963.

MSNBC.com-*Newsweek,* October 3, 2002. Copyright 2002 Newsweek, Inc. All rights reserved. Reprinted by permission.

Negroponte, Nicholas. From "Get a Life?" © 1995 by Nicholas Negroponte. This article originally appeared in *Wired.* Reprinted by permission of the author.

Netscape. Netscape Communications browser window and Netscape Composer © 1999 Netscape Communications Corporation. Used with permission. Netscape Communications has not authorized, sponsored, endorsed, or approved this publication and is not responsible for its content.

New Student Services. Screen shot from <www.utexas.edu/depts/dos/nss> reprinted with permission of The University of Texas at Austin, Office of the Dean of Students.

New York Times on the Web. "Search" page from <www.nytimes.com>. Copyright © 1998 by the New York Times Company. Reprinted by permission.

News Service. "News Service Usenet Access,"<http://www.news-service.to/>.

Nuland, Sherwin B. "Medical Fads: Bran, Midwives, and Leeches," *The New York Times,* June 25, 1995, p. E16.

Olds, Sharon. "The One Girl at the Boy's Party" from *The Dead and the Living* by Sharon Olds. Copyright © 1987 by Sharon Olds. Used by permission of Alfred A. Knopf, a division of Random House, Inc.

The Onion, Onionhumorgraphic, The Fast-food Lawsuit. Reprinted with permission of *The Onion.* Copyright 2002 by Onion, Inc. <www.theonion.com>.

Orphans III, Listening to Orphan Films, September 26–28, 2002. <www.sc.edu/filmsymposium/orphanfilms.html>.

Patoski, Joe Nick. "Three Cheers for High School Football." Reprinted with permission from the October 1999 issue of *Texas Monthly.*

Professional Communications Center Brochure. Reprinted by permission of the Professional Communications Center at the University of South Carolina College of Engineering & Information Technology.

Quindlen, Anna. "Between the Sexes, a Great Divide" from "Life in the 30's" column, *The New York Times Magazine,* March 24, 1988. Copyright © 1988 by The New York Times Company. Reprinted by permission.

Ravitch, Diane. "Educational Insensitivity." Originally published in *The New York Times,* June 5, 2002. Copyright The New York Times. Reprinted by permission.

Ramage, John, and John Bean. *Writing Arguments.* New York: Allyn & Bacon, 1995, Third Ed.

Reid, T. R. From "Sumo," *National Geographic*, Vol. 192, Issue 1, July 1997. Reprinted by permission of the National Geographic Society and the author.

Roland, Alex. "Leave the People Home," *USA Today Online*, July 3, 1997. Reprinted by permission of the author.

Rose, Mike. *Lives on the Boundary*. New York: The Free Press, 1989.

Sagan, Carl. *The Demon-Haunted World*. New York: Random House, 1995.

Schriver, Karen. *Dynamics in Document Design*. New York: John Wiley & Sons, 1977.

Samaras, Thomas T. "Let's Get Small," *Harper's*, January 1995, p. 32. Reprinted from *The Truth About Your Height: Exploring Myths and Realities of Human Size and Its Effects on Performance, Health, Pollution, and Survival*. San Diego: Telecote Publications.

Santiago, Chiori. "The Fine and Friendly Art of Luis Jiménez," *Smithsonian*, 1993.

Schor, Juliet. *The Overworked American*. New York: Basic Books, 1991.

Shapin, Stephen. *The Scientific Revolution*. Chicago: University of Chicago Press, 1996.

Shoales, Ian. From "Napster," *Byte*, May 22, 2000. Reprinted by permission of the author.

Shrum, Robert. "The Nikes Jumped Over the Moon," *Slate*, December 13, 1996. Reprinted by permission of United Feature Syndicate, Inc.

Sigma Tau Delta Newsletter. From the Spring 2000 issue of the *Sigma Tau Delta Newsletter*. © 2000 by Sigma Tau Delta International English Honor Society. Reprinted by permission.

Smith, Lamar. "Midnight Basketball Is Winner on Street," *The Los Angeles Times*, August 19, 1994.

Stern, Barbara Lang. "Tears Can be Crucial to Your Physical and Emotional Health," *Vogue*, June 1979, Condé Nast Publications.

Stevens, William K. "Prairie Dog Colonies Bolster Life in the Plains," *The New York Times*, July 11, 1995.

Stone, Deborah. "Work and the Moral Woman," *The American Prospect 35* (November–December 1997), p. 83.

Summer Orientation 2000. Brochure reprinted with permission from the University of Texas at Austin, Office of the Dean of Students.

TakeNote! Web pages. *TakeNote!* by Dichiara. Copyright 2000. Reprinted by permissions of Pearson Education, Inc., Upper Saddle River, NJ.

Tenner, Edward. From "Chronologically Incorrect," *The Wilson Quarterly*, Autumn 1998. Reprinted by permission.

Texas Business and Education Coalition. "School Gains, 1999." February 27, 2000. <http://www.tbec.org/gains>.

Toulmin, Stephen. *The Uses of Argument*. New York: Cambridge University Press, 1991. Originally published 1958.

Urban Latino Web page. <www.urbanlatino.com>.

Urquhart, Brian. *Ralph Bunche: An American Life*. New York: W. W. Norton & Co., 1993, p. 435.

U.S. Unemployment rate. From *Governing* (Sourcebook 2000), p. 101; also U.S. Bureau of Labor Statistics.

UT Library Online. "UT Net CAT" web page reprinted by permission of The General Libraries, University of Texas at Austin.

Utne Reader. "homepage."

van der Plas, Robert. *The Mountain Bike Book*. San Francisco: Bicycle Books, 1993.

Walker, Alice. *In Search of Our Mothers' Gardens*. Orlando: Harcourt Brace Jovanovich, 1983.

Walker, Janice R., and Todd Taylor. *The Columbia Guide to Online Style*. Copyright © 1998 Columbia University Press. Reprinted by permission.

Walt Whitman Web page. <www.poets.org>.

The Weekly Standard. "homepage."

Weiner, Jonathan. "Glacier Bubbles Are Telling Us What Was in the Ice Age Air," *Smithsonian,* May, 1989.

West, Cornel. *Race Matters.* Boston: Beacon Press, 1993.

Wheeler, John. "Black Holes and New Physics," *Discovery,* University of Texas at Austin, Winter 1982.

Wilbon, Michael. <www.washingtonpost.com>, June 18, 2002, p. D01.

Wilde, Oscar. *The Picture of Dorian Gray,* 1891.

Williams, Ted. "Only You Can Postpone Forest Fires," *Sierra,* July/August 1995, p. 42.

Wilson, William Julius. *The Truly Disadvantaged.* Chicago: University of Chicago Press, 1987, p. 156.

Women in Science. Web pages reprinted by permission of Women in Science at the University of Texas at Austin.

Wright, Richard. *Native Son.* New York: Harper & Brothers, 1940.

Yahoo! Web page. Reproduced with permission of Yahoo! Inc. Copyright 2000 by Yahoo! Inc. Yahoo! and the Yahoo! logo are trademarks of Yahoo! Inc.

Yankelovich, Daniel. "The Work Ethic Is Underemployed," *Psychology Today,* May 1982. Ziff-Davis Publishing Co.

Zinsser, William. *American Places.* New York: HarperCollins, 1992.

PHOTO CREDITS

2 Dan Bosler/Getty Images Inc.–Stone; 3 Cynthia Johnson/Getty Images Inc–Liaison; 11 SPIN; 11 Harper's Magazine; 11 Richard Strauss/Smithsonian Institution/Supreme Court Historical Society; 16 James Prosek; 19 Corbis Digital Stock; 25 Gruber-Fashion Wire Daily/AP/Wide World Photos; 27 Justin Cone; 35 Justin Cone; 36 Erika Barahona Ede/Guggenheim Museum Bilbao; 52 Key Color/Index Stock Imagery, Inc.; 52 Library of Congress; 56 Brad Stratton; 63 American Honda Motor Co. Inc.; 70 Wally Mc-Namee/CORBIS; 78 Justin Cone; 85 Mark Pett; 93 Christy Friend; 104 TimePix; 104 American Family Physician/Family Practice Management; 111 Jose Luis Pelaez/Corbis/Stock Market; 113 Corbis Digital Stock; 128 Gary Conner/PhotoEdit; 133 Christy Friend; 137 Joseph Sohm/Chromosohm/Unicorn Stock Photos; 140 Jeff Greenberg/PhotoEdit; 141 Ray McManus; 145 Christy Friend; 149 Arcieri/ROPI/ Newsweek; 156 Jonathan Elderfield/Getty Images, Inc–Liaison; 156 New York Times Pictures; 158 Xerox Corporation; 158 PH ESM; 165 Michael Boynton; 176 Christy Friend; 179 Christy Friend; 191 Corbis Digital Stock; 207 Richard Chambury/Globe Photos, Inc.; 208 The Granger Collection; 211 The Museum of Modern Art/Film Stills Archive; 213 Christy Friend; 214 Christy Friend; 223 Christy Friend; 232 Jerry Bauer; 234 Lee Bauknight; 235 Charlie Archambault/Corbis/Sygma; 235 Lini Kadaba; 236 Tony Korody/Corbis/Sygma; 236 AP/Wide World Photos; 237 Jean Weisinger; 237 Don Carraco Photography; 238 AP/Wide World Photos; 238 Sara Barrett/Alfred A. Knopf, Inc.; 239 Mark Jenkinson/Corbis/Outline; 244 Jerry Bauer; 245 Ng Han Guan/AP/Wide World Photos; 247 Jennifer Lewon/Jennifer Lewon Photography; 247 John T. Edge; 248 Jerry Bauer; 249 KC Culver; 252 Ng Han uan/AP/Wide World Photos; 253 AP/Wide World Photos; 253 Bob Burgess/AP/Wide World Photos; 255 Ruggero Vanni/Vanni Archive/CORBIS; 257 James M. Kelly/Globe Photos, Inc.; 260 Jerry Bauer; 261 Nancy Crampton; 268 Don Carraco Photography; 269 Steven L. Hopp/Barbara Kinslover; 270 Ellen Domke/Algonquin Books; 271 Michael Rose; 271 Dominique Nabokov/Open Society Institute; 274 Pacha/CORBIS; 278 Stephan Shapin; 278 Marion Ettlinger; 281 Ng Han uan/AP/Wide World Photos; 282 Chris Cole/Duomo Photography Incorporated; 286 NASA/NASA/John F. Kennedy Space Center; 287 American In-

Index

index

index

index

index

index

index

Summary of Changes to the *MLA Handbook for Writers of Research Papers*, Sixth Edition (2003)

The *MLA Handbook for Writers of Research Papers* was recently published in a new sixth edition. Some forms of documentation and citation have been changed. This insert is intended to detail these changes and provide you with the most up-to-date information about MLA style. Be sure to speak with your instructor if you need additional clarification.

PREPARING THE LIST OF WORKS CITED

Full-Text Databases

Most college and university libraries subscribe to full-text periodical and book databases such as the *New York Times Online* and *American National Biography* and to general databases such as JSTOR, InfoTrac, and Lexis-Nexis that provide a wide range of bibliographic and full-text sources. When you cite works from databases, observe the following changes in MLA style.

1. *URL-Specific Document:* When you cite an online source that can be accessed by a short and logical URL, include the full URL in your citation of the source. An article from the *New York Times*, for example, can be easily accessed by the reader using the URL specified in your Works Cited list.

   > Petersen, Melody. "A Respected Face, but Is It News
   >
   > or an Ad?" <u>New York Times on the Web</u> 7 May
   >
   > 2003. 8 May 2003 <http://www.nytimes.com/2003/
   >
   > 05/07/business/media/07DRUG.html>.

2. *URL of Search Page:* If the URL of your document is long and convoluted, it will be quite difficult for your reader to access the source. Consider this example of a URL from a journal accessed through JSTOR.

   > http://links.jstor.org/sici?sici=00290564%28197512%
   >
   > 2930%3A%3C305%3AATSOPJA%3E2.0CO%3B2-5

When this problem arises, MLA suggests that it is more convenient to supply the URL of the database's search page, as shown here.

Hart, Francis R. "The Spaces of Privacy: Jane Austen."

    <u>Nineteenth-Century Fiction</u> 30.3 (1975): 305-33.

    <u>JSTOR</u>. 5 Feb. 2003 <http://www.jstor.org/search>.

3. *No URL:* If your source does not have an accessible URL or the URL is unique to the library, cite the URL for the home page of the subscription service that you used to find your source.

Youakim, Sami. "Work-Related Asthma." <u>American</u>

    <u>Family Physician</u> 64 (2001): 1839-53. <u>Health</u>

    <u>Reference Center</u>. InfoTrac. Bergen County

    Cooperative Lib. System, NJ. 14 Mar. 2003

    <http://www.galegroup.com/>.

Internet Sources

The new edition of the *MLA Handbook* does not change the style for Internet citations, but it does expand the information to be included. The following citation exhibits the necessary components of an Internet citation.

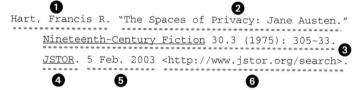

❶ Name of author, editor, translator, or compiler of the source.

❷ Title of the article or other short work, enclosed in quotation marks. For a posting to a discussion list or forum, use the subject line as the title.

❸ Publication information for the print version of the source.

❹ Title of the Internet site (scholarly project, database, online periodical, or Web site, underlined).

❺ Date of access.

❻ URL of the source or URL of the site's search page if the URL is exceptionally long.

Remember to include the following details in your citation if such information is given or available for your source.

- Include the name of the editor, translator, or compiler of the source in addition to the author's name.
- Note the name of the editor of the Web site.
- Include the date of electronic publication, latest update, or posting.
- Give the name and location of the library if your site was accessed through a library subscription service.
- Name the list or forum, if your source is a posting to a discussion list or forum.
- Include the name of the site's sponsoring institution or organization.

Other Important Points Concerning the List of Works Cited

1. *Work from a Library Subscription Service:* When you cite material from a library service, be sure to cite the name of the database used, the name of the service, the name and location of the library, the date of access, and the URL of the subscription service home page if it is available.

   ```
   Dutton, Gail. "Greener Pigs." Popular Science
        255.5 (1999): 38-39. ProQuest Direct.
        Public Lib., Teaneck, NJ. 7 Dec. 2002
        <http://proquest.umi.com>.
   ```

2. *Work from a Personal Subscription Service:* To cite a source that you found via a personal subscription service that allows you to retrieve information through a keyword search, end the citation with *Keyword,* followed by a colon and the date of access. If you used a series of topic labels rather than a keyword end the citation with *Path,* followed by a colon, and the sequence of topics that you used to locate your source. Use semicolons to separate the topics.

   ```
   Futurelle, David. "A Smashing Success." Money.com
        23 Dec. 1999. America Online. 4 Oct. 2002.
        Path: Personal Finance; Business News;
        Business Publications; Money.com.
   ```

THE MECHANICS OF WRITING: ELLIPSES

The most significant difference between the fifth and sixth editions of the *MLA Handbook* is in the style of ellipses. The fifth edition required that ellipses (three spaced periods used to indicate an omission from quoted material) be enclosed in square brackets. Now the style is to omit the brackets. You should, however, check which ellipsis style your instructor prefers.

*Preferred Ellipsis Style of the **6th** Edition:*

In her article "Living in Two Cultures," Jeanne Wakatsuki Houston notes: "My husband and I often joke that the reason we have stayed married for so long is that we . . . mystify each other with responses and attitudes that are plainly due to our different backgrounds" (191).

*Preferred Ellipsis Style of the **5th** Edition:*

In her article "Living in Two Cultures," Jeanne Wakatsuki Houston notes: "My husband and I often joke that the reason we have stayed married for so long is that we [. . .] mystify each other with responses and attitudes that are plainly due to our different backgrounds" (191).

Exception: Do enclose ellipses in square brackets if the original passage you are quoting contains its own ellipsis points. The brackets will distinguish your ellipses from those in the source.

Original Source:

In "Living in Two Cultures," Jeanne Wakatsuki Houston discusses her early questions about marital roles. She notes:

> When we first married I wondered if I should lay out his socks and underwear every morning like my mother used to do for my father. But my brothers' warning would float up from the past:

don't be subservient to Caucasian men or they
will take advantage. So I compromised and laid
them out sporadically, whenever I thought to do
it . . . which grew less and less often as the
years passed. (224)

Quoted Source:

In "Living in Two Cultures," Jeanne Wakatsuki
Houston discusses her early questions about marital
roles. She notes:

> When we first married I wondered if I should
> lay out his socks [. . .]. But my brothers'
> warning would float up from the past: don't be
> subservient to Caucasian men or they will take
> advantage. So I compromised and laid them
> out sporadically, whenever I thought to do
> it . . . which grew less and less often as the
> years passed. (224)

The following paper by first-year student Chassey Wilkins-Hicks
demonstrates the changes to MLA guidelines. The format shown in
this paper is reflective of MLA style but has been slightly modified to
accommodate the space limitations of the trim in this book. Note
that MLA-style student papers should be double-spaced throughout.
As always, see your instructor if you have any questions regarding the
arrangement of this paper.

Hicks 1

Chassey Wilkins-Hicks

Professor Ezzell

English 112

17 April 2003

Peace by Prescription

"Sit down at the dinner table!" "Stop
fidgeting and finish your homework!" "Didn't
you hear a single word I said?" Do these
demands sound familiar? Perhaps you remember
hearing those same words as a child, or
maybe you have even spoken them to your own
son or daughter. They are not uncommon
phrases in the home of a lively, vivacious
child doing nothing more than enjoying life
and burning the energy many adults wish they
could bottle. Yet many adults are beginning
to view any type of bubbly, rambunctious
behavior as unacceptable. More parents are
being swayed toward the idea that if you
have to speak to your children in such a
manner, there must be something wrong with
them. Enter attention deficit hyperactivity
disorder (ADHD). In the past two decades the
diagnosis of ADHD has been on a steady rise.
Independent academic studies as well as
numerous years of research by organizations
such as the National Institute on Drug Abuse
(NIDA) place the proportion of the general
public affected at approximately 3 to 5
percent (United States). The American

Academy of Pediatrics reports that 4 to 12 percent of the nation's school-age children are affected (1).

A considerable number of the diagnosed children are prescribed some form of psychostimulant, such as methylphenidate, to treat their symptoms. One brand is so commonly used, it has practically become a household name--Ritalin. These drugs, however, do not pave the path to recovery. Instead, they chemically alter some of the behavior symptoms associated with ADHD. As I intend to prove, behavior therapy is a much safer alternative than psychostimulants in treating children diagnosed with ADHD. The process can also prove to be a learning and rewarding experience for children, as well as their parents.

A comprehension of exactly how the diagnosis of ADHD is determined is needed to understand the treatments offered. Even with the countless hours of research dedicated to the study of ADHD, the cause remains a mystery. Zwi, Ramchandani, and Joughin attribute the symptoms to a collection of neurobiological problems in the function and makeup of the brain rather than just one disorder (975). Unfortunately, none of my research reveals a conclusive opinion that the brains of those classified with ADHD function differently than the brains of those who are considered normal. And, because there is no proven medical examination or test that can confirm ADHD, the chance of misdiagnosis remains high.

Jaydene Morrison, a nationally certified school psychologist and teacher, does a fantastic job of outlining the standard practice of diagnosing ADHD in her book Coping with ADD/ADHD. It requires several steps and a wide range of IQ and aptitude tests. A doctor may first want to rule out any medical disorder or learning disability (9). The frustration experienced or what may appear as lack of attention due to a hearing impairment can be a misconception of an unruly student. Teachers are often requested to assist by completing lengthy questionnaires on the child's behavior as well as study habits and moods. The next step is determining whether the child falls within the academic level of his or her peers. Reading, writing, spelling, and mathematic capabilities are analyzed for correctness as well as speed. IQ testing such as problem and puzzle solving is utilized in a verbal and hands-on setting. These different aspects of testing demonstrate the process by which the mind computes the problem and transfers the information to paper (11).

Hicks 4

Symptoms of ADHD include a wide variety
of behavior and learning traits. Some of
these include being inattentive, easily
distracted, unable to organize, forgetful,
overtalkative, fidgety, and impatient. Many
argue that this list also describes most
typical, healthy children at some point in
time. In an October 2000 issue of US News
and World Report, Nancy Shute quotes Dickie
Scruggs as saying, "[T]he diagnosis of ADHD
would fit every child in America."

Ritalin, a central nervous system
stimulant, is used to treat ADHD based on
the speculation that it increases the
release of dopamine in the brain. This
assumption is founded on laboratory research
performed on healthy adults. The InfoFacts
sheet on methylphenidate (Ritalin) explains
that by use of a type of brain scan called
positron emission tomography (PET),
researchers confirmed an increase in dopamine
levels in what were considered normal,
healthy subjects administered with

←— 10 —→ therapeutic doses of
  spaces
          methylphenidate. . . . The
          researchers speculate that
          methylphenidate amplifies the
          release of dopamine, a
          neurotransmitter, thereby
          improving attention and focus in

Hicks 5

individuals who have dopamine
signals that are weak, such as
individuals with ADHD. (United
States)

Like many others who disagree with the
use of psychostimulants as a primary
treatment for ADHD, I am not out to disprove
the effects of these drugs. In fact, as
described in the research above, Ritalin and
similar drugs can improve attentiveness and
concentration in almost anyone. In a
personal interview, Thomas Mates, PhD, a
respected child psychologist here in
Wilmington, North Carolina, told me that
many college students have admitted taking
these types of pharmaceuticals to improve
their study habits. Improving only the
ability to focus, however, does not teach a
child good learning habits. The chemicals
merely subdue the individual and the
undesirable behavior. David Stein, PhD,
author of Ritalin Is Not the Answer and an
advocate for behavior therapy, asserts, "The
drugs do control the behaviors, but then
they serve to mask the problem behaviors and
thus block the way for effective change"
(35). What parent would envision spending
quality time with an eight-year-old child
that was under the influence of cocaine?
Amazingly enough, though, parents of

millions of children have been convinced
that giving Ritalin to their child is
acceptable. The comparison with cocaine is
not so outrageous when you consider that the
NIDA has placed a Schedule II narcotics
control label on methylphenidate.

As with any drug, the risks of
adverse reactions are always present. A
long list of side effects accompanies these
stimulant medications, including "decreased
appetite/weight loss, . . . transient tics,
stuttering, increased blood pressure or heart
rate, and growth delay" (American Academy of
Pediatrics 12). I can speak only for myself,
but I hope I represent all cautious parents
when I say that I would take dealing with my
child's behavior problem over inducing these
side effects in her.

I question, is the tranquility these
drugs create for the children or for the
parents? The choices between two minutes
of the parents' day to administer the dose of
a tiny pill versus the countless hours of
one-on-one attention needed to find the root
of the problem could appear too easy. The
answer is obvious for those who are willing
to take the time. I don't deny that there
may be children with extreme cases of
inattentiveness and/or hyperactivity that may
require a medical approach. This, however,

should be the last option and used after all
other means, methods, and programs have been
exhausted. Mind-altering drugs are not a safe
alternative in treating children for what is
more often than not a behavior problem.

Behavior therapy does work. Stein notes
that the treatment of Helen Keller by Annie
Sullivan is the "first documented behavior
modification case" (13). Helen Keller's
motivation and drive were eliminated by a
family who pampered her and overcompensated
for what they thought were her inabilities
to function for herself. Ms. Sullivan
removed Helen from these detrimental
surroundings and required her to perform
activities necessary to everyday existence.
In doing so, Helen was able to gain and
retain the knowledge to lead a self-
fulfilling life.

I recently took my nine-year-old
daughter to a psychologist. I was relieved
to hear that she does not exhibit the
characteristics or enough of the symptoms
to be diagnosed with ADHD. Why then was I
prompted to have her tested? More than
likely it was for the same reasons most
parents are succumbing to this decision. She
was almost unmanageable at times and seemed
easily distracted or frustrated when it came
to schoolwork or long projects. Thinking

back, I was looking for the easy way out.
The term "spoiled" now looms in my mind.
After reviewing the results of her tests
and discussing the doctor's analysis, we
concluded she needs more direction in
controlling her behavior, study habits, and
thinking patterns. The doctor also explained
that I may be too lenient with her at times,
allowing her to feel entitled to get what
she wants. In looking for a way out, I,
probably like many other parents, was
searching for a cause rather than looking at
my parenting skills. We are looking,
however, in the wrong direction if looking
for a medical answer. Stein writes,
"I deeply believe that nothing medical
causes children to not pay attention and to
misbehave. They simply do not pay attention
and they do misbehave" (22). Behavior
therapy, therefore, can be a learning and
growing experience for the child and for the
parent, as well.

There are many behavior therapy
treatment programs geared toward and
created specifically for children suffering
from ADHD. The programs may differ in
structure, but are based on modifying the
child's current behavior by applying the
techniques frequently and consistently.
Some programs set goals and rewards for

good behavior and have consequences for inappropriate behavior. These rewards and consequences vary depending on the present and long-term goals set by the parent and child. The program is individualized to the child by allowing him or her to participate. Recognizing behavior, both good and bad, is an important step in allowing the child to assist in setting goals and choosing punishments.

Another program, the Caregivers' Skill Program, works "by first getting [children's] behavior under control, so we can get their full attention, so we can inspire their motivation" (Stein 41). Lack of interest, and thus motivation, can cause anyone to be inattentive, fidgety, forgetful, and easily distracted. No, it is not a coincidence that you have heard these descriptions before. This only reinforces the fact that these are not symptoms of ADHD alone. As stated above, the first goal is to get a handle on the current behavior. This is achieved in a manner similar to other programs by identifying the problem behavior and using reinforcements such as spending more time with the child and praising the child. Material reinforcements such as special privileges and objects are also an option, but their effects are

Hicks 10

short-lived and can cause another form of
entitlement expectancy. Immediate
reinforcement of positive behavior leads to
a much more pleasant atmosphere than
discipline for bad behavior. Ponder this:
If your employer only pointed out the
shortcomings of your work performance
without praising your accomplishments,
would you not have a bad attitude?

Stop and smell the roses. The roses in
this story are the children. We would not
unnecessarily poison our roses just as we
should not poison our children. Drugs such
as methylphenidate and amphetamines used
needlessly are poison to a child's mind and
body. Encouragement, interaction, and
positive reinforcement are the keys to a
healthy, motivated child. Who knows? Many
parents may find their children need them
more than anything a prescription could
ever offer.

1"

↕ ½"

Hicks 11

Works Cited

← 1" → American Academy of Pediatrics.   ← 1" →

← 5 → <u>Understanding ADHD</u>. Elk Grove
spaces

Village: American Academy of

Pediatrics, 2001.

Mates, Thomas. Personal interview. 27 Mar.

2003.

Morrison, Jaydene. <u>Coping with ADD/ADHD</u>.

New York: Rosen, 1996.

Shute, Nancy. "Pushing Pills on Kids?" <u>US</u>

<u>News and World Report</u> 2 Oct. 2000:

60. <u>Academic Search Elite</u>. EBSCO.

Cape Fear Community Coll. Lib.,

Wilmington, NC. 24 Mar. 2003

<http://www.epnet.com>.

Stein, David B. <u>Ritalin Is Not the Answer</u>.

San Francisco: Jossey-Bass, 1999.

United States. National Institute on

Drug Abuse. <u>NIDA InfoFacts:</u>

<u>Methylphenidate (Ritalin)</u>. 17 Mar.

2003 <http://www.nida.nih.gov/

infofax/ritalin.html>.

Zwi, Morris, Paul Ramchandani, and Carol

Joughin. "Evidence and Belief in

ADHD." <u>British Medical Journal</u>

321.7267 (2000): 975-76. <u>Academic</u>

<u>Search Elite</u>. EBSCO. Cape Fear

Community Coll. Lib., Wilmington, NC.

20 Mar. 2003 <http://www.epnet.com>.

The boldface chapter and section numbers to the right of each symbol and explanation direct you to relevant places in this book.

abbr	Problem with an **abbr**eviation.	45a
adj	Problem with an **adj**ective.	33b–d
adv	Problem with an **adv**erb.	33e–f
agr	Problem with subject-verb or pronoun-antecedent **agr**eement.	25, 30
apos	An **apos**trophe is missing or misused.	28b
art	An **art**icle is misused.	28d, 36b
awk	**Awk**ward. Sentence reads poorly, but problem is difficult to identify.	19f–i, 20a–c
cap	A word needs to be **cap**italized	44b, 44c
case	A pronoun is in the wrong **case**.	31
coh	A sentence or paragraph lacks **coh**erence.	15a, 15b,
cs	Sentence contains a comma **s**plice.	38c
div	Word **div**ided in the wrong place.	43b
dm (or dang)	**D**angling **m**odifier. A modifying phrase has nothing to attach itself to.	33a
frag	Sentence **frag**ment.	38a
ital	**Ital**ics needed.	44a
lc	Use a **l**owercase instead of a capital letter.	44b, 44c
mm	A **m**odifier is **m**isplaced.	33a
num	Problem with the use of **num**bers.	45b
p	Error in **p**unctuation.	35, 37–41
pass	A **pass**ive verb is used ineffectively.	20a, 26e
pl	**Pl**ural form is faulty.	28a
pron	**Pron**oun is faulty in some way.	29–31

ref	Not clear what a pronoun **ref**ers to.	29
rep	Word or phrase is **rep**eated ineffectively.	20c
run-on (or fs)	A **run-on** sentence or fused sentence.	38d
sexist	A word or phrase is potentially offensive.	18d-1
sp	A word is mis**sp**elled.	5b
sub	**Sub**ordination is faulty.	19g
trans	A **trans**ition is weak or absent.	17
vb	Problem with **v**er**b** form.	26, 35
w (or wrdy)	A sentence is **w**ordy.	20c
ww	**W**rong **w**ord in this situation.	18
¶	Begin a new paragraph.	15
no ¶	Do not begin a new paragraph.	15
⊙	Insert a period.	37a
⌄	Insert a comma.	39a–39c, 39e
no ⌄	No comma needed.	39d
⌄	Insert an apostrophe.	28b
⌃	Insert a colon.	40b
⌃	Insert a semicolon.	40a
⌄	Insert quotation marks.	41a
//	Make these items parallel.	19h
ʌ	Insert.	
↗	Cut this word or phrase.	
#	Leave a space.	
◯	Close up a space.	
✕	Problem here; find it.	
∿	Reverse these items.	